Lifelong Learning and its Impact on Social and Regional Development

Contributions to the
First European Conference
on Lifelong Learning
Bremen, 3-5 October 1996

Collected Papers

Edited by Peter Alheit
and Eva Kammler

Donat Verlag · Bremen

Deutsche Bibliothek – CIP-Einheitsaufnahme

Lifelong Learning and its Impact on Social and Regional Development : Contributions to the First European Conference on Lifelong Learning, Bremen 3-5 October 1996. Collected Papers / Peter Alheit and Eva Kammler (Publ.). – Bremen: Donat, 1998
ISBN 3-931737-53-5 Paperback

Druck: R & C-Service, Bremen

Contents

Section 3
Universities as Open Learning Centres

Section 4
The Information Technology Challenge to Lifelong Learning

Section 6
Social Movements and Adult Continuing Education

Section 7
Multiculturalism and Ethnicity

Preface

The *European Year of Lifelong Learning* has impacted upon discussions within adult continuing education. Although its effect in raising public awareness may only be of a short duration, the public and political authorities decision to focus on a European Year enabled the issues to be readdressed within adult continuing education.

The European Conference on *Lifelong Learning and its Impact on Social and Regional Development* which took place at the University of Bremen from 3-5 October 1996 focused on a series of problems that adult continuing education faces today. Modern Europe, on the threshold of the 21st century, has to meet considerable challenges:

- to preserve freedom and democracy which was built up during the post-war-decades
- to remove social inequality which still exists and prevent the emergence of new inequalities
- to deal with the structural problems which accompany the growth of our industrial societies, in particular mass unemployment.

Throughout Europe existing standards of wages and living are endangered. The welfare state has reached its limits and social peace has become fragile. Our natural resources are about to be destroyed. With growing globalisation the pressure for economic decisions oriented towards market efficiency increases in order to preserve Europe's competitiveness. At the same time we are confronted with growing corruption and violence in Europe.

Such challenges can only be met if Europe becomes a learning society, that is if education and training become the centre of a common policy. Only a Europe which practises lifelong learning, has a chance to deal with the problems of the present and the future in a humane and civil way.

However, what does 'lifelong learning' mean? What type of political action is needed to ensure the establishment of lifelong learning? The conference proceedings will follow up these questions and show that lifelong learning takes place not only as formal learning, but also to a large extent as informal learning. A learning society will be aware of the importance of both issues. The information society demands both as it is aimed basically at the autonomous learner who has to handle a large amount of knowledge. Under such conditions it is important to realise that the natural processes of learning take place in a concrete life world, in a specific local and regional setting.

If lifelong learning is to be taken seriously, it has to be supported by the regionalisation of adult continuing education. Regional adult continuing education will be able to react to the specific needs of communities, thus enabling individuals to take responsibility for their own learning and to fulfil the potential of full citizenship.

We would like to thank all who have contributed to the objectives of this conference through speeches, papers and discussions. We would also like to thank the Board of Advisors, namely Professor Paolo Federighi (Firenze), Professor Staffan Larsson (Linköping), Professor Wilhelm Mader (Bremen), Professor Maria Slowey (Glasgow), Professor Richard Taylor (Leeds), and Senatsrat Ralf Wilken (Bremen) for their serious and efficient work.

We would like to thank particularly our cooperants Gabriele Reinhart-Hansen and Sabine Reeber who were responsible for the layout of this book.

Furthermore we would like to thank very much our colleague Barbara Merrill, University of Warwick, for the proof reading of the manuscript.

Last but not least we would like to express our gratitude to those institutions which supported this conference actively through financial grants:

The European Commission,
Bruxelles

Bundesministerium für
Bildung, Wissenschaft, Forschung und Technologie,
Bonn

Deutsche Forschungsgemeinschaft, Bonn
Senator für Wirtschaft, Bremen
Senator für Bildung, Bremen
Universität Bremen

The conference proceedings are work documents which express the serious wish to build a democratic Europe of tomorrow in which full citizenship guarantees sustainable development.

Bremen, July 1997

Peter Alheit　　　　Eva Kammler

Rita Süssmuth

Senator Kahrs,

Mr O'Keefe, Representative of the European Commission and Co-ordinator of the European Year of Lifelong Learning,

Vice-President Prof. Lichtenberg,

Dean Beck,

Professor Alheit,

Ladies and Gentlemen:

This conference entitled, 'Lifelong Learning and its Impact on Social and Regional Development', at which I am speaking as President of the Association of German Adult Education Centres, has prompted me to start with a few preliminary remarks.

We are dealing today with an old issue and yet a very topical one. In my own time as research assistant, lecturer and professor, we had at the UNESCO institute in Hamburg up-to-date bibliography on further education or on lifelong learning. However, this mostly focused on a subclass in the area of adult education; it characterised one of the realities of adult education yet it was in no way related to the social and, hence, political pressures of our times.

Reference has been made to the period when Bremen university was set up and to the importance universities had - and were to have - for regional locations during the phase of reform. Much doubt has been cast on this in the meantime. I must point out that in many cities universities are the biggest employers, and I think that once again we will have to become much more active at regional level. Although the projects - the word 'project' itself says it all - have been described as one-sidedly emancipatory and estranged from reality, they have lost none of their importance.

On the contrary we are finding our way back to much that existed previously.

I am one of those who owe their livelihoods as university professor to the 1960s. Without the opening up of education at that time we women would have had no opportunity to increase that small contingent of university professors who were women. I believe that many women grasped those opportunities. Today, it is even more difficult, in view of the dwindling number of places, to obtain access at all.

I would like to continue my preliminary remarks with a wish. In fact, it may seem like a small dream or even a big one. Professor Alheit has said that he prefers to jump in not at the shallow end but at the deep end as it is worth being confronted with more severe criticism. We had the educational reform movement in Germany from 1890 to 1930, abruptly ended by National Socialism. And something now tells me that we are facing a new beginning. After the extreme neglect of education, I do not mean in the sense of teaching and learning, I seem to sense something new stirring, and it appears not to be atypical. I have taken a look at where the presenting papers for the conference come from, and which country has the largest share. I have been struck by the fact that there are very strong delegations from the United Kingdom and the Scandinavian countries. This reminds me of the last century.

And the Adult Learners' Week? Well, I try to imagine us doing something like that in Germany. It might come off but, at the moment, in politicians' Sunday speeches - even on adult education centres and adult evening classes - I repeatedly hear a condescending remark I find quite annoying: 'We're not at some adult evening class!' meaning something like: 'This is not a kindergarten!' - implying that serious learning does not take place in such centres. This notion brings us close to our topic, that is, the link between informal and formal learning, which evidently the British, yet again, tackle and practise in a much more unconventional way than we now do. Our idea, in contrast, seems to be that if you do not follow on rigorously and systematically from classical education, that is, from a content-related education, it cannot have much to do with learning.

What I find important in the issue of lifelong learning, which certainly derives its current relevance for social policy from the radical changes in society brought about by the acceleration in the growth of new knowledge and in the obsolescence of old knowledge, is that we must now face up to the fact that people can no longer expect to spend their whole lives in one job; they must re-train even within one and the same occupation, and constantly move on to new fields of activity. I venture to suggest that our education researchers in the various fields, although we have always asked what the key qualifications are, are simply unable to say what knowledge people really need. And, maybe, compared with curriculum research in the 1970s - on whatever approach it was based - we are now more cautious about wishing to lay things down centrally and systematically for one and all. Nonetheless, I feel that there are certain approaches which, despite regionalisation, do have some universal features. I wish to endorse what has been said, and ask: for whom is lifelong learning really important, and who are those involved? We are not even clear about that. We are discussing lifelong learning in a situation where, on the one hand, we claim that we have a highly differentiated education system, but, on the other, are obviously reluctant to talk about illiteracy. We think that illiteracy is confined to the third world but it is to be found right in the middle of highly developed states.

The second point is: who participates in the further development of the learning society? That is what people in the world's poorest countries ask when they are told, whether with reference to established universities in South Africa, like Johannesburg, or to institutions in the very poorest states: 'Now don't you start with computers'. For people are only too aware that those who do not share in the spread of knowledge are cut off from it. And, in a narrower sense, this also means that they have no opportunities for participating in society and not only when it comes to the question of entry or re-entry into gainful employment; they can then play little or no part in social developments in general. That is why this participatory aspect is of central importance and harks back to development of adult education, which emerged after all from a popular movement that claimed education as a civil right and as the only way out of the predicament of working people. Adult education was always associated with worker education and to that extent, there was a close link between people's opportunities for personal and social advancement and democracy. The 19th century provides many examples.

I have already mentioned the Scandinavian countries but now I would like to take as example developed by the French; the *école active*. It had a different basis from the Kerschensteiner approach. It was project-related. The project-related learning approaches, whether in-school or out-of-school, were set in students' immediate life context whilst transcending its narrower confines. Some of this we took up in the second half of the 60s and 70s; some of it was lost again in the 80s and 90s. All these projects fell victim to a rigorous qualifications strategy. There is one more aspect that did not exist in quite the same form in the 19th century. Professor Alheit has just referred to the 18 to 25 age groups but if one looks around our adult and further education centres, one now finds a growing number of elderly people with quite important resources for the learning community. And for me, in a civil society they are no less important than young people. On no account do I wish to view the question of lifelong learning only from the standpoint of its utility for the economy and for democracy. The idea of empowerment is a lifelong notion; it applies not only to younger people but to those of a more advanced age as well. As I see it, empowerment is the change that is determining employees' new outlook. If you compare the vocational training of past decades with the present-day situation, you will find a qualitative change emerging in the employer/employee relationship. In an address this morning I said that until now we had subscribed to the notion that industry was split into two sides - employers and the trade unions - each with its own specific interests. But, in fact, industry consists of employers *and* employees, and both need empowerment. More and more forward-looking firms have long since grasped that their productivity depends entirely on the empowerment, participation and decision-taking capacities of their young 'human resources', their workers.

Empowerment is equally important for all other areas of our work. In your planning for this seminar you have taken account of social, regional and gender-specific aspects. In our various life contexts - age-related, gender-related, occupation-related - depending on our ability to influence events, we experience vigorous participation or impotence. We have a society that is once again in phase of change; the civil society. Communitarianism has developed further in other countries than in Germany, whether in Scandinavia, the USA - probably once more with the approach represented by Professor Fischer from Boulder - or in Italy. Italy is a country with more and more volunteers joined together under the motto 'We tackle our problems ourselves' and this concept has evolved much further than in my country. But for my own country, too, I would like to say that the number of people taking the initiative and innovative action in seeking to shape their own lives is not on the decline, but on the increase. In our published opinion, however, it is often asserted that nobody is willing to 'get involved' these days. In the Federal Republic, there are 200,000 initiatives with more than two million members (we are not quite sure just how many), with a rising trend, alongside the eight to ten million citizens traditionally involved in associations and clubs. So you cannot say there is a decline. There are definitely some areas where we have a rise. Admittedly, the most rapidly growing area is sport but that area, too, can be used very well for both informal and formal learning.

It was important for me to outline the larger picture of what we are discussing at this seminar because, if we do not develop the concept in contexts, we will get no farther than the ideas of education functionaries, if I may use that term. And then it will be a very narrow, one-dimensional concept. We need this for Germany as an economic location. But it is too little if we do not link it to the field of civil society and the issue of empowerment for the individual. In developing out concept, we must also overcome the feeling of impotence engendered in people by the tremendous acceleration in the expansion of our store of knowledge. We are all aware that we have never had so many researchers, so much new knowledge at any one time in the world, and we ourselves know that every day we are confronted with new concepts and ideas. I imagine somebody dying 50 years ago and coming back to the various countries of Europe and the world - and try to visualise how he or she would cope with everything that has happened in the meantime.

In this connection, I would like to return to what Professor Dohmen wrote recently in a paper for Germany's Ministry of Education and Science. In applying the English concept of lifelong learning to Germany, he described lifelong learning as a strategy that promotes self-controlled, skills-building learning, which is another word for empowerment. Taking up the sceptical diagnosis formulated in 1973 by a high-ranking preparatory commission for the UNESCO, he says that the classical educational facilities like school, college and university, vocational and general further education, may be activating little more than 50 % of the skills that are lying dormant in a population. In solving the problems at hand, however, we will have to tap a considerable portion of this unexploited potential. This follows on directly from the findings of intelligence research. We are accustomed to thinking of our brain as already overtaxed, but are told by brain researchers that we are apparently only at the start of what the human brain is capable of achieving. Sometimes I find this hard to imagine. However, it does mean that people are able to engage in new creative and intelligent solutions and learning processes. This includes information processing; it includes openness, creativity and flexibility in finding personal responses to new and unexpected situations. Let me say in passing that I am a great admirer of Socrates and must confess that I learned more from him than from anyone else. One thing I have grasped: genuine mobility starts in the mind. If you do not have it there, you can travel the world and still not be mobile - or only geographically.

That is why I would like to come back to my point: if we fail to overcome the present confusion between the accumulation of information (I call this 'data graveyards') on the one hand and human education on the other, then the blessings of growth in information will tend to be Mephistophelian. I would like us to tackle this issue and have the courage to draw from old sources, both those of Antiquity and those of Humanism, for I do not believe that we have made much progress hitherto in our conceptual thinking. We have extended it; people have changed; much more has changed in social and technical fields but not in the anthropological and philosophical domains. This being so, it seems to me to be important - as Professor Lichtenberg, I believe, said - that we view innovative thinking again in contexts and not pursue a single path. When politics hit upon the idea of setting up ethics commissions, it became clear how far our ethical landscape had disintegrated. Today - I merely take as an example the recent debate in the

Council of Europe on what used to be called 'bioethics' and is now called 'bioethics and medicine' - we see that we cannot carry on like this, using these crutches, when it comes to re-integrating ethical questions into learning and into education. It seems to me to be important that lifelong learning must consider this from the outset and choose a different approach.

This brings me back to my second point: the information society generates job opportunities as well. I am not quite as pessimistic as my colleague Professor Alheit. I am familiar with McKinsey's studies and Späth's hypothesis. They are correct from a uni-dimensional point of view. The crucial point is that in order to produce two and a half or three and a half times more of a given good, I need hardly any more people; in many cases fewer and fewer; and in some cases no people at all any more. But for the development of these production techniques I do need people and increasingly so. We then have the question of where to acquire the intelligence needed to produce goods with so few people. We have jobs in new areas. Here I would like to include one figure that is little heeded in the Federal Republic. If one looks at the data for Europe (I am keeping to Europe because I am not familiar with the data from other regions) and asks where will jobs emerge, the answer is usually in services. But the fact is that, although the service sector will continue to develop, the highest growth has been noted in other areas, in particular in information technologies. This is a market where we in Europe have had too small a share so far. So when I look at the forecasts, the strongest growth in jobs, 38 %, is in that sector. Europe's share is 8 % at present. Employment is mainly located in the United States and Japan, at all events outside Europe. We will also have to see where new areas of work emerge in the areas of environmental technology and health care. This is more a question of funding. The crucial and important point is the question: how do I organise lifelong learning in a learning society? Above all, how do I get people who are either frustrated with learning or have never grown accustomed to learning in a positive sense to the point where they have fun in this area? Much of what has been developed in the British and Scandinavian concept goes back to and recalls Dewey: the 'problem approach' in real-life context. This brings us back to the German tradition of Kerschensteiner, to take a good case in point. Since it has to do with praxis in an ever more abstracted world, it brings people in, driven by the pressures of everyday life or by curiosity. It need not be a matter of pressure. People *are* still interested after all; we have not lost all our curiosity.

There is a third important point in this connection. The media have helped to create the impression that learning should not involve effort. But besides all the fun, learning does require a willingness to work hard. It would be wrong to tell everybody: I invite you to learn, but it will be organised in such a way that you do not even notice you are making an effort, as this would give learning the character of entertainment. I hope this will not be the case in the society of the future since effort has always been part of learning, and education calls for hard work, perseverance and shifting goals. Why is it that Asians have overtaken us in some fields? The question may be answered by taking Harvard as an example. In recent years, Harvard professors have again and again reported that, in the 1950s, it was the Europeans who had a greater motivation to learn and produced the best students and graduates. Then came the Israelis and, more recently the Asians, and they have outstripped all the rest. What has enabled them to do so? Not higher intelligence, but in fact secondary attitudes to learning: perseverance, postponing wants, getting along on less during your studies, etc. I think all of that is part of the issue: how do I get through on a budget; how do I spend my money; how do I deploy my resources? People must be won over to the idea that this effort can be fun, too.

As far as the regional question is concerned, you could say that, by regionalising, you are accommodating those people who are not keen on moving. I think that this decentralising approach is the right one. In Germany the federal system organises society from the smallest unit upwards. From the point of view of manageability, including the manageability of problems and solutions to problems, and the accessibility of people, it is no coincidence that in the Federal Republic the Federal Labour Office has been decentralising its approach, also in the fields of further education, retraining, employment promotion measures, and is now saying: 'Look to the regions, organise things yourselves, decide for yourselves.' This applies by analogy to lifelong learning as well, not only in the world of work, but also in social, cultural, environmental projects, and in all forms of living together. After reading an American like Lisbeth in 'Civil Society', you might be feel it would be fun to get involved. In Germany, learning is always associated with duty, and you ask: how can I dodge it? I would like to hope, especially with this decentralised regional approach, that there will be a desire for self-development and learning. At the same time, however, regional development work, too, must be done, for there is a trend in Germany at the moment to run our country down as an economic location. I personally am convinced that it is high time we talked more of our locational strengths, and also of the infrastructure at regional level; of the knowledge and learning potential available, not only in urban environments but specifically in rural area; and also of the possibilities that are now available, much more than in the past, of creating work in rural areas. We can then bring many strands together - local people, forms of co-operation and networks.

If we take this concept as our point of departure, I think we will enter a phase in which what has hitherto been confined to studies by adult educationalists and those fully or partly employed in the area of adult and further education will evolve into a social movement. I am glad that the European Union is developing initiatives in this area: we need both the national and the European component if we are to move forward. The first thing to be done is to translate into practice - and not just in pilot projects - what has been taken up only as a concept so far at federal level in the *Kultusministerkonferenz* (the standing conference of ministers of education and cultural affairs of Germany's *Länder* or states). It is my conviction that the new approach will help shape events and that it will also take much greater account of the anthropological dimensions of people as learning and evolving beings. In this connection, allow me to say that I wish not only this conference, but also the cause itself much success. Perhaps this time around, taking adult education in particular as its point of departure, that second great reform movement may emerge which we in Europe urgently need. Thank you.

Michael Young

Can Lifelong Learning Prevent the Breakdown of Society?

Thank you very much for that introduction. I will start with apologies. I did intend to be here for the whole conference. And I wish I had. And if I had been, I would not be so liable to repeat what other people have said before me, probably much better. And I hope you will make allowances for that.

I am here because of my mother. My mother was a remarkable woman. And she left me in quite a lot of delightful doubt for most of my life on whether my father was an Australian violinist, he died rather early, or a Russian revolutionary who went across Germany with Lenin in 1917 in the famous Sealed Train to the Finland Station in St. Petersburg and who probably died early too. I think a certain tension has been built up on the back of this delightful doubt. I am delighted, of course, that my mother's granddaughter is in the audience today.

I have been told by my chairman today that one of the issues that has come up several times in different guises in the last few days is about individualism versus collectivism in lifelong learning. Should lifelong learning be devoted to development and advancement of individuals, individual achievement, qualifications, degrees, diplomas, certificates and so forth? Or, should it be devoted to the building of group life, community and solidarity, to community benefit, to trust and the building up of trust?

In approaching this dilemma I hope you may be prepared to forgive me for being to start with somewhat autobiographical because I want to illustrate in reasonable humility the schizophrenia, the split mind, the conflict which must be fairly common in adult education, between what might be called the Australian tendency to individuality, vying with what perhaps could be the Russian tendency to a more collective view. I have to admit or perhaps I should say, I have to confess, that a good part of my life has been spent on the promotion of open learning and distance teaching. And I think that hardly anything could be more favourable to individual learning than that, where a lot of the learning happens at home. People are on their own in their own kitchens or sitting rooms or bed-rooms, struggling on, as isolated as many students of the world-wide open universities in their millions have done so far; even if it takes six, seven or eight years to get a full degree. So I have sheered very strongly to that extreme in much that I have done.

It started because one of the few times I had the misfortune of being in an ordinary university was in Cambridge in 1959/63 where I taught my own subject of sociology. I got fairly fed up with the university, because it only operated for seven months of the year, the other five months being vacation. I put forward the idea that in that five months there should be a second university on the same campus. The students who could not get to the ordinary Cambridge would be kept going with correspondence courses and cassettes and so on during the seven month period. The reaction was horror. There were only two supporters out of the many thousands of teachers. I was told over and over again that the important work of the university was not done when the students were there. The students were really secondary. The important work was done when people were writing their books, doing their research, travelling around getting stimulation for the next year's lectures. When I suggested that an entire staff could be brought in from a Polytechnic for the summer vacation, the horror was even greater. It was a disaster. So I did turn my mind to the prospects of a university standing on its own, an open university with no attachments to any existing university, and started a college, called the National Extension College, as a pilot project for an open university. That was in 1962. Then I had perhaps the greatest bit of luck of my life from the point of view of those who are in favour of individual learning. Harold Wilson took on the idea and I think really believed or at least believed ninety percent that the idea was entirely his. I decided then that the golden rule of innovation which I tried to practise for most of my life is if you have a good idea, try to father it on someone else more important than yourself. The university opened in 1969.

That was one story. It is the largest university in Britain now. Almost every university has opened an open learning bit of it for some or other activities. There are 30 open universities in the world. Some are much larger than the British. The Thai Open University has 450,000 students, South Korea has an open university of about the same. The Indonesian is even bigger and 3 million students have been claimed for the Chinese Open University.

So it has hit a gusher and beyond that there are thousands of institutions particularly in the developing world that have taken on open learning to try to meet some of their needs, specially at the level of secondary education.

I do not know whether the Internet version of the Open University, which I think is on the way, is going to have a more personal touch than the original one. If it does, it might at least meet some of the criticisms of the open university which is that people having to study on their own are in greater difficulties than acknowledged. Sometimes it has harmful effects on families and since it takes so many years, it can take a big slice out of a person's life. Married women have been to the fore. There have been students as old as ninety as well as teenage students. It has been lifelong learning.

I have added to the Open University an International Extension College for the development of open learning methods in Africa and Asia and also more recently, 10 years ago, an open college of the arts for teaching almost all the arts at a distance. People did not think it possible to teach painting and sculpture without a live tutor. We have shown it can be done, but so far it is not completely sure that it can be done economically. There has never been a government subsidy for any of these ventures except the open university. The Open College of the Arts is looking for any partners in Europe who are engaged in the arts, adult education especially, who might join with us in common programmes and among several things joining the Internet Art Gallery that we launched last week for amateur artists who can display their work to each other, who can invite families showing the work on the Internet and who can also sell their works to each other, to others and to commercial firms that may be on the lookout for new designs. We like partners. We have one in Australia, the Open College of the Arts there, and we would like some in Europe.

I have also moved the other way. Towards the goal which I think is much more important, towards an education which emphasises collectivism.

The first venture is slightly bizarre. It was a Community Study Clubs on commuter trains into London. It was called the Brain Train, colloquially by British Rail, when it was still British Rail. We survey every person on a train before starting it anywhere, and usually find that God is on our side. We ask everyone what they like to study, and we ask everyone what they would like to teach; extraordinarily there is usually a pretty close match. I remember talking to one person who said he was an architect and would like to teach architectural history and there were three people travelling regularly on the same train who all wanted to study that. He taught it rather brilliantly, by asking people to look out of the train window as they rushed through the country, it was from Cambridge to London, and gave a quick lecture on that little building and that church and so on. The students got so keen that on Saturdays and Sundays they went to visit the churches and buildings to get a longer view of what they were seeing so fleetingly on the train. The Brain Train has gone on for twenty years.

There is also the Tower Hamlets Summer University which works just for five weeks in the summer, provides a very wide range of courses and activities - dancing, drumming, singing, physics, canoeing, drama, chemistry - and the object has been good racial relations between the Bangladeshis, who are now almost 50 percent of the population of the district where I work, and white people. The racial groups are largely segregated in schools, but they would not be in these out-of-school activities. Some success has been achieved, but not nearly enough.

The last thing is a Mutual Housing Association in Bradford. Tenants who come into it will have to commit themselves in a mutual aid clause to the tenancy, to helping disabled people, elderly people, single parents, mothers and others, and accept training for the purpose. There will be employment generation schemes and houses will be maintained and repaired by local people who will get training for the purpose. There will be community care contracts. We are hoping to introduce a new kind of currency just for the housing scheme which will, we hope, smooth the relationships between the people.

So there is the problem. There is the mix. Was the open learning chapter in my life a mistake? Was it the right mix? Was it wrong?

The most important question, as I see it, is a general one for the future: which way will things go? I would say that unless there is a change in the mental climate the future will be with individual learning. But if it goes the other way and there is more collective learning for the benefit of the collective, then I think that in the course of time the climate could change further in that direction. What would bring this about, I think, although it does have a gloomy aspect to it, is that I believe that Western society is heading towards collapse. And why should lifelong learning play a small part in the averting of that collapse? One has to be somewhat optimistic to think it will. I have risked a date for the breakdown when it's going to happen because in a book I wrote in 1957, 'The Rise of the Meritocracy', I prophesied that on a particular day, in 2033, there would be a revolt in England and a revolt that might spread through the world. A revolution brought about by a coalition of long-term unemployed men and feminists. We will see. We will not all see. I myself will be anxiously watching the very day from a safe distance, hoping that I am wrong.

In some part I do put the blame for what has happened on front-end education for individual advancement and individual fulfilment. Education is supposed to open our minds more generally, not just for information technology or computer science or Latin or physics or whatever, and to give us a chance to explore the depths in our souls. The hidden depths and hidden energies in all of us, unconscious and conscious, which need to be tapped and sometimes are, whoever your father is. But the emphasis of it all has been on the individuals.

The worst of it is, where this sort of education has been locked into a cyclical system, schools and training systems turn out people whom the economy demands and the managers in the economy by and large determine the sort of people whom education turns out. Education and economy are like lovers in an embrace. But you see that the lovers cannot detach themselves from each other. You cannot get out of the clinch. You cannot even take a breath.

And so education goes on being focused on individual capacities and exam qualifications which are required by employers. Teachers, unwittingly or wittingly, have become recruiting sergeants for the economy. People who are unlikely to pass muster are the worst off of all. They are not likely to succeed, if they are not thought to be likely to succeed. People made to look foolish, become foolish. If it is thought they are likely to become unemployable, they are likely to become unemployable. Teachers' prophesies become self-fulfilling. In class, there is usually an under-class. The growth of the corresponding under-class in society as well as school is not all the fault of ordinary education. Every country has its unique experience of sorting the sheep from the goats. Economies become more complex. Unskilled and semi-skilled jobs have been cut down or disappeared. Two hundred years of mechanisation have been topped up by computers, we have been talking about that earlier today. Manual strength is no longer an advantage, except in sport, and men have lost their age-old advantage.

The result of all this is, as I see it, to bring back a Marxist notion, that there is a large and growing reserve army of the unemployed, which looks like becoming ever larger with more and more young people in it. That is the most disastrous thing about it. More and more men and more and more long-term unemployed, and no-one knowing what to do about it. The European Union and the single currency is likely to make things worse in my view with its emphasis on keeping down inflation. Anyway, the course of events is going pretty well as I predicted it would in the meritocracy book. The final explosion came because the elites of each nation took it for granted that without intelligence in their heads the lower classes are never menacing, even if sometimes mercurial, not yet completely predictable. The elite was wrong and eventually there was a successful revolt in favour of collective solidarity, the non-meritocratic life.

As for the standard of living, bad as the outlook was in 1957, the prospects have worsened since then. The machine-based collective of the global economy has to find and stress the motivation which remake people into willing slaves of the economy. The appeal has been to give paramountcy to what is called the 'individual standard of living'. The standard of living is judged not by the quality of life, but by the quantity of commercial goods and services which people can acquire. Marx, again, has something to say on this subject. When in the first volume of his great book he spoke about the 'fetishism of commodities', which he thought, when he was writing, was even then on the way to capturing the mind of his contemporaries.

People have become more choosy about themselves and their partners. Partly because they have been encouraged to be more choosy about the great things that technology has presented them with. Technology has individualised the activities of the home. 'Heimat ist individuell.' This is a rather new development. In the days when there was a marked division of labour between the sexes, many of people's activities were outside the home, because the prevailing products of technology were on the scale of the community. Industry has produced smaller and smaller machines with which to automate the home. At first it brought people back into the home. The public laundry gave way to the washing-machine, public bars to individual bars, ice-making factories to small refrigerators in the kitchen, heated homes became more and more comfortable, the bus and train were challenged by the car, the cinema was largely replaced by television. To watch sports people did not have to go into a large stadium anymore.

But I think there have been important changes in going down from the mini to the micro and adding to them micro-machines. The collective of the family has flipped over into the individual. The two-car-family changed that. Husbands and wives did not have then to go out together when they went out at all. When families were lucky enough or unlucky enough to have three cars, the car has been even more the centrifuge. So also inside the home. When my mother was middle-aged and I was a youngster, in the thirties, once upon a time, one could hear something, that by now seems extraordinary. The BBC came into existence in 1928. By 1930 you could still hear this kind of announcement of an evening: 'This is the BBC. Nine o'clock news and Alva Liddel is reading it. There is no news tonight so I will play music for the next quarter of an hour.' That would be so extraordinary now if it happened. I wish it would. Once upon a time people sat around the radio, then around the television. But now the family no longer need to ensconce themselves or so in a circle around the telly looking at the latest instalment of a Soap Opera. They can have television sets in different rooms. Along with the High-fi, they can use the video to attach themselves in the collective just as they can use their very personal computer not necessarily to access the Internet, but to play extraordinary games about monsters all by themselves. The disintegration in families has sometimes gone so far that people do not even eat their meals together. The microwave has come into prominence. Quick meals for different members of the family at different times. The microwave has hit Max Weber on the head. Max Weber believed that eating together was one of the central secrets of human solidarity. It is not only eating together that could go. A model family of the future could sit in the same room each with its own Walkman to which it is plugged in listening to different pieces of music gazing rather blankly at each other. The paradox in this display of greed is that after a quite moderate level of material wealth has been reached there is not much to gain in satisfaction from getting more. Once you are securely above the bread line there is very little relation between income and happiness. The relationship may be turned on its head: the more income the less happiness, partly because the rich even more than the rest of us are ever more driven by the demon of time: they are always trying and always failing to put more than is possible into every second in a run of 24 hours or a week. What is the point of it if things take over from people and abundance of things makes people into husks bright enough on the outside but with souls suffering from the shortage of spiritual oxygen. Greed has to be centrally stimulated, the industrial machine has to be kept going. Can it really go on forever? If the answer is no and the heart of society becomes more or less empty, something of a new start will have to be made.

The individualism which has divided people within the family has gone along with a much more fundamental weakening of the family ties between people, between husband and wives, between grandparents and children. Lifelong learning with the same people has become less common. Samuel Butler said the question whether you get married is just the question of how to ruin your life in one way rather than another. People are choosing more often to ruin it not by getting married. A growing number of children have to put up with the consequences. There is evidence in the British longitudinal studies which started with a cohort of people in 1946 and followed them through the years. Children whose parents had divorced before they reached fifteen had a lower level of attainment, more disruption, more delinquency, lower incomes and were more prone to divorce or separation. Take that trend much further up to 2033 and the lack of family stability could have produced by then a generation without the inner stability which can come from a secure and affectionate childhood. The central problem of every city and town in Europe, even Bremen, could become the crowds of emotionally homeless children roaming the streets and seeking to get their own back for the neglect they have suffered in their earlier lives.

So I have tried to make out a case, plausible I hope, for believing we may be actually heading for breakdown. Education so far has helped to promote it rather than hold it back. In my argument the overemphasis on the individual has been the villain of the piece. Individual development, individual choice, individual destiny, and all this while the scale of the world economy to which all of us belong willy-nilly is getting more vast and more impersonal by the day. A frightening paradox in itself. The conclusion which in my view follows is that the future may well be on the side of lifelong learning which needs to become less individualist and more collectivist. Long before 2033 it needs in one way or another to stress the value of bringing it home to as many people as possible that we are all members of the one interlinked humanity in the same ecological and social environment. I shall end with one of those prophetic statements for which Alexis de Tocqueville is famous. Referring to the aftermath of the French revolution, he said: 'I see each citizen standing apart like a stranger'. In a society of strangers even children can be strangers. Such a society cannot survive indefinitely. Learning and lifelong learning focused on collectivism could at least point the way to a different future.

Peter Alheit

Two Challenges to a Modern Concept of Lifelong Learning[1]

Introduction

Individual demand for education during adulthood has ceased for some time to be a privilege of culturally interested and well-educated citizens. The perspective of a *'Lifelong Learning Society'*, as is now being witnessed in Japan[2], seems to be turning into an economic and social policy necessity of the first order. Not only is the need for parallel further and continuing education rising in all developed industrialised countries - the 'life time' available for education has also undergone considerable expansion.

This process also involves certain risks, however. The new and enlarged 'time budget' is a consequence of the substantial reduction in the time that must now be spent in gainful employment in post-industrial societies. At the same time, the number of wage-earners in secure jobs is declining dramatically, to be replaced either by deregulated employment, forms of temporary employment and highly insecure forms of hidden wage labour, or by mass unemployment on a scale that social policymaking has little chance of coping with. The image of a flourishing labour society in which all members who are fit for work spend 40 years of their lives working 40 hours a week has finally become a thing of the past, if indeed it was ever reality in the first place.

Even dramatic reductions in working hours, as is now provided for in the well-known collective bargaining agreement between the German Metal Workers Union and *VW* to reduce the working week to 28.8 hours, are only able to maintain the status quo as far as workforce size is concerned, but without creating a single new job. On the basis of figures provided by McKinsey experts, Lothar Späth, the ex-Prime Minister of Baden-Württemberg and today the Managing Director of *JENOPTIK*, claims that 'if the best

1 Slightly modified version of a keynote given to the European Conference 'Lifelong Learning and its Impacts on Social and Regional Development' (Bremen, 3-5 October 1996).
2 See McCormick 1989; Miura et al. 1992; Kawanobe 1994; Maehira 1994; Jütte 1996.

available technology were to be deployed wherever possible, 9 million of the 33 million jobs that still exist in Germany would be destroyed. Unemployment would rise to 38%.'[3] I assume that the forecasts for the UK would not be much better. In other words, we are living in societies in which fewer and fewer people produce more and more goods and amass more and more 'riches' that, aside from the environmental and social costs, are of questionable social benefit.

There is every indication at present that preference is being given to *neo-classical* solutions for redistributing the time that has been 'won': solutions which tolerate a societal split between the privileged and the marginalised, the over-employed and the under-employed, the highly skilled and the deskilled. Regulation of the social and environmental risks of modernisation is being left more and more to market mechanisms alone. The Japanese example shows that *more intelligent* (and more democratic) solutions are at least feasible, namely a progression from a 'labour society' to a 'learning society'.

I would like to explain the need for such a progression in two ways and which I call the two challenges to a new concept of Lifelong Learning:

- firstly, with reference to *new findings* on learning processes in adulthood, the challenge of 'individualisation' in late modern societies (1);
- and then the challenge of building up a new practical sense of public-spiritedness and communitarianism which I shall try to demonstrate through a *scenario* that deliberately abandons the conventional pathways for organising education and which cautiously moves on to 'utopian terrain' (2).

1 The need for a paradigm shift: biographical learning

We have got used to hearing that we are living through a dramatic transformation of society. From the macrosociological perspective the classical

3 Quoted in Zoll 1994, p. 81

descriptions of modern societies are losing their power of conviction. We stopped attaching the old label of 'working' or 'class' society long ago. Even the modern 'welfare state' would appear to be on the way out. Instead terms such as the *one-third, two-thirds society*, the *risk society*[4], or more recently and surprisingly the *event society*[5] are claiming central positions within the alternating scenarios.

'Microsociology' also appears to be losing its bearings somewhat. People's social behaviour within their immediate social nexus is losing any distinct contours it may have had. Relationships, intergenerational orientations, the gender roles and traditional social milieus are all in a process of dissolution[6]. If we are to sum up the secret drama of modernisation in modern societies with an appropriate and fashionable term, then we would almost certainly choose the concept of *individualisation*, a term that the German sociologist Ulrich Beck in particular has influenced[7] and which has now established itself within the sociology of the English-speaking world as well[8]. The concept is certainly not new. But as Beck or Giddens use it, it suggests a fascinating combination of phenomena at the micro- and macro levels. On the one hand, it stands for interesting changes in the immediate social sphere, in family constellations, kinship or gender relations. At the same time it also refers to the standardisation procedures within social institutions, and even embraces in more recent times the increased need of isolated individuals for new forms of collectivity.

No pattern of interpretation in contemporary sociological discussion has expanded into the public forum with such ease. None has also proved itself to be compatible with politics with quite the same success. If the popular slogan of the women's movement, *'the personal is political'* were to be expressed as a sociological formula, then the 'individualisation thesis' would be the ideal choice. The decision made by an 18-year-old daughter to move out of her parents' middle-class home and insist on her own pad is a *political* decision, because it exacerbates the catastrophic situation on the housing

4 See Beck 1986, 1992; Beck, Giddens & Lash 1994.
5 See Schulze 1992.
6 See Alheit 1994a.
7 See again Beck 1986, p. 205ff.
8 See in particular Beck 1992, p. 87ff.

market. The teaching couple's conscious decision not to have children is similarly political, because it has a bearing on the pensions policies of the next century. The plan of a 35-year-old nurse to do a university degree is doubtlessly political, because it disrupts the official planning of qualification levels in society as a whole. Finally, the decision made by a 14-year-old girl from a broken family background not to break off her pregnancy and to risk instead a fate as a 'welfare mother' is also political. At least then she is standing on her own two feet.[9]

Those dramatical changes expressed by the individualisation theses are, of course, not without consequences to education. Moreover, systematic or institutional intervention is less and less a guarantee that individuals will be activated to take part in continuing education. What is really needed is an approach that centres exclusively on the learning subjects themselves.

This is precisely what the basic idea behind the strategy of lifelong learning could be. One of the main recommendations in the January 1996 paper presented by the OECD to the Conference of Ministers of Education[10] is the idea that lifelong learning should combine formal and informal learning. This is based on the realisation that people in modern society, regardless of their class origins, race or gender, are all engaged in lifelong learning, not in schools with teachers, but in their everyday lives, at work and through communication. This 'natural' form of everyday learning is an important starting point for any lifelong learning for all.[11] It is the real basis for activating individual demand for education. Moreover, there are two decisive arguments at the conceptual level in support of this view:

(a) new systematic findings about *how* people learn and

(b) the by no means trivial discovery that we learn in the context of our *life-span*.

(to a) Unlike schoolteachers, adult educators are well aware of the fact that learning by adults is always 'supplementary'.[12] Yet there still remains an

9 See Alheit 1994b.
10 See Dohmen 1996, pp.11ff.
11 Alheit 1983; Dohmen 1996, p.13.
12 See Schmidt & Weinberg 1978.

educational fantasy that interpretation patterns could be 'exchanged' or that new action orientations could be stimulated, old skills revived or innovative competencies implemented. Such exaggerated visions of educational input seem to be an integral component of professionality.

Careful analysis of educational biographies shows that adult learning (and probably every kind of learning) functions very differently indeed.[13] External impulses are not irrelevant, but they are not necessarily processed in quite the way that adult educators might like to think. Every stimulus or idea, every form of educational intervention is translated into the learner's 'experiential language' and assessed accordingly. Not until such external input has been integrated into the individual's body of experience is the impact of teacher input actually determined. Seen in this way, learning is not an input-output process, but much rather a form of *'intake'*, a process of autonomous processing of external impressions.

This discovery about the learning biographies of adults is congruent with recent finding in biology, especially the work of Humberto Maturana and Francisco Varela, the Chilean neurobiologists.[14] Their concept of reality processing is based on the observation that the human organism behaves like a closed system towards its environment. It perceives external 'perturbations', then processes them with an internal and independent logic. The determining aspect is not the external stimulus, but the inner logic of the system.

Learning could, therefore, be seen as a creative construction of reality from the perspective of the learner that communicates with similar creative constructions of other learners. The activation of education in this context would involve the provision of a fertile climate for similar processes of 'self-managed' learning and to support the 'natural' process of self-learning.[15]

(to b) Of course, the potential of the learners is not arbitrary, but is based instead on an 'internal history' constituted from a chain of external

13 See Alheit & Dausien 1985, 1996; Alheit 1993, 1998; Dausien 1996.
14 See Maturana & Varela 1987.
15 See Dohmen 1996, p.25.

influences - conditioning impressions that in theory can be recollected and narratively reproduced at any time.[16] In other words, the unique biographical construction in each case has its own internal form, with unmistakable roots in society.

What is more, every biographical construction has a kind of 'shell', namely the life course, which Martin Kohli was perhaps right in comparing to an 'institution'.[17] An institution because the life course is shaped by institutional procedures and constructions of normality, and sometimes by historical disasters and cohort effects. Individual learners are always linked to the collective through their life course.

When the latest statistics on unemployment in Europe[18] refer to an average unemployment among young people under 25 of well over 20%, as much as 34.9% in Italy and an incredible 41.7% in Spain, then we can speak not just of a severe cohort effect, but in a certain sense of a change in the life-course regime - a quarter to almost half of young people must reckon with the status passage between education and employment turning into a kind of 'time out' period. Social risks are not only distributed unequally in the social space. They are also 'temporalised'. The mere fact of being a child on the threshold to working life involves a major risk situation.[19]

Such an experience must also be processed by the subjects themselves, of course; and it is astounding how creatively many of those affected actually cope with this risk phase in their biographies. However, this very example is a clear illustration of the urgency that is implicit in the concept of lifelong learning. It could operate as a kind of framework for subjective learning and coping processes, a framework that could be available to everyone in risk situations.

16 See Schütze 1981, 1984; Habermas 1981,II, pp.206f.
17 Kohli 1985.
18 See EUROSTAT (Januar 1996).
19 See Alheit et al. 1994.

2 *The idea of the 'second sector'*

I would hope that these arguments show, at least implicitly, that a policy for activating the individual demand for education cannot be a small-scale affair nowadays. Instead, what is needed is a European debate on 'macrosolutions'. This would be an appropriate way to tackle the pending educational reforms, and a necessary step given the severe socio-political problems that exist.

I see my own ideas in this context as such a 'macro-level' proposal. I am well aware that it is precisely this aspect that makes the proposal open to attack and criticism, but I accept this 'vulnerability' because it enables the concept of lifelong learning to be placed in the context of pragmatic political action. My idea relates to three separate dimensions of the debate:

- the concept of a second, non-commodified sector of activity[20];
- the idea of a citizen's wage for socially essential activities[21];
- the idea inherent in the concept of lifelong learning, namely that links are needed between educational processes and everyday practice, between formal learning and informal learning[22].

More pressing than the question as to how we could increase individual educational activity in the context of lifelong learning is how to prevent larger groups in society being squeezed out of the labour market on a long-term or permanent basis. This enforced release from the labour market does not necessarily increase the willingness to engage in continuing education. More probably, it leads to social disintegration, even to a greater susceptibility to anomie among certain groups.

Many industrial sociologists, economists and technology specialists share the assumption that the difficult situation on the labour markets will become increasingly critical[23], so it is essential that potential solutions be sought

20 See Benseler et al. (Eds) 1982; Berger et al. (Eds) 1982; Offe 1984; Offe & Heinze 1990, to name but a few references.
21 See Gorz 1989; Offe 1986, to name but the most prominent writers.
22 See again Dohmen 1996.
23 See Beck 1996.

after as a matter of urgency. The relatively well-known idea of a basic social insurance for all is problematic, because it would reinforce and consolidate the current system of job distribution and marginalise those who are forced to live on this basic income over a protracted period of time. Models of state-organised '*workfare*', that is, the public-sector financing of second and third labour markets, has essentially the same effect. Careers below the primary labour market raise the threshold for re-entry to the labour market to a drastic extent. Marginalisation is the rule here as well.

A possible way to counter this would be to establish an *autonomous 'second sector' of non-commodified activities* that are essential for or at least desired by society. Suggestions and ideas which could be integrated into the concept range from the publicly financed educational year in Denmark, to various proposals of a voluntary 'social year' in Europe, or the established practice of civilian service (as opposed to military service) in Germany. The basis for reproduction would be an adequate level of 'citizen's pay', to which all those active in the *second sector* would be entitled.

Unlike compensatory workfare measures, which only affect those who have already been pushed out of the primary labour market, involvement in the *second sector* during a certain biographical phase (leaving school would be a suitable point) should be a duty that all citizens, men and women, would have to perform. The activities would comprise social, environmental and cultural services, on the one hand, or participation in lifelong learning initiatives, in self-learning centres or 'internet cafés', for example, in senior citizen clubs or study circles. The linkage between practical work and self-directed studies would comply with the idea of making lifelong learning an established activity in society that continues after leaving the *second sector*.

The obligatory status of such a period would not only develop public-spiritedness and communitarianism. It would also make 'learning to learn'[24] a feasible objective for all and in that way lead strata that are more 'remote' from the educational process to participation in self-organised educational

24 See Simons 1992; Smith 1992.

practice. The activating effect this would have on the individual demand for education could scarcely be over-estimated.

Those completing a two-year period in the *second sector* would acquire 'vouchers' for vocational training and education in companies or universities. Everyone would have the right to receive citizen's pay during such training. Voluntary extension of work in the *second sector* would be possible at all times. A return to the *second sector* at a later stage, as part of a sabbatical for instance, would be explicitly encouraged. Conceivable modes would be self-determined cycles of education and work, alternating with phases in waged labour.

The advantages of such a system are indisputable. It would eliminate the problem of mass unemployment, have a civilising impact on social conflicts and lead to a collective rediscovery of communitarianism. It would also establish a type of learning based on the 'natural' everyday learning that people engage in, and which, therefore, takes everybody into consideration and places nobody at a disadvantage. It would be the optimal instrument for motivating individual participation in education. The financial mechanism, for which there are certainly some interesting concepts[25], would probably depend on national and cultural traditions. In any case, it would obviously be a good investment and possibly lead to an inspiring 'learning society'.

References

Alheit, P. (1983), Alltagsleben. Zur Bedeutung eines gesellschaftlichen 'Restphänomens', Frankfurt, New York.

Alheit, P. (1993), 'Transitorische Lernprozesse: Das „biographische Paradigma“ in der Weiterbildung' in Wilhelm Mader (ed) Weiterbildung und Gesellschaft, pp. 343-417, Bremen.

Alheit, P. (1994a), Zivile Kultur. Verlust und Wiederaneignung der Moderne, Frankfurt, New York.

Alheit, P. (1994b), 'Arbeit und Bildung im Modernisierungsprozeß: Entkoppelung oder neue Synthese?' in Alheit, P. et al. (eds) Von der Arbeitsgesellschaft zur Bildungsge-

25 See, for example, Scharpf 1994, to indicate but one.

sellschaft? Perspektiven von Arbeit und Bildung im Prozeß europäischen Wandels, pp. 23-47, Bremen.

Alheit, P. (1995), 'Individual modernisation': Changing intra-action environments in late modernity' in Skevos Papaioannou et al. (eds) Education, Culture and Modernisation, pp. 119-141, Roskilde.

Alheit, P. (1998), Biographieforschung als Herausforderung der Sozialwissenschaften? in Dausien, B. (ed), Biographie und Lebenswelt. Zugänge zur subjektiven Rekonstruktion des Sozialen, Frankfurt am Main (forthcoming).

Alheit, P. and Dausien, B. (1985) Arbeitsleben, Frankfurt, New York.

Alheit, P. and Dausien, B. (1996), 'Bildung als biographische Konstruktion? Nichtintendierte Lernprozesse in der Erwachsenenbildung' in Report 37/1996, pp. 33-45.

Alheit, P., et al., (1994), Die Kehrseite der 'Erlebnisgesellschaft', Eine explorative Studie, Bremen.

Beck, U. (1986), Risikogesellschaft. Auf dem Weg in eine andere Moderne, Frankfurt am Main.

Beck, U. (1992), Risk Society, London.

Beck, U. (1996), 'Kapitalismus ohne Arbeit' in Der Spiegel 20/1996, pp. 140-146.

Beck, U., Giddens, A. and Lash, S. (1994), Reflexive Modernization, Oxford.

Benseler, F., et al. (eds), (1982), Die Zukunft der Arbeit, Hamburg.

Berger, J., et al. (eds), (1982), Kongreß Zukunft der Arbeit. Materialienband, Bielefeld.

Bourdieu, P. (1987), Die feinen Unterschiede, Frankfurt am Main.

Dausien, B. (1996), Biographie und Geschlecht. Zur biographischen Konstruktion sozialer Wirklichkeit in Frauenlebensgeschichten, Bremen.

Dohmen, G. (1996), Lebenslang lernen - aber wie? Eine Einführung in Bernhard Nacke and Günther Dohmen (eds) Lebenslanges Lernen. Erfahrungen und Anregungen aus Wissenschaft und Praxis, pp. 11-22, Bonn.

Gorz, A. (1989), Kritik der ökonomischen Vernunft, Berlin.

Giddens, A. (1990), Consequences of Modernity, Oxford.

Habermas, J. (1981), Theorie des kommunikativen Handelns, 2 Vol., Frankfurt am Main.

Johnstone, J. W. C. and Rivera, J. R. (1965), Volunteers for Learning, Chicago.

Jütte, W. (1996), 'Lerngesellschaft: Notwendige Umwelt für das lebenslange Lernen' in Nacke, B. and Dohmen, G., (eds) Lebenslanges Lernen. Erfahrungen und Anregungen aus Wissenschaft und Praxis, pp. 28-41, Bonn.

Kawanobe, S. (1994), Lifelong Learning in Japan in International Review of Education *40* (6), pp. 485-493.

Kohli, M. (1985), 'Die Institutionalisierung des Lebenslaufs. Historische Befunde und theoretische Argumente' in Kölner Zeitschrift für Soziologie und Sozialpsychologie *37* (1), pp. 1-29.

Maehira, Y. (1994), 'Patterns of Lifelong Learning in Japan' in International Review of Education *40* (3/4), pp. 333-338.

Maturana, H. R. and Varela, F. J. (1987), Der Baum der Erkenntnis, Bern, München.

McCormick, K. (1989), Towards a Lifelong Learning Society? The Reform of Continuing Vocational Education and Training in Japan' in Comparative Education *25* (2), pp. 133-149.

Miura, S., et al., (1992), Lifelong Learning in Japan. An Introduction, Tokyo.

Offe, C. and Heinze, R. G. (1990), Organisierte Eigenarbeit. Das Modell Kooperationsring, Frankfurt, New York.

Offe, C. (1984) 'Arbeitsgesellschaft'. Strukturprobleme und Zukunftsperspektiven, Frankfurt, New York.

Offe, C. (1986), 'Sozialstaat und Beschäftigungskrise. Probleme der Sicherung sozialer Sicherung' in Alheit, P., et al. (eds) Wie wir leben wollen. Krise der Arbeitsgesellschaft, Widerstand, Reform und Perspektiven, pp. 29-44.

Recum, H. von (1978), Bildungsökonomie im Wandel, Braunschweig.

Scharpf, F. (1994), 'Negative Einkommenssteuer - ein Programm gegen Ausgrenzung' In Die Mitbestimmung 3/1994.

Schiersmann, C. (1995), 'Zielgruppenforschung' in Tippelt, R. (ed) Handbuch Erwachsenenbildung/Weiterbildung, pp. 501-509, Opladen.

Schütze, F. (1981), 'Prozeßstrukturen des Lebensablaufs' in Matthes, J., et al. (Eds) Biographie in handlungswissenschaftlicher Persperpektive, pp. 67-156, Nürnberg.

Schütze, F. (1984), 'Kognitive Figuren des autobiographischen Stehgreiferzählens' in Kohli, M. and Roberts, G., (eds) Biographie und soziale Wirklichkeit. Neue Beiträge und Forschungsperspektiven, pp. 78-117, Stuttgart.

Simons, P. R. J. (1992), 'Theories and priciples of learning to learn' in Tuijnman, A. and Max van der Kamp (eds) Learning Across the Lifespan. Theories, Research, Policies, pp. 159-171, Oxford.

Smith, R. M. (1992), 'Implementing the learning to learn concept' in Tuijnman, A. and Max van der Kamp (eds) Learning Across the Lifespan. Theories, Research, Policies pp. 173-188, Oxford.

Strzelewicz, W., H.D. Raapke, and Schulenberg, W, (1966), Bildung und gesellschaftliches Bewußtsein, Stuttgart.

Taubman, P. J. and Wales, T. J. (1972), Education as an Investment and a Screening Device, New York.

Vester, M., et al., (1993), Soziale Milieus im gesellschaftlichen Strukturwandel. Zwischen Integration und Ausgrenzung, Köln.

Zoll, R. (1994), 'Staatsbürgereinkommen für Sozialdienste. Vorschläge zur Schaffung eines zweiten, nicht marktförmig organisierten Sektors der Gesellschaft' in Oskar Negt (ed) Die zweite Gesellschaftsreform. 27 Plädoyers, pp. 79-96, Göttingen.

Section 1

Skill Enhancement and Community Development in Regions of Economic Decline

Rob Humphreys / Theresa McGoldrick

Widening Access to Higher Education in a Former Coalfield Region: Institutional and Student Perspectives on Policy, Practice and the Learning Experience

Introduction

The South Valleys, like many coalfield and so-called 'older industrial regions' of Western Europe, have experienced rapid and far-reaching economic, social and cultural change in recent years. In South Wales, the initial post-1945 years were ones in which the regional economy had to a considerable extent recovered from the mass unemployment of the 1920s and 30s, but this was underpinned by the nationalisation of the coal and steel industries, and by new employment opportunities in the service sector, which were equally dependent on the state. The election of successive Conservative Governments from 1979, which were committed to cutting public expenditure, led to major job losses in the steel industry, and to the near disappearance of deep mining in the region. Coupled with the absence of alternative employment opportunities, this has led to the return of high rates of unemployment and social deprivation, and to the return of a prevailing image of the South Wales Valleys as a so-called 'problem region', and a succession of regional development strategies in which latterly, education and training have been central (Cooke and Rees, 1981, Rees, 1990, Rutherford, 1991).

A further prevailing image of the region, however, is that of adult education being a central part of its culture. The travel writer H. V. Morton, in his 1932 best-seller, *In Search of Wales* tells of his encounter, on a street corner of the Rhondda town of Tonypandy, with two young miners engaged in a discussion about Einstein's Theory of Relativity (Morton, 1932: 247). John Ormond's elegiac 1961 film, *Once There Was a Time*, focuses solely on two elderly Rhondda men counter-posing respectively the explanatory powers of Christianity and Marxian social analysis. The film achieves its effect in part because it does not have to be explicit about adult education being a part of the men's cultural heritage; it makes the assumption that the audience is already aware of this[1]. Some of the leading political and trade union figures of twentieth century Britain, such as Aneurin Bevan, James Griffiths, Arthur Horner and Wil Paynter, were (and remain) identified in the public imagination as being products of a working class culture of learning in South Wales. And miners' libraries and institutes are rightly seen as an integral part of the history of coalfield culture and politics in the region (Francis, 1976).

These popular images, albeit romanticised at times, have their roots in a real history, which saw the rapid industrialisation of the coalfield giving birth to a cosmopolitan, yet still self-consciously Welsh, society and culture, in which autodidactism, trade union education, and political education were central. Much of this grew out of local communities themselves and was a result of the activities of such bodies as trade unions and co-operative societies, as much as it was the result of outside organisations. It has been argued elsewhere that the relationship of the University of Wales and its constituent Colleges to the coalfield was at best an ambivalent one, though at the same time not insignificant (Francis and Humphreys, 1996, Morgan, 1996). In the case of adult education as a whole, however, it is impossible to understand the history of politics and political leadership of the coalfield without also having a grasp of the role of adult education, which was both an agent, and a site of, political argument and action. (Lewis, 1993) That history, especially so in the case of the inter-war period, has been described in terms of an 'inheritance', and a 'series of legacies' (Lewis, 1986) and it is still sufficiently part of a popular memory that it can be invoked in latter day debates and discussions about policy making in adult education and in areas of wider social policy. (Reynolds and Francis, 1988).

An emphasis on the continuity or tradition of adult education can, however, mask discontinuities, and new developments which have arisen in the context of social, cultural and institutional change since 1945, and since the mid-1980s in particular. In this paper, we discuss a new initiative in university adult education in South Wales, which in one sense might be seen as part of the tradition of adult education in the coalfield, but which at the same

1 For a brief discussion of the film, see Berry (1994), pp 290 - 294.

time represents a sharp break with that tradition. The initiative is the Community University of the Valleys (CUV), which is a programme developed and run by the University of Wales Swansea (UWS), and which is currently based at Banwen, a former mining community in the north-west of the coalfield.

The CUV is a small development if measured in terms of student numbers, but it might be argued that it has a far larger symbolic significance in terms of the changing nature of higher education in the region, and of education being central to economic development strategies. It contains, or is a product of, many of the most significant new developments in UK higher education in recent years: the move towards a mass HE system; the growth of part-time study; the Access movement; and an enhanced role for HE institutions in their local region[2]. As well as outlining the nature of the scheme and its provision, we seek to analyse its development from two key perspectives.

First, we seek to locate the CUV within institutional social and economic contexts in South Wales, and within changes in higher education in the UK more generally. This approach itself involves two levels of analysis. We first follow Scott's argument that recent fundamental changes in higher education, 'must be interpreted in the context of the restless synergy between plural modernisations - of the academy, polity, economy, society and culture' (Scott, 1995: 10). Scott's argument is one made in the context of a wide-ranging discussion and analysis of the HE sector as a whole in the UK. This is the 'macro-context' into which any discussion of the CUV must be placed. But the local and regional particularities of South Wales, in terms of society, economy, polity, and HE must also be interrogated if a full and rounded analysis of an initiative such as the CUV is to be developed. As Martin has recently argued:

> The literature of community education tends to be both ahistorical and partial. Community education is treated as a free floating and timeless concept..... In its relation to education, 'community' should be viewed as an ideological construct which is both historically and contextually specific. 'Community education' therefore only makes sense if it is

2 For analyses of this latter development, see Goddard *et al* (1994), and Elliott *et al* (1996).

located historically and situated in relation to state policy in a systematic and discriminating way. Analysis is therefore directed towards the dynamics of the tensions and contradictions that are generated both between and within policy and practice (Martin, 1996:109; see also Martin, 1993).

This kind of framework of analysis might be termed the 'micro-context', and it is in seeking to fully explore the CUV at this level of analysis that we approach the project from our second key perspective. We report on the early stages of qualitative research which seeks to understand the *student perspective* of the provision, and of its place in regional development more generally. We hope to show that neither perspective alone is sufficient in gaining a rounded understanding of the CUV, and that it is by no means certain that the strategies of institutions and funding agencies (at a national or local level) will be understood in the same terms, or utilised in the manner expected, by those for whom they are designed and put into operation.

The Setting

The CUV offers *community-based* higher education, up to undergraduate level. In its most developed form, it is located at Banwen, a former mining community in the north-west of the South Wales coalfield. The CUV provision is delivered at the local community by the Department of Adult Continuing Education (DACE) of UWS, in partnership with the DOVE Workshop[3], a locally based training organization, and with Onllwyn Community Council[4]. This partnership has been central to the origins and continued development of the project. The CUV is designed to attract adult students who, for whatever reason, would not be able to take up educational opportunities on the main Swansea Campus. It therefore specifically targets those who are unemployed, those who have caring commitments (for older or

3 The acronym stand for 'Dulais Opportunities for Voluntary Enterprise', but the full title is rarely used.
4 A Community Council is the lowest tier of local government in Wales (and is the equivalent of a Parish Council in England).

younger relatives), lone parents, and those who are on low incomes or without transport.

As this is an area in which there has historically been a male-orientated labour market (most obviously in the mining industry), women returners are especially targeted. This is an aspect of the provision which requires very careful strategic planning, and will be influenced by a number of different, at times contradictory, factors. Opportunities for women in an area like Banwen have historically been limited, because of prevailing labour market conditions and cultural patterns. Furthermore, women's employment in Wales as a whole is marked by part-time, often low-skilled, work, and low pay, so education and training opportunities for women are a necessity (Istance and Rees, 1994). But recent research has suggested that in a general Welsh context of high numbers of school leavers with few or no qualifications, particularly in South Wales valley areas (in contradiction to another myth of the Welsh 'educational tradition'), long term unemployed and economically inactive men face especially difficult problems in the labour market (Istance and Rees, 1996). Thus far, the CUV has been very successful in attracting female students, less so in attracting men. It is not our purpose in this paper to offer an explanation for the differential in terms of gender in the take-up of educational opportunities, but we note that research is needed into the reasons for unemployed men appearing to be less likely than women to participate in education and training.

Banwen and its adjacent communities of Dyffryn Cellwen and Onllwyn, are at the head of the Dulais Valley, where anthracite coal was mined, rather than steam coal, as in the central and eastern valleys of the coalfield. The population of the Onllwyn ward (which comprises the three communities) is 1318, and the population of the Dulais Valley as a whole is 5676. Both figures show an overall decline since 1951. In terms of political culture, the area shares with the rest of the former coalfield an overwhelming support for the Labour Party, but in the past there has also been minority support for the Communist Party (Francis and Smith, 1980, Matthews, 1993). It should be noted also that the Welsh language is still widely spoken in the area. The

1991 Census of Population revealed that within the Dulais Valley, 29.5 per cent of the population over three years of age are able to speak Welsh.

The settlement pattern of this part of the coalfield is somewhat different, however, to the more densely populated central valleys, such as the Rhondda, which have become identified nationally and internationally as the quintessential topographical image of South Wales[5]. Banwen, and other anthracite communities, are semi-rural in character, with little of the civic and economic infrastructure which marks out areas like the Rhondda. This has left communities in the area particularly vulnerable in the post-coal era, with little alternative employment opportunities, and poor transport links to nearby urban settlements such as Neath and Swansea. Recent research has revealed that new spatial patterns of inequality which have emerged within South Wales, even within the area of the former coalfield, with communities at the heads of the valleys faring most poorly. Recent inward investment in South Wales has been overwhelmingly concentrated on the southern coastal strip, particularly within the east-west arc from Newport to Bridgend (Morris, 1995, Adamson and Jones, 1996). The declining population figures for the Dulais Valley are indicative of the overall economic and social decline of its communities, and by 1991, Onllwyn was placed twenty-fourth of 908 wards in Wales ranked in order of relative deprivation (Welsh Office 1991)[6].

The rapid social changes in the region are the context in which all adult education providers are having to fundamentally re-assess their provision and curricula (Trotman and Morris, 1996). It was in the specific contexts of the disappearance of the coal industry, following the year-long miners' strike in 1984 - 85, and a recognition that existing provision was inappropriate or inadequate, that DACE, and hence UWS, began to reformulate its relationship with the coalfield. One of the features of the strike was that women were active in support of the miners and their own communities - and at the same time contested some of the pre-existing notions of nature of these

5 For a historical outline of Banwen and the Dulais Valley specifically, see, respectively, Evans (1977), and Sewell (1975), pp 3- 10.

6 The tables are calculated from data on the following: unemployment; low economic activity; low socio-economic groups; population loss; numbers of permanently sick; overcrowding in housing; lack of housing amenities; standard mortality rate.

communities. As Rees has argued, the active participation of women in support of the miners' strike can be explained in part by reference to their growing role in the labour market in the post-1945 period (Rees, 1985).

In the Dulais Valley, the women's Miners' Support Group had continued to exist after the strike, and sought to play a role in the future of the valley. This led to the setting set up of the DOVE Workshop, a small voluntary training organisation for women, which was funded initially by the Urban Aid scheme. After gaining premises for its activities in the form of the Community Centre at Banwen (a former coal board building), DOVE began to seek out educational providers, such as the WEA, Neath College, and DACE, in order to enhance its portfolio of provision[7].

After initially providing short liberal adult education classes and information technology classes (the latter funded by the European Social Fund), DACE set up a community-based Access course[8] at the Banwen Centre in 1989, the first of its kind in Wales. Once the case had been made for community-based Access provision, on the grounds that it targeted students who could not otherwise avail themselves of similar provision on the main Swansea Campus, a key and pressing question was inevitably posed: *access to what?* The barriers which had prevented potential Access students from taking up opportunities on the Swansea Campus would still exist after completing an Access course. The need for continued educational progression routes became clear, and consultation began with existing and former Access students at the Banwen Centre, as part of a one year project funded by the Universities Funding Council (UFC). Local organisations such as the DOVE workshop and Onllwyn Community Council were also involved in this process. The result of the consultation exercise was the identification of a need for a *community-based* undergraduate curriculum. The eventual development of such a curriculum, in the form of the CUV, requires an understanding of the new set of institutional and funding relationships for higher education in Wales and the wider UK, which pertained in the 1990s, together with

7 For discussions of the formation of the DOVE Workshop, see Francis, M, (1988 & 1995).

8 Access courses are those specifically created for adults in order to enable them to gain entry into undergraduate level higher education. They are particularly designed to attract students with few or no previous qualifications.

an understanding of institutional and other *constraints* which were equally influential in shaping the project.

Funding, Governance and Institutions: Opportunities and Constraints

The CUV has in part been the product of a changing system of governance of higher education in Wales, and of a plurality of funding regimes for infrastructural developments. The creation of a separate Higher Education Funding Council for Wales (HEFCW) in 1993 meant that there was a potential degree of flexibility in the funding of higher education in Wales which did not exist previously (though the degree of divergence should not be exaggerated). A concern of HEFCW since its creation, is that continuing education opportunities should be provided in all parts of Wales. This criterion applies to the funding of some continuing education provision, and would appear to mark out the Welsh Funding Council from its counterpart in England. In addition, strategic goals of further and higher education funding in Wales are shaped by, and increasingly linked to, Welsh Office policy on economic development. The fact that an area like the Dulais Valley was an area which was targeted by a number of Welsh office initiatives, most notably the 'Valleys Initiative'[9], launched by the Secretary of State for Wales Peter Walker in 1988, meant that the proposal for the CUV fitted into wider strategies for economic regeneration. The recent Welsh Office document *People and Prosperity* identifies education and training as central in the development of the Welsh economy, and uses a discourse of 'lifelong learning' in this context (Welsh Office 1995) . It would appear that such a discourse, which is now prevalent within UK policy making circles, and is utilised across the political spectrum, is sufficiently broad and flexible to enable an essentially free-market orientated Welsh Office, and a more centrist or left-leaning adult education profession to share objectives in a project

9 The full title of this programme was *The Valleys: A Programme for the People*.

such as the CUV[10]. The proposal was approved by HEFCW on a recurrent funding basis, calculated on an orthodox full-time student equivalent (FTE) basis. The first cohort of students enrolled in October 1993.

The CUV benefited also, however, from the availability of European funding. UWS was successful in bidding for money from the European Regional Development Fund (ERDF), in order to substantially enlarge the Centre at Banwen. Other funds at the 'start-up' stage were forthcoming from Neath Borough Council, British Coal, the Coal Industry Social Welfare Organisation (CISWO), and Onllwyn Community Council. These various funding bodies and agencies, together with the DOVE Workshop and the other educational providers which utilise the Centre at Banwen, might be seen as a coalition of interests which temporarily came together under the overarching theme of economic and social regeneration. Inevitably, there were, and continue to be, differing nuances and emphases within this coalition, not least tensions between community development and individual student achievement, and between those outcomes measured in terms of employment for students, and those measured, more intangibly, in terms of individual and social well-being. There are, of course, occasions when these issues are not in any way oppositional, but there are also occasions when they can appear to be contradictory, and, as is to be expected, the various providers and funders have differing views as to the priorities of this kind of provision, in terms of outcomes. In addition, it cannot be assumed that the students of the CUV will articulate such matters in the same manner, or use the same discourse(s), as we show later.

In the specific case of UWS, the inclusion of an enhanced regional role as part of its developing mission statement, meant that the CUV became both a real and symbolic feature of an institution undergoing real change. The *Strategic Plan* of the institution specifically refers to its regional mission:

> The University has a vital role to play in the economic and social regeneration of its region...We anticipate a growing trend towards students

10 It is interesting to note that the term 'lifelong learning' appears in the *People and Prosperity* document, but did not appear as recently as 1988 in the *The Valleys: A Programme for the People* document. In the latter, the older discourse of 'education and training' was used.

> studying at their home university, some of whom might wish to study whilst working part or full-time... To meet these needs, we have extended the range of our part-time degree provision and a part-time degree in science is being planned to complement, from 1997/98, the successful scheme in humanities. This planned development also builds on the success of the Community university of the Valleys, now broadened in partnership with the Open University and the University of Glamorgan (University of Wales Swansea 1996: 8).

It is vitally important also to note at this point that a development such as the CUV is not the straightforward implementation of a proposal contained in the institution's mission statement. That statement itself is the product of pressures and politics within the institution. Whilst a new emphasis on home-based students and the local and regional role of the University has been a product of government moves towards a mass higher education system in the UK as a whole, the shaping of this policy, and to some extent the speed of its implementation, at a local level, will be a product of the politics and organisational culture of the institution itself. In the case of UWS, DACE has been a key player in developing the CUV and then seeking to broaden the mission statement subsequently. Scott has recently described continuing education departments as having worked within the 'interstices' and 'creative spaces' of their parent institutions, and it would appear that DACE at Swansea fits into this pattern (Scott 1996). In particular, the development of the CUV has been largely an incremental one, in which it has to some extent been a response to events and changed circumstances, as much as it has been a worked out strategy from the start.

The nature of the provision at the CUV is, to some extent, inevitably constrained and influenced by the existing internal organisation and culture of UWS. Providing modules from the part-time degree in Humanities has been relatively straightforward, for example (though certainly not problem-free), as these require little technical support or special equipment, and are relatively low cost; moving the curriculum into applied science as the institution proposes for the main Campus at least, will clearly be a more difficult task.

But if the provision is the product of a plurality of funding sources, of internal institutional politics, and of funding and institutional constraints, its very existence is acting in subtle ways to re-shape the institution as a whole. Formal meetings of the University, library provision, staffing, and indeed the Students' Union, have each been affected by the fact that there is now a not insignificant body of students who are registered members of the University, but who may well never have to visit the main Campus. Most of all, in this context, the creation of partnerships at local level has influenced university policy, and the processes by which policy is made, even if only at the margins.

Students and Provision

Modules from the BA Degree in Humanities (which is offered on the main Swansea Campus) are made available at the CUV at Banwen, and students there have access to library and other facilities on site. It is possible to complete a degree, including the sitting of examinations, within this community setting. In 1996-97, the scheme was in its third year of operation, and there are fifty-five students enrolled on the BA scheme at Banwen, with a further nine enrolled on the one year pre-degree foundation programme. These students are overwhelmingly female, with an average age in the mid-30s. Many are women returners, a number are lone parents, and a number having caring responsibilities for older relatives. Around twenty per cent of the students are working part-time, including six who work in the nearby Lucas SEI electrical components factory (situated in the upper Swansea Valley town of Ystradgynlais), which has been very supportive of those of its employees who have enrolled on the CUV. The students come overwhelmingly from the Dulais Valley, the upper Swansea Valley, and the Neath Valley, although the day-time provision and crèche has attracted some students from as far afield as the outskirts of Swansea. There is a small number of retired students, but most have enrolled on the scheme with the specific aim of improving their employment prospects, though there are few illusions about local job opportunities in the short-to-medium term. It is interesting to note, in the context of recent debates in the field of continuing education in the UK about the desirability of accreditation of provision, that the CUV has been successful in attracting students who are active (or potentially active) in the labour market, and who have enrolled for an undergraduate programme, with all the commitments, in terms of time and intellectual effort, which that involves.

Teaching on the undergraduate and foundation programmes takes place during the day on weekdays, and the timetable is organised around school times. There is always a half term, in line with local school half terms, in order that parents (and particularly lone parents) are not deterred from enrolling and attending. Modules on the BA programme often include an additional day school, which is usually on a special theme, and can involve guest tutors from other higher education institutions. These day schools are held on a Saturday, and are always open to the wider general public, and advertised locally. This aspect of the provision is intended to increase local 'ownership' of the CUV as a whole, and, of course, serves to create a potential starting point in an educational progression route.

A number of UWS staff are permanently or partly located at the Banwen Centre. These include a Tutor in Community Education, the Co-ordinator of the CUV scheme, a secretarial assistant, and a library assistant. The holders of the two latter posts are themselves products of short courses held at the Banwen Centre. At present, teaching on the CUV is undertaken on a 'face-to-face' basis, but plans are in place to develop a plurality of modes of provision, by the utilisation of video-conferencing and other distance learning technologies. This will create opportunities to widen the curriculum.

It is often the undergraduate level provision at the CUV which has aroused most interest from others working in the field of continuing education, as it is this, perhaps, that is the most innovative feature of the scheme in terms of actual course delivery. But the plurality of levels of provision, which is designed to create in turn a plurality of potential progression routes, plus the fact that UWS is not the only provider at the Banwen Centre, are also vitally important parts of the scheme. The range of provision offered by DACE at the Banwen Centre includes; short accredited and non-accredited courses in a variety of subjects and from art to information technology. In addition, an innovative Return to Learn class has been developed which runs all year round, which students can attend on a 'drop-in' basis. Whilst students can gain direct entry to the BA scheme of the CUV, these different levels of potential starting points have been very important. In addition to those who have opted for the direct entry route, the undergraduate modules have also attracted students who first came to the Centre to follow non-accredited art or language classes, and IT courses.

Given that the CUV provision is targeted, student support mechanisms are vital. Educational guidance is embedded in the provision, and a DACE Guidance Worker is present at Banwen one day per week, and at other times by appointment. In addition, one of the DOVE employees is also a qualified educational guidance worker. UWS counselling and careers services are also made available to CUV students by appointment. Students enrolled on the undergraduate scheme attend study skills sessions, which are designed to assist with the processes of studying. A bursary system is in operation, which gives students on the BA scheme the opportunity to apply for some remission of course fees (in 1996, the fee levels were £140 per module). At least as important in terms of student support, however, is that free crèche facilities are made available to CUV students. The crèche is run by qualified staff of the DOVE Workshop, and has proved to be a vital resource for students.

Working in partnership

It could be argued that the nature of the provision at the CUV is innovative, given that the BA scheme is offered in a community setting, but the nature of the local partnerships is equally, perhaps more, innovative, and it is the nature of these partnerships which mark out the CUV from the work of UWS in the coalfield in the past. As noted above, the recent work of UWS at Banwen arose in the specific context of the aftermath of the 1984-85

Miners' Strike, and the creation of the DOVE Workshop out of the local Women's Support Group for the miners and mining communities. Set up in order to provide training opportunities for women, the DOVE Workshop also works with the local branch of the Workers' Educational Association, and with Neath College (the local further education College) in creating a varied portfolio of education and training opportunities. In 1995-96 (the most recent figures available), there were over 200 students per week using the Centre for educational purposes. The Centre is also the local community centre, and is owned by the local Onllwyn Community Council. UWS, through DACE, works with both these organisations in seeking to widen educational opportunities locally. A Community Development Strategy Group consisting of representatives of the various providers and agencies which use the Centre, meets once per term in order to plan future provision, and to respond to student or public demand for courses.

The Banwen provision is not the only form of community-based education provided by UWS. In addition, again through DACE, UWS provides community-based provision elsewhere in south-west Wales at Foundation level, and a wide range of short courses, of both an accredited and non-accredited nature, in many centres in the region. Here, too, partnership with community-based groups is a key component of the work. It is anticipated that in time, modules of the BA programme will be offered in the other locations which are currently running the foundation programme.

The focus in this section of the paper has been on the development of the CUV, partnerships with local organisations, and current provision at *Banwen*, but it should be noted that the CUV has a wider meaning other than community-based HE at any one physical location. In terms of strategy for UWS, it also serves as a *metaphor* for a rolling strategy of building community-based educational provision throughout the South Wales coalfield, in collaboration with other educational providers and locally based groups.[11] Other HE institutions involved in the CUV include the Open University in Wales and the University of Glamorgan, and, UWS works with other pro-

11 For a discussion of community provision elsewhere to which DACE has contributed, see S. Reynolds (1995).

viders in the wider region, through the Valleys Initiative for Adult Education (VIAE), a 'network of statutory and voluntary organisations concerned with the role of Adult Education in the survival and development of valley communities' (VIAE 1990: 2). The membership of VIAE includes Local Educational Authorities, the University continuing education departments of UWS and University of Wales Cardiff, the WEA, and community-based and national voluntary organisations. In the future, UWS and its partners seek to provide a plurality of locally based educational opportunities available for adults in the coalfield, delivered in a variety of ways, by a network of educational providers, rather than single institutions.

Thus far, we have attempted to both describe the development and practice of the CUV initiative in South Wales, and to place it within an analytical framework which takes into account the economic and social changes within the region, the changes within higher education in Wales and the UK, and the institutional opportunities and constraints which pertain at UWS. We turn now, however, to the student perception and experience of the CUV, and we report on the early stages of qualitative research on the student body. Regional Development policies, and the more specific educational programmes which are a part of such policies (whether framed in a discourse of 'lifelong learning', 'skill enhancement', 'community development' or otherwise) are ultimately created for the people of the region in question, as individuals and as social groups. In the same way that an initiative such as the CUV can be both a product and a shaper of its parent institution, it would appear to be the case that students will shape, as well as be shaped by, any educational or wider regional development scheme in which they are participants.

The Qualitative Research

The CUV is a radical initiative in educational terms, but is perhaps even more so in social terms (in as far as these can be separated). The no entry-qualification which pertains at the CUV is not new - it has been established in the Open University in the UK for more than twenty-five years, but the coming together of industry, educational institutions, local and national government, and what we might term the European State in its establishment contains elements of social engineering, and it forms a part of a wider set of social and regional development policies for South Wales. The impact of low-cost, no entry qualification degree study within a valley community and culture may have unforeseen social and economic outcomes which may in turn affect the shape and self-image of individuals, families and ultimately the wider community.

Adult educators in Britain (and doubtless elsewhere) are well aware of anecdotal accounts of the impact on individuals and their families of such changes, but this is now being supported by a growing body of research (Aslanian and Bricknell, 1980, Barnett, 1996, Blair, McPake and Munn, 1995, Blaxter and Tight, 1993, 1994, 1995; Britton and Baxter, 1994, Cox and Pascall, 1994, Edwards, 1990, Haselgrove, et al 1995, McGivney, 1990, 1996; Munn and MacDonald, 1988; Sargant, 1991, Wakeford, 1994, West, 1995, 1996). The aim of the qualitative research reported on in this paper is to undertake a tracking study of a cohort group of students for each of the first three year groups of the CUV and to follow them through to graduation or cessation of studies. The fieldwork commenced in the academic year 1995-96, when the original student cohort were in Year Three of an anticipated six year part time degree programme, commencing Part Two of their degrees.

The research comprises five broad strands:

- to develop a framework of best practice concerning selection and guidance procedures;
- to examine students' motivation for entering and continuing to participate in the degree programme and to establish if such motivation changes in any significant way over time;
- to relate students' perceived aspirations to their economic, social and educational backgrounds and to assess the nature of these aspirations;

- to assess the CUV and University of Wales response to the students' aspirations;
- to record any major life changes which students may experience during their period of study, which they perceive as being related to their joining the CUV.

It is hoped to continue this work as a longitudinal study, following the first three graduate groups beyond the Community University experience, to observe subsequent life changes attributable to their learning experience.

However, this paper seeks to focus on the experiences of students so far, their attitudes towards education in general, and towards the CUV and higher education in particular. It will also examine the students' perception of the notion of community and regional development and their place within it. Discussion will be offered on the apparent disjunctures, where they occur, between student views on and experiences of policy issues, and the institutional perspective on such issues.

The entire student body of the three year groups within the study consists of 55 students. A new entry has been added for the year 1996-97, but this and subsequent year groups fall outside the remit of this paper. Women considerably outnumber men on the programme 44:11. After much consideration and discussion it was decided that it was not feasible to obtain a so-called 'representative' sample of this student group. The total numbers are relatively small and, superficially at least, there are striking similarities among them in terms of culture, social background and age ranges. However, there is a noticeable lack of male students in the CUV, so from the outset efforts were made to draw as many men into the study as was possible. Similarly, there are few students at the younger end of the age range. The 1995-96 intake attracted more younger students than either of the previous years, and again, attempts were made to include them. Participation of the others was almost random, but because of the apparent evenness of the student group, it was decided that this was not a weakness in the study.

The research has involved wide-ranging questionnaire and interview surveys on a cohort of twelve students from each of the three year groups. Each interview is scheduled to last approximately one hour. Questions are designed to elicit responses within the five strands of the research, but the interviews are conducted to allow and encourage students to talk about themselves and their lives without the constraints of category headings.

For the purposes of this paper, the tapes and transcripts of the interviews have been analysed to assess students experiences of education before embarking on the part time degree; their experiences of higher education within the CUV and the impact these experiences have had on themselves and their families; their views of their own place within regional development policies. It should be stressed that the research is still in its early stages, so although the first interviews have been used by some students as an opportunity to reflect widely on their lives prior to higher education, for many it has been their first time considering these matters within an analytical framework of the kind drawn up for the research under discussion.

The Region

The South Wales Valleys have constituted a region of enormous demographic and cultural change in the past hundred and fifty years. The years of industrialisation and in-migration from the mid-nineteenth to the first two decades of the twentieth century have been described as a 'klondyke' and a 'frontier region' (Williams, 1985). The society and culture which grew out of that process was described in 1921 as 'American Wales' (Zimmern, 1921), an image which has been utilised more recently by historians of region to explain and characterise the historical experience of the people of South Wales (Smith, 1993, Williams, 1995). But amidst the turbulence of massive in-migration, and, later, out-migration, and of economic boom and deep recession, an identity and culture has been produced and shaped which has held the notion of place, community and region at its centre. As Smith has pointed out, 'the valleys' is a 'mindscape' as much as it is a landscape; it is a term which 'floats free from its moorings' (Smith, 1993:92). Similarly, the idea of *community*, often encompassing tradition and continuity, though in fact never static, has been an especially strong one in the South Wales coalfield, which has been produced and reproduced as a consequence, in part, of rapid change. It is also a cultural construct which has been deeply enmeshed with notions of social class, and one which has been utilised as a rallying point in times of crisis, such as the 1984 - 85 Miners' Strike (Williams,. 1985, Gilbert, 1992, Roberts, 1995).

One of the most recent pieces of research on the region investigates the effects of very recent economic change on the patterns of social organisation, leisure and consumption in the Valleys (Adamson and Jones, 1996). The research identifies key changes within the economy and class structure of Valleys society, characterised by where people live and which result in the emergence of economically and culturally diverging communities. The working class in the Valleys can now be characterised as comprising three distinct groups, which are largely marked off from each other both in spatial terms, and in terms of patterns of income and consumption: first, the *traditional working class communities* which reside in the terraced housing of the valley floor, and which still retain many of the traditional values of the coal communities; secondly are the n*ew working class communities* which will typically reside in the new private housing developments which are often located very close to the old council housing estates; thirdly the *marginalised working class communities* (as Adamson and Jones describe them) which in the Valleys are located in housing (largely council estates) on hilltops away from the valley floor. Of course, these categories are not intended to be overly prescriptive, and it is possible to place individuals in more than one of these categories.

In attempting to define the social class of the respondents in the present research (on the CUV), if their current level of educational attainment alone is used for this purpose, following Gardiner (1986), then overwhelmingly, as undergraduates, they are now middle class. However, this is clearly inadequate, given the background and place of residence of the students, and if the definition is arrived at by the more traditional means of occupation and father's occupation, then of the thirty-six students in the study, almost all would be described as working class. Certainly almost all have working class backgrounds, and most regard themselves as remaining within that socio-economic and cultural group at the present time.

If measured by place of residence, then the students in the study reflect the spatial patterns identified by Adamson and Jones. Twenty students belong to the first group, that is, the 'traditional' working class; six to the second group of the 'new' working class; four to the third group of 'marginalised'. The other students either live outside of the Valleys in Swansea, or do not fit the working class definition. Caution must be exercised here, however, as the research of Adamson and Jones was conducted in the densely populated Rhondda and Cynon Valleys, which, as we noted earlier, have a different settlement pattern to the Dulais Valley and other parts of the anthracite coalfield.

Students' views of education

In examining the students' views and experiences of education prior to enrolling with the CUV, few of them had mainly negative experiences of school. Of the older students most had either been to grammar school or had at least gained a place there which they had subsequently not taken.[12] However, none of this group had gained qualifications at grammar school, most of them having left school at the age of fifteen or sixteen. There was a strong sense among this group of 'not fitting in', as Diane explained:

> I always handed my homework in...always participated in school... I just came of age at the wrong time ...Her father - he's a teacher... hers's a vicar ... hers's a doctor ...

Because going to grammar school had separated her from most of the children from her own village, as an adult Diane now finds that there are only two to three other adults in the community who went to school with her, and

12 Grammar schools were part of the former UK system of educational selection by examination at the age of eleven. Children who passed the 'Eleven Plus' examination gained a place in grammar school, while the others were given different choices, which were widely perceived as inferior.

these are 'other drop-outs'. Diane seems to feel a sense of loss, even in her forties over this.

In a few cases, as with Angela, individuals were not allowed to take up a grammar school place:

> I loved school .... devoured the library .... excelled at school ... always winning prizes ... little holy pictures, and sixpences, ... And then I passed my eleven plus and, as I said, we were a big family ... and my mother had had another baby ..and she needed help at home. That was basically it.

Angela left school at fifteen, went to work in a factory and started her part time degree in her fifties.

Of the students who had attended comprehensive schools, comments like 'they told me I was too thick' were common. Paradoxically, as Blaxter and Tight have remarked with regard to their own research with mature students, very few students seemed to feel that they had lost out or been let down in any way by school (Blaxter and Tight, 1993). In the case of the CUV respondents, Mary's comments are fairly typical:

> I can't say I was unhappy with the *school* as such, I was just unhappy with school full stop ... didn't see the point in it...

After leaving school, one third of the study had undertaken further education (including Access courses), including some to the minimum higher education entry level. In one case (Kay) the student had experienced adult education from both sides, as she had been a vocational teacher in the WRENS (the women's naval service in the UK).

Few of the students had been consciously preparing themselves for higher education, however. Angela is fairly typical here. She had undertaken an A Level each year at the local tertiary college, and only considered the part time degree after being coaxed by her tutor there. 'I couldn't do that' had been her first - and second - reaction.

Students' views of the CUV and higher education

There was widespread surprise among the students over how much 'easier' than expected the academic work is. Given that some of them were already at HE entry level their ability to cope with academic work shouldn't really be surprising, yet many of them continue to express this view.

Overwhelmingly, the success of the CUV is described by all but one of the students as being due to the following: its small scale size; the approach and approachability of the academic staff; the supportiveness of the students themselves towards each other; the relaxed atmosphere; the study skills support; student services support; flexibility of all staff; the use of a shared kitchen.

A typical comment from Norma, a mother of six, in her forties, who relies on the availability of the crèche: 'If I can do it anywhere, I'll do it here...'. Harriet, in her mid thirties, commented, 'Now I feel like a grown up....'. John, a retired police officer, appreciates the non-competitive nature of study compared with staff development within the police force:

> There's a bit of coaxing from fellow-students ... a bit of pull here and a push there, you know the way ... and we, we've come through it.

Dennis developed this line further:

> You kept thinking, you know, well where's the catch? I'm expecting to be treated like a school-kid and I'm not. I'm being treated like an adult and I thought ... this is strange...

Although this is an overwhelming view, the valuing of the small-scale of the CUV was not unanimous. Two students (both of them men, including Dennis) moved to the CUV partner institution, the Open University, in order to take advantage of the wider range of course options.

Dennis was also very critical of the extent of student support offered at the CUV, arguing that there was over-provision in this area:

> As the Good Book says, 'Let the dead bury the dead' ...you know...? Let the students sort out students' problems, yeah?

However, this view has been countered by *all* of the others. John suffered a serious illness shortly after completing Part One of his studies:

> I was in Intensive Care. Their phone went day and night from students ... from staff ... from everybody ... it was wonderful.

Harriet had a series of traumas immediately before starting; a car crash, a burglary, plus some personal problems:

> -----was marvellous, sending me copies of everything. They have been very supportive.

One student was sharply critical of the CUV. He argued that the scheme was too small, the library was inadequate, there was too much work, and that the scheme as a whole should have been located in the centre of Swansea. This student left the CUV half-way through the first term of Year III. However, within a matter of weeks he had returned, deferring one of his two course modules, still complaining about the location, but back on board.

It has been mentioned that two students have left the CUV, possibly temporarily, to study with the OU (students are able to do this as there is facility for credit transfer between UWS, the Open University, and the University of Glamorgan). On being questioned about their preference of locations, very few expressed a wish to move from the CUV. Two of the younger students - one male and one female, expressed an intention to move. The male wants to study on the main campus in order to complete his degree more quickly and to benefit from a wider choice of options there. Additionally, though, he wishes to enjoy the full-time student experience. The female hopes to transfer to another institution offering different provision for the same reasons. Some of the younger women, and one in her forties, would like to be able to transfer to the main Swansea Campus, but only, they explain, to study full-time in order to obtain their degree more quickly. Two other women in their forties, both from Swansea, would also like to transfer to Swansea to study full time, and admit to a sense of 'losing out' on the campus experience. The remainder wish to remain in Banwen. Although in terms of barriers the circumstances of some of this group have changed sufficiently to allow them to continue full-time at Swansea, they reject this option. In fact, some of them seemed quite alarmed by the question. From a staff and institutional perspective this is an interesting, and to some extent, unforeseen, development. One of the stated aims of the process from the outset was individual empowerment, and it was anticipated that some of the CUV students would wish to transfer to the Campus. Their refusal to consider this was seen in the main by staff as a negative outcome. Discussion with staff elicited views ranging from lack of confidence, to evidence of a 'dependency culture'.

While universities have always known 'mature' students, and over the last 10-15 years, have had to make considerable adjustments and concessions to the needs of this student group, the picture that emerges of those studying with the CUV is one of a very different and distinct group. They are also quite different from the Swansea Campus based part-time degree students.

When questioned, all but one of the students stated that they would not have embarked on higher education at the time they did, had not the CUV been available. Additionally, most of them believe that they would *never* have taken the step. It is possible therefore, perhaps probable, that these are students we would never have seen in higher education at all; only the fact that they can study in a community environment makes participation possible at all. This would appear to demonstrate clearly that the CUV is successful in attaining one of its main objectives.

Individual and Community

Within the UK, there has been a rich body of theory and practice in adult education which has sought to target the disadvantaged, or the working class (or whatever form of words is chosen), and which has sought also to empower *communities*, as well as individuals (for example, Jackson, 1976,

Lovett, 1988, Northmore, 1986). However, other community educators have questioned this view and assert that such provision also needs to be able to offer participants 'accessible routes out of the community' (Gardiner, 1986).

Even when such accessible routes out of the community have not been designed with the provision, students have in practice tended to find them for themselves, posing 'empowerment of the community' educators with the dilemma of having created elites. Individuals who rise out of their social class and who move out of their communities have been familiar to adult educators in a whole range of educational provision - from trade union studies to present-day accredited adult education.

In theory, the CUV students may be different. It is possible that by creating and nurturing a 'student-type' which wants (or has little option but) to remain within her or his own community *throughout their higher education*, the scheme may unwittingly or even unwantingly succeed in keeping them there afterwards.

On this particular issue, the vast majority of the CUV respondents, especially those who live in the Valleys, express no interest in leaving their area, either to follow their higher education or a subsequent career. There are a number of factors at work here, such as family commitments and employment, as well as the straightforward desire to remain within a familiar community. We should note also that students future plans may change during the course of their studies. However, if these generations of graduates do remain largely within the community, their own education and social development will inevitably become embedded in the community itself, with all the concomitant advantages to that community. If this does turn out to be the case, then the CUV could have a profound impact on the social and regional development of the area, though the exact nature of the relationship between qualified members of a local labour market, and increased economic investment, particularly in causal terms, is very hard to predict. We should note also that due in the main to some of the institutional constraints mentioned earlier in this paper, the CUV students will graduate in the first instance with a qualification (BA in Humanities) which is not of an explicitly vocational nature, although a number of students (albeit at a relatively early stage) have expressed an interest in undertaking some kind of short vocational course once they have graduated (such as a post-graduate teaching qualification).

Social and Regional Development

As already indicated, all of the students are aware of the immediate impact of the CUV on their own personal development. It is perhaps not surprising, then, that almost all are able to identify some kind of wider social development accruing from the scheme. But thus far, the majority is unable to discern evidence of regional economic development, or to locate the scheme (or indeed themselves) within such development. The fact that they associate regional development with evidence of increasing economic growth largely colours this view.

In terms of social development associated with the CUV, almost all the students have a very positive view, from John's brimming, all-embracing enthusiasm:

> It's a standing joke in the car between my wife and I (travelling to Abergavenny), 'Oh look, it's the Centre of Excellence! It's Onllwyn! It's Dyffryn Cellwen! What's Oxford or Cambridge got on it?

to Ruth's more gender-specific comments:

> Lots of women other than ...sort of *students* use the place... Whereas the old miners used to have the old Welfare Library to go to ... at least now ... and it is for women really, it's not *for* men, even though men go there ... They've got a place of their own where they can learn new skills. So, yeah, I think it's done good.

Ruth's remarks are particularly interesting. They utilise one of the most prominent images of the pre-war tradition of adult education in the valleys (the Miners' Institute Library), in order to show how things have changed. They also lay bare the changed gender relations within South Wales - and

Valleys - society. But in addition, whilst they point to the fact that the DOVE Workshop was, and remains, a women's initiative, they also articulate what appears to be a relatively common misconception that the CUV provision is predominantly for women. This is a misconception which is of concern to some CUV staff.

For other students, though, perceptions of social development are elusive:

> Hm...I think most people are aware of it and ...I'm not sure what they think about it to be honest (Beverley).

Although some see longer term outcomes, none see any direct relevance so far to regional economic development. Diane's view is typical:

> ...Well, it hasn't brought any jobs, has it? Oh wait...let's see [counts imaginary heads] ...one...two...three...well maybe a few...

Perhaps we should not be so surprised by this, as the question of a regional development role for the CUV, as we explained in the earlier section of this paper, has in one sense only arisen incrementally. It has been the product of changing institutional structures and funding regimes, and of the 'politics' of UWS, in which the continuing education department has worked creatively in the 'interstices' of its parent body. But it is in part also the product of the community itself, again in a very incremental manner, arising as it did from partnerships and alliances with the locally based DOVE Workshop.

The incremental nature of its development, its local rootedness, and at least its potential in wider social and economic developments, was articulated by one of the respondents:

> It's a vehicle. It's up to the individuals to use it - no ifs and buts about that. I feel that it's ...er...something which the community can and will be proud of. The fact that ordinary folk can go there, pursue what they want to pursue ... achieve a standard which they want to achieve ... And it's come from - let's face it, it's come from a building which was dilapidated... and a group of women saying 'Hell we got to do *something*! The pit ... has gone' And from that ... a University has come

> which reflects the community. I mean, yeah ... people *will* knock it, especially in its formative years, but once the results start coming ... It's burning through, and as each year goes by it ... the light will get a little stronger.

This, though, is not a typical view. The majority of respondents were focused on their own individual prospects and possible opportunities. It does not follow that this entails a negation of the very strong sense of community in the area, one which remains strong in spite of (or perhaps because of) very rapid change. Rather it is possible that the very security of the respondents' sense of community and their place within it, means that these are 'worn' unselfconsciously, so that it will inevitably be the individual which is the focus of attention. This, however, will be explored further as the qualitative research progresses. Some of the other research of this kind cited earlier, reveals shifts in identity for mature students, particularly those from working class backgrounds. As this research progresses, it is intended that these issues will be further addressed, if and when they arise.

This paper must remain tentative in its conclusions, as the qualitative research on the students of the CUV is in its very early stages. But, in addition to reporting what we believe are interesting findings from this research, we have attempted to show that a complete analysis and rounded view of a project such as the CUV requires not only an analysis of its origins in an institutional and economic and social context, but also an exploration of student perceptions of the scheme. It is our contention that a reciprocity exists between the two sides of this equation. The nature of the scheme (and indeed the constraints which have given it shape) will, by definition, channel students into certain pre-determined directions, but the students will also influence the future shape of the scheme. And as for the wider issues of social and regional development, in time, these can be measured (to some extent) using employment data and other economic indicators. But here too, the reciprocity already mentioned must be a factor: those involved in educational provision are social actors, rather than mere passive recipients.

References

Adamson, D. and Jones, S. (1996), The South Wales Valleys: Continuity and Change Occasional Papers in the Regional Research Programme: Paper 1, Glamorgan, University of Glamorgan.

Aslanian, C. B. and Bricknell, H.M. (1980), Americans in Transition: LifeChanges as Reasons for Adults Learning New York, College Entrance Examination Board.

Barnett, R. (1996), 'Being and becoming: a student trajectory', International Journal of Lifelong Education, Vol 15, No 2.

Blair, A., McPake, J. and Munn, P. (1995), 'A New Conceptualisation of Adult Participation in Education', British Educational Research Journal, Vol 21, No 5.

Berry, D. (1994), Wales and Cinema: the First Hundred Years, Swansea, University of Wales Press.

Blaxter, L. and Tight, M. (1993), 'Rolling with the flow: the prior educational paths of part-time degree students', Journal of Access Studies, Vol 8.

Blaxter, L. and Tight, M. (1994), 'Juggling with Time: How Adults Manage their Time for Lifelong Learning', Studies in the Education of Adults, Vol 26, No 2.

Blaxter, L. and Tight, M. (1995), 'Life transitions and educational participation by adults' International Journal of Lifelong Education, Vol 14, No 3.

Britton, C. and Baxter, A. (1994), 'Mature Students' Routes into Higher Education' Journal of Access Studies, Vol 9.

Cooke, P. and Rees, G. (1981), The Industrial Restructuring of South Wales: the Career of a State Managed Region, Swansea, University of Wales Institute of Science and Technology Papers in Planning Research, No 25.

Cox, R. and Pascall, G. (1994), 'Individualism, self-evaluation and self-fulfilment in the experience of mature women students', International Journal of Lifelong Education Vol 13, No 2.

Edwards, R. (1990), 'Access and assets: the experiences of mature mother-students in higher education', Journal of Access Studies.

Evans, C. (1977), Blaencwmdulais: A Short History of the Social and Industrial Development of Onllwyn and Banwen-Pyrddin, CFP.

Francis, H. (1976), 'The Origins of the South Wales Miners' Library', History Workshop Journal, 2.

Francis, H. and Humphreys, R. (1996), 'Communities, Valleys and Universities' in Elliott et al (eds) Communities and Their Universities: The Challenge of Lifelong Learning, London, Lawrence & Wishart, pp 230-249.

Francis, H. and Smith, D. (1980), The Fed: A History of the South Wales Miners in the Twentieth Century, London, Lawrence & Wishart.

Francis, M. (1988), 'Dulais Opportunities for Voluntary Enterprise', in Reynolds, S. and Francis, H. (eds) Learning From Experience: The Future of Adult Education in the Valleys, VIAE.

Francis, M. (1995), Women and the Aftermath of the 1984-85 Miners' Strike: A South Wales Analysis, unpublished Msc Thesis, University of Wales Swansea.

Gardiner, J. R. (1986), 'Working with Women', in Ward, K. and Taylor, R. (eds) Adult Education and the Working Class: Education for the missing millions, London, Croom Helm.

Gilbert, D. (1992), Class, Community and Collective Action: Social Change in Two British Coalfields, 1850 - 1926, London, Clarendon Press.

Goddard, J., et al, (1994), Universities and their Communities, CVCP.

Haselgrove, S. (1995), The Student Experience, Buckingham, Society for Research into Higher Education/Open University Press.

Istance, D. and Rees, T. (1994), Woman in Post-compulsory Education and Training in Wales, Equal Opportunities Commission.

Istance, D. and Rees, G. (1996), Lifelong Learning in Wales: A Programme for Prosperity, Leicester, NIACE.

Jackson, J. (1976) The Strome & Maukinhall Informal Education Project - a Greenock Experiment, Scottish Journal of Education.

Lewis, R. (1986), 'The Inheritance: Adult Education in the Valleys between the wars', in Francis, H., (ed), Adult Education in the Valleys: the Last Fifty Years, Llafur.

Lewis, R. (1993), Leaders and Teachers: Adult Education and the Challenge of Labour in South Wales 1906 - 1940, Swansea, University of Wales Press.

Lovett, T. (1988), 'Introduction' in Lovett, T. (ed) Radical Approaches to Adult Education: A Reader, London, Routledge.

McGivney, V. (1990), Education's for other People: Access to Education for Non-Participant Adults, Leicester, National Institute of Adult Continuing Education.

McGivney, V. (1996), 'Staying or Leaving the Course: Non-Completion and Retention', Adults Learning, Vol 7, No.6.

Martin, I. (1993), 'Community education: towards a theoretical analysis', in Edwards, R., Sieminski, S. and Zeldin, D., (eds), Adult Learners, Education and Training, London, Routledge, pp 189 - 204.

Martin, I. (1996), 'Community education: The Dialectics of Development', in Fieldhouse, R. and Associates, A. History of Modern British Adult Education, Leicester, NIACE, pp 109 - 141.

Matthews, I. (1993), 'Maes y Glo Carreg ac Undeb y Glowyr, 1872 - 1925', yn G.H. Jenkins (gol), Cof Cenedl VIII, Gomer, pp 133 - 164.

Morgan, K. O. (1996), 'Y Brifysgol a'r Werin: the People's University', in J. Elliott et al (eds) Communities and their Universities: the Challenge of Lifelong Learning, London, Lawrence and Wishart.

Morris, J. (1995), 'McJobbing a Region: Industrial Restructuring and the Widening Socio-economic Divide in Wales', in Turner, R., (ed), The British Economy in Transition: From the Old to the New? London, Routledge, pp 44 - 66.

Morton, H. V. (1932), In Search of Wales, London, Methuen.

Munn, P. and MacDonald, D. C. (1988), Adult Participation in Education and Training Scottish Council for Research in Education.

Northmore, S. (1986), 'A Community Development Model of Adult Education', Community Development Journal, Vol 21.

Rees, G. (1985), 'Regional Restructuring, Class Change and Political Action: Preliminary Comments on the 1984 - 1985 Miners' Strike in South Wales' Society and Space, 3.

Rees, G. (1989, 'The State and the Transformation of a Region: Thatcherism in South Wales', in Alheit, P. and Francis, H., (eds), Adult Education in Changing Industrial Regions, Verlag Arbeiterbewegung und Gesellschaftswissenschaft.

Reynolds, S. (1995), 'Amman Valley Enterprise: a Case Study of Adult Education and Community Revival', in Mayo, M. and Thompson, J., (eds), Adult Learning, Critical Intelligence and Social Change, Leicester, NIACE.

Reynolds, S. and Francis, H., (eds), (1988), Learning From Experience: the Future of Adult Education in the Valleys, VIAE.

Roberts, B. (1995),'Welsh Identity in a Former Mining Valley: Social Images and Imagined Communities', in Day, G. and Thomas, D., (eds), Contemporary Wales, Volume 7, Swansea, University of Wales Press.

Rutherford, T. (1991), 'Industrial Restructuring, Local Labour Markets and Social Change: the Transformation of South Wales, in Rees, G. and Day, G., (eds), Contemporary Wales 4, Swansea, University of Wales Press.

Sargant, N. (1991), Learning and 'Leisure': A Study of Adult Participation in Learning and its Policy Implications, Leicester, National Institute of Adult and Continuing Education.

Scott, P. (1995), The Meanings of Mass Higher Education, Buckingham, Open University Press.

Scott, P. (1996), 'The Future of Continuing Education', paper presented to the UACE Annual Conference, Leeds, March.

Seaman, A. (1921), My Impressions of South Wales, London, Mills and Boon.

Sewell, J. (1975), Colliery Closure and Social Change, Swansea, University of Wales Press.

Smith, D. (1993), Aneurin Bevan and the World of South Wales, Swansea,University of Wales Press.

Trotman, C. and Morris, S. (1996), Communities in Transition: The Role of Adult Continuing Education, DACE Resaerch Papers in Continuing Education, Swansea, University of Wales.

University of Wales Swansea, (1996), Strategic Plan, University of Wales Swansea.

Welsh Office, (1991), Index of Socio-Economic Conditions.

Welsh Office, (1995), People and Prosperity: An Agenda for Action in Wales.

Wakeford, N. (1994), 'Becoming a mature student: the social risks of identification', Journal of Access Studies, Vol 9

Ward, K. (1996), 'Community Regeneration and Social Exclusion: Some Current Policy Issues for Higher Education' in Elliott, J., et al, (eds), Communities and their Universities: The Challenge of Lifelong Learning, ,London, Lawrence & Wishart, pp 204-215.

West, L. (1995) 'Beyond Fragments: Adults, Motivation and Higher Education', Studies in the Education of Adults, Vol 27, No 2.

West, L. (1996), Beyond Fragments. Adults, Motivation and Higher Education: A Biographical Analysis, London, Taylor & Francis.

William's, C. (1996), 'Searching for a New South Wales', History Workshop Journal

William's, G. A. (1985), When Was Wales?, Harmondsworth, Penguin.

William's, R. (1985), 'Mining the Meaning: Key Words in the Miners' Strike', New Socialist 25, March.

Jens-Jörgen Pedersen

EU Job Rotation: One means to a lot of ends!

'Nothing is as powerful as an idea whose time has come'

In the beginning of 1995 EU Job Rotation was created by 7 Danish WEA divisions. They had had experiences with job rotation in Denmark since the birth of job rotation around 1990 and they were some of the first organisations to try out the concept. The time had come to see whether or not the idea could catch on internationally.

After six months all reservations were gone and it was obvious to everyone that job rotation was an interesting tool in Labour Market Policy all over Europe.

The background for the popularity was the widespread need for an integrated strategy which dealt with both growth and employment. So far the two elements have primarily been seen as two isolated problems and unfortunately not integrated in a single strategy as it is proposed in the job rotation model.

Unemployment

The battle against unemployment has for a long time been one of the greatest social challenges of our time. In spite of relatively comprehensive efforts in the battle against unemployment there are still large numbers of people trapped in an unemployment spiral which will, as time passes, alienate them more and more from the labour market. There is a need for new initiatives which will ensure a higher employment rate and a gradual absorption into the labour market. There must be an active use of the idle hands, not just as a social necessity but as a labour market political prerequisite for keeping up with the economic growth.

Economic growth and the technological development

We are in a situation and an epoch where lifelong education and training is a necessity and an accepted prerequisite for the future development of human resources and thereby the growth and competitiveness of Europe. Further training is not only relevant for people who have had little vocational training but it is even seen today as part of the strategic planning of a number of leading European industries.

The gloomy future

The European future does not look too bright within the next 10 years if no action is taken. The population in Europe is getting older, which means that an ageing labour market is a European reality within a few years. In the year 2005 the number of young people (under 30 years) will have dropped by 17%, at the same time there will be 7% more of the 30-50 year olds and 12% more of the 50-60 year olds.

Conclusion: a very pronounced movement in the pyramid of ages.

The participation rate has in the same period increased from 69% to 74%. If the number of workplaces are the same as today, the total unemployment will in the same period increase from 17 to 34 millions.

Presently the content of work is changing very rapidly with an increasing content of knowledge in the production. The new technologies generally are expanding rapidly.

Year 2005:

- 80% of the technology is less than 10 years old, that is unknown today.
- 80% of the workforce will have an education that is more than 10 years old

Conclusion: a lot of new technology and a lot of out of date knowledge.

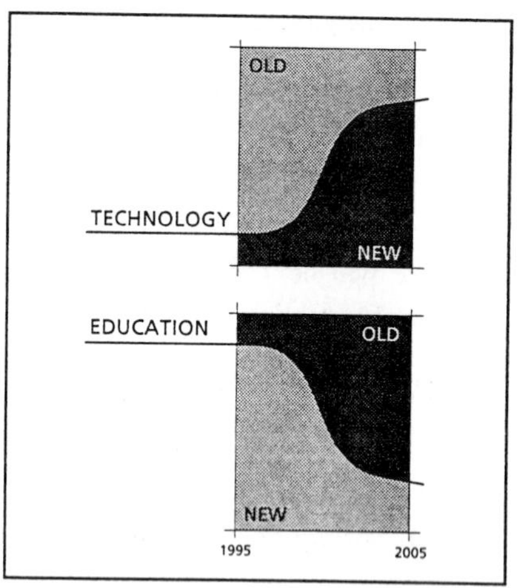

The perspective is both frightening and fascinating. The fascination is, that the renewal is happening so fast, that we will be faced with new challenges. The frightening perspective is of course, that we do not know who will be 'hurt', when the 'renewal-train' is thundering through our back-yard. Will we get on the train in time? What will the new technology look like? Will we be able to learn in time when we cannot make any predictions?

The lack of qualifications will be so tremendous and historically unique, that it will become a real substantial threat to the European economies. Today only 5% of companies are planning with a perspective of 10 years or more. So it is very likely that companies will not be able to take on the challenge by them selves.

The General Director of DGV has on several occasions - like the Danish Prime Minister - mentioned, that we must have an operational standard for an acceptable unemployment-rate in Europe. Allan Larsson has suggested 5% as the upper limit, like the situation t now in U.S.A, and by doing this he has also indicated what kind of initiatives will be necessary. We have to create jobs for 17 million people in the EU during the next 10 years, and it is suggested doing this through creating 10-12 million new workplaces and 5-6 million places within further training.

Creating that number of new workplaces is not that overwhelming. If the European jobcreation rate continues, as we have known it for the past 10 years, it is possible that companies will take care of this part of the challenge.

The future looks rather more gloomy when looking at further training. There still are too few traditions of investing in human resources, in spite of the best intentions. We have to speed up our work in order to establish new further training places, if we are to improve our international competitiveness; our faith in being in front is unfortunately not a fact.

Whether the standard necessarily has to be 5-6 million more places in further education, we do not know. However, we have to plan a strong offensive further training strategy if the European economy is going to survive in the global society.

Danish and European companies may ask: 'How will we be able to find the time and money for all that further training?' With Job Rotation as a tool, we can give a very realistic answer:

- because of the unemployed substitutes, the production will stay intact,
- the economy of further training is the cheapest possible, because the resources are already there; passive money is turned into active money.

EU-Job rotation does not have the answer to all the questions, but we intend to contribute to the development which we see as necessary. Job rotation can contribute with:

- a substantial increase in the amount of further training,
- a significant improvement of the quality of training and its implementation,
- dissemination of results and experiences, nationally and internationally.

Those who are employed must receive continuing vocational training if they are to keep their jobs whether it is because of economic growth or the introduction of new technology.

An integrated strategy: Job rotation

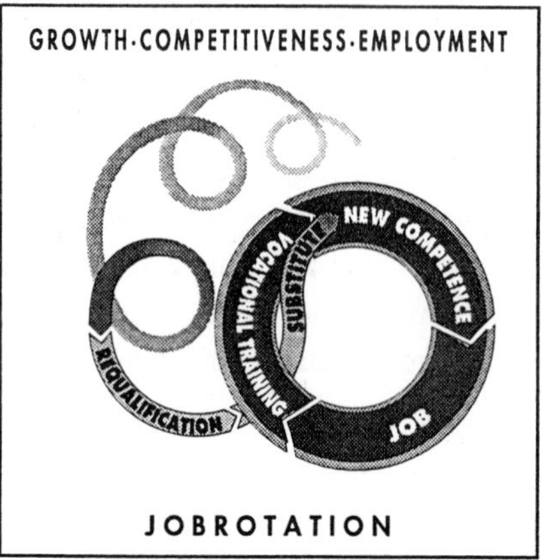

The solution is obvious: why not combine the two problems and they will turn out to support and solve each other? The model and the thinking is very simple. An unemployed person is trained to become a substitute in a company for an employed person who in the meantime gets further training.

The advantages are obvious. The enterprises obtain an upgrading and qualification of their employees typically caused by either organisational or technological changes without any reduction in their workforce and they get contacts who may be candidates for later employment: no loss of production and if the substitutes do not stay in a job, which at least 71% of them do, they go into a job bank. For the unemployed it is a chance to get a real job experience which for the vast majority turns into permanent jobs and for those who do not stay in the enterprises there is a fairly good chance that they will get the chance at the first possible job opening.

The labour market effects will be increased flexibility, improving the unemployment situation, and finally it will prevent bottleneck problems either internally or externally in relation to the company.

'It is common sense - it has to work'. Rarely has anything been so simple and at the same time only had winners: the employed, the employers, the unemployed, and the society.

Job rotation experiences in Denmark

Job rotation is to an increasing extent used as a labour market political tool. This can be seen from the development in the number of participants in job rotation projects from 1994 to 1995, in which period the number increased by approximately 63%.

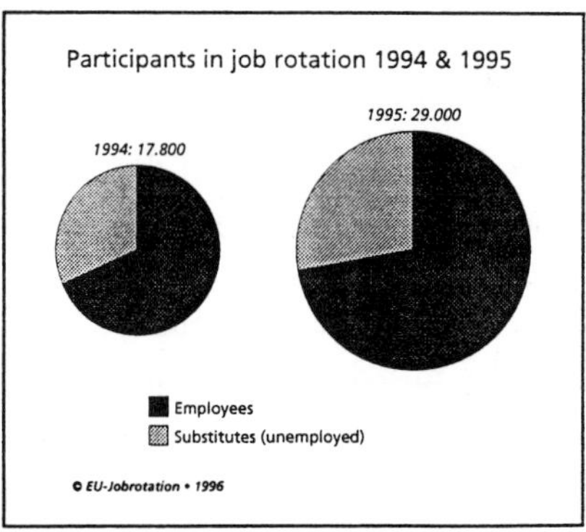

Even though job rotation started in the public sector in Denmark the situation today is radically different as approximately 78% of all Danish job rotation is carried out in the private sector.

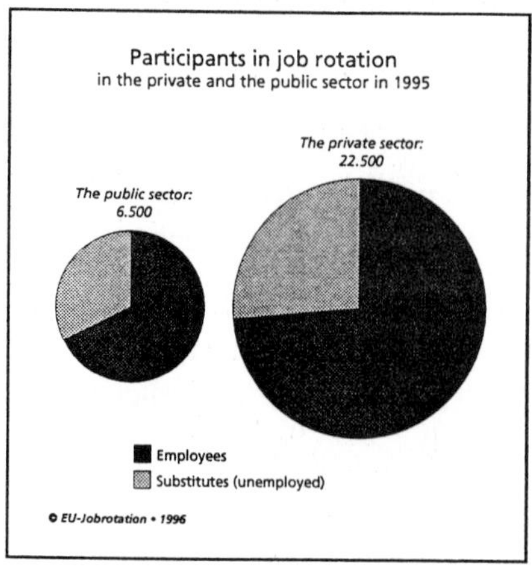

The effects of Job rotation is very noticeable.

For instance in Danish Telecom, a company with about 16,700 employees, one of the effects on the employees back at work was a 41% reduction in absence.

With regard to the unemployed the regional results of job rotation was according to the Public Employment Service in Århus County that 71% were in ordinary employment 6 months after completion.

The results signal that the recruitment basis of the enterprises is improved considerably through participation in a job rotation project and the job rotation projects have contributed to reducing the vulnerability of the participating enterprises and increased the adaptability and the flexibility. In this way job rotation also contributes to reducing the bottle neck problems on the labour market, and as it has been put: 'The difference between success and failure is the right employees'

EU Job Rotation gets on the track

Officially the network was started at a conference in Vienna in March 1996 under the slogan of Job Rotation a new track in Europe. 150 people from all European countries met together at the Palais Ferstel in order to discuss job rotation. The partnership agreed on the following workplan:

Together the partners of the EU Job Rotation network have agreed to develop a common European Job Rotation Model. This model will:

- nationally develop specific models
- transnationally develop a common European content of the elements within the training modules through the transfer of know-how with respect to the best practices, and
- at Community level to develop the model and mainstreaming of the results.

Below is what the partnership looks like today and ever since the beginning the network has been using a bottom-up strategy.

The network is a powerful base of European knowledge and possibilities in the future and the ambition of the network is very explicit: we will increase our efforts during the next three years in order to bring 100,000 EU citizens into job rotation. This will of course involve a lot of resources but fortunately between 80 and 90 percent of the necessary funding is already available in the system today through passive money used for inactive purposes. Job rotation should be part of a new and more active labour market policy.

Through common efforts and a strong commitment the network will contribute to the development of lifelong learning in the EU and at the same time play an active role in the battle against unemployment.

The tracks have been laid down and the network will try to be of support to European Growth, Competitiveness and Employment through the use of existing resources: combining the need for lifelong learning with the need for new employment initiatives, the two problems will become each other's solution.

This 'common sense' concept is right now being tested and implemented all over Europe and the Secretariat plays the co-ordinating role in both the national and the transnational projects.

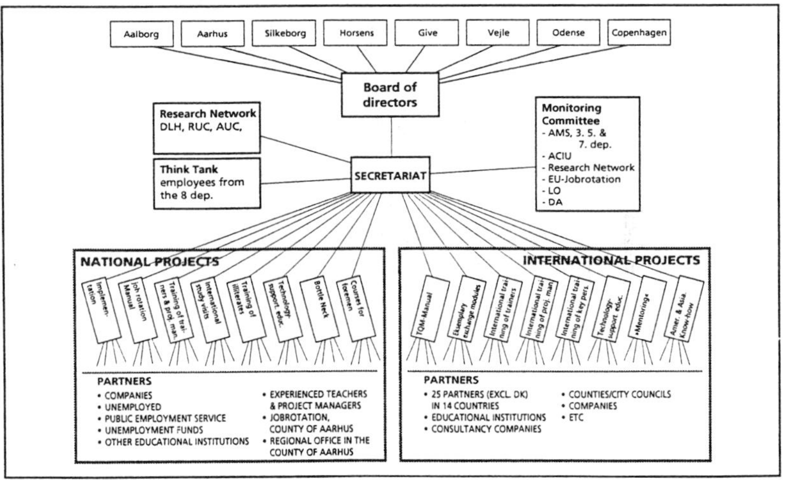

As a co-ordinating unit we supply the network with channels of communication using modern technology through the internet and a closed computerised conference for the partners of the network as a tool for the transnational co-operation. The Secretariat publishes a newsletter, News on the Fax, which is sent out to the partners on the fax quite regularly, once or twice a month and a series of seminars are organised in Denmark of two to four days duration on the theme of 'Job rotation in theory and practice: Introduction arrangement for EU Job Rotation partners' for either key persons, project managers or supervisors, middle managers, shop stewards and trade union representatives.

Representing the EU Job Rotation network we are of course pleased that in the year after Lifelong Learning in Europe the Commission has asked the Danish Government to host a European conference on JOB ROTATION. We too see it as a natural continuation.

Recently the EU Job Rotation network met at a Country Presentation in Edinburgh with the following mission statement:

Anyone who thinks of her/himself as too small to make a difference has never been to bed with a mosquito!

Ulrike Nagel

Second Chances in a Risk Society

There seems to be a growing agreement among social scientists that the modernising processes of the western world have not led to a higher degree of social equality, but instead to a development that might even lead to a further 'encrustment' of the social structure of industrial societies (Mayer, 1990).

That is to say, that the determinative power of the social structure is still operating as a reproductive mechanism of inequality. British researchers have thus coined the notion of 'structured individualisation', meaning that traditional mechanisms of allocation continue to govern the distribution of chances and risks among social strata.

On the other hand, and at the same time, there is an agreement that also when adopting a micro-sociological perspective and looking at the individual lifecourse, at families and households, the dynamics within the social strata are unmistakable.

In trying to conceptualise these two seemingly contradictory observations, two German scholars (Berger and Sopp, 1995) have noted that 'the force behind tradition is being substituted by a necessity for individual choice'. They argue that this necessity for individual choice does not imply a neglection of the determinative powers typical of modern industrial society. What they wish to convey is that at the same time that the determinative powers of social structure have decreased, the range of options and thus the flux of movement within social structure increases.

The consequences of this state of affairs are illustrated by two scenarios:

For one part of the population, increase in social mobility, individualisation of the life course and differentiation of life worlds and milieus turn out to be a gain and are accompanied by new and broader experiences of social structures and social positions, providing new chances for participation, new ideas. All this results in an increase in flexibility; contributing to an image of modern society as open and pluralistic. On the whole, the processes of social change lead to a better understanding of social inequality as well as of different strata and milieus, thus allowing for more tolerance; the overall result is depicted as a better integrated, more coherent society.

The contrasting scenario depicts the situation of the other part of the population; here the necessity for individual choice turns into risks, and social mobility works out to be a matter of detachment and isolation from traditional sources of security and from traditional certainties. Here the individual is disoriented, suffering from status inconsistencies, pressurised by the growing necessity for self-reflexivity, and, finally, may be doomed to collapse. The result on the macro-level of society is desintegration. Included in this scenario is the prospect of fundamentalist orientations spreading more widely, and a development towards what Ulrich Beck (1993) has called 'anti-modernity'.

The ambivalence of the modernising process that is mirrored by these scenarios can also be traced in recent discussions on processes of identity formation; at issue is whether contemporary industrial society gives rise to new forms of participation and, thereby, of identification as illustrated by the first scenario, or rather is a source of fragmentation and deconstruction of the individual self (Welzer, 1995).

Less fundamental but equally interesting is the empirical question concerning the ratio of these scenarios, that is, their distribution among populations. Though there is no proper answer to this question, from time to time figures are presented, mostly as a means of social criticism and very often as a weapon directed against governmental politics.

One such figure which has agitated the German discussion was the slogan of the 'two-thirds society'. It was used in 1984 by the opposition party, the social democrats, and expressed the conviction that the utopia of modern society, the utopia of a continuous increase in social equality, had to be given up and had to be substituted by the concept of a two-thirds division of wealth, thus highlighting the brute fact that no matter what the rates of productivity would be like, still a section of about one third of the population would remain marginalised (Leisering, 1993).

Today, even this figure tends to be outdated, at least when we look at the United States and at a prognosis that appeared recently in a German magazine. The latest data showed a ratio of 20:80, meaning that in the near future 20% will be living well while 80% will more or less be on the margins of poverty. Even if one doubted this ratio as a prospect for Europe, there seems to be little reason to doubt such a trend.

The reason for this development can be illustrated by the image of a pair of scissors, scissors of national indebtedness here and structural unemployment there, as Oevermann (1983), a Frankfurt School sociologist, has put it. In accordance with this scissorlike movement, the central mechanism of integration and legitimation of the European welfare state, namely its politics of subsidising and securing social equality, is under deconstruction.

One of the most discomforting outcomes of the retreatism of the state is that it allows social problems to spread on a large scale, especially problems such as integrating the younger generations into the socio-economic system. While still socialised into the ethics of the credential society and equipped with achievement orientations, they are at the same time, excluded from participation in the labour market and yet are not endowed with norms and values which would allow them to decide an alternative way of life, alternative to the traditional one of modern society, namely the making of a professional career through participation in the labour market.

The crux is, and again I draw from Oevermann (1983), the absence of alternative forms of self-realisation or, to put it positively, the dependency of self-realisation on professional achievement.

These circumstances, together with an overall retreatism of the state from securing social equality, may explain not only growing rates of deprivation and of violent crimes but also the fact that the average delinquents today are younger than they used to be only a few years ago.

But this is only part of the story. At the same time that the spiral of national indebtedness and structural unemployment has increased the individual's risk of facing the second scenario outlined above, so-called grey areas of the labour market (Osterland, 1993) and third arenas of political culture

(Habermas, 1985) have emerged, that is, a way of life both outside the scenarios mentioned above, securing income neither by a permanent job nor by unemployment benefit. This grey area or third arena, based on a shadow or informal economy, on self-employed work and networks, is neither less demanding than the first scenario nor is it to be mistaken for the world of tramps, hobos or any other dropouts. It is comparable to the first scenario inasfar as flexibility plays a prominent role, and from its personnel it demands solidarity, readiness for risk-taking, consumption abstinence. All of these characteristics can in no way be expected to flourish in the climate of the second scenario. But flexibility here has a different source than the one exercised in the first scenario. While in the context of the first scenario flexibility is derived 'par force', that is, by the force of labour market conditions and as a result of discontinuous employment patterns, in the context of the third arena it derives from individual choice of an alternative way of living and making a living. Thus, this third arena has been discussed in terms of a dissident arena, of intelligent self-imposed moderation (Habermas, 1985), of heightened/enhanced individual autonomy (Oevermann, 1983).

Since the same political economy that has brought about an increasing number of second scenarios has also brought about the phenomenon of the third arena, and given the fact that there is a state guaranteed minimum standard of social security, it seems to be mostly a matter of attitude, of outlook on life whether third arena activities come into the individual's reach.

The conclusion I would like to draw is that education and qualifications directed towards members of second scenarios can no longer be judged according to standards like credentials and employment rates only, but should equally be judged with respect to what might be called their third arena aptitude, that is with respect to the convergence of curricula with the demands and requirements of third arena infrastructure.

Since the third arena too reproduces itself through work, skills enhancement remains to be the primary goal. But likewise it means creating awareness of activities within the third arena and introducing them as options for participation and identification. This pedagogical task implies training for coping with discontinuous lifecourse patterns, with loss of formal status and with status inconsistencies. It also means training for multiple or mixed participation patterns including commuting between the first scenarios, third arenas and stately benefits (Even if this mixed pattern of individual reproduction may not appear to be very original, its impact on the agenda of further education might not yet be apparent).

My thesis is that to the extent that the third arena is acknowledged and even advocated as an alternative to the first scenario, adult or further education and training may be looked at as providing second chances in a risk society. That is, as a second chance of participation and identification after dropping out of the first scenario and as an alternative to ending up in the second scenario.

This thesis may also apply to the project from which I borrowed the title of my lecture. Presently set up by the European Commission (Directorate General XXII - Education, Training and Youth) as a measure to combat exclusion, the 'Second Chance School' project, as it is called, is directed at those groups most disadvantaged by economic development and social change, that is, people beyond compulsory education and without formal qualifications ('dropouts'), usually to be found in depressed areas. The second chance school project aims at improving *access* to skills, thus providing reentrance into the labour force.

Facing 18 million unemployed people in Europe, the second chance school project appears to be far too pretentious. But if reinterpreted as a means of heightening awareness of and access to third arena job markets and ways of living, it may be made workable. Since the project is founded on the idea of strengthening personal stability, enhancing skills, and encouraging participation in local cultural events, sports, and other such activities, it appears to be very likely to realise what it promises to establish: second chances in risk societies.

References

Beck, U. (1993), Die Erfindung des Politischen. Zu einer Theorie reflexiver Modernisierung, Frankfurt am Main.

Berger, P. A. and Sopp, P. (1995), Dynamische Sozialstrukturanalysen und Strukturerfahrungen in Berger, P. A. and Sopp, P., (eds), Sozialstruktur und Lebenslauf, Opladen, pp 9-24.

Habermas, J. (1985), Die Krise des Wohlfahrtsstaates und die Erschöpfung utopischer Energien in Habermas, J. Die Neue Unübersichtlichkeit. Kleine Politische Schriften V, Frankfurt am Main, pp 141-163.

Leisering, L. (1993), Zwischen Verdrängung und Dramatisierung. Zur Wissenssoziologie der Armut in der bundesrepublikanischen Gesellschaft, Soziale Welt 4, Jg. 44, pp 486-511.

Mayer, K. U. (1990), Soziale Ungleichheit und die Differenzierung von Lebensverläufen in Zapf, W., (ed), Die Modernisierung moderner Gesellschaften. Verhandlungen des 25. Deutschen Soziologentages in Frankfurt am Main, Herausgegeben im Auftrag der deutschen Gesellschaft für Soziologie, Frankfurt am Main/New York, pp667-687.

Oevermann, U. (1983), Kann Arbeitsleistung weiterhin als basales Kriterium der Verteilungsgerechtigkeit dienen? (unpublished paper).

Osterland, M. (1990), 'Normalbiographie' und 'Normalarbeitsverhältnis' in Berger, P. A. Hradil, S. (eds), Lebenslagen, Lebensläufe, Lebensstile, Soziale Welt, Sonderband 7, Göttingen, pp351-362.

Wenzel, H. (1995), Gibt es ein postmodernes Selbst? Neuere Theorien und Diagnosen der Identität in fortgeschrittenen Gesellschaften, Berliner Journal für Soziologie 5, pp113-131.

Gunnar Sundgren

Popular Education - Regional Crisis and Social Integration

Abstract

Study circles in Sweden have a history of more than one hundred years. Roughly 75 per cent of the adult population have at one time or the other participated in a study circle. Almost 25 per cent do so every year. For about ten per cent of the participants it has become part of their lifestyle. The topics of the study circles vary from traditional studies to leisure and sports studies. Some studies form part of a trade union's or a social movement's strategy for promoting social change.

In a broader study called 'The Circle Society' (Cirkelsamhället) a case study of a small town of 6,600 inhabitants, Norberg, 200 kilometres north-west of Stockholm, was conducted. Until 1986 Norberg was a regional centre for mining and the steel industry. Today there are no large industries left. The community itself is the largest employer and some three hundred small private employers struggle to survive. Nine hundred citizens of Norberg travel everyday to nearby towns to work. In this study there were 15 informants and 22 participants of different study circles in Norberg were interviewed. The main focus of the interview was to map out the participants' subjective meanings towards the study circle. However, it also included identifying the objective functions it served for the local community.

The results indicate that there are a great variety of meanings and functions. The participants' aims are less collective and political than they may once have been. Instead they meet a large number of different individual needs. In the local community it seems as if the study circles not only broaden the views of the participants but also contribute to important civic virtues. Putnam, in his Italian study '*Making democracy work*' (1993), specifies them to be honesty, sincerity and trust. The study circle seems in fact to contribute to the socialisation of participants in this way. Moreover, it appears to foster a specific sense of restricted intimacy, a circle 'tact', where virtues such as patience, openness, willingness to reformulate opinions on the world and self-control develop.

Being neither part of the lifeworld nor part of the systems for power and economy in the way that Habermas defines them, the study circles seem to belong to an area where socially controlled interaction between equals under relative freedom establishes a specific public domain with its' own logic and grammar. In the local community it means that the study circle contributes both to cultural reproduction and to social change, to individual autonomy as well as local identity. It allows specific groups to formulate their interests in a socially acceptable way and thereby contribute to social integration. At the same time they offer a public domain that is relatively free from official regulation and control.

The circle society[1]

In 1995 the State Department of Education in Sweden launched an evaluation programme to look at popular education. It was intended to be a basis for policy proposals from a government commission appointed to consider if and how they should be reformed. Since 75 per cent of the adult population have participated in a study circle at one time or another and almost 25 per cent of the same population enroll in a study circle every year this is a rather important issue in Sweden.[2] Officially popular education receives state support on the basis that it contributes to democracy and equality:

> State support to popular education should aim at supporting people in their attempts to change their life situation and at fostering engagement for their participation in the development of society.
>
> Activities that aim at reducing educational differences and to raise the general level of education in the society should be given priority as well

1 This is the title of a government report by Eva Andersson, Ann-Marie Laginder, Staffan Larsson, Gunnar Sundgren published in 1996. The Swedish title is *Cirkelsamhället. Cirkelns betydelser för indvid och lokalsamhälle. SOU 1996:47.*

2 Statistics from Jonsson & Gähler (1995) *Folkbildning och vuxenstudier.*

as activities organised for those who have been educationally, socially and culturally neglected (Jonsson and Gähler, 1995).[3]

With the intention to evaluate whether or not popular education in Sweden fulfils these aims the state Department of Education contacted different researchers and research groups asking them to look at different aspects of Swedish popular education. The researchers were free to formulate their own research problems but they had to present their results primarily to the commission within a year. At Linköping University we proposed a research project entitled 'The circle society'. It looked at the relationship between popular education, nota bene, the study circles, and the local community and, more specifically, the significance of the study circles for the individual and for the local community.

Three different regions were chosen; a modern suburb of Gothenburg, a small traditional town, Nyköping and a small community formerly a centre for heavy industries but now in a stage of transition, Norberg. Using qualitative methods, partly inspired by hermeneutics and ethnomethodology, the three regions were described on the basis of observations, informant interviews and participant observation in the community. Twenty -twenty-two participants in different study circles were then interviewed in each region (22 in Norberg). The interviews were on average an hour long and were recorded and transcribed to text. They were semi-structured and covered three main areas; background and current life, motives for and experiences of being a study circle participant and finally views on education, the local community and future plans. On a very general level the results indicated that the study circle is seen by most participants as a way of combining personal interest with learning while also offering the opportunity to socialise. In the study circles participants exchange experiences on a topic but they also interact and enter a specific social sphere that is not exclusively a part of their private life nor of their strictly regulated public life.

3 Proposition 1990/91:82 *Om folkbildning* (On Popular Education). Translation is mine.

Norberg - a region in transition

I shall now move on from looking at individual meanings given to study circles to the meaning they have for the local community. In this case it is the small community of Norberg, formerly a regional centre for mining and steel industry. The number of inhabitants today is roughly 6,600. The unemployment rate is just above 14 per cent. More than 900 travel back and forth to nearby communities to work each day. The municipal has been able to keep up the number of inhabitants, in spite of the fact that almost all of the old heavy industries have closed since the late sixties. In fact for almost one hundred years the population has been roughly the same in terms of numbers. Why then are people staying in Norberg although there are few jobs available and the future of the community is endangered as a result of this?

Norberg is still dominated socially by the old working class tradition. Until the last election the social democratic party had been in political power for more than a generation. Quite a few of the politicians within the social democratic party have held leading positions within the mining companies, in the steel industry or in the community office. On the whole, Norberg has been fairly homogeneous. There is still no clear segregation in the community in relation to housing or social life.

During the years of industrial decline there were two major attempts by the population to find alternative employees. Together with their political representatives they launched two campaigns under the name of 'The Norberg Model' and 'The new Norberg Model'. The first one was partly successful in that it led to the establishment of a mechanical plant delivering parts to the multi-national company ABB which has its national centre in the county capital, Västerås. The other campaign was less successful but both of them engaged many citizens in different activities and may well have contributed to a common feeling of community membership. The life of the community is, on the whole, an active one. Statistically speaking every adult in Norberg belongs to not less than four different associations.[4] Many of these associa-

4 According to local statistics and informants, for detailed references see the report Cirkelsamhället.

tions have both regular activities and organise study circles in one form or another.

A typical study circle often has five to ten participants who meet regularly once a week for two or three hours, eight to ten weeks in a row during a school-term. There are eleven different organisations through which you can arrange a study circle if economic and administrative support is needed. Most of these organisations are associated with popular movements. The largest ones are associated with different parts of the labour movement including the two socialist parties. Another one is connected with traditional organisations for peasants. Others are associated with the conservative or the liberal party. There are also organisations for leisure groups, environmental groups and a central organisation for sport activities, as well as two Christian organisations one of which is connected to the state church and the other to the different free churches in Sweden. All of them distribute information and organise a large number of study circles. In fact the state support is channelled through the corporative organisation 'Folkbildningsrådet' (The National Board of Popular Education) to the different organisations. This means in practice that the participants often have to pay less than the full cost of the circle. In the case where the study circle leader is also one of the participants, participating in the study circle is free of charge. Sometimes even the study material is free. The local community usually gives additional support to the organisations and circles.

In Norberg many of the study circles are associated with ABF (Workers Association for Popular Education). Quite a number of them are associated with the largest association for retired people in Sweden PRO (Retired People's National Association) but most of the other organisations also organise study circles in Norberg.

Three study circles in Norberg

Before analysing the possible contribution of the study circles I will outline three examples of study circles that were active in spring, 1995 in Norberg:

1. 'My farm in EU'

On the outskirts of the town lives a part-time farmer (Erik). He is in his sixties and is handicapped as a result of farm and industrial work. Previously he used to combine working for a company that installed industrial railways with farming his own land. Today he has a small pension which he lives on at the farm with his wife. Their daughter recently took over the main building on the farm and lives there with her family. Except for one horse, two meat-cows and a few pets there are no longer any animals on the farm but he is growing his own food, harvesting the land and looking after the forest and the wild life in it. When he was a boy he had seven years of schooling but he never continued with his studies partly because he had some difficulties with reading and writing. Instead he spent a few years working in a town 200 kilometres away but came back to the small village where he was brought up and where his father had a tenant farm. He combined farm duty with producing a certain amount of charcoal every year for a big mining company in Norberg.

Erik now participates in two study circles. Sweden recently entered the European Union bringing with it new conditions for Swedish farmers. A lot of technicalities had to be learned about how land and production should be registered so as to get a maximum of support from the union and the state. Erik entered the study circle entitled 'My farm in the EU' partly to manage the new paperwork but partly, as he stated clearly in the interview, because it is his way of getting out and meeting other farmers in the nearby region. He participates also in a second study circle with almost the same people. The second circle is about how to care for the forest and its wildlife. Farming and forestry is for Erik much more than making a living, it is a lifestyle and he has strong feelings for the land, the forest and the wild animals. In fact farming is both his occupation, hobby and a basis for his social life. The study circle is organised by the farmers' regional association which is part of a national wide association for farmers. Formally the study circle is organised by the regional division of Vuxenskolan (The School for Adults), one of the eleven organisations for popular education in Sweden. In this context Erik meets his colleagues once a week almost all the year round. They discuss the official topic of the course but they also dwell on different subjects of interest for the members of the group. The topics can range from family issues, technical advise, local politics to the question of whether Sweden really should have entered the European Union. Erik stated that he had changed his opinion during this time from being positive to negative. This was the result of testing his arguments with the group and being convinced by a few of the more critical members. There is, however, no pressure to reach consensus in the group, every person has the right to her/his own opinion.

2. 'On our way towards the future'

The second example illustrates a middle-aged woman, Anna, who is educated as a nurse's assistant and is working at a service-home for elderly people run by the community. She lives in Norberg with her husband and her dogs in a small house of their own. Her union has started a series of study circles, 'On our way towards the future', to discuss the change over from centrally decided salaries related to age and experience to local ones decided by the employer, based on judgement of individual competence and value. The initiative for the change came from the employers central organisation and was accepted by the national union. Although Anna, like most of her colleagues, found the new system a bad one she entered the study circle hoping to be able to make the level of the individual salary more fair and also to be sure that she would not be over-looked. The circle was organised by the union through the Workers Association for Popular Education (ABF). The study circle leader was also the chairman of the local union. When Anna describes her motives for, experiences of and expectations in relation to the study circle it is clear that it has multiple meanings for her. She is not only guarding her own interest by participating but she is also finding an oppor-

tunity to discuss the change over in management and goals that took place when the responsibility for the service-homes passed over from the county and its health organisation to the local community and its social service. The change meant a new work policy. Social welfare was seen as more important than bodily care. This meant assuming new work tasks and a loss of security when the hierarchy of the hospital organisation was broken up. From Anna's point of view this meant that she might be ordered to do work for which she was not properly trained, both less and more advanced than before. Furthermore, no one could be sure of how many assistants would be needed. These topics were not the official ones in her study circle but for a great deal of the time the members talked about their work tasks, comparing experiences and discussing how to act in the new situation.

3. 'Medieval song and dance'

My third example is a young woman in her late twenties who has been working in local industry for a few years. Today she is unemployed due to rationalisations and cut- backs. She has economic support from the community for the days she studies to improve her formal education from primary to secondary level so that she can apply to university. Her plan for the future is to become a social worker. As a child she came to Norberg from a more northern part of Sweden with her mother and brother. She now lives alone in her own apartment in the centre of Norberg. A few years ago she joined a local theatre group. The theatre group presented a play about the history of the labour movement in Norberg, focusing particularly on the events of a significant strike by workers in the old mining company. She worked backstage with the make-ups for the amateur actors in the play. Her interest for history was awakened and a year ago she joined a study circle entitled 'Medieval song and dance', which was also organised by the Workers Association for Popular Education (ABF). Singing has always been a life long interest. In the circle she meets regularly with a group of women of different ages and one middle-aged, unemployed industrial worker. The group studies medieval history, songs and clothing, sings and dances, and makes their own medieval dresses while they prepare a small show to be performed at a historical site in Norberg. During the interview it became clear that she finds Norberg a dull place for young people as there are few activities and joining the study circle was for her one way of filling her leisure time with a meaningful social activity. As in the other circles discussions are often topic-related but at the same time the participants exchange opinions and experiences from other aspects of life, both private and public.

Contributions to community life - autonomy, social network and identifying common interest

Study circles contribute to community life in a variety of ways. They socialise and foster autonomous and self-regulating citizens. By offering a time and a place where citizens can meet and get acquainted the study circles also act as social networks. Furthermore talking to other people on specific and general topics is also a prerequisite for identifying common interests.

Quite a few of the participants interviewed, the retired, young students and middle-aged mothers, stated that they go to the study circle to 'get away from home for a while'. The circle can be seen as a device to balance the pressure of everyday life. In this respect it is part of a citizen's self-regulatory activity and contributes to their mental health. Furthermore some informants stated that the alternative to the study circle would be a much more passive life at home. For the unemployed or the retired, particularly, there is the risk of social crisis in the absence of a meaningful activity like the study circle. The well-behaved and self-controlled citizen will her/himself be able to identify a threatening crisis and regulate her/his life so as to be able to avoid them or treat them properly. She/he will also seek socially acceptable forms to express her/his discontents as do the young people who organise themselves into rock-circles. In the raw music and texts they can attack the establishment in a socially acceptable way. Participating in a study circle can be a part of this self-regulatory activity. We can, for example, find topics like 'healthier sports'. A study circle was set up by members of a sports club to study how to avoid injuries from training and, as my informant explicitly stated, to prevent seeking help from hospitals when injured. In another circle we found a recently widowed man who attended a study circle on cooking so that he would be able to manage his new life. Many of the circles, mostly those organised for retired people, in dancing, singing and handicraft, will help to keep the participants physically fit.

The material also indicates that, for some of the participants at least, the study circle contributes to their social network. For example, for the retired and the unemployed it seems as if the participants in the same study circle take some kind of social responsibility for one another by contacting a member if they miss a meeting. Other kinds of study circles, such as singing in a choir or making pottery will tend to bring together young and old as well as people from different social backgrounds. In some of the circles you will also find a conscious effort by the participants to broaden their views by talking to people of a different age, sex, class or culture. The study circle offers a time and a place where citizens of different backgrounds can meet regularly. We can of course not be certain about the kind of conversations that take place inside the circles. Our informants indicate that they talk mostly about the subject matters. However, during coffee breaks and in small talk in study circles in, for example handicraft, they talk about life outside the circle and about local matters of common interest. In the examples given it is evident that both Erik, the farmer, and Anna, the nurse's assistant, use their study circles to deliberate in a true sense. They dwell on what must be considered as common interests, for and against the European market or changing the policy for the care of elderly people and the relationship between employer and employee in the local workplace.

Deliberative democracy and civic virtues

Bernard Manin, a French researcher, discusses the connection between the legitimacy of the state and the possibilities that the population has to ponder over and to talk about political issues and decisions. Following Rousseau he says that there must be some kind of social contract between citizens that will give the state legitimacy. Manin is, however, critical towards Rousseau in that he does not pay attention to what has to forego the shaping of opinions; the 'deliberation of all':

> ... (it is) necessary to alter radically the perspective common to both liberal theories and democratic thought: the source of legitimacy is not the predetermined will of individuals, but rather the process of its formation, that is deliberation itself... a legitimate decision does not represent the *will* of all, but is one that results from the *deliberation of all* (Manin, 1987: 351-352).[5]

This, he goes on to say, is what constitutes a deliberative democracy. The concept of deliberation has both an individual and a collective meaning. Individual in the sense that each citizen has to deliberate with her/himself, seeking arguments and judging them. Collective in the sense that these arguments and judgements are discussed and reformulated together with others. The actual point where decisions are made is not as important for the democracy as is the discussion, the political dialogue. It is in this situation that democracy can be conquered and secured in a never ending process.[6] The Swedish political debate has also brought attention to the deliberative aspect of democracy. Recently the so-called, Board of democracy, consisting of prominent social scientists has released a report called 'Democracy as dialogue'. They state that a democracy must rest on citizen rule, on acceptance, law and with power enough to enforce political decisions. The trick is to find a working balance in between these three factors. To find that balance we have to compromise and it is while working out those compromises that citizens must deliberate with one another. Establishing citizen rule becomes important. We then have to get 'control of the political diary',

---

5 Deliberative democracy is defined in a similar way by Miller (1992 p. 55): 'The deliberative ideal also starts from the premise that political preferences will conflict and that the purpose of democratic institutions must be to resolve this conflict. but it envisages this occurring through an open and uncoerced discussion of the issue at stake with the aim of arriving at an agreed judgement. The process of reaching a decision will also be a process whereby initial preferences are transformed to take account of the views of others.'

6 I discuss at length what implications a democratic view like this would have for teaching in regular schools in my book Knowledge and Democracy, see Sundgren (1996) Kunskap och demokrati. Om elevers rätt till en egen kunskapsprocess.

have an enlightened understanding among citizens, good participation in elections and a well functioning life of associations and local self control. Social scientists state that:

> Democracy as citizen rule is the political method by which independently reflecting people in equal conditions through discussions reach decisions in questions they themselves have recognised as being common issues.[7]

In his book, '*Making Democracy Work: Civic Traditions in Modern Italy*' Robert D. Putnam discusses what the true basis for democracy in a society might be. He compares two regions in Italy. Statistical data about citizens' participation in society is included but he also questions people about their opinions on democracy and their views on local politics and politicians. The conclusions are that it is the communicative network of exchange between citizens in a civil society that is the ground for a well-functioning modern democracy and not, as we might have expected, the level of education or the degree of urbanisation. Nor is it the degree of consensus in society, its social stability or modernity that is the key explanation to a communicative democracy where the citizens deliberate on common affairs, have confidence in their politicians and are ready to limit their personal needs on behalf of common interests. The crucial factor, it seems, is if the citizens are members of civil groups where people from different social classes and with different views on life and politics can meet and exchange ideas, modify them and form opinions in social interaction with each other.

Participation in civic organisations incalculates skills of co-operation as well as a sense of shared responsibility for collective endeavours. Moreover, when individuals belong to 'cross-cutting' groups with diverse goals and members, their attitudes will tend to moderate as a result of group interaction and cross-pressures. These effects it is worth noting, do not require that the manifest purpose of the association be political. Taking part in a choral

7 See Rothstein (1995 p. 13) *Demokrati som dialog.*

society or a bird-watching club can teach self-discipline and an appreciation for the joys of successful collaboration (Putnam, 1993:115).[8]

It is evident that popular education provides places and situations were people can meet and interact in an informal way. They are in themselves a specific public sphere where individual aims and opinions can be confronted with others, be fused together or more clearly stated with the result that a basic element in democracy is established and enforced. Moreover, the study circle is a kind of public arena and an opportunity for individuals to transform their individuality to citizenship just by participating. By entering the study circle you are already something else than just an individual, you are acknowledging the fact that you can share interests and goals with other men and women. Leaving the closed privacy of life at home but, as I will elaborate on later, at the same time keeping out of the more official role-playing of public life outside the sheltered study circle. Putnam argues that democracy functions first when there is a basic socialisation of the population. Members of a democratic society have to attain certain civic virtues.[9] Most researchers agree, he says, that the most important of these virtues are honesty, trust and law-abidingness. Moreover it is of great importance that the individual recognises the social limits of her/his own freedom, a prize we all have to pay if we want to belong to a community.[10] We could add that there are other valuable virtues for a citizen similar to those virtues we would like to see our students have. These are communicative virtues like tolerance, patience, having an open mind, being willing to admit mistakes, readiness to change ones' world view, self-control and last but not least, being a good listener.[11] What then is the relationship of these democratic and communicative virtues, the interaction in the study-circle and society at large?

---

8 Putnam (1993) *Making democracy work: civic traditions in modern Italy.* Princeton university press. Princeton. New Jersey. Quotation from Putnam's discussion of theory (p. 90) but he uses almost the same formulations when presenting his results (p. 115).

9 Op. cit. p. 111

10 Relying on what Barber (1984) says about the necessity of personal limits he discusses the prize the individual has to pay in termsof restricted freedom if s/he wants to become member of society in his Strong *Democracy: Participatory Politics for a New Age.*

11 These are student virtues mentioned by Burbules (1993 p. 36 ff.) in *Dialogue in teaching - Theory and Practice*, here from Roth 1996.

The study circle as a social phenomena

The relationship between the state and the individual is a central topic for almost all social research as is the constitution of modern society. Habermas analyses the latter in terms of lifeworld and systems.[12] He argues that the lifeworld is separated from the systems and that the lifeworld is constituted by personal experience and emotionally loaded relations, unique and authentic. The systems of power and of money transactions on the other hand rely on impersonal, neutral, exchangeable and non-authentic relations. Socialisation of the individual, the integration of society and cultural reproduction are all affected by the systems. The individual is socialised to become autonomous and to function like any other object on a market. Integration of society then is mainly obtained by establishing functional hierarchies that distribute power and money. Cultural reproduction rests on physical and mental disciplining.

But, might we ask, where does the study circle belong, to the intimacy of the lifeworld or to the neutral and impersonal systems? The likely answer is that it both exceeds the relatively narrow limits of the lifeworld, based as it is on strictly personal relationships, experiences and communication as well as being different from the official and instrumental role-playing and neutral communication of the systems. The study circle does not belong to any hierarchy of power nor has it any economic significance to speak of either for the participant or for the market.

Should we try to characterise the interaction, communication and relationships developed in a study circle based on what our participants say; friendly but not intimate? In fact it seems to be marked by a certain restricted intimacy. The participants bring to the study circle some material from their lifeworld, interact authentically to some extent inside the circle but at the same time they are fairly restricted when meeting fellow members of the study circle outside the time and place where it belongs. If participants meet

12 See for example Habermas (1981) *The theory of communicative action. Vol 1. Reason and rationalization of society and Vol. 2. The critic of functionalist reason* or the Swedish volume from 1990 with texts from different periods: *Kommunikativt handlande. Texter om språk, rationalitet och samhälle.* For a critical review see for example Outhwaite 1994, *Habermas. A critical introduction.*

in the village shop they would of course normally say hello to each other but they would not behave as close friends included in their lifeworld. Another indication of the same character is that a couple of participants state that they like the study circle because there they can be sociable without having to gossip. The content of gossiping, I would argue, belongs to the intimacy of the lifeworld. Although we might look upon gossiping as something negative it consists of the same kind of value statements we exchange with close friends. Personal comments then, addressed not to a close friend but to someone relatively distant we call gossip. Gossiping can be understood as communicating value judgements and not knowing or respecting the limits of when, where and to whom to give them to. If so, the relative freedom from gossiping in the study circle tells us perhaps that the intimacy of the relationship there has its definite limits and that the participants recognise this and tend to respect those limits. Other statements from study circle participants reinforce the impression that there are certain expectations as how to behave in a study circle. You should neither be too passive, refuse to interact, or be too dominant. On the whole then, a study circle participant ideally should show some pedagogical tact, let us call it 'circle tact'.[13]

Not only Habermas but several others have tried to make a distinction between private life and official, impersonal interaction in the society at large. Tönnies has also characterised differences between gemeinschaft und gesellschaft.[14] The integrative element in gemeinschaft is the close relationship between people and their commonly shared values. Gesellschaft rests on integration within the division of labour in the sense that you can not do without the other person because you have to rely on her/his production or service. Putnam (op. cit.) also discusses Tönnies' views and criticises him for idealising the past. It is not, says Putnam, the historical dimension in itself nor is it the degree of modernity that is the crucial basis for integration, it is the character of the interaction between the members of a particular society. Interaction then is seen as an independent factor that has to be ana-

13 In a conference paper *Reflectivity and the Pedagogic Moment* Van Maanen (1990) discusses pedagogical tact as something teachers have or have not. Very likely all social situations requires some sense of tact, it may well be that educational situations do so even more than many other situations.

14 Asplund (1991) elaborates on this in his essay *Essä om Gemeinschaft och Gesellschaft.*

lysed in its own right. A Swedish social psychologist Johan Asplund, following Mead's theory of symbolic interaction, has elaborated a theory of man's drive to interact both with objects and with other humans.[15] When s/he interacts with other people, says Asplund, man is socially responsive. In many of his books Asplund re-analyses classical experiments. He uses social psychology to try to show that this urge to interact socially is so strong that it explains many otherwise morally questionable behaviours. Moreover he analyses several everyday interactive situations and finds that they have their very delicate and specific rules. My conclusion is that social interaction of any kind that has some cultural regularity will have its own specific grammar. So also does the study circle. For most Swedes it is a well known, easily recognisable and well structured socially interactive situation.

The study circle is a place for social interaction but is it also a place where planned and co-ordinated action originates? The way in which people co-ordinate their acts is a central topic for Habermas. According to him acts are co-ordinated either through external pressure from systems of power and money distribution or through agreement between individual subjects in a shared lifeworld. In the first case acts tend to be associated with a strategic and instrumental attitude that hinders genuine interaction between equals. In the second case interaction is associated with open dialogues among people searching for truth, deciding what is good in an ethical sense, striving to express themselves correctly and in a reliable way.

The rationality guiding the co-ordination of acts is in the first case instrumental and in the second communicative. Normally we would understand the study circle as being voluntary and free. In fact these specifications are part of the official definition of popular education in Sweden. Most study circles will also answer to this. Quite a few of those interviewed stated that they regard the fact that they themselves decide whether to participate or not is part of the attraction of study circles. They also appeal because there are no tests or examinations connected with study circles. It may well be then that the study circle participants foster a communicative rationality rather

---

15 See for example Asplunds *Det sociala livets elementära former* (1987) and *Storstäderna och det forteanska livet* (1992).

than an instrumental one. However, the degree in which they use this communication to co-ordinate their act to reach common goals can be questioned. It is evident that they co-ordinate their acts in that respect and this keeps the circle going by sticking to a common subject and meet regularly. The remaining question, however, is whether you could say that the participants get together, communicate and co-ordinate their acts on a common ground of shared interests to improve their collective situation. Neither in the examples given here nor in the material at large does this seem to be the case. Very likely this was once true for the study circles initiated by the popular movements at the beginning of the century but not today.

Study circles seem to offer a specific public arena where you can be a citizen among others and where you can develop a communicative rationality which is not immediately connected to the co-ordination of acts directed toward goals of common interest. The study circle is, it appears, mainly a place for what we could call 'communicative learning', for pursuing a personal interest but it is also a place for deliberation. Community members, to some extent, deliberate about common affairs. In that respect the study circle contributes to the forming of citizenship, to local democracy and to the integration of the local community. The study circle, therefore, may well be a stabilising factor in times of regional crisis.

References

Andersson, E., Laginder, A. M., Larsson, S. and Sundgren, G. (1996), Cirkelsamhället. Studiecirklars betydelser för individ och lokalsamhälle, SOU:*47*, Stockholm, Fritzes

Asplund, J. (1992), Storstäderna och det forteanska livet, Göteborg, Korpen.

Asplund, J. (1987), Det sociala livets elementära former, Göteborg, Korpen.

Asplund, J. (1991), Essä om Gemeinschaft och Gesellschaft, Göteborg, Korpen.

Barber, B. (1984), Strong Democracy: Participatory Politics for a New Age, Berkeley, University of California Press.

Burbules, N. (1993), Dialogue in teaching - Theory and Practice, Teachers College Press.

Habermas, J. (1981/1984/1991), The theory of communicative action. Vol 1. Reason and rationalization of society, Boston, Beacon Press, Cambridge: Polity Press.

Habermas, J. (1981/1991/1992), The theory of communicative action. Vol 2. The critic of functionalist reason, Cambridge, Polity Press.

Habermas, J. (1990), Kommunikativt handlande. Texter om språk, rationalitet och samhälle, Göteborg, Daidalos.

Jonsson, J. and Gähler, M. (1995), Folkbildning och vuxenstudier. Rekrytering, omfattning, erfarenheter, SOU, pp141. Stockholm, Fritzes.

Manin, B. (1987), On legitimacy and political deliberation. *Political Theory, 15,* 3, pp338-368.

Miller, D. (1992), Deliberative democracy and social choice. *Political Studies,* XL, pp 54-67.

Outhwaite, W. (1994), Habermas. A critical introduction, Cambridge, Polity Press.

Proposition, (1990/91:82), Om folkbildning, Stockholm, Fritzes.

Putnam, R. D. (1993), Making democracy work: civic traditons in modern Italy,

Princeton, New Jersey, Princeton university press.

Roth, K. (1996), Möjligheternas praktik: Den fria individen i gemenskap. En pragmatisk attityd till och i utbildning, Lärarhögskolan i Stockholm.

Rothstein, B. (1995), Demokrati som dialog, Stockholm, SNS förlag.

Sundgren, G. (1996), Kunskap och demokrati. Om elevers rätt till en egen kunskapsprocess, Lund, Studentlitteratur.

Van Maanen, M. (1990), Reflectivity and the Pedagogic Moment, HSR Conference, Laval, June 9-13.

Tom Schuller

Human and Social Capital: Variations within a Learning Society

Introduction

'Training is regarded by many politicians and policy-makers as the answer to many of our economic ills. It is seen by some as vital to our economic future. If we fail to invest sufficiently in the nation's 'human capital' - the brains and skills of the current and future workforce - we are told, then we will continue to lose ground in the competitiveness race. Some commentators have suggested that the technologies involved in the future of work mean that the gap in wealth between low and high human capital countries is set to widen.' (Machin and Wilkinson, 1995:1).

Such a statement, from the Commission on Public Policy and British Business, is made on the UK context, but it could be matched by similar statements in almost every Western country (see Reich 1991, Benoit-Guilbot 1995; European Commission n.d.). Even in those whose position in the world economic league has not declined as rapidly as the UK, investment in education and training has moved to a more and more central role in the debate over future economic prospects.

Economic competitiveness is not the only policy sphere in which investment in learning is given primacy. Concerns about social equity and the personal and social problems caused by the exclusion of large segments of the population, notably the unskilled and unqualified, mean that calls for greater investment at all levels, from nursery education to technical training, command broad-based support. Over the last decade or so, the rhetoric of the need for lifelong learning has become so insistent that it seems to have squeezed out critical appraisal of exactly what effects ever-increasing participation in education and training has on the life chances of students, on the institutions where they are to be found, and on the wider social and economic context.

In this paper I want to approach the issue in a non-rhetorical spirit, and to pursue one line of thinking which adds a different dimension to the debate. I argue that in some respects the adoption of the human capital approach, implicitly or explicitly, has led to an unduly narrow focus, not in the content of the learning (which is a fairly common claim, especially amongst the defenders of more liberal approaches to education) but in the way 'investment' is conceived, and benefits measured. I suggest that the notion of 'social capital', although still far from being tightly defined let alone easily analysed, is potentially extremely fruitful, for it shifts the focus from learning as an essentially individual activity towards learning as a function of social relationships. Such an approach has major implications at several levels, from the conceptual to the policy-making. It demands a broad approach to lifelong learning which goes beyond the acquisition by individuals of formal qualifications.

The issue is of direct significance to the theme of the relationships between lifelong learning and regional and social development, in a number of ways. I want to add my voice to the small chorus of people warning against an over-reliance on lifelong learning as the solution to our economic and social problems. We are in danger of repeating the errors of the 1960s, where initial education was so strongly touted as the route to social justice and equal opportunity. Too much was claimed for the potential of schools, and as a consequence expectations were not met. On its own, learning, however powerful and however broadly conceived, is not the solution to problems of unemployment, depression or backwardness, individually or collectively. There are major points of comparison and reflection here between the two periods, especially for educational professionals and policy-makers.

One implication of my argument is that we need in any case to look carefully not just at the quality of lifelong learning as well as at the quantity of provision and participation; but also at the way diverse patterns of learning achievement, varying between groups and geographical locations, affect the overall balance of development. The impact of (quantitatively) enlarged and (qualitatively) enhanced access to learning will depend on how it ties in with a whole set of other relationships: within organisations, families, communities and economic sectors. The notion of *balance* is crucial here, though it is hard to define. I draw a speculative parallel with highly significant work done on health, which relates overall health levels in a population to general patterns of inequality within societies rather than to absolute levels of material well-being.

Educational Expansion and the Temporary Triumph of Human Capital

'Probably the most important and most original development in the economics of education in the past 30 years has been the idea that the concept of physical capital as embodied in tools, machines and other productive equipment can be extended to include human capital as well. Just as physical capital is created by changes in materials to form tools that facilitate production, human capital is created by changes in persons that bring about skills and capabilities that make them able to act in new ways.' (Coleman 1988:S100). Coleman cites, predictably and reasonably, Theodore Schultz and Gary Becker as the originators of this development with their work in the 1960s (Schultz, 1963; Becker, 1964).

Since then, huge amounts of research and analysis has been built on the notion of human capital (see e.g. Carnoy 1995 passim). This has not been uncontested, methodologically or politically. In the ideologically riven era of the 1960s and 1970s, there was at first considerable resistance to the notion itself, mainly on the grounds that it reduced learning to some type of commodity to be acquired, and imbued with unsavoury business overtones an activity - learning - which ought rather to be seen as something of intrinsic cultural merit. The ideological edge to the debate has dulled, not (*pace* Bell and Fukuyama, those aspirant terminators of political debate) because there are no longer any fundamental political divisions, but because the end of what the French call *les trente glorieuses* - the exceptional 30-year period of post-war prosperity and stability - has focused minds on what might be done to sustain as far as possible the benefits of employment and economic growth; and because newly industrialised countries arrived on the international scene with remarkable records of comparative success based at least in part on their high human capital formation. The weaknesses of many educational systems and institutions were exposed, opening up the ground for reform.

There are trenchant critics of the 'new vocationalism', as the dominant ethos of current policy has been dubbed. But the opposition arguments fall into two rather contradictory camps, which are not always distinguished: on the one hand against the subordination of more liberal forms of education to training geared to business needs, and on the other hand attacking the inefficiency of current provision even from the economistic point of view. The subordination view challenges the values of new vocationalism and rejects the view that there should be closer links between education and the labour market; the inefficiency view broadly accepts the goals but denies that current strategies are the right ones for achieving them. One of the reasons for the dominance of a rather narrow human capital approach is the frequent failure of these schools to articulate their position fully.

A further reason for the spread of human capital as an analytical construct is that it lent itself well to the application of sophisticated modelling and statistical techniques. Large banks of data became available which included information on length of schooling and qualifications achieved, on the one hand, and income and occupational levels on the other. This offered a rich vein for the emerging technical tools of the econometricians and of quantitative analysts of social mobility (Erikson and Goldthorpe, 1992). It became possible to measure all kinds of relationships between schooling and subsequent economic success, pointing almost unanimously to the fact that the more education someone had the more likely they were to earn above the national average (Ball, 1991). At the macro level the same appeared to be true, with countries whose populations stayed in school or college longer outperforming those, such as Britain, where large numbers left school without any qualifications and where relatively small proportions of the relevant age cohort continued into higher education.

All of this seemed to point in one direction only: any individual, and any society, that did not invest heavily in education and training was consigning themself to economic underachievement, or at least increasing the probabilities that they would lose out in the competitive race for position, power or material well-being. Occasional dissident voices were raised, most notably by those who pointed to the downside of the qualifications chase - the diploma disease, as Ronald Dore notably termed it (Dore, 1976) - though such critics were not setting themselves against education itself, but against the proliferation of certificates. The argument here was that wholesale expansion of education, in a society where the supply of 'good' jobs was finite (though not fixed), would lead inevitably to an inflation of the credentials required for jobs, without the jobs themselves being done better in many cases. Such voices were mostly drowned in the flood of technological change, as traditional manual jobs disappeared, and a soaring proportion of occupations required, or at least demanded, higher forms of literacy and skill.

Most readers will have detected in this account a note of scepticism about the quality of all this activity; surprising, perhaps, from someone who has actively propagated the doctrine of recurrent education for two decades (CERI/OECD 1975; Schuller 1978; Schuller and Megarry 1980). I am not about to recant. But I use the term 'quality' advisedly. For although quality is one of the most common buzzwords in the current British educational vocabulary, it is generally applied to mechanisms for assessing educational provision and the institutional structures which sustain it. Very rarely has it been deployed at a general level to question the quality of investment in human capital. In short, whilst the relationships between educational levels and economic success appear undeniable at a general level, the question of how efficiently and effectively the former have generated the latter has been far less frequently raised.[1]

The most obvious manifestation of this is the headlong competition between countries to raise the rates of those staying on to complete upper secondary schooling, and thus gain access to higher education. The 1980s saw regular announcements on the international scene of intentions to improve participa-

1 I use 'efficient' here in the broad traditional economic sense of achieving an end using the fewest resources possible, and 'effective' similarly to refer simply to the extent to which an end is achieved.

tion in post-compulsory education. At the secondary school level France set herself the target of 80% of school leavers achieving the baccalaureate, entitling them in principle to enter higher education. In the UK the goal for higher education participation was raised first to over 30%, then to 40% and now some influential quarters are talking about 50% of the age cohort going on to higher education.[2] Objections to these ambitions have been mainly about their resourcing, rather than the forms it has taken. Higher education institutions have accepted huge increases in student numbers in order to secure the finance which accompanies them, mainly from governmental sources, but have found their units costs cut dramatically. Few have wanted, and fewer been able, to resist this pursuit of sectoral or institutional interests, even where it has been of distinctly mixed value to them. The discrediting of the radical deschoolers on the one hand and the conservative 'more means worse' attitude on the other has led to a shortage of fundamental critiques of the way in which current systems have ballooned.

There has certainly been a significant increase in the numbers of adults enabled to return to college or university, and this is encouraging. But the effect on their labour market chances is far from unambiguously positive, and claims that a transformation of the system has occurred are exaggerated. The rise in the average age of students is mainly due to initial students staying on longer, for example to do postgraduate work, and the overall effect has arguably been to institutionalise the dependence of young people, achieving no better overall balance between initial and continuing education than existed previously. Quantitative expansion has triumphed - perhaps because the educational system itself, as the natural source of social critics, has been the vehicle of growth. Despite the friction between government and universities, it is arguable that they have connived in promoting immediate growth at the expense of longer-term remodelling of the system.

The growth of the formal education system has been paralleled by a growth in expenditure on training, by governments, individuals and companies. There is no doubt that this represents not only an expansion in learning

2 'Higher education' is, incidentally, generally understood to refer to degree programmes, although technically students pursuing certificates and diplomas are also in higher education; this is a crucial blurring.

opportunities but also a shift in the distribution across the life cycle. It has also generated a large number of innovative initiatives, in the shape of company learning or employee development schemes, which offer an interesting challenge to the formal education system. However, there are similar questions to be raised in this sphere in relation to the efficiency and effectiveness of the preoccupation with individual qualifications, and the impact of expansion on the social distribution of learning.

In short, the expansion of the formal system has generated enormous strains, in the secondary and tertiary institutions and in the budgets sustaining them. Has the effort involved paid the dividends that might have been expected? Such a question is necessarily counterfactual, and it would be perfectly reasonable to counter it by saying that any country which had not made such an effort would have found itself plummeting down the league table. My purpose here is not to say how it might have been done differently. But I do wish to raise the issue of whether a different conceptual framework, underpinned by notions broader than that of human capital, might lead to very different conclusions. In short, I wish to argue that the focus on individual achievement of extra years of education, and higher levels of qualification - in the formal sense of individually certificated achievement - biases investment in certain directions at the expense of others; and the notion of social capital might be one way of achieving a broader focus which opens up very different lines of thought and possible policy options.

Before going further, I should make it clear that this is not a wholesale attack on the human capital school, either ideologically or technically. Coleman's judgement quoted above is quite accurate. There are important respects in which it makes sense to think of education and training as investments, and to think about who bears the cost and who reaps the benefit of them. Many of the technical analyses are beyond my competence. They build spectacular edifices of equations on assumptions which are heroically unstable.[3] This in itself is not necessarily damaging, providing the

3 See for example the exposition by Mulligan and Sala-i-Martin of a labour-income-based measure of human capital. The problem with their first LIB measure was that 'we had to assume that the zero-schooling worker (which we took as the unskilled worker) had the same amount of skill always and everywhere.... We also had to assume that this worker was a perfect substitute for all the others... A second problem was that when the relative wages among workers changed for reasons other than

limitations are recognised. The problem occurs when a particular conceptual framework and methodology drives out alternative, possibly complementary approaches.

Social Capital: Three Conceptions

I shall give some definition to the notion of social capital by reference to three prominent scholars. The first two, Robert Putnam and Francis Fukuyama, are political scientists, the third, James Coleman, a sociologist. It is not their disciplinary identities which are important, but the communalities and contrasts in their approaches.

In a recent article in *Prospect*, Putnam defines social capital as 'the features of social life - networks, norms and trust - that enable participants to act together more effectively to pursue shared objectives.' (Putnam, 1996). This is indeed broad, but he proceeds quickly to give this empirical substance, drawing on extensive time-budget surveys of Americans in succeeding decades: 1965, 1975 and 1985. Most forms of collective political participation, both in the direct sense of political such as working for a political party or more broadly such as attending meetings about town or school affairs, have declined by between a quarter and a half. These findings are complemented by opinion surveys which show a decline in the last two decades of social trust. Only nationality groups and hobby clubs run counter to this trend.

Putnam examines possible causes for this civic disengagement. He looks, for a possible explanation, to such items as longer working hours, participation by women in the workforce, or the decline of traditional communities through slum clearances. The main conclusion is that the 'culprit' is television. He contrasts newspaper reading, which is positively associated with participation, and television, where 'each hour spent viewing is associated

technological shocks, then our measures would unrealistically reflect movements in the stock of human capital.' (1995 p3). The solution was to invent a model Geographical Traveling Salesman who passes through 48 different economies within a year, apparently representing a better measure of human capital. Exclamation marks fail me.

with less social trust and less group membership.' Television privatises leisure time, and therefore erodes social capital. He finds, surprisingly, that although participation is usually associated with higher levels of education, and educational levels have increased, the decline in social capital has affected all levels:

> 'The mysterious disengagement of the last quarter century seems to have afflicted all educational strata in our society, whether they have graduate education or did not finish high school.' (p67).

On this he concludes that the rise in education has mitigated what would otherwise have been an even steeper decline, but it has not succeeded in reversing it.

Putnam's approach is overtly normative. His measures may seem to be excessively encompassing - how solid is a type of capital of which 'social visiting' is a basic component? But his deployment of empirical data is substantial and compelling as an identification of a significant trend. The failure of rising educational levels to halt the decline in social capital is a powerful indication of a rather different form of instrumentalism than that which is usually pointed to. Moreover, the differentiation, crude as it is, between different types of mass media - some as positively informative, and encouraging participation, others as sapping social energies - opens up important avenues for exploration in relation to the information society.

Fukuyama's book on *Trust: The Social Virtues and the Creation of Prosperity* has a global scope, as he sets out to explain national differences in economic performance by reference to cultural factors, and especially the relationship between the development of large or small scale enterprises on the one hand and the family or other relationships which characterise society on the other. He defines social capital as follows:

> 'a capability that arises from the prevalence of trust in a society or in certain parts of it. It can be embodied in the smallest and most basic social group, the family, as well as the largest of all groups, the nation, and in all the other groups in between. Social capital differs from other forms of human capital insofar as it is usually created and transmitted

through cultural mechanisms like religion, tradition, or historical habit.' (1995: 26). Fukuyama contrasts the development of trust, and of social capital, with standard economic arguments about self-interest:

> While contract and self-interest are important sources of association, the most effective organisations are based on communities of shared ethical values. These communities do not require extensive contract and legal regulation of their relations because prior moral consensus gives members of the group a basis for mutual trust. (ibid.)

And he draws a corresponding contrast between human and social capital:

> The social capital needed to create this kind of moral community cannot be acquired, as in the case of other forms of human capital, through a rational investment decision. That is, an individual can decide to 'invest' in conventional human capital like a college education, or training to become a machinist or computer programmer, simply by going to the appropriate school. Acquisition of social capital, by contrast, requires habituation to the moral norms of a community and, in its context, the acquisition of virtues like loyalty, honesty and dependability...Social capital cannot be acquired simply by individuals acting on their own. It is based on the prevalence of social rather than individual virtues.' (ibid. pp26-7)

It is hard to extract from Fukuyama's text specific measures which might be used as Putnam has done for assessing growth and decline in social capital. This does not necessarily detract from the argument; I would certainly not wish to argue that only those theses which include 'hard' or quantitative measures have merit. To some extent, Fukuyama seems to want to establish the centrality of the notion of 'trust' by attributing to it a whole range of other social phenomena. However the general thesis is of evident relevance to any debate on the relationship between education, economic performance and social success, and the brief passage quoted goes to the heart of the difference between human and social capital.

James Coleman can probably claim to be the originator of the term, so we can turn to him with some expectation of a starting definition. He acknowledges the diversity, if not the diffuseness, of the concept:

Social capital is defined by its function. It is not a single entity but a variety of different entities, with two elements in common: they all consist of some aspect of social structures, and they facilitate certain actions of actors - whether persons or corporate actors - within the structure (1988 :S98).

So far so vague, but Coleman goes on to specify three forms of social capital. The first deals with the level of trust which exists in the social environment and the actual extent of obligations held. Social capital is high where people trust each other, and where this trust is exercised by the mutual acceptance of obligations. Coleman gives the example of Egyptian markets where neighbouring traders help each other by bringing commissions or providing finance without entering into legal or financial contracts. The second form concerns information channels; here Coleman cites a university as a place where social capital is maintained by colleagues supplying each other with ideas and information (he does not pause to reflect how far this has declined recently - nor how far other organisations maybe now approximate more closely than universities to this idea of a learning organisation). Thirdly, norms and sanctions constitute social capital where they encourage or constrain people to work for a common good, forgoing immediate self-interest.

Coleman then turns to examining the effect of social capital in creating human capital, in the family and in the community. Family background plays a large part in educational achievement (Coleman concentrates on schooling), first through financial capital - the wealth which provides school materials, a place to study at home and so on; and secondly through human capital, measured approximately by parental levels of education and influencing the child's cognitive environment. To this Coleman adds social capital, defined in terms of the relationship between parents and children. By this he means not so much the emotional relationship as the amount of effort parents put directly into their children's learning, and he cites John Stuart Mill's father and Asian immigrant families in the US as examples of high social capital. On this reckoning, one could have high levels of financial and human capital but low social capital, for instance in a high-status dual-earning household where both parents were too busy with their careers to provide direct support for the children, though presumably direct parental effort can be substituted for to some extent by relatives or paid help.

At the community level, social capital involves the extent to which parents reinforce each other's norms, and the closeness of parents' relations with community institutions. Where households move frequently, and little social interchange occurs between the adult members of the community, social capital is likely to be low. This may occur even where financial and human capital levels are high (which Coleman uses to explain why some Catholic schools in poor but relatively stable neighbourhoods outperform many private schools : 'the choice of private school for many of these parents is an individualistic one, and, although they back their children with extensive human capital, they send their children to school denuded of social capital.' (1988:S114).

Coleman goes on to test out this approach with some empirical data, using a random sample of 4000 school students and looking at variables such as the following: socio-economic status, number of siblings, number of changes in school due to family residential moves, mother's work patterns, frequency of discussion with parents about personal matters and presence of both parents in the household. This is not the place to examine the results, nor even the methodology in detail. But it is interesting to note how complex the methodology becomes, for instance in interpreting high sibling numbers as denoting a probably decrease in social capital (because the parents will have mathematically less time with each child). And it would be particularly interesting to explore the impact of domestic technology - especially Putnam's villain, the television - on parent-child interactions as a form of social capital.

It is time to summarise, and then to relate these several statements to the issue of lifelong learning. First, all three are quite straightforward about the normative content of their conceptualisations. The emphasis may be different, with Fukuyama seeking the secret of the creation of prosperity, Putnam to regenerate political health and Coleman to explain social patterns, but they all give primacy to the role of norms. Secondly, there is a clear commitment to collective values. This may appear to sit oddly with Fukuyama's previously proclaimed *End of History* ideology of the triumph of capitalism over alternative ideologies (to my mind an infinitely inferior thesis to that put forward in *Trust*), but he is seeking here to establish some kind of social base for that liberal capitalism. For the others, it is a self-evident truth that social relations are in themselves a good. Coleman, for example, does not pause to consider whether the imposition of norms by the Catholic church, aligning itself with parents to achieve educational success, might through its authoritarianism undermine non-conforming forms of social capital. Personally I have no trouble in endorsing this kind of communitarian stance at a general level, but the complexity of how and how tightly norms are enforced needs to be recognised.

Thirdly, and crucially for the purposes of this paper, the three call into question the value of human capital when it is divorced from wider social relations. All challenge the individualism and the assumed rationality of orthodox human capital approaches. Coleman draws on economistic notions of utility-maximisation as well as on sociological models of socialised behaviour, but he concludes by identifying social capital as a public good, and pointing out that the social structural conditions that overcome the problems of supplying it as a public good, strong families and strong communities, are less in evidence than in the past, and we can therefore expect a decline in human capital as a consequence. Finally, Putnam and Coleman offer rather different sets of specific measures by which the accumulation or erosion of social capital can be assessed. These certainly have their weaknesses, but they make a striking contrast to the narrowness of the assumptions made in most human capital computations.

Technology and Organisational Change: the Relevance of Social Capital

In this section I want to treat, quite summarily, some of the aspects of change in working life, and relate these to the issues raised above. The general argument is that against the background of ever-increasing overt demands for skill, organisational changes have mixed implications for investment in learning. The individualisation of employment contracts and the fragmentation experienced by many in their working lives has shifted the emphasis towards individual acceptance of responsibility for this investment. But some organisational changes are at odds with such an individualised approach, and suggest that investment decisions cannot sensibly be seen to belong to a marketplace peopled by individual actors. The place of information technology in this is central.

The relevant characteristics can be stated quite simply. In many industries and many organisations, although certainly not evenly across industries or organisations, there is a trend towards a reduction in core staff and a change in the nature of employment contracts, away from permanence and towards flexibility. There is no need here to rehearse in detail the various arguments about flexibility. There is quite rightly some scepticism about how far the flexibilisation of the workforce is an empirical reality or a piece of managerial ideology, but the numbers of people working part-time or on fixed-term contracts has grown almost everywhere; large workforces have been downsized, either through redundancies, contracting out or both; and functional flexibility has followed in the wake of new technologies and the re-division of labour in many economic sectors.

Several consequences follow from this which are relevant to the debate on human and social capital. The first is that the brute fact of large-scale unemployment has meant a loss of much human capital, however that is measured. It is not only the unskilled that have lost their jobs: unemployment affects all levels of the occupational hierarchy, though not equally. One particular feature of the collapse of full employment has been the loss of the human capital embodied in older workers, whose economic activity rates (at least amongst males) have dropped precipitously over the last two decades

(Kohli et al 1991). This human capital, it should be noted, was often not recognised in formal qualifications, as older workers did not benefit from the post-war expansion of schooling. Secondly, contracting out has in part been motivated by a desire to cut labour costs and overheads, including not only costs such as pension payments but expenditure on training. The notion of training as an 'investment' has not percolated through to accountancy practices, where it figures as a cost with no corresponding increase in the asset sheet.[4] Responsibility for maintaining existing skills and acquiring new ones has been shifted, to smaller supplying firms or to the individuals where these operate on a freelance or consultancy basis.

As far as the internal organisation of work is concerned, there is generally agreed to be a trend towards flatter hierarchies, shorter chains of command, and a greater emphasis on teamwork. This is deemed to require not only multiskilling in the technical sense, with more people capable of carrying out several different functions, but also higher level communication and interpersonal skills necessary to allow teams to work together effectively. Once again, we need to distinguish the rhetoric from the reality. Teamworking, quality circles and the like are hardly new concepts, and there is a long history of managerial fashions which owe more to public relations than anything else - accentuated by the scramble by commentators to coin the next winning phrase (winning, that is, for their book sales and consultancy scales more than for the majority of organisations referred to, or the people working in them). But even if we do not take all such pronouncements at their face value, there is still a strong demand for abilities to do with forming relationships. The issue is whether we push the question back one stage further, and ask whether such characteristics are primarily those of individuals, and to be acquired as such, or are reflections of social contexts and relationships.

Nowhere is the proneness of business to reversals of fashion clearer than in the sudden switch from downsizing to loyalty as the next centrepiece of

4 See the ambitious and importnat fifth objective of the European Commission's White Paper, *Towards a Learning Society*, which proposes that capital investment and investment in education and training should be treated on an equal basis (EC, n.d., pp49-52). The possibility of serious human resource accountancy is an intriguing one, but fraught with both technical and social difficulties.

managerial strategy. Here we come directly into contact with the tension between investment in lifelong learning and some of the trends referred to above. How can firms secure loyalty, if employees are seen to be easily disposable, temporarily or permanently? One answer could be, by investing more rather than less in their skills and knowledge; but it is rather more likely that the costs of such investment are actually being externalised, that is, put out to the flexible employees themselves.

New information technologies have played a major part in these trends. At a fundamental level, the shift towards more knowledge workers - symbolic analysts, in Robert Reich's much quoted phrase - has been powered by the huge growth in the availability of information-handling machines and the systems which allow information to be transmitted almost irrespective of geographical or temporal location. Much data-processing takes place in countries where there is a ready supply of cheap skills, which may be thousands of miles from the centre of production; Western insurance and banking services, for example, taking advantage of the huge stocks of computer skills in the Indian sub-continent.[5] Within countries we can see, for example, a town such as Chester in the north of England becoming one of the fastest-growing centres of financial services (from a very small base), far away from the traditional metropolitan centres of such operations as companies take advantage of cheaper office and labour costs.

Such trends have quite contradictory implications for analyses of human and social capital. One the one hand there is the image of the impressively qualified and lavishly equipped symbolic analyst, enjoying a pleasant lifestyle untroubled by the stress of metropolitan life and still able to exercise their skills in a labour market disembedded from any clear geographical context. On the other hand there are large numbers of workers struggling to retain a hold on employment of any kind, with no organisational support or protection, and with poor access to fresh sources of human capital. They have neither the time to acquire new skills, because only their immediately pro-

5 A recent UK policy document, the Labour Party's *The Skills Revolution*, quotes the chief executive of the HongKong and Shanghai bank, John Bond, as saying that his enterprise draws on 68 different education systems across the world to meet the challenge of economic change, as technology enalbes them to use their learning and skills thousands of miles from their home base.

ductive time is paid for, nor the social contacts through whom skills can be acquired as part of regular working life.

The thrust of my argument is this. Even where workers are exercising skills acquired in the general expansion of education and training, they may be struggling to maintain these skills because of social or occupational fragmentation and isolation. And where they are still employed in workplaces alongside colleagues, the emphasis on personal qualifications pushes to one side the collective knowledge and skills which are supposedly the key to success in a contemporary economy. A human capital approach may continue to register growth; but a social capital approach which takes a broader view based on relationships at work (personal or corporate) may give a very different picture.

Naturally, this requires a closer examination of what constitutes social relations. The Internet opens up huge possibilities of fast and frequent communication with large numbers of people, free from physical or temporal constraints. For academics, this signals a huge expansion of the possibilities of forming collegial communities. Moreover the nature of the Internet allows individuals to choose quite precisely what they wish to share with their unseen colleagues, and therefore allows some relationships of trust to evolve naturally. It is up to individuals to decide how much they wish to share, and on what basis. The scope for freeloaders, who receive messages and tap into web pages but never contribute to the common pool is enormous. On the other hand, they may find that the resources of the worldwide information system tend to be more effectively mobilised by those who do form some kind of bilateral or, more likely, multilateral relationships, even with those whom they have never met. There is not a simple divide to be made between relationships which are purely technologically mediated - stereotypically involving social isolates who can communicate only via the keyboard and screen - and those which are deemed to be social because they involve physical co-location.

Individualisation and Human Capital

These shifts in economic and organisational structures are part of a wider trend towards greater individualisation of personal biographies. There is some debate over how far lifecourses are becoming more or less standardised (Kohli, Meyer). In a longer-term perspective, many societies have witnessed a growing standardisation and homogenisation of biographies, with the introduction of age norms defining the location and role of individuals on the social structure. Against this must be set the decay of traditional employment structures and family patterns has meant the erosion of defined sequences of stages and a blurring of the transitions between stages. The tension has been well described by Jansen and Van der Veen:

> On the one hand, the traditional social and ideological ties of family, class, neighbourhood, church, etc are weakened, which gives more freedom of choice and decision to the individual. This means that individuals become more 'self-responsible' for the planning and organisation of their lives.....On the other hand, should this development be equated, not unproblematically, with a growing autonomy and emancipation of the individual subject? (1992:278-9).
>
> Jansen and Van der Veen go on to identify the pitfalls facing adult education in embracing too enthusiastically the individualisation of biographies: the substitution of material values for religious and political ones, the lack of preparation for making effective choices, the problems caused by the blurring of recognised transitions, and the spread of new forms of social inequality in what has been called the democratisation of social insecurity.

Many of these arguments are derived from Beck's characterisation of the risk society (Beck, 1992), two features of which deserve particular mention here. First, there is a shift from unequal control over the means of production in classic industrial societies to a generalised uncontrollability of industrial and technological innovation. (Beck concentrates on the environmental effects, but the risks are more general even than these.) Secondly, struggles for power move from being related to ownership of the means of production and distribution to control over information and the definition of what counts as useful knowledge.

This raises a host of issues, of which I want to concentrate on only two: the individualisation of competence; the social mix of competence; and the recognition of the sources of competence.

The individualisation of competence is inherent in the preoccupation with increased levels of formal qualifications. Certificates are awarded almost exclusively to individuals, and this has a number of consequences. It means that teaching is geared to individual achievement, possibly at the expense of collective learning. It defines learning in terms of what is immediately measurable, at the expense of other forms of learning which may be equally valuable but which cannot be demonstrated as such by the end of the specified learning period. And it tends to exclude the types of learning which occur outside formal institutions, whether or not these are part of the formal education system.

This is, of course, a sweeping generalisation. It is worth recording, for example, that although National Education and Training Targets in the UK concentrate on levels of individual qualification, they include targets for organisations attaining Investors in People status, and IiP is a scheme which encourages corporate approaches to human resource development. Nevertheless even within such schemes progress is largely measured in terms of qualifications achieved at different levels within the workforce.

Individualisation focuses attention on the supply side. It assumes that increasing the supply of qualified people is the primary requirement for improving economic performance. But there is some scepticism about this. It is not clear that employers are actually making use of the enhanced qualifications of the labour supply, as opposed to merely raising the levels of qualification required for jobs which remain essentially the same, or which have changed but do not necessarily demand enhance skills (Regini 1995). Politically, it places the responsibility for change on the shoulders of individual members of the labour force, implying that those who cannot contribute to the economy are not just lacking in skills but are not conforming to modern norms. In short, there are serious questions about the balance between the supply side and the demand side, and the rhetoric about lifelong learning may be giving undue primacy to the former.

Such observations have been made by people operating explicitly or implicitly within the human capital framework. But there is a further consideration., which follows fairly clearly from the earlier discussion of social capital. There are many other components, beyond the provision of overt learning opportunities and the acquisition of recognised competencies, which contribute to the accumulation of social capital (or, to put it another way, to the building of a learning society). Coleman and Putnam refer to some of them, in families and communities. There are many other possible candidates, depending on the coarseness or fineness of mesh used. To take just one example: newspaper-reading, identified by Putnam as strongly contrasting with television in the impact it has on social participation, surely depends on the quality of the newspapers. Coming from a society which sports some of the most uninformative (to put it mildly) press in the world, I find it hard to give an unqualified endorsement of newspapers as a positive element in the social capital equation. Nevertheless, the point is that if learning cannot be compartmentalised, and if qualifications are more likely to be obtained by those who are also learning outside the college and the workplace, we cannot ignore the other, highly invasive, sources of information and learning which exist, beyond those tailored to individually certified achievement.

The Distribution of Learning: Health and Relative Inequalities

I come now to the issue of the social distribution of learning, and an analogy with the work of Richard Wilkinson. Put simply, Wilkinson argues, using global epidemiological data that health in the developed countries is no longer affected very much by improvements in material prosperity, but by the quality of the social environment. In countries such as Brazil and Britain, where social inequalities are very marked and the gap between rich and poor has grown significantly in the last two decades, mortality and morbidity rates for the poor are very high compared to those at the bottom end of the social pyramid in less hierarchical societies. That much may be unsurprising, but it is also the case that the well-off are unhealthier - not only than their counterparts in more equal societies but even - and this is the startling finding - than the poorer in other countries. The health of the wealthy in Britain is worse than the health of the poor in Sweden. Social cohesion, or its absence, is a crucial factor affecting the health of a society *at all levels*.

The link to the notion of social capital is potentially fascinating. I have not had time to think this through in any detail, but here is a preliminary exposition of the analogy with Wilkinson's findings on health. A society may expand its levels of human capital formation in gross terms, just as it may raise its overall GNP and income per capita. But if no attention is paid to the distribution of human capital, the impact of this rise may be very different to what might have been anticipated. Obviously those who individually fail to raise their levels of qualification are excluded from the gains (unless the trickle down theory is operating in a way which would be wholly contrary to the evidence thus far); but even those who seem to be in a position to benefit may not in fact be doing so. Within the given society, or region, they will be relatively well off, as human capital theory would predict. But not only are they worse off - in learning achievement, if not materially - than those who are at the high end of the human capital spectrum in countries or regions with a more equal record of learning achievement; they may also be learning less than the lower achievers in those more equal societies.

Intuitively this does not make much sense, and it is tempting to dismiss the analogy outright. How can successful executives, judges or university professors (or whatever position we take to exemplify higher levels of learning - the modern polycompetent) in one developed country be less well qualified than unskilled workers in another? In terms of labour market position, almost certainly not. But when we broaden the notion of learning so that all forms of social relationships are included, the parallel maybe does not seem so far-fetched. What are those who are earning large amounts but who are always under stress in their own lives and increasingly isolated from the lives of others exercising in the way of savoir vivre? Are they developing the kinds of skills which are needed primarily to safeguard their own position as far as possible in a society where increasing numbers are unable to safeguard theirs, and if so how do such skills affect their daily lives? What competencies do they have to assure themselves of the futures of their children, who may not attain the same position as themselves (the classic dilemma, which explains much of why most middle-class parents support comprehensive education, since they cannot be sure that their children will make it into the elite)?

There are no data sets equivalent to those which enabled Wilkinson to reach his momentous conclusions. But I maintain that the notion of social capital at least points to the types of information which we should be considering in order to explore some of these issues. By its stress on relationships and values, inherently social phenomena, it takes us beyond the individual acquisition of formal qualifications, or even of real and undeniable skills and competencies.

Comparative Studies on Social Capital

These are some of the issues which John Field and I are setting out to explore in a comparative study of Scotland and Northern Ireland: two small countries where participation in learning (education and training) by adults appears relatively low, especially when compared with achievement in initial education (Field and Schuller, 1996). We shall be looking at several economic sectors in both countries - agriculture, electronics, healthcare, finance and tourism - and using focus groups to discover whether stakeholders consider this low participation to be a significant issue, and if so what they think should be done about it. In carrying out the study we hope to develop a framework for measuring social capital, covering some of the issues sketched out above. We would be delighted to hear from fellow researchers who are doing similar work.

References

Ball, C. (1991), Learning Pays, Royal society of Arts, London.

Beck, U. (1992), The Risk Society: towards a new modernity, London, Sage.

Becker, G. (1964), Human Capital, a theoretical and empirical analysis, with special reference to education, Columbia University Press.

Benoit-Guilbot, O. (1995), 'Introduction', *Sociologie du Travail* XXXVII:4, pp 495-502.

Carnoy, M. (1995), Encyclopaedia of Economics of Education

CERI/OECD, (1975), Recurrent Education: Trends & Issues, Organisation for Economic Co-operation and Development, Paris.

Coleman, J. (1988), *American Journal of Sociology*

Dore, R. (1976), The Diploma Disease: Education, Qualification and Development, London Allen & Unwin.

Erikson, R. and Goldthorpe, J. (1992), The Constant Flux: a study of class mobility in industrial societies, Oxford: Clarendon Press

European Commission (no date) *Towards a Learning Society*, Brussels.

Field, J. and Schuller, T. (1996), *Scottish Journal of Adult and Continuing Education*

Fukuyama, F. (1995), Trust: the social virtues and the creation of prosperity, London, Hamish Hamilton.

Jansen, T. and Van der Veen, R. (1992), 'Adult education in the light of the risk society', International Journal of Lifelong Education, Vol. 11, No. 4, pp. 275-286.

Kohli, M., Rein, M., Guillemard, A. M. and Herman van Gunsteren (1991) Time for Retirement, Cambridge University Press.

Kohli, M. and Meyer, J. (1986), 'Social Structure and Social Construction of Life Stages', Human Development, Vol. 29, pp. 145-180.

Machin, S. and Wilkinson. D. (1995), Employee Training: Unequal Access and Economic Performance, Institute for Public Policy Research, London.

Regini, M. (1995), 'Demande en ressources humaines et institutions de formation dans quelques regions européennes', *Sociologie du Travail* XXXVII:4, pp 645-660.

Reich, R. (1991), The Work of Nations Simon & Schuster

Schuller, T. (1978), Learning Through Life Young Fabian pamphlet 47, Fabian Society, London.

Schuller, T. and Megarry, J., (eds.) Recurrent Education and Lifelong Learning, World Yearbook of Education, Kogan Page.

Schultz, T. (1963), The Economic Value of Education, Columbia University Press.

Wilkinson, R. (1996), Unhealthy Societies: The Afflictions of Inequality, London, Routledge.

Gerhild Brüning

The Project REGIO: Aims and First Results

Introduction

German society is undergoing a social structural change historically unparalleled in its quantitative and qualitative dimension. Technological change, globalisation of markets, changing conditions of production and so on have led to a crisis in employment. Societal and individual loss of orientation and uncertain future prospects are the results. The collapse of the former German Democratic Republic and the subsequent difficulties of the transformation make especially clear the necessity of new paradigms for society as a whole. The comprehensive structural models developed in the 1970s, irrespective of their ideological orientation, were based on a growth model of correspondingly increasing scope of allocation. As growth rates of the 1970s became unachievable, the structural supra-national models developed along these principles proved no longer viable. One solution seems to be an orientation towards regional development concepts.

The discussion about goals, range, significance and the legitimacy of advanced vocational training has once again been touched off under the conditions of the transformation process. During the post-unification period it seemed almost as if the structural change and economic alignment of the two German states could be overcome solely through advanced training programmes. Job-related further training has indeed accomplished much on the labour market and at the socio-political level. The hope attached to further education, that it would contribute to the creation of sorely-needed jobs in the former East German states have, however, exceeded the possibilities of further education. This is an essential instrument for mending structural ruptures, but it is only one of several.

Against this background a number of questions arise:

What effect can further training, and vocational training in particular, have when considering the situation on the labour market?

How can further training be utilised under these conditions?

What possibilities does vocational training have in forging links between the job market and publicly-sponsored employment measures?

What form should it take regarding concept and content in order to fulfil the expectations of reintegrating the unemployed into the primary labour market?

In times of mass employment can advanced vocational training find its sole legitimacy in providing individuals with access, or greater ease of access respectively, to the job market? Or is a new strategy necessary, one that reaches beyond the concept of gainful employment?

What educational and development opportunities exist, not only for the individual but also for the region when employment is combined with job qualification measures?

Project REGIO's Approach

These questions are the points of reference for Project REGIO, whose official title is 'Training Pedagogical Personnel in Labour Market Policy Measures in the Context of Regional Co-operation'. The German Institute of Adult Education (Deutsches Institut für Erwachsenenbildung/DIE), located in Frankfurt am Main, is responsible for conducting the project on behalf of the German Ministry of Education, Science, Research and Technology in Bonn between the beginning of 1995 and the end of 1997.

The project has two main approaches. One is the further training of pedagogical and supervisory personnel working in qualification and employment organisations. The training programme contents are, therefore, selected so as to address the above-mentioned questions. The project's second approach is to initiate networking relations among persons in both the primary and secondary labour market, those active in the regional structural development and job market on a local and regional level. Vocational training plays an important role in this.

Plan of Action in the Project

Choice of Location

Operating throughout Germany in selected locations, the REGIO Project co-operates with employment and qualification organisations, that is, with organisations that enable the jobless to re-enter the primary job market through public-financed job and job qualification programmes. Initial considerations in the choice of project locations were to consider shared characteristics but also to allow differences.

The choice of locations was based on the following criteria:

- three locations in the 'new' states of former East Germany (Neustrelitz in Mecklenburg - Vorpommern /Western Pommerania and Zwickau and Scharfenstein in Sachsen/Saxony) and two locations in the 'old' West German states (Saarbrücken in Saarland and Taunusstein in Hessen/ Hesse);
- three locations of a predominantly rural structure (Neustrelitz, Scharfenstein and Taunusstein);
- two locations where industrial production has massively decreased in recent years (Zwickau and Saarbrücken);
- four locations which show an above-average unemployment rate between 15-20% (Neustrelitz, Zwickau, Scharfenstein and Saarbrücken);
- at all five locations work is going on with employment and job qualification organisations.

The points in common for the East and West locations, which had been carefully selected in order to make a comparison relevant for research purposes and to be able to determine corresponding plans of action, proved somewhat unimportant. Common to the organisations, however, was the difficulty in accomplishing the tasks and functions of reintegrating jobless persons into the primary labour market and increasing productive performance in an economic sense.

An additional commonality was the lack of discussion about the employment organisations. As long as there is no discussion about future prospects, areas of activity and social and job market policy possibilities within the context of the current political framework, these organisations will have no comprehensive or workable future prospects.

Further Training Offerings and Methods of Action

The seminars offered by Project REGIO at the various locations have two focal points. Standard topics of adult education are offered for the pedagogical personnel (instructors, teachers, and social-guidance counsellors). Particularly in the new German states, many persons from non-teaching fields are entrusted with teaching responsibilities. In addition, fluctuation in this field is very high due to the system of work-creation measures (on limited short-term contracts) which necessitate repeatedly offering courses dealing with basic issues in adult education and advanced vocational education.

In the face of a lack of jobs and multiple vocational qualifications acquired by unemployed persons through job-training schemes, further education per se has been plunged into a crisis of legitimacy, but not because a lack of job qualification hinders re-entry. Re-entry is hindered rather because the potential supply of manpower on the labour market exceeds the demand. Seminar themes include dealing with the goals of further training measures against a background of social change. The thematic choice did not come as a result of theoretical reflections by the project staff, but rather from discussions by educational practitioners. This type of seminar is oriented towards the key skills approach as formulated by Mertens in the early 1970s. He postulated that in addition to conveying functional qualifications, further education has another task, that of conveying extra-functional qualifications which contribute to an individual's personal development and support her/him in assuming social responsibility.

In the face of the current mass unemployment phenomenon, this approach has been expanded. Further training, especially vocational further training, is supposed to both maintain and extend the individual's vocational competence, whereas 'competence' in this sense cannot be viewed exclusively under vocational aspects but is as well an integral approach to one's life orientation.

The project's procedural approach regarding the needs survey and conceptual contents of seminars is founded on a research approach, which, based on action theory, includes both macro- and micro-didactic levels. Also included are the biographical experiences of the participants and the societal norms. It is particularly in the field of further vocational training, that research conception must consider economic, labour market and politico-educational, and legal issues and how these affect willingness to learn and potential self-realisation of employed and unemployed persons as well as other target groups.

Needs surveys concerning seminar offerings were conducted on the basis of experience gained from projects and work which established the relationship between participants' interests, goals of the sponsoring organisations and the conditions of financial sponsorship.

Although there are standard topics in the field of vocational training, the curriculum planning was tailored to the participants' specific situation and the location. Since projects increasingly contain conceptual variations, the content of the seminars offered can even change during a course itself. Such seminars thus display special regional characteristics as well as being of varying length and course content. Systematic feedback by means of reflection and evaluation on the part of participants, organisations, and project and scholarly experts is necessary to be able to achieve this.

The second focal point of the seminar is directed towards the supervisory personnel of the participating employment organisations. Solidly established classical topics include 'Project Management' and 'Time Management and Self-Management'. Workshops within the fields of organisational development and discussion of models have shown themselves to be especially valuable. Developing a model has proved to be essential to employment organisations as a pre-requisite for on-going development and safeguard for the future, since the official task designation for the employment organisations is self-contradictory. Their main goal is to integrate persons back into the primary job market, the assumption being that the primary job market can provide employment and that persons are unemployed only because they lack functional qualifications to get a job. These premises are no longer valid. The employment organisations have increasingly taken on a socio-political task of providing employment to the jobless, the long-term unemployed, and also welfare recipients. In addition, the employment organisations are supposed to display high-quality performance in the absence of basic given conditions. By creating jobs on the primary labour market through the establishment of new business enterprises, they are supposed to be working towards phasing themselves out as quickly as possible. Discussion and definition of goals thereby become absolutely essential in order to reach a consensus about the actual content of the work and about possibly necessary structural changes of the employment organisations.

Regional Structural Development

The project's second approach, to collaborate with local and regional networking systems, has been carried out in Neustrelitz in Mecklenburg-Vorpommern and in Taunusstein in Hessen. The networking began on a level quite different from the original project planning.

In order to realise workable regional co-operation, seen as helping to strengthen the primary labour market, it had been planned to bring participants important to regional development together into work groups. To be included in this activity on-site were representatives from training and employment organisations, employers' and employees' associations, the local political scene, labour office, socio-political associations and so on. Concepts for regional development and strategic planning were to be worked out in round-table discussions. This approach has not been realised to date.

Experience from regionally-based projects of other states shows that networking and co-operation are effective only when they address participants' varied interests at each location. Common interests can only be developed when these various positions are taken into consideration.

New opportunities for co-operation, communication and negotiation can be planned and tried out within the framework of development-based research. However, the role of the adult educator is less as a teacher than as a moderator, adviser and individual accompanying the process.

Based on these experiences, a project group was formed in Neustrelitz (Eastern location) in which for the first time only the local employment organisations of the county and the 'Oberzentrum' of Neubrandenburg were represented. The goal of this project group is to:

- help the employment organisations to understand their own role;
- determine the project areas relevant to the future of the employment organisations;
- move forward integration of the planning and executive activities of regional structural development.

Although the employment organisations consider themselves an important element of the social and economic structure, this potential has too seldom been actively put to use. Now the regional structural development plans, often existing only in piecemeal approaches and not as an over-all concept, are to be examined in terms of their relevance in terms of economic and labour market policy and then adapted accordingly. Furthermore, the employment organisations want to be established as a structural factor of regional development to the greatest extent possible in both regional and local economic programmes.

This structural integration is supposed to ensure political acceptance, make possible planning horizons and open scopes of activity.Following this phase of consolidation, the project intends to intensify co-operation with the remaining participants active in determining regional labour market policy.

In Taunusstein (Western location) co-operative efforts between the project and the regional headquarters in co-ordinating the job market and local employment policy have resulted in the formation of various work groups. These groups want to contribute to regional economic development according to a procedural model characterised by individual suppliers, who develop economic potential through mutual co-operation, the so-called 'from the bottom up' model. Projects to promote tourism in the Rheingau-Taunus-Kreis are planned in which the concentration of individual interests widen the scope for co-operative opportunities and result in economic synergy and job creation. These activities include creating a network of tourist sector enterprises in the region, developing year-round tourist attractions, marketing local wine and agricultural products directly, and reviving village stores.

At both locations the project has assumed supportive, advisory and moderating roles.

Project Results to Date

The training programmes offered to pedagogical personnel within the employment and job qualification organisations have been well-received. Both the content and the didactic methods of the seminars have met needs but have also revealed other specific gaps as well. In addition to this effect of providing additional job qualification, the seminars have also served as a 'job performance bonus' for participants, particularly in the new German states. The chance to participate has meant an additional recognition of work and provided motivation for the difficult everyday work routine.

The lack of long-term continuity on the part of pedagogical personnel (as a rule they have only limited term contracts and are often insufficiently qualified and unprepared for their new activity) would necessitate concomitant job training. The employment office often meets this need by combining employment measures with job qualification measures. However, the pedagogical personnel are still too rarely integrated in this form. Sufficient training provided by Project REGIO for these groups is impossible for lack of time, financing and personnel. The project has therefore initiated the idea of colleague-based consultation groups. These various professional groups meet regularly to gain information from each other as well as from outside expert sources. The exchange of information results in mutual support in this type of work involving difficult target groups and also helps in developing new problem-solving strategies.

The recently expanded approaches of self-organisation and self-accessed learning are useful here. The length of time needed until this colleague-based consultation becomes self-supporting and no longer dependent on Project REGIO is still unclear at present.

The vocational further training offerings of the project have been adjusted to the framework of the employment and job qualification organisations. Part of this is the training of supervisory staff, an area of further education considered especially important for several reasons:

- The concept 'employment organisation' is also a short form for 'Society of Labour Support, Employment and Structural Development' (Gesellschaft für Arbeitsförderung, Beschäftigung und Strukturentwicklung/ABS). Employment organisations are an important element in the regional economic structure, but have too rarely intervened actively in the planning process. Calls are increasing to examine the task designation of these employment organisations and to eliminate the field of regional structural development from the list of responsibilities. The call for concentrating, or limiting responsibilities respectively, are heard frequently because supervisory personnel are insufficiently prepared for these. Every employment organisation must conduct for itself this discussion regarding areas of responsibilities and opportunities for taking action. It must however also keep in mind opportunities for co-operation with other organisations and persons from the primary labour market in order to take advantage of possible synergy effects.

- The reform of the Labour Support Law has restricted the conditions for support of the employment organisations and thereby also for the unemployed. Only the long-term unemployed have a chance of receiving support. A support policy of this kind often results in the commonly observed effects of long-term unemployment, such as addiction, illness and in the origin of new problem groups. Special competence, which is not always available, is required of both supervisory personnel and social guidance counsellors, of whom especially in the latter group more are needed.
- The employment organisations see themselves increasingly confronted by a demand for improved measures, to be understood in this connection as measures that can be continued after the support programmes have ended and represent economic and social benefits for the region. Drafting concepts of benefit analysis necessitates business and financial knowledge which supervisory personnel often first have to aquire.

In all of these areas the project has offered support to the employment organisations in the form of organisational consultation and coaching. The need for consultation has heretofore dealt with internal and external structural discussions, working out models and prospects, project development and management, and regional networking.

Regional networking and the creation of co-operative efforts are only possible on a long-term basis and are dependent on staff continuity. Both requirements contradict the framework of the employment organisations whose political goal is to phase themselves out. Due to uncertain working conditions, there is high staff fluctuation which causes a constant drain on qualifications. Despite numerous discussions and innovative approaches, acceptable solutions for these contradictions have yet to be found.

Project REGIO has sponsored high-level discussions among experts concerning the future of employment and job qualification organisations. The results of these 'strong point-weak point' analyses have yet to be discussed in order to reach definite conclusions about the conceptual and structural form of these employment organisations.

In future the employment organisations will retain their socio-political function despite all difficulties since a continuing high unemployment rate is to be expected. However, these organisations will have to adapt to huge changes.

Integration into the primary labour market will prove impossible for many, more so from a lack of job opportunities than from a lack of job qualifications.

The target groups have changed to the extent that the ranks of the jobless now increasingly consist of older persons, women and, in a tight job market, the insufficiently-qualified applicants.

The project contents of the employment organisation will have to adapt to changing target groups which, under the current framework, will result in a loss of quality. The given goals of the employment organisations, to initiate business start-ups and to work in a product- and market-oriented fashion, will be even more difficult to attain.

Employment organisations are, therefore, increasingly stressing a greater socio-political role for themselves. While they are still a gathering place for the unemployed, there is a tendency in rural areas towards socio-cultural projects to counteract the desolation and depopulation of these areas. Numerous projects with this slant have been carried in Neustrelitz in Mecklenburg-Vorpommern. Their goal is maintaining vocational competence among unemployed persons while at the same time improving the region's social and cultural infrastructure.

Example: The Chroniclers

In 1995 Mecklenburg-Vorpommern celebrated its 1000th anniversary. The 'Chroniclers Project' originated as part of the preparations for the numerous planned festive ceremonies. The original idea was to critically examine regional historical documents for possible information gaps and falsifications, particularly in more recent history, and then to correct these. The project was sponsored by the employment office. Equally divided between measures for employment and job qualification, provisions were made primarily for job-related training in project management, computer work, use and analysis of historical sources, archival documentation, typing, multimedia techniques, documentation, and so on. An individual goal for the participants in this critical examination of history became that of facilitating the search for self-identity and thereby bolstering self-confidence, thus contributing to personal stability. The project was so successful that all the participants for the theoretical section registered for an external examination, a nationally-recognised professional qualification as a documentation assistant, which was a development unplanned-for originally. As a point of interest, all the participants passed the examination.

Socio-political and labour market policy impetus can be expected as a result of this chroniclers project. The depiction of historical events, listing of sightseeing attractions and the development of additional materials are to be included in regional tourist promotion activities, thus making the area more attractive to both local residents and outside visitors. Even if the project has not yet generated any jobs on the primary labour market, project participants could experience that meaningful work is possible outside regular forms of gainful employment. Under present social and economic conditions it is necessary to expand the concept of 'work' from the exclusive aspect of gainful employment to include the idea of 'socially useful work', 'community work', or 'public work' in the discussion as well.

Here, under the aspect of further education, is a good example of how general, political, cultural and vocational education can forge meaningful links with each other and result in greater competence not attainable through purely functional job qualification programmes.

Still another aspect of learning and motivation is significant. On-site learning that integrates the whole person through active individual participation was made possible by way of excursions, work with original historical sources (often found by chance), interviews and discussions with local residents (often the participants themselves).

In conclusion, advanced vocational training must submit to self-scrutiny against this background of labour market conditions. Technical and functional job qualification as an aid to reintegration into the primary labour market is no longer enough. A broader view of qualification - more oriented towards combining training with active work - is necessary. Further vocational training measures linked to employment and which consider a region not only as an investment option but also as over-all social and cultural entity in whose formation an individual can actively participate, have the best chance of making vocational learning into a socially meaningful personal experience.

Peter Faulstich

Summary

The author points out that most of the programmes supporting regional development are guided by the priority of economic development, thus defining a specific function for continuing education. He in turn poses the question which regional structures will have to be created or preserved in order to enable the personal development - and that includes education and training - of people in a specific region. Region is therefore understood as the cultural context of living together, from which experience will help to develop an identity. Thus the author analyses the prevailing arguments for prioritising economic development under the aspect of global competition versus regional policies. He shows that at present we can observe signs of return to a regional strategy and develops new strategies for adult continuing education in this context. This he does considering the basic question of economic ratio and personal identity. This question is definitely linked to the problem of a regional cultural identity which the rather complex German term of 'Heimat' could eventually cover. He finally pleads for an adult continuing education which is aware of indigenous resources and utilises the opportunities which are innate to a regional identity.

„Heimat“ als Problem regionaler Qualifikationspolitik

Regionalorientierte Ansätze finden derzeit bei den Akteuren in der Weiterbildung wachsendes Interesse. Die Wirtschaftsförderung der Städte und Kreise setzt auf regionale Qualifikationstrategien; Länder initiieren regional orientierte Förderschwerpunkte; zahlreiche Programme und der Sozialfonds der EU fördern Weiterbildung für die Entwicklung strukturschwacher Regionen.

In solchen regional orientierten Strategien ist Weiterbildung in der Regel ein Faktor im Rahmen übergeordneter Politikfelder. Weiterbildung wird als

Instrument für die Wirtschafts-, besonders die Arbeitsmarktpolitik eingesetzt. Indem aber in dieser Weise nach der Funktion von Weiterbildung für wirtschaftliche Entwicklung gefragt wird, erfolgt von Anfang an und oft unbemerkt eine Unterordnung unter ökonomische Interessen.

Demgegenüber will ich den Vorschlag unterbreiten, bei der Betrachtung des Verhältnisses von Wirtschaftsentwicklung und Weiterbildung die Denkrichtung umzukehren. Demgemäß ist nicht zu fragen, was denn Weiterbildung beitragen kann oder soll zur regionalen Ökonomie, sondern welche regionalen Strukturen gesichert oder geschaffen werden müssen, um die Entfaltung der Personen, die in einer Region leben - also auch ihre Bildung -, zu ermöglichen.

Region wird dabei gesehen als der kulturelle Kontext erfahrbaren Zusammenlebens, in welchem sich Identität entwickeln kann. Ein solches Problem kann man in Deutschland nicht aufwerfen, ohne über den Begriff Heimat zu stolpern - ein Wort mit einer spezifischen Sondertradition, das in andere Sprachen kaum übersetzbar ist. Der Schriftsteller Max Frisch hat darüber nachgedacht: „*My country* erweitert und limitiert Heimat von vornherein auf ein Staatsgebiet. *Homeland* setzt Kolonien voraus.“(Zit in Cremer/Klein 35). „*Feeling home*“ überbetont den emotionalen Aspekt. Vielleicht können aber beim gemeinsamen Nachdenken verallgemeinerbare Einsichten gewonnen werden.

Ich werde im ersten Abschnitt unserer Überlegungen versuchen, die vorherrschende Argumentationsfigur einer Unterordnung von Regionalpolitik unter Versuche zur Standortsicherung angesichts von Globalisierungstendenzen zu überprüfen. Die regionalen Akteure geraten dabei m.E. in Spiralen von Hilflosigkeit. Zweitens werden Anzeichen für eine Rückkehr zu regionalen Horizonten belegt. In diesen Zusammenhang werde ich drittens resultierende Strategien für die Weiterbildung einordnen. Viertens müssen, um eine solche Strategie zu fundieren, Grundsatzfragen im Verhältnis von ökonomischer Rationalität und persönlicher Identität aufgeworfen werden. Dabei stößt man - fünftens - auf das Problem der regionalen kulturellen Identität und eben - wie gesagt - auf das schwierige, fast unübersetzbare, deutsche Wort

Heimat. Abschließend - sechstens - plädiere ich für eine Erwachsenenbildung, welche sich besinnt auf Chancen von Identität in der Region.

1. Regionalpolitik zur Standortsicherung?

Wenn man die vorherrschenden Leitlinien ökonomischen und auch politischen Handelns betrachtet und in ihrer letzten Konsequenz ernst nimmt, muß man sich eigentlich wundern, daß es die Frage nach den Regionen noch gibt. Die Ökonomie wird weltweit eingeebnet.

Wenn man den Versuchen, weltweit gleiche und bessere Möglichkeiten der Verwertung des Kapitals herzustellen, widerspricht, steht man fast hoffnungslos im Abseits. Die hegemoniale Denkbewegung geht in die entgegengesetzte Richtung. Wenn man die Äußerungen der ökonomischen und politischen Akteure zusammensieht, so sind sie insgesamt gekennzeichnet durch zwei Begriffe, welche die Rahmenbedingungen für anstehende Handlungsrichtungen abgeben: „Weltmarkt“ und „Standort“. In der „Zeit“ vom 5.Juli 1996 findet man die große Überschrift: „Alles Standort, oder was ?“ Region kommt dann nur noch ins Blickfeld als - prinzipiell immer auswechselbarer - Standort.

Die „Zukunftssicherung des Standortes Deutschland“ - oder Großbritannien, oder Italien, oder Dänemark u.s.w. - im Rahmen sich weltweit vollziehender Modernisierung und Globalisierung wird oberste Handlungsmaxime gegenwärtiger Politik.

Dabei geht es um die Durchsetzung eines Entwicklungspfades, der explizit von wohlfahrtsstaatlichen Prinzipien Abschied nimmt. Letztlich geht es darum, Akkumulationsbedingungen herzustellen, welche als Investitionsanreize im jeweiligen Inland und in den einzelnen Regionen wirken. Dem dient eine aggressive Deregulierungs- und Privatisierungspolitik. Die nationalen Gesellschaften und regionalen Gemeinschaften werden in internationalen Wettbewerb getrieben. Die wichtigsten Schritte dahin waren drastische Maßnahmen zugunsten des Freihandels, das Ende der Währungskontrollen und die Liberalisierung der Geldmärkte. Es gibt auch einen Starttermin für diese Durchsetzung dieses unbegrenzten Freihandels: die GATT-Konferenz von Punta del Este (Uruguay) 1986.

Kern der Strategie ist, uneingeschränkte, gnadenlose, absolute Konkurrenz zu ermöglichen. Standortpolitik ist dann der Versuch, über Senkung von Löhnen, Steuern und Sozialleistungen und damit letztlich der Preise Anteile auf dem Weltmarkt zu erobern. Das Ausland wird allerdings das gleiche tun mit der Folge einer Abwärtsspirale für alle. Regierungen, die versuchen sich dieser Logik zu entziehen, werden bestraft. Der Motor der zu Glaubensbekenntnis erhobenen Marktwirtschaft ist die Konkurrenz. Die regionalen Ökonomien werden in einen Prozeß getrieben, den man als „Hypercompetition“ bezeichnen kann. Regionale Identität kommt im weltweiten Wettbewerb nicht vor.

Die Konsequenzen sind absehbar: Wenn Märkte international wirklich „frei“ werden, zwingen sie zu weltweiten Investitionsstrategien, zum Wegzug von Kapital und resultierender Destruktion von Arbeitsplätzen. Die globalen, streunenden und zudem kurzfristigen Fluktuationen des Geldes zerstören die territorialen Institutionen der einzelnen Staaten und die historisch gewachsenen Solidarsysteme. Soziale Konstruktionen wie die labilen Wohlfahrtssysteme, die sich erst in langen Verhandlungen und Machtkämpfen in unwahrscheinlichen Gleichgewichten des Sozialstaates etabliert haben, sind weltweit „freien“ Märkten schutzlos ausgeliefert. Die Dynamik einer apersonalen, sachlichen und anonymen Regulation ist gegenüber demokratischen und sozialen Prinzipien rücksichtslos. Dies gilt auch gegenüber den Institutionen der Erwachsenenbildung.

Ein Weitergehen auf diesem Weg führt letztlich ins Bodenlose. Je mehr sich die regionalen Wirtschaften auf den Export von Waren und Dienstleistungen ziehen lassen, desto stärker müssen sie sich den auf dem Weltmarkt herrschenden Bedingungen anpassen und desto stärker schlagen Weltmarktschwankungen auf den Binnenmarkt durch. Aus dieser Sicht ist der Abbau des Sozialstaates zwangsläufig und unumgehbar. Eine auf den „globalen Sektor“ ausgerichtete Wirtschaftspolitik, welche ausschließlich auf die Entlastung der Kostenseite setzt, vernachlässigt darüber hinaus die Tatsache, daß Arbeitseinkommen gleichzeitig die kaufkräftige Nachfrage für Binnenmärkte darstellen. Die Vergangenheit hat gezeigt, daß Kostenentlastungen und immense Gewinnsteigerungen keineswegs zu Arbeitsplatzsicherung und -erweiterung mit den dafür nötigen Investitionen geführt haben. Vielmehr unterstützt eine solche angebotsorientierte Standortpolitik ein ökonomisches Wachstumsmodell, das verstärkt auf Technikeinsatz, Arbeitsreduktion und erhöhte Arbeitsintensität setzt. In letzter Konsequenz ist diese Strategie aber chancenlos. Horst Afheldt hat in seinem Buch „Wohlstand für niemand?“ drastisch formuliert, daß weltweit Arbeit billig ist wie Dreck. So führt der radikalisierte Marktliberalismus zu absehbaren, unausweichlichen Konsequenzen:

- im Kampf gegen den Rest der Welt geraten die nationalen Staaten und regionalen Akteure in eine Überbietungsspirale bezogen auf verbesserte Gewinnchancen;
- gleichzeitig resultiert daraus eine Unterbietungsstrategie bezogen auf Gewinnschranken im Rahmen einer nach oben gerichtete Verteilungspolitik;
- ein Teil dieses Gesamtansatzes ist der schrankenlose Abbau des Sozialstaates mit allen Gefahren für sozialen Konsens und Demokratie.

Verlierer der Globalisierungspolitik sind letztlich in allen Regionen die Arbeitskräfte, die den Geldströmen nicht folgen können. Es besteht eine prinzipielle Asymmetrie der Mobilität zwischen Kapital und Arbeit.

Allerdings bleiben die Vertreter des Neoliberalismus von solchen Argumenten weitgehend unbeeindruckt, weil unterm Strich die weltweiten Kapitalprofite steigen. Die Einkommen aus Vermögen explodieren seit 1986. Fragen der Verteilungsgerechtigkeit werden nicht mehr gestellt. Die Arbeitseinkommen stagnieren. Der Sozialstaat degeneriert zum Konkurrenzstaat. Es ist Teil herrschender Ideologie, diese Entwicklungsrichtung als unausweichlich darzustellen.

Bei genauem Hinsehen ist der scheinbare Sachzwang der Weltmärkte aber auch Resultat von Politik der zentralen Akteure - der internationalen

Banken, der transnationalen Konzerne und auch der nationalen Regierungen, die durch Deregulierung der internationalen Geldströme und Handelswege dem Spekulationsdruck auf den Kapitalmärkten nicht nur nachgegeben, sondern ihn überhaupt erst ermöglicht haben. Dadurch wurden die fatalen Kapitalstrategien einer Ausnutzung unterschiedlicher nationaler Standards und regionaler Faktoren bei internationalen Investitions- und Produktionsentscheidungen überhaupt erst möglich.

Diese Entwicklung ist aber keineswegs zwangsläufig und unumkehrbar. Die teuflischen Ergebnisse werden spürbar und Gegenstimmen lauter. Ich zitiere dazu Paul Kennedy, der mögliche Tendenzen für das 21. Jahrhundert untersucht. „Das System wird angesichts der demographischen und technischen Vorhersagen des weltweiten freien Marktsystems nicht lange halten, und es wird einen backlash gegen den Kapitalismus des freien Marktes geben."

2. Rückkehr zu regionalen Horizonten

Es ist zumindest möglich und in Ansätzen bereits feststellbar, daß nationale und regionale Politiken wieder die Oberhand gewinnen werden, welche auf mehr Ordnung, mehr Kontrolle und mehr Schutz setzen. Es beginnt eine Denkweise stärker zu werden, welche gegen weitere globale Entgrenzung des Güter- und Kapitalverkehrs angeht. Die Globalisierung ökonomischer Aktivitäten ist keine unaufhaltsame Tendenz, sondern selber Ergebnis politischer Entscheidungen. Es existieren Handlungsspielräume, in denen geprüft werden kann, wie der ökonomische Wildwuchs in politische Kontrolle mindestens supranationaler Konstellationen oder sogar in nationale und regionale Verfügung zurückgeholt werden kann, um Schaden für Arbeit, soziale Sicherheit und Umwelt abzuwenden.

Ein Strang der Reorientierung ist eine Wiederentdeckung regionaler endogener Potentiale.

Die zentralen Problemkomplexe - fortdauernde Arbeitslosigkeit, technologische und ökonomische Umbrüche und die sich noch verstärkende Umwelt-krise - finden räumlich verteilt unterschiedlich starke Ausprägungen. Die regionalökonomischen Entwicklungen der letzten Jahre haben resultierende Disparitäten keineswegs gemildert, sondern eher verstärkt. Berufs-, Bildungs- und Lebenschancen sind ungleich verteilt, und die Diskrepanzen wachsen. Ein starkes Gefälle mit deutlichen Grenzlinien zwischen industrialisierten Ballungskernen und ländlich strukturierten Regionen ist weiter vorhanden.

Die traditionelle Regionalpolitik, welche darauf beruhte, industrielle Wachstumsüberschüsse in ländliche Problemregionen zu lenken, hat nicht verhindern können, daß sich räumliche Ungleichgewichte eher noch verstärkt haben. So verbreitet sich ein Plädoyer für eine Rückbesinnung auf endogene Potentiale. Von daher richtet sich das Augenmerk besonders auf vorhandenen qualifikatorische Ressourcen. Die Stärke einer Region beruht sicherlich auf ihrer Lage in internationalen Verkehrsströmen, auch auf natürlichen Vorkommen, letztlich aber vor allem auf den Fähigkeiten der Menschen.

Wenn Region in den Fokus ökonomischer Strategien genommen wird, heißt das abzustellen auf die Qualifikation der Arbeitskräfte und die Innovation zur Schaffung von Arbeitsplätzen.

3. Mittlere Systematisierung und regionale Institutionen

An dieser Stelle kommt dann die Weiterbildung und ihr gegenwärtiger Zustand ins Spiel. Wir haben mit dem Begriff „mittlere Systematisierung“ zur Kennzeichnung des Entwicklungsstandes ein Stichwort in die Debatte geworfen, das großen Anklang und Aufmerksamkeit gefunden hat. Diese Begrifflichkeit ist theoretisch anschlußfähig an Giddens Theorie der Strukturalisation, besonders zu den dort zu findenden Hinweis auf „degrees of systemness“ (Grad der Systemhaftigkeit).

Bezogen auf den Grade der Systemhaftigkeit ist der Weiterbildungsbereich immer noch ein „weiches“ System. Dies gilt zunächst bezogen auf die

Systemgrenzen, wo einerseits ein fortschreitender Prozeß der Herausverlagerung von Lernaufgaben aus primären gesellschaftlichen Institutionen voranschreitet, gleichzeitig aber auch eine Ausbreitung, Zerstreuung und Entgrenzung stattfindet. Das System der Weiterbildung befindet sich in einem permanenten, flexiblen Prozeß von Kristallisation und Verschwinden.

Weiterbildung ist auch ein „weiches" System bezogen auf die strukturierenden Regulationsmechanismen: im Spannungsfeld von Politik und Ökonomie stellt es ein „gemischtwirtschaftliches" System dar. Darüber hinaus sind die Bedarfe an Weiterbildung „weich", weil Interessen und Motive häufig latent bleiben und deshalb oft Ersatz- und Ausweichfunktionen greifen. Schließlich gibt es auch widerstreitende Prinzipien für die Gestaltung der internen Struktur bezogen auf Institutionalisierung, Professionalisierung, Finanzierung, Regionalisierung usw..

Bezogen auf Indikatoren wie Institutionalisierungsgrad, Professionalisierungsgrad, Programmhorizonte u.ä. erweist sich die interne Struktur der Weiterbildung als dem unterstellten Bedeutungszuwachs inadäquat. Es müssen deshalb Regulationsmechanismen verstärkt werden, welche Funktionalität und Leistung des Systems erhöhen. Dabei bringt es wenig, sich auf die ordnungspolitische Auseinandersetzung um das Verhältnis von Markt und Staat zu begeben. Beide extremen Regulationsmodelle sind in ihrer „sauberen" Form den vielfältigen Anforderungen und Interessen unangemessen. So hätte ein Marktmodell nach den neoklassischen Visionen vollständig informierter und unbedingt rational handelder Akteure für den Bildungsbereich fatale Konsequenzen. Schon lange ist die bildungsökonomische Diskussion zu dem Ergebnis gekommen, daß es unmöglich ist, Konsum- und Investitionsaspekte von Bildung voneinander zu trennen, und daß systematisch externe Effekte in Form von sozialen Erträgen unberücksichtigt bleiben. Dies müßte letztlich zu einer Unterausstattung in der Weiterbildung führen. Auch ist deutlich geworden, daß der Allokationsmechanismus des Marktes keineswegs einer eindimensionalen Zweck-Mittel-Rationalität folgen kann. Ohne kommunikative und moralische Voraussetzungen käme ein nur über Geld koordinierter Austausch gar nicht zustande. Die immer wieder nachgewiesenen Beteiligungs- und Angebotslücken im Weiterbildungssystem können geradezu als Paradebeispiele für „Marktversagen“ herangezogen werden.

Aus der theoretischen Kritik des Marktmodells folgt aber nun keineswegs, daß der Staat überall ordnend, kontrollierend oder steuernd eingreifen müsse. Das Weiterbildungssystem ist auch ein Paradebeispiel für die beschränkte Verarbeitungskapazität staatlicher Politik angesichts der Überkomplexität der spezifischen Möglichkeitshorizonte. Dies gilt für

- die Ordnungsfunktion, wo lückenlose juristische Regeln die Flexibilität und Dynamik der Weiterbildungsaktivitäten gefährden würden;
- die Leistungsfunktion, da eine umfassende Gewährleistung von Weiterbildungsangeboten angesichts der Finanzkrise des Staates nicht durchzuhalten ist;
- die Gestaltungsfunktion, da fehlende informationelle, organisatorische und finanzielle Ressourcen sowie ungeklärte Prioritätenprobleme eine Umsetzung vieler Planungskonzepte unmöglich machen.

Es ist daher schon lange eine Erosion der Vorstellung von einer hierarchischen Überordnung des Staates über ausdifferenzierte gesellschaftliche Teilsysteme erfolgt und lange gehegte Omnipotenzillusionen mußten aufgegeben werden.

Interessant werden demnach Überlegungen über intermediäre Organisationen - Institutionen und politische Aktionsfelder, in denen weder der Markt, also dezentrale Unternehmensentscheidungen, noch ein hierarchisch steuernder Staat erfolgreich sein können. Es bestehen immer schon Netzwerke korporativer Akteure, mit Konstellationen von Interessen und Macht, welche das stereotype Bild einer klaren Trennung von Staat und Gesellschaft und vom Staat als höchstem Kontrollzentrum widerlegen. Dabei wächst die Problemlösungskapazität durch eine dezentrale Form der Entscheidungsselektion und Handlungskoordination.

Die in der Erwachsenenbildung schon lange diskutierten Probleme der Kooperation und Koordination erhalten aus dieser Sicht neues Gewicht. Modisch formuliert geht es um polyzentrische regionale Netzwerke, welche ein Zusammenwirken von staatlichen, kommunalen und privaten Institutionen, Vertretern der Sozialpartner, der Lehrenden und Lernenden sowie staatlichen Verwaltungs- und Förderungsinstanzen ermöglichen.

Vor diesem Hintergrund haben wir in verschiedenen Gutachten - für Hessen, Bremen, Schleswig-Holstein und Nordrhein-Westfalen - Weiterbildungsräte als entsprechende Gremien vorgeschlagen. Diese müßten sowohl die Erwachsenenbildungsträger, die bisher getrennt davon operierenden Verwaltungsausschüsse der Arbeitsämter sowie die regionalen Berufsbildungsausschüsse und weitere Repräsentanz unter Einbezug von Förderern umfassen. Zu den Aufgaben solcher regionalen Weiterbildungsbeiräte können gehören: Bedarfsklärung, Planung und Empfehlungen für Schwerpunktsetzungen; Abstimmung der Angebote und Erstellung regionaler Programme; Anregungen zur Kooperation und zur Sicherung der Kontinuität von Angeboten; Beratung über die öffentliche Weiterbildungsinfrastruktur; Mittelbeantragung und Vergabe öffentlicher Initiativprojekte; Verknüpfung mit der Wirtschaftsförderung.

Solche Initiativen bleiben allerdings solange zerbrechlich, wie nicht die notwendigen „Support-Strukturen“ zur Verfügung stehen, welche träger- und einrichtungsübergreifende Aufgaben sicherstellen. Deshalb spricht einiges dafür örtliche Weiterbildungszentren einzurichten. Zu deren Leistungen gehören: Information, Beratung und Werbung; Curriculum- und Materialerstellung; Qualifizierung des Personals; Bereitstellung dezentraler Ressourcen; Koordination gemeinsamer Projekte; gemeinsames Marketing für die Weiterbildung; Qualitätssicherung und Evaluationsansätze.

Angesichts der diskutierten Probleme des staatlichen Handelns im Weiterbildungsbereich ist hier ein neues strategisches Konzept angelegt, das sich der Alternative von staatlicher Trägerschaft versus Subsidarität entzieht und auf die Gestaltung der Rahmenbedingungen abstellt.

Gerade angesichts der negativen Effekte der Globalisierung ist eine stärkere Berücksichtigung der Region als Handlungsebene naheliegend. Kooperationen auf regionaler Ebene sind Ansatzmöglichkeiten für eine Reorganisation der Unternehmen wie auch für einen Rekonstruktion des Wohlfahrtsstaates.

Regionale Entwicklungen durch Innovation und Qualifikation sind dafür die wichtigsten Stichworte. Die Anpassung der Weiterbildung an regionale Bedürfnisse soll Kostensenkung, Stärkung der Eigenverantwortung der Regionen, größere Bedarfsnähe, stärkere Gruppenorientierung der Weiterbildungsinstitutionen gewährleisten. Weiterbildungsverbünde kombinieren die Funktionen von Beiräten, nämlich demokratische Prioritätensetzung, und von Zentren, nämlich die effizientere Ressourcennutzung.

Im Zentrum einer Sicherung und Erneuerung des Sozialstaates muß auch regional die Rückkehr zur Vollbeschäftigung stehen. Bevor man dies als Illusion abtut, müßten die schon länger vorliegenden Ideen genau geprüft werden. Allerdings bleiben Zweifel, ob Strategien im Bereich der Tarifparteien - wie sie in der Bundesrepublik Deutschland unter dem Stichwort „Bündnis für Arbeit“ diskutiert werden - tatsächlich eine ausreichende Lösung der Beschäftigungsaufgabe bewirken können. Nach wie vor geht es neben Initiativen zur Umverteilung von Arbeitszeiten um den gezielten Aufbau eines Sektors öffentlich geförderter, organisierter und finanzierter Beschäftigung. Dies meint nicht nur einen „zweiten Arbeitsmarkt“, sondern Bereiche gesellschaftlich notwendiger, sozial geschützter und qualifizierender Arbeit im Non-Profit-Sektor. Es gibt gesellschaftliche Bedarfe, die sinnvoll bearbeitet werden müssen, aber einzelwirtschaftlich nicht profitabel sind. Diese bislang unverrichtete Arbeit unter dem Einsatz von Arbeitslosen mit Hilfe einer alternativen Verwendung der Kosten der Arbeitslosigkeit gilt es zu organisieren. Das Institut für Arbeitsmarkt- und Berufsforschung der Bundesanstalt für Arbeit benennt die Höhe der fiskalischen Kosten der registrierten Massenarbeitslosigkeit in Deutschland für 1995 auf 143 Mrd. DM. Es geht also um einen veränderten Einsatz der z.T. sowieso verausgabten sozialstaatlichen Mittel auf eine verstärkte Förderung vom Arbeit statt der passiven Finanzierung von Arbeitslosigkeit.

Dies bedeutet auch ein Herauslösen der Sozialstaatspolitik aus der neoliberalen Standort-Logik und eine Rückkehr zur regionalen Perspektive. Im Zusammenhang der Beschäftigungssicherung sind dazu zwei Schritte notwendig:

(1) die Einschränkung spekulativer Kapitalströme, um den Spielraum für eine beschäftigungsorientierte Wirtschaftspolitik zurückzugewinnen;

(2) die Entwicklung von beschäftigungspolitischen Instrumenten zum Beispiel durch den Ausbau eines öffentlich verantworteten und finanzierten Non-Profit-Sektors.

Regionale Beschäftigungsgesellschaften in der Kombination von Arbeit und Bildung - etwa Recycling-Zentren u.ä. - sind Beispiele in diese Richtung. Deutlich muß aber gesagt werden: Es handelt sich nicht nur um Probleme sogenannter „Benachteiligter" oder von „Randgruppen". Die Risiken, welche in der kurzen Phase des Wohlstands nur von Ausgegrenzten und Stigmatisierten getragen wurden, werden mittlerweile zur Normalität wachsender Bevölkerungsgruppen. Deshalb sind Beschäftigungsgesellschaften als normales wirtschafts- und arbeitsmarktpolitisches Instrument einzuordnen.

Es ist notwendig, dies zumindest als Möglichkeit zu denken, um sich deutlich zu machen, daß der gegenwärtig immer noch mächtiger werdende „globale Sektor" keineswegs automatisch alle gesellschaftlichen Bereiche durchdringen muß. Der „Standort"-Druck ist allein diesem Sektor geschuldet, der unter Weltmarktkonkurrenz auf globalen Märkten arbeitet. Das Fatale ist, daß er „freigesetzt" jede andere Form des Wirtschaftens zerstört. Wenn man das erkannt hat, muß notwendig nach anderen Möglichkeiten gesucht werden. Dabei ist deutlich geworden, daß es durchaus Alternativen gäbe. Warum greifen sie dann aber nicht oder bleiben zumindest marginal?

4. Menschenbilder: Ökonomische Rationalität und persönliche Identität

Die Antwort ist, daß die Alternativen zu spät einsetzen. Sie akzeptieren ungefragt eine Logik ökonomischen Handelns, aus der zwangsläufig eine Dominanz der Ökonomie über die Moral resultiert. Die traditionelle Ökonomik unterstellt, daß soziale Ordnung sich über die unsichtbare Hand des Marktes herstellt. Sie setzt auf Eigennutz und Rationalität der Individuen.

Der Markt vermittelt die individuellen Nutzenkalküle über die Preise. Die sich ergebenden Gleichgewichte sorgen für die Beschränkungen individuellen Handelns und führen nach diesem Modell soziale Ordnung herbei.

Diese Denkweise setzt sich, gegenwärtig wieder einmal verstärkt, als Grundmuster der Interpretation menschlichen Handelns durch, indem alles Handeln grundsätzlich als rationale Entscheidung in Knappheitssituationen betrachtet wird. Der Homo oeconomicus optimiert mit unbarmherziger Rationalität und unfehlbarer Präzision seinen Gewinn. Dies kennzeichnet einen „ökonomischen Imperialismus“, der gleichzeitig die Ökonomie der Marktwirtschaft zum grundlegenden ethischen Prinzip erhebt. Der Prophet der „Neoklassik“ Milton Friedman hat dies in der Überschrift zum Ausdruck gebracht „The social responsibility of business is to increase its profits“.

Nun hat sich aber in der Wirklichkeit der Unternehmen in der Marktwirtschaft gezeigt, daß die rigorose und konsequente Verfolgung individueller Interessen organisatorisch wie sozial und ökologisch „unerwünschte“ Folgen produziert. Das grenzenlose Erwerbsstreben erzeugt einen Vektor der Maßlosigkeit und ein Klima der Raffgier. Die Folge ist Zerstörung sozialen Nutzens durch egoistische Interessen. Der kollektiv beste Zustand wird nicht erreicht, wenn die Akteure ausschließlich individuellen Präferenzen folgen.

An diesem Dilemma kann die Beschränktheit des Rationalitätstyps „homo oeconomicus“ gezeigt werden. Ohne die Herausbildung sozialer Normen ist auch ökonomisches Handeln letztlich nicht möglich. Überall sind implizite Handlungsordnungen vorhanden, welche die Wirksamkeit von Organisationen überhaupt erst herstellen. Kommunikation und Koordination wären ohne solche Ordnungsmuster überhaupt nicht möglich. Dies hat der amerikanische Ökonom Granovetter mit dem Begriff der „sozialen Eingebundenheit“ gekennzeichnet. Dahrendorf hat parallel zu der sprunghaften Ausweitung von Optionen die notwendigen orientierenden Sinneinbettungen menschlichen Handelns als „Ligaturen“ gekennzeichnet. Dies ist nichts anderes als der einfache - aber in den neoklassischen Modellen verdrängte - Gedanke, daß die Wirtschaft ein Subsystem einer viel umfassenderen Totalität von Gesellschaft ist. Während das neoklassische Modell der Ökonomik eine egoistische Individualität und instrumentelle Rationalität voraussetzt, ist menschliches Handeln immer schon eingebunden in kulturelle Konstellationen und Kontexte. Eine Gesellschaft, die konsequent auf atomisierte, isolierte und ihren egoistischen Interessen folgende Individuen setzt, untergräbt ihre eigenen Grundlagen.

Die radikale Durchsetzung eines sozial entpflichteten Individualismus muß notwendig zu sozialen Krisen und einer Erosion von Demokratie führen. Charles Taylor hat in seiner grundlegenden Arbeit „Quellen des Selbst“ gezeigt, daß sich menschliches Handeln in unseren Gesellschaften immer moralisch konstituiert,d.h. es gibt unvermeidliche Rahmenbindungen für menschliche Handlungsordnungen. Diese entfalten einen Raum, in dem sich das Selbst verortet. Dieser ist selbstverständlich kulturell gefärbt. Das punktuelle Individuum, wie es in den Modellen ökonomischer Rationalität unterstellt wird, ist demgemäß eine Fiktion. Etzioni fragt in seinem Buch „Die faire Gesellschaft“: „Sind Menschen nichts anderes als kalte, nur auf ein Ziel programmierte Rechner, die nichts anderes im Sinn haben als ihr Wohlbefinden zu maximieren?“ (1996, 11)

Diese Frage so zu stellen, heißt sie zu verneinen. Demgemäß ist es notwendig, eine Idee wieder zu verstärken und rückzugewinnen, in welcher Verantwortung und Menschlichkeit wieder deutlich werden. Die intensiv geführte Debatte über moralische Grundlagen moderner Gesellschaften unter dem Stichwort „Kommunitarismus“ zeigt, daß dieses Problem nicht zu umgehen ist. Die zunächst von den USA ausgehende Debatte unter Intellektuellen, die sich communitarians, „Gemeinschaftler“ nennen - Etzioni und Taylor sind diesen zuzurechnen - geht zentral um die Verantwortung des Einzelnen in der Gemeinschaft.

5. Kulturelle Identität und Heimat

Gemeinschaft stellt sich nun aber meist regional her. Sie entwickelt sich im Verhältnis zwischen Personen durch Kontakt, Kommunikation und Kooperation.

Eine Bezugnahme von Menschen auf den regionalen Kontext kommt nun aber im Deutschen nicht aus ohne den Begriff Heimat - ein unangenehmes , eher despektiertliches Wort. Es ist hochbelastet im Verwendungszusammenhang im Spannungsfeld von Romantik und Nationalismus.

Ausgehend von Heimatrechten einer stationär - feudalen Gesellschaft wurde der Begriff zusätzlich aufgeladen durch Kompensation gegenüber einem um sich greifenden Kapitalismus. Fatal wurde das Wort durch nationalistische Engführung von Heimat und Vaterland.

Dabei verweist die Ambivalenz des Heimatbegriffs zugleich auf Probleme des neuzeitlich-europäischen Fortschrittsprozesses. Es ist eine Reaktion auf eine alle Lebensbereiche umfassende gesellschaftliche Modernisierung. In ihm bündelt sich das Unbehagen an der Moderne angesichts der Erosion lebensweltlicher Traditionen. Dies hat den Individuen einerseits vorher ungekannte Wahlmöglichkeiten und Freiheiten gebracht. Andererseits entstehen daraus Entscheidungszwänge und Unsicherheiten. Dies läßt sich mit dem Begriff Heimatlosigkeit bezeichnen.

Wenn man aber nun heute, abgesetzt gegen einen letztlich hilflosen Antimodernismus, wieder den Begriff Heimat aufgreift, muß er von traditionalistischen, nationalistischen, antimodernistischen und xenophoben Gehalten bereinigt werden. In einer posttraditionalen Gesellschaft ist Heimat nicht mehr der warme Gegenstand eines passiven Gefühls, sondern aktiv gestaltete und angeeignete Welt.

Heimat konstituiert sich in einem regional definierten sozialen Raum. Sie entsteht in personaler Kommunikation. Menschliche Interaktionen haben selbstverständlich immer einen Bezugsrahmen in der Region (Giddens 170). Diese liefert den kulturellen Kontext, in dem sich die Menschen auskennen, erkannt werden und mitwirken. Dies meint nicht nur Lokalisierung sondern auch Differenzierung. Erst im Unterschied zu anderen ist Identifikation mit der Region möglich. In der Wahrnehmung und Anerkennung des Fremden entsteht eine reflexive Konstitution eigener Identität.

Erst in einem solchen Kontext gibt es auch wieder Orientierungen bezogen auf die Frage von Bildung, wenn damit die Selbstentfaltung des Individuums in einer Gesellschaft gemeint ist. Es geht um die Chancen und Horizonte von Identität. Die wichtigste Erkenntnis bei Charles Taylor ist, daß das Ich sich moralisch konstituiert durch Integration in die Gesellschaft.

Dabei hat Arbeit nach wie vor eine zentrale Rolle. Axel Honneth hat unlängst noch einmal auf die fundamentale Bedeutung von Anerkennung für die soziale Konstitution aufmerksam gemacht und darauf hingewiesen, „daß sich die soziale Wertschätzung einer Person weitgehend daran bemißt, welchen Beitrag sie in Form formal organisierter Arbeit für die Gesellschaft erbringt".

Arbeitskräfte aber sind eben nicht nur Wanderarbeiter des Kapitals. Sie sind Menschen, die nach Identitätschancen suchen. Wenn es richtig ist, daß sich dies immer in regionalen Kontexten vollzieht, im Austausch mit bekannten Anderen, folgt daraus ein Recht auf Immobilität.

6. Erwachsenenbildung als Chance für Identität

In regional gestalteten Landschaften ist für die Entfaltung der Menschen Bildung ein zentrales Moment. Es geht also darum, eine Infrastruktur miteinander vernetzter Bildungsangebote zu sichern und zu entwickeln. In der Bundesrepublik Deutschland hat zuletzt die Kommission „Zukunft der Bildung - Schule der Zukunft" beim Ministerpräsidenten des Landes Nordrhein-Westfalen diese Idee propagiert. Ich selbst habe bei der Zuarbeit dafür plädiert, Weiterbildung als einen zentralen Fokus einzubeziehen. Es geht darum, Bildungszentren und Qualifizierungsnetzwerke aufzubauen. Die verschiedenen Stufen und Bereiche von Bildung sollen zusammengefaßt und auf regionale Perspektiven bezogen werden.

Zweifellos spielt dabei die berufliche Bildung im Hinblick auf die regionale Wirtschaftsentwicklung ebenso wie bezogen auf Chancen menschlicher Identität eine bedeutende Rolle. Regionale Innovationspolitik ist ohne gezielte Qualifizierungsstrategien letztlich nicht möglich. Weiterbildungsverbünde zwischen Unternehmen, öffentlichen und privaten Trägern können ein solches kooperatives Konzept in Netzwerken institutionalisieren. In einigen der fünfzehn Strukturregionen in Nordrhein-Westfalen haben sich Arbeitskreise gebildet, um die Erfordernisse regional orientierter Bildung zu identifizieren. Sie übernehmen Aufgaben der Bedarfermittlung, der Entwicklungsplanung und der gemeinsamen Durchführung.

Allerdings erschöpft sich ein regional reflektiertes Konzept von Weiterbildung - das ist meine Hauptbotschaft - nicht in der Funktion für die Ökonomie. Vielmehr kommt es gerade darauf an, eine personorientierte Perspektive einzunehmen und zu fragen nach den Chancen kultureller Identität in der Region. Dafür sind Zentren der Bildung als Stätten der Begegnung unverzichtbar. Es ist ebenso banal wie relevant, darauf hinzuweisen, daß Menschen sich in ihrer Leiblichkeit nicht auflösen in monetäre oder auch mediale Prozesse. Wir leben körperlich in sozialen, zeitlichen und räumlichen Kontexten. Insofern braucht die individuelle Biografie als Chance für Identität immer einen Ort. Als Versuch, solche Orte - Betriebe, Stadtteile, Gemeinden und Regionen, zu nutzen und herzustellen zur Entfaltung von Persönlichkeit, hat Erwachsenenbildung einen umfassenderen Sinn.

Wieder kann ich nicht vermeiden, zu schließen mit einem Zitat, das das utopische Potential des deutschen Begriffs Heimat klassisch zusammenfaßt:

„Die Wurzel der Geschichte aber ist der arbeitende, schaffende, die Gegebenheiten umbildende und überholende Mensch. Hat er sich erfaßt und das Seine ohne Entäußerung und Entfremdung in realer Demokratie begründet, so entsteht in der Welt etwas, das allen in die Kindheit scheint und worin noch niemand war: Heimat.“ So Ernst Bloch im letzten Satz von „Prinzip Hoffnung“ (S. 1628). Dies hat nicht zu tun mit enger Provinzialität, sondern ist umgekehrt die Voraussetzung eines reflektierten Kosmopolitismus.

Hinweise

Afheldt, Horst: Wohlstand für niemand? München 1994

Bloch, Ernst: Das Prinzip Hoffnung. 3 Bde. Frankfurt/M. 1977

Cremer, W./Klein, A.(Hrsg.): Heimat. Bonn 1990

Etzioni, Amitai: Die faire Gesellschaft. Frankfurt/M. 1996

Faulstich, P. u.a.: Bestand und Perspektiven der Weiterbildung. Weinheim1991

Giddens, A.: Die Konstitution der Gesellschaft. Frankfurt/M. 1992

Kommission „Zukunft der Bildung - Schule der Zukunft“: Denkschrift. Neuwied 1995

Taylor, Charles: Quellen des Selbst. Frankfurt/M. 1996

Section 2

Access Strategies for the Education of Adults

Richard Taylor / Tom Steele

European Access Network
Lifelong Learning and its Impact on Social and Regional Development

Has a new Grand Narrative of Continuing Education now replaced the older one of adult education? It used to be said that, since its emergence as a formation in the mid- nineteenth century, adult education was a strategy for the education of working men and the extension of the benefits of university education to the lower classes generally. This was an essentially democratic movement designed to redress social injustice and break down the barriers of privilege in which the university degree system largely functioned as a rite of passage for the adolescent children of a wealthy elite to attain the qualifications for their destined place in social life. Current research in Continuing Education, however, seems to indicate that this heroic dimension of adult education has given way to something much more pragmatic. We hear, increasingly, that participation in higher and continuing education favours the already well-educated; that rather than alleviating them, higher and continuing education reproduces social inequalities; that the lowest third to one half of the population are excluded from any form of higher and continuing education and that no political party aspiring to government has any educational strategies to change the status quo.

In the section devoted to 'Access Strategies for the Education of Adults' which we are reporting on here, this perspective was largely confirmed, but with important reservations that innovative schemes and projects were continually being invented to break the mould. On the pessimism-of-the-intellect side, the reports of participants established that higher and continuing education continues to service the better-off ; that despite the announcement of 'mass' higher education it still continues to reproduce social inequality and has failed to alter the nature of the university as a social institution and that continuing education is used by the already well-educated to advance their own professional development and thereby increase their differential over the excluded classes. On the optimism-of-the-will side however, the reports revealed that more women and adults now participate in higher education (although it has to be said they are still largely drawn from the traditional social strata) and that access as an issue of social justice is (uncomfortably) on the agenda of higher education. Most promising of all is that despite the current discouraging climate in education, adult educators are still devising innovative schemes to include previously excluded social groups.

The range of contributions, which included a Europe-wide study of Access to HE, and five specific studies drawn from Finland, Switzerland, Belgium, Scotland and England, and a German philosophical overview, was most impressive. Despite the limitations of having to write and make presentations in what for many contributors was their second-language, English, non-native speakers grappled eloquently with complex problems and comparisons.

In the first contribution of the series, Maggie Woodrow, from Westminster University, reported on a research project on *'Access and under-representation in European Higher Education'*. Her conclusions were that despite its intense commitment to change, the Access movement had substantially failed to alter the institutions and culture of higher education. It was still oriented towards school-leavers from privileged backgrounds who would spend three or four years in full-time education (often away from home). The likelihood of school-leavers and adults from the lower social classes, ethnic minorities or lower income groups participating in HE had improved only marginally and finally, participation in higher and continuing education was largely the preserve of a middle-class and well-educated elite. Despite this, she argued that Access should continue to be interpreted as an Equal Opportunities issue intending wider participation in HE. The fact, however, that it is still viewed largely as a parcel of 'special arrangements' perpetuates and legitimates an overall inequitable system. The Access movement has still not been accepted by HE as challenging its entire *raison d'être*. The discourse of 'standards' is continually raised against widening access to excluded groups and the argument that these groups have lower completion rates often masks a reluctance to accommodate non-traditional students, who are more likely to suffer from financial hardships. The hegemony of government-inspired market-orientated policies in HE and CE has encouraged many universities to offer programmes of professional development on grounds which are more orientated to income generation than educational need. In the traditional field of liberal adult education, similarly, the need to charge higher fees in the face of altered funding priorities perpetuates a middle-class student body and discourages low-income groups from part-time study.

The contribution from Lynn Tett, of Heriot Watt University, Edinburgh, *Making a difference? - Including excluded groups in higher education: a case study* reported on an innovative project devised by her department aimed at drawing community activists into HE. This was what she called an 'apprenticeship scheme' which was a newly devised Access route through which activists could study a degree in Community Work and so obtain professional qualifications. This was conceived as deliberate reversal of conventional privilege by targeting low-income and ethnic-minority students, who, under the scheme, get extra tutorial and financial help. Conceptually, the programme is intended to represent a shift from an individual to a community focus and lays great stress on the importance of partnerships with external bodies and associations. The rationale for the scheme also draws on research which shows that funding inequalities have halted moves to mass expansion of the HE system in Britain. There is also a stratified unevenness in the way HE institutions have incorporated Access. They can be divided broadly into three approaches as follows: for a few institutions (usually 'New' universities, converted from the polytechnic sector in 1992) access is central to their mission; for others (older civic redbricks) it is bolted on as a gesture to equal opportunities but, in many of the most ancient universities, there is no discernible culture of access. In the group discussion, it was argued that traditionally, the British education system, has been premised on *failure* associated with class, gender, age, race and disability and that no substantial move to equality of opportunity will take place until a political will enforces major changes in its structure and ethos. The principles involved in the initiative described here, (known as the LAST initiative) encourage working-class activists to take charge of their own educational needs. Students, with appropriate skills for HE are recruited from local community groups (18 from 150 applicants) and those who are not successful are offered educational guidance. Collective experience is highly valued and developed into critical awareness and understanding. Qualifying students are encouraged to remain in their communities as paid activists.

By contrast, René Levy from the University of Lausanne in Switzerland described his research project *Six Years of Continuing Education at Swiss Universities: evaluation and perspectives*. This was a study of special 'impulse' funding to universities by the Swiss government for the purpose of establishing a culture of CE broadly and, specifically, of establishing university centres with programmes of learning in CE. The outcome of the study revealed that the funding had established 285 courses with more than six thousand students taking part. Participation in the centres was mainly by well-educated professional people who were extending their range of professional 'tools'. The centres were informed more by a logic of accumulation and status maintenance than compensatory mobility, with CE being viewed by participants as a form of cultural capital. Dr Levy concluded that although it indicated a new middle class was emerging, CE tended to reproduce existing structural inequalities of class and income. However, it was clear that women were strongly represented in the courses which indicated a shift in gender participation and many students had no previous experience of HE. Students with low purchasing power were noticeably absent though and Dr Levy argued that new forms of external funding would be necessary if any serious empowerment of these students was to take place. He recommended a credit and certification system on the European model and fiscal incentives to firms to subsidise demands from employees.

Another approach to get more adults into continuous learning was suggested by Professor Dr Günter Dohmen, of the University of Tübingen in what was the most discursive contribution to the seminars. He made the radical suggestion that, in the face of the current social crisis of humanity in critical transition, HE should be 'deschooled' (in the Illich idiom) in order to cope with the sheer variety of learning needs. In the current historical moment, which could be termed (in Daniel Bell's idiom) as that of the 'end of ideology', new key competencies were required by social actors. In place of traditional educational processes, such as formal courses of instruction,

HE should now promote experiential learning. This should be based on constructivist approaches which focused on new patterns and formations of knowledge and problem solving. Lifelong learning, he emphasised, was not the same as lifelong *schooling*, since a much greater degree of self-direction was implied which did not fit into routine courses of instruction. Seventy five per cent of all learning is experiential and this form of 'natural' learning takes place outside schooling systems, so what is required is not just access to existing *institutions* but generating increasing self-reliance of learners. This implies that the 'Learning Society' is a natural counterpart to lifelong learning and as such educational institutions must be radically reconstructed. Universities may have to lose their traditionally closely-guarded independence but should still exist for periods of more concentrated learning and offer research and training to the outside world. Much greater emphasis has to be placed on educational guidance systems and development of new competencies which the older institutions may not be able readily to service. In the following group discussion, the problem of how to prevent people being locked into narrow self-interest or parochial concerns and lack of civic awareness was raised, which Prof. Dohmen saw being resolved by guidance and greater institutional openness.

Dr Jukka Tuomisto of the University of Tampere, Finland, addressed the question of *Access strategies for the education of adults in market-orientated adult education policy - a Finnish perspective*. He described the historical stages of the development of adult education in Finland (which seemed to have a generalised resonance throughout Europe). The first stage, between 1925 and 1969, was one of liberal adult education, where the institutions of adult education had significant autonomy over their own educational policies. In the 1970s through to 1985 this was replaced by a planning-centred, interventionist policy which emphasised vocational education and training. This, in turn, was supplanted by a market free-for-all in the late 1980s (but maintaining the rhetoric of vocational and professional education) in which educational decision-making became increasingly *corporate*, involving employers, local authorities and the adult learners themselves. In the post-modern society it was argued, everything is commercialised (price has replaced value) and adult education has had to demonstrate its economic usefulness; state funding has been frozen and decentralised, and economic individualism has been aggressively promoted.

The net effect of the current policies in Finland has been to increase the participation of the professional classes in CE (although this has remained static in the 1990s) and also the already well-educated. Another consequence is that the Finnish Open University has grown by recruiting unemployed matriculating school-leavers. Dr Tuomisto's conclusion was that lifelong learning has been co-opted and harnessed to specialised vocational training programmes for experts to aid economic growth and consumption, and to legitimate market orientation. As a consequence those who cannot pay for CE have been further marginalised. There is also a need for general citizenship education which is not being met under the current policies. In the group discussion it was suggested that, whatever the drawbacks of market-orientation, it had encouraged adult educators to become more goal orientated and had possibly even led to higher quality education, although this was disputed.

Jean Luc Guyot from the University of Louvain in Belgium described a joint comparative project that he was carried out with Etienne Bourgeois at Louvain and Chris Duke and Barbara Merrill of the University of Warwick *Comparing Access chances in Belgium and UK: Warwick and Louvain as institutional case studies*. They had constructed a typology of admissions conditions ranging from the least-open to the most-open access policies and practices. Despite the fact that access policies varied widely between faculties and departments in both universities, the authors identified some trends common to each. They identified two prevailing categories of adult student: firstly, the 'second chance access' group who, although they possessed appropriate qualifications, due to economic and cultural factors, did not enter university immediately after leaving school. The second category was of adults already qualified with a degree who required further specialisation or complementary training in another topic.

Some departments showed no interest in adult programmes at all; these were labelled the least socialised and included science departments. Those that welcomed adult students - generally the Humanities and Social Science faculties were the most socialised (although there was some disagreement between which actual departments were socialised; philosophy for example although in the Humanities was taught in an elite way and not sensitive to adult needs). Among the professional departments, Nursing and Law were seen as more socialised. The authors offered an explanatory framework for their conclusion which emphasised the role played by 'academic tribes'. They concluded that both sociological levels and epistemological levels were factors in determining the policies and heterogeneity of adult access. Some of their conclusions were disputed in the following discussion, which offered counter-examples to the stance taken by departments of philosophy, which do not, generally, seem to relate to any sociological or epistemological pattern.

Finally, Geoff Layer of the Department of Access and Guidance, Hallam University, Sheffield, in his paper *From the ghetto to the mainstream*, addressed the very important and much neglected theme of access for disabled people. Dr Layer noted that, generally speaking, access for disabled people had a low priority and HE institutions tended to operate a 'deficit model' of provision rather than positively addressing their overall policies and practices. Sheffield received HEFCE special needs funding to develop their programme with the intention of increasing by one hundred the numbers of disabled students, enhancing staff awareness, producing guidance material, preparing students for work and most importantly embedding the operation within the university . They adopted the approved social model of disability which advocated removing 'disability' from the individual to the institution.

Hallam University appears to offer an enviable model for enabling this form of access. In the first place, the author maintained, it was necessary to see disability as a social construction and that society itself actively disables individuals. To overcome this, institutions needed to change their patterns of recruitment, revise their curricula and institute learner support systems, employment preparation and staff development.. Hallam University adopted a policy of positive action for the disabled and a recruitment target of four per cent (that is, one percent above the minimum required). They created an applicant support culture which included taster courses, induction programmes, learner agreements stipulating level of support needed, support groups, buddy schemes and staff development programmes. A Disabled Student Support Service was established which devised a handbook for disabled students, recruited interpreters and notetakers, investigated methods of assessment of needs, a drop-in internal support programme, established schools and colleges link and secured specialist equipment. The actual increase in numbers of disabled students at Hallam has risen from three per cent in 1989-90 to five per cent in 1994-95, to around one thousand students in absolute numbers. Hallam's example, arguably, offers a model of best practice in the area of recruitment of and support for disabled students which should be carefully noted by other institutions who want a serious programme of access for the disabled.

Conclusion

As revealed in this section's seminars, the less optimistic conclusion about the current state of Access provision, is that what began as a social movement to extend higher education to the deprived majority of the population and to challenge the elite mature of universities, currently appears to have been pragmatically incorporated into the mainstream. As a consequence, although the number of mature and 'non-standard' students has grown significantly, the proportion of students from disadvantaged and socially-excluded backgrounds has not significantly increased. While the increase in the number of mature students and women students is to be welcomed, universities seem reluctant to initiate wide-ranging programmes of recruitment for students from excluded communities. Thus the ideal of 'mass' higher education still waits to be meaningfully extended to mature students from the lower socio-economic groups, including ethnic minorities. Nevertheless the Access movement still retains considerable creative and innovative vitality, as was demonstrated by the reports from Edinburgh and Sheffield, and has thrown up impressive models which other institutions could meaningfully emulate. If, however, higher education systems are to be diverted from their historical role of reproducing social inequalities, the whole nature of the three- or four-year residential degree, which has been historically constructed as a rite of passage for a privileged social elite, has to be radically deconstructed. The innovative programmes of the Access culture and the historic practices of adult and continuing education offer plenty of models of how a genuinely democratic and inclusive system might be achieved.

Maggie Woodrow / David Crosier

Access, Adults and Under-representation in European Higher Education

Access and Lifelong Learning

The European White Paper on education and training argues that the economic prosperity, social cohesion and personal development of the people of Europe depends on a major commitment to involve everyone in learning throughout their lives. This is the message at the heart of the European Year of Lifelong Learning, but what has this message to do with the universities? What is the relationship between lifelong learning and access to higher education? Given the scarcity of resources, who has the priority in getting what kind of lifelong learning? Where do they get it and who pays?

The meaning of 'access'

This paper begins with a call for greater precision in the use of the word 'access', particularly in a European-wide context, where different interpretations contribute to the construction of different political realities and outcomes. 'Access' used merely as a synonym for 'participation' highlights the positive, reporting on those who *are* participating, thus representing the status quo in a favourable light and justifying the continued allocation of resources to those groups already well-established within the system. On the other hand, 'access' interpreted as *wider* participation, encompasses exclusion and non-completion, exposing immediately the limitations of current systems and the marginalisation of mature students, many of whom are late starters in the life-long learning process.

The Council of Europe interpretation of 'access'

The interpretation employed by the Council of Europe for its project, *Access to Higher Education in Europe*, (1) on the work of which this paper is based, is a distinctive one which sets the framework for the project, within three inter-related elements:

- greater participation in higher education of good quality
- the extension of participation to include currently under-represented groups
- a recognition that participation extends beyond entry to successful completion.

Thus 'access' is inextricably associated with an equality of opportunity which encompasses under-represented groups, and embraces not only entry, but also successful completion, with all that this implies.

Who gets higher education in Europe, and who does not?

The recent extensive increase in participation in European higher education is often taken as evidence of a widening of provision. This is certainly the case in respect of more equitable gender participation, but regrettably not otherwise. The failure of mass higher education to effect significant change in the relationship between educational opportunity and socio-economic status is instead evidence of *maximally maintained inequality*, that is, that those of low socio-economic status will only benefit when the enrolment of advantaged groups is already so high that further expansion is only possible by bringing in students from disadvantaged groups; an optimum point apparently not yet reached.

So who does get higher education in Europe? As a generalisation, and taking Europe as a whole, the main beneficiaries are members of the following groups.

Group A. Beneficiaries

- those from medium to high income families
- those whose parents have had experience of higher education
- those from dominant ethnic groups
- those without disabilities
- those who are 18+ with high marks in school-leaving examinations

Those who are most likely to be excluded from higher education in Europe fall within the following group.

Group B. Least likely to benefit

- those from low income groups
- those whose parents have no experience of higher education
- those from minority ethnic groups
- those with disabilities
- those who have experienced earlier educational disadvantage

There is likely to be a stronger correlation among the five categories in each group than with those in the other group. Those from Group B who do enter higher education, would be more likely to drop out for financial reasons than those from Group A, and their performance is more likely to be affected by the need to earn an income while studying. Those from Group B would be more likely to be taking their higher education course at a less prestigious university, or in a professional/vocational institute than those in Group A. Since these institutions are often less generously resourced, the higher education of those in Group B would cost less, but they would be more exposed to the disadvantage of under-funding, for example, in respect of staff/student ratios.

Access strategies in higher education

Access strategies have evolved side by side with interpretations of equality of opportunity in higher education. Progress can be charted in the following stages (2):

Stage 1: Unequal rules for entry to higher education, which overtly exclude all but the most privileged.

Stage 2: The firm application of equal rules to everyone, without recognition of their unequal socio-economic or cultural background, or that this would exclude from higher education many with the potential to benefit.

Stage 3: Making special arrangements for a minority of non-traditional entrants - a well-intentioned move, which however often serves to legitimate and perpetuate inequitable systems.

Stage 4: The application of inclusive entry policies, designed to meet the needs of those historically marginalised or excluded, where equality of opportunity is systemic.

Some European countries are starting to appreciate the value of moving towards Stage 4, but in Western Europe Stage 3 is the most common model and in the most Eastern countries Stage 4 remains the norm.

Access and adults

Adult and continuing education is a particularly important part of access, because so many who have experienced early socio-economic and/or educational disadvantage are unavoidably late starters in entering higher education. They already fall within the B Group above. What is provided for them in higher education?

Adults in the Mainstream

There is no generally accepted European age at which a student becomes an adult student and this makes comparisons between countries problematic. Yet it is clear that one contribution to lifelong learning that higher education is already making in a few countries, is a significant increase in the proportion of adults on first degree or diploma courses. In the UK for example, mature students now comprise the majority of full-time first year undergraduates, but this is unusual and in Spain for example, relatively few adults enter higher education full-time. Here, as in Germany and in most central and eastern European countries their normal attendance pattern is part-time (3). Sometimes, as in the Russian Federation, experience in employment is an admission requirement for mature students. In several countries, including Belgium, Spain and the UK, Open or Distance Universities have had a major impact, all the more effective for being designed to meet the learning needs of adults.

Alternative entry routes

The increase in the number of mature students has been facilitated by the development of alternative entry routes, many of them initiated by higher education institutions. Such 'second chance' programmes are often in reality the first chance that these students have had. They include special entrance examinations such as the Diplômes d'Acces aux Etudes Universitaires (DAEU) in France and in the Netherlands, the colloquium dictum; short preparatory, foundation, or access courses, for example, .in the UK, Spain and the Russian Federation; and in several countries, including France, APEL, the Accreditation of Prior Experiential Learning. While there is thus no shortage of good examples, these entry routes for adults remain on the fringes of systems still dedicated primarily to school leaver participation.

An adult elite

Although the increased number of mature students on mainstream courses represents a success for second chance education, and especially for women, there is a disappointing tendency for these students to be drawn mainly from backgrounds similar to those of Group A entrants. It appears that even the alternative routes by which many adults enter higher education are more useful for integrating into the system those who are most similar to traditional entrants, than for encouraging participation by new groups of students from different socio-economic or cultural backgrounds. The likelihood of adults from more diverse backgrounds ever participating in any post-school education, let alone lifelong learning, seems remote, unless their needs can be prioritised.

Financial constraints

In particular, financial barriers to participation for those from low-income groups need to be overcome if lifelong learning is to be anything more than a slogan. In Germany and the Netherlands, adults are not eligible for student grants; elsewhere grants do not take account of the additional financial commitments of mature students, many of whom give up paid work to return to study and/or have dependants to support. In Western Europe, fees are generally charged for part-time and evening courses, and their introduction for full-time courses appears to be imminent. Open University courses are expensive, and there is some evidence linking non-completion rates in higher education, to financial hardship among mature students (4).

A juvenile learning environment

In general, higher education institutions have been slow to provide appropriate measures of organisation, guidance, and counselling for adult entrants, and except in some eastern European countries, crèche facilities for students with young children are still only optional extras. Curriculum delivery methods designed for 18 year olds frequently fail to take into account the wider experience, greater motivation and maturity of adults, requiring them to undergo a juvenilisation process to conform to norms of learning behaviour. Open or Distance University learning methods are generally a notable exception and demonstrate the particular potential for adults of computer-based learning. Elsewhere, a grown-up learning environment in higher education to meet the needs of adult students, would be one of the best access outcomes of the European Year of Lifelong Learning.

Professional updating

Postgraduate and professional updating covers an enormous variety of provision and represents quite a different approach to adult learning in higher education, not least because it is perceived as part of the income-generating strategy of institutions. Fees are high, with courses often being tailored to meet the requirements of particular employers, and sometimes run jointly with them. The curriculum is often dynamic, giving a high priority to meeting the specific learning needs of adult clients, who are in the Group A category, being predominantly male, white, well-educated, and in full employment of a skilled or professional nature. They are also at present the group most likely to experience the advantages of lifelong learning.

Non-vocational adult education

This is the Cinderella of higher education for adults, although it is part of the old extra-mural tradition of European universities and provides one of the main means by which they involve their local communities. Despite the wide curriculum range, which includes extensive foreign language provision, all aspects of the liberal arts and many practical subjects (in the UK, for example, a fifth of all students aged 65+ are learning about computers), non-vocational courses are not well-subsidised by the state, particularly when they resist pressures for accreditation. In consequence their high fees contribute to the perpetuation of a largely middle-class student body, despite the potential for wider participation as leisure time increases.

There is an acute short-sightedness in this failure to recognise that higher education has a responsibility, not only to educate for leisure but to redefine and restructure it; to rescue it from the banalities of the media; to counteract the moronic, manipulative influence of the entertainment industry; to ensure that *delinquency and crime are not seen as a natural concomitant of it;* to *give back some purpose to those millions of people who are unemployed, especially those who have not known what it is like to have a job,* and to *ensure that self-worth and self-esteem are not so defined and determined by regimentation through work that in a condition of worklessness an overwhelming anomic and ontological displacement occurs, with suicidal consequences for some (5).* Nevertheless education for leisure comes at the bottom of the pile. Labelled as non-vocational adult education, it is deprioritised by a negative categorisation which not only devalues, disparages and downgrades it, but ignores the outcomes of such neglect.

Conclusion

Overall, the verdict on universities access offer to adults must be could try harder'. Except where income generation potential is high, as with professional updating, the assumption is that adults must adapt to meet the norms of higher education, rather than the other way around. Such attitudes, together with high fees, ensure that those adults in Group B above, are likely to find that the European Year of Lifelong Learning has not been designed with them in mind either. If this is to be avoided, priorities and resources need to be allocated to those still outside the system, rather than to those to whom it has so far been dedicated.

References

Woodrow, M. (1996), Quality:Equality, Report of the Project on Access to Higher Education. Council of Europe.

Armour, M. (1995), Transcultural International in Proceedings of the 5th EAN Convention. Amsterdam.

Woodrow, M. and Crosier, D. (1996), Access for Under-Represented Groups in European Higher Education, Council of Europe.

The Scottish Citizen's Advice Bureau, (1995), Poverty by Degrees.

Gus, J. (1995), Coming Back from Oblivion. Economy, Race and Education - Towards the Millennium' London.

Lynn Tett

Making a Difference? Including Excluded Groups in Higher Education: a Case Study

Introduction

In this paper I report on the initial findings of a project called the Lothian Apprenticeship Scheme Scotland (LAST) designed to enable community activists from the working class, disabled, and minority ethnic communities to participate in higher education. The project 'seeks to achieve equality of outcomes for people whose circumstances, geographic, physical or cultural, would not permit them to consider becoming professionally qualified' (LAST, 1994:2). A degree in community education is the entry qualification to the community education profession. This project aims to enable these groups to enter this profession whilst working in their own communities and studying part-time. As now implemented at Moray House Institute (Heriot Watt University) the 'apprentices' take some modules from the Community Education degree alongside full-time students and study other modules as a group outside the normal institutional 'term' times. The project provides extra tutorial support and finance for travel, books, dependants' care and disability costs. I will be looking at the pre-course and initial on-course experience of the eighteen participants in the project all of whom are working class, two are disabled, three are black and none have the standard entry qualifications for the course. Before I describe the project in more detail, however, I will draw on findings from the literature to consider what leads adults to participate in HE and what steps institutions can take to encourage under-represented groups to access their provision.

Adults' participation in Higher Education

More adults in Scotland are participating in higher education institutions than at any time in the past. From 1990 to 1993, the number of entrants to full-time higher education in Scotland aged 25 and over increased, on average, 19% per year to 10,396 in 1993 (SOED, 1995). However, those that do participate are drawn from a limited grouping and generally exclude 'those groups who have been least well-served by the school system ... These include ethnic minorities, especially the black communities: women, especially those who, through early parenthood or the need to work, had to abandon their education; and working class adults, especially the unemployed, whose talents may not have been fully recognised at the secondary stage.' (Further Education Unit 1987) In addition Uden (1996) has argued that funding inequalities for adult students, including the loss of the mature students' allowance and the lack of support for part-time students, most of whom are adults, have halted the moves towards mass expansion of the system.

Institutions can do much to combat this continuing inequality through explicit access policy frameworks. Smith et al (1993) found, however, that there was great disparity between institutions for which access was a central tenet in strategic planning; institutions where access was seen as a 'bolt-on' extra; and institutions where the culture of access was altogether absent from mission and planning statements. In these latter cases, the standards of traditionally qualified students at point of admission was stressed over the value added by the institution at point of exit. Such divisions are broadly reflective of the different ethos prevailing in the 'old' and 'new' universities with the latter much more likely to 'take a higher percentage of lower socio-economic groups ... (and those) with non-standard entry qualifications' (Uden 1996:17).

The reasons for certain groups' non-participation has also been explored in some depth, and are generally explained in terms of situational, dispositional and institutional 'barriers' (Johnstone and Rivera, 1965, Cross, 1986, Darkenwald and Merriam, 1982, Hayes and Darkenwald, 1988) as well as structural conflicts between potential learners and the educational and social systems (McGivney, 1990, O'Shea, 1979, Jarvis, 1985, Keddie, 1980) with which they are interacting. Such barriers prompted Halsey (1991) to argue that the outcome of expansion in higher education is the *absolute* but not *relative* gain of disadvantaged groups in relation to advantaged groups, because ascriptive forces continue to determine patterns of participation.

Numerous studies (Johnstone and Rivera, 1965, Kelly, 1989, May 1985, Houle, 1961, Morstain and Smart, 1974, Cross, 1986, Aslanian and Bricknell, 1980) have examined why adults choose to return to education and have concluded that it is the product of an interplay of forces in a complex social, cultural and educational context. Perhaps the most key of these forces is the knowledge of educational opportunities, for if potential participants do not know that the opportunity to return exists, then other barriers become irrelevant. Whilst adults are considering a return to higher education institutions can most helpfully offer guidance and advice. Yet guidance at this stage is often not available from higher education institutions (Blencowe, et al, 1996, Howieson, 1992).

In summary, if traditional non-participants are to return to higher education then major changes must be made on the part of institutions in terms of structure and ethos and ways must be found of overcoming the dispositional and attitudinal barriers of potential learners. How LAST has done this is the subject of the rest of this article.

The Lothian Apprenticeship Scheme - Selection and Recruitment

An important way in which the LAST project has tried to overcome some of these barriers has been through its recruitment policy. (Figure 1).

Figure 1

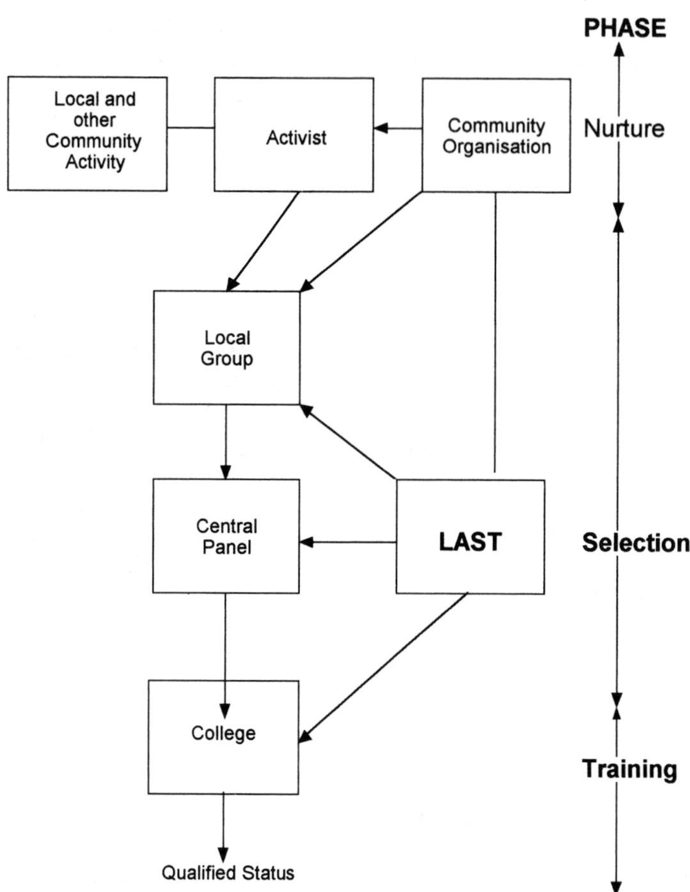

For some activists this process has taken almost two years, beginning with early contact with a community organisation or individual community worker and progressing through to selection for the LAST scheme. The role that community work staff have played in the generation of demand from local activists has been crucial. Without early guidance in relation to informal experience and progressive opportunities activists were unlikely to become involved. The local community education worker in each of the Urban Aid areas then established a local group drawn from community activists, representatives from local community work organisations and employers. Since community activism was an entry requirement for selection these local groups were able to nurture potential applicants and convince them that they could apply for these places.

On Course

Once participants had started the course and again after three months, they were interviewed in order to ascertain their experience of, and attitudes to, education and their initial impressions of the course. The interviews were transcribed and analysed and this information was used to identify common themes. The themes that emerged from this analysis were: 'academic and financial support' 'school experience'; 'learning experiences which had resulted in change'; and 'attitudes to higher education'. The ways in which these factors affected the 'apprentices' experience is reported on below. Throughout the text the person being quoted is identified by her/his first initial.

Academic and financial support

Institutional factors such as academic support, financial support and a positive culture are all provided through LAST. These include: each student having an individual tutorial each week; a student/tutor ratio of 9:1; there are 6 lap-top computers available which apprentices can take home as well as computers in the Institution; and there is a fund for travel and dependency-care costs. The group also provide informal support to each other both through study groupings in their own geographical area and through the tutorial groups.

When asked to identify the factors that they found supportive the apprentices were appreciative of their tutors. For example 'He always listens to and values what I have to say but he is also critical in a way which does not make you feel stupid' (J) They were also positive about the facilities such as computers which were available to them. 'The computers are brilliant for the likes of me because I'm starting from the basics.' (A) Finally, the meeting of child-care costs enabled some people to participate. 'I'm a single parent with two children. I couldna have come if I wasna able to pay the child-minder out of the LAST funds' (T)

School Experience

All of the apprentices were negative about their own school experiences as the following representative quotes show:

'I was selected out of school by the teachers'. (J.) 'The teacher was only interested in the five or six clever, well-behaved ones who might pass the 'bursary' exams' (A.).

'I was always in trouble at Secondary school and kept on being suspended. That was fine at the time though because it meant I could hang about with my older friends who were all unemployed' (N.).

Similar experiences of schooling have been found by researchers investigating non-participation in post-compulsory education. For example, Veronica McGivney has argued that: 'People who have ostensibly 'failed' in the school system do not wish to repeat that failure. Many are consequently suspicious of education in any form ...' (1990:20).

What then has led this group of apprentices to participate in a degree programme? Perhaps the next theme provides some clues.

Learning Experiences

Although all of the eighteen 'apprentices' described their experience of school negatively they were able to give positive examples of learning which had taken place at a later point in their lives. These experiences were often associated with their involvement in community action. For example:

'What I' ve learnt since school has been through being involved in campaigns especially the one to keep the Accident and Emergency Department open at our local hospital' (D). 'Learning for me took place through Trade Union and Labour Politics and through working at the grassroots with the tenants' movement' (A.). 'I ended up meeting a group of black women that were beginning to challenge a lot of stuff that I hadna really thought about but I was able to connect it to my experience so I learnt something that's always stayed with me' (Z.).

For some apprentices their life experiences changed the way they thought about themselves. For example:

'Real learning for me was when I went on a Youth Exchange to Italy. I'd never left Scotland before and it was meeting a whole lot of great people and finding we could communicate' (S.). 'I was taken to court after a fight in a pub. I was innocent but the bouncer said it was me. I learnt from that that it's easy to get labelled and I've never forgotten it' (N.).

It can be seen from the above quotes that 'learning' is very broadly defined, is derived from their life experiences and associated with their community activism. This informal learning has, in addition, provided the entry requirements for this course. This in turn means that early negative experiences of school and an understanding that HE is 'for folk who arena like us' (A) can be overtaken by removing some of the attitudinal barriers and by being part of a cohesive group. By privileging experience of community activism over academic qualifications the 'apprentices' are helped to value their own strengths. This suggestion is supported by the interviews where the 'apprentices' overwhelmingly identified their experience as their main contribution to the course.

Attitudes to Higher Education

The apprentices all suggested that higher education was for middle -class people with money. The only exception seemed to be 'really clever people' whose families were willing to make enormous sacrifices to support them through this experience. The students who were over 35 considered that 'it's for young folk'. One student summed up the general view 'I think that higher education works well for people who have got the money or the status and because of that they are able to make the time to do what they want to do' (Z). In other words their view is that 'education is for other people' (McGivney 1990).

However, they were all themselves now participating in HE so what had led them to change their view? It appears that this was because the way in which they were recruited emphasised the end result of participation, the professional qualification of a degree in Community Education, rather than the process of getting the degree. This means they did not see themselves as participating in higher education as such. Moreover, making up a large part of the year group (eighteen out of a total undergraduate year of 55) they were able to maintain their own identity. In addition, by privileging experience of community activism over academic qualifications the 'apprentices' are helped to value their own strengths. This suggestion is supported by the interviews where the 'apprentices' overwhelmingly identified their experience as their main contribution to the course. For example:

'I have got all my practical experience of living and working in W to offer the course, so I know what it's like to be poor because I have to live it day after day' (J). 'I bring my experience of being working class and knowing that I have something to offer ... Being working-class isn't just about being 'deprived' (S). 'My life is richer where I am than it would be elsewhere so I'm not intimidated by all these middle-class people' (A).

Conclusion

It has been argued (Benn and Burton 1995) that Britain has an education system premised on failure and that the resulting educational inequalities are directly related to class, gender, age and race. One reason for this may be because people from the non-participating groups are expected to fit into the existing education system rather than the system being changed to suit excluded groups. The LAST project has attempted to bring about social change through education targeted at working-class communities which has prioritised the development of critical awareness and understanding. In many ways the project has resisted the focus on individual progress and development evident in many access programmes by privileging community activism and emphasising the continuing role of participants in their communities. It has done this by selecting participants not just on their individual attributes, but on their collective involvement and activism, and by recognising the value of their experience.

References

Aslanian, C. B. and Bricknell, H. M. (1980), Americans in Transition: Life Changes as Reasons for Adults Learning, New York, College Entrance Examination Board.

Benn, A. and Burton, R. (1995), Access and targeting: an exploration of a contradiction In *International Journal of Lifelong Education,* Vol 14. No 6, 444-458.

Blencowe, L., Denning, P. and Tett, L., Adult Educational Guidance in Higher Education (Edinburgh: MHIE).

Cross, K. P. (1986), Adults as Learners: Increasing Participation and Facilitating Learning, San Francisco, Jossey-Bass.

Darkenwald, G. and Merriam, S. B. (1982), Adult Education: Foundations of Practice, New York, Harper and Row.

Further Education Unit, (1987), Access to Further and Higher Education: A Discussion Document, (London: Further Education Unit) .

Halsey, A. H. (1991), An International Comparison of Access to Higher Education, *Oxford Studies in Comparative Education*, Volume 1.

Hayes, E. and Darkenwald, G. (1988), Participation in Basic Education: Deterrents for Low Literate Adults, *Studies in the Education of Adults,* 20 (1), 16-28.

Houle, C. O. (1961), *The Inquiring Mind,* Madison, WI, University of Wisconsin Press.

Howieson, C. (1992), The Guidance Project (Edinburgh: Teh University of Edinburgh).

Jarvis, P. (1985), The Sociology of Adult and Continuing Education, London, Croom Helm.

Johnstone, J. W. C. and Rivera, R. J. (1965), Volunteers for Learning: A Study of the Educational Pursuits of Adults, Hawthorne, New York, Aldine.

Keddie, N. (1980), Adult Education: An Ideology of Individualism, in J. L. Thompson (ed), Adult Education for Change, London, Hutchinson.

Kelly, P. (1989), Older Students in Education, Adults Learning, September 1 (1) 10-13.

LAST (1994), Recruitment and selection Pack (Edinburgh: Lothian Apprenticeship Scheme Trust).

May, S. (1985), Shall I Go to Class this Evening? *Adult Education,* 58, 6-13.

McGivney, V. (1990), Education's for Older People: Access to Education for Non-Participant Adults, Leicester, National Institute for Adult and Continuing Education.

Morstain, B. R. and Smart, J. C. (1974), Reasons for Participation in Adult Education Courses: A Multivariate Analysis of Group Differences, *Adult Education,* 24, 83-98.

O'Shea, J. (1979), Surviving Adult Education, *Adult Education,* 52 (4), 229-235.

SOED (1995), Scottish Higher Education Statistics 1992-1993 Edn/J2/1995/6 (Edinburgh: The Scottish Office).

Slowey, M. (1988), Adult Students - The New Mission for Higher Education? *Higher Education Quarterly,* 42 (4), 301-316.

Smith, D., Scott, P. and Mackay, L. (1993) Mission Impossible? Access and the dash to growth in British Higher Education *Higher Education Quarterly,* 47 (4), 316-333.

Uden, T. (1996), Widening Participation: Routes to a learning society. (Leicester: NIACE)

R. Levy

Six Years of Continuing Education at Swiss Universities: Evaluation and Future Perspectives

Since 1990 the Federal Government in Switzerland has promoted continuing education in universities through providing subsidies for impulse programmes. This paper outlines the scheme, effects and current perspectives.

1. About my position

Although I am involved in academic continuing education I am not willing to forget my main profession as a sociologist. This means that I will:

- focus on academic continuing education,
- not consider the social desirability or even necessity of continuing education, but just assume it,
- proceed first in an analytical-descriptive vein and then change to a more political-normative one,
- consider continuing education as a part of the social production and distribution of knowledge and skills in general.

I will briefly outline the institutional framework within which my topic is located.

2. The federal impulse programme in the context of the Swiss university system

2.1 The institutional structure of the Swiss educational system

In comparison with other European states, including those with a federalist structure, the Swiss educational system differs because it is very decentralised. The sovereignty of the federated states (cantons) is more preserved in the field of education than any other. Thus, it is no exaggeration to say that Switzerland has as many educational systems as it has cantons, that is, twenty-six. The classical universities function with cantonal resources and depend on cantonal authorities whereas the two technical universities are run by the federal state. Seven of the 26 cantons have their own university, most since the 19th century (with the exception of Basle and Geneva). An eighth canton, St. Gallen, created an economic university - it should be called a monoversity - in the sixties. Thus, there are ten universities in Switzerland at the present moment. All of them are either German or French speaking; a new one is being planned in the Italian speaking canton of Ticino. Support for education, especially at the academic level, varies historically among legislative politicians. Generally education is supported more at the federal level than the cantonal one. This is one of the reasons why federal activities and initiatives in relation to universities are quite significant despite the cantonal sovereignty in that matter. Among others, there is a more or less strict division of labour in the sense that public subsidies for academic research comes only from the Confederation, the university cantons limit themselves to financing teaching and the infrastructure. They also receive financial compensation through students from other cantons. The Confederation can encourage other academic activities through special measures although these have to be accepted by Parliament.

It is easy to imagine that in such a context the landscape of institutional actors in the area of science policy is complex. The university cantons are represented by their ministers of public education at a national conference for the universities (Schweizerische Hochschulkonferenz, Conférence universitaire suisse) which has functions of co-ordination between universities and of representation vis-à-vis the federal state. In terms of the latter, the federal agency of education and science (Bundesamt für Bildung und Wissenschaften, Office fédéral de l'éducation et de la science) is the main 'contracting party' of the universities and their cantons. The situation of the two technical universities is different as they are directed and financed by a 'school council' and a state secretary for science and research who depends directly on the federal minister of the interior. The same ministry also houses the Swiss national foundation which is in charge of subsidising scientific research like the German DFG.

2.2 The federal impulse programme for continuing education

After a prehistory the federal Parliament accepted adopting in 1989 an impulse programme aimed at developing professional and academic continuing education as well as the diffusion of CIM in the firms. This paper addresses only the academic programme.

In the context of this programme it was possible to finance centres of continuing education in universities (salaries and part of the current expenses), courses if these were recommended by an expert commission on the basis of a number of fixed, formal criteria and other, less formalised ones of more pedagogical, substantive and strategic content.[1] The decision- making process reflects the complexity of university policy in Switzerland: the expert commission was instituted by the intercantonal conference for the universities, the final decisions where taken by the federal agency of education and science which also administrates the funds.

1 The initial fund reserved for the six years' duration of the program amounted to 75 million francs; it was cut to 45 million by subsequent economy measures. The *formal criteria* required an orientation towards specialisation, acquiring interdisciplinary or new scientific knowledge, or the professional reintegration especially of women, an explicit and detailed program, an organisation allowing to follow the courses while maintaining a professional activity, and a minimum of 40 hours and 10 participants. *Additional criteria* where the substancial and practical relevance, the coordination between universities, and a reasonable rate of direct financing by the participants.

The programme was clearly conceived as an impulse or initiating action with the aim to establish continuing education as a principal activity in the universities. In the long term these would be integrated into their current budgets. The initial programme lasted from 1990 to 1996. The last courses were decided upon at the end of 1995 with the last of the accepted ones starting in 1997 or 1998. The part of the programme subsidising the centres has been prolonged by gradually reducing the finance to facilitate their transfer to the regular budgets, that is, from the federal to the cantonal level. By the year 2000 the contribution will be zero.

The cantons with universities have reacted differently to this federal initiative as each university has responded to the new task in a divergent way. Only a few cantons decided straightaway to develop this new activity (for example, Bern), others limited themselves for structural or conceptual reasons to create minimal structures but still allowing them to receive subsidies (Neuchâtel, Fribourg, Basle and Zurich). However, all of them participated in one way or another, and a certain dynamism developed in all the classical universities. In the economic university of St. Gall, the situation was different as it had been developing continuing education for quite some time as a self-financing activity. The situation for the two technical universities was different as they had their own financial regime. They developed post-diploma courses which they were able to finance with their own funds. This helped them to develop continuing education. In these three cases, therefore, centres of continuing education were functioning before the impulse programme. None of the university cantons accepted explicitly an obligation to integrate this new activity into its financial plans. This is why in the transitional phase there was some uncertainty as to the future of the centres that had been created. Several of them are now under strong pressure to become self-financing.

3. Continuing education at universities and the impulse programme

3.1 Overview

It is impossible to present a complete picture of the development of continuing education in Swiss universities because of the lack of information. A recent survey and other studies have provided some nation-wide knowledge about the development of continuing education but knowledge is limited to those courses subsidised by the federal impulse programme'in the nineties.

I will illustrate with an example of the development of continuing education under this particular programme at Lausanne.

The commission of the Swiss conference for the universities has recently published an evaluation of the effects of the impulse programme. I largely agree with it and wish to quote it: 'The Confederation's impulse programme has been successful at all cantonal universities and has led to the hoped-for extension of continuing education. On the one hand, it has been possible to create centres for continuing education at these universities relatively quickly, simultaneously and in a co-ordinated way, and to equip them with personnel and the necessary infrastructure. On the other hand, the federal funds helped to produce 285 complementary courses by the end of 1995 in a great variety of disciplines. (These courses have reached more than 6700 participants. - Complement and translation RL)' (SHK 1996: 1).

3.2 Development of the offer

Let us start by looking at the development of the number of courses since the inception of the impulse programme (graph 1).

With a little bit of good will, it is possible to distinguish the three stages: a launching stage roughly 1990-1993, a phase of stabilisation 1993-1996, and a finishing phase 1996-1998. Unfortunately, we have no overall figures about the development of non-subsidised courses during the same period; we shall see such figures later in relation to Lausanne.

Graph 1: Number of subsidised courses of continuing education 1990-1998, by university

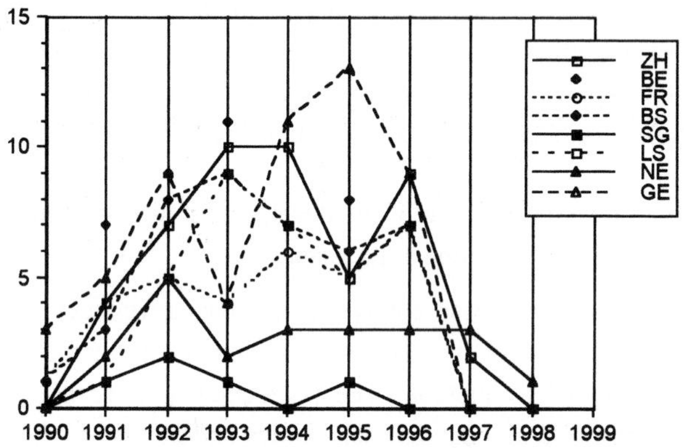

Universities: Zurich (ZH), Bern (BE), Fribourg (FR), Basle (BS), St. Gallen (SG), Lausanne (LS), Neuchâtel (NE), Geneva (GE).

We can see that in the *first stage* the train rapidly speeds up, with those universities who have undertaken some preparation (Bern and Geneva) joining in earlier than the others. However, the latter catch up quickly with the exception of St. Gall. We can also see that the smallest and least well equipped universities with respect to continuing education, that is, Neuchâtel and Fribourg, reach and afterwards maintain a level that is lower than for the other universities. Institutional factors, among which the sheer size of the university, seems to play an important role for the capacity to become an actor in the game initiated by the Confederation. The specific structure of the centres seems to be of lesser importance if one considers the similarities between the curves of Zurich with its very decentralised structure and those of Geneva, Basle and Lausanne which have clearly more centralised services.

During the *second stage* the number of subsidised courses develops differentially but generally on a rather high level with the differences related to university size. There is also a slowly decreasing tendency that is most probably related to the transition to non-subsidised courses.

The radical decrease in the *third stage,* after 1996, reflects the anticipated ending of the impulse programme; it is without doubt more than compensated by the simultaneous development of non-subsidised courses in all universities.

This is, of course, not a profound analysis with a systematic validation of interpretations. Nevertheless, on the grounds of all formal and informal information I have, it appears to be sufficient to justify the rather optimistic conclusions I have quoted from the commission's final report.

3.3 Case study of the social composition of participants: Lausanne

The University of Lausanne did not have any prior inter-faculty co-ordination of activities in continuing education. These were left to the initiative of individual faculties or professors, mostly in medicine, economics and to a lesser extent also in law. The service of continuing education was created ex nihilo with the help of the federal subsidies, which is all the more remarkable as this university, contrary to Geneva, lacks studies in pedagogy, especially in adult education. From 1991 to 1995, 37 courses with a total of 1,234 participants took place.

Graph 2: Development of the number of subsidised and non-subsidised courses at the University of Lausanne, 1990-2000

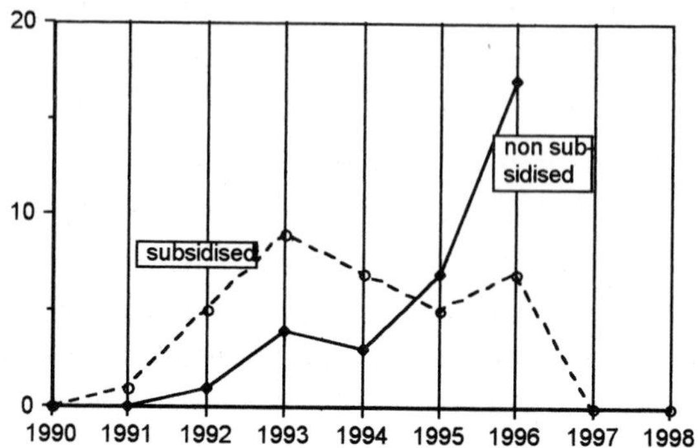

According to graph 1 it has been possible to reach a volume of subsidised courses that corresponds roughly to the university's size, which indicates that the objective to reinforce activity in the realm of continuing education has been attained to a reasonable extent. Graph 2 shows that it has also been possible to create the hoped-for spill-over effect towards self-financed courses. Continuing education has been introduced in hitherto less active disciplines as practically all faculties have participated, reaching an audience that had little or no prior contact with the university.[2]

Graph 3: Age of participants, University of Lausanne 1991-1995

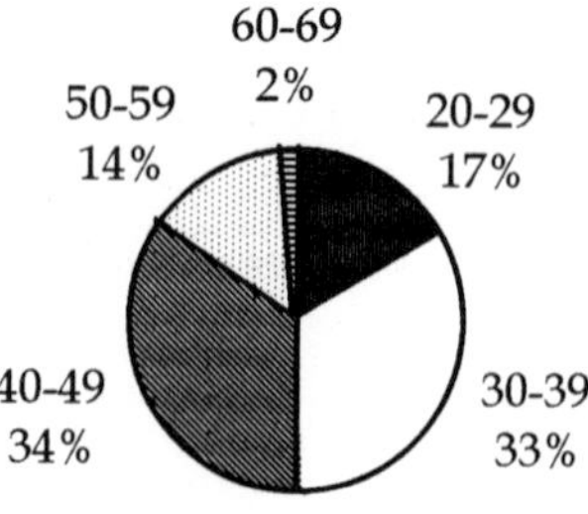

2 Graphs 3 to 7 concern only the subsidised courses.

Graph 3 makes it plain that the new initiative has attracted mainly the career-intensive *age* groups between 30 and 50, which may be related, among others, to the fact that the younger people have left their initial education not very long before. According to the survey this age structure holds also for continuing education in general.

According to Graph 4, there are almost as many men as women among the participants, which means that women's participation, at least in the working area of this university, has been more intensive than men's, since women's labour force participation is clearly lower than men's, including those in the higher professions to which participants of university lifelong learning mainly belong.

Graph 4: Participants by gender, University of Lausanne 1991-1995

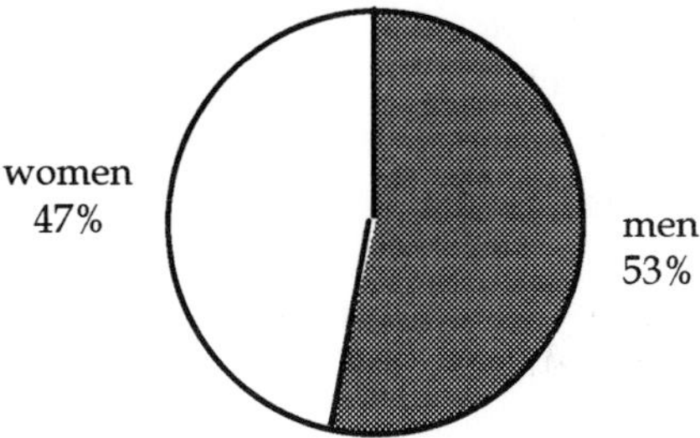

One of the main objectives of the federal impulse programme was to open the universities to non-university graduates. Graph 5 shows that this has been the case to quite some extent at Lausanne as one third of the participants have *no academic degree* (total population: about 12%). The second largest group's initial education has not gone farther than to the apprenticeship diploma.

Graph 5: Participants' level of initial education, University of Lausanne 1991-1995

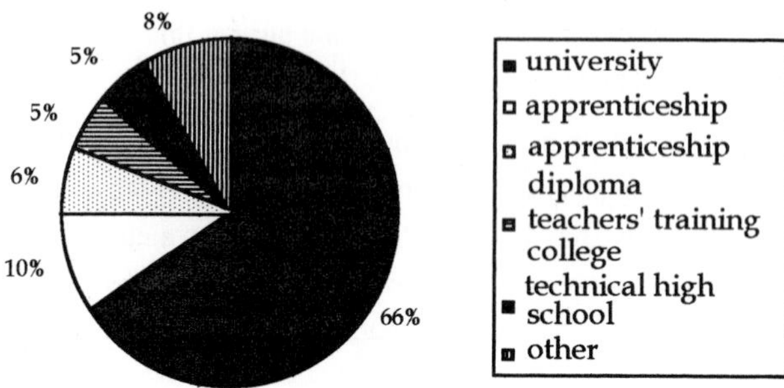

The *professional fields* from which participants have been recruited are fairly wide-spread (Graph 6), again in accordance with the programme's aims. However, we have to note a large proportion of the various categories of participants from the public sector (health, education, public administration and enterprises) with respect to their proportion in the work force; this finding corresponds to other results.

Graph 6: Participants by professional fields, University of Lausanne 1991-1995

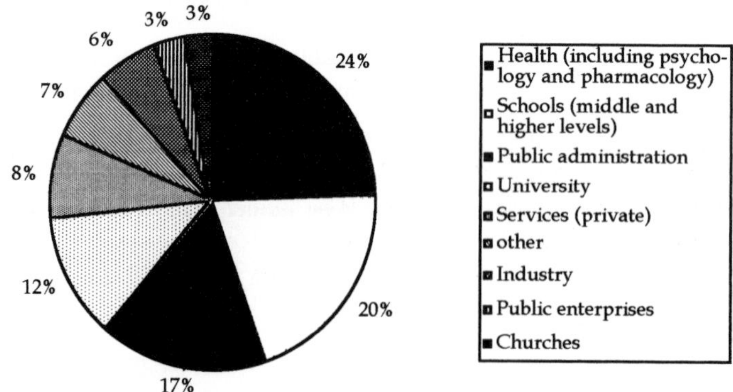

We can speculate about this fact being related to a general sympathy for continuing education in the public sector that is supposed to be higher than in the private sector, or rather to the two sectors' different composition, implying that the public sector comprises a higher proportion of those professions and positions that are interested in this possibility to renew knowledge. Probably, both effects combine: on the one hand, state functions are more directly related to professional profiles that are strongly based on knowledge and expertise (Fluder, 1996: 92), on the other hand, state agencies invest more in long-term strategies of human capital formation than private firms. Another factor that may intervene is again structural: firm size. The Swiss economy has a very strong component of small firms, whereas state agencies focus on middle or large organisations.[3]

Graph 7: Participants' professional position, University of Lausanne 1991-1995

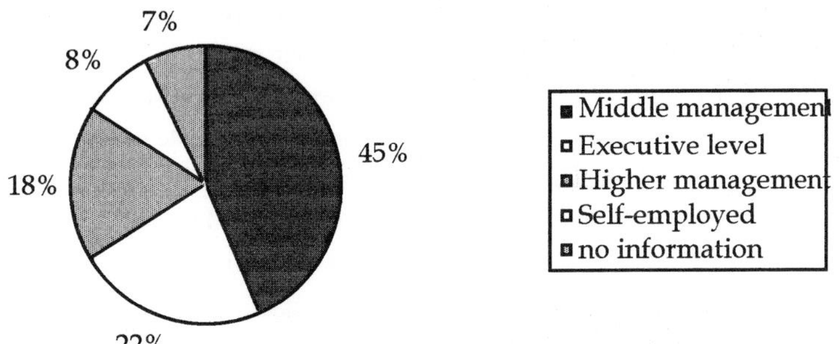

Concerning *hierarchical (class) position,* graph 7 shows a relationship between continuing education and hierarchy that we shall take up again in the next section: almost half of the participants belong to the middle management, almost a fifth to the higher management, that is, almost two thirds come from higher positions. Of course, this fact alone would not be very

3 In the survey that will be used in the following section, the proportion of the professionally active in firms of 25 or more is 36.6% in the private sector, 48.8% in the public sector.

astonishing in relation to academic continuing education. However, we also find the same relationship for other levels of continuing education; therefore, it can hardly be explained by the level of the offer.

On the whole it is safe to say that, at least in the case of Lausanne, the federal impulse programme has helped to realise an offer of continuing education that corresponds rather well to the objectives to make university knowledge available to a large array of participants who are not exclusively former university graduates.

3.4 The use of the existing offer of continuing education

Let us now have a deeper look at the question of who uses continuing education. The available data stem principally from a survey by the Federal office of statistics in 1993 (BFS 1995, Rychen & Schmid 1994, Rychen 1995). Unfortunately, the published results do not say a lot about academic continuing education, we shall have to enlarge our interest to the whole field of lifelong learning. Another source of information is a survey on social stratification I conducted in 1991 with a nation-wide sample of 2,030 people (Levy et al. 1996); again, it concerns all aspects of lifelong learning and does not single out its academic part, but it allows for finer-grained analyses of its use according to a great number of social criteria.

3.4.1 Continuing education among university graduates

Results about lifelong learning practices among university graduates - who are the main target group of academic continuing education despite more generous objectives - show that only a fifth of the courses they take are specifically geared to academics. Moreover, they recur less often to such courses than graduates from non-university tertiary schools. Part of this difference is certainly explained by the larger definition of its audience by most of academic continuing education. However, it may also have to do with university graduates having specific non-academic needs for complementary education.[4] These explanations notwithstanding, it seems likely that the low proportion of university courses among those taken by university graduates also indicates that the universities are still far from having explored all their market potential. Courses offered by public agencies (18% in the general public, 22% among academics) is relatively modest, those offered by universities even more modest (11% among academics).

Another important finding concerns the reasons given for *not* taking courses of continuing education. Adults with tertiary education mention much more frequently than others autonomous forms of continuing education such as reading, going to congresses and the like. Instead of going to courses, they organise their lifelong learning on their own. This fact may explain an intriguing statistical peculiarity shown by graph 8.

Graph 8: Ratio of participation in continuing education by level of initial education (survey 1991, N=1976)

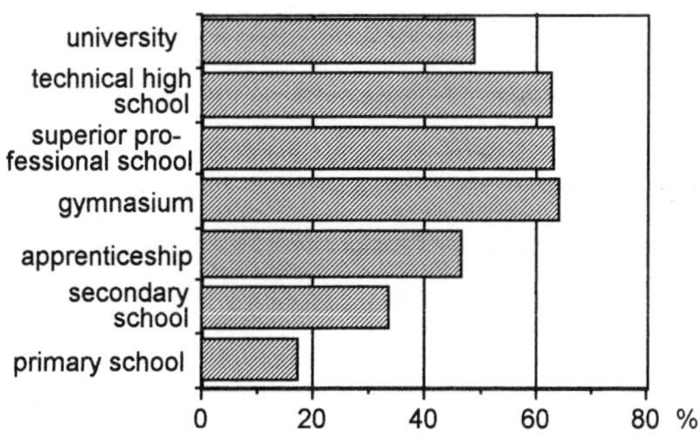

A closer look at the relationship between participation in courses of continuing education and the initial educational level shows that there is a general, quite clear-cut positive correlation (to which we shall come back), but that university graduates deviate from the statistical association (graph 8). Their

4 Findings from periodical surveys of university graduates corroborate this interpretation (Diem 1994).

ratio of formal lifelong learning is lower than people with non-academic tertiary education. The reasons that university graduates advance more often than others for not going to such courses indicates quite clearly that absence from these courses must not be identified with not practising lifelong learning at all. Their autonomous activities in this field probably explain to a very large extent the academics' deviation concerning institutionalised lifelong learning as shown by graph 8.

One practical conclusion from these results could be that in the future, academic continuing education should address itself more to non-academics and especially to target group with less than a tertiary education because among these groups autonomous forms of lifelong learning are much less frequent and the university label may have more appeal to them. Another, more interesting conclusion would be to improve the pedagogical format of the courses offered to university graduates on the basis of these results and to integrate their autonomous forms of learning.

3.4.2 Lifelong learning in general

The basic result about the social use of continuing education is without doubt the main tendency in graph 8 we have already seen: *the higher the level of initial education, the more continuing education is practised.* This finding is confirmed by others stemming from my study on social stratification. The distinction of interviewees by their socio-professional categories yields similar, but more differentiated results. The highest participation rate is amongst members of top management (75.0%). Apart from these, the highest rates are found in the middle professional categories (64%), the lowest ones among both the lowest and the best-located categories (liberal professions 41%, unskilled 22%). If one considers simultaneously the professional position and the initial level of education, it appears that the participation rates among the overqualified tend to be higher than among the underqualified. *The more modest initial education is compared to the professional position, the less frequent is lifelong learning.*

This is a strong hint at lifelong learning being used specifically by the 'new middle classes' that are often difficult to identify empirically. These social categories occupy intermediate professional positions implying little decisional competence but important expert functions, which accounts for the most crucial qualification being the ability to use various kinds of knowledge and for a strong motivation to maintain and develop this knowledge.

Still other results add credibility to this interpretation. We found a strong differential according to *hierarchical position* between persons with executive functions (39% participants in lifelong learning activities) and those with middle and higher management positions (70% and 68%). Lifelong learning is more often used by employees in *public* than in private enterprises - it has already been said that expert functions in a large sense are more important in the public sector than in the private one - and also more often in the more *dynamic sectors* of the industry and the services.[5] Distinguishing finally (with Kohn & Schooler 1983) according to the *nature of work,* we find analogous, but more differentiated differences between persons with mainly manual work (30%), mainly relational work or work with a mixed profile (55%), and those who mainly work with symbols, that is, who plan, write, calculate, analyse, draw etc. (66%).

This confirms the impression that lifelong learning finds its best clients among the so-called knowledge-workers for whom knowledge, analytical and reflective capacity are the most important professional tools - and maybe also their most important foundations of identity.

All this indicates that education and its maintenance by lifelong learning has the meaning of a specific form of capital, the enlargement of which during adult life - much like the constitution of its initial volume during initial education - follows a logic of accumulation and rewards and not so much a logic of compensation or of the equilibration of incoherent positions. This reminds one of another result of the survey about motivations to participate; among these, 'adaptation to changing conditions' is clearly more important than

5 On a more precise level this means that lifelong learning is especially little asked for in such sectors as textile, wood and furniture, paper, synthetics, leather, shoes, stones and earth, but also in hotels and restaurants, whereas it especially appreciated in the branches of graphics, metal, banks, insurances, education, culture and leisure.

'upward mobility' or other reasons. In the area that interests us, forces of status maintenance play a more important role than forces of compensatory mobility. Thus, compared to other criteria of social status, education has a more pronounced component of power than its seeming institutional openness and accessibility makes us usually believe.[6]

This is tantamount to showing (at least for Switzerland) that - contrary to its constitutive values - lifelong learning is in fact firmly anchored in the classical mechanisms of inequality and its reproduction in modern society, especially in the economy. It turns out to be a first rate resource of social positioning, its accessibility is controlled accordingly, especially by way of privileges conferred to high-placed collaborators by their employers as the survey shows.[7]

This fact has its most immediate practical consequence for the question of the extent to which access to lifelong learning should be regulated by the market mechanism. It follows that the universities' function as producers of public goods (and not purely as profit centres) in the realm of continuing education can only be secured by measures that financially empower those potential clients who have a low purchasing power and by the integration of fund-raising as a regular task into the professional repertoire of centres of continuing education.

4. Transitional stage

Lifelong learning in Switzerland is actually in the transition stage between the finishing regime of subsidised courses and the upswing of the regime of self-financed courses. Most likely, the situation of the various lifelong learning centres in the universities will become more diverse and loose its

6 This interpretation is further confirmed by our findings about social mobility. In Switzerland, attainment of professional positions is as strongly determined by prior education as in Germany and clearly more so than in Anglosaxon or Scandinavian countries (Levy et al. 1996).

7 Cf. the results of the microcensus concerning the hierarchical and gender differences of the encouragement by the employer (BFS 1995, Rychen 1995).

actual transparency - as we have seen, we already know very little about the development of the non-subsidised courses. This opaqueness may be typical of such stages, but efforts are needed to secure a minimum of documentation of course development in Switzerland on the basis of a common grid.

It may also be typical of such a situation that the attempt to evaluate it tends to yield the trivial image of the half full and half empty glass. I shall of course not allow myself to filter out the problems by opting for the pink-only vision, and rather consider both the elements belonging to the full half and those belonging to the other; however, the panorama will by no means be complete.

I treat the half *full* part rather briefly. Among its elements, there is a) the positive development of self-financed courses in all universities, b) the solid collaboration of practically all university centres of lifelong learning, since their directors have a clear vision, despite the potential competition between them, of their common interests and the fact that these can only be defended by common action (for example, the elaboration of a common quality code, common marketing for the academic label, more practical forms of collaboration in the area of course information, etc.). Another positive element is c) the improved institutional integration at the universities as compared to the launching phase, be it in the field of presidential policies or in the field of legal bases.

However, the latter subject also belongs to the *empty* half, for a) at most of the universities and despite real progress, institutional consolidation of lifelong learning has still a substantial way to go. I shall come back to this. An additional difficulty comes from b) the actual financial situation that becomes dramatical for several universities in the very moment of the necessary take-over of lifelong learning into their ordinary budgets. The university cantons have never explicitly accepted an engagement to do so, and in the present situation, they seem very unprepared to do it. The university authorities' temptation is to extend the principle of self-financing not only to the courses, but to the services as well. This would be the final step towards the function as a profit centre, and the university would renounce its function as a public service in this field. Still another difficulty is c) the blocked possibility to participate in the educational programmes by the European Union.

I think that even in the face of great local differences most of the difficulties can be overcome, provided a minimum of financial and strategic autonomy remains granted. This brings me to the last section:

5. Perspectives and strategies

Many practitioners of continuing education in Switzerland have spent a fair part of the last years at working out and realising strategies and measures to develop and consolidate lifelong learning at the universities. Thus, what I can present here reflects more or less directly the present state of thinking in this field and may not be particularly original. I shall limit myself to spot those aspects that seem to me most important in the next years and shall group them in two categories: first, the realisation of good courses for lifelong learning, second, the institutional consolidation of continuing university education.

5.1 High quality offer

The most important element in any development strategy is evidently the production of good courses that satisfy the participants. What 'good' means should not be restricted - especially at the university level - to the pragmatic criterion of the effective demand (following the slogan 'Good' is what people are willing to pay'), but it should be based on criteria of formal and substantive quality. As mentioned before, one policy in this field in Switzerland consists of working out a common quality code of the university services of continuing education.

The quality of university lifelong learning must also become publicly known. In that respect, the main line should not be usual publicity, but rather other, well-targeted forms of PR and information. From this perspective, it has been helpful that the services in Switzerland were able, with the help of the Confederation, to participate collectively in two educational fairs. Here also it is important after the end of the impulse programme not to fall back on purely local strategies, but to find an equilibrium between a necessary heightening of the profiles of the individual services with their respective strengths and areas of competence, and the common engagement for the 'label' of academic continuing education. In the area of information, a good precondition has been realised in the form of a nation-wide, publicly accessible data base on the actual offer of courses that is presently being transferred to internet. Increased integration of various techniques of distance learning may also be helpful to reduce practical barriers, although the problem of the isolation of the individual, atomised learners, that may well neutralise the advantages of their active engagement (especially in the case of adults who 'come back' to learning), is not always clearly tackled.

Another new instrument in the professional tool-kit of practitioners has not yet been sufficiently developed and put to use: fund-raising. I am convinced that finding external financial resources must become an integral part of their professional identity and knowledge.

5.2 Institutional consolidation

To reinforce institutionalisation is a second strategic orientation that is at least as important as the first one because it is more slow to take shape and because the practitioners in the services of continuing education have an understandable tendency to neglect it, as they have to be primarily preoccupied with the production of courses. A first and crucial component of this line of action is the maintenance of the exchange of information between all the partners, especially the ones who represent potential participants, but also all those who influence some part of the relevant environment. Even if external policy is usually seen to be a privileged task, even as a monopoly of the steering boards of the universities, it seems clear to me that political lobbying and contacts with the media in favour of university continuing education must not be left to rectors and presidents, and that the practitioners should not restrict themselves to making suggestions to them. They have to engage in this activity on their own, be it at the local, regional (cantonal) or national level. Here is another field of possible and necessary co-operation between services. Part of it can be realised on the level of an already existing working group uniting the directors of the university services, another aspect calls for the intervention of an official commission for strategic questions that has the necessary status to interact with relevant public actors.

A large number of more concrete and local measures of institutionalisation has been discussed for several years: official acknowledgement of continuing education as a major task of universities, of equal importance as their more conventional ones; integration of this activity into the job descriptions and time-budgets of university teachers; consolidation of a critical mass (of manpower and soft money) for continuing education in the ordinary budgets; effective integration of the services in all relevant procedures in the universities (for example, external presentation, access to equipment, decision-making, internal flows of information etc.). Once a university has made the decision to engage in continuing education the system should run by itself. However, there still exists an important need for action. There are also substantial differences between universities.

Other important strategic objectives remain pending. I think above all of the two related questions of certification and of the establishment of a permeable credit system based on the European model. This again is an area where purely local strategies can quickly become counterproductive for all parts.

Last but not least, I should like to mention a ceterum censeo of mine. It is of crucial importance to realise in the near future measures that are apt to give equal purchasing power to all potential participants in lifelong learning, be it by help of subsidised and protected educational leaves, of fellowships, educational credits or vouchers with favourable conditions of reimbursement, of fiscal incentives for firms that encourage lifelong learning of their personnel, and for people who pay for themselves. To care about such questions does not belong to the usual self-image of producers of continuing education, but in the present political and institutional constellation they are the only actors who have a legitimate say on such initiatives.

Contrary declarations notwithstanding, it seems to me that in Swiss university policies on initial education are still largely predominant, not only with respect to the acquired volume of resources, but also concerning planned for developments. Let me cite only one illustration of the fact that continuing education practitioners need to be anything but modest in the present situation. Even if, after the end of the impulse programme, that is, in the year 2000, the canton of Waadt would add the total amount of the subsidies to its university budget, this amount would represent no more than a fifth of a percent of that budget; not really a generous resource allocation for one of the four main goals in the university's official mission.

Concerning changes, it seems evident that much more thinking and resources go towards initial education. One last example: The board of coordination between the French speaking universities, called Conférence des universités de Suisse occidentale (CUSO), has recently established an official label and also some financial means for post-graduate studies; analogous requests concerning continuing education have not been answered and even less been planned for. This calls for a last question: should we not aim at uniting, the universities, continuing and post-graduate education into one single organisational unit, as is already the case in the two technical universities (under the heading of 'post-education')? This could be an efficient structural measure to prevent energy-consuming conflicts for resources and to secure the effective realisation of synergy, for instance, in the form of common modules.

References

BFS (Bundesamt für Statistik, 1995), La formation continue en Suisse, Enquête de 1993, Bern.

Diem, M. (1994), La situation des diplômés universitaires sur le marché de l'emploi en 1993. Office fédéral de l'éducation et de la science, Berne.

Fluder, R. (1996), Interessenorganisationen und kollektive Arbeitsbeziehungen im öffentlichen Dienst der Schweiz. SEISMO, Zürich.

Kohn, M. L. and Schooler, C. (1983), Work and Personality: An Inquiry into the Impact of Social Stratification, Norwood, NJ, Ablex Publishing Co.

Levy, R., et al. (1996), Tous égaux? De la stratification aux représentations, SEISMO, Zürich.

Rychen, D. S. (1995), La formation professionnelle continue, Vie économique 12, p. 40-46.

Rychen, D. S. and Schmid, B. (1994), Einblick in das Weiterbildungsverhalten der AkademikerInnen. Referat vor der Weiterbildungskommission der SHK, Bern 27. 5. 1994.

SHK (Schweizerische Hochschulkonferenz, 1996), Sondermassnahmen universitäre Weiterbildung, Schlussbericht (1.10.1990-31.12.1995) - Entwurf. Bern.

Günther Dohmen

Another Approach to get more Adults into Continuous Learning

Raising the interest and commitment for lifelong learning by a promotion of informal learning

1. The necessity of an extension of 'lifelong learning' for a broader development of human abilities

Mankind is in a critical period of crises and transition. We are challenged by dramatic transformations:

– in the economy (through global market competition),

– in ecology (because of a continuous devastation of our natural life-base),

– in labour markets (caused by rising unemployment and substitution of expensive human labour),

– in politics (from growing social gaps, violence and distrust of parliamentary democracy),

– in personal life-styles (affected by fast changes of reference systems and values).

Obviously these challenges cannot be adequately mastered by familiar methods, approaches, skills, abilities and competencies any more. We need new ideas and new capabilities for the maintenance of a peaceful human survival.

Especially required will be key-qualifications and corresponding situations:

– for a sensitive and constructive comprehension of new information,

– for an open and creative development of new patterns for action and behaviour,

- for the implementation of communicative tolerance and fair democratic agreements and
- for the strengthening of a reasonable responsibility for the common wealth.

However, it will not be enough to develop the abilities, skills and competencies of an elite group of leaders. We need a broader development of the latent potential of everybody because our standard of living depends on having able persons and teams at every level and in every sphere of our personal, social and professional life.

Rigid hierarchical structures are not flexible enough for immediate adequate reactions to fast changing challenges. Decentralised decisions, qualifications and competencies are therefore needed. This is why the 25 ministers of education of the OECD-States agreed in January 1996 in Paris on the necessary promotion of 'lifelong learning for all'.

It is certainly difficult to develop the necessary capabilities of mankind on a broader scale. A feasible way to promote new abilities has always been learning provoked by new tasks and actual problems which cannot be solved with familiar strategies and competencies. Those situations force us to think about new approaches and new ideas and this means; to become creative.

This 'innovative learning' refers to a constructivist learning theory which understands human learning as a constructive processing, comprehension, interpretation and assessment of information and experiences. It aims at new knowledge, better understanding and more suitable notions and behavioural patterns related to the actual problems of a sustainable future. Learning in this innovative context can efficiently initiate the development of new abilities and qualifications.

As we continuously meet new challenges in a fast changing world we must develop new potentials by new learning. This means: we must learn as long as we live in order to master our personal and social life and to reasonably influence our destiny.

As *everybody* is confronted with those challenges during his or her life the crucial factor to overcome the actual crisis in human development is really 'lifelong learning of all'. But how can we adequately promote it ?

2. *The rationale of self-directed lifelong learning*

Learning is already a vital function of every human life. We cannot survive in a permanently changing world without lifelong learning. However, this does not mean that we must be channelled through organised courses of instruction 'from the cradle to the grave'.

There are mainly two reasons why a 'lifelong learning of all' cannot be organised as a lifelong schooling for all.

(1) Adult learners will not and should not be subjected to formal learning throughout their life. The most precious aim of education in our cultural tradition is personal emancipation to thinking and deciding on one's own, which also means to more and more people independent learning.

(2) Lifelong schooling for all could not be organised and financed by society.

(3) It is desirable as well as necessary to conceive of 'lifelong learning for all' more as self-directed learning than as something organised by special institutions for pupils of all ages.

Self-directed learning is connected:

- with a daily effort for understanding and mastering actual challenges in individual life and work
- with a fundamental interest in openness to new experiences,
- with a behavioural disposition towards thinking on one's own, self-directed acting and responsible participation and
- with a longing for independence from dominant leaders.

3. *Informal learning as a base for the accomplishment of a 'lifelong learning of all'*

In order to get more people into continuous learning we should pay more attention to their informal learning in practical life situations. This is where 'lifelong learning of all' is already an existing reality. Everybody is learning whenever he/she takes up, processes and assimilates new impressions and information in order to cope with new tasks and challenges.

This 'natural' learning is a fundamental but often an unconscious function of everybody's life which is developing independently of educational provisions in society. About 75% of human learning is this informal experiential learning in everyday life situations.

Nevertheless teachers and educational policy-makers are used to seeing and promoting only the smaller but more conspicuous part of human learning which is organised in school-like educational institutions.

However, in these traditional teaching-learning-settings it seems to be impossible to raise considerably the interest and commitment of school-frustrated adults for deliberate lifelong learning. Promotion of lifelong learning of all is not just part of the problem of opening access to the existing educational institutions, it is also an impetus for fundamental changes of the functional patterns of these institutions.

At any rate the 'natural' 'original' learning of everybody in his/her professional life and daily living world should get more social acknowledgement and professional support; last but not least because it is a fundamental potentiality for the development of dormant 'human resources'.

We need to look for new feasible approaches to widen the access to continuous learning for those large groups of the adult population who still do not participate in continuing education.

Could not the informal learning processes, which are already familiar to most people, be a better base for the necessary development of the lifelong learning of all ?

The international discussion seems to be influenced by two different concepts of lifelong learning, one of which accentuates more a lifelong organised *education* and the other a more informal lifelong self-directed *learning.*

The 'lifelong education' concept is more interested in establishing adult continuing education as an equally institutionalised and supported part of the public education system. Everybody will have a lifelong chance to obtain admission to a publicly acknowledged and supported adult education institution where they will receive professional teaching and guidance and

Organised learning thus provides the social benefits of approved educational certificates.

This approach led to a strengthening of adult learning institutions but the success of this strategy was limited by the reluctance of many adults to participate in education institutions. It was also impossible to finance an institutionalised system of lifelong learning for all.

The 'lifelong learning' concept emphasises more the independent learning of mature persons and its mobilisation and promotion. It takes learning more as everybody's lifelong fundamental striving for understanding and competency to master actual challenges and to maintain personal self-assertion and self-determination in a fast changing complex world. In this context the ideal way of human learning is 'self-directed learning' in challenging life situations.

I think these two different concepts of lifelong *education* and lifelong *learning* should not be treated as excluding alternatives. The necessary development of adult education institutions should be integrated into a larger concept of human learning which comprises many different formal and informal ways and forms of lifelong learning.

This means that the education institutions have to change their tasks and their structures. Just to enlarge them in their traditional functional patterns is not appropriate within this innovative perspective.

4. The 'learning society' as the environmental counterpart of a 'lifelong learning of all'

It is a characteristic of informal and of self-directed learning that it is not organised by educational experts but that they are personal activities provoked by practical challenges in stimulating environments. The adequate way to promote and support this more experiential learning is, therefore, the development of learning incentives, learning opportunities and learning support in the learners' environment.

This leads to the concept of a 'learning society' in which everybody can find learning opportunities almost everywhere and in every period of his/her life. A learning society is an environment which offers motivating learning chances in any possible situation and produces a broad interest in continuous learning on one's own.

In a learning society the formal education institutions are special places for complementary more coherent and systematic learning in broader learning networks with different sorts of formal and informal learning situations.

In a *modern* learning society the new technologies offer new possibilities to get information and learning support 'just in time'; whenever one needs them.

The most important change emerging from this broader lifelong learning pattern in a learning society is a change in the mental attitude of people. To understand learning as being no longer primarily as something which has to be directed by society for the people but as a more self-directed activity which selects and uses adequate learning opportunities in numerous networks of learning challenges, learning situations and learning supports which are available in a learning society is important.

If this self-directed learning needs some temporary help and guidance there must be open counselling services and different modular learning materials for individualised learning available on the spot or on the computer. A general mutual commitment on sharing one's knowledge and competence with others should shape a new 'culture of learning'. This is probably the essence of a vivid learning society.

5. *Consequences for the university*

The perspective of increasing self-directed lifelong learning processes of larger numbers of people in a learning society necessitates that the functions of all existing education institutions will have to change.

They will have to concentrate their know-how and their facilities on the foundation, animation, support and completion of individual learning processes in different life and work situations and environments.

Some of the consequences for the universities can be for instance:

- a wider opening of research and teaching to the outside world and its actual problems,
- the concentration of educational research and training on different lifelong learning processes and the possibilities and problems of their adequate support,
- the picking up of informal learning activities in fields of personal interest (and success) as starting points for the acknowledgement and further development of individual learning processes,
- the acknowledgement and crediting of experiential learning and its results (documented in portfolios),
- a stronger orientation towards the promotion of self-directed learning of the students,
- the establishment of open services for all adults interested in scientific learning accomplishments,
- a transformation of subject-oriented systems of study towards more interdisciplinary and problem-oriented approaches,

- a diversification of the arrangements for individualised studies, for example, on the basis of 'contract learning',
- the implementation of electronic technologies for the promotion of self-directed learning,
- the support of distant studies and the development of a 'virtual campus' and
- the development of modular unit-credit-systems.

In the lifelong learning phase of human evolution the university will have to give up a traditional self-sufficiency. It has to open its mind to a new role as one special support system of higher learning in a large diversified network for numerous self-directed lifelong learning processes in a modern learning society.

Geoff Layer

From the 'Ghetto' to the Mainstream

1. Introduction

This paper reviews the changes made in disabled student support within a UK university tracing the developments that have taken place between 1989 and 1995. This period has seen the proportion of disabled students increasing from 0.3% to 5.4% of the student population at the same time as student numbers have also rapidly increased.

Whilst the increase in student numbers may appear significant the real challenge to any Access development is ensuring that once opportunities have been created students are able to succeed. This is often seen as requiring the introduction of different support models. The danger of such a strategy is that it can reinforce the elitist view that Access strategies provide students that 'have to be helped' to achieve. In effect this can lead to the creation of 'ghettos' where what are perceived as 'students needing help' are supported. The projects reported on in this paper have tried to ensure a move away from the concept of the 'ghetto' to one where disabled students are recognised as an integral part of the student community, where staff are aware of those needs and can respond to them without constant referral to another agency. In other words, the University becomes 'disability friendly' as an entity.

Such a move requires a number of changes in the following areas:

- Recruitment strategies
- Curriculum development
- Learner support
- Administrative processes
- Preparation for employment
- Staff development

and, most importantly, there is a requirement to ensure a 'culture change'. Without a general recognition that disability is part of everyday life then the development of an institution-wide approach is more difficult to achieve if not impossible.

2. Background

The University is one of the largest in the UK with just over 22,000 students. Its mission is

> to provide opportunities for the development of intellectual, professional and practical skills and qualities; to encourage national, regional and international access to higher education; and to contribute to the economic and cultural development of the region.

It promotes itself as a vocational university serving business and the professions. This can be demonstrated through its high level of graduate employment (65% on completion in 1995), the work experience element in all courses and the professional body recognition that is linked to the degrees and diplomas.

The University has a major commitment to widening participation and to supporting students. The co-ordination of this activity is located within the Student Services Centre where the Access and Guidance team have developed an approach which integrates learner support and educational guidance for all, with particular activities designed to widen participation. It was from within Access and Guidance that the initiatives to develop an integrated approach to disabled student support developed and where the co-ordination of the work is located.

The University has always encouraged the recruitment of students with disabilities. The early initiatives were developed through the Sheffield Local Education Committee (1), particularly in respect of support for Hearing

Impaired students. It is interesting to note the language used to describe the students:

1982	-	'Handicapped'
1985	-	'Students with Disabilities'
1995	-	'Disabled Students'

This demonstrates the changing awareness of the issues involved and this is referred to later. The University set up a working party on Disability in 1985 from which emerged the Committee on Disability which advised the Principal. The advisory nature of the committee posed a number of problems as although the group had a number of interesting and radical ideas there was no resource, financial or staff, to put the ideas into practice.

Students with particular needs, hearing or visually impaired, were supported from the Sheffield-wide service and paid for from Disabled Students Allowances which students could receive over and above any standard financial grant. This model meant that individual students with a demonstrable need could be supported. It was, however, provision that was 'bolted on' to the traditional support model and was not integrated into a general model of learner support. For example, the support staff came into the university to provide assistance in class and were not necessarily available at other times. Support was on an individual basis with limited collective sharing of issues and problems.

(1) A number of UK Universities were formerly known as Polytechnics and were part of a unified education service for a particular area and were managed by locally elected councils through an Education Committee. This formally changed in 1989 but had been 'management from a distance' for a number of years.

3. Impetus for Change

Like many other developments and strategies related to Access, change is difficult to introduce without additional resources or one-off investment.

In 1993 the Higher Education Funding Council for England (HEFCE), which funds English universities, announced an initiative under which £5 million would be available for projects 'to encourage widening participation for students with special needs' for the academic year 1993/94. The University successfully applied for funding with a project with the following planned outcomes:

- increasing the number of students with disabilities by 100 for the 1994/95 academic year
- improving the performance of students with disabilities
- increasing the awareness of staff
- producing guidance handbooks and materials
- enhancing the preparedness of students with disabilities for work experience programmes
- seeking to embed the support for students with disabilities within the University.

This project was followed by a similar initiative in 1994/95 whereby the University was again successful with a project that aimed to enhance the level of support provided for students particularly in respect of orientation and within the curriculum.

These two projects were housed within Access and Guidance and came about at an opportune moment; the Guidance function was just developing and therefore disability could be seen as an integral part rather than a 'bolt on' service.

4. The New Approach

With the appointment of a project team in 1993 the University had its first opportunity to utilise staff whose primary role was to develop support for what were then described as students with disabilities.

The first action of this new team was to clarify the language within the University and from that re-definition came the guiding philosophy that informed future work. The Project Team persuaded the University to adopt the social model of disability which is based on a recognition and acceptance that:

> disability is the disadvantage or restriction of activity caused by contemporary social organisation which takes little or no account of people who have an impairment or medical condition and subsequently excludes them from mainstream social activities. *Disability* is therefore imposed *upon disabled people* and can, with a re-organisation of society, be removed.

By accepting that disability is socially constructed, the onus is clearly on the University to identify what barriers and obstacles are presented to disabled people and to determine how to remove them. Hence the use of the term disabled students.

This approach reflects a radical change from previous definitions and imposes a sense of clarity over the role of the University in responding to student need.

The University's concern is not so much with a student's condition or impairment but with the obstacles which are subsequently placed before the student. The aim is to provide the support services, equipment and physical adaptations which remove these obstacles and enable a student to integrate into mainstream University life and to be able to use all the facilities and services. In adopting this approach, the University is clearly committed to recognising, and makes every effort to meet, the 'Seven Needs for Independent Living', a set of principles outlined by disabled people's organisations that enable genuine independence. They are to be found in Appendix One.

As the Guidance Service within Access and Guidance developed the Disability Project Team was strengthened as rather than having a specialist, stand-alone service, it became part of the general service. The philosophy of the Guidance Service is that all staff are aware of general student issues and the particular needs of certain groups. Disabled students, therefore, approach the Guidance Service. Only if the needs are particularly complex does the student need to see a specialist adviser, as all advisers should be able to help the student achieve their objectives. This philosophy is fundamental to the aim of ensuring that the support model becomes more 'normal'.

5. What has Changed?

Recruitment

In order to ensure that more disabled people had the opportunity to participate in HE a recruitment and admissions policy was developed. Part of the recruitment strategy included the University setting a target of 4% of the student population for all Schools. The target of 4% was identified because UK employment legislation requires large organisations to employ at least 3% of its workforce from registered disabled people. It was felt by the University that there was an obligation to provide a graduate disabled workforce larger than the minimum required by employers.

This recruitment target was then supported by an admissions policy and procedure designed to assist disabled applicants (Appendix 2). Much of the process is constrained by the national application procedure through the Universities and Colleges Application System (UCAS), and use was made of the national definitions and codes. The key part of the process is a guarantee that disabled candidates from certain categories of disability (that is, UCAS codes 1, 2, 3, 4, 5, 6, and 8 - attached as Appendix 3) who meet the *minimum* academic requirements for admission should be guaranteed an interview, thereby having the opportunity to provide additional evidence in support of their application.

This process has led to the development of an applicant support culture where students are helped throughout by ensuring that they visit the University and that they are appropriately supported during that period.

The strategy has achieved some success with the following increase in disabled student numbers

1989/90	0.3% of student population
1992/93	1.5%
1993/94	2.0%
1994/95	5.0%

These figures relate to students who have voluntarily declared themselves as disabled on the University enrolment form. Part of the increase is undoubtedly due to a greater awareness of the issues and people therefore feeling happier about disclosing their impairment. Much of the increase though does reflect new students.

Learner Support

As indicated earlier specific support has been provided for certain individuals. There was however no mechanism for co-ordinating services and there was duplication and a lack of direct lines of communication. It was also felt necessary to ensure that the curriculum changed to reflect disability issues and how students were supported on courses. Given the philosophy of integration across the University and the involvement of all staff it was decided to focus on the transition process of admission, the development of transparency of support needs and the utilisation of students in the support process as a peer group.

To achieve this a number of activities were put into place:

(i) a taster course is offered each year for disabled people thinking of applying to the university. This has always attracted about 40 people who are then given an insight into how they can maximise the opportunities available to them.

(ii) all disabled students are invited to a special three day induction programme prior to the start of the new year to help them meet fellow disabled students to introduce them to the University.

(iii) a learner agreement was drawn up between the University and the student which stipulated the level of support the student required. This would be finalised at induction if all the appropriate assessments had taken place.

(iv) disabled student support groups were established so that students could meet and discuss issues on a regular basis.

(v) a 'buddy' scheme was established under which existing disabled students met, welcomed and assisted the integration of new students.

(vi) a model for the development of disability issues was produced with the School of Engineering which can be translated into other programmes of study.

Staff Development

This is the key factor in ensuring that cultural changes takes place and the University was fortunate that so many staff were interested and wanted to participate. This meant that their energies could focus upon developing sessions and materials that were owned across the institution. Consequently a Disability Handbook has been produced which is used in regular staff development sessions and has proved to be extremely popular.

6. From Project to Permanency

Once the project funding came to an end the University was faced with the dilemma of how to continue its commitment. Although strict budget constraints exist in the HE sector in the UK the University decided that its disabled students would receive more appropriate support from a developed in-house service. The benefits of this are:

- it is available on site
- staff and students are more involved in University life and therefore able to influence change more easily
- staff are able to utilise group work activities
- the team has a greater role in staff development so that the issues were owned by more staff
- enhanced accountability to the University and the student.

The University therefore established a Disabled Student Support Service within the Guidance Service. This new aspect of the Guidance Service was funded by the University on the expectation that students would contribute through the Disabled Student Allowance (see Appendix 4) and that eventually it would break even.

The service was established in February 1996 and to date has:

- produced a new student handbook
- ensured that disabled students were supported during the admissions process
- re-established the taster courses for disabled people
- employed a team of communication support workers
- provided a note-takers training course so that students can be supported
- developed an assessment of need process that makes sure that appropriate support is in place before disabled students arrive
- organised a learner support tutorial programme so that disabled students can 'drop in' for specific support

- promoted links with local schools and colleges so that the transition to HE is more planned
- further developed and supported disabled student support groups
- established an enhanced orientation programme for disabled students
- enhanced the level of specialist equipment.

A number of these activities are enhancement and consolidation from the projects. The major new developments are the provision of learner support sessions and trained support workers. The challenges being addressed for the next year are a review of assessment practices and a further drive on staff development.

Although these are early days there is considerable evidence that the University is beginning to respond to disabled students, recognising that it is we who have created the barriers and not a deficiency of the individual. It will be a slow process but the goal is too important to be allowed to slip.

References

Disability Development Project, Final Report 1994, Sheffield Hallam University.

Disability Discrimination Act, 1995.

Access to Success for Students with Disabilities in Higher Education in Scotland, Scottish HEFCE, 1995.

Access to Higher Education: Students with Learning Difficulties and Disabilities - A report on 1993/94 and 1994/95, HEFCE Special Initiatives to Encourage Widening Participation for Students with Disabilities, HEFCE, 1996.

Guidelines on Guidance and Learner Support, Higher Education Quality Council, 1995.

Appendix 1

The Seven Needs for Independent Living

1 Information

All materials, and methods of communication take account of the needs of disabled people ,for example, large print, braille and sign language.

2 Peer Support

Disabled people are able to learn from and benefit from the support and experiences of other disabled people.

3 Accommodation is available and physically accessible to disabled people.

4 Equipment and Adaptations

Equipment and technical aids are available when appropriate.

5 Personal Assistance

Personal assistants are available to those disabled people who need the help and support.

6 Environmental Access

All buildings are accessible to disabled people.

7 Transport

Transport, public and private, should be accessible to disabled people.

Appendix 2

Access and Admissions

The University operates a seven-stage admission procedure for disabled students designed to guarantee full and fair consideration of applications from all disabled applicants and to ensure that they are able to present comprehensive information in support of their application and to gain insight into the range of available academic and non-academic support. At each stage of the process data is gathered to ensure that future recruitment is targeted effectively and appropriate adjustments are made to practice and procedures.

Stage One - Information to Applicants Disabled applicants by virtue of their particular circumstances are likely to request more information than other groups of students. Each applicant is likely to have a unique set of requirements and time is taken by staff to find out at this initial stage what specific responses are needed from the University. All requests from potential disabled applicants are passed to a designated member of staff in the Central Admissions Office.

Stage Two - Receipt of the Application Currently candidates applying through the national full-time application systems and institutional applications for direct entry to years 2, 3 and 4, are asked to indicate on the form, using a code, whether they have a disability. On receipt of application forms the Admission Office staff screen applications carefully, identify those from disabled people and highlight the relevant sections on the form that is, the code, personal details and further information. Monitoring forms are then attached to all applicants´ forms before they are passed to Admissions Tutors.

Stage Three - Consideration of the Application The Admissions Tutor makes a decision against the established criteria for admission. Tutors must ensure that consideration of academic ability is separated from considerations centred on an applicant´s other requirements and take account of the following positive action strategy agreed by Academic Board in July 1994:

- Disabled candidates who have entered codes 1, 2, 3, 4, 5, 6 and 8 and who meet the minimum academic requirement for entry should be guaranteed an interview during the two year monitoring period, thereby having the opportunity to provide additional evidence in support of their application.

- Schools are asked to achieve a recruitment target of 4% disabled students.
- Applications from disabled people are monitored in order to track the success or failure rate of such applicants and to ensure that rejections are made against clear criteria.
- Any disabled candidate who is judged to meet the academic criteria should not be refused admission on the grounds of disability without compelling reasons.

When Admissions Tutors have considered the application, the decision is indicated on the monitoring form and all papers returned to the Admissions Office. At this stage, information is collected on rejection and entered on the database. The information collected is used as a basis for future developments in the admission of disabled people.

Stage Four - Interviews/Open Days In addition to the usual papers sent out, disabled candidates in categories 1, 2, 3, 4, 5, 6 and 8 who are being invited to interview or open day are sent a letter offering an informal session with an adviser prior to the more formal session with other candidates. Wherever practical, the informal session is held on the same day and prior to the interview or open day. The informal session offers the opportunity for disabled candidates to find out what the University can offer, discuss any specific requirements for support, view the facilities of the University and assess the situation with appropriate staff. The needs identified by the applicant are recorded by the adviser on a proforma. The completed proforma is sent to staff in the Admissions Office who will attach it to the application form. At this stage information will be collected on those rejected after interview, along with the reasons.

In addition to the letter, one of the following information leaflets is sent to the candidate:

- Information for Dyslexic Applicants or those with a Specific Learning Difficulty
- Information for Hearing Impaired/Deaf Applicants
- Information for Physically Disabled Applicants

- Information for Applicants with ME (Myalgic Encephalomyelitis/ Chronic Fatigue Syndrome)
- Information for Visually Impaired Applicants - in this case staff ascertain whether applicants have need of a large print, braille or taped version of the leaflet.

On receipt of an affirmative reply and the appropriate form, the Admissions Office passes the request to the Education Adviser (Disability) who makes the necessary arrangements and informs the candidate, admissions tutor and appropriate adviser.

Stage Five - Offers Offers to disabled candidates are made in the usual way and the application form and proforma completed at open day or interview is held by the designated member of staff in the Admissions Office until the applicant indicates firm acceptance. On firm acceptance, copies of all papers are sent to the Education Adviser (Disability). On the basis of the proforma prepared at the interview or open day a profile of the disabled applicant is prepared, along with an outline of how the requirements will be met. When this has been agreed and signed by the candidate, the profile is circulated to relevant Schools and facility managers.

Stage Six - Entry to the University As soon as the candidate has indicated firm acceptance, an invitation to the special Induction Programme for Disabled Students is offered. This programme is designed to give any disabled student who requires it, a chance to meet with a range of staff and gain support for claiming the Disabled Students' Allowances and full information on how to access services. In addition, the opportunity is offered to meet with programme staff, check access arrangements and ensure that all practical support/equipment is in place for the beginning of Semester One.

Stage 7 - Monitoring and Evaluation

In order to maintain and enhance the quality of the admission process for disabled students a range of indicators has been developed against which the procedures can be monitored. In addition, detailed information on the progress of disabled applicants is routinely and systematically collected at each stage of the recruitment and admission process, analysed and used as a basis for future development.

Appendix 3

UCAS Codes - Disability

1 Dyslexia.
2 Blind/Partially sighted.
3 Deaf/Hearing impaired.
4 Wheelchair user/mobility-related disability.
5 Personal care support.
6 Mental ill-health.
7 An unseen disability ,for example, asthma, diabetes, epilepsy.
8 More than one disability.
9 A disability not listed above.

Appendix 4

Disabled Students Allowances

The following grants/allowances are examples of financial support which may be available to disabled students.

Disabled Students' Allowance (DSA)

DSA is only available to full-time students who are eligible for a mandatory student award. The allowances are means-tested so not all students qualify.

This allowance is to assist disabled students to benefit as fully as possible from a course of study. If you are eligible, the allowances are available from your Local Education Authority (LEA). The LEA must consider all cases where extra costs are incurred in studying because of a physical, hearing, visual impairment or a specific learning difficulty.

The allowances only covers costs relating to disability which are incurred as a result of being a student.

There are three parts to the allowance:

a) Non-medical personal assistance - up to £4,975 each year
b) Equipment - up to £3,745 for the course
c) General allowance - up to £1,245 each year

The general allowance is for 'other extra costs' and usually covers minor items such as tapes and braille paper, but can also be used to top up the other two allowances if needed.

Applying for DSA

LEA´s will not normally accept an application for DSA unless it is supported by the University.

When applying for the Allowance, students are required to supply the following information:

a) Evidence of disability, which can be one of the following:
    i) proof of registration as a disabled person
    ii) copy of SEN statement from school
    iii) assessment by a suitably qualified or experienced person, ,for example, a chartered or educational psychologist
b) An assessment of the student's need for specific items of equipment/non-medical personal support. This needs to take into account:
    i) the extent of disability
    ii) the demands of the course
    iii) the suitability of the particular piece of equipment/support

   iv) any training which the person may require to use equipment

c) Quotes for the cost of equipment and support (the number of quotes required varies from LEA to LEA).

Details of how to apply can be obtained from the Student Awards Officer of your Local Education Authority.

Jukka Tuomisto

Market-Oriented Adult Education Policy
- a Finnish Perspective

From liberal adult education policy to market services

According to Alanen (1993: 13-18), we can distinguish three different stages in the role of the state with regard to planning and supporting adult education in Finland. The first stage was one of a liberal adult education policy (1925-1969), influenced by ideas in the 1920s. Liberal thinking maintained that subsidised organisations providing liberal adult education (folk high schools, adult education centres, and study centres of cultural organisations) had to be allowed a certain degree of autonomy. The task of the state was to support studying which was based on citizens' personal interest. In this stage, the task of adult education was to establish and support a society of citizens.

The rapid changes in the structure of industry and production technology in the 1960s brought with it the need to develop vocational adult education. The Adult Education Committee, set up in 1971, was expected to draw up a proposal for a comprehensive development of adult education. This marked the beginning of the period of planning-centred adult education policy (1970-1985). Emphasis was put on advancing vocational adult education which at that time was still quite undeveloped. The economic recession and the simultaneous reforming of the school system slowed down the plans for advancing adult education in the 1970s. In fact, true development only got started in the early 1980s, when several committees were set up in this field, producing a large number of reports.

The transition to the period of market-based adult education policy (1985) did not happen overnight, but only gradually as a result of a number of reforms. However, in the 1990s the adult education policy of the state has emphasised the role of market forces. The aim has been to develop adult education in such a way that it would accommodate the changing demands of the labour market as flexibly as possible and improve the economic competitiveness of Finland (Tuomisto, 1992: 55). Market mechanisms have been used in reforming the system of control and financing; educational organisations today compete with each other for the same tasks. The expressed goals of this new adult education policy are primarily related to quantity and instruments, even though the quality of education and its assessment have also been a much discussed topic in the last few years. But as Wexler (1987: 71) points out, the movement for 'quality in education' hides the reconstitution of education as an object of commodity exchange.

The social context in which adult education has had to operate in the last ten years or so is characterised by the following factors: new technology and the new possibilities offered by it; keen international competition; emphasis on image policy in economy and other areas; economic recession which has forced the state and municipalities to make considerable cuts in order to balance their economy; European integration; the collapse of the Soviet Union; new distribution of decision-making power between the state and the municipalities; the 'rundown' of public economy and increasing privatisation; high unemployment, especially among the young and those near retirement; ecological problems and harsh criticism of continuing growth, aiming at sustainable development.

Can the present market-oriented policy be an answer to all the above problems, or is it simply a symptom of the fact that no one knows what should be done? When development work is left to the markets, whose interests does this serve in the end? Tuijnman (1992: 210-219) lists the following features as characteristics of the 'market model' in adult education:

1) Economism: trust in the economic usefulness of education.

2) Vocationalism: increased emphasis on vocational education.

3) Financial austerity: education costs of the public sector can no longer be increased.

4) Decentralisation: a weakened role of the state in decision-making related to education.

5) Individualism: focus on meeting the educational needs of individuals.

6) Accountability: calculating the effectiveness of all education should be possible.

7) Politicisation: all decision-making related to education happens more and more as a joint effort of corporations, while local authorities, employers, trade unions and individual adults themselves represent the most important decision-makers.

8) Fragmentation: the range and variants of learning possibilities have generally increased in the industrialised countries. They now vary from classroom learning to collaborative group learning, open learning networks and support for self-directed learning.

9) Skills shortages: the economic situation at present encourages firms to strengthen their concern with human resource development. There is also an increasing demand for people with 'the skills employers want'.

All the above features can clearly be identified in Finland, too. It is easy to see that the central ideas of traditional adult education (promoting humanism, equality, emancipation and democracy) have, at least in part, been rolled over by the market forces (Tuckett, 1991, Ball, 1993). Many adult educators are worried, even frustrated, about this trend, while others see it as a possibility of adding to the social 'value' of adult education.

Goals and the data used

We know from several cross-sectional studies of adult participation in study activity that people with a long education and a good social status study more than those with a shorter education and a lower social status (Rubenson and Willms, 1993: 14-16, Berichtssystem, 1993: 65-66). However, we know very little about how this 'self-evidence' or 'natural law' has developed over the years; in other words, how big these differences are and whether they have increased, decreased or remained the same. If there are changes, which sectors do they concern, which direction are they taking and why?

This article examines

1) Changes in participation by adults in study activity:
   - overall participation rate (1972-1995),
   - adult education related to one's work or profession (1980-1995),
   - inservice education (1982-1993),
   - social and interest-based studies (1980-1990);
2) Some developmental features of certain sectors of adult education,
3) Advantages and disadvantages of the principle of market-oriented planning.

The first national study of adults' participation in Finland was made in the early 1970s on the initiative of the Adult Education Committee (Lehtonen and Tuomisto, 1975). Since then the Central Statistical Office has conducted a national survey in the early 1980s (Havén and Syvänperä, 1983, Katajisto, 1984) and in the 1990s (Simpanen and Blomqvist, 1992). The most recent study is from last year, but only some preliminary results are available so far (Blomqvist and Simpanen, 1996). In addition to general surveys, various sectors are involved in special projects in their own fields (for example, statistics of liberal adult education, labour market education, apprenticeship education, inservice education, etc.).

Changes in participation

Increased participation in adult education is a universal phenomenon. In Finland, the growth was especially great in the 1980s, while in the 1990s the growth seems to have stopped. Does this mean that we have now reached some kind of a 'saturation point' in participation?

Table 1: Overall participation in adult education in 1972, 1980, 1990 and 1995 by basic education (population aged 18-64) (Lehtonen and Tuomisto, 1975, Adult education 1993, Blomqvist and Simpanen 1996).

	1972	1980	1990	1995	Change (1972/95)
Comprehensive school	17	23	31	33	+16
Secondary education	35	39	53	50	+15
Higher education	44	53	78	75	+31
All	20	32	47	48	+28

Participation has increased in all groups representing different levels of basic education, but the increase has been the greatest among those with a higher education degree (the increase in 1972/90 being 31 percentage units). However, among these people it is quite natural that they have reached some kind of a ceiling. Conversely, people with just a comprehensive school education would still have a lot of room for growth, but studying does not seem to be part of their life style. These people are often older and/or already marginalised from the labour market. The development of adult education has consequently resulted in greater educational polarisation. In the other industrialised countries, too, the process of polarisation seems to be the prevailing trend. Educational polarisation in Germany is slightly greater than in Finland (Berichtssystem, 1993: 140-146), while in British Columbia, Canada, it seems to have been much stronger in the early 1990s (Rubenson and Willms, 1993: 15).

Table 2: Participation in adult education related to the work or profession in 1980, 1990 and 1995 by socio-economic group (employed population aged 18-64) (Blomqvist and Simpanen, 1996).

	1980	1990	1995	Change (1980/90)
- Executives	48	74	71	+23
- Clerical workers	38	60	62	+24
- Workers	13	28	35	+22
- Farmers	11	12	32	+21
- Other entrepreneurs	12	27	24	+12
All	25	45	50	+25

In the 1980s, vocational adult education increased among executives and clerical workers, in particular. However, this trend has not continued in the 1990s. Growth has continued with workers and farmers in the 1990s, although their participation is still only about half that of executives and clerical workers.

Inservice education represents that part of vocational adult education which has increased the most in the last decade. It also represents the largest individual area of education (Rinne et al, 1995).

Diagram 1: Participation in inservice education by employed population by socio-economic status in 1982-1993 (%)

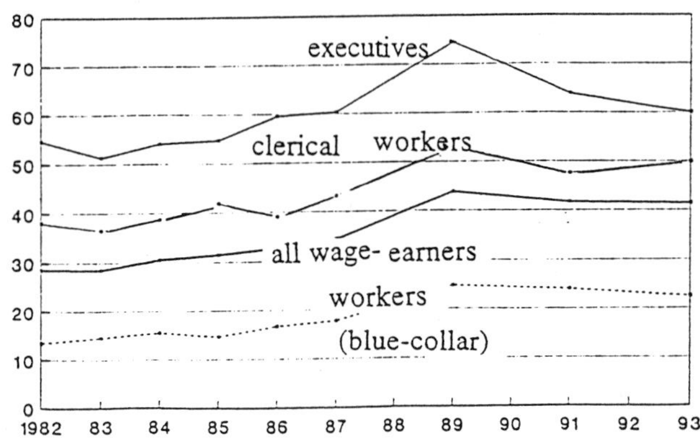

The diagram shows that during this period employers have provided education primarily for their executives and clerical workers. Education for workers has been rather limited. The situation is similar in many other countries (Rubenson 1991, Ball 1993). The statistics in Finland show that private employers provide considerably less inservice education for their staff than public employers. In 1993, private employers provided inservice education for about 36% of their staff, municipalities for about 47% and the state for about 56% of their staff (Kivinen and Rinne 1995: 122).

Changes in social and interest-based studies were considerably smaller in the 1980s (Table 3). With executives and clerical workers, participation in fact seems to have decreased somewhat, while with other groups some growth can be seen.

Table 3: Participation in social and interest-based studies in 1980 and 1990 by socio-economic status (employed population aged 18-64), (Simpanen and Blomqvist, 1992: 96-97).

	1980	1990	Change (1980/90)
-Executives	24	23	-1
-Clerical workers	29	25	-4
-Workers	13	12	-1
-Farmers	13	25	+12
-Other entrepreneurs	10	12	+2
All	17	18	+1

In all, social and interest-based studies are fewer than vocational studies and the changes in them are smaller. Polarisation thus seems to be the problem of the labour market and vocational adult education, in particular. This tells something about a deepening division of society into successful experts and marginalised, uneducated workers who no longer belong to the active work force.

Adult education in universities

In connection with the open university, people have always talked about promoting educational equality. The fact is, however, that the proportion of students without a student matriculation examination has diminished all the time. Among other things, this results from the following factors:

(1) Educational inequality. The proportion of students with a student matriculation examination in the whole population has increased. This is

clearly visible in the younger age groups of whom about half nowadays take this examination.

(2) Removing the age limit. Earlier, open university favoured adult students by setting the age limit at 25 years and work experience. Because of the high unemployment rate, especially among young people, the Finnish government removed the age limit in 1993 and has in many other ways encouraged young people to participate in education. This has resulted in the open university now being full of young people, newly graduated from the upper secondary school.

(3) Student selection. Since age and work experience can no longer be used as the criterion for selection, open university students are now accepted in the order of registration. As a result, the most eager applicants, equipped with their sleeping bags and sandwiches, arrive to queue up for a student place the night before registration begins. They want to ensure that they will be among the first to enter when the doors are opened in the morning, and will thus be selected. This system of selection favours those young people who are not working. It measures the eagerness of applicants, of course, but at the same time puts them in an unequal position in the competition for student places.

(4) Tuition fees. In the early 1980s, tuition in open university was free. Today students must pay a moderate fee, which is still clearly smaller than those of commercial profit-making schools. (For example, a block of studies which will produce an approbatur qualification costs about 800 marks.) Surprisingly, the fees have not been criticised much, not even by students. It seems that those who participate are prepared to pay for their tuition, while those who do not participate do not worry about the fees either. It is mostly the unemployed who have criticised the system, because for them the fees are high. The system has changed the type of open university student: they are now mostly individuals who can afford to pay for their studies and who will clearly benefit from the education in view of their career.

The amount of vocationally oriented continuing education provided by universities has increased steadily over the last few years. However, this form of education has always been specially commissioned, so in this respect it has not actually changed. It is worth mentioning, though, that the proportion of courses commissioned by employers has clearly increased in the 1990s. In 1992, one fourth of the courses were commissioned by employers who were also responsible for selecting the students.

Labour market adult training

Former employment training is now called labour market adult training, (LMT). The change in the name refers to profoundly changed attitudes and ways of thinking. In the past this training primarily aimed at finding employment for people, while today it is more openly used for storing the unemployed. This way not only the unemployed but their educators, too, are kept off the unemployment registers. This is of great importance for the present government of Finland which has promised to reduce the present high rate of unemployment (15-20%) by half. For this reason training is arranged, even though it is common knowledge that many of those in training will hardly find jobs afterwards. Youth unemployment in particular is of great concern, so young people are now pressed hard to participate in labour market training. Of course, young people cannot be forced to attend these courses. However, the options available to them can be reduced by the authorities in such a way that they see training as the only way out of their bleak situation. The Finnish government decided that young people under the age of 20 with no vocational education will no longer receive labour market benefits but will be directed to vocational studies or work practice. This decision has been in force since the beginning of 1996. From the beginning of 1997, the age limit will go up to 25. In practice this means that compulsory education of young people with no jobs will be extended to that age. Obviously the aim is to train and educate the population even more than today, openly 'recommending' training as an alternative to unemployment. Such action, however, is more like social work than educational activity.

This seems to be the price that society has to pay for the 'flexibility' demanded by the labour markets (Hyyppä, 1996: 204-207).

The proportion of employment education, together with entrepreneur training, also increased in universities in 1991 and 1992, when special funding for this purpose was available (the so-called Relander funding). This type of education doubled in one year, as measured by both the number of participants and the amount of instruction. The government had approved a special employment and industry scheme which aimed at finding jobs for the academically educated unemployed. In part, the scheme only managed to embellish the statistics related to unemployment: it brought a break in a long period of unemployment and temporarily 'stored' work force in a half-way house (Kivinen and Rinne, 1994: 257). At the moment, the proportion of employment education for the academically educated is about 10% of all employment education. Academically educated people are thus gaining ground in this sector of education.

Adult education centres

The traditions of liberal adult education are kept alive by the adult education centres which focus on leisure time and voluntary studies. They have received considerable financial support since the 1920s, based on the law on state subsidies. In the 1990s, the state launched a so-called withdrawal strategy in its funding policy, with the aim of reducing drastically the costs of state sponsored education. This strategy has been applied in financing the activities of the non-corporate public sector since the beginning of 1993. In the past all acceptable expenses were reimbursed more or less automatically. After the introduction of the new system, municipalities now receive a lump sum of state subsidy which they must use to provide all educational services. Since this money is no longer divided between the different sectors as it used to be, elected trustee persons have more freedom in deciding about its use. Adult education centres belong under municipal administration for education and culture, and each municipality organises its administration as it sees best. Many adult education centres have now been integrated with other organisations dealing with education and culture (for example, culture, education, youth work, etc.). Nowadays the centres can decide freely which kind of courses they provide. They can also arrange vocational courses. In the past it was not allowed. Students must pay a fee for their instruction, whereas in the past all teaching was practically free of charge. The incomes of the education centres have increased, which has given them more flexibility. In developing the adult education centres, quantity and economic efficiency have become the most important goals (Jääskä, 1994).

Conclusions and future visions

Finnish adult education has been strongly labour market oriented in the 1980s and 1990s, and the volume of adult education has continued to grow. The situation is similar in most European countries (Lichtner, 1991). The disadvantages resulting from this trend are that the cost of education has gone up. The emphasis has shifted to vocational education, and polarisation of education is a reality, especially in education related to working life. The reasons for students' participation have been instrumentalised. Young people are burdened with compulsory education until the age of 25 (if a young person does not accept employment offered, he/she will lose his/her unemployment benefit). Older age groups have had several periods of training but have not found jobs afterwards. All this means that education more and more often provides a half-way house for temporary 'storing' of the work force.

The new policy also has its advantages. Studying is now more goal-oriented and fewer people drop out. The quality of teaching has generally improved, although the provision of trivial or substandard education has also increased. Teachers must concentrate more on their work and its quality: students expect to get their money's worth now that they have to pay fees. Competition forces schools to ponder their strengths and their mission in greater depth.

The market-oriented planning strategy, however, has limitations which prevent it from serving as an adequate foundation for adult education planning. Here are some of them:

(a) The logic of the markets. Those who support the market-oriented educational system claim that with well-functioning markets the quality of education improves for all concerned. However, it is obvious that this has not happened. Educational services are now highly concentrated, while large groups of citizens have become ‘marginalised’. The process of polarisation is reality in most industrialised countries. This is something that adult educators and adult education planners cannot accept. One of the goals of adult education has always been to reduce educational inequality. How far is polarisation allowed to go before something is done to prevent its harmful effects?

(b) The values of adult education. Should we be satisfied with a situation in which adult education only serves the needs of economic life and employment policy? Where are the basic values of adult education, such as the promotion of democracy and equality? Adult education has always involved tasks related to civic education, individual growth and emancipation, and it has struggled to perform these tasks well. In fact, these tasks have been considered the primary goals of adult education. In the market-oriented model of planning there is no room for such goals.

(c) The target groups of adult education. Society, particularly one living in a market economy, will always have groups of people who are threatened by the risk of being marginalised from normal social life. We need educational planning and training which also takes into account marginalised people in a weak social position.

(d) The content of education. The emphasis should be shifted from specialised vocational education for experts to more general education from larger groups of citizens, enhancing their skills and preparedness to manage their own lives.

(e) The principle of lifelong education/learning, too, has now been harnessed to serve the ideology of continuing growth and consumption: it is used as an instrument to legitimise market-oriented education. This is especially enforced by industry and trade, in other words the representatives of market forces. Adult educators must be able to bring forth alternative ways of thinking that rely on more sustainable ecological ideas.

There is no returning to what we had before, but unfortunately the present direction does not seem promising either. Adult educators must become aware of today's situation and where it will lead us. We must start developing a new education strategy in-between the models of centralised planning and market-oriented planning. The new model should combine the humanistic traditions of adult education and the dynamics of the markets. It is not an easy task, but certainly a great challenge.

References

Alanen, A. (1993), Aikuiskasvatuksen organisaatiomuodot (Forms of organisations in Adult Education), Tampere, University of Tampere. Department of Education. Report B 7. Aikuiskoulutuksen tilastot vuodelta 1991(Statistics of Adult Education 1991), Opetushallituksen julkaisusarjat, Raporttisarja 17/1992.

Ball, S. J. (1993), Education Markets, Choice and Social Class: the market as a class strategy in UK and USA, British Journal of Sociology of Education, Vol. 14, No. 1.

Berichtssystem Weiterbildung, (1991), Bundesministerium für Bildung und Wissenschaft, Schriftenreihe Studien zu Bildung und Wissenschaft 110, Bonn 1993.

Blomqvist, I. and Simpanen, M. (1996), Aikuiskoulutustutkimus 1995 (Participation in Adult Education 1995), Ennakkotietoja. Tilastokeskus. Koulutus 1996.

Havén and Syvänperä (1983), Aikuiskoulutukseen osallistuminen (Participation in Adult Education), Tilastokeskuksen tutkimuksia 92, Helsinki, Tilastokeskus.

Hyyppä, H. (1996), Aikuisten päivähoitoa (Day-care for adults), Aikuiskasvatus 3.

Jääskä, P. (1994), Tulos vai vapaus (Outcomes or Freedom)?, Näkökulmia kansalaisopistojen toiminnan tuloksellisuuden arviointiin, Aikuiskasvatus 1.

Katajisto, J. (1984), Osallistumismuutokset Suomen aikuiskoulutuksessa 1972-1980 (Participation chances in Adult Education 1972-1980 in Finland), Aikuiskasvatus 2.

Kivinen, Osmo and Rinne, R. (1994), Korkeakoulujen aikuiskoulutus (Adult Education in Higher Education). Teoksessa Jakku-Sihvonen and Yrjölä (toim.), Aikuiskoulutus 1990 -luvun Suomessa, Opetushallitus, Helsinki, Hakapaino Oy, Lehtonen and

Tuomisto 1975, Participation in Adult Education in Finland, Adult Education in Finland, Vol. 12, No 1-2.

Lichtner, M. (1991), Labour Market Strategies and Adult Education in Europe, Studies in the Education of Adults, Vol. 23. No. 2, October.

National Board of Education (1993), Adult Education in Finland, Helsinki.

Rinne, R., Silvennoinen H. and Valanta, J. (1995), Työelämän aikuiskoulutus (Working-life Adult Education), University of Turku, Research Unit for the Sociology of Education, Report 29, Turku.

Rubenson, K. (1991), Aikuiskoulutuksen kehittŠminen - markkinvoimien ohjattavaksi vai tavoitteiseen politiikkaan ? (Participation in adult education and training - between the market and policy), Aikuiskasvatus 2.

Rubenson, K. (1993), Adult Education Policy in Sweden 1967-1991. In Edwards, Sieminski & Zeldin (eds), Adult Learners, Education and Training, London, Routledge.

Rubenson, K. and Willms, J. D. (1993), Human Resources Development in British Columbia, U.B.C. Vancouver, Centre for Policy Studies in Education.

Simpanen, Matti and Blomqvist, I. (1992), Aikuiskoulutukseen osallistuminen (Participation in Adult Education). Tilastokeskus. Tutkimuksia 192, Helsinki: Hakapaino Oy.

Tuckett, A. (1991), Counting the Cost: Managerialism, the market and the education of adults in the 1980s and beyond. In Westwood, S. and Thomas, J. E., (eds), The politics of Adult Education, Leicester, NIACE.

Tuijnman, A. C. (1992), Paradigm Shifts in Adult Education. Teoksessa Tuijnman (ed), Learning Across the Lifespan, Theories, Research, Policies, Oxford, Pergamon Press.

Tuomisto, J. (1992), Aikuiskasvastuksen perusaineksia (Basics of Adult Education). University of Tampere, Institute for extension studies, Publication serie B 2. Tampere.

Jean-Luc Guyot / Barbara Merrill

Departmental Cultures and Academic Disciplines: Implications for the Access of Adults in Universities

Introduction

In recent years policy changes, particularly in Britain, have increased the number of adults entering higher education (HE). Access issues, primarily at the point of entry and participation, are high on the research agenda in Britain. Access to higher education within a European context is also an issue of growing importance but less well addressed by research. This paper presents the findings of a Belgian/UK institutional case-study research project on the policy and practice of the access of non-traditional adult students to universities. The research was undertaken by the Department of Education at the Catholic University of Louvain (UCL), Belgium and the Department of Continuing Education, University of Warwick, United Kingdom. Working comparatively and collaboratively the two research teams were interested in examining the following question in relation to adult access and universities: what makes an institution accessible?

By concentrating on a comparison at the macro, meso and micro levels of policy and practice within universities the research aimed to identify national, institutional and educational arrangements and strategies for facilitating the access and achievement of adult students. This paper focuses on the meso level; the impact of departmental cultures and academic disciplines in relation to the access and experiences of adults in universities. Adult students are located differentially across university disciplines and departments. Why are some departments more open than others? Why are adult students attracted to certain disciplines? The first part of the paper outlines the findings of the case-studies at UCL and Warwick. Theoretical issues are addressed in the second part.

Quantitative and qualitative approaches were combined to obtain a comprehensive picture of departmental life and adult student experiences. For example, a survey of key arrangements, admissions conditions, time and location of teaching, together with the adult student participation rate was undertaken at departmental level in both institutions. These aspects were compared with the perceptions, experiences and behaviours of lecturers and adult students in relation to access issues. Most adults at Warwick study broader degree programmes than younger students. They had to participate in and negotiate with several departments during their student career. In doing so, many perceived departments differently in terms of their attitudes and behaviour towards adult students, even within the same faculty. We could also not ignore the effect of the status and epistemology of academic subjects in relation to access issues. Academic knowledge is shaped by both the university and external social, economic and political factors. The attitudes of adult students and lecturers towards disciplines were partly influenced by such elements.

Some results from the UCL case study

In the process of the Warwick/UCL research, the Belgian team tried to present a comprehensive description of the UCL programmes. This description concerns mainly the accessibility of such programmes for adults. Two major aspects were given priority. First, formal admissions conditions and arrangements (scheduling and location of courses) designed to make the programmes more accessible to adults and, second, the number of adults enrolled on the programmes studied. Our analysis concerned the degree programmes offered by UCL in the 1992/93 academic year.

The programmes analysed were:

- the first year of the first level programmes ('premières candidatures')
- the first year of the second level programmes ('premières licences' and assimilated programmes)
- the level I programmes that consist of only 1 year ('candidatures uniques', 'baccalauréat', 'épreuve préparatoire de premier cycle', etc.)

- the level II programmes that consist of only one year of study ('licences uniques', 'épreuve préparatoire de second cycle', etc.)
- the level II complementary programmes or specialisations; and
- the level III (i.e., graduate level) complementary programmes or specialisations.

In total 293 programmes were analysed with regard to the first line of investigation. For the second line of investigation we considered only full-time enrolment taken by Belgian students (principal studies). Only 235 programmes were finally included in the study of adult participation because 53 programmes did not meet our nationality and/or enrolment selection criteria. Some did not have any enrolment, others had only foreign students and/or Belgians registered for complements to their main courses of study.

For purposes of comparison with Great Britain, we must point out that in Belgium, unlike Great Britain, there is no official administrative definition of an adult student. Consequently, we had to draw up our own definition. This takes the level of study being considered and, to a certain extent, the line of study into account. We thus considered the students to be adult students if they met the following criteria:

- students enrolled in first year of the first level and students enrolled in one-year candidatures and their equivalents who are 23 years old and up
- students enrolled in first year of the second level (première licence or its equivalent) or one-year licence (or its equivalent) who are 26 years old and up (this cut-off was raised to 27 and up for students in the first year of level II in medical studies); and
- students 29 years old and up who are enrolled in level II or III complementary programmes and specialisations, the exception being specialisations in medicine, for which this age limit was raised to 35 and up (it was not possible to break down the curriculum of level III medical specialisations into separate years).

To have a more accurate picture of reality, it would have been interesting to have been able to allow for possible breaks in the students' academic careers as well as their ages. Unfortunately, such information cannot be extracted from the UCL data base as it currently stands.

Analysis of Formal Admissions Conditions and Time and Space arrangements

General remarks

The 293 programmes were analysed according to an analytical grid designed using three of the variables that are considered crucial for adult admissions and easy to single out from the UCL course catalogue for the 1992/93 academic year. These three variables were:

- the type of formal admissions criterion
- flexible scheduling; and
- off-campus teaching.

With regard to the formal admissions conditions, we first drew up a typology of admissions conditions. This typology was built on a continuum of accessibility from the least open type (type A) of access to the most accessible (type F). The time arrangement category includes evening courses, weekend courses, and programmes that intentionally bunch courses together on certain days of the week. With regard to the teaching sites, we made a distinction between programmes offering off-campus teaching and the other programmes, as we felt that the principle of decentralisation or relocation to be an important element of a policy to broaden adults' access to university education. Analysis of the programmes and their characteristics in the university's various faculties also yielded interesting information.

The faculties

Before presenting this information, some clarifications about the Belgian university system must be made. The organisation of teaching and research in Belgian universities is characterised by a faculty structure. Each faculty is concerned with a scientific field and is composed of a various number of departments which deal with scientific sub-fields. For instance, the Catholic University of Louvain includes the following Faculties:

- Sciences (SC)
- Engineering (FSA)
- Agronomic Sciences (AGRO)
- Veterinarian Sciences (VETE)
- Medicine, including Pharmacology, Physical Education and Physiotherapy (MED)
- Philology and Literature (FLTR)
- Theology (TECO)
- Economics, Politics and Social Sciences (ESPO)
- Psychology and Education (PSP)
- Law (DRT)
- education units not attached to faculties (EUEN)
- research units not attached to faculties (not analysed in this research).

We, therefore, analysed the situation of each faculty with regard to the three types of arrangements (admission, time and space) in order to show the differences across faculties. Graphs 1 and 2 summarise the faculties' position for the time and space arrangements.

If all the programmes of all the faculties are grouped together, 71 % have conventional (type B) or closed (type A) admissions policies. AGRO, ESPO, EUEN, PSP, SC and TECO are below this value. They are thus the faculties that tend to have less restrictive admissions policies. From these, SC appears to have some restrictions. Many of the SC programmes were identified as belonging to the F category of admission conditions because they formally offer the possibility to people without any previous qualifications to enter if they pass an entrance examination. In practice, no one takes advantage of this possibility and, therefore, these programmes should be considered as belonging to the B or even A category. From this point of view, this makes SC mostly closed to adult access.

As shown on graph 1, of the group of the faculties with less restrictive admission conditions, the proportions of programmes with time arrangements offered by ESPO, EUEN and PSP are above the U.C.L. global figure (10,9 %).

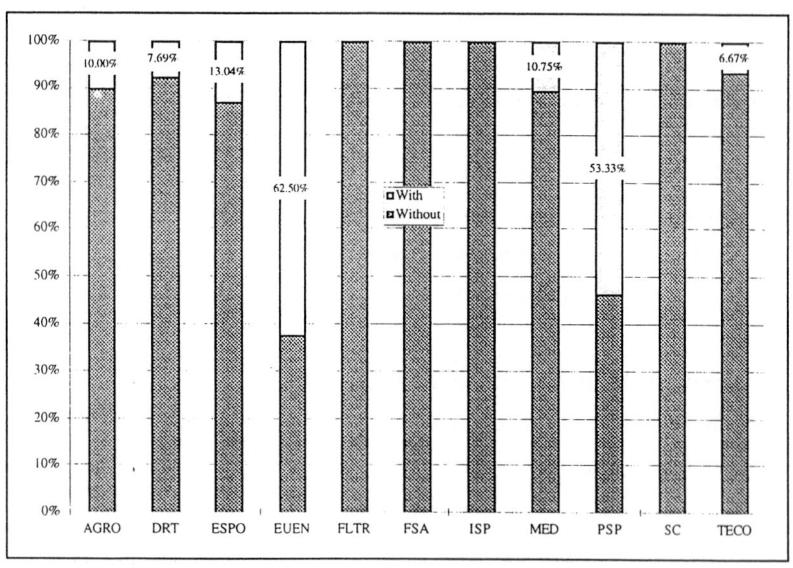

Graph 1. Proportion of programmes with and without special time arrangements in each faculty.

Only EUEN offers off-campus teaching (graph 2). The faculties that seem to be most attuned to the needs of adult students from a purely formal perspective, therefore are EUEN, ESPO and PSP, in descending order.

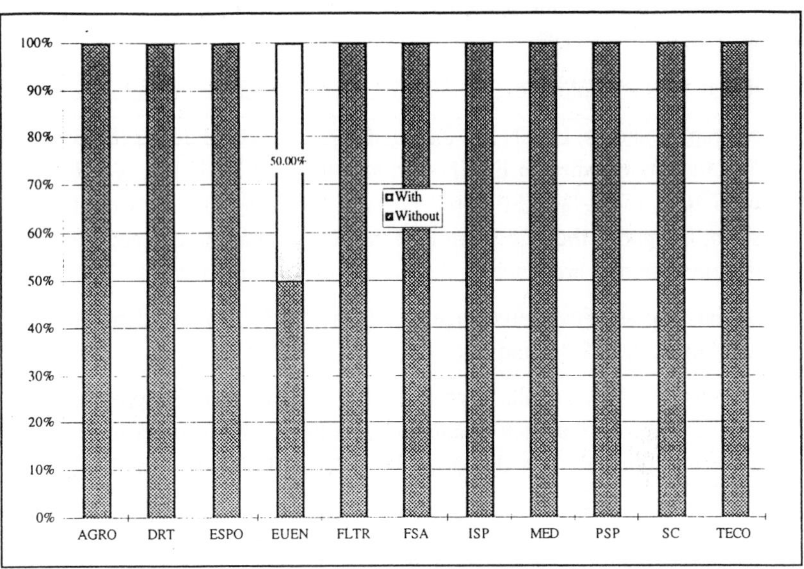

Graph 2. Proportion of programmes with and without off-campus teaching in each faculty.

Adult enrolment in programmes under consideration

General remarks

To see the impact of admissions conditions, time and location arrangements on adult participation in the programmes considered, we studied the number of Belgian adults enrolled in each programme (principal studies or majors).

The faculties

We will not present the results of the analysis of the impact of the arrangements on adult participation. Instead we will focus on the situation of each faculty with regard to this participation. From this perspective the analysis revealed that:

1. for UCL as a whole, close to one out of ten students is an adult student.
2. as graph 3 shows, EUEN has the highest proportion of adults (81.6 % of the students enrolled in EUEN's programmes are adults). It is followed by TECO (55.6 %), ISP (36.8 %) and PSP (19.2 %). It would thus seem, in light of the EUEN programme scores, that the university initiative programmes are reaching their adult participation target.
3. SC has the smallest percentage of adults (1.6 %); followed by AGRO (2.5 %), FSA (2.9 %) and DRT (3.3 %).
4. as graph 4 shows adults choose EUEN, TECO and ISP programmes more frequently than their younger counterparts. On the other hand, they are proportionately less drawn to the FLTR, AGRO, FSA and SC programmes.

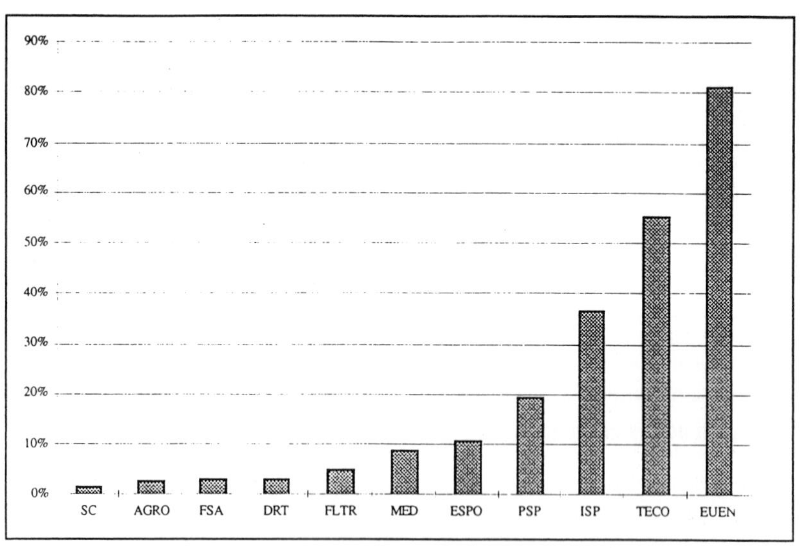

Graph 3. Proportion of adults in the programmes in each faculty

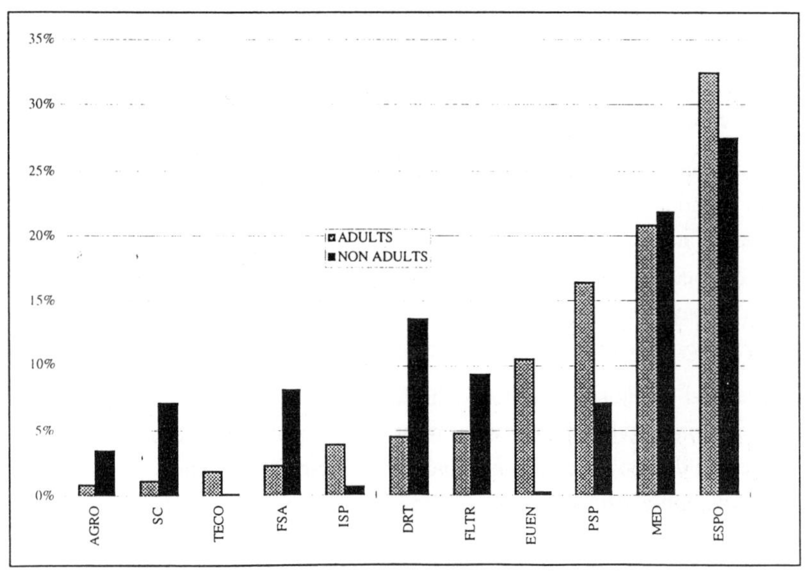

Graph 4. Distribution of adult and non-adult students in the programmes across the faculties

Other empirical elements and conclusions

The quantitative approach presented here was the first part of the description of adult access and accessibility at UCL. The second stage consisted of a qualitative analysis of how the three types of arrangements (admission, time and space) were put into practice. We also analysed other types of arrangements that are more difficult to quantify (curriculum structure, teaching approaches, assessment and services available for adult students). The third stage was a large survey of the adult student population at UCL in order to characterise it and to understand the way that the different arrangements were perceived and used by these students. It would be too long to give the details of the results of these two steps; the major point is that they reinforced the feeling that, first, the situation was quite heterogeneous between and within the faculties, but secondly, some trends could be identified. These trends were also present at Warwick. In fact it is possible to distinguish two categories in the adult audience at university.

The first one could be labelled as 'the second chance access' category. It refers to adult students who do not have a previous university diploma. These are adults who did not have the opportunity to enter university after secondary education at the age of 18 despite having the appropriate qualification because of economic and cultural factors. Others have had some form of university education but did not achieve certification.

The second category refers to adult students who already have a previous degree from university but who want to get complementary training in another field or to specialise in a particular topic. These adults may also be found on non-certificated courses (this has not yet been analysed in this research).

These two categories of adults are different. They do not enter the same programmes. The second category is mostly located in the complementary or specialisation programmes of the second and third study levels and in the non-certificated training designed for professionals, such as medicine or engineering.

The descriptive analysis of the programmes and the survey conducted on the adult student population showed that some departments are not interested in 'second chance access' adult programmes: the arrangements are few and the adult participation rate is very low, for example, science, philosophy, literature, agriculture and veterinary sciences. Theology could be put in this category as the high adult participation does not match with a particular interest in adult access but is due to the specificity of its students (priests).

In contrast, other departments are more interested in second chance access adult training and provide arrangements for this audience. Adult participation is quite high. Most of these departments are in humanities: economics, politics and social sciences, psychology and education, and education units not attached to faculties. Similar experiences were also found in more professional faculties, such as, medicine (nursing and public health programmes) and in law. Finally, some departments must be pointed out for their effort to provide specific vocational training for adults who already have a previous university degree. These are mostly non-certificated courses, such as medicine and engineering.

Some results from the Warwick case study

Warwick is a strongly departmental university. There are about 30 departments, supported for research by about 40 interdisciplinary research centres and institutes and organised into three faculties (four before autumn 1994). Four departments were identified for the purpose of this study; Biological Sciences, Arts Education (a subject degree plus a teaching qualification), Law and Sociology. These departments provided a range in terms of adult student numbers from low (biological sciences) to high (sociology). Like Louvain, we undertook a quantitative survey of admissions conditions, time and teaching location and the adult participation rate. Some similarities existed between the two institutions, for example, few adult students were found in the science departments.

To obtain a fuller picture of mature student life at Warwick we interviewed staff and adult students (undergraduates) in the four departments. Adult students in the UK are aged 21 years and over at undergraduate level and aged 25 years and over at postgraduate level. At Warwick there are three categories of adult students; full-time, 2+2 and part-time. The 2+2 degree programme is aimed at non-traditional adult students who have been out of the education system for a long time and who may also lack formal qualifications. The first two years of the degree course are taught in local further education (FE) colleges. FE colleges are post-16 institutions. Many part-time degree students are also engaged in full-time employment. Warwick is a highly-rated research-led university that has also committed itself to promoting lifelong learning opportunities and access for non-traditional adult students. Not all departments, however, embrace the policy for widening access. 'Certain departments within the University tend to be more conservative than others' (Duke and Merrill, 1993:11). Among some departments there is a concern that opening doors to non-traditional adult students lowers standards. Others are supportive of such initiatives.

Cultural differences, therefore, exist between departments or 'academic tribes' as referred to by Becher (1989). The following extracts help to give a flavour of the 'academic tribes' at Warwick. In Biological Sciences there is a consensus that the subject area is unsuitable for adults, particularly those who have been out of education for a long time. This belief is reinforced by the fact that the Department teaches microbiology, a specialism within biology:

> They have to be committed to do a science degree. Science moves rapidly and 5-10 years away is a long time. In arts this is not a problem - you do not forget how to read a book (lecturer, biological sciences).
>
> If you have been out of biology for a period of time then you will not have heard about this and what you did in school 15 years ago was traditional biology. It is so different from what we do now and so in this department the adult students do struggle (lecturer, biological sciences).

Young (1971), in discussing knowledge and education, points out that: 'academic curricula in this country (UK) involve assumptions that some kinds of and areas of knowledge' are more 'worthwhile than others' (1971: 34). Science is viewed as 'high knowledge' with different sciences being placed near or at the top of the academic hierarchy within universities. For Becher (1989) academic cultures are related to the nature of knowledge:

> It would seem, then, that the attitudes, activities and cognitive styles of groups of academics are closely bound up with the characteristics and structures of knowledge domains with which groups are professionally concerned (Becher, 1989: 20).

Adult student numbers at undergraduate level are very few in biological sciences, rarely more than six, and the majority of these are in their twenties. It is hard for an adult who has not got A levels (the standard entry requirement for university) and who is over thirty to gain entry to biological sciences. Although Access (a programme designed for adults for entry into higher education) is a recognised route into higher education it is no longer formally accepted as a mode of entry by the Department. Access and non-traditional students are considered to be more suitable for the 'new' universities. 'New' universities referring to the former polytechnics before the ending of the binary system:

> As far as the University is concerned, it is of course important to give equality of opportunity, but because the University is high in the Research Ratings and because it may not be able to be top at everything it should accept that in some areas of study some of the adults might be better served at another institution which is able to put on more the kind of course on which they can succeed (lecturer, biological sciences).

Becher (1989) observed the following behaviour amongst academics:

> The tribes of academia, one might argue, define their own identities and defend their own patches of intellectual ground by employing a variety of devices geared to the exclusion of illegal immigrants (Becher, 1989: 24).

Although Becher (1989) is alluding to behaviours between groups of academics the model is applicable to academic staff in relation to non-traditional adult students. The goal of Biological Sciences is to maintain and expand a high academic reputation. Teaching non-traditional adult students is not part of this strategy. Adult students are not 'real' students. Consequently Biological Sciences may be oversensitive about the presence of 'soft' adult students in the Department as they do not match comfortably with the image as a high status academic Department. Young (1971) offers another explanation. He argues that what is valued as knowledge in society is defined by those with power:

> those in positions of power will attempt to define what is to be taken as knowledge, how accessible to different groups any knowledge is, and what are the accepted relationships between different knowledge areas

> and between those who have access to them and make them available (Young, 1971: 32).

Within this framework science can be viewed as a knowledge area whose access is denied at degree level to non-traditional adult students in a university like Warwick.

On the other side of campus, metaphorically and literally in terms of geography, the world is different, at least with some departments such as Sociology, Arts Education and, surprisingly, Law. Here there is a welcoming attitude towards adult students. The Law Department at Warwick provides an interesting case. Traditionally within European universities law has a high academic status and is closely associated with the legal profession and hence is socially exclusive and elitist. Law at Warwick does not follow this pattern as its emphasis is on social law which studies law in context. Law provides a good example of Becher's (1989) theory whereby the nature of knowledge shapes the culture of the department.

Academics in Sociology, Law and Arts Education are positive in their attitudes towards the participation of adults, to the point of some stating that they would like to see a larger number in their Departments. Sociology, at 21% (1994-95), has the highest undergraduate adult participation rate in the University. For these three departments adult students enrich the culture as 'mature students make the whole life of the Department healthier in some sense. In that latter way it has made the whole experience of teaching more rewarding. This is a universal view throughout the Department' (sociology lecturer). Many lecturers outlined the benefits of teaching adults with younger students in seminars:

> Adults dominate seminars in a quantitative sense but domination in a very welcoming sense as they do talk. They do have something to contribute. They will draw on their own experience. Somehow they have the confidence to admit when they are stuck which is good. Also attitudinally confronted with a group with a collective task, perhaps because of their maturity, they see it as part of their responsibility to make the group a success (professor, sociology).

This is matched by the adult students' perceptions as they find these departments supportive. Academic staff here view the University in less exclusive terms than Biological Sciences. Unlike the latter, mature students are not perceived as lowering the academic standard of the Department or the University. For them widening access is an acceptable part of the mission for an 'old' (universities under the binary system) university like Warwick:

> I think that Warwick would see itself as an institution that wanted to participate in a process of people having opportunities and also because we would see ourselves as an institution that wanted to be rich and diverse and not homogeneous. We would see that fitting in to the approach to the study of law and the overall educational experience of everybody that is there (law lecturer).

Negotiating Departmental Cultures: The Adult Student Experience

Most of the adult students experienced the cultures of several departments within the Social Studies Faculty as part-time and 2+2 degree programmes are broad-based. Departments were soon categorised by adult students in relation to their openness and support. Participants encountered, in Becker and Geer's (1961) term, 'problematic situations' both at university and at home. To deal with the problematic situations they faced the adult students developed group perspectives. Individual problems became collective ones. At university problematic situations arose at departmental level. Lecture and seminar times were central areas of concern for women students with children. Classes had to be chosen to fit in with the school day. This limited course choices. Participants pointed out that although the University's policy was to encourage the access of mature students the structure did not always accommodate them:

> The only thing for me is the lack of childcare facility which feels like a lack of support for students with children. It is not a welcoming univer-

> sity for children. It does not feel like they want children here and if you are a mature student with children it is very important. I do have to come in and bring him even if it is to run into the library. Quite often I have to bring him in when I have a meeting with a lecturer. So I hurry (Avril, part-time).

Many women declared that during school holidays the only solution to childcare problems was to take children with them to lectures and seminars. Sociology staff were supportive in allowing children to attend seminars. In the absence of institutional change many women took action to solve the immediate problem by negotiating with individual lecturers and departments. In doing so they learnt to manipulate the system to meet their needs. If seminar times were not suitable the women negotiated a new reality with the lecturers concerned. As a subcultural group they were affirming strategies within the confines of organisational regulations. Sociology staff were the most accommodating in changing seminar times. However, some departments were not. Pamela had wanted to major in politics but the attitude and culture of the Politics Department forced her to change to sociology:

> I think that the Politics Department has got a lot of catching up to do. They disappointed me greatly. They are so rigid and strict in their petty rules. The Sociology Department I found so warm, affectionate and they treat you as a human being. Lecturers in Sociology are more supportive (Pamela, 2+2).

Joyce received a sexist response from a Politics lecturer. In making a request to change her seminar times the lecturer replied, 'we do not want to hear anything about childcare arrangements. If you cannot fit in, just do not come'. Another 2+2 student commented; 'Sociology are accommodating but with Politics you would think that you were in a different university'. Jayne concluded that the Politics Department were not as helpful as the Sociology Department. 'If you go and ask about anything it is as if you should know, why are you asking us?'. Cathy acknowledged the institutional difficulties in designing a timetable to meet the needs of students with children:

> Where it is possible teaching hours should fit in with school hours. On the whole it did but I also recognise that putting together a timetable is a mammoth task as you have to get people together from different departments. On the whole I think they were accommodating as they could be. In Education there were quite a few lectures from four to six. I managed to get round it but it was probably more difficult for other people. I have got family living nearby who can help (Cathy, full-time).

Participants in this study observed and experienced the tribes of academe at Warwick.

Towards An Explanatory Theoretical Framework

Research at UCL and Warwick revealed the heterogeneity of the adult student population. Differences of gender, ethnicity, age and mode of study affects the experiences of mature students in universities. For example, the learning needs of part-time adult students are different to those studying full-time. This study also highlights the diversity of access policies both between and within universities. The existence of academic tribes ensures that access policies vary from department to department, even within the same faculty. In general, however, social science and humanities departments are more accessible to non-traditional or second chance adult students than science departments. To what extent, therefore, is there a relationship between the nature of an academic discipline and the access of adults? More specifically how does the type of knowledge constructed and taught in the different disciplines influence policies on the widening of access for adults?

Universities interact with the external world (Rothblatt, 1985, Elzinga, 1987, Barnett, 1987, Becher, 1989, Bourgeois, 1990, 1991). As Barnett (1988) writes, 'higher education in the modern world is inescapably bound to its host society'. Departments depend economically upon research funding from governments, agencies and organisations. Such economic relationships are not value-free. In return for funding universities are expected to develop 'useful' scientific outcomes thus shaping the type of knowledge produced.

Becher (1989) notes that pressures from society on a university, for example in research and development, can sometimes lead to the creation of new departments in order to progress in research fields which do not correspond with traditional scientific paradigms and are not efficiently covered by existing departments. In this way there is a parallel with the creation of education units or programmes specifically designed to meet the needs of adult students. In Belgium, for example, the influence of civil society upon the development of new departments has been particularly strong (Bourgeois, 1990). The design of new programmes, in some cases, may result from the interaction between a university and society. Becher and Kogan (1980) identified this process in relation to vocational courses such as nursing or accountancy, 'whose establishment depends on their being seen both as academically acceptable and as viable in terms of student numbers'.

At UCL we are examining further the relationship between adult access policies and the impact of society upon the University. First, we will identify the disciplines which are the most 'socialised' , that is to say, those which have the most important connections with the outside world, for instance, with regard to funding of research, collaboration with social, economical or political actors and contacts with external professionals. The results of the descriptive analysis of the programmes and of the adult student population will be compared with the results of the analysis of the level of socialisation of the discipline. One could then test the hypothesis that adult programmes and access are more common in the most socialised disciplines. The diversity of adult programmes (academic and vocational) and the category of adults targeted could also be understood by taking the socialisation process of disciplines into account.

For example, humanities develop more adult access programmes because these disciplines are more in touch with the social and political actors from the outside world Professional studies, such as medicine and engineering, are more interested in developing programmes for adults who already have a university degree. These disciplines have more connections with external professional and/or economic agents. Disciplines which have minimal interaction with external organisations, for example, mathematics, philosophy and literature, may not be open in terms of adult access. The next step will be to verify our hypothesis in another national context, for example, the UK.

At Warwick departmental cultures and the discipline knowledge are more influential than external factors in determining adult access policies. The theories of Becher (1989), Young, (1971) and Kuhn (1970), Pantin (1968) provide a useful framework. According to these authors it is possible to build, from an epistemological point of view, a typology of different disciplines. The typology includes two axes (hard verses soft and pure verses applied disciplines). Within this hierarchy the hard and pure sciences are placed at the top. As discussed earlier the science disciplines, except engineering, at Warwick have a low adult participation rate. Most lecturers in these departments feel that the sciences are inappropriate for adults. The 'soft' disciplines, in contrast, are more open to non-traditional adults in terms of policy and practice. These departments have a greater involvement and commitment to adult programmes such as part-time and 2+2 degrees.

The culture of a department is partly determined by the subject matter of a particular discipline (Becher, 1989). This may be another factor that influences adult access in universities. The subject matter of sociology, education and, at Warwick, law, for example, look at issues of inequality in society. Lecturers in these departments were more aware of the inequalities of the British education system and hence the need to provide second chance education for adults. 'Often adults are people who could not afford university at an earlier age and I do not believe that it should be now or never at 18' (law lecturer). Social science subjects are also more appealing to adults as they relate to the 'real world' and are hence less abstract than the sciences. 'People want to do sociology because it is raising the issues that are important to them. It is more acute than with the younger students' (sociology lecturer).

Our research at UCL and Warwick indicates the importance of the sociological (the level of socialisation of the disciplines) and epistemological (the hierarchy within the types of discipline) factors in determining the policies and the heterogeneity of adult access. This theoretical framework needs to be developed further before applying it to other universities in different national contexts.

References

Barnett, R. (1988), Limits to academic freedom in Tight, M. (ed.) Academic Freedom and Responsibility. Milton Keynes, Open University Press.

Becher, T. (1989), Academic Tribes and Territories, 2nd edition, Buckingham, Open University Press.

Becher, T., Kogan, M. (1980), Process and Structure in Higher Education, London, Heinemann.

Becker, H. S., Geer, B., Strauss, A. and Hughes, E. (1961), Boys in White: Student Culture in Medical School, Chicago, University of Chicago Press.

Biglan, A. (1973), The Characteristics of Subject Matter in Different Scientific Areas, *Journal of Applied Psychology*, Vol. 57, No. 3, pp. 195-203.

Bourgeois, E. (1990), University Politics: Adult Education in a Belgian University, PhD thesis, Chicago, University of Chicago.

Bourgeois, E., Duke, C., de Saint Georges, P., Guyot, J. L., Merrill, B. (1994), Comparing Access Internationally. The Context of the Belgian and English Higher Education Systems, Working Paper 13, Continuing Education Research Centre, Warwick, Department of Continuing Education, University of Warwick.

Bourgeois, E., Guyot, J. L. (1995), Access and Participation of Adults in Higher Education in Belgium, in Davies, P. (Ed) 'Adults in Higher Education: International Perspectives on Access and Participation', London, J. Kingsley Publishers, pp. 61-83.

Bourgeois, E., Duke, C., de Saint Georges, P., Guyot, J. L., Merrill, B., (1995), Comparing Access Internationally. Admission, Provision and Adult Participation in Two Universities, Working Paper 14, June 1995 Continuing Education Research Centre, Warwick, Department of Continuing Education, University of Warwick.

Guyot, J. L., -sous la direction scientifique de Bourgeois, E., et de Saint Georges, P., - (1995), Résultats d'une enquête auprès des étudiants adultes de l'Université Catholique de Louvain, Working Paper polycopié, Louvain-la-Neuve, FORG-FOPES, UCL.

Duke, C., Merrill, B. (1993), The Winding Road: Widening Opportunities for HE, Department of Continuing Education, University of Warwick/Employment Department.

Elzinga, A. (1987) Internal and External Regulatives in Research and Higher Education Systems, in Premfors, R., (ed) Disciplinary Perspectives On Higher Education and Research, Report No. 37. Stockholm, University of Stockholm GSHR.

Kuhn, T.S. (1970), The Structure of Scientific Revolutions, 2nd edition, Chicago, University of Chicago Press.

Pantin, C. F. A. (1968), The Relations Between the Sciences, Cambridge, Cambridge University Press.

Rothblatt, S. (1985), The Notion of an Open Scientific Community in Scientific Perspective, in Gibbons, M. and Wittrock, B., (eds) Science as a Commodity, Harlow, Longman.

Young, M. (ed), (1971), Knowledge and Control, London, Croom-Helm.

Section 3

Universities as Open Learning Centers

Ramon Flecha / Barbara Merrill

Universities as Open Learning Centres

Introduction

The six papers in this section focused on lifelong learning within the context of universities. In general the papers were concerned with exploring and implementing new approaches to teaching and learning to meet the requirements of adult students in higher education. More broadly they addressed the need for organisational change. Universities were perceived as being too elitist and traditional in their structures, particularly in relation to teaching and learning. Change strategies are necessary if universities are to become open learning centres. All were critical of the didactic teaching methods currently used in universities. On the whole both the papers and the group discussions centred on practice rather than theoretical approaches. Practical examples of universities as open learning centres at regional, national and international levels were outlined by presenters. Participants in the group discussions compared and contrasted these examples to their own experiences. Comparative perspectives were enriched by the presence of participants from eastern, southern and northern Europe. Despite the diversity of cultural and geographical backgrounds several common strands were identified.

Five papers emphasised the necessity for a closer relationship between education, training and work while one paper considered universities as open learning centres within the tradition of radical adult education and social transformation. The role of adult education and adult learning was considered within the context of a changing economic, social and political climate within Europe. Adult education has to respond to a shifting Europe if it is to meet the needs of adult learners. In particular, the economic transformation of European countries was something that could not be ignored by adult educators and universities. The traditional employment pattern is being eroded. Presenters pointed out that a job was no longer for life. Individuals will have to change jobs, be re-trained and re-skilled throughout their working lives. Within this framework it is, therefore, important that individuals learn to take control of their own learning and career paths. Although many focused on the vocational aspects of adult education and hence the professional development of adult learners, learning was also perceived as being about community, personal and self-development. Vocational training is not the unique aim of universities, but is one of its dimensions. Acting as open learning centres, they should respond to the set of intellectual and scientific challenges of the present world such as the development of the information society, the overcoming of inequalities, the opening to new forms of life and identities and the critique of all kinds of discrimination, for example, racism, sexism and ageism.

All the papers stressed the need to provide a learning environment which enables adults to be self-directed and self-motivated in their learning. One of the key roles for adult educators is, therefore, to equip adult students with the ability of how to learn which can then be applied to a range of thinking and disciplines. In doing so adult learners are endowed with the skills to continue with their own learning beyond the boundaries of universities. Implicit in this approach is the necessity to make learners aware of how they learn. Experiential learning is an important ingredient for this practice. These examples are attempts to move away from the position of universities setting the parameters for learning, such as deadlines for essays, courses, examinations etc.

For some adults geographical location and/or employment commitments mean that distance learning is the most suitable mode of learning. Examples of distance learning models were included amongst the papers presented in this section. All centred on postgraduate level of study aimed at professional adults. These distance learning courses were not aimed at non-traditional adult students but at adults who already had previous higher education qualifications or considerable professional experience. However, one paper explicitly addressed the needs of disadvantaged adults through the creation of an adult learning centre in a socially and economically deprived urban area.

Outlining The Papers

This section outlines the key issues of the papers delivered in this section of the conference. Space allows only for a summary and flavour of the ideas presented.

a) *Lifelong education and training - executed by AKAD's Adult Continuing Education Organisation*, Horst Möhle, Leipzig University, Germany

This paper focuses on vocational adult education and training and the unity between employment and learning. Möhle argues that adult education needs to respond to changes in the employment structure. Lifelong learning is, therefore, discussed within the context of economic changes within society and the requirement for a skilled and 'thinking workforce'. Employees will increasingly embark upon a series of short-term contracts throughout their working lives. For Möhle, 'the education and training of highly qualified personnel as part of human resource development remains the main task of educational institutions' (1996: 2).

AKAD have developed integrated distance learning models which are rooted in the self-directed learning of adults in the field of vocational education. Three levels of distance learning study are available; pre-degree, undergraduate and postgraduate. They are all short-cycle programmes in business management, business-related information technology and economics-oriented industrial engineering. Entry is possible for those who lack the appropriate qualifications provided they complete a foundation course and successfully pass the course examinations. All three levels are assessed by examinations. There is no room for flexibility such as assessment by Assessment of Prior Experiential Learning (APEL). However, students do have the opportunity of choosing the timing of their examinations.

Teaching approaches are student-centred. The assumption is that adult learners need to become autonomous and independent learners thereby taking responsibility for their own learning. In such a learning environment personal as well as professional development will be achieved. The distance learning courses rely heavily on the adults having access to various forms of media and technology which may exclude certain groups of adults. Participation on the courses equips students with research and developmental work skills. A number of core competencies relevant to the work situation are embedded within the curriculum such as conceptual thinking skills, problem-solving skills and critical thinking skills. AKAD promote the need for closer co-operation and collaboration between industrial firms and educational institutions. This they view as essential for lifelong learning within a learning society.

b) *Lifelong Learner As Career Orienteer*, Pamela Houghton, University of Central Lancashire, UK

Like Möhle, Houghton links learning and employment, emphasising that one career for life will no longer be the pattern. In future individuals will increasingly have to plan and determine their career through 'career orienteering'. The focus is very much on individual responsibility. The role of universities is to equip adult students with the skills and knowledge to enable them to 'career orienteer' by providing them with a lifetime learning strategy which they can employ beyond university. This paper, therefore, lies within the domain of human resource development, drawing on the McKinsey 7S framework. The approach draws on psychology, promoting consensus values. Individual student learner's needs are assumed to be the same as the organisation's needs.

Learning and self-development are inter-related but a critical factor is that the individual must be motivated to learn. A learning strategy involves self-diagnosis, goal setting, risk assessment, designing a learning strategy and assessing performance. The individual learns how to be in control of their own learning. This approach challenges the institutional led approach to learning. In this situation the learner rather than the institution sets the boundaries for learning by deciding when assessment will take place. It, therefore, calls for a more flexible approach to the curriculum. The ideas have been put into practice in the Business School at the University of Central Lancashire, UK. A new course, as part of the undergraduate degree programme, has been introduced entitled career management. It includes reflective learning from experience. Implicit in this approach is the notion that learners learn in different ways and individuals need to choose the best learning methods for them.

c) *Open Learning Systems - Regional, National and International Co-operation,* Ernst Raters, university of Bremen, Germany

Using a practical example of a European MBA course, Raters promoted the notion of a mixed mode of learning within universities. A mixed mode of teaching and learning utilises open/distance learning materials on campus. This calls for greater flexibility in course delivery. The use of new technologies as multimedia learning resources are also important ingredients.

For cost-effective reasons Raters argues for 'institutional co-operation on a regional, national as well as European or international level'. The European Master of Business Administration provides an example of transnational co-operation and networking. The course, aimed at managers, combines distance and residential learning. Six European universities participate in the project. The distance learning element is supplemented by video-conferencing, fax, e-mail and telephone. Students, therefore, do require access to such facilities. Assessment remains formal by examinations. Such courses, according to Raters, are an essential component for lifelong learning and the trend towards a European Information Society.

d) *Adult Education Open University - New Agendas for Lifelong Learning,* Henning Salling Olesen, Roskilde University, Denmark

Working at Roskilde University, Olesen offers another example of open learning in a new university within the framework of lifelong learning. In this case it is an Adult Education Open University programme studies at masters' level aimed at part-time adult students who have some academic and/or professional experience. It is a three year programme. Operating since 1990 the course now attracts about 300 students. The aim of the programme is to 'connect practical milieus with academic research'.

The focus of the curriculum is on reflection of practices. Although largely based on collective group work assessment remains by formal examinations.

Weekend teaching sessions are interspersed with residential camps. The adults work in self-managing work groups. Most students are professionals in education, health education or social work and many are women. The programme enables students to reflect critically upon their professional practices rather than assuming that present practice is the norm and hence a closed circuit. In conceptualising the issues students are encouraged to transcend the closed circuit by reflection in 'a mirror room'. The students' expectations on the outcome of the course are for both professional and personal development. At an institutional level such programmes demand innovative ways of teaching and learning, challenging the traditional outlook of old, elite universities. This type of teaching also requires universities to reorganise into interdisciplinary centres of learning and research, hence 'modernising' the university.

e) *Non-Teaching Cases of University As Open Learning Centres: The Communicative Formulation of the Law of Adult Education,* Mercè Espanya, University of Barcelona, Spain

This paper looks at adult learning from a collectivist perspective. Access to university in Spain for adults, particularly non-traditional adults, is very limited. Adults have to pass a formal examination. Universities remain elite institutions in terms of its students and culture. Adults are socially excluded. In some universities centres, such as the Centre of Research for the Education of Adults (CREA) at Barcelona, initiatives have been implemented to try and transform this situation.

CREA has set up an adult school in Verneda, a socially and economically deprived area of Barcelona. The centre is based on the principles of social participation and transformation. At present there are 1, 500 students and 90 volunteers, mostly university graduates, professors and members of different social movements. Community development activities in the local community have emerged from the demands of adult students at the school. The school is run collaboratively by the students and volunteers. Participation is high because courses relate to the experiences of the students.

Using life history approaches CREA have undertaken research on the participation and non-participation of adults in education. Since 1990 CREA have been involved with regional governments, such as Valencia, in creating laws of adult education. The process of formulating laws was also used as an opportunity for communicative action and research, drawing on the theories of Freire, 1990, and Habermas, 1984. Opening university access is a two-way learning process. It is not just about presenting university knowledge to adults but about sharing knowledge and learning from learners and non university people in a democratic way.

f) *The Specific Role of Universities in High Level Training Offered in France,* Alexandre Meliva, CEREQ, Marseille, France

The final paper outlined the findings of a research programme which looks at how vocational training is carried out and its effects upon the labour market. Both pedagogical and financial aspects were researched. Adult education is utilised to look at the problems confronting employment and the labour market. The paper attempts to clarify the role of universities in relation to training. During the 1960s trade unions promoted the participation of adults in university further education programmes in France. However, the growth in numbers of younger students during the 1970s diminished the number of places available to adults.

New training systems were developed by non-university institutions, such as companies and the state, offering diplomas both for those in work and for the unemployed. Universities, although facing competition, offer higher level courses. University diplomas also have higher prestige on the labour market and provide greater flexibility in course delivery. The teachers of such programmes tend to come from less academic backgrounds than lecturers in universities. Adult education in France has adopted a pragmatic approach, responding to the needs of the market at the expense of a collective, humanistic one.

Group Discussions: Concepts and Issues as a Learning Experience

Vocational adult education and responding to the needs of the labour market from the perspective of the individual learner was very much the focus of the papers in this section. The open learning models presented are aimed at mostly professional adults, many of whom have previous educational qualifications. In this sense they are, therefore, traditional students. Discussion opened out into considering ways in which universities could meet the needs of non-traditional adult students such as those who are unemployed, working class people, minority ethnic groups. Underpinning these debates was the question of what is the purpose of adult education within the framework of lifelong learning? Is adult education divided into two camps, vocational versus academic and social development? Is it possible to reconcile the two approaches?

There was a recognition that teaching in universities had become more innovative. However, this is not matched by more creative assessment methods. Universities remain traditional and rigid in this sense as programmes continue to be assessed by examinations. Formal assessment can be off-putting to non-traditional students. How do we change the attitudes of academics and administrators to encourage the access and presence of non-traditional adult students in universities? The need to break down barriers between different disciplines was also felt to be part of the process of facilitating more open and innovative ways of learning.

Several of the examples of distance learning rely on the access to and use of multi-media technology. Participants discussed the role of the university within an information society and the consequences of this for learning and learners. Who has access, as learners, to such technology? Does it exclude certain groups of adults from participating? Many of the open learning programmes are run jointly by several institutions either on a regional, national or international basis. Strategies for enhancing collaborative approaches were discussed. Participants also highlighted the differences between northern and southern Europe and it was felt that southern European countries were often excluded from such opportunities.

In summary the following key points dominated the group discussions:

The starting position was the recognition of the importance of university adult education within a changing economic and social environment in Europe. European countries have become information societies and universities play a key part in this process. However, it is important that in responding to the learning needs of an information society that the socially excluded are not forgotten, particularly as both north and south Europe are now experiencing greater social and economic inequality. Education at all levels is becoming increasingly associated with market forces and an individualised approach to learning. Vocational education is viewed by governments as the solution to the economic problems in society. While professional and vocational education is valuable it is important to ensure that the social and personal benefits of education at both individual and group levels are not forgotten.

As universities develop as open learning centres there is the danger that the adults who benefit will be mostly those from the middles classes with previous educational qualifications. At the moment distance learning courses are concentrated at postgraduate level, aimed at professionals in employment. Open learning provision needs to be broader than postgraduate study and provide for the learning needs of non-traditional adult students at pre-degree and degree level.

Universities remain traditional in structure and in the delivery of programmes. Such structures make universities inaccessible to those without the 'cultural capital'. Adult educators need to research ways of changing university structures and identify strategies which would encourage the socially excluded to participate. Knowledge is not the exclusive preserve of universities. Learning is a two-way process whereby teachers and learners learn from each other. Universities have to learn to change if they are to become learning universities and avoid society from becoming further divided into the 'haves' and 'have-nots'.

The papers and discussions gave members in this section a lot of stimulus for reflection and thought about theoretical issues and practices at individual and institutional levels. Participants welcomed the opportunity to have time to stand back and reflect about learning processes, how adults learn and the significance of creating a framework for the self-reflection of learners. The focus was very much on the individual learner but as adult educators we need to look at ways of enabling social groups to transform and change through the learning process.

The papers focused overwhelmingly on practical examples. Participants expressed the need to develop a theoretical framework to further enhance good practice. Finally an important outcome for this section was that it widened our knowledge and understanding of differing cultural contexts in relation to open learning and universities across Europe.

Horst Möhle

Lifelong Education and Training - Executed by AKAD's Adult Continuing Education Organisation

Introduction

Throughout 1996, the European Year of Lifelong Learning, a wide ranging debate aimed at the objective 'to prepare Europeans to pass smoothly to a society based upon the acquisition of skills, where one continues to learn ... throughout life ..., to a learning society' (European Commission, Edith Cresson/Pádraig Flynn: White Paper, 1995) took place. This international conference at the University of Bremen is a culminating event in this discussion.

The German Academic Society for Adult Continuing Education (AKAD for short) is evaluating its past development as a contribution to lifelong learning and the creation of a new institution at university level for qualifying working graduates up to the university diploma and the doctoral degree as an innovative step. International research and developmental results are being creatively used for the further improvement of AKAD's model. Furthermore, AKAD is contributing with its innovative experience of its consequent development during 36 years of its existence to enhancing the international development of distance education for adults.

According to EU's 'Leonardo da Vinci programme' a more integrated approach' in education is needed in order to facilitate innovation (European Commission, Education, Training, Youth, 1995). Therefore, we pay particular attention to AKAD's 'integrated distance education model':

- its unique lifelong learning concept;
- its learner-oriented concept, typical of adult distance education;
- its didactic combination of self-learning of adults from media and learner support measures (including using technical media);
- the growing links between learning, studying and working, between the respective institutions.

AKAD's basic distance education concept is distinguished by its integrative character thus ensuring a high quality of education. The higher the grade of integration of the different and sometimes contrasting elements, the higher the quality.

1. A unique lifelong learning concept

At the moment there is a period of worldwide dramatic change. The internationalisation of the economy, the creation of the global information society, the accelerated scientific and technical progress are characteristic of this period. This revolution 'changes the way we work together and the way we live together' (Recommendations to the European Council, 1994). Industrial production and also the service sector are becoming knowledge- and skill-based. A 'thinking work force' is needed.

We are now confronted with questions of the further existence of careers. Lifelong careers might disappear. Everyone will have several different jobs not only over time but also at any one time. People may increasingly become project employees, contracted to undertake a project or a succession of projects (Godsell, B, 1996).

In this context, lifelong education and training play a central role. The education and training of highly qualified personnel as part of human resource development remains the main task of educational institutions.

The advent of the information or learning society involves encouraging the acquisition of new knowledge which ought to be the top priority (European Commission, White Paper, 1995). As the knowledge which is acquired during initial training is becoming rapidly obsolete, the need for further and continuing education is growing rapidly because knowledge and skills must be updated and renewed from time to time. We prefer subjects which help develop the intellectual capacity of learners; the learning to learn.

As is well known, the present model of concentrated learning and studying for a limited period is being replaced by lifelong learning. However, it is necessary to closely combine initial, further and continuing learning, they must be totally harmonised. Both open access to education and its permeability from the early beginnings to its highest level must be ensured.

AKAD's policy has always been oriented towards lifelong learning and now includes three levels. The first level is formed through its programmes in the field of general education, continuing professional education with the aim of passing state-recognised examinations of the Chambers of Industry and Commerce and foreign language studies in English, French, Spanish and Italian culminating in final examinations recognised by the Universities of Cambridge, Salamanca and Perugia and by Alliance Française.

AKAD's second level of continuing education involves degree programmes at short-cycle institutions of higher education (Fachhochschulen) in business management, business-related information technology and economics-oriented industrial engineering, as well as continuing education courses in economics for academics from non-economic fields. These are all fields of importance for European economic development. Now there are three state-recognised AKAD institutions of higher education (Fachhochschulen) for working adults in the North, South and East of Germany together with 7,500 diploma students.

Nowadays the third level of AKAD's higher education concept is being set up. An academic institution for the continuing education of graduates of short-cycle institutions preparing them to take a university diploma or the doctoral degree in economics and the social sciences is being created in the Southern part of Germany. AKAD is thus the only private German institution of education with such a complex profile oriented towards lifelong learning.

Distance education is regarded as having an important role in expanding the opportunities of adults to take part in education, especially higher education, thus helping to equalise the educational chances of all citizens. Distance education is often a second chance for those who had no opportunity to attend traditional programmes of general or vocational training.

AKAD has altered its entry requirements for working people. This innovative amendment is based on applicants' professional qualification and work experience over a long period. AKAD has introduced a 'higher education probationary study' ('Hochschulprobestudium'). Working adults can take a basic course of four semesters which concludes with a set of examinations. After having passed them successfully, the working students may proceed to the special course leading to the award of a diploma after two more semesters (Diplom der Fachhochschule).

Working people without a normal vocational training certificate can pass a foundation course (of a duration of four semesters) including independent further training examinations run by the Chamber of Industry and Commerce. We call these basic studies 'vocational training integrated studies' ('berufsausbildungs-integrierte Studien'). The EU's Leonardo da Vinci programme is orientated towards the close combination of vocational and general education and their equal standing. Hence AKAD is contributing to this connection of practice-oriented vocational or professional training and academic theoretical studies.

As Germany is characterised by its adherence to formal academic entrance qualifications for higher education, there are different ways of preparing working adults to attain these entrance conditions. AKAD, for example, offers Abitur courses of a different duration or so-called aptitude tests for short-cycle institutions ('Fachhochschuleignungsprüfung'). These preparatory programmes ensure the well-assessed entrance level of the future working students. Higher education is thus opened up to working people.

2. The learner-oriented concept typical of adult distance education

In a world of radical social and economic change as described above, the importance of personal development and lifelong learning is increasing. In contrast to traditional universities at single mode distance education institutions of higher education, the basic orientation is student-centred, as can be seen when analysing the worldwide educational development during the last few years (Möhle, 1996). The adult learner as a person with life and professional experience is at the focus of attention when designing study programmes and courses, and when organising the study process. Adult students who are in employment ought to be autonomous and independent learners whose aim is optimum active learning. They are willing to take an increased degree of personal responsibility for their learning. Adult learners also like to be regarded as partners of their teachers. This year we wish 'to highlight for Europe's citizens the need to go on learning throughout life' (European Commission, DG XXII, 1995). Citizens must at the same time be provided with the special tools to learn in an information society.

AKAD's distance education programmes and courses are oriented towards the users who will become self-learners using the media available and the support services. Subjects are preferred which help to develop the students' necessary self-responsibility to fully use their intellectual capacity. The students' personal responsibility in choosing and performing their studies as well as self-monitoring their study progress is also decisively increased. The working students may individually determine the pace and length of their studies, therefore they may fix their dates for written tests and examinations themselves. This means the 'time semester' has at AKAD been replaced by the 'achievement semester'.

AKAD's design of distance learning strategies also stimulates effective conditions for students' creative work. It is the aim to qualify distance students to do research and developmental work. After an introductory course on research, students are closely involved in research work on topics which are of importance both for the development of their place of work and the research programmes of their distance education institution. Experienced distance students in employment always form a crucial element of the existing but limited research capacities. Full-time students of traditional universities do not possess the requirements for being included in research work at an early stage of their studies.

At AKAD's short-cycle institutions of higher education, the research work of adult students is closely integrated into the distance learning process.

Knowledge and skills acquired on the basis of the curricula are creatively used for recognising and solving the academic problems of professional practice. The best research results presented at one of AKAD's institutions by working adults are analysed and then published every two years in the form of reviewers' copies (Schönherr and Möhle, 1994).

3. The didactic combination of self-learning of adults from media and learner support measures (including using technical media)

The precondition for distance education and training adults at a high qualitative level is also a well - designed didactic concept - in correspondence with the coming information society.

One of the main tasks is to enhance the social, professional and personal relevance of the content of programmes and courses.

'Ensuring a European dimension' (European Commission, Memorandum, 1991) as far as content is concerned means including European politics, economics and cultures in the curricula; it means disseminating knowledge about the European Union. AKAD, for example, offers an optional special subject amongst others entitled 'European business studies'. European language courses are also delivered at AKAD. It is becoming necessary for everyone to be able to acquire and keep up his/her ability to communicate in two foreign languages in addition to their mother tongue (European Commission; White paper, 1995). These are preconditions for working actively across national boundaries within the European Single Market. The European dimension is integrated into AKAD's nationally oriented aims and content of distance education. Thus it may be ensured that future generations are educated in a European context.

According to the new demands of the information society we need a broad and complex basis for the initial education of young citizens. Continuing education programmes and courses are usually organised in a multi-disciplinary or interdisciplinary way in order to enhance the flexibility of studies.

At AKAD's new continuing higher education institution a general studies programmes is organically combined with the academic content. It contains European-oriented political, philosophical, sociological and psychological subjects forming a strong theoretical basis for practice-oriented studies.

By broadening the intellectual and practical capacities of adult distance students it is necessary to ascertain the 'key qualifications' formed by a limited number of generic and practical skills, supplemented by analogous job-related skills.

Skills of self-directed learning, concentrated on skills of working creatively within the framework of complex and dynamic situations are accentuated. Attention is paid to conceptual thinking skills, problem-recognising and solving skills and critical thinking skills. Enabling students to perform academically is a typical quality: verbal skills are needed to participate in tutorials or teleconferences, especially communication skills. Skills for writing academic papers are also necessary. Process skills of observation, measuring, hypothesising, interpreting, drawing conclusions, building scientific concepts and models are required. Job-related skills form a crucial part of open and distance learning programmes and courses. There is a set of key competencies which are required by all citizens to enable them to perform life-roles. Skills, however, that are especially needed for living and working in the coming information society are not adequately met at the moment, including the skills of using computers and television. These skills must be integrated into all subject-bound knowledge systems.

Normally, systematic knowledge is delivered in a systematic way because people acquire knowledge best in this mode. Fundamental knowledge is being increasingly presented in the form of case studies. A reduction of knowledge-based content is to make way for skills development (in order to develop the citizens' generic and professional skills). We are, therefore, increasingly integrating case-bound knowledge into subject-bound knowledge. Having learnt how to analyse cases, people are able to improve their basic skills for solving problems. This is a most effective way for developing adult education.

Self-learning from media and using student support services are and remain the 'conditio sine qua non' of successful distance education of adult learners. The types of media chosen are those which encourage adults to use their intellectual capacity and develop their independent learning.

At present three media approaches are to be found in distance education: the print-based, the broadcast-based and the computer-based concept. Other media are combined with these basic media. Co-operation and communication between learners and tutors should also be stimulated, be it by correspondence, by telephone, by facsimile, by computer or face-to-face.

Seventy to eighty per cent of distance education programmes and courses are print-based. Broadcast-based systems including radio and television are preferred in a few countries. A precondition is that learners are taught to watch television effectively. Video conferencing is a particularly excellent means of higher education. Computer-mediated distance education in the form of electronic mail and computer conferencing characterised by written longer lasting instruction is also a flexible means. In contrast to the print-based media, televisual- and computer-based distance education can be organised in an interactive way, which is no doubt more demanding, stimulating and activating. The results gained in such an interactive process are much better.

At the moment multi-media based segments or modules are integrated into print-based courses. The telephone conference for example is featured for the presentation of the teachers' and students' comments and a general conversation. Students use the fax machine to submit assignments which are corrected by the teachers. Telephone tutoring is also quite common.

Maintaining its basic distance education concept, AKAD is now completing its mostly print-based programmes and courses by computer-based distance learning segments and modules (Schönherr, 1994). It is not the aim to depersonalise the distance education process. At AKAD's institutions of higher education for working adults, face-to-face sessions (mostly seminars of a different level) are and remain integrated into the self-study process of different media. The trend in a few institutions to cut support services is indeed wrong.

In the framework of open and distance learning a special mode for self-testing and self-evaluation is closely combined with testing and evaluation and with the students' learning and research process. Testing through self-answered questions, multiple-choice questions (though sometimes regarded as 'pedagogical infantilism'), interest- and task-driven exercises and tutor- and computer-marked home assignments and projects as well as examinations at the end of modules and courses are an exact source of not only students' interests and achievements but also their learning difficulties. AKAD also uses these forms of assessment specifically for distance education.

4. The growing links between learning/studying and working, between the respective institutions

The open and distance learning process of working adults is being increasingly integrated into their work process. Working and studying form an ever-closer unity. This connection is based on the life and professional experiences of adult working people. Their experiences are an inherent part of the distance education content. A stimulating 'learning environment' is based on close co-operation between firms and educational institutions. The topics of research work of working students are of interest for both.

AKAD also co-operates successfully with enterprises or branches of professional work. AKAD, for example, offers courses in the framework of the BAYER-AKAD distance education programme. (BAYER is one of the largest chemical concerns in Germany.) In the fields of specialisation, for example banking, AKAD is co-operating in course design and delivery with the German consortium of Volks- und Raiffeisenbanken for its employees.

AKAD is ensuring its territorial and international co-operation via its fifteen study centres. General academic knowledge and skills are transferred to local needs especially via the territorial seminars by the help of the local tutors who thus become mediators between theory and practice.

AKAD's study centres in Switzerland and Austria are the starting points for their integration in international networks in order to broaden international co-operation in the interest of ensuring high quality. AKAD is, therefore, ready to participate in the EU's projects for the further development of open and distance learning.

References

Commission of the European Communities, 'Open Distance Learning in the European Community' (Memorandum COM (91) 388 final).

European Commission, (1995), White Paper on Education and Training, Foreword by Édith Cresson and Pádraig Flynn, Brussels.

European Commission, (1995), Education, Training, Youth: Leonardo da Vinci Programme, Vademecum.

European Commission, (1995), DG XXII 'Education, Training, Youth: European year of lifelong learning, Brussels.

Godsell, B. (1996), Keynote address: 'Managing and Developing People' at the 10th International Meeting of University Administrators, Cape Town.

Möhle, H. (1996), Leonardo-Volet IV-Using the results of worldwide distance education to execute the Leonardo da Vinci programme, Stuttgart.

Recommendations to the European Council: Europe and the global information society, Brussels, 26 May (1994).

Schönherr, K. W. and Möhle, H. (1994), Learning the Doing, Doing the Learning in a most effective way, when Studying at a Distance; Montreal.

Schönherr, K. W. (1994), Der Heimstudienplatz 2000 (The home study place 2000), Karriereführer Hochschulen II.

Pamela Houghton

Lifelong Learning - a Compass for the Career Orienteer™

A colleague (Brooke 1996) recently remarked that: 'an individual can no longer expect to follow a career path. Any path that there is will be made of crazy paving - and you lay it yourself!'

In future, before an individual can follow any career path, its shape will have to be determined by the individual, the route planned and then plotted. The career planner thus becomes a 'career orienteer'. Responsibility for checking one's position along the way, in relation to the situation and the surroundings, lies with the individual. Such a check may necessitate a change of direction. In career terms such a change of direction may necessitate self-development, re-modelling or an intellectual 'make over'. How well does higher education prepare its students for this periodic 'prismatic' planning?

This paper uses as a starting point the McKinsey 7S framework (Fig l) (Mintzberg and Quinn 1995). The central idea is well-known; effective organisational change stems from the interaction of, and the relationship between, several factors; *structure, systems, style, staff, skills, strategy, and shared goals*. It was developed by the consulting firm McKinsey in the 1970s where its three authors, Waterman, Peters and Phillips, worked at the time.

It is the author's view that its central ideas have relevance not only for effective organisational development, but also effective individual development. The author adapts this framework to focus attention on the individual, and provide a holistic view of self-development through change, by replacing the *staff* factor by *self*.

(4) The framework can be seen as a set of compasses. The effort involved in redirecting an organisation is to ensure that all the factors are aligned. 'When all seven needles are all pointed the same way, you're looking at an organised company' (Mintzberg and Quinn 1995).

This analogy is continued in this paper. The McKinsey 7S self-development framework is intended to be used as a compass by the 'career orienteer'. Thus the curriculum in higher education must provide both the course and the skills required to use the compass for lifetime learning and career planning (Fig 1).

Strategy - What do I Want to Achieve?

An organisation's *strategy* is the set of actions that a company plans in response to, or in anticipation of, changes in its external environment (Mintzberg and Quinn 1995). It is the company's chosen route to competitive success and encapsulates those factors that will create its unique value.

Similarly, in terms of the 7S self-development framework (Fig 1) the career orienteer will be required to, or wish to, develop a *learning strategy* at some point along the career route. How much practice does higher education currently give the students within its care in the preparation of a learning strategy? It should be the aim of all learning organisations, and particularly higher education, to give practice in developing a lifetime learning strategy.

Fig. 1 - The McKinseys 7s framework remodelled as a compass for the Career Orienteer™

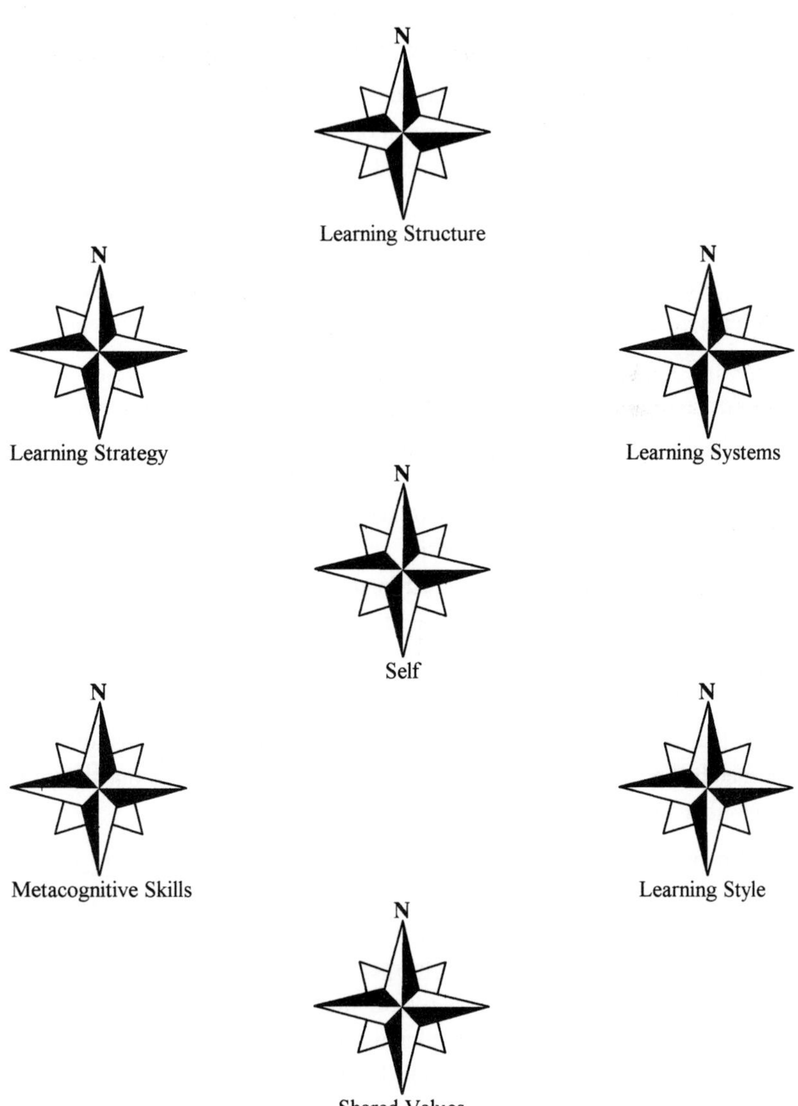

For those who have already established such a strategy this will involve merely a checkpoint review, testing out the compass needles to ensure that the position matches their current situation to their surroundings, and that they can move purposefully along their chosen career route.

For others a *learning strategy* may be enforced by circumstances. Some individuals find themselves in a situation with which they are currently uncomfortable and need to move forward.

Megginson and Pedler (1992) state that a learning strategy starts with self and the desire to learn. 'Without this desire self-development cannot start. This desire usually stems from some dissatisfaction or feeling of discomfort with present state. It is not necessary to know what you want to learn nor what you need to learn'.

This desire to learn is an issue for those working in higher education. How can we enhance student motivation? As argued by Elton (1996) 'some students' motivation for learning may differ from what their teachers would like it to be, at least in the order of importance given to them'. He points out that motivation can be intrinsic, extrinsic, achievement-oriented or social with intrinsic motivation related to interest in the subject (Entwistle and Waterston (1987). Students will require assistance to assess their own motivation and teachers must recognise and then appeal to those factors which are likely to produce higher commitment.

When the career orienteer has reached a point at which the situation does not match the surroundings Megginson and Pedler (1992) set out the path for plotting a *learning strategy*:

(l) The first step is *self-diagnosis*, the aim for the individual is to understand the source of dissatisfaction. In the view of Pedler, Burgoyne, and Boydell (1986) different people will prefer different methods of self-diagnosis. Some by simple introspection; others by conversing with members of their learning network, maybe a partner, colleagues or friend; or by completing self-administered questionnaires found in the many books now published on self-development.

(2) Complete a *risk assessment* in terms of those forces that are likely to help or hinder achievement and build them into the *learning programme*. Once the ability to take risks, survive them and profit from them has been developed then the self-development process will be strengthened.

(3) Design a *learning programme* and find the appropriate resources aimed at developing the *skills* necessary to achieve the *learning goals*, encapsulating *individual learning style* and a *successful learning system* within a *supportive learning structure* with *shared values* of success.

(4) *Assess performance* against original goals. Such an assessment will provide another checkpoint to evaluate whether the Career Orienteer™ is on track, and whether future goals need review. It also provides incentive to plan the next target.

Skills - What do I Need to Get There?

When organisations face a mismatch between the business environment and their current situation they must do more than shift in strategic focus. They need to add a new capability, new winning *skills* (Mintzberg and Quinn 1995). *Skills* represent the link between the organisation's strategy and the new era. Whilst at the same time they define changes that need to be made in the other six factors in the 7S framework.

This is so for the career orienteer. Responsibility for checking one's progress along a career path lies with the *individual*. As mentioned earlier once a *learning strategy* has been devised this may necessitate a change of direction. In career terms such a change may necessitate development, or remodelling, in other words, adding *new capabilities*, *new winning skills* or simply *undiscovered capacity* (Lusty 1996). Depending on the career orientation of the orienteer these skills could be personal, academic, professional, or entrepreneurial. For the purpose of this paper the author will reflect on the metacognitive skills that will assist the other six factors in the 7S self-development framework.

Some psychologists maintain that one factor unique to human thinking is metacognition, which is the ability we have to reflect on our own thinking process (Fisher 1990). These are the *skills* required to learn how to learn. How much do our students know about their own learning process when they have finished their studies in higher education? How often are they able to identify the thinking processes involved in the work on which they are assessed?

(1) Knowledge acquisition (input), for example, sensory experience, attention, memory, perception.

(2) Metacognition and decision making (executive control), for example, planning, predicting, checking and controlling.

(3) Strategies for using knowledge and solving problems (output), for example, reflecting, generating ideas, problem solving.

Fisher (1990) divided thinking skills into three:

(1) Creative thinking

(2) Critical thinking

(3) Problem solving.

His view is that thinking is involved in any mental activity that helps to formulate or solve a problem, to make a decision, or to seek understanding. It involves critical and creative aspects of the mind, both in the use of reason and the generation of ideas. It is through thinking that we make meaning out of life.

(1) *Creative thinking* is largely rearranging what we know in order to find out what we do not know. Thus, to think creatively we must be able to look afresh at what we usually take for granted. Creative thinking supplies the context of discovery, provides a hypothesis, using insight and inspiration. It is also called divergent thinking and researchers have suggested that there are four aspects to divergent or creative thinking skills.

(a) *fluency of thinking* is the ease with which we use stored information when we need it.

(b) *flexibility* is the ability to overcome mental blocks, to alter the approach to a problem.

(c) *originality or novelty* is shown by an unusual or rare response to provide a vision for the future.

(d) *elaboration* is the number of additions that can be made to some simple stimulus to make it more complex.

(2) *Learning to think critically* is to learn how to question, when to question and what questions to ask. Critical thinkers develop certain attitudes such as:

(a) *a desire to reason* which requires learning how to reason, when to use reasoning and what reasoning methods to use

(b) *a willingness to challenge*

(c) *a passion for truth*

For Bloom (1956) critical thinking was synonymous with 'evaluation'. In his taxonomy of cognitive goals of education evaluation was the pinnacle. Table l (Fisher 1990) sets out his hierarchy of thinking levels.

Table 1 - *B S Bloom's Taxonomy of Cognitive Goals*

Category	*Thinking Process Cues*
1. Knowledge (remembering and retaining)	Say what you know, what you remember, describe, repeat, define, identify, tell who, when, which, where, what
2. Comprehension (interpreting and understanding)	Describe in your own words, tell how you feel about, say that it means, explain, compare, relate
3. Application (making use of)	How can you use it, where does it lead you, apply what you know, use it to solve problems, demonstrate

4 Analysis (taking apart)	What are the parts, the order, the reasons why, the causes, the problems, the solutions, the consequences
5, Synthesis (putting together)	How might it be different, how else, what if, suppose, develop, improve, create in your own way
6. Evaluation (judging and assessing)	How would you judge it, does it succeed, will it work, what would you prefer, why do you think so

Fisher (1990)

(3) Many models are available to help *problem solving*. Fisher (1990) provides three sets of interacting factors:

(a) attitude which include *interest*, *motivation* and *confidence*

(b) *cognitive ability* which includes knowledge, memory and thinking skills

(c) *experience* to provide familiarity with content, context and strategies.

Style - Which is my Preferred Method of Learning?

Karlof (1993) states that *style* is one of the lesser known implements in the management tool box when consideration is made of the process of managing change. It can be said to consist of two elements; personal style and symbolic actions. Thus management style is not a matter of personal style but of what the executives in the organisation do and how they use their personal signal system.

When relating *style* to the 7S self-development framework no one learning style is considered better than another. Each will have particular strengths and weaknesses and these will be different depending on the particular setting in which they are used, and the task to which they are applied. Are students in higher education aware that some analysis can be made of their personal learning style and that learning strategies can be adapted to take account of this?

The Open University (1992) link Honey and Mumford's *learning styles* with the various stages of Kolb's learning cycle.

The *Activist* learns best from constant exposure to new experiences. *Reflectors* learn best from activities that allow them space to ponder over experience and assimilate information before making a considered judgement. *Theorists* learn best from activities that allow them to integrate observations into logically sound theories. They are less comfortable with subjective opinion or creative thinking. *Pragmatists* learn best from activities that have clear practical value and allow ideas and approaches to be tested in practical settings.

The Open University states that *learning styles* provide opportunities for students to think about the way they learn, help them describe the learning they do and assess its effectiveness. However, how many students in higher education are aware of their learning styles? They are understood by the teacher, but not the learner! They also utilise the abilities associated with each of the four stages of the *learning cycle* as part of the *learning system* to which the 7s self-development framework now turns its attention.

Systems - How do I get There?

The *systems* of any organisation are all the formal and informal procedures that make organisations work day by day and year by year.

The *systems* identified in the 7S self-development framework concentrate on the *learning process*. The Open University (1992) defines learning as the ability to process information, insights and experience into new learning.

In his article 'Action learning and excellence in management development' (Margerison, 1994) sets out the differences that have occurred in the last 30 years between traditional learning and action learning (Table 2)

Table 2 - *Differences Between Traditional Learning and Action Learning*

Traditional	*Action Learning*
Classroom based	Work based
Individual orientation	Group orientation
Input orientation	Output orientation
Knowledge orientation	Action orientation
Passive	Active
Historical focus	Concern with the here and now and future
Cost investment	Investment return required
Producer oriented	Market/customer oriented

C. J. Margerison (1994)

In 1984 D. A. Kolb published a book called 'Experiential Learning - Experience as the source of learning and development'. Before developing his four-stage model of learning by doing the author sets out the issues of significance for the teacher and learner (Cotton 1995). Learners must be committed to the process of exploring and learning:

- the teacher imposes some structure on the learning process so that the learners are not left to *discover* by random chance
- there must be scope for the learner to achieve some independence from the teacher
- exposure to experience is necessary for the learner
- the learner is involved in the active exploration of the experience

- the learner must feel safe and supported so that they are encouraged to value their own experience
- the learner must reflect on their experience in a critical, selective way.

Cotton (1995) states that there is a difference between learning how to do something and the process of learning from activities and personal experience. The process of active learning and work experience is called 'experiential learning'. This is developed later.

Gibbs states that learning can be described as either practical or theoretical as both involve doing or involve thinking. However, it is not enough just to do, neither is it enough just to think. It is also not enough simply to do and think. Learning from experience must involve links between the doing and the thinking. Kolb's Experiential Learning Theory places four stages in sequence to form the experiential learning cycle. The cycle can be entered by the learner at any point, but its stages must be followed in sequence. This has significance not only for the *learning system* but other factors in McKinsey re-modelled:

(1) *Learning style* - Individuals will have their preferred learning style. However, each stage on the Kolb cycle will benefit from different abilities and approaches and individuals should be encouraged to experiment with a mix of styles.

(2) *Learning structure* - Experiential learning follows a link cycle so the teacher must provide appropriate learning activities and teaching methods to support each stage. Cotton (1995) makes some suggestions:

(3) Active experimentation suggests that planning a *learning programme* and preparing a learning contract ensures that learning needs are diagnosed; learning objectives specified; learning resources and strategies put in place; and that there is validated evidence of learning.

(4) *Learning strategy* - Cotton (1995) quotes Carl Rogers' theory '... get on with optimistic learning and self-development'. Every event and personal experience can provide a learning opportunity. Thus an attitude of

learning opportunism makes it possible to view all experiences as a potential area for useful learning.

Structure - Where to do I go to Learn?

The *structure* of an organisation refers to the way business areas, divisions and units are grouped in relation to each other (Karlof, 1993). The challenge is to be in a position to focus the dimensions of the organisation that are currently important to its evolution and to be ready to re-focus as the critical dimensions shifts. Divisions and units are grouped in relation to each other.

Structure has been interpreted in the 7S self-development framework as where the career orienteer will go to learn or rather, where learning will be delivered.

Margerison (1994) has identified the changing processes in management education and development from experiential to existential. These are characterised as follows:

- From *teaching* to *resourcing,* that is, personal consulting and counselling
- From *programmes* to *contracts* based on intra-organisational assessment of problems and opportunities
- From *individual* to *group orientation and learning*
- From *standard* to *real up-to-date cases*
- From *delegating* to *developing* that is, managers acting as developers
- From *top-down appraisal* to *bottom-up appraisal* , that is, self-appraisal and team appraisal
- From *product-centred* to *marketing-centred orientation*, that is, part-time Masters degree, tailored to suit the needs of the organisation; National Vocational Qualifications (NVQ) and competency based qualifications gained as an integral part of work; work based learning

- From *inputs* to *outputs* , that is, relating knowledge and skills to tasks that have a purpose rather than teaching as an end in itself
- From *fixed* to *continuing education*, that is, lifelong learning
- From *experiential* to *existential* management development.

Much has been written about the advent of the 'learning organisation or the learning company'. For the career orienteer 'learning organisation' has to take on a different meaning. Pedler, Boydell and Burgoyne (1988) set out their working definition of a learning company: 'an organisation which facilitates the learning of all its members and continuously transforms itself.'

An organisation is defined in the dictionary as an 'organised body or system or society.' In turn a society is defined as 'any social community'.

The career orienteer will not remain a member of a single organisation during working life. Thus the learning organisation will be replaced by the learning community. This community is likely to evolve into a learning network providing support through the learning process. We return to the *learning strategy* and the first step of *self-diagnosis*. Different people will prefer different methods of self-diagnosis. Some by conversing with members of their learning network, maybe a partner, colleague or friend. A learning community provides support. It may be the University, the employer, but it may be the pub, family, or friends.

Shared Values - Who Will be my Mentor?

The effect of this view of the future is to place more emphasis on the final factor in 7S self-development framework shared values.

For the organisation *superordinate goals* related to guiding concepts, a set of values and aspirations, often unwritten, that go beyond the conventional formal statement of corporate objectives. The shared values of an organisation are things that everybody is aware of as being specially important and crucial to the survival and success of the organisation (Karlof 1993).

The career orienteer, without an organisation, will need to create individual *superordinate goals* and ensure that values are shared within their own learning community.

Parikh (1991) acknowledges that the role of management has now changed and the essence of the new paradigm is to create within the organisation 'a climate, a culture, and a context in which corporate enrichment and individual fulfilment collaborate and resonate progressively...'. He provides a very useful model (Table 3), contrasting the old management paradigm with the new paradigm, in which the focus is the individual 'the concept of self - our real identity.' This has been extended by the author to include self as learner within the new paradigm.

Table 3 - *The Learning Paradigm*

Characteristic	*Old Paradigm*	*New Paradigm*	*Learning Paradigm*
Focus	Institution	Individual	Self
Source of strength	Stability	Change	Self-development
Leadership	Dogmatic	Inspirational	Developer
Strategy	Planned	Entrepreneurial	Self-development
Structure	Hierarchy	Network	Learning Organisation
Systems	Rigid	Flexible	for learning
Staff	Title and rank	Being helpful	Individuals
Style	Problem solving	Transformational	Learning
Skills	To complete	To build	Metacognitive
Shared value	Better sameness	Meaningful difference	Learning network

Parikh (1991)

The Learning Paradigm in Table 3 shows that the focus of management turns its attention to the individual; the source of strength of an organisation is self-development; the role of leadership is as developer.

In a learning community everyone is a learner and everyone is a developer. The role of a member of a learning community could vary from critical or developmental friend, monitor, motivator, or in a more formal setting, authenticator of claims for competence (The Recording Achievement and Higher Education Project 1991 - 1993).

The career orienteer takes responsibility for individual career progression and self-development. The 7S self-development framework provides a set of compasses to ensure that the learning strategy, the learning system, the appropriate skills, learning style, supporting learning structure and shared values of the learning community all convey a clear pathway to the goals set and the personal targets to be reached.

Course and Compass

In an attempt to provide both the course and the compass for its students the Lancashire Business School at the University of Central Lancashire in the UK has developed a new subject, career management, as part of its Combined Honours programme. Students will take this subject alongside those offered by the Faculties of Health, Science, Design and Technology, Cultural, Legal, and Social Studies, as well as Business. The subject comprises historical and theoretical aspects of career management, personal development, career planning and reflective learning from experience.

The learning outcomes of the subject propose that at the end of the programme students will be able to:

- demonstrate skills appropriate to the needs of successful career management
- be skilled practitioners of reflective learning

- undertake self-analysis and personal audit using an appropriate range of techniques
- prepare a personal development plan
- apply a model of career management
- compare and contrast theories of career choice
- describe the historical development of and the contribution of various disciplines to the development of career education and career management
- demonstrate knowledge and understanding of trends in the labour market
- demonstrate knowledge and understanding of the use of occupational classification systems
- explain recruitment and personnel selection processes

It is the hope of the course team that in the words of Carl Rogers these students will '... get on with optimistic learning and self-development' and that every event and personal experience can provide a learning opportunity along the pathway to an effective career route to the goals set and personal targets to be reached.

References

Bloom, B. S. (1956), Taxonomy of Education Goals, New York, David McKay.

Brooke, S., Quality Manager, GEC Alsthom Traction.

Cotton, J. (1995), The Theory of Learning, London, Kogan Page.

Elton Lewis (1996), 'Strategies to Enhance Student Motivation' Conference on Student Motivation held at University of Central Lancashire April.

Fisher, R. (1990), Teaching Children to Think (Simon and Schulster)

Gibbs, G. Learning by Doing - A Guide to teaching and learning methods, Further Education Unit.

Karlof, B. (1993), Key Business Concepts, London, Routledge.

Kolb, D. A. (1984), Experiential Learning - Experience as the Source of Learning and Development.

Lusty, J. (1996) Pro Vice Chancellor, University of Central Lancashire.

Megginson, D. and Pedler, M. (1992), Self-Development - A Facilitator's Guide, London, McGraw Hill.

Mintzberg, H. and Quinn, J. B. (1995), The Strategy Process - Concepts, Context, Cases, European edition, London, Prentice Hall 2nd edition.

Open University, (1992), A Portfolio Approach to Personal and Career Development Workbook.

Parikh, J. (1991), Managing Yourself, London, Blackwell.

Pedler, M., Burgoyne, J. and Boydell, T. (1986), A Manager's Guide to Self-Development, London, McGraw Hill.

UCAS and Employment Department, The Recording Achievement and Higher Education Project 1 September 1991 - 31 August 1993.

Ernst Raters

Open Learning Systems - Regional, National and International Co-operation

1. From conventional mode to mixed mode model in higher education

Higher education has traditionally focused its attention on conventional modes of course delivery. Courses have required students to attend at predetermined times in order that direct interaction may take place with the teacher. The application of this model has evolved to yield a variety of approaches. In the majority of institutions some combination of lectures, seminars and tutorials are the norm. The model requires that there will be direct contact in location and time between the persons responsible for course delivery and the students.

For such conventional settings in the educational process a special learning environment is required with all the physical and infrastructural implications like real estate requirements, equipment needs, student relocation and support.

Besides the conventional higher education model we have had for about 20 years the foundation of institutions, in which the students and teachers are separated by distance and also by time. Such distance teaching institutions are found in nearly all European countries: like the Open University in Great Britain, the Open Universiteit in the Netherlands or the Fern Universität in Germany.

The key orientation of these distance teaching universities is placed on the development and quality control of the learning resources: the production and evaluation of learning materials. The distance learning model also places substantial demands upon the student, who must display significant self-motivation and drive, and appropriate study skills.

The conventional (on-campus) and the distance approaches have come together in some universities mostly in a version, which is best described as 'dual mode'. On-campus students are taught in the conventional manner whilst separate programmes utilise open learning approaches for off-campus students.[1]

In German universities we find the open learning model only for courses in continuing education, while the graduate courses follow, with very few exceptions, the conventional learning model.

At the moment the European discussion leads to a fourth approach, which may be described as a mixed mode model, as the methods and materials created for open/distance use are also utilised by on-campus students. The mixed mode model also implies a strategy of incorporating learning materials prepared elsewhere as well as the idea of co-operation with other institutions. This very flexible approach to learning has been put forward largely by the development of the so-called *'new media'*, the discussion of the *European Information Society*, and the role of distance learning within it. Another 'driver' is the movement towards *lifelong learning*.

2. European Information Society

The Bangemann Report on the Information Society (1994) claims significant benefits from the development of information: communication- and knowledge-systems for Europe's regions in terms of cultural expressions and closer integration for the more peripheral areas, and for governments and administration operating closer to local needs.

The challenges facing the European Union in making distance learning one of the motors of the information society are considerable.

The current situation, however, indicates how relatively little is currently spent on open/distance learning in the EU. Within the current European Union there are approximately 85 million people taking part in some form of education and training every year, which accounts for just over one third of

1 Fallows, S. and Robinson K. (1995) , Developing a mixed mode university: some issues and problems, in: One World many Voices - Quality in Open and Distance Learning, Volume 1, Selected papers from the 17th World Conference of the International Council for Distance Education, (pp. 407 - 410), Birmingham, United Kingdom, Edited by David Sewart.

the current population of the EU. The total European expenditure on education and training is estimated at 250 billion ECU's.

Expenditures on open and distance learning add up to 1,7 billion ECU's. This is only 0,68 % of the total expenditure on education and training.[2]

Nevertheless some building blocks for the educational dimension to the European Information Society have been put in place:

- Research and development into using new learning and communications technologies;
- Developments towards the idea of a European Training Network;
- Developments towards the idea of a European Open Learning Network.

In the context of the first building block the DELTA-programme has achieved key results through 30 projects and other concerted actions and studies within the telematics for flexible and distance learning. The results become more relevant as the tools for telematics in distance learning are now more widely available, such as computer- and video-conferencing, satellite-based delivery and computer-networking-systems like the Internet, which will lead to an increasing market in distance education.[3]

Nevertheless we should not forget, that studying within a distance education context is still largely based on printed learning material. Besides this, one important result of the DELTA-projects was that 'positive learning outcomes were observed in these pilot applications particularly where distance teaching and learning were combined with periodic face-to-face interactions in the form of seminars and residential meetings.'[4] (DELTA: Developing European Learning through Technology Advance).

2 Robinson, A. H. (1995), Policy Implications for Distance Learning in the European Information Society and the Widening EU, Open University, United Kingdom (4p.)

3 Info 2000, Deutschlands Weg in die Informationsgesellschaft, (1996), Bericht der Bundesregierung, hrsg. v. Bundesministerium für Wirtschaft.

4 Telematics for Flexible and Distance Learning (DELTA), Final Report, EU Research and Technological Developments Programme (1991 - 1995), Written and edited by Peter J. Bates, European Commission, Directorate -General DG XIII

3. Structural requirements for organisation and co-operation

This leads to the understanding that it is necessary to generate different teaching-/ learning environments, pedagogical practices and organisational infrastructures of high quality. If the power and sophisticated array of new technologies in education are to be exploited, an appropriate organisational development strategy is required that is cost-effective.[5]

To enable more cost-effective methods to be utilised for the design, the production and the dissemination of multimedia learning resources, institutional co-operation on a regional, national as well as European or international level is necessary. Co-operation is the base for an appropriate administrative and technical infrastructure. This fits the 'ideal model' formulated by Tony Bates, one of the well known experts of information technologies in open learning and distance education, as he said the ideal model is 'based on the idea of high-quality, pre-produced, modular multimedia materials, available on demand, that can be adapted and modified by both teachers and learners to suit individual needs. The 'heart' of the teaching system is the remote teacher or mentor, who negotiates with and guides the learner, its 'brain' is a multimedia relational database, and its 'veins' and 'arteries' are wide-band telecommunications networks'.[6]

The last part of my contribution will give some examples and experiences of co-operation and institutional networking in the field of open and distance learning, in which my institution is involved.

5 Taylor, J. C. (1996), Perspectives on the Educational Uses of Technology, Report produced for the International Council for Distance Education Standing Conference of Presidents, Lillehammer.

6 Bates, A. W. (1994), Hello, technology! Goodbye, distance teaching institutions? Open praxis, The Bulletin of the International Council for Distance Education, Volume 2, (pp. 5 - 7) , Edited by Ros Morpeth, Cambridge, United Kingdom.

4. Co-operation and networking by the Centre for Continuing Education at the University of Bremen in the fields of open and distance learning

I am working at the Centre for Continuing Education, a central academic sector at the University of Bremen. One department of the centre is dealing with activities in the fields of open and distance learning. This department has the status of a distance study centre, which is engaged in different forms of regional, national and international co-operations and networks.

One basic co-operation is the connection with the Fern Universität in Hagen (Northrhine-Westfalia), the German 'Open University'. Advising and supporting students of the Fern Universität, who are living in the Bremen region is one of the main tasks of the Bremen study centre, as this is also the main task for other distance study centres all over Germany. Many of them are co-operating with other distance-education institutions and are working together with the faculties of their universities, concerning the development, adaptation and integration of courses for open and distance learning.

There is a close relationship between the study centres at universities all over Germany. A special networking system has been established as well as a Euro Study Centre - North West Germany (ESC-NWG). The ESC-NWG is one of the Euro Study Centres, nominated by the European Association of Distance Teaching Universities (EADTU), representing four autonomous distance teaching and open universities in Spain, Germany, the Netherlands and the United Kingdom as well as several other national associations and consortia for higher distance education.

The mission and the aims for Euro Study Centres on their European dimension are defined as:

- to give better service to learners and potential learners in open and distance education,
- to improve inter-operability and to create quality assurance in an European context,
- to provide student support to different target groups and to open up opportunities for new clients,
- to improve dissemination of good practice,

- to enhance access to a European market for distance learning courses and services,
- to promote transnational course delivery by the application of new technologies and
- to improve the transnational networking of study centres.[7]

The Euro Study Centre - North West Germany has been in operation since 1992 and is engaged in different European projects, graduate courses as well as courses for continuing education.

5. A project example: the 'Euro-MBA' course

I want to present one of these projects because I think that it is a good example for new transnational forms of co-operation and networking as well as referring to open and distance learning.

The objective of the project is the course 'Euro-MBA', which provides an opportunity for managers to complete a programme focused on management in Europe and to earn the degree of an 'European Master of Business Administration'.

The course consists of a combination of distance and residential learning and true international arrangements as there are:

- international composition of the student groups with at least five different nationalities,
- international composition of the faculties by six well known European universities and business schools,
- international spread of residential sites over six different parts of Europe,
- international content of the course material and

7 Pronk, N. (1993), Networking of Study Centres: An International Approach, in: UNED - EADTU, The Proceedings of the UNED/EADTU Conference and Workshops, Madrid 11th - 12th February 1993, the Open University Network: Course Delivery, Student Support and Study Centres, EADTU, (pp. 101).

- international in both the theoretical and practical dimension of international management.

Some central parts of the course materials have been produced by an EADTU-working group and has been funded by the COMETT-programme.

The other parts were written by different international authors under the control of the Dutch Open universiteit.

The 'Euro-MBA' is delivered by a consortium of institutions representing different European countries:

- Open universiteit of the Netherlands,
- Institute of Business Administration of the University of Marseilles in connection with the Euro Study Centre Nantes, France,
- Advanced Management Education Centre of the University of Jyväskylä, Finland,
- University College Dublin, Ireland and
- Euro Study Centre North-West-Germany in connection with the University College Delmenhorst, Germany.

The 'Euro-MBA'-course contains 1,800 study hours over 2 years. The contents of the course are delivered mainly through written course materials. Some of the distance learning courses are combined with video-programmes and computer conferencing. Centralised tutoring services are available by telephone, fax, e-mail and video-conferences. Provisions are made for the students to communicate electronically. Besides that counselling is available through the network of study centres maintained by the consortium partners.

The objectives of the six residential weeks are not the repetition of the course contents but the promotion of cultural immersion and of international team building, leadership skills training, specialised information in a regional context and issue-oriented teaching about central management questions like 'Innovation Management' or 'Total Quality Management'.

Students, who have passed examinations in all modules, and have completed all the associated tasks and assignments, will receive the University degree 'European Master in Business Administration'. This degree will be jointly awarded by the Open Universiteit of the Netherlands and the Institute of Business Administration of the University of Marseilles.

6. Conclusions

(1) We see a development in the direction of mixed mode universities, promoted by growing educational demands in the process of lifelong learning and by new possibilities in using new learning and communication technologies.

(2) Open and distance learning will play a bigger part in this process but will be most effective in the combination with some elements of conventional higher education like seminars and face to face tuition.

(3) It is not sufficient to make available good study material for open and distance learning. The effective organisation of the learning processes and the distribution of a course is of high complexity and, therefore, needs an effective organisational infrastructure.

(4) A nation-wide or international distribution of courses in higher education requires organised co-operation between qualified (university) institutions to guarantee effective delivery of the course. It is, therefore, very important to have established institutional networks, to transfer and transform decentralised produced courses and make them operational towards the 'European Information Society'.

Henning Salling Olesen

Adult Education Open University- New Agendas for Lifelong Learning

This paper is not an academic contribution, but deals with a very practical discussion of the status and reference of the concept of lifelong learning.

My idea is to present an experience of lifelong learning in our university as a case study. The Open University is not exactly one of the principal aspects of the concept of lifelong learning; neither in terms of participants, contents, or function. However, it will be my argument, that it represents some important trends, that deserve our open-minded consideration, when discussing lifelong learning; trends that differentiate and modify the landscape of adult education and learning. The social structures of society are changing, the composition of the work force is changing, and the cultural and psychological setting is a melting pot. Universities study this as an interesting object of academic research but we are also in the middle of it.

Brief Presentation

The Adult Education Open University programme:

- is a study programme at Masters level
- offered for part-time mature students
- with some academic and/or professional background
- 1 -5 full work years for 3 study units in a 3-year programme.

The programme is located in an inter-institutional organisation as it is offered jointly by the University of Copenhagen (the old, traditional education department), the Royal Danish School for Educational Studies, the University of Aalborg (the young, regional university) and the University of Roskilde (the young, alternative university in the metropolitan Copenhagen).

The programme started in 1990. It has been a huge success in terms of applications. At the moment there are 300+ students enrolled, which is a lot in Denmark. It has become the adult education centre, connecting practical milieus with academic research, concentrating education in adult education.

The framework is an open education legislation. The students have to pay, unlike ordinary higher education, a moderate fee (equivalent of 550 DM per year), which automatically triggers a state grant to the institution per paying student (4 x student fee).

It is also an alternative type of masters programme:

- it is largely based on collective project work. Each study unit has an examination based on project work
- every study unit consists of 6-7 intensive weekend seminars, self-managing study groups, and self-managing project group meetings with an appointed supervisor.

The weekend seminars take place in the university at sessions that are a mixture of wildlife camps, residential meetings and continuing education. They are very intense, very informal, and very dedicated as the students (mature students!) meet Friday afternoon until Sunday afternoon, sleep in classrooms in field beds, receive food from a diner transportable, and work intensively.

The programme consists of three units with the following titles:

- Socialisation and Learning Processes
- Adult Education and Society
- Educational Planning and Organisation.

Each unit includes core literature (1500 pages), background lectures and reading, and a project work on a theme within the subject area of the study unit.

The definition of relevant themes is quite open: the students are not only allowed, but encouraged to work on themes of subjective interest which are sometimes related to professional experiences or sometimes to theoretical.

Who are the students, and why are they coming?

The students are 'all types of people'. Most of them having some kind of professional background in education, training, planning of training, staff development, social pedagogy, etc. A large number are teachers in continuing education, health education, social workers and teachers in social work, staff development officers. Their formal educational background varies as some have very little formal education, but possess a qualifying professional experience including in the field of continuing education as many academic professionals go for a supplementary qualification. Probably the largest proportion have a non-academic higher education qualification.

The majority are women (2/3). The unifying motivation seems to be, that they have tried a lot of sector-related continuing education and training and now they are looking for something deeper, more theoretical, less applied and operational. On the other hand, they are not looking for traditional academic study as it is also a personal development project. It is important for them, that the study respects and makes use of their professional experience, and gives space for personal development etc.

So the typical student is in employment that is in a personal-professional area. They are, therefore, not necessarily in job transition or career change although a few are.

Most students spend their leisure time on this study. They are strongly devoted to it. As a result they are a pleasure to teach. However, it is a difficult situation for the students and quite a few give up during the three year period. Most leave because of 'unrelated' reasons like changes in their work situation, pressures of family life, etc. For many the break is temporary.

The Professions' Perspective: Opening the Mirror Room

Most participants have a professional experience in areas that are not really professionalised in the traditional sense, but they are in a professionalising process such as teaching in adult and continuing education, nursing, social work, and (social) pedagogy. To the extent that this professionalisation has an aspect of educational expertise, the study in itself contributes to professionalisation. And to the extent, that projects may very well focus on professionally relevant problems, it is the case for other professions as well.

This is an important process, because most of these sectors need professionalisation for the quality of their services. In some cases they are also fighting for the independence and relevance of their profession (for example, nursing). Professionally relevant problems are very good drives in this process.

The Adult Education Study programme supports this professionalisation process but not within a traditional technological paradigm, where theoretical knowledge is supposed to provide the basis for rationalised action. We have deliberately resigned from defining the study programme as a teacher training or planners training, and as a result give little emphasis to methods and prescriptive knowledge. By definition it is defined as a basic theoretical and reflective programme. The core is the project work with its pragmatic, problem-solving dimension and its emphasis on problems and experiences picked out of everyday life of professional people, supporting an elementary processing of knowledge in the perspective of analysing problems, contexts and possible actions. In this way we hopefully contribute to professional quality. This is mainly confined to professions with an educational content in a broad sense such as teaching, planning of education and training etc. but because of the flexibility of the project work it also relates to some extent to more distant professions, for example, nursing, social work, labour market administration. Recent discussion in theories and concepts of professional knowledge, knowledge-in-action and reflection-in-action (Schön, 1983) and tacit knowledge (Polanyi, 1966), focuses on concepts related to the everyday experience stressing that practical skills and competencies are more than the verbal, discursive knowledge connected with the formal basic disciplines and methods of that profession. I think, that the project work, to the extent that it directly relates to practical fields of experience, to a large extent is including the types of knowing and the type of reflection that Schön and others are dealing with. The type of problems being addressed in our students` work is of the type, which in Schöns' terminology, gives rise to 'reflection-in-action', that is, the surprising or puzzling aspects of the practical experience.

However, this way of conceptualising the practical experience tends to harmonise and naturalise the circuit of vocational practices, basic vocational education, continuing education and training, sectoral networks and fora of discussion, and a sample of theoretical references fitting into or providing the basis of the professionalism also tend to be a closed circuit. Sometimes even research activity related to the specific area and the problems of that profession is a part of this closed circuit.

It is too simple to describe the professional sphere in this way primarily because it is not free of contradictions. However, it is a reasonable assumption, that the contradictions of the practical task and the conditions of the professions and semi-professions, give rise to an active defence mechanism, and produce a collective consciousness which is a core part of professional knowledge and routine, defining the possible and present professional practice and thinking as the normal and rational way of dealing with the tasks of the profession. In other words it is a professional ideology, recognising and respecting that a professional ideology is in fact based on a certain rationality but also criticising and relativising historically its self-understanding.

We have labelled this closed circuit of rationality, consisting of interrelated discursive knowledge, practical paradigms and attitudes a mirror room because the analysis of problems and experiences, and the possible actions are always reflected back upon each other.

Traditionally vocational education and most continuing education and training remain within this closed circuit. An academic study of problems within the field using theoretical and critical reflection might, in the best cases, break through the closed circuit. Such research might conceptualise some of the contradictions and dynamics in a way that also transcends the circuit. It is a matter of content, of sociology of knowledge, and of ways of thinking. Within the metaphor: to turn some of the mirrors in the professional mirror room, to break the closed circuit but still looking on the problems inside the mirror room, and still partly looking at them through the modes belonging to that mirror room.

The Institutional Perspective: What the Universities may Learn

Danish universities represent the German/Humboldt-type university. They have successfully resisted basic changes in their structure and function until the early 1970s. At this time one factor was changing; mass enrolment and the inclusion of new types of students.

Instead of reforming old institutions new universities were built, including Roskilde. They had by definition a different and more open relation to society (distinguishing them as red universities), and were excluded from access to some of the institutional and elite privileges of the older universities. The old universities resisted and still continue to resist basic changes, although the institutional culture has changed a lot. Nevertheless, to some extent, the new and the old universities (were) uniform in one aspect: they concentrate on the basic teaching of ordinary students, coming through the 'gymnasium', and taking a full academic programme. Access was not seriously widened. Extramural activities, open university, professional continuing education and similar types of expansions have never been highly represented in Danish universities. Complementary to the universities' role, two institutional developments must be mentioned. One is the widespread and high quality of the adult education system, supported by private organisations, but with a high degree of public funding building on the self-confident and anti-academic folk high school tradition. Another is the system of independent higher education for professional and semi-professional vocations which also deals more openly with continuing professional education and training, particularly for engineers and primary school teachers.

To be comparative: Danish universities are less German than German universities, and much less elitist than most continental universities. On the other hand, it is obvious that we could learn something from the British approach to access problems, but more particularly from the North American framework of higher learning.

However, today there is a relatively well preserved academic tradition in conservative or in progressive versions, but nevertheless academic. To involve these two sectors in the teaching of students with a professional background and a highly personal involvement necessitates a mutual learning process. Even in our very progressive university there is a lot of hesitation and uncertainty about the institutional outcome which is understandable but it is obvious that we may acquire a lot of inspiration and new challenges from this contact.

In Adult Education, for example, it means that suddenly we have students representing all possible important fields and institutions outside the universities as part-time students inside the universities. It means that we learn about their views and problems. They also give us access to new areas of research and practical experience.

In terms of content the classic challenge of theory to prove fruitful in practical thinking and problem solving has assumed a new and friendly dimension. It is now not an anti-academic aggression, and it is also not an instrumentalist reduction of science and theory. It is a very committing challenge to utilise different perspectives on knowledge, and prove how fruitful academic skills, knowledge and virtues may be.

We often say, that the teachers ought to pay for the job of teaching. At the institutional level, the universities might be grateful for this task, though we must express it in taking money instead of paying money.

This type of teaching commitment may contribute to a curricular and research paradigm development, reshaping universities in interdisciplinary centres on research and learning instead of disciplinary and disciplining institutions defending their own status and perspective. It could be an important factor in a modernising universities, something that has been delayed for decades in many countries.

This type of modernising has the very attractive quality of being relatively democratic. The overall impression is that when continental universities are modernising, it is by commercialising part of the activities or by renewing the links to the establishment in the sense of linking elitist science with the power centres of the capitalist economy. I do not think that modern learning can easily compete with this. However, it is important to build up links with society on a democratic basis, rather than establishing a corral defence for the academic virtues, which are in reality a renewal of elitism.

I referred earlier to professional experiences in relation to our open university programme. I think it is important to emphasise the difference between the role of universities in a traditional profession like law or medicine where universities have been institutionally and scientifically integrated into the closed circuit of professions. It makes a difference, whether the university programmes are in this sense 'internal', or whether they represent a broader aspiration for the students, and in terms of curricular orientation. I think it is important for professional development too.

The Life Long Learning perspective: Self-managed, personal and professional

In the use of lifelong education and lifelong learning a small cultural battle has taken place. On the one side the liberal adult education sector, emphasising the autonomous learner and goals like personal development and political education, and regarding the institutional independence as the protection of these perspectives and on the other the continuing education sector, emphasising learning in everyday life rather than institutions, therefore giving priority to the important learning interest of everyday life, connected with work and the professions.

I like to see our small example as a mediating case in the sense of bridging professional and personal education, closely related to everyday life experience but primarily a very self-managed type of continuing education.

Lifelong learning as a political concept is depending on a new definition of the relation between political education and work/profession.

Our mature students represent different versions of a new orientation, where work/profession does not only play a different role to wage labour or the traditional professions, but where it also changes over the life course. Many students are in a career or job change, even more are in a kind of personal re-orientation (life crisis/transition). Tow-thirds are women but we are not dealing with women re-entering the labour market after motherhood (generally Danish women do not leave the labour market in their children's' first years) but in some cases a re-orientation in life takes place in the phase when the children are older and demand less attention and energy.

Behind these phenomena is the condition of modernity, that you must create your own life; you must not only choose and arrange it, but you must also interpret it and assign a meaning and a continuity in it. You may call this the biographicity as a generalised life condition (Alheit, 1994). In the working classes this may still not primarily lead into adult education, but surprisingly frequently you do see such orientations in traditional education for workers and especially for those in marginal situations such as unemployment. Our mature students are not working class; they are mainly middle class although it is not always so clear. As I mentioned, the participants are very different, including some groups that are culturally working class though they may by profession approach middle class (teachers of vocational training, social workers, and others).

Behind this is also a reshaping of the social classes. This makes it much less clear who would benefit from which types of adult education.

The concept of lifelong learning must encompass these changes among the social classes; general cultural orientations, and the structure of learning motivation, including the interrelation between personal, professional and political education.

The core of lifelong learning seems to be the autonomy of the learner, and if viewed in relation to the educational supply, offers facilities for self-managed learning.

Instead of a conclusion:

There is no conclusion on these reflections. It may have seemed as if I argue that our specific case represents or proves the necessity to act in specific ways. This is not my point as it would at least have demanded a more detailed and documented presentation of the empirical basis.

I am concerned instead about inspiring some new agendas in the university institutional policies, in professional knowledge development and in the political discussion under the headline of lifelong learning. By accepting the plausibility of the case you already open a discussion of these new agendas.

References

Alheit, P. (1974), Zivile Kultur. Verlust und Wiederaneignung der Moderne, Campus.

Polanyi, M. (1966), The Tacit Dimension, Gloucester, Mass.,Peter Smith.

Schön, D. (1983), The Reflective Practitioner, New York, Basic.

Merce Espanya

Non-Teaching Cases of University as Open Learning Centres: The Communicative Formulation of the Law of Adult Education

1. The Closed Doors of the Spanish University

We have to start by saying that currently in Spain universities provide mostly for traditional students. Adults who want to access to a University have great difficulties in doing so because they have to pass an examination that is very academic in content. Only people up to 25 years old can do it. These examinations are totally decontextualised from their daily lives as they do not take into account the reality of the lives of adults.

Assessment of Prior Experimental Learning (APEL) does not exist in Spain. either as a means of accreditating their practical knowledge nor for facilitating entrance to higher education.

Nowadays, the role of university extension in Spain is extremely limited and reduced. When the university extension scheme was created at an International Pedagogic Congress in Madrid in 1892 (Léclere, 1893) it was conceived as a way to enable all citizens to have access to higher education as universities were monopolised by a minority in society. Nevertheless, the civil war (1936) destroyed these kinds of democratic cultural projects.

There are very few further practices that could be called University Extension and most of the activities performed on its behalf, respond to purposes and impulses that are not related to it. For instance, now we can sometimes see in Spanish newspapers a few advertisements for University Extension courses, but what they offer are courses like *Techniques of Exploration of the Pulmonary Function* or *Nephrology and Dialysis Applied to the Cure of the Renal Sick.*

The resources allocated to the university extension scheme are being used in some cases for giving specialised university courses and in other cases for paying end of course trips. It is in this manner that the circle of the Matthew

Effect is repeating itself, giving more to those who have more and giving less to those who have less (Merton, 1973).

The University has not achieved educational equality. On the contrary, it sometimes helps to increase cultural inequalities. In the present information society, there is a dramatic fragmentation between those having regular jobs and those who are socially excluded. The increasing cultural inequalities reinforce such social exclusion by choosing the 'best' to be trained in high knowledge and putting the others out on the borders.

CREA (Centre of Research for the Education of Adults, University of Barcelona) and other progressive groups of the universities have a global project of transformation of this situation. The general idea is to open universities not only through teaching, but also in other areas, such as research. Open learning of non-traditional students could come not only from courses, but also from their participation in different kinds of university activities.

2. Some Transformative Experiences

2.1 Adult School La Verneda

La Verneda is a unique adult school because of its high popular participation. There are 1,500 students and 90 volunteers, most of whom are university graduates, professors, people from different social movements and former participants. For example, there is the case of a university professor who studied adult basic education at La Verneda after dropping out of the traditional educational system and who is currently teaching at the University.

The higher education programme in this school is due to a long and constant fight for working in a project following principles of social participation and transformation that were begun by the present professor and director of CREA.

In the centre we are not there exclusively for instruction but to create knowledge through dialogue. The quarter where the school is located has gained some health, education, communication, leisure and other improvements, thanks to popular demands emanating from the school.

In La Verneda we have overcome the traditional counterposition between university experts and 'cultural dope' (Garfinkel, 1967) image of participants. All of us are creating and transforming together. The design and contents of the curriculum and the management of the centre is carried out collaboratively. Participants of La Verneda co-operate as members of the research team in the investigations carried out.

The Verneda case demonstrates that if university extension is far from achieving its principles it is not because of a lack of popular demand or the lack of motivation of people participating in higher education. Participation generates participation and to enter into this circle it is necessary that somebody begins offering courses that are fully adapted to the public to whom they are offered and not to the interests of those who have power to do it.

Currently the University possesses the legitimacy and power for creating knowledge and science to open the way. We cannot continue to blame the lack of motivation as the cause for not participating because a real demand exists.

Returning to the access examination for entry to university mentioned at the beginning of this paper we find that at La Verneda we have the contradiction of preparing people for an examination that has not taken into account the practical and cultural knowledge of particular groups of people, such as adult psychology nor his/her reality. But as it is the only way to gain access at present so we have we have to provide this type of teaching. Most participants fail and abandon the adult school.

Another case worth considering is the Literary Gatherings the school offers. People who, two or three years ago, could not read or write are now discussing works by Kafka, Cervantes, etc. In this way we have managed to create a dynamic communicative interaction whereby people can express their knowledge freely, but always being open to criticism, and where they seek to come to a common understanding.

2.2 Adult Education Participation Research

CREA has developed a research programme on adult education participation and non-participation using quantitative and qualitative methodology, such as, surveys, gatherings, life stories, case studies and comparisons.

This research has been sponsored by UIE (Hamburg's UNESCO Institute of Education), Governments of Catalonia and Galicia and CIDE (belonging to the Government of Spain).

A new orientation to qualitative research has been created by using four kinds of theoretical work:

a) reviewing the most usual methods in qualitative research and the most representative literature in social sciences;

b) reflecting on both activities from a study focused on those sectors of culturally excluded population which considers such people as persons rather than as 'cultural idiots';

c) discovering that, in the new information society, we should look for the most determining factors for cultural participation or non-participation in people's daily life context;

d) the permanent corroboration of the researchers' ontological assumptions are not more complex than those that we impute to actors.

(a) We found important differences among the most usual methods in qualitative research and the present literature in social sciences. Since Goffman (1959) developed the dramaturgic action or Garfinkel the communicative one, there have been other contributions, such as, the theory of communicative action of Habermas, the structuration theory of Giddens, the Scribner

(1988) studies on practical intelligence and others that have given a new dimension to the studies of adult education. They are the basis of qualitative methods.

(b) Social research is in permanent danger of instrumentalising people and of not taking into account that they are individuals who interpret and build their own lives. This danger increases with excluded people. Qualitative research has taken important steps forwards as it considers people persons as actors who interpret their situation and who are not, therefore, 'cultural idiots'. However, in the usual methodological development itself a deep presence of deficit theories which claim that these people do not know how to build a debate, can be seen. This methodological development must be replaced with concepts (like practical conscience and practical intelligence) so that individuals are considered as actors. This should be evident in the

(c) Actors in daily life in the present information society are slightly different from the ones taken from implicit considerations in the usual qualitative research, especially when they are taken from perspectives, like the psycho-analytical-structuralist ones, based on institutions and social life typical of industrial society. Nowadays, in many social settings, issues concerning cultural participation or non-participation are related to social relations formed in markets, cafes, work places or community centres rather than the determining factors of school or family history. In fact, participation and non-participation depend on those interpretations permanently built up in daily life and the information about the past changes according to those interpretations.

During the process, all the elements of the research have been open to public debate because of the nature of the theoretical basis to the interpretation of the findings of qualitative methodologies. Through this way, a lot of participants in adult basic education have learned much more that what they could learn on university extension courses.

3. The Communicative Elaboration of Laws of Adult Education

During two centuries of adult education in Spain, we have not had any laws in this field. Since 1990 there have been four approved already and there are more in process. The formulation of the last one, already approved (Ley de Formación de Personas Adultas de La Comunidad Valenciana), gave CREA the opportunity to act as an university open learning centre.

CREA received from the Government of Valencia the request to formulate the foundations and development of the law. Usually, those kind of processes are managed as a teleological action grounded on instrumental rationality (Habermas, 1984). In other words, the group of experts act without any connection and collective reflection with citizens. The latter are reduced to the role of *cultural dopes*, as if they knew nothing interesting about the education they need and want.

In this case, we made an agreement with the Government to conduct the process as communicative research. On the one hand, we were looking for a communicative formulation of the law as part of the needed radicalisation of modernity (Giddens, 1991) and democracy. On the other hand, we wanted to link such formulation to the development of a process of open massive learning of both the non-university public and our university centre.

The work was based on communicative action (Freire, 1990, Habermas, 1984). All the foundations of the law were subject to public debate: unlevelling effect, overcoming of ageism, adulthood and adult learning, information society, educational equality which includes difference, co-ordination of resources and initiatives and participants. These debates included the involvement of trade unions, city councils, neighbourhood associations and the federation of associations of participants in adult education.

Communicative learning is not hierarchical but horizontal. CREA teaches something to the public, but we also learn a lot from them. The federation of associations of participants was in fact the main protagonist of the process before, during and after the formulation of the law. Opening the doors of the university is not only makes it possible for the public to share our knowledge; it also, and mainly, develops new knowledge through a collaboration between the university and non-university people and institutions.

As an example, the debate about the unlevelling effect was an incredible learning opportunity for all. Many politicians, professors, professionals and participants had before the process a compensatory conception of adult education; they thought that this field was a decreasing one as it related only to those adults who had not enough schooling at the 'appropriate age'. During those processes of formulation of the adult education legislations such a conception was mostly overcome. Many participants explained their experiences of completing schooling when they were children and their educational needs now as adults. A lot of learning was developed about the information society and the key changes it produces in our lives. A lot of knowledge was also created about how to face these changes.

Even the most delicate items were the subject of open debates. The movement fought during these years for an Institute of Adult Education. But, in the moment of the debate, it was impossible to obtain it, because the Government was reducing the number of institutes. It was necessary to renounce this objective. We did not want to do it without the consensus of citizens and so we held a general assembly. No one was against the change. Participants demonstrated how mature people could act in assemblies when they are not waylaid with perlocutionary effects (Austin, 1962). The law was approved by the Parliament of the Community of Valencia.

Now analysing the experience we can say that people from the University, from the Government and social movements all learnt together, one from the other. Creating communicative spaces where all participants learn, research, and generate culture in a horizontal and democratic way is important.

References

Austin, J. L. (1962), How to Do Things with Words, Oxford, Oxford University Press.

Freire, P. (1970), The pedagogy of the oppressed, New York, Herder & Herder.

Garfinkel, H. (1967), Studies in Ethnomethodology, Englewood-Cliffs (N.J.): Prentice-Hall.

Giddens, A. (1991), Modernity and Self-Identity. Self and Society in the Late Modern Age, Cambridge and Oxford, Polity Press and Basil Blackwell.

Goffman, E. (1959) The presentation of Self in Everyday Life, New York, Anchor Press Doubleday.

Habermas, J. (1984), The Theory of Communicative Action, Vol.I: Reason and the Rationalization of Society, Boston, Beacon Press (Original work published 1981).

Leclère, L. (1893), Las Universidades Populares en los Países Anglosajones. Boletín de la Institución Libre de Enseñanza, t. XVII; p.119-125, 139-140, 179-182,.Madrid.

Merton, R. K. (1973), Sociology of science: theoretical and empirical investigations, Chicago, Chicago University Press (v.c. en Alianza Universidad, Madrid, 1977).

Scribner, S. (1988), Head and hand: An action approach to thinking, Teachers College, Columbia University, National Center On Education and Employment, (ERIC Document Reproduction Service No. CE 049 897).

Alexandre Meliva

Summary

The Development of Further Education Programmes for Adults in French Universitites

In France the universities provide approximately 5% of further education programmes. The fact that universities deliver such programmes is important as it is a special sector. They are concerned mainly with higher education which is disciplinary in character and which leads to a certificate. Target groups are employees or individuals for whom evening courses are organised. This education sector is largely shared with the CNAM.

The financial support of the government and companies, initiated by laws passed in 1971, has drastically changed the nature of their services and their participants. Before the introduction of the laws the role of universities in further education is unclear. Besides the graduate work the training and diploma work now occupies an important part of their activities. This work of the universities is non-graduate. There are some training courses which do not lead to a degree and also short placements for professional updating and long qualifying activities for professional training. These trainings have been developed since the application of the laws passed in 1971. There is a demand of people working in the economy who have identified their needs and contacted the universities. Besides these training courses the universities continue to offer training of a general nature. Here you find the 'universities' of leisure and for the retired people. Furthermore the universities who specialise in sciences tend to offer a much broader range of programmes such as engineering, applied research, consulting, technology transfer, training of the trainers etc.

The position and the conditions of the universities to deliver further education are different and depend upon whether the course is degree or non-degree level. If a degree can be taken the universities assume their usual mission: they control the validation and awarding of the certificate of the diplomas. They dispose of a quasi-likeable market and the salaries in question meet the demands they make.

As they find themselves confronted with a demand, the training programmes for qualifications appeal to the characteristic qualities of the universities, for example, the particular competences of the academic staff, access to research etc. The user pursues an aim and attends the university either full- or part-time.

In this case the demand imposes concrete requirements which the universities alone cannot meet but the competitors can take measures to meet. They have to anticipate the demand and develop a programme which meets precise requirements. This bringing in of the universities into commerce makes it necessary to create marketing and engineering capacities.

This splitting of the delivery between universities and non-universities divides institutions in terms of the disciplines they offer, the levels of programmes, the kinds of people who participate, the financial means and the type of academic staff who can be involved.

On the basis of the results of the study made by the CEREQ in 1993, the present study proposes to analyse the evolution of the forms of further education in universities by comparing the specifications of the delivery of further education in universities with the type of programmes offered globally and the changing internal heterogeneity of this structure.

De la Formation Permanente à la Formation Continue: L'évolution de l'offre de Formation Universitaire Pour Adultes

Sur la base des résultats tirés de l'enquête menée par le CEREQ en 1993[1], la présente communication se propose d'analyser successivement l'évolution

1 enquête menée par le CEREQ auprès de 645 organismes de formation continue réalisant au moins un million de chiffre d'affaire (soit 12% d'entre eux); cf. méthode et résultats dans CHARRAUD A.-M., MELIVA A., PERSONNAZ E.: 'Continuing training providers : activities, aims and publics' in Training and Employment n°24, summer 1996

des composantes de l'offre universitaire de formation continue en termes de publics, de niveaux et de spécialités dispensées, de modalités d'intervention pédagogique et de moyens dont disposent les universités.

I. L'institutionnalisation de la Formation Permanente des adultes

Dans un contexte de croissance de l'emploi et de pénurie relative de diplômés issus de la formation initiale, où les opportunités de mobilité professionnelle ascendante sont réelles, complétées éventuellement par une formation sanctionnée par un diplôme, la formation permanente des adultes à l'université jusqu'aux années 80 répond le plus souvent à un besoin de promotion sociale ou d'épanouissement/émancipation des personnes et s'opère principalement sous deux formes[2]:

- la reprise d'études dans les cursus de la formation initiale; l'attente en matière de reconnaissance suit le plus souvent une logique diplômante qui atteste d'une qualification négociable sur le marché du travail, notamment dans les conventions collectives et statuts professionnels et permet en général au salarié d'obtenir ou d'améliorer une situation professionnelle;
- l'adhésion à un programme de 'formation de promotion sociale' dans des instituts universitaires (Nancy, Toulouse, Strasbourg, Grenoble, Lille); ceux-ci sont nés pour la plupart au début des années 60 de la volonté de l'Etat d'organiser un '*droit à la deuxième chance*' en offrant les possibilités d'un rattrapage éducatif à ceux qui n'ont pas eu accès à des études initiales. Ils font le plus souvent l'objet d'une gestion syndicale paritaire. Les prestations tiennent compte des besoins de l'économie locale, dont les acteurs font appel aux universités pour bénéficier,

2 pour une plus large approche de l'idée de promotion sociale cf.:
- P.MEHAUT: 'Se former tout au long de la vie ?' in Bref n°120, mai 1996
- Dossier in 'Actualité de la Formation Permanente', n°141, mars-avril 1996
- revue 'Pour', n°148,1995

en dehors comme en cours d'emploi, de formations longues, diplômantes, de niveau supérieur (ingénieurs notamment).

Mais le blocage progressif des embauches, la réduction des opportunités de promotion, le rétrécissement de l'horizon économique des entreprises, des restructurations industrielles et une mobilité inter-entreprise qui s'accompagnent souvent d'un passage par le chômage, des grilles de classification devenues plus floues voire obsolètes du fait de la montée des activités tertiaires... les diverses manifestations de la crise de l'emploi et les évolutions qui affectent le marché du travail vont sensiblement altérer le mythe de la promotion sociale et le rendement des formations correspondantes.

Parallèlement, l'allongement de la scolarisation, l'accès plus massif à l'enseignement supérieur, la concurrence que mènent les nombreux sortants de formation initiale à la fois aux salariés dans l'emploi et aux bénéficiaires de la formation permanente contribuent à rendre moins impérative et moins attrayante la formation de promotion sociale.

La conjugaison de ces deux mouvements va profondément bouleverser le dispositif français de formation permanente.

Dans les années 70, les pouvoirs publics votent une série de lois qui précipitent le paysage éducatif français dans deux voies principales: à côté d'un système de formation initiale qui perdure, la formation permanente se concentre sur deux types de publics: les 'victimes' de la crise de l'emploi et les salariés, et contribue à l'émergence de deux principaux acteurs: l'Etat et les entreprises sur lesquels se recentre l'économie générale du système de formation permanente, devenue 'formation professionnelle continue' (FPC).

Dès lors on assiste à l'arrivée d'une multitude d'opérateurs venus d'horizons institutionnels très divers qui créent leur propre structure de formation et dont l'offre forme aujourd'hui un quasi-marché[3]:

3 En 1993, 47000 organismes sont déclarés auprès des services de l'Etat mais seulement 70% d'entre eux sont en activité, forment 9 millions de stagiaires et réalisent 34 milliards de francs (source Ministère du Travail).

- les associations à but non lucratif, la plupart versées auparavant dans la promotion sociale, l'éducation populaire, l'animation culturelle; en 1993, elles représentent le tiers du marché en CA et nombre de stagiaires accueillis[4];
- proches des entreprises, les branches professionnelles développent sous l'égide du CNPF leurs propres structures de formation (ASFO); de même les centres internes d'entreprises s'ouvrent à un public externe; ce secteur capte aujourd'hui 15% du CA total et forme 20% des stagiaires;
- les structures consulaires: CCI, Chambres d'agriculture et Chambres de Métiers représentent 8% du marché en 1993 (CA et stagiaires);
- les structures privées à but lucratif (SA, SARL, individuels) se sont multipliées; elles concentrent 20% des financements et accueillent le quart des stagiaires en 1993;
- divers Ministères tels que Education Nationale, Agriculture et Travail accompagnent leur mission première de structures de formation professionnelle, respectivement: GRETA, CFPPA et AFPA; en ce qui concerne les établissements d'enseignement supérieur, une loi formalise ce processus en 1984 en leur ouvrant tout l'espace de la formation continue par la possibilité de création de services de FPC en leur sein, principalement chargés d'assurer le financement des formations et d'enregistrer le public transitant par le canal de la FPC; en 1993, le secteur public pèse pour environ 20% des ressources et des stagiaires de formation continue, dont 6% relèvent des services d'établissements d'enseignement supérieur relevant de l'Education Nationale: CNAM, grandes écoles, et services universitaires; ces derniers, qui nous intéressent ici, contribuent pour environ 4% du CA total, 8% des stagiaires accueillis et 5% des heures dispensées en formation continue.

Si la plupart des organismes présents avant les lois de 1971 exploitent un savoir-faire déjà prouvé en matière de promotion sociale (associations,

4 Les chiffres cités, tirés de l'enquête CEREQ, ne concernent que les organismes qui réalisent plus d'un million de CA en 1993, soit 20% des organismes qui représentent 80% du marché.

CFPPA, CNAM, secteur consulaire, branches professionnelles, certaines universités), l'entrée de l'Etat et des entreprises dans leur financement va profondément changer la nature de leur public et de leurs prestations et bousculer les anciennes acceptions et contours de la formation permanente; c'est le cas des services universitaires qui, à côté d'une logique diplômante, se dotent d'une logique qualifiante.

L'évolution des formes de la formation permanente dans les universités sera abordée successivement en situant l'offre de formation continue dans leur activité globale puis en restituant la spécificité et l'hétérogénéité de l'offre universitaire dans l'offre globale de formation continue.

II. D'une Logique Diplômante à une Logique Qualifiante - Place et forme de la formation permanente des adultes dans l'offre de formation des universités.

Pour cerner la place et la forme de la formation permanente dans l'offre globale des universités, nous devons simultanément croiser deux dimensions:

- une dimension produits;
- une dimension publics.

La dimension 'produits'

L'arrivée de nouveaux financeurs a confronté les établissements d'enseignement supérieur à deux logiques coexistantes et souvent complémentaires en matière de formation continue, mises en évidence dans un rapport du CNE[5].

La première concerne toutes les formations diplômantes, qui débouchent sur des diplômes reconnus; elles relèvent de la mission traditionnelle des uni-

5 cf. Comité National d'Evaluation : 'Universités : les chances de l'ouverture. Rapport au Président de la République', juin 1991

versités et occupent naturellement une place essentielle dans l'activité, qu' elles conduisent à la délivrance d'un titre national ou d'un diplôme propre à l'établissement.

La seconde logique est celle des formations non diplômantes, c'est-à-dire qui ne visent pas un diplôme reconnu. Elles recouvrent une grande variété de situations d'un établissement à l'autre. On peut distinguer:

- les stages courts d'actualisation des connaissances et de perfectionnement professionnel, les actions qualifiantes de formation professionnelle. Ces formations se sont développées en application des lois de 1971. La demande émane d'acteurs de l'économie qui, face à des besoins identifiés, font appel aux universités;
- les formations de culture générale, dont les 'universités' du temps libre et du troisième âge; les publics en attendent moins un diplôme que la 'valeur ajoutée' que confère la fréquentation de l'université, voire une amélioration de leur qualité de vie.[6]

Par ailleurs, les universités à vocation scientifique interviennent souvent dans un ensemble plus vaste qui regroupe aussi l'ingénierie, la recherche appliquée, le conseil, le transfert de technologies, la formation de formateurs...

La dimension 'publics'

Une enquête du Ministère de l'Education Nationale (MEN) menée auprès de 10 universités en 1992 [7] distingue et évalue trois types de public:

- le public traditionnel étudiant inscrit en formation initiale, autour de 70% du public total accueilli;

6 cf. FOND-HARMANT L. 'Cycles de vie et fonction sociale de l'offre universitaire de formation d'adultes' in Actualité de la formation permanente, n°141, mars-avril 1996

7 cf. BEDUWE C. et ESPINASSE J.-M. 'L'université et ses publics' in Education et Formations,1995, n°40.

- le public de la formation permanente; il représente environ 30% de l'offre globale moyenne et se compose:
  - d'adultes en reprise d'études inscrits auprès des services administratifs de l'université dans un cursus de formation initiale diplômante; ce public se distingue du précédent par son âge supérieur à l'âge normal, un parcours laissant souvent apparaître une interruption d'études, et un statut sur le marché du travail 'actif'; il correspond à l'ancienne forme de promotion sociale en université; l'enquête MEN l'évalue entre 7% et 32% du public total selon le nombre de critères retenus mais l'estime en moyenne autour de 28%; dans l'enquête CEREQ il représente environ 55% du public formation permanente;
  - des stagiaires de la formation professionnelle continue, aux caractéristiques identiques à celles du public précédent, mais distincts par le seul fait qu'assurant le financement de leur formation à partir de leurs fonds, d'une prise en charge de l'Etat ou de leur employeur, ils s'inscrivent directement auprès du service de FPC de l'université. Selon l'enquête MEN, ils ne représenteraient qu'environ 2% du public total, soit selon l'enquête du CEREQ 40% des publics de formation permanente: les salariés d'entreprises comptent en moyenne pour 20%, les demandeurs d'emploi pour 10% et les 'individuels', bien qu'ils soient confondus au public adulte, pour environ 15%.

Le champ et les formes de la formation continue universitaire

Par croisement des dimensions 'produits' et 'publics', on aboutit à une délimitation et une compréhension de la diversité des formes de la formation permanente en université (cf. tableau 2.1). Si le public d'adultes en reprise d'études est concentré sur les formations initiales diplômantes, les publics de la formation professionnelle continue évoluent:

- dans des formations diplômantes, qu'il s'agisse
  - des formations initiales (FI) où il se confond généralement au public étudiant; l'organisation pédagogique des cursus fait dans ce cas l'objet d'adaptations de nature diverse aux nécessités du public adulte (préparation des diplômes à temps partiel par regroupement des enseignements ou aménagement des horaires, enseignement à distance...);
  - de formations créées spécifiquement pour ce public et débouchant sur des diplômes identiques à ceux délivrés aux étudiants -dans ce cas la demande émane du marché et la FPC donne un banc d'essai de nouvelles formations (Maîtrise Sciences et Techniques, diplômes d'universités par exemple); la plupart du temps, ces formations, initiées par les services FPC, sont financées par les individus eux-mêmes lorsqu'ils ne relèvent pas d'un dispositif de financement.

  L'activité de formation continue en matière de formations diplômantes se rapproche de l'ancienne activité de formation de promotion sociale.

- dans des formations non diplômantes:
  - les actions qualifiantes sont plutôt destinées à des salariés en formule inter ou intra-entreprise, ou des demandeurs d'emploi; on touche là au 'noyau dur' de la FPC;
  - les formations de culture générale, le plus souvent financées par les individus eux-mêmes, s'apparentent à l'ancienne activité d'éducation permanente.

Tableau 2.1: Diversité des formes de la formation continue en université

		Formations Diplomantes - titres nationaux -diplômes d'universités	Formations non Diplomantes	% FPer *	% TOT **
FI	Etudiants typiques	Formation initiale	-	-	68
F P	Adultes en reprise d'études	Formation initiale (Promotion sociale)	-	55	30
E R M A N E N T E	Stagiaires FC sur financement - d'entreprises: salariés inter ou intra - de l'Etat: demandeurs d'emploi - individuel	Formation initiale ou Cursus spécifiques (Promotion sociale)	Stages courts Actions qualifiantes ('noyau dur' FPC) Culture générale Hors âge Temps libre (Educ. permanente)	20 10 15	2

*enquête CEREQ **enquête MEN

Comme le souligne le rapport du CNE, les modalités d'intervention des universités dans la formation professionnelle continue sont différentes selon qu'elles opèrent dans l'une ou l'autre logique.

Dans le cas des formations diplômantes, les universités assument leur mission de toujours: elles maîtrisent l'offre comme elles le font en matière de formation initiale et assurent la délivrance du diplôme. Elles disposent d'un marché quasi captif et les salariés concernés satisfont aux exigences qu'elles édictent.

Se situant plus directement dans une logique de la demande, les formations qualifiantes font appel aux qualités propres des universités: compétences particulières des enseignants, label, accès à la recherche... L'utilisateur poursuit un objectif dont il '*sous-traite*' tout ou partie à l'université. (...) Dans ce cas, la demande impose des exigences concrètes que les universités ne sont pas seules à pouvoir satisfaire et la concurrence peut jouer avec plus ou moins de vigueur. Elles doivent aller au devant de la demande et construire une offre adaptée à des besoins précis. Cette insertion de l'université dans la société marchande requiert la mise en oeuvre de capacités de marketing et d'ingénierie.

Les universités qui auparavant s'étaient engagées dans des programmes de '*formation de promotion sociale*' se repositionnent le plus souvent en prenant appui sur leur expérience passée, les autres en innovant complètement.

Les composantes de droit et de sciences économiques constituent un ensemble aux pratiques distinctes avec une relative autonomie d'action. L'antériorité et la structure même de leurs activités contribuent à pérenniser leurs spécificités. C'est ce qui se passe par exemple dans les sciences économiques avec les Instituts d'Administration des Entreprises, qui bénéficient d'un double amarrage, à l'université qui offre ses ressources, au tissu économique qui garantit l'assise de la demande.

Ce clivage va traverser les différentes composantes de l'offre: les disciplines et les niveaux dispensés, les types de publics accueillis et de financement perçus mais aussi les ressources pédagogiques mobilisées.

III. L'activité de fpc des Services D'universités: L'évolution des Composantes de la Formation Supérieure des Adultes en termes de publics, de niveaux et de spécialités dispensées, de modalités d'intervention pédagogique et de moyens dont disposent les universités.

Les résultats, tirés de l'enquête du CEREQ, présentent les spécificités des prestations des universités dans l'offre de formation continue mais aussi l'hétérogénéité interne de cet ensemble composite. Car les universités ne s'investissent pas également dans la FPC et les deux logiques n'y sont pas également présentes.

Disciplines proposées

En matière de formations initiales, les disciplines ne sont pas toutes pareillement sollicitées par la FPC: les sciences exactes, la gestion, les langues vivantes sont des spécialités très présentes alors que les lettres classiques, la sociologie, la philosophie, l'ethnologie, certaines langues concourent peu à la formation professionnelle continue. Les sciences exactes confèrent un relatif monopole aux universités (28% des heures totales dispensées en FPC) alors que la gestion et les langues subissent une concurrence rude (respectivement 14% et 8% de part de marché).

A contrario, les formations à l'informatique, celles de l'enseignement ou de la santé constituent de véritables actions de formation continue. Ces spécialités comportent un public actif -salarié ou demandeur d'emploi- plus important que les premières et confèrent aux universités une part de marché confortable (respectivement 10%, 27% et 15% des heures totales dispensées en FPC).

Niveaux dispensés et certifications délivrées

Les services universitaires accueillent en moyenne 90% de leurs stagiaires et dispensent 80% des heures sur des formations aux niveaux supérieurs au bac, dont plus de la moitié au niveau bac+4; niveau auquel, jouissant d'un quasi-monopole (40% de part de marché), ils rencontrent principalement les prestations du CNAM, des organismes privés, de certaines associations proches des entreprises et des CCI.

Ces tendances sont à nuancer en fonction de la part que prennent l'une et l'autre logique, les actions qualifiantes et les actions diplômantes dans l'offre des établissements.

Dans certaines structures, les formations supérieures représentent en effet moins de 50% des heures, celles-ci sont alors dispensées sur des niveaux intermédiaires ou sans référence à un niveau quelconque.

S'agissant des formations qualifiantes, le client peut exiger de n'avoir qu'un seul fournisseur pour des formations destinées à des salariés de tous niveaux. Dans ce cas, pour obtenir un marché qui comporte certaines formations situées à son niveau, une université peut être amenée à intervenir dans des formations éloignées de son espace de compétence. On verra par exemple le service de FC d'une université assurer des formations de niveau V parce que celles-ci font partie d'un projet global d'entreprise qui comporte aussi des formations de niveau supérieur.

Si tous les services assurent une validation des acquis, celle-ci se fait principalement sur des diplômes d'université qui concernent en moyenne 42% des stagiaires alors que les diplômes d'Etat en concernent en moyenne le quart.

Les diplômés sur titre d'Etat sont proportionnellement plus nombreux dans les sciences exactes et dans les services d'universités où prime un public salarié et un financement d'entreprises; les diplômés d'universités, plus fréquents dans les disciplines de sciences humaines, de gestion, d'enseignement et de formation, sont aussi plus nombreux dans les services où prime un public demandeur d'emploi et un financement public.

Publics, financeurs et environnement socio-économique

Si la plupart des stagiaires inscrits à titre individuel -c'est-à-dire ne relevant d'aucun dispositif- acquittent leurs droits directement auprès des services administratifs des universités, ceux qui suivent sur leurs propres moyens des formations spécifiques initiées par les services de FPC génèrent en moyenne 15% des ressources de FPC, ce qui est supérieur aux autres organismes.

Les fonds publics représentent en moyenne 40% de leurs ressources. Les services universitaires entretiennent des relations avec toutes les institutions publiques; cependant, en matière de financement, ce sont les régions qui sont leurs principaux bailleurs de fonds; en moyenne, elles financent les universités à hauteur du quart de leurs ressources (contre 7,3% dans l'ensemble des organismes) alors que l'Etat n'intervient que pour 15% en moyenne. De même, à part les organismes d'accueil, d'information et d'orientation, les universités s'investissent peu dans des relations avec des acteurs sociaux tels que des organismes d'aide aux handicapés, des bureaux d'aide sociale, des associations culturelles et sportives,...

Dans leur contractualisation avec les employeurs -qui représentent en moyenne le tiers de leurs ressources-, les universités préfèrent les conventions directement conclues avec les entreprises (22% de leurs fonds) à la contractualisation avec des établissements publics (7%) ou avec une fédération ou une branche professionnelle. En général, les entreprises avec lesquelles traitent les universités sont plutôt de grande taille (plus de 500 salariés) que des PME-PMI. Elles évoluent le plus souvent dans des secteurs de pointe: industries agro-alimentaires, énergie, biens intermédiaires, services marchands, organismes financiers. Si la plupart des services universitaires ont réalisé des actions intra-entreprises, celles-ci contribuent pour une faible part de leur CA (17% en moyenne).

Si la plupart des universités sont en relation avec des organismes mutualisateurs de fonds, elles recourent peu à leur médiation en matière de financement; représentant 6% du CA, ils sont surtout des donneurs d'ordre de prestations occasionnelles pour des universités portées vers un public salarié.

L'équilibre des actions n'est jamais garanti. L'évolution des règles qui président à la participation des entreprises au financement de la FPC et les modifications dans les responsabilités respectives de l'Etat et des régions dues aux lois de décentralisation apportent un supplément de complexité et d'instabilité. Bien que peu d'universités aient mis en place une comptabilité analytique et que les charges prises en compte dans l'établissement des coûts soient très variables d'une université à l'autre, les universités pâtissent en général d'une forte proportion de charges afférentes à l'administration et à la gestion; celles-ci représentent en moyenne 25% du coût des actions conclues avec l'Etat.

Les stratégies d'équilibre des actions vont alors sensiblement différer selon les logiques de formation.

Les universités les plus attentives à l'équilibre financier des actions oeuvrent principalement en formations diplômantes alors que celles où prime l'activité de FPC peuvent concevoir un possible déséquilibre financier. Celles qui traitent avec les bailleurs publics motivent ce déséquilibre par l'assurance de bénéficier d'un financement pérenne alors que celles qui sont plus portées vers un financement privé y voient un moyen d'une implantation sur un nouveau marché ou le sentiment d'une utilité sociale.

Dans un souci d'équilibre financier des actions, les universités où prime une logique diplômante feront plus souvent appel aux fonds publics dans le cadre d'un dispositif, engageront des actions à publics multiples, signifiant plusieurs financeurs, ou des actions inter-sectorielles ou encore privilégieront des formations générales disciplinaires.

Alors que celles où prime une logique qualifiante mettront plutôt en place des actions courtes et de perfectionnement professionnel pour un type de public unique, notamment les salariés, privilégieront les actions de branche, et les formations tertiaires et administratives et celles des services.

Durée des actions et modalités pédagogiques proposées

La durée des actions est très variable selon les publics: tournant autour de 270 heures en ce qui concerne les demandeurs d'emploi (soit la moyenne des autres organismes), elle oscille autour de 145 heures pour les salariés, ce qui est dépasse les durées enregistrées dans l'ensemble des organismes.

Peu distinctes des autres organismes en matière d'alternance, ou d'enseignement à distance, les universités tirent leur spécificité pédagogique d'une certaine disponibilité en cours du soir. Cette pratique est adoptée par plus de la moitié d'entre elles et est en relation positive avec un public constitué de salariés.

Tandis que les universités financées sur fonds publics pratiquent plus souvent l'alternance des lieux de formation université/entreprise.

Seules les universités où domine une logique qualifiante (forte proportion de salariés et demandeurs d'emploi) assurent un suivi des stagiaires après formation; il est mené le plus souvent par les associations d'anciens élèves qui maintiennent un contact d'au moins six moins avec les stagiaires.

Eléments de stratégie et démarche qualité

Dans une perspective d'amélioration de leur stratégie, contrairement à l'ensemble des organismes, les universités ne cherchent pas en priorité à maintenir ou développer leur part de marché.

Elles s'attachent en premier lieu soit à une diversification de leur gamme de produits et de leurs prestations (40%), soit à recentrer leur activité sur des produits et des prestations majeurs (30%), ou encore à différencier leurs prestations par rapport à celles de leurs concurrents (20%).

Alors que la première stratégie correspond à des services plus portés vers une activité de formation initiale diplômante, les deux dernières caractérisent les services plus orientés FPC: la deuxième correspond à ceux qui s'adressent en priorité à un public demandeur d'emploi, la troisième est plus le fait de services dispensant des formations pour les salariés.

La plupart des universités appliquent des normes de qualité; elles sont le plus souvent internes à l'université et mises au point à partir d'une réflexion de l'équipe pédagogique. Cette pratique semble être notamment plus répandue dans les universités portées vers un public d'individuels qui suivent des formations diplômantes.

Politique de communication et démarche commerciale

Toutes les universités mènent une politique de communication externe. Leur spécificité tient à la cible visée par les messages qui, à côté des entreprises, privilégient les stagiaires potentiels des formations.

Le contenu des messages porte à la fois sur la qualité des prestations et sur des informations pratiques ayant trait aux actions de formation mises en place par l'organisme; les premiers sont plus le fait des universités oeuvrant dans une logique diplômante alors que les deuxièmes sont le fait de celles versant dans une logique qualifiante.

Si les supports restent traditionnels -catalogue des stages et plaquette d'information sur le service-, les universités se distinguent des autres organismes par la spécification des coûts des stages.

Au delà de la politique de communication, la promotion du service passe par deux démarches essentielles: le mailing et la réponse à des appels d'offre publics; la visite et l'information auprès des entreprises d'un secteur spécifique arrive en deuxième lieu.

Là encore, le clivage diplômant/qualifiant semble discriminant des pratiques de promotion: quand l'université table sur le prolongement de son savoir-faire traditionnel, le service ne développe pas de fonction d'ingénierie ou de marketing; à l'inverse, les services qui opèrent le plus pour le marché sont obligées de s'organiser pour aller au-devant de la demande. Ainsi le mailing auprès des stagiaires potentiels est plus souvent le fait des universités à public individuel majoritaire, alors que les deux autres modes sont caractéristiques de services opérant dans une logique qualifiante: la réponse à des appels d'offre publics est le mode de promotion caractéristique des services comportant un public demandeur d'emploi important, la visite auprès d'entreprises étant la démarche privilégiée par les universités tournées vers le public salarié.

Ressources pédagogiques

En matière de ressources pédagogiques, la gestion du personnel enseignant en formation continue dans les universités procède fortement d'un appel à des ressources extérieures à l'établissement: vacataires ou contractuels. Les intervenants extérieurs en université sont principalement des enseignants dans la formation initiale employés par un recours aux heures supplémentaires; ce profil est notamment plus important dans les formations destinées aux demandeurs d'emploi et financées sur fonds publics. En moyenne générale, le quart des professeurs contribue à la FPC, avec une variation entre 10 et 90%, suivant l'importance des deux logiques.

La raison principalement invoquée à ce recours est le besoin de compétences non disponibles dans des domaines d'expertise ou sur un plan pédagogique alors que le souci de s'adapter aux fluctuations de l'activité est en général peu invoqué par les universités; les universités n'ont en effet qu'une autonomie partielle en matière de recrutement et de rémunération des personnels.

Si la première raison est surtout partagée par les services comportant en majorité un public hors FPC, les considérations de nature économique sont davantage avancées par les services à composantes qualifiantes.

Parmi les universités enquêtées, la majorité des services sont dirigés par un professionnel de la formation (formateur, responsable pédagogique ou directeur d'organisme de formation) et oeuvrent dans une logique qualifiante alors que les services dirigés par un enseignant de la formation initiale évoluent plutôt sur une logique diplômante. Selon le CNE, le niveau auquel le directeur ou le responsable de formation du service se situe dans la hiérarchie des grades universitaires conditionne pour partie le degré de considération et la collaboration de la communauté universitaire; une collaboration insuffisante engendre un appel massif à des vacataires avec le risque de voir le service devenir un corps étranger à l'université.

Bien que l'importance des non-réponses aux tarifs pratiqués en matière de prestations externes n'autorise pas un traitement de cette question, l'enquête révèle des traitements supérieurs à la moyenne dans les universités; ce qui n'est pas sans poser de problèmes entre les enseignants de l'université et les formateurs externes où des distorsions amples existent dans les systèmes de rémunérations, entre les enseignants de FI et ceux qui évoluent en FPC dont l'activité n'est pas prise en compte dans l'évolution des carrières. Dans le domaine des formations qualifiantes, plus ouvert à la concurrence, l'université ne se présente pas à armes égales avec le secteur privé qui peut aller jusqu'à attirer ses enseignants avec de meilleures rémunérations.

Ressources matérielles

L'attribution de moyens et de locaux par le Ministère ne tient pas compte de la FPC dans ses ratios. Aussi surgissent des problèmes dus à la concurrence entre formation initiale et FPC, d'autant plus aigus que le service se développe, que les cursus s'allongent, que le public augmente. Dans le domaine des formations qualifiantes, des conditions d'accueil inférieures à ce qu'offrent les organismes concurrents peuvent être à l'origine d'une moindre fréquentation.

Les investissements pédagogiques des universités ont augmenté entre 1991 et 1993; en 1993, la plupart, essentiellement constituées de publics de la FPC, en avaient réalisé entre 5 et 10% de leur CA; au-delà de 10% du CA, on trouve essentiellement des services opérant sur fonds publics. Ces dépenses ont surtout porté sur des équipements et outils pédagogiques.

En matière de locaux, où est particulièrement vive la concurrence entre FI et FPC, les surfaces dont disposent les services universitaires sont en moyenne plus élevées que dans les autres organismes.

La majorité d'entre eux disposent d'un centre de documentation, d'équipements audiovisuels, de salles informatiques. Si les deux premiers sont particulièrement présents dans les centres où évolue un public individuel, le troisième est caractéristique de services orientés vers les salariés. Les laboratoires de langues, plus composés d'individuels, sont moins représentés.

Alors que les services davantage portés vers les salariés ont tendance à louer leurs locaux, ceux destinant leurs formations vers des demandeurs d'emploi les acquièrent sur subventions publiques, tandis que ceux qui évoluent plus sur une logique diplômante déclarent financer leurs propres locaux.

CONCLUSION: Entre une logique institutionnelle et une logique économique, quel modèle organisationnel des universités pour une formation tout au long de la vie?

De l'exploration des divers aspects que revêt l'offre de formation permanente universitaire, on est frappé par la singularité des services dispensés par les universités et en même temps l'extrême hétérogénéité de cet ensemble composite. Les situations sont contrastées sur de nombreux points, depuis la définition de la politique générale jusqu'au suivi et à l'évaluation des résultats. Les structures, moyens et activités offrent un nombre considérable de cas de figure: chaque université est particulière.

Cette hétérogénéité est largement portée par le clivage diplômant/qualifiant qui lui-même recoupe à bien des égards celui de l'institution et du marché; il soulève des problèmes de politique interne qui renvoient à des questions de régulation institutionnelle et de coordination économique que partagent aujourd'hui la plupart des organisations publiques qui évoluent sur un marché concurrentiel, que ce soit dans le domaine des télécommunications, du logement[8] ou des transports[9].

C'est sans doute tout autant un problème organisationnel qui guette la question de la formation tout au long de la vie. En recentrant l'action sur des formations diplômantes, répondant au besoin de l'individu, et dispensées sur des durées relativement longues, l'idée d'une formation tout au long de la vie rejoint le concept français de la formation de promotion sociale.

Sur ces formations les universités semblaient être les mieux placées; ayant abordé la formation professionnelle continue par les formations diplômantes, ne serait-ce que par leur capacité à attribuer des diplômes ou le fait qu'elle sont les seules à disposer de la plus large palette de savoirs mis à jour et enrichis par la recherche, elles se sont délibérément placées dans une logique de l'offre et ont développé leur action sur un marché semi-captif.

Or cette activité aujourd'hui fait justement problème en matière de formation continue: l'examen des différentes composantes de l'offre universitaire met en évidence une relation positive entre une logique diplômante et une régulation de nature institutionnelle, ou négative avec une coordination de nature marchande. Le rapport du CNE relève plusieurs points où apparaissent ça et là les contradictions.

Ainsi, au-delà de l'ampleur des problèmes qui occupent les dirigeants en matière de formation initiale, n'invoque-t-il pas, pour expliquer le manque de visibilité et l'intérêt inégalement porté à la FPC par les différentes universités, 'des structures administratives peu adaptées' -contrairement à l'enseignement secondaire où la question de la FPC est nettement mieux prise en compte, l'autonomie et le caractère disparate des établissements universitaires se prêtent mal à une appréhension homogène et commune de la FPC-, la

8 cf. EYMARD-DUVERNAY F. et MARCHAL E.: 'Les règles en action : entre une organisation et ses usagers', Centre d'Etudes de l'Emploi, Oct. 1993

9 cf. HATCHUEL A., JOUGLEUX M., PALLEZ F.: 'Innovation de produit et modernité publique', Ecole des mines de Paris, avril 1993

'rigidité des règles internes' et le 'difficile jeu entre formation initiale et FPC' qui accroissent les obstacles liés à la mobilisation et l'allocation des ressources de tous types, 'un marketing déficient par rapport à celui des organismes privés, des rigidités bureaucratiques qui entravent l'essor là où la souplesse est requise'?

Et cette contradiction inhérente à l'organisation formatrice risque de s'accentuer d'autant que la tendance que prennent les universités ne semble pas aller en faveur d'une rencontre des deux logiques.

Dans ces conditions, la question est bien de savoir de quelles régulations, de quel modèle, quelle forme, choix et conditions organisationnels nouveaux peut être porteuse l'idée d'une formation tout au long de la vie dans les universités.

Section 4

The Information Technology Challenge to Lifelong Learning

Peter von Mitschke-Collande / Frieder Nake

The Information Technology Challenge to Lifelong Learning

It is generally assumed, and somehow taken for granted, that information and communication technology will cause a leap forward for lifelong learning. This assumption has its root in the fact that computers are becoming widely available: they are used in many private homes, in an increasing numbers of workplaces, and in many public institutions, and are being built into all sorts of technical systems. The world-wide spread of the Internet during the last three years has produced even greater expectations as to the direct, immediate, and limitless access to 'knowledge'. To the extent that lifelong learning is an open and uncontrolled activity outside of formal institutions, information technology appears to many as a tremendous support for, if not the best of, all media.

The information technology challenge could therefore be understood as a technical impulse for an improved performance that has to be taken up by educators organising or delivering units of lifelong learning opportunities. Aspects of information technology that people think of in this context are: learning on demand (or just in time), multimedia software, world-wide access to linked information structures, interactive educational software, and more.

Given the tremendous attention that information technology attracts in the press and other public media, the number of just 15 participants in this section may be disappointing. If it is true that information technology is the future, that all learning processes in the near future will comprise some use of networked computers, then why do not more educators take an interest in a discussion of precisely this topic? One possible explanation is that educators do not really put too high hopes on the thesis of technology shaping the future. Perhaps they still believe that technology is not all that interesting, or that simply using a computer for text processing, file management, an occasional drawing exercise, and perhaps some surfing of the vast storage accessible by the Internet, can easily be mastered by anybody, and therefore does not warrant any special attention.

The section was highlighted by five paper presentations and much dedication to lively discussion. The papers were:

Kate O'Dubhchair (University of Ulster, Northern Ireland)
Information technology – a gateway to lifelong learning

In a rural situation with high unemployment, a need for higher education was felt, and an attempt was made, to leapfrog to the fore-front of the information society by making available to the public university-level courses, technical equipment, and even a whole building with plenty of opportunities. Computers are used as a means in teaching three modules.

Tilman Hartenstein (Association for Adapted Adult Education, Norway)
Open and distance learning – a second chance for disabled persons

A large European project with participating institutions from six countries has just been launched that tries to give people with various kinds of disabilities an easier access to higher education. Computers are used for the distribution of materials via the Internet, perhaps for adjusting materials, and to build and maintain a large database (even after the project finishes).

Eero Pantzar (University of Tampere, Finland)
Using communication and information technology in university level adult education

Despite the great opportunities that information technology offers today, its infrastructure is not maximally exploited in Finland. Barriers to a broader implementation were identified as: cost, lack of services, computer illiteracy, traditional thinking, lack of enthusiasm among providers, low data transfer rates, and lack of time and effort.

Norbert Siggelkow (Universität Hannover, Germany)
Information technology as a subject and medium for professional development of civil engineers

A study programme leading to a certificate has been established and formally approved by the authorities. The programme will help civil engineers to brush up their know-how, particularly in using computer software for modern ways of structure calculation (by the finite elements method). The computer is also used as a means to facilitate communication between the many different experts that are involved in planning a building. In the study programme, students get their materials through electronic channels. They work from a distance, but occasionally meet for a seminar. Under current economic pressure, however, these seminars are no longer popular, since small companies cannot afford to send engineers to such training.

Gerhard Fischer (University of Colorado, Boulder, USA)
Making learning a part of life – beyond the gift-wrapping approach of technology

Against the background of many projects carried out in the Centre for Lifelong Learning and Design, a broad view of lifelong learning was given. It should not be restricted to adult education, and, in fact, should become the general activity in education. When computers are used, and they should be used extensively; they should disappear in the cognitive background. Nobody should have to struggle with the medium more than with the problem. The gift-wrapping approach would put the old, but untouched contents, marked by Skinner's and F.W. Taylor's concepts, into an attractive technological parcel. Instead, a great variety of different approaches should become available, if the use of high technology in learning is going to make sense. In other words, computers by themselves do not change education; just offering information via a new medium does not change the information. The new medium turned into a usable form and applied by good educators would, however, make a difference.

In the discussion, it became clear that learning is about adjusting values, gaining experience, and acquiring information. It can be, and often is, organised according to these three layers. In general, it is about changing a person's behaviour. Traditionally, this is organised in a great variety of person-to-person situations. When information technology is introduced into learning situations (particularly, if these are isolated learning situations), emphasis may easily be placed on the lower of these three layers of learning. It should be clear that these layers are interdependent. Therefore, isolating information acquisition, and putting it onto a machine, destroys the major orientation of learning for the sake of its most basic facet. All the knowledge of the world is at your fingertips, and easy connections to everyone and to the best of all, are typical propaganda slogans for computers in learning. It is the propaganda for the information superhighway.

If this rather exaggerated claim was true at all, it would presuppose a transformation of implicit (tacit) knowledge into some explicit form. Otherwise, it could not become part of software. The transformation of some entity or process from an implicit to an explicit state, necessary for any software development, could also be viewed as the transformation of subjective into objective forms of knowledge.

But such a transformation is not knowledge-preserving. It changes knowledge in fact, it reduces knowledge to information, and it further reduces information to data. What a computer can store, process, transmit, and output, are only signals. Signals are the physical forms of signs. Signs are what gets moved in thinking (as Carles Sanders Peirce, the American philosopher and founder of modern semiotics, once remarked: 'we cannot but think in signs'). In the case of the computer, signals coincide with data. So we do not get any knowledge out of any computer. All we get is data, and it is up to us to use those data and construct knowledge from them.

All the hope surrounding information technology boils down to nothing but quantity: get faster access to more data. This may be interesting in certain learning situations, but it is definitely not interesting in all situations. The myth of information technology is that its subject matter was knowledge or intelligence, not data and computable functions. It is disappointing to realise how many still blow the horn of that myth though they should know better.

Information technology may facilitate some processes, and it does so, indeed. But it is still endangered by mistaking the techniques of data storage and data access for contents which is a rather stupid idea. The idea is so stupid that it must be wrapped into the repeated announcement of 'knowledge storage and access'.

Ever since the writings of Humberto Maturana and Francisco Varela, it should have become clear that knowledge and information are not commodities; they do not come in pieces, and they cannot be transferred from one place to another. Learning is a deeply situated process of high context-dependency, two aspects that totally evade the computer.

T.S. Eliot once wrote: 'Where is the wisdom we have lost in knowledge, where is the knowledge we have lost in information?', and we could continue this by the line, 'where is the information we have lost in data?'. Each of the steps hinted at here marks a higher degree of explicitness but learning takes place implicitly, it is only supported by explicit artifacts.

The contradiction that marks the limits of the use of information technology in learning processes, could also be rephrased by the tension between closed and open systems. Technical systems are always closed, even if used interactively. Learning systems are always open. This contradiction determines the use of information technology in learning. It follows from here that information technology (software, in particular) can play only a very limited role in any learning situation. The situation has to be arranged such that the technical system can be easily accessed and used by the learner whenever the learner has a need for this.

The great motivation many children and adults experience when freely using the computer comes from its immediacy, its reliability, speed, imagery, directness, fast feedback, and lack of human intervention (at least superficially). When a learning environment is characterised to a sufficient degree by elements of an explicit, objective, yet non-material nature, it may be worthwhile to turn them into software and offer that software (consisting of data and programmes) as one additional component of the environment to learners. This would be an enlightened position vis-à-vis information technology. You would not totally rely on the artefact, but trust the human's motivation and activity, and you would still make an effort to produce a rich, stimulating medium.

Knowledge remains part of our experience in life. Data is a commodity. Propagandists want to set the two into one. Educators should not allow them to do this, they should nevertheless use information technology, and should stress the difference between human knowledge and machine data.

We do not gain better access to knowledge, rather the nature of knowledge gets changed in a certain way. It gets trivialised when it becomes data on a machine. One-way physical exchange of data between a human and a machine is different from two-way semiotic exchange of information between two persons, which, in turn, is different from communication of two or more people trying to use their knowledge.

One further issue was raised during the section's sessions. Why are national governments, and the EC, promoting information and communication technology programmes so strongly? The way it gets published, and the effort given to technology-aided self-controlled learning, raises a suspicion that the public sector is trying to transfer to the individual the responsibility for learning, particularly for continuing education and training. This seems to be in line with the policy of private employer's associations. In consequence, learning and the risk of economic survival would become more and more privatised; a development that would be in line with the strive to turn knowledge and information into market commodities.

The section made it quite clear that education organised as a separate, institutionalised effort could (in part) be turned into lifelong learning as something happening while you live your life. It should be rewarding to organise an intensive workshop of educators and computer scientists to hammer out, in great detail, some of the issues that surfaced in this discussion.

Kate O'Dubhchair

Information Technology - A Gateway to Lifelong Learning

Introduction

This paper documents a unique partnership which brings together university and community in an effort to open up the University to the community and facilitate collective and individual learning in support of community economic development.

This partnership builds on an existing relationship and the developments recorded here are set against recent Rural Development Initiatives and against the potential growth of the Information Society and the role of Information Technology in society.

The region I am discussing is that of the county of Fermanagh, Northern Ireland, which lies on the extreme west of Northern Ireland and epitomises all the needs and difficulties of peripherality in an area renowned for it's unspoilt beauty.The immediate area has a population of approximately 55,000 with a wider catchment area in excess of 250,000. Led by Fermanagh District Council the people of the region are very proactive and over twenty years a substantial network of community groups and community activity has been established.

The University involved in the relationship is the University of Ulster which, as many of you will know, has an ongoing commitment to community outreach and continuing education. The University has recently amended it's mission statement to specifically include provision of lifelong learning and rural outreach.

This story begins ten years ago when the Special Telecommunications Action Programme for Remote Regions (STAR) was launched in the European Union, with an overall aim of bringing peripheral regions 'up to speed' in terms of Information Communication Technology (ICT) by the provision of both infrastructure and services and stimulation of uptake by users. Two years later, in 1988 Northern Ireland became involved and a call for bids for funding was launched. The lion's share of monies available went to British Telecom for a fibre optic network to support Integrated Digital Services Network (ISDN) but small grants were available to encourage providers and potential users. With considerable insight and vision the Chief Executive of the council approached the University's Faculty of Informatics to put forward a bid centred around the regional vocational ethos of tourism and craft and design. The bid was successful and led to the creation of the Fermanagh STAR Centre and to five years of productive work. I would like to emphasise at this point that the focus of the work was always drawn from the community and that throughout great care was taken not to compete with local providers but to work with all the other players in the field to add to the total sum of activity. At the end of the funding period there was evidence of real economic development associated with the project; creation of jobs. In addition the Centre had moved to viability and was making a small profit. Two independent assessments placed the Fermanagh Project first among all the STAR projects in Northern Ireland.

As the STAR project reached a natural conclusion the University and Fermanagh District Council met to consider their relationship and whether it should continue and in what form and with what role in the community. The process was carried out formally and thoroughly as a part of the derivation of a five years Regional Economic Development Strategy. The result showed access to higher education and telecommunications as key factors in future economic development of the region.

The challenge, of course, has been how to deliver these overarching themes in an imaginative and constructive manner. Effort went into devising an appropriate model for delivery still firmly rooted in community ownership, complementarity and a broad view of University activity. The result has been the creation of the University Partnership Board and the physical plans of the Fermanagh Higher Bridges project.

The remainder of this paper will explore the mechanisms used in the early relationship that we believe fostered a spirit of co-operation and community ownership, the realities of implementation and the conceptual outline of what we hope to achieve through the Board and by this expanded presence of the University of Ulster in Fermanagh.

Background

Over the last decade many writers have expressed views on the changing nature of society and in particular the effect of information technology. There is something of a consensus that we are moving into the 'information age' or era and this is reflected in recent EU initiatives all centred on the 'Information Society, Europe's Way to the Information Society, An Action Plan' (1994), Europe and the Global Information Society [1994]. In fact some regions notably in Finland and Denmark have already put in place regional plans for implementation of the information society, 'Developing a Finnish Information Society', (1995), 'From Vision to Action, Info-Society 2000', Danish Government, March 1995. The latter initiatives seem to me something to be heartily welcomed as they bring us back to a model where the people and the individual are again in charge of shaping society. Prior to this there was a distinct feeling that the common belief was that technology was deterministic. This view was strongly reinforced by the plethora of studies of impact and effect.

Computer literacy or technology literacy is talked of as a need to understand and communicate more in society but seldom as a vehicle through which to develop and shape society. Yet we have writers from the seventies advocating us 'to use the best technology that we know, but to make it an aid to those who work with it, so that their work becomes an enrichment of their humanity, and so that the resource which their abilities represent is used to the highest degree'. Similarly dictums of both the OECD (1986) and the Standing Conference of European Ministers of Education (1991) cause us to reflect on the sociological implications of information and communication technologies: 'The important issue remains then to understand the modalities of growth of information and to maintain its development so as to master the consequences... the role and responsibility of education in this respect are indisputable, and 'Education should now take a more proactive stance towards society, the new information and communications technologies... should not be rejected but accommodated through a more critical approach based on the fundamental values of personal choice, equality and protection of cultural life'. The latter pronouncement particularly draws us back to the concept of citizenship and particularly social citizenship which is concerned with equal distribution of, or access to, the social benefits of the community and to consideration of our definition of community. T. H. Marshall, the author of the seminal work on social citizenship, noted over forty years ago a great conflict between the development of social citizenship and the demands of free market competition. The former calls for greater co-operation and equality and the latter greater competition and inequality.

Ardigo describes the potential for information technology to advance the cause of social citizenship in terms of three general areas to:

- to ensure a fair distribution of the social benefits of technological progress;
- to improve the efficiency and effectiveness of public administration and the liberal professions;
- to enable the best possible exercise of citizen's rights to information and their participation in decision making.

Another commentator highlights the fact that information is now a commodity. We seldom now talk of knowledge, wisdom and skills but rather of information, a value added concept dependent only on access and navigational skill and subject like any other commodity to market forces assessing worth.

Our definition of community is also changing. Traditionally we belonged to our local community, our national community etc. Globalisation gives the individual a sense of multiple allegiance and choice. It is hoped by many that these new dimensions of community will herald a re-growth of pride in community and commitment to community. Vice-President, Al Gore speaks of The Information Highway promising a renewed sense of community, connecting us rather than atomising us, while elsewhere there is talk of electronic communities flowering through individual choice. The realisation of these aspirations needs a wider definition of communication from simply the extension of messages over geographical distance to a drawing together of people through commonality and fellowship.

Accepting as Funston (1993) says, that 'technology therefore is shaped by the society that produces it then its direction and application is not predetermined and it can be moulded by beliefs in democracy, equality and social justice'.

In terms of impact rural communities must offer a high potential arena for the implementation of technological solutions. Along with inner city 'black spots' rural regions display the greatest inequities in our society. In this I am thinking of instances where, for example, in my experience there is absolutely no childcare provision, where families have one or no car and there is little or no public transport and where access to education, particularly higher education is dependent on travel to locations in excess of sixty miles away. To use the current phraseology - you have communities marginalised and socially excluded through factors that are beyond individual control. The results of course, we all know, are loss of population/emigration; lower than average working population; high levels of deprivation and young people, leaving for Higher Education, often never return.

If we are entering a new era, moving from an industrially based society to a knowledge based society it is important that the whole community does so and again in particular that the weakest parts are given the opportunity to leapfrog to the fore. In this year of lifelong learning it is apposite that a major report from the European Union should highlight education as a key catalyst for progress, 'Building the European Information Society for us All, The First Reflections of the High Level Group of Experts', assembled by the Directorate General for Employment , Industrial Relations and Social Affairs (1996). The move to lifelong learning is a cultural shift. Recent figures have been published on participation in learning throughout the UK.

Northern Ireland is devastatingly low in the league with 53% of the population not involved in any form of learning. We feel this is a reflection of the geographic distribution of people and of the points made above. In recent years the two universities have been investing in efforts to move out to the regions. I have already mentioned the updating of my own university's mission statement. The University of Ulster has been active in over twenty centres throughout N. Ireland but the Fermanagh Higher Bridges project represents an acceleration of that process and a real commitment to this social movement of which I speak.

The overall aim of Fermanagh Higher Bridges, therefore, is to bring the multidimensional presence of the University of Ulster into the Fermanagh region to act as a catalyst for social cohesion, social inclusion and community economic development. I would wish to stress at this point that offering mainstream programmes is one string in the 'bow' of the project. Other equally important strings are those of community programmes, Technology Transfer to Business, access to the University's research and development resource, professional development and programmes to address social inclusion of those disaffected or disenchanted with education.

At the beginning of this paper I said that all our work in Fermanagh is firmly rooted in the community, reflects community need and is intended as complementary to any other higher education provision. That is the corner stone of our model of operation.

The University is servicing a local need and the project belongs to the local community. In our preliminary discussions with colleagues in Fermanagh District Council they also felt it was important that the project was not perceived of as dominated by the Council so we sought to create a modus operandi that would free us from these constraints. The result was the formation of the Fermanagh University Partnership Board (FUPB). Membership of the Board reflects all local interests including the Further Education College, Agricultural College, Training and Employment Agency, Fermanagh Business Initiative and a number of nominated representatives of different sectors of the community. We are in the process of establishing FUPB as a charitable company, this will give the university a specific legal entity with whom to deal. The Council is represented on the Board and provides the secretariat and the university with a non-voting member.

In thinking of a building programme or physical location for the various activities, we were fortunate in that the Council decided that this would be an excellent use for a building they had acquired and that they would donate it to the project. The building in question is a historic building within the conservation area of the county town of Enniskillen. The building can be sympathetically renovated maintaining its historic facade and providing 6,380 square feet of accommodation on four floors. We first began to plan an Interactive Technology Centre with three specific suites, an open access floor and a degree of overlap in common services and meeting rooms. The three specific suites were:

– The Flexible Learning Suite, consisting of a hi-tech lecture theatre (75 seats) a multimedia tutorial room (40 seats) and dedicated seminar rooms with videoconferencing facilities; the Community and Economic Development Suite, a collection of flexible space to be used for short term projects ranging form cultural to economic development; the Sme Support Suite with Trade Development Unit, Consultancy Unit, IT Training Unit, Computer Services and a Europoint.

As dialogue on planning continued it became apparent that the project was perceived of as having a great deal of local significance. Fermanagh and particularly Enniskillen have suffered during the 'troubles' in Northern Ireland and many will remember the 'Poppy Day' bomb blast that claimed the lives of eleven local people. The site of this tragedy, the reading rooms of St Michael's Catholic church coincidentally is directly opposite that of the Orange Hall/INTEC Centre. For some time the Council had been aware that there was a need for a neutral venue within the county and for good conferencing facilities. The project team entered negotiation with the parish authorities and, based on long term lease plans have gone ahead to create a new building housing conference and exhibition area, meeting rooms, restaurant and thirty study bedrooms. This is, of course, a very important development in moving towards meeting our aims of social inclusion and cohesion. It also makes the project a very symbolic landmark in moving from the past to the future. All these physical plans are the subject of funding applications and the overall cost is in the region of £7 million. We hope to undertake the work in two phases, the renovation of the Orange Hall in 1997 and the new building completing in 1998.

Having launched the idea and tested public opinion it was felt very important that academic and programmatic planning proceed in parallel. This is not the building of just another university campus therefore the work can be carried on irrespective of premises. The work plan for 1996/7 includes the enrolment of the first cohort of students, introduction of technology enterprise programme, continuance of the IT consultancy role, progression of a major research project in community economic modelling, link-up between the local Business Initiative and a University Research Centre in Food Processing, design of a new degree in Equine Studies to be jointly offered between Fermanagh Further Education College, Fermanagh Agricultural College and the University of Ulster Faculty of Science, involvement in inward investment drive and design of an ongoing formal academic plan.

Collective and individual learning is at the heart of our work. The courses we are offering this year reflect three themes addressing our core objectives:

Widening access - particularly for mature students with experiential learning. Initial target groups are those interested in community development for whom we are offering a first step certificate in community development studies, and those less certain of the route they wish to take but keen to consider further study. For the latter we are mounting a series of modules from basic information technology to the accessing information (the INTERNET etc.) and a learning to learn, study skills module backed by advice and support on choice of course or career.

Increasing existing HE Provision

The Fermanagh Further Education College is being supported in significantly expanding its range of business management courses into Year 2 modules of two business studies degrees and Masters in Business Administration. Staff at the FE College will become 'recognised teachers' of the University, and the University will work with the college administration to facilitate access to higher level modules by videoconferencing and distance learning.

Professional development

A programme is being prepared for the second semester period, January to April, introducing Postgraduate Diplomas/Masters Degrees and also accredited short courses again in topics reflecting local interests.

As I hope you can gather what we are doing is novel and exciting and a very real challenge for all concerned.

Recently the Partnership Board spent some time in trying to verbalise its mission and vision. Let me conclude with an extract from those deliberations:

– The Higher Bridges Project focuses on the creation of a central structure - a physical, social landmark to the new millennium in a rural community, a monument to revitalisation and a commemoration of an entry to a new era - The Information Age. Our vision is of a community revitalised, individually and in partnership, with enthusiasm in the future.

References

Council of State, 1995, Developing a Finnish Information Society, Finland, Helsinki.

European Commission, Europe's Way to the Information Society, An Action Plan, Com.(94) 347 final, Brussels 19/7/94.

European Commission, Europe and the Global Information Society, European Commission, Directorate General for Industry, June 1994.

European Commission, Building the European Information Society for Us All, Directorate General for Employment, Industrial Relations and Social Affairs, January 1996.

From Vision to Action, Info-Society 2000, Danish Government, March, 1995.

Tilman Hartenstein

Disabled Adults - a Second Chance in Adult Education

I am discussing a project which was only begun a few weeks ago, so please forgive me for referring to fleeting goals more than to achieved results.

The project brings together eight organisations from six European countries, and has been established under the European SOCRATES programme within the subprogramme 'Adult education'. It will last for three years and so far we have received SOCRATES funding for the first year.

The title of the project is 'Disabled Adults - a second chance in adult education'. This title asserts the need to define some terms, for example, the term 'disabled adult'. We all know who an adult is as we work in the field of lifelong learning. But who is a disabled adult?

What is disability?

There are no clear scientific definitions of the term 'disabled', and the question of who is a disabled, is a political question to answer. As the Second Chance project was initiated by Norway, our starting point was the definition given by the Norwegian authorities in the Norwegian Plan of Action for the Disabled in 1990:

'Disablement is a discrepancy between the capabilities of the individual and the functions demanded of him/her by society in areas which are essential to the establishment of independence and social life.'

In addition, disablement is often defined to be of a permanent nature. Temporarily impaired mobility because of a broken leg due to skiing is no disablement in that sense. However, a temporarily disabled person may also benefit from efforts taken for permanently disabled persons. So, in education, we look at disabled persons in an even larger perspective than the system of social benefit does, and we define them like this:

'Disabled persons in education are persons who need a special kind of assistance or adjusted material to take part in any kind of education provided by public institutions, schools, or others.'

When dealing with the term 'disability', it is very important to have in mind that the phenomenon 'disability' in a crucial way relates to society and culture, and to the individual's role in it. For example, allergies or writing and reading difficulties often do *not* derive from physical dysfunctions, but are caused by environmental and psycho-social factors. Further more the way disabilities are treated in society in general is significant to the individuals' way to deal with them, and to the degree of disability the individual experiences. So are educational traditions and thinking structures which can define different disabilities to range on the whole scale from being relatively unimportant to being essential for all does or don'ts.

Our definition therefore includes a wide range of temporary or permanent disabilities.

Disabled persons are people who have:

- defects of the senses or the motory abilities, that is mental handicaps, impaired mobility, impaired hearing, impaired vision, and concealed disabilities such as diabetes, mental disturbance, coronary disorders, or allergies caused by environmental influences
- learning difficulties such as dyslexia, aphasia or other types of brain misfunction, and reading and writing difficulties caused by specific social relations between an individual and the society around
- serious emotional problems or social problems
- or combinations of these, which is very often the case, especially in connection with emotional or social problems.

Disabled people in Norway and Europe

The official Norwegian Health Survey of 1985 shows that there were about 19% permanent disabled persons in Norway at that time, and about 16%

were of working age, that is between 16 and 66 years old. The authorities estimate that about 1 in 10 persons of working age receive disability benefits and/or basic supplementary benefits.

At the first look this seems to be many. But, as a matter of fact, there is every probability that the real number is even higher.

It is important to keep in mind that there is no complete statistical record of the number of disabled people in any country. That is due to several problems. Very often, data based on peoples' own assessments result in lower numbers of disabled persons than surveys based on the specialist's assessments.

On the other hand, very often the official surveys do omit disabled persons living in institutions. So does the Norwegian Survey of 1985, at a time when there still were institutions for disabled people in Norway. This is not the case today.

In addition there are disabled people outside institutions who miss corresponding status because they have had no diagnosis. A good example are elderly people who often aren't considered as disabled, but just as old.

Nor do all disabled persons who have a diagnosis, receive treatment or benefits.

Some of them will not even apply because they fear being socially downgraded or stigmatised. Others do not apply because of the lack of information about their rights. Many are in jobs although they may need technical aids, others may incur no extra expenses which could entitle them to basic grants.

The real amount of disabled people is therefore probably much higher than the official number, especially among adults, who often have to decide by themselves whether they should call for help or not. As long as disablement is connected to low social status, many adults will refuse to call themselves disabled.

Estimations made by adult educators who work in adapted adult education, show that the actual number of permanently disabled people in Norway may be around one million, that is *25% of the overall population*. When including temporarily disabled persons, the number will be even higher.

We think that this situation can be transferred to other industrial countries in Europe. The official statistics tell us that about 34 million people in Europe have disabilities or impairments which entitle them to social benefits. That is about 1 in 10 persons, the same as in Norway. In the wider perspective of education for disabled persons than I describe here, and the knowledge of the Norwegian experiences, at least 25 % seems to be realistic on an European scale.

What can adapted education do?

Within the goal of lifelong learning it is therefore evident that adapted education for disabled adults has to fill different roles for those who participate in it. We do not only talk about education as a public field which should be accessible for all. A main task of adapted adult education must be to encourage more people to realise their disablement, and in the second step to accept and frankly stand up and show it. The status of disabled persons can not be improved if there are insufficient educational offers to this group among other accepted target groups.

We believe that the existence of an extensive adapted educational offer not only improves the educational situation of the disabled directly, but also contributes to the social acceptance of disablement among the non-disabled, that is, promoting a more *enabling* environment.

Adults who have special needs are often entitled by experts to education at the basic school level. This is correct for many groups of disabled adults who did not have the chance to go through an adequate school period, and who need a second chance.

This right to basic education also applies to non-disabled adults who need to renew their training in fundamental areas, for instance as a result of illness or injury.

But - and this is important to the Second Chance project - the possibility to attend adapted higher education has to be developed too. Even though - or just because - the call for higher education is considered not to be as strong among disabled persons as among others, a far-sighted policy for the disabled should emphasise the significance of a higher education goal for disabled adults, both younger and elder ones.

Last but not least a model of adapted education can also be a Second Chance for the educational institution by itself, implementing a chance to renew the sight upon disablement as an obstacle to education.

Disabled peoples' educational access situation

The main task for the SECOND CHANCE-project is to improve the access for disabled adult persons to adult education in general. As we know, the access is difficult and in many respects illusory.

This is due to several reasons:

1. missing physical arrangements or adjustments, that is, unacceptable and unsuitable localities at schools, universities and other education institutions
2. few adjusted materials in an exploding educational and distant teaching marked, included multimedia devices
3. little knowledge about and consciousness around disabled adults and different kinds of disabilities among the lecturers and staff within the educational institutions in general
4. partly missing knowledge of, and use of new Information and Communications Technology (ICT) and Open and Distance Learning (ODL) for the benefit of disabled adults.

This situation is more or less common for all European countries. So what should be done?

The White Paper on Education and Training, issued by the European Commission in 1995, says:

'Adapting and improving education and training systems has to be strengthened through partnerships: no single institution, school, or company can claim to be able to develop the skills needed for achieving employability.'

As one of the main goals of the European Social Fund is to employ more disabled people, education of course is crucial to this initiative, as the so called HORIZON programme has shown. The need to develop conditions not only for distance work, but also distance education, should therefore lead to a common European strategy towards adapted education.

The several different groups of disabled people have a variety of needs in relation to adapted education. There is no point in trying to solve all specific problems in general at the green table.

We know that local co-operation often is of prime importance in enhancing accessibility to adult education for local groups with specific diagnoses. But we think that the local projects in European countries can benefit from each others experiences, and they can contribute to the development of common standards of accessibility to adapted education, similar to other standards being developed in the European Union.

Focus on ICT and ODL

As the European programme for lifelong learning is focusing on Information and Communication Technology (ICT) and Open and Distance Learning (ODL), we do the same in relation to disabled adults. Experiences show that ICT and ODL are of even greater importance for disabled people than others.

There are groups of disabled persons who are depending on ICT to be able to communicate in the private and public area.

There are groups of people with impaired mobility which depend on ODL to achieve contact with far away schools or even the university in their neighbourhood.

And, of course, ICT and ODL are complementary fields where actions in one field should correspond to actions in the other. The main point is to exploit the potentially qualitative advantages in the fields of ICT and ODL as a supplement and to some degree a substitute to traditional stationary education. It must be possible to offer virtual mobility and a certain freedom of remote choice to people with impairments who really are in need of it, when the same thing is offered to persons without these needs.

In addition, ICT can be used to develop advanced adjusted ODL methods for different target groups. Here we see a developing field of possibilities, the real dimension of which one can hardly imagine.

The Second Chance partners

The project is initiated and co-ordinated by the *Association for Adapted Adult Education in Norway (ADA).*

This may be surprising since Norway is not a member of the European Union. But, fortunately, to be a non-member of the EU is not the same as to not cooperage. In the European SOCRATES programme, countries outside the EU can participate on level with countries inside.

Despite the formal political defiance of the Norwegian people, Norway is a country with long traditions of international co-operation. The relatively well developed standards of integration politics towards the disabled in Norway, makes the country a good starting point for a project like Second Chance.

To complete the resources of ADA which is a quite small organisation, two other Norwegian partners join the project. The *Norwegian Federation of Organisations of Disabled people (FFO)* is , like ADA, a partly governmental financed, non-governmental organisation (NGO). The FFO has fifty member organisations and has long experience in adult education for disabled people, mainly on a basic educational level. They also cooperage internationally at the European and UN level.

At the University of Oslo there is a *Section for disabled Students (SDS/ UiO).* This organisation assists disabled students of all kind in and through their studies. The SDS has some experience in the field of ICT and ODL, due to co-operation with the section of informatics at the University of Oslo.

Then there are five organisations from countries of the EU participating in the project. The *North East Wales Institute of Higher Education (NEWI)* is a Higher Education Corporation with a wide spectrum of faculties. The NEWI has no specific knowledge of the target groups, but a strong willingness to improve access. On the fields of ICT and ODL the NEWI does have main activities, for example, on electronic access towards educational resources.

The *Association for Higher Education Access and Disability (AHEAD)* is an all Ireland voluntary organisation whose membership includes all colleges of higher education and students with disability in the country. The AHEAD staff is by as much as 70% made up by disabled people. The AHEAD has experiences from former international projects and special knowledge of adjusted educational assistance for deaf adults and persons with impaired hearing.

The *Co-operative Body of Organisations for Disabled in Sweden (HSO)* is an umbrella organisation for twenty eight Swedish organisations. The HSO has a special project on ICT and adjusted ODL which has achieved results as ,for example, a network for disabled persons ('The Fruit Tree'), which will be made available for the Second Chance project.

At the *University of Athens* in Greece the *Counselling Centre (CC/UoA)* does career counselling interventions for disabled students, research and surveys, such as the HORIZON project on the integration of deaf students.

And in Spain the *Federación ECOM* is a non-governmental organisation with 91 member associations. ECOM gives advice to organisations, professionals and individuals in several fields, among them educational integration and accessibility matters. ECOM has experience with both ODL and ICT, as among others computer training for physically severe motor handicapped students.

All the partners in the Second Chance project do participate in several other European programmes, such as the HELIOS programmes, the LEONARDO programme, the ERASMUS and LINGUA programmes, and the HORIZON project. It is important to defend the rights of disabled people in many fields of which the SOCRATES programme is just one. For the problems of the disabled to become visible, we need a wide range of activities within Europe, and surely beyond European borders too.

The Second Chance project structure

The main activities of the Second Chance project are split up in several steps.

Firstly, the project will start to create a *Second Chance database.*

This database will be used as a communication and work tool by the project, but will also be the medium of presentation when the project is finished. Together with the Swedish data network 'Fruit Tree' it will be developed as a resource of communication possibilities, documents, software, mailing lists, and educational catalogues especially adjusted and designed for use by disabled people, and available for all on Internet.

Secondly, we will establish *work groups* which will concentrate on several topics or target groups. Development of adjusted ICT and ODL will be one of the topics, and deaf adults or physically disabled adults some of the target groups.

Thirdly, the partners are supposed to start *national projects* to develop new models of accessibility, or do research work and surveys on special topics. As the Second Chance project is going on, the models must be tested and evaluated.

Fourthly, the *outcomes* of the national projects will be gathered by the work groups, and will result in a paper edited both on-line and on paper, called the Second Chance Handi-guide. This guide will benefit planning authorities, educational institutions and the disabled people and their associations in Europe. We also want to produce some more popular result presentations, like television-programmes, and we do hope that there will be some new products to be used in adapted education at the end of our work.

Main goals of the Second Chance project

The main goals of the Second Chance project are the following.

- A strengthening of partnerships between institutions dealing with adapted adult education in Europe, in order to develop a common 'European standard for education accessibility for adults with disabilities', is hopefully one outcome of the Second Chance project.
- The establishment of the Second Chance database as an allover tool for communication and information within Europe, is another goal of the project. We hope that the database can be continued when the project is finished after three years, and can be used not only by institutions, but also by the disabled people themselves.

Altogether, we want to strengthen the European dimension within the different educational institutions in general and a European consciousness towards the disabled students as well.

The possibility of contact between disabled adult students in Europe, or even the exchange of disabled students as supposed by the ERASMUS part of the SOCRATES programme, is one of the specific ideas to develop.

Eero Pantzar

Experiences of Using Information and Communication Technology in Teaching and Learning at the Adult Higher Education Level

1. Introduction

Since the 1980's there has been an explosive increase in adult education in all European countries. The growth has been dramatic. The issue, unlike the past, has not centred on the increasing number of students in general. Instead the challenge has been about the fact that the masses entering adult education, in Finland also at the university level, are increasingly less selected. This growth has been so immense that traditional teaching systems have been unable to respond to the new requirements. Therefore, for example, in university adult education (adult higher education) - open university, vocational further education and retraining - there is an on-going quest for more flexible forms of teaching and learning to supplement conventional teaching (Pantzar, 1995b). Although, for example, the enrolment to open university (70,000 students per year) is outnumbered by many traditional Finnish adult education institutions (Rinne et al 1992, Parjanen, 1993), distance education and also information and communication technology-based distance learning, is bigger than the other sectors of adult education.

Coinciding with dramatic educational changes, there has been tremendous progress in the field of information and communication technology; especially the storage, documentation and transfer of information have gained entirely new dimensions. In principle, it seems that humans are now capable of solving more and more difficult questions faster and more easily than ever before. On the other hand, the ease of information handling seems to create new, real or imaginary, needs for knowledge. Meeting the educational needs set by the society and individuals calls for increasing efficiency and flexibility on the part of the education system and learning environments. In this development, the application of information and communication technology (ICT) plays a central role (Pantzar, 1995a).

The impact that the fast development in ICT has had on distance education and learning and on the utilisation of computer-aided learning in face-to-face education has played a significant role in the recent developments in modern learning environments. This change is not just about the new requirements set in education and learning. The huge increase in the amount of available information is not necessarily the primary reason for the creation of new efficient learning environments. The big question is how to filter the necessary information from the information flow. The main challenges for the development of learning environments will be presented by the rapid outdating of knowledge and the dramatic growth of education, especially in permanent education which will involve adults for an extended part of their lives (Pantzar, 1994). For adults, the problem has always been finding open and flexible learning opportunities. Today, judging by technological facts, the opportunities seem to be better than ever. From the pedagogical point of view, however, things are not quite as simple. It will be interesting to see how adults, whose learning history is normally focused on the classroom and the teacher as sources of information and knowledge, will be able to relate and participate in the changing learning environments. The youngsters of the computer generation, on the other hand, will find it much easier to adapt (Pantzar, 1995c).

2. Lifelong learning and ICT-based learning environments

One concrete outcome of the idea of lifelong learning is the expanding studies pursued by adults which have been influenced, above all, by changes in working life and are due to educational challenges. When estimating today's educational challenges, one must not forget the fact that learning is an inherent part of man's activity and, therefore, a lifelong process. The fundamental function of learning has been to provide individuals with a means of coping in situations encountered in their current environments. The pragmatists (Dewey et alii) were among the first to emphasise that learning is adaptive by nature and geared towards helping the individual in his or her struggle for coping (von Wright, 1996, cf. Jarvis, 1988).

In prehistoric times, man's basic coping assumed a capability of acquiring nourishment and shelter as well as the power of reproduction and taking care of due responsibilities. In today's complex world, an idividual's life is regulated by an infinite number of things. The environment which we have to live within and which determines our learning needs as a social community is not restricted to nature and the family. For the modern man, problems of coping are strongly concretised in his relationship with the built environment and with a social environment which has become considerably more complex than ever before (De'Ath, 1976, Pantzar, 1991 and 1993).

Throughout man's history, informal forms of learning have been decisively more significant than formal education institutions whose history is, in fact, rather brief. During this brief historical period, universities have played a major role as the seeker and promoter of scientific knowledge and wisdom. The university with its centennial tradition has, however, offered study opportunities to only a fraction of the population who after having been educated as clergymen, for example, distributed the acquired message within the framework of eccelesiastical teaching. It was not until popular education commenced that adults were given a more substantial opportunity to access formal education. However, it was not until the late 20th century that universities expanded their responsibilities to such an extent which allowed the mentioning of university adult education as well. This expansion is part of formal education's response to the challenges created by the need for lifelong education.

The increases in adults studying, along with the lengthening of basic education during childhood and adolescent years have also imposed new challenges on learning environments. The study needs of adults working and the related teaching and study arrangements are most commonly perceived as a particular challenge. Universities too have been compelled to meet the challenge. Traditionally, universities have been rather conservative with regard to their teaching. This has sometimes seemed to have contributed to the fact that, within the framework of the higher education, the opportunities offered can only be exploited by those adults who can participate in conventional education. On the other hand, experiments in various countries around the world have produced results that have encouraged universities to understand their role as institutions of higher learning on the one hand and as institutions for the entire nation on the other. Hence, in the best instances, it has been adult education that offered the best prerequisites for the development of university teaching. This also applies to the implementation of modern learning environments. It must be said, however, that there are marked differences in university resources, in Europe. Similarly, the structural solutions of adult higher education seem to affect the results. The wide-scoped activities of the UK's Open University or Germany's Fern Universität comprise excellent research and development activities in relation to learning environments and teaching environments (Kmi, 1996, Kanselaar, 1996).

From the Finnish viewpoint, it is easy to see that the use of ICT is also connected to the size of the market area. It is obvious that the Open University and Fern Universität with their potential for dozens of millions of students is of an entirely different category than the one million Finnish-speaking adult education participants. The required investment cost per student here in Finland has frequently constituted the stumbling block for solutions which have been considered reasonable in all other respects.

3. ICT and the learning theories

The task of an ideal learning environment, ICT, based learning environment, is to support effectively the learning processes of a student. Theorists of learning have more and more committed themselves to the constructivist learning theories. These theories seem to be very well suited, for example, to ICT-based learning environments. Earlier, in the programmed learning and also to some extent in computer-aided education, the practical work was based on a behaviouristic view of learning. The differences of the main learning theories could be summarised as follows. To the behaviourists, the internal processing is of no interest, to the cognitivists, the internal process is only of importance to the extent to which it explains how external reality is understood while on the contrary the contructivist views the mind as a builder of symbols, the tools used to represent the knower's reality (Euler, 1994).

When looking at learning in information- and communication-based learning environments from the constructivist perspective, we are mainly interested in the learner's activity and the factors of the learning environment that promote learning. The meaning of interaction in general are emphasised when looking at learning from a constructivist perspective. The expansion of ICT in education has made interaction a very complicated concept, since the potential interacting parties in a learning situation can be defined in many different ways, and the meaning of these interactive situations in human learning can be interpreted in many different ways (Resnick, 1989, Koivunen, 1993).

Defining learning as an interactive process or as a phenomenon that requires interaction seems to be the established practice (Wagner, 1994). The interaction between the different participants in ICT-based learning environment can be divided into learner-learner interaction, learner-computer interaction and learner-interface interaction, or into human-human and human-machine interactions (Hillman et al, 1994). In addition to this, the main theories on distance learning (Moore, 1989) emphasise the significance of learner-content interaction. In the learning process, learner-content interaction is primarly intra-personal.

The growing significance of ICT in education and learning changes the interactive relations and their meaning in the learning process. In the realm of human interaction, an essential part of educational activities in universities, both learner-learner and learner-teacher interaction are undergoing a constant change. Collis (1990) states that the use of ICT is more generally becoming associated with some encouraging trends in the social organisation of learning. According to her, although the majority of software packages are designed around the assumption of a single user interacting for some period of time with a computer, the reality of a limited number of machines and also limited telematic on-line connections, for example, in universities, has fostered the development of groupwork with ICT tools.

The essential factor of interaction, for learning, is the quality and quantity of information and its processing made possible by the interaction. In this respect , human-human interaction differs from human-machine interaction. The quality and quantity of information depends upon the resources of the learner or machine involved, and vary in different cases. For the present we may be persuaded that the processing of information can reach its deepest scope (learning) in a human-human interaction.

4. ICT and Universities in a Finnish information society

The term 'Finnish Information Society' has been used in reference to a Finland of the future, with an essential part of the societal basic infrastucture based on the existence of modern communication and information technology, and the utilisation thereof. Applying the idea of an information society to educational policies requires, as a goal, that schools and universities must be provided with modern communication and information technology. The Finnish state is prepared to invest considerable sums of money for the said purpose (cf. European Commission, 1995, Cochinaux et al, 1995). In the current situation, many Finnish universities, have an up-to-date infrastructure for technology-based teaching and learning. At present this infrastructure is not exploited to the maximum. This is due to a number of reasons, for example:

- teachers' average skills and capabilities of planning and implementing teaching within this framework are limited, at present.
- teaching and learning materials are available for conventional teaching mainly.

Young students are clearly better prepared to participate in technology-based learning than their teachers. This is natural as most of them have had the opportunity to became familiar with modern learning environments at school (Pantzar, 1996).

These central ICT implementation problems in university teaching apply to basic education and university adult education alike. Surveys carried out in European universities support the stated view. The surveys have shown that only a small portion (in 1995) of European universities have used computer-aided teaching, even though universities and research centres have made substantial investments in modern teachology (Desk Study, 1996). The amount seems to be unrealistically low, but is, however, supported by extensive German research, for example, Hopkins, 1996. In addition, research has indicated a number of obstacles that slow down ICT implementation in learning environments. In addition to the ones stated above, the most common reasons include:

Costs: Initial costs, although soon recoverable, are often substantial and, at an early stage, the advantages may be outweighed by the disadvantages. Networking and telecommunication technologies must be cheaper and faster. The high cost of a connective infrastructure coupled with slow data transfer rates is seen as a major handicap in the development of networking and telecommunications applications.

There is a fear, however, that the costs of purchasing the necessary equipment cannot be considered as an investment for the future as developing technologies change so rapidly and there is a constant need for updating.

Traditional thinking: Universities may tend to consider their growth in terms of new buildings and physical size rather than in progress through ICT development. The belief that reducing costs through developing ICT translates into reducing the number of faculties and increasing the student-faculty ratios: the traditional view that good teaching makes more learning than a mechanical act.

Lack of services: There is a lack of availability of inter-operable network services.

These services are based on available technology but in Europe use is hindered by a number of problems that only a joint effort between all concerned actors may help to overcome.

Tariffs: Long connection periods are needed for distance learning, resulting in high communication tariffs.

Data transfer rates: The problem of slow transfer rates is one which has to be addressed by developers while the high cost obstacle has to be overcome by administrations, politicians and governing bodies.

Time and effort: Some HE institutions may feel that ICT requires too much time and effort, creates too many distractions and yields too little value for the investment (Desk Study, 1996).

Naturally, the problems stated above are not always encountered simultaneously. However, each of them can form insurmountable obstacles to efficient utilisation of ICT in teaching. Furthermore, it must be observed that, within each nation, the character of the problems is different from that encountered in co-operation between universities of various countries. Student relations between European universities have been intensified through various ODL projects, for example, National ICT infrastructures. The number and quality of computers used in universities, and the students' capabilities and opportunities of using telecommunication may cause problems in collaboration. Problems may arise from the students' different possibilities in using personal electronic mail, for example Open to Europe, 1996.

To carry on with the stated ICT utilisation problems, I would like to point out a common way of thinking. It appears that the various parties involved in university teaching, that is, the decision-makers and implementers, in conventional teaching and adult education alike, are cautious in taking a stand due to the fact that any knowledge of the investment's life-span and profitability, for example, is mainly based on guesswork.

Universities have carried out several experiments on ICT-based teaching. I shall illustrate the situation using a few examples.

The Hypermedia Laboratory of Tampere University has made a programme for teaching financial administration. Primarily, this material is used for adult education at the higher level but it is applicable to university basic education as well. This computer-aided teaching material package is based on the idea that its contents form an inherent part of the rest of the education and will be integrated into other forms of teaching. Successful use of the material depends, above all, on the teachers' and education planners' capacity for creating rational, complete learning environments (Koivula, 1996).

The use of electronic mail has fairly long traditions. At Jyväskylä University, electronic mail has been used, among other things, for discussing the contents of basic studies in sociology. A special object was to develop the participants' argumentation skills. According to a follow-up study, the students experienced electronic mail discussions as mainly positive. This was perceived as a motivating method which inspired argumentation, for example. The study results also verified improvements in argumentative skills. In addition, it was established that the central problem in electronic mail discussion is tutoring which is time-consuming and requires much work (Marttunen, 1996).

At Jyväskylä University, information technology-based solutions have been tested within the realm of natural science. Prime examples are the computer simulations applied to biology teaching. The teaching cost savings made in biochemistry teaching may be seen as the chief motive for the use of simulations. Research-connected ethical reasons also support the use of simulations. In addition, it was stated that part of the modern biochemist's experiments do in fact take place in silico, not in vitro or in vivo as in the past. The follow-up study which complemented the study indicated that simulations have positive effects on learning. On the other hand, it was emphasised that the programmes require a great deal of work, planning and design, the benefits of which are best seen over a long period of time (Vuento, Laitinen and Vihinen, Ranta, 1996).

Recently the interest of Finnish universities seems to have been focused on a more comprehensive use of the Internet for teaching. Meanwhile, the development of computer-based multimedia materials, such as CD-ROMs, has mainly been quite slow. The small market area and high development costs form efficient obstacles. In several instances, production of the said materials has been boosted by the possibility of using them for both basic and adult education in universities.

Pedagogically, multimedia materials (CD-ROMs) provide more versatile possibilities for presenting the subject matter than the Internet's WWW pages, which, through the present main cable technology, are available to the majority of students only in the form of hypertext enriched with still pictures. This, however, does provide an opportunity for new teaching and learning solutions.

Many universities have used WWW pages as teaching material. Two methods have been used. The conventional method has been to offer the lecture material as a network version, without intra-textual links, in its most rudimentary form (Sams, 1996).

More advanced applications are reprensented by WWW pages with links to external materials, in addition to intra-textual and picture links (Tilastollinen tietojenkäsittely, 1996). The experiences gained and studies conducted have proved that, as such, WWW pages are functional teaching material. However, abundant resources are required to produce high-quality pages (Raportti, 1996).

5. Experiences of using information and communication technology-based learning environments in adult higher education

In Finnish universities, the various modern forms of open and distance learning seem to have been adopted most quickly by the units working with adult higher education. On the other hand, it should be remembered that in Finland higher education for adults, for example European university education, is provided by conventional universities. This has meant close planning and implementation co-operation between the before mentioned units and faculties.

All Finnish universities (21) have an institute for academic further education. The oldest of these is the Institute for Extension Studies of the University of Tampere. This institute pioneers methods of open and distance learning. Teaching and instructional material have been conveyed through radio and television, audio and video conferences, using computer-aided methods (in the form of CD-ROM diskettes), and through the Internet. At present, however, modern learning environments only cover a fraction of the teaching programme. This portion is continuously increasing, however. Also other universities have been very active in developing learning environments for adult higher education.

The modern communication and information technology is also used for other communication purposes between teachers and students. Feedback on achievements and written assignments, study guidance and tutoring (Verkkotutor, 1996) has been provided extensively through electronic mail or the WWW, for example.

The main obstacles for a more extensive use of information technology-based learning environments in adult higher education include the following:

Instructional design and preparation resources are insufficient, particularly with regard to teaching quality and instructional material quality development.

There is a shortage of technical assistance personnel. On average, the faculties have shown relatively little interest in developing teaching within the framework of adult education.

University teachers' efforts to participate in learning environment and material development have not been supported sufficiently.

I have personally participated in different research and development projects connected with using modern communication and information technology (ICT) in adult higher education. In connection with these projetcs I have noted that:

- Using ICT, for example, in Open and distance learning, enhances educational equality.

- ICT-based learning environments give students more freedom of choice for planning and implementing their learning. This also supports the ideology of 'from teaching to learning'.
- State-of-the art technological infrastructure also enables efficient, co-operative learning.

The designing of learning environments and the use of new ICT in mediating learning material requires abundant resources and a new type of didactic thinking, of which the basic insights are as follows:

- some of the essentials for designing ICT-based learning environments are different to those of conventional education: changes in the role of the teacher and the student, different style of communication and interaction, etc.
- using ICT in education and learning requires greater planning input than conventional education. The more technological the output (learning environment) is, the more planning it requires.
- the share of team work and interdisciplinarity is greater in ICT-based education and learning material production than in conventional frameworks.

Before succeeding with really flexible learning environments characterised by ICT we have to solve many problems of educational planning and instructional design. First of all we should develop learning theoretical arguments as to why those modern learning environments are better than conventional ones.

6. Conclusions

The use of information technology and communication technology in adult higher education (AHE) will certainly increase. The rate of implementation, in Finland for example, will depend on several factors. The development of teaching implemented in the form of adult education has been partly dependent on the development of university basic education. This means that the trends followed by university basic education give a number of guidelines for the entire development. The development of university basic education into an ICT-based form of teaching is determined, at least, by the following factors:

- financial situation which affects the willingness to invest.
- teachers' professional competence, above all the universities' willingness to develop this competence in such a fashion that the staffs' capacity to implement.
- ICT-based teaching and to participate in teaching material production would always be up-to-date.
- up-to-date infrastructure; computers, data networks and teaching materials.
- students' capability of active participation in ICT-based teaching and learning.

The development of adult higher education into ICT-based education is also affected by the following factors which are indepedent of basic education:

- the willingness of external financiers and other interest groups to develop ICT-based teaching.
- the preparedness of students coming from outside the university to participate in it.

ICT-based teaching and learning

Available networks and other connections from the university to the world outside, for example, for open university teaching; other technological equipment such as student computers, availability of teaching materials suited for teaching adults.

The state and development lines of teaching in European universities as well as the implementation state of ICT-based teaching may well be summarised by a quote from the (unpublished) report of the Council of European Rectors' University Restructuring Team which centres on universities and IT-based teaching. The report's SWOT analysis deals with weaknesses, strengths, opportunities and threats.

The strengths of university teaching are seen by the fact that:

- the universities are proud of their dedication to non-interest study and guard their academic autonomy. The universities are also confident that their concern with the personal development of the student is well-paced.

As for *the weaknesses*, it is stated that

- there is a recognition that the student-teacher relationship is not always what it should be. Many universities are deemed to have failed in establishing a strong rapport between teacher and learner.

  Rapid changes in educational technology are perceived as an *opportunity* to change the higher education offer from a teacher-centred, paper-based environment to learner-centred, electronic-based model. Multimedia gives more choice of learning paths and so better accommodates the pace of different students moving towards the same goal.

With regard to *the threats* it is said that

- advances in technology and an increase in the amount of information available to everybody provoked fears of a non-structured mass of information not being managed by the university. With this came some recognition that universities indeed no longer held a monopoly on the creation of knowledge and on its transmission.
- Most importantly for the universities there is the danger that the use of technology may increase rather than reduce the gap between student and teacher (CRE-report 1996).
- From the point of view of adult higher education, the emphasis on strengths, weaknesses, opportunities and threats is different from that of

ordinary basic teaching. As I see it, there are more reasons to worry about educational equality and opportunities for lifelong learning. The decisions to be made concerning ICT-based solutions in AHE, will, provided that they are successful, increase educational equality and provide better lifelong learning possibilities. On the other hand, unsuccessful choices and solutions will result in the opposite situation. The coming choices to be made by European and national education politics and its underlying societal values will determine which of the two directions development will take in the dawn of the next millennium.

References

Cochinaux, P. and de Woou, P. (1995), Moving towards a Learning Society. A CRE-ERT Forum Report on European Education.

Collis, B. (1990), Using information technology to create new educational situations. Prospect XX(2), pp 173-186.

CRE-Report (1996), Universities and new technologies, The CRE Working Group on Restucturing the University, Research report.

De'Ath, C. (1976), Anthropological and ecological foundations of lifelong education in Dave, R. (ed.), Foundations of lifelong education, Exeter, Pergamon Press pp 235-285.

Desk Study (1996), Higher Education and Research, Unpublished report.

Euler, D. (1994), (Multi)mediales Lernen - Theoretische Fundierungen und Forschungsstand, Unterrichtswissenschaft 22(3), pp 263-284.

European Commission (1995), White Paper on Education and Training, Teaching and Learning. Towards the Learning Society, COM (95) 590, Brussels.

Hillman, D., et al. (1994), Learner-interface interaction in distance education, American Journal of Distance Education, 8(2), pp 30-42.

Hopkins, J. (1996), Information Technology and the Information Society in Europe: Expectations and Barriers to the Implementation of New Media in the Higher Education and Research Sector, Deploy Project Summary Report, Http://www.csc.fi/forum/JH/iteurope.html. 20.11.1996.

Jarvis, P. (1988), Adult and continuing education, London, Routledge.

Kanselaar (1996), Lifelong learning with and without new media, Lifelong Learning in Europe, 1(1), pp 18-25.

KMi (1996), KMi Research Preview, Http://www.open.ac.uk/kmi-misc/kmi-research-preview.html, (2.10.1996).

Koivula, P. (1996), Hypermediaohjelma taloushallinnon opetukseen. Peda-forum 1, pp 11-12.

Koivunen, M. R. (1993), Ihmisen ja tietokoneen vuorovaikutus in Hyvönen, P., et al (toim), Tekoälyn ensyklopedia.

Marttunen, M. (1996), Korkeakouluopiskelua sähköpostilla, Peda-forum 1, pp 12-13.

Moore, M. (1989), Three types of interaction, American Journal of Distance Education 3(2), pp 1-6.

Open to Europe 1996, Http://www.salford.ac.uk./iti/ote/homepage.html. (2.10.1996).

Pantzar, E. (1994), The Human-computer Interaction from the Point of View of the Learning Theory in Linna, M. and Ruotsala, P. (ed), Hypermedia in Vaasa '94, Vaasa Institute of Technology pp331-337.

Pantzar, E. (1995a), Towards a Critical Theory of Open Distance Learning in Seward, D. (ed), One World Many Voices, 17th World Conference for Distance Education.

Pantzar, E. (1995b), Study Circles - a critical phase in learning at a distance in Klasson, M., et al (ed), Social Change and Adult Education Research, Linköping, UniTryck, pp 228-239.

Pantzar, E. (1995c), Theoretical Views On Changing Learning Environments in Pantzar, E., et al (ed), Theoretical Foundations and Applications of Modern Learning Environment, Tampere, University of Tampere Computer Centre Publication Series No. 1, pp 85-101.

Pantzar, E. (1996), Open and Distance Learning - Experiences at a Finnish University, Paper presented in Dresden at the CRE Meeting on ODL. 29.-30.4. 1996.

Pantzar, E. and Väliharju, T. (1996), Kohti virtuaalisia oppimisympäristöjä, Ammatti-instituutti, Tutkimus 1, Helsinki.

Parjanen, M. (1993), Adult Higher Education on the Peripheries of Europe, in Finland and Ireland in Parjanen, M. (ed), Outside the Golden Gate, Tampere, University of Tampere, Institute for Extension Studies, Publications A, pp 3.60-83.

Raportti (1996), Raportti kvantitatiivisten menetelmien kehittämisprojektista, Http://www.helsinki.fi/valttdk/optek/kvbanrap.html. 19.11.1996.

Resnick, L. (ed), (1989), Knowing, Learning and Instruction, Essays in honour of Robert Glaser, Hillsdale, Lawrence Erlbaum.

Rinne, R., et al (1992), Aikuisten kouluttautuminen Suomessa, Research Unit for the Sociòlogy of Education, University of Turku.

Sams, M. (1996), Neuropsykologia, Http://www.uta.fi/laitokset/psyk/studies/opetmat/ Neuro96.html. 19.11.1996.

Tilastollinen, tietojenkäsittely (1996), Http://www.helsinki.fi:80/~valt_www/stat/pruju. html. 19.11.1996.

Wright von, J. (1996), Oppiminen selviytymiskeinona (Learning as a coping strategy), Psykologia 31(5), 351-358.

Verkkotutor (1996), *Http://www.uta.fi/tyt/verkkotutor. 12.11.1996*

Vuento, M., Laitinen, M. and Vihinen-Ranta, M. (1996), Tietokonesimulaatiot biokemian opetuksessa. Peda-forum)1, 14-15.

N. Siggelkow / G. Nitsche

Information Technology as a Subject and Medium for Professional Development of Civil Engineering

The following article will give an insight into continuing education in civil engineering at the university of Hannover. There will be a brief outline of the themes and the use of information technology in continuing education in relation to how it is used today and future developments.

With the passing of the „Hochschulrahmengesetz“ (HRG) and the amendment of the HRG for the Federal German States, the legislators have given the universities an important social-political task: the universities are also responsible for continuing education outside of the standard graduate and post-graduate curricula and should participate in appropriate educational events. This commission means that the universities are available as partners in all fields of business and society for the further education of employed people. Their resources of scientists, personnel, equipment and laboratories can be made available to interested parties who are already in employment.

Further education has found its own place in the study programme at the University of Hannover. In addition to the internal further education for employees which is realised by the ‘Central Department for Further Education’ using external lecturers in some cases, I would like to mention the continuing education programmes in the field of ‘Department of Work Sciences ‘and in the field of engineering science the continuing education course ‘Rubber technology’ and the workgroups ‘Technological co-operation with developing countries’ and ‘Continuing education course for civil engineers’ (WBBau).

A very rapid development has taken place within the last 10 years in civil engineering in the fields of theoretical methods and data processing. Network-based personal computers and workstations now have the computing capacity of mainframes. The associated wide scale application of modern DP equipment is already visible in civil engineering offices in their eagerness to apply these new technologies hand in hand with the restructuring of previous company organisations and personnel structures. To maintain competitiveness, the decision-making engineers need to focus clearly on these new developments, to get acquainted with the possibilities that they offer and to acquire the basic knowledge which is needed as a foundation for extensive innovative decisions.

From the business viewpoint, a qualified undergraduate education is a prerequirement for coping with the structural changes that will take place. However, to an increasing extent the undergraduate studies must be qualified by additional education. The present-day short half-life of knowledge must be continuously updated by a lifelong process of learning. The aim of universities is to apply continuing education to transform the scientific results into practical usage in dialogue with the business world, to monitor the transformation and to enrich research and training with study topics which are of practical use to the professions. In the engineering sciences particularly, it is necessary to resolve a deficit in the field of applied information processing. This applies both to undergraduate studies and, in particular, to continuing education. At many German Universities, this development has resulted in the founding of departments of computer science in civil engineering, but the available continuing education courses in this field are not sufficient by any means.

Continuing education for civil engineers

Continuing education for civil engineers (WBBau) is a course at the University of Hannover with a government approved examination structure. It is available for persons in employment as a distance learning (correspondence) course with personal attendance seminars and is available for technical personnel from the field of engineering and associated fields. The WBBau is subdivided into the fields of 'civil engineering design' and 'water and the environment'. 'Civil engineering design' was integrated into the newly founded Department of Computer Science in Civil Engineering in 1993. This shows the importance that is placed at the University of Hannover on continuing education for civil engineering information technology.

'Continuing education course for civil engineers' is designed as a distance learning course with personal attendance phases. This allows the course to be offered throughout the whole of Germany independently of access to universities. This is particularly important because engineers are often not able to take time off from the daily work process and their travelling costs are not met by the company. Accordingly, normally only two personal attendance seminars are scheduled per semester. In comparison to a conventional full-time course, this approach gives students more flexibility while ensuring a continuous advance of their studies. This is helped by individual tutoring and intensive support.

The teaching structure of the course 'Civil Engineering Design' is subdivided according to content and needs into introductory, basic, intensifying and project courses which are modular. This satisfies the need for a different starting-out level, a continuous study process and the need to teach special technical knowledge.

WBBau has engaged university lecturers from various universities and educators from the professional world with appropriate technical qualifications to prepare the teaching material and to carry out the courses. The course contents are orientated towards practical aspects of the profession. Each course is allocated a tutor who can answer questions about the training material even during non-attendance phases, for example, by e-mail. The personal attendance seminars, which are held twice a year, offer the possibility of discussing training material with the authors and tutors.

The courses, each of which extend for one semester, can be assembled into a complete study course according to individual needs. Each of them are so conceived that the students need to invest about 4 to 6 hours per week. Successful participation is awarded by a detailed certificate. The study course is concluded with an oral examination after submitting a written paper, generally after six semesters. The University of Hannover issues a graduation certificate.

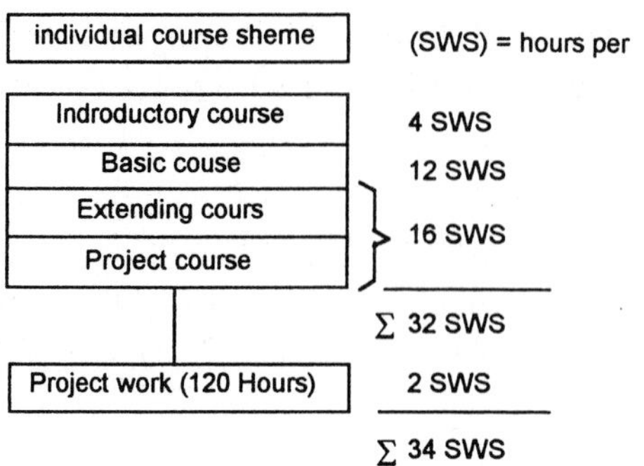

Fig: Example for a possible study course

Courses are currently available on the following topics:

- Finite element analysis
- Numerical methods, finite element analysis
- Non-linear methods in static calculations for trusses, load bearing methods
- CAE applications through to practical programming
- Computer communication
- Technical optimisation and expert systems
- Civil engineering design including changes required by Eurocode, construction physics and dynamics

The Participants

The WBBau advertises throughout German-speaking countries in technical journals, in periodicals from the engineering academies and in the local press. Information is also available on the institute's internal server and can be found using appropriate search engines. The range of participants consists of engineers with university degrees (53 %), engineers with technical college degrees (36 %) and technical personnel with appropriate qualifications (11 %). Most of the students are motivated to take part in the further education courses in order to adapt their technical knowledge to the current scientific status; further reasons are the acquisition of basic knowledge in the fields of computer-aided engineering in order to get an overview of the latest technologies, to ensure the possibility of professional promotion or to learn how to programme a computer.

Example of a study course

A student with particular interests in the fields of numeric methods and finite element analysis could assemble a study course from the following modules (figure).

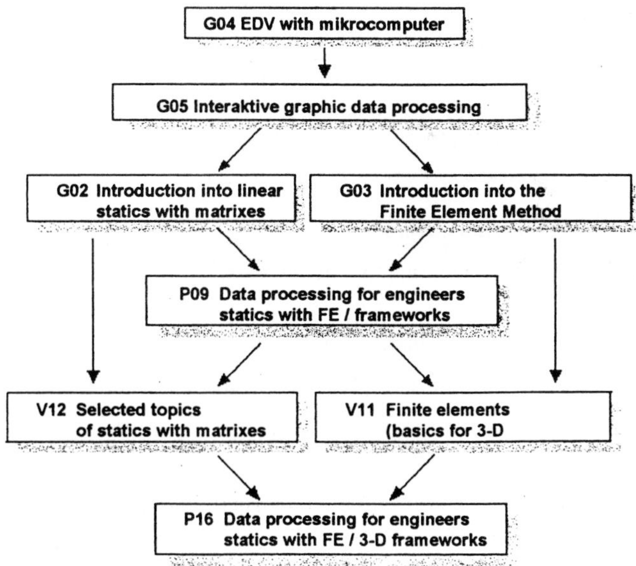

Fig: Individual study plan (Example)

Examples of courses available in the WBBau program

Project course FEM applications for surface structures (P16)

The classical analytical methods of solving calculation of surface structures are bound to simple geometric structures. The finite element method opens the possibility of describing and solving the calculation of complex structures in a more comfortable way. The practical application, therefore, of the finite element method is becoming ever more important in the daily work of engineers. However, extreme care must be taken before applying such software tools without appropriate background knowledge, since the finite element method of approximation can produce incorrect results if insufficient attention is paid to the model design and the FE network on which it is based. Within the framework of the WBBau program, the course P16 'The application of FEM to surface structures' is designed as a follow-up course to basic and intensifying courses on the theme of finite element analysis.

Appropriate FEM software tools are used to teach the meaningful and responsible application of the finite element method to the calculation of surface structures. Particular attention is placed on suitable discretion of the task, on the possibilities of processing the input data and on the responsible analysis of the results of the calculations. The course considers two shell elements, a plate element and a combined shell/plate element. The theoretical background is explained where this is necessary.

The following topics are covered:

- the meaningful transformation of an existing problem into a discrete network,
- the choice of suitable generating strategies,
- the execution of appropriate controls for error estimation,
- practical experience to improve the students' confidence in the method of finite element analysis,
- the practical use of various programmes and the characteristics of different types of elements,

- qualification with respect to reliability assessment of solutions to complex partial problems (coupling of different types of elements, eccentric couplings etc.),
- an understanding of the numerical structure of an FEM programme in order to be able to estimate the technical possibilities and limitations.

In addition, participants have access to teaching software which was developed at the institute and helps them to get to know and to assess the main methodically-based characteristics of the finite element method using practical examples. This software was awarded the German Universities Software Prize in 1990 as the best software aid in the field of civil engineering.

The importance of communication in networks for civil engineering practice

The introduction of computers to the engineering community has led to the situation where data, plans and calculations are usually now available in digital form. Architects designs and technical drawings from the design offices are usually now made using CAD. Standardised data exchange formats allow the system-independent exchange of digital drawings and documents. The information which is currently available to the partners participating in the construction project and a knowledge of the current planning status are major resources which are now accessible to the engineers. The continuous process of world-wide networking, for example, Internet and ISDN communication and the transfer of data, open up new possibilities for the civil engineer too. The flow of data from the architects to the static engineer and the quality assurance department can continue digitally right through to the construction site. Changes to the design can be communicated from the planning department to the site in the shortest possible time. The spatial separation between the partners involved with planning and those involved on-site with the building itself are no longer of any significance. This also changes the significance of construction projects for the employment situation in the local region. With the introduction of European standards in the field of building construction and the acceptance of these standards in countries outside of Europe too, planning activities can be carried out independently of the location with the help of the new communication technology. In the future, price and ability will compete more strongly with companies who are located close to the construction site. Dealing with the new communication technologies has become a challenge for engineering offices and their employees, a basic technology in a competition throughout the European marketplace. Even without local offices, engineering capacity can now be offered throughout Europe or even world-wide. This is not only true for the engineering activities themselves. The classical concept must be rethought in the case of continuing education for engineers, too. The Internet and the newly available methods to propagate knowledge will influence training and further education more and more in the future.

Project course: 'The application of communication technology in Computer Aided Engineering' (E21)

In order to implement integrated project processing, it is vital to intensify communication through networks. This is particularly important because it's not only necessary to be able to exchange information in the form of ASCII data, but also to exchange engineering drawings made with CAD between the partners using the high performance networks of the Deutsche Bundespost (for example at a data transfer rate of up to 32 Mbit/s).

The course E21 'The application of communication technology in Computer Aided Engineering' covers this topic within the framework of WBBau. The course was developed 1989 in co-operation with lecturers from the Universities of Berlin, Munich and Bochum with the help of the Deutsche Forschungsnetz (DFN). The aim is to give the students some experience in using modern communication technologies and to demonstrate the possibilities which they offer,for example:

- the transfer of input/output files,
- the use of software installed on other host computers with the help of a remote login,
- the exchange of information and messages,
- data compression, for example, when exchanging graphical information.

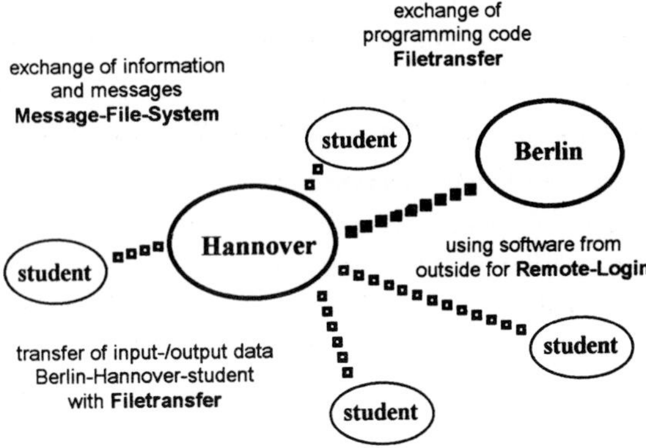

Fig: Usage of DFN services

The participants are able to connect to the communication server in Hannover using the telephone network (telephone modem) and to use the various services which are available and/or get information on the courses and to complete their homework etc. It is also possible with this communication server to reach partners in Berlin and Bochum by using, for example, the Deutsche Forschungsnet (DFN).

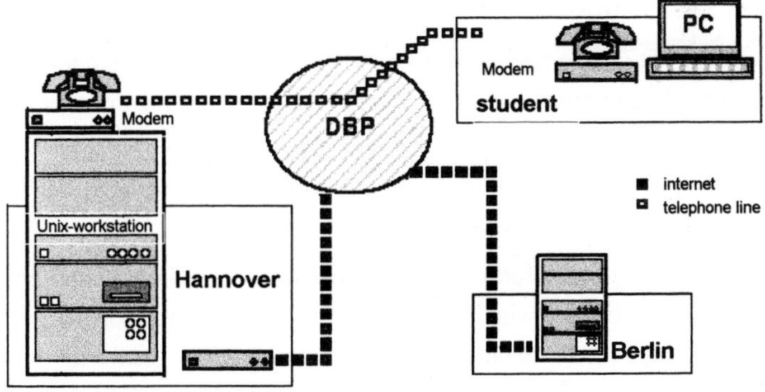

Fig: Usage of communications in continuing education

As an example, during course preparation the study material was created with a standard DTP system and transferred to the participants.

To save costs, the communications method chosen for this course was based on telephone modems and standard telephone lines. Due to the quantity of data and the technological pre-requirements it was not possible to consider the transfer of graphical data at this stage. However, new cheaper hardware and the ready availability of ISDN connections now allow the transfer of large quantities of data.

The significance of communication facilities for continuing education

However, for continuing education, the data networks are not only a means of transmitting training materials and communicating with and supporting students. During the development of the Internet, new software has become available which changes the whole approach to working with documents. Of particular note in this connection are browsers which allow the user to page through an appropriately formatted document using so-called hyperlinks, in order to access additional topics of interest. The transfer of knowledge is supported by individual interaction and by graphics. With this multimedia aid, the user can select particular themes from the document to fill in gaps in his or her personal knowledge.

In this connection, it is also necessary to mention the 'Learning on demand' which is promoted by companies. The network user retrieves the information which is needed individually, i.e. he or she accesses information and knowledge on the problem which is currently being worked on and retrieves the information necessary at the time point when it is required.

In addition to the usage of information in global networks, this technology can also be used in networks which are internal to the company for the purpose of internal training or to access in-house knowledge databases (for example, standard forms, appointment scheduling, advertising information, in-house business data etc.)

Integration of the new media in continuing education

The rapid change of technology in the field of networking and the new possibilities of transferring knowledge have motivated the department of computer science in civil engineering to introduce the training and continuing education topic 'Communication and data processing in networks' within the framework of a co-operation with other universities. The aim is not only to teach the new technology as a topic, but also to use it for the training itself. Within the framework of the project, the course is available as a voluntary intensifying course within the framework of a continuing education co-operation between technical colleges and universities. The following topic will be covered:

Networks

- Network technology
- Communication in networks
- Data storage in networks

Databases

- Access to scientific networks
- Basic concepts and applications
- Relational
- Programming
- Applications of networks
- Basic principles of abstraction
- The JAVA programming language

Execution

As far as possible, the continuing education programme should be carried out using a Wide Area Network. Dial-up nodes allow students to access the Internet, to get their own e-mail address and to use on-line training materials and software. Scripts and tutorials are available to give the participants experience with text, graphics and programs with the help of multimedia. Programmes with integrated checking and protocol mechanisms will be developed to correct the student's work. Methods of communication between lecturers and other students will be tested. Knowledge of the technologies of communication in networks, data storage, and the implementation of communication techniques should be taught and tested. Key areas are themes such as the preparation of information material with hypertext links, data storage in databases and even the programming of simple graphics for multimedia applications in networks using the object-oriented programming language JAVA.

Gerhard Fischer

Making Learning a Part of Life – Beyond the 'Gift Wrapping' Approch of Technology

Abstract

The previous notions of a divided lifetime – education followed by work – are no longer tenable. Learning can no longer be dichotomised, spatially and temporally, into a place and time to acquire knowledge (school) and a place and time to apply knowledge (the workplace). Professional activity has become so knowledge-intensive and fluid in content that learning has become an integral and inseparable part of adult work activities. Professional work can no longer simply proceed from a fixed educational background; rather, education must be smoothly incorporated as part of work activities fostering growth and exploration. Similarly, children require educational tools and environments whose primary aim is to help cultivate the desire to learn and create, and not to simply communicate subject matter divorced from meaningful and personalised activity.

Lifelong learning is a continuous engagement in acquiring and applying knowledge and skills in the context of authentic, self-directed problems. The research in lifelong learning in our Centre for 'Lifelong Learning and Design (L3D)' at CU Boulder is grounded in descriptive and prescriptive goals such as: (1) learning should take place in the context of authentic, complex problems (because learners will refuse to quietly listen to someone else's answers to someone else's questions); (2) learning should be embedded in the pursuit of intrinsically rewarding activities; (3) learning-on-demand needs to be supported because change is inevitable, complete coverage is impossible, and obsolescence is unavoidable; (4) organisational and collaborative learning must be supported because the individual human mind is limited; and (5) skills and processes that support learning as a lifetime habit must be developed.

We claim that most current uses of technology to support life-long learning are restricted to a gift wrapping approach: they are used as an add-on to existing practices rather than a catalyst for fundamentally rethinking what education and learning should be about in the next century. Old frameworks, such as instructionism, fixed curriculum, memorisation, decontextualised learning, etc., are not changed by technology itself. This is true whether we use computer-based training, intelligent tutoring systems, multimedia presentations, or the World Wide Web (WWW). We are engaged in developing computational environments to support new frameworks for lifelong learning such as: integration of working and learning, learning on demand, authentic problems, self-directed learning, information contextualised to the task at hand, (intrinsic) motivation, collaborative learning, and organisational learning.

1. Introduction

There is general agreement as we approach the next century and next millennium that our society is changing into a knowledge and information society. We will face new opportunities and new challenges in all dimensions of our lives. But the future is not out there to be discovered: it has to be invented and designed. Our research agenda is focusing on 'making learning a part of life', and the implications this has on how, under the influence of new media, new social structures, and new objectives for a quality of life, human beings will think, create, work, learn, and collaborate in the future.

2. Learning: Current Theories

Current trends in educational theory make the following fundamental assumptions about learning (arguments supporting this view can be found in the books by L. Resnick '*Knowing, Learning and Instruction*', D. Norman '*Things That Make Us Smart*', and M. Csikszentmihalyi '*Flow*'):

- Learning is a process of *knowledge construction*, not of knowledge recording or absorption.
- Learning is *knowledge-dependent*; people use their existing knowledge to construct new knowledge.
- Learning is highly *tuned to the situation* in which it takes place.
- Learning needs to account for *distributed cognition* requiring knowledge in the head to combine with knowledge in the world.
- Learning is affected as much by *motivational issues* as by cognitive issues.

3. Lifelong Learning

Lifelong Learning: A Ubiquitous Goal. Lifelong learning has emerged as one of the major challenges for the world-wide knowledge society of the future. A variety of recent events support this claim: (1) 1996 is the 'European Year of Lifelong Learning' [Otala 1993], (2) UNESCO has included 'Lifetime Education' as one of the key issues in its planning, and (3) the G7 group of countries has named 'Lifelong Learning' as a main strategy in the fight against unemployment. Despite this great interest, there are few encompassing efforts to tackle the problem in a coherent way. Lifelong learning cannot be investigated in isolation by looking just at one small part of it, such as K-12 education, university education or worker re-education.

Learning as a New Form of Labour. The previous notions of a divided lifetime-education followed by work are no longer tenable. Learning can no longer be dichotomised, spatially and temporally, into a place and time to *acquire* knowledge (school) and a place and time to *apply* knowledge (the workplace). Professional activity has become so knowledge-intensive and fluid in content that learning has become an integral and inseparable part of adult work activities. Professional work can no longer simply proceed from a fixed educational background; rather, education must be smoothly incorporated as part of work activities fostering growth and exploration. Similarly, children require educational tools and environments whose primary aim is to help cultivate the desire to learn and create, and not to simply communicate subject matter divorced from meaningful and personalised activity.

Lifelong learning is a continuous engagement in acquiring and applying knowledge and skills in the context of authentic, self-directed problems. L^3D's theoretical framework for lifelong learning is grounded in descriptive and prescriptive goals such as: (1) learning should take place in the context of authentic, complex problems (because learners will refuse to quietly listen to someone else's answers to someone else's questions); (2) learning should be embedded in the pursuit of intrinsically rewarding activities; (3) learning-on-demand needs to be supported because change is inevitable, complete coverage is impossible, and obsolescence is unavoidable; (4) organisational and collaborative learning must be supported because the individual human mind is limited; and (5) skills and processes that support learning as a life-time habit must be developed.

4. Lifelong Learning and Design

Lifelong learning integrates and mutually enriches the cultures of work and education. Central to this vision in our own research is the notion of design activity, a model of work that is open-ended and long-term in nature, incorporates personalised and collaborative aspects, and combines technical and aesthetic elements. Design is an argumentative process, involving ongoing negotiations and trade-offs; it is also a collaborative process making increasing use of new social structures brought about by the advent of computer networks and virtual communities. The communality that crucially binds these and other design activities together is that they are centred around the production of a new, publicly accessible artefact. Engineers and architects design infrastructure and buildings, lawyers design briefs and cases, politicians design policies and programmes, educators design curricula and courses, and software engineers design computer programmes. It is impossible for design processes to account for every aspect that might affect the designed artefact. Therefore, design must be treated as an evolutionary process in which designers continue to learn new things as the process unfolds. The relationship between learning and design provides the impetus for the work done at the L^{3}D Centre. Because design is an essential aspect of all problem-solving activity, and since designers are constantly learning and communicating with each other, the research done at the L^{3}D Centre seeks to ground educational theory within the domain of technology that supports design and communication.

5. Beyond the 'Gift Wrapping' Approach of Educational Reform-Rethinking, Re-inventing, and Re-engineering Education

A deeper understanding and more effective support for lifelong learning will contribute to the transformation that must occur in the way our society works and learns. A major finding in current business re-engineering efforts is that the use of information technology had disappointing results compared to the investments made in it (Landauer 1995). While a detailed causal analysis for this shortcoming is difficult to obtain, it is generally agreed that a major reason is that information technologies have been used to mechanise old ways of doing business rather than fundamentally rethinking the underlying work processes and promoting new ways to create artefacts and knowledge.

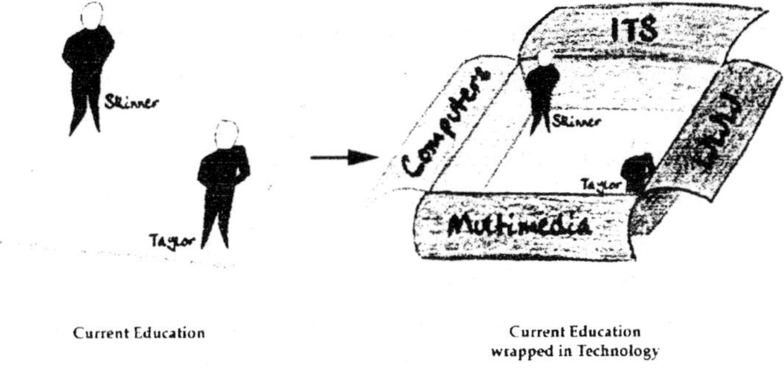

Current Education

Current Education wrapped in Technology

Figure 1: The 'Gift Wrapping' Approach

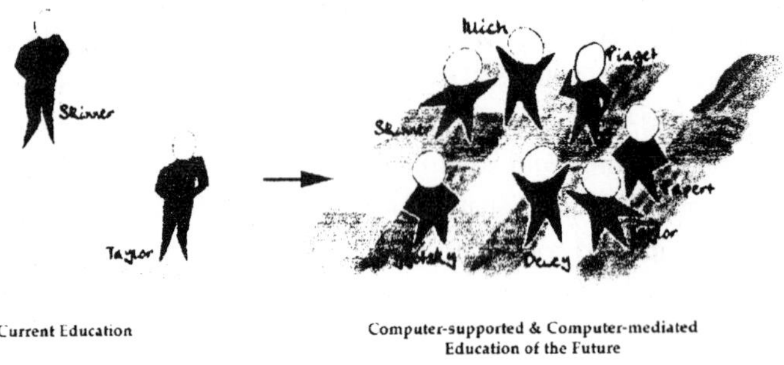

Figure 2: Re-thinking and Re-inventing Education

We claim that a similar argument can be made for current uses of technology in education: it is used as an add-on to existing practices rather than a catalyst for fundamentally rethinking what education should be about in the next century. For example, the innovation of making transparencies available on the WWW rather than distributing copies of them in a class takes advantage of the WWW as an electronic information medium. This may change the economics of teaching and learning, but it contributes little to introducing new epistemologies. Old frameworks, such as instructionism, fixed curriculum, memorisation, decontextualised learning, etc., are not changed by technology itself. This is true whether we use computer-based training, intelligent tutoring systems, multimedia presentations, or the WWW.

We need computational environments to support new frameworks for education such as lifelong learning, integration of working and learning, learning on demand, authentic problems, self-directed learning, information contextualised to the task at hand, (intrinsic) motivation, collaborative learning, and organisational learning. Figure 1 illustrates the gift-wrapping approach in which technology is merely wrapped around old frameworks for education. Figure 2 indicates what is needed instead: a richer conceptual framework, leading not just to the addition of technology but to the weaving of technology into learning and working.

Figure 3 tabulates the major changes required. It shows strong similarities between the behaviourist learning theory of B.F. Skinner and the models of industrial work of F.W. Taylor, and contrasts these with the lifelong approach to learning.

Skinner/Taylor		L^3D
there is a "scientific," best way to learn and to work (programmed instruction, computer-assisted instruction, production lines, waterfall models)	--->	*real problems are ill-defined and wikked; design is argumentative, characterised by a symmetry of ignorance among stakeholders*
separation of thinking, doing, and learning	--->	*integration of thinking, doing, and learning*
task domains can be completely understood	--->	*understanding is partial; coverage is impossible*
objective ways to decompose problems into standardisable actions	--->	*subjective, situated personal interests; need for iterative explorations*
all relevant knowledge can be explicitly articulated	--->	*much knowledge is tacit and relies on tacit skills*
teacher / manager as oracle	--->	*teacher / manager as facilitator or coach*
operational environment: mass markets, simple products and processes, slow change, certainty	--->	*customer orientation, complex products and processes, rapid and substantial change, uncertainty and conflicts*

Figure 3: Beyond Skinner and Taylor

6. Myths and Misconceptions

The current debate about the ability of computation and communication to fundamentally change education are (in our opinion) based on a number of fundamental myths and misconceptions. The most prevalent ones are:

- *Computers by themselves will change education*–There is no empirical evidence for this assumption based on the last 30 years of using computers to change education (such as computer-assisted instruction, computer-based training, or intelligent tutoring systems). Technology is no 'Deus ex machina' taking care of education. As mentioned before, making slides available over the World-Wide Web rather than giving paper copies to students can be valuable, but will not change education. Instructionist approaches are not changed by the fact that information is disseminated by an intelligent tutoring system.

- *Information is a scarce resource* –Dumping even more decontextualised information on people is not a step forward in a world where most of us already suffer from too much information. Instead, technology should provide ways to say the right thing at the right time in the right' way. In our research, we have explored problems associated with high-functionality applications (such as operating systems, word processors, spreadsheets, etc.). Our empirical findings (which are universally true for all systems) are illustrated in Figure 4 (Fischer 1993a). These systems provide challenging problems for a research agenda for 'Learning and Intelligent Systems,' because if future progress is achieved only by extending D4 to D4', there will be no benefits for users. Instead of increasing the tool mastery burden of users even more, we need new concepts such as learning-on-demand, information delivery, and task-based unfolding, so users can incrementally explore and master such systems according to their needs.

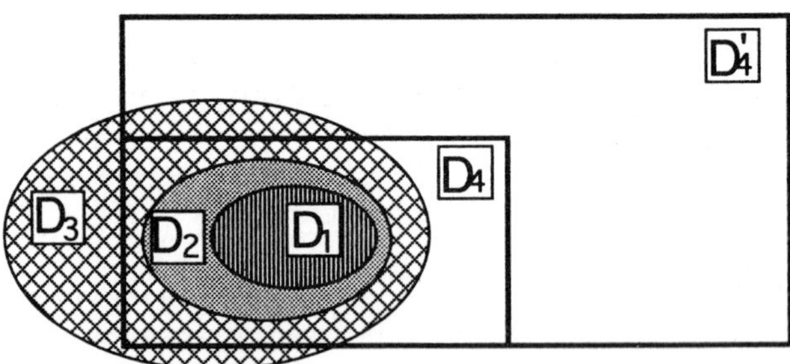

Figure 4: Levels of Users' Knowledge About a System's Information Spaces

The rectangle (D4) represents the actual information space of a system and the ovals represent users' knowledge about the system's information space.

D1 represents concepts well known and easily employed by the users. D2 contains concepts known vaguely and used only occasionally, often requiring passive help systems. D3 represents concepts users *believe* to exist in the system, some of which lie outside the actual information space. In the case of increased functionality (as illustrated by D4'), the area D4-D3 (representing the functionality users are not even aware of) increases to D4'-D3, not that of the ovals.

- *The content, value, and quality of information and knowledge is improved just because it is offered in multi-media or over the WWW*– Media itself does not turn irrelevant or erroneous information into more relevant information (as indicated by Figure 5). We must create innovative technologies (such as simulations, visualisations, critiquing, etc.) to let people experience knowledge in new ways.
- *'Ease of use' is the greatest challenge or the most desirable goal for new technologies* –Usable technologies that are not useful for the needs and concerns of people are of no value. Rather than assuming people should and will be able to do everything without a substantial learning effort, we should design computational environments that provide a low threshold for getting started and a high ceiling to allow skilled users to do the things they want to do.

Figure 5: The Existence of Information Alone is Not Good Enough

- *The 'Nobel Prize winner' myth: Every school child will have access to a Nobel Prize winner* – This was one of the selling points for the information superhighway. While this argument is true (or will be true soon) at the level of technical connectivity, it is doubtful that Nobel Prize winners will look forward to getting a few thousand e-mail messages a day.
- *The single or most important objective of computational media is reducing the cost of education* – Although we should not ignore any opportunity to use technology to lessen the cost of education, we should not lose sight of an objective that is of equal if not greater importance: increasing the *quality* of education.

7. Requirements for Systems Supporting Lifelong Learning

To operationalise and substantiate the preceding theoretical framework we have articulated six hypotheses which frame the design and development of the computational artefacts in our proposed research.

- *Hypothesis 1: User-directed and supportive.* In any computational system supporting lifelong learning, the choice of tasks and goals (including the learning opportunities offered) must be under the control of the user/ learner and support contextualised to the user's task must be provided.

Implication for System Building. Creating a system that supports user-directed tasks within a chosen domain implies that such an environment covers an extensive range of potential projects. Such a system needs to provide rich additional structures, that is, all the components of our domain-oriented design environments (DODEs) (Fischer 1994a): domain-specific construction tools, catalogues (or on-line libraries) of examples, and so forth.

Potential Challenges or Pitfalls. Any DODE that is rich enough to support realistic projects is likely to present significant complexity to the user. A major challenge in designing such environments is to allow users to encounter the complexity of the system gradually. Mechanisms such as self-disclosure (DiGiano, Eisenberg, 1995a), in which a system allows users to perform simple tasks by direct means while simultaneously suggesting other (ultimately more powerful) ways of accomplishing the same tasks, offer promise in meeting this challenge.

- *Hypothesis 2: Contextualised presentation.* A system supporting lifelong learning, when it presents information to the user must do so in a way that is maximally relevant to the user's chosen project or task.

Implication for System Building. A DODE is not merely a tool for design but is more like a knowledgeable assistant (Collins, Brown, Newman 1989)-sharing, when possible, system knowledge relevant to a particular design task. It should not only provide more information, but say the right thing at the right time in the right way (Nakakoji and Fischer, 1995).

Potential Challenges or Pitfalls. The feasibility of a knowledgeable assistant crucially depends on how users can communicate their intentions and task descriptions to the system and whether they can do so in a way that does not itself require inordinate expertise. Systems that support the articulation of partial task specifications, such as Janus (Fischer and Nakakoji, 1991), and ProNet (Sullivan, 1994)) suggest means to address this challenge.

- *Hypothesis 3: Breakdowns as opportunities for learning.* A system supporting lifelong learning will be sufficiently open-ended and complex so that users will encounter breakdowns. The system must provide means for allowing users to understand, extricate themselves from, and learn from breakdowns; turning them into opportunities rather than failures.

Implications for System-Building. As any professional designer knows, breakdowns, (Dede, 1995; Fischer, 1994b; Popper, 1965) although at times costly and painful, also offer unique opportunities for reflection and learning (Petroski 1985). This is also expressed by Norman: 'The way we learn is by trying something, doing it and getting stuck. In order to learn, we really have to be stuck, and when we're stuck we are ready for the critical piece of information. The same piece of information that made no impact at a lecture makes a dramatic impact when we're ready for it' (Norman, 1993). This insight provided the rationale for exploring learning on demand (Fischer,

1991). Critiquing systems (Fischer et al. 1991) offer advice and information to the user precisely at the problematic moment and by supporting reflection-in-action (Schön, 1983), allow users to explore the argumentation and design rationale associated with their actions. Our future design environments will be equipped not only with catalogues of exemplary or illustrative work (as suggested by Hypothesis 2), but also with catalogues of illustrative failures.

Potential Challenges or Pitfalls. In many design domains, the notion of breakdown is imbued with so much context and common-sense knowledge that it precludes easy identification by a computational system. New and creative mechanisms are required to allow the user and system to engage in a form of dialogue centring on understanding those breakdowns that neither the user or system is able to identify independently.

- *Hypothesis 4: End-user modification and programmability.* A system supporting lifelong learning must provide means for significant modification, extension, and evolution by users.

Implications for System-Building. Design environments deal with complex and open-ended domains in which long-term users build extensive catalogues of personalised creative work. In contrast, non-programmable systems-systems in which the user is compelled to make choices by selection among fixed sets of alternatives (for example, via menus or dialogue boxes) are rarely capable of providing users with the means for achieving their work; users' tasks eventually outstrip the capabilities provided by such systems. As a result, DODEs need means by which users can extend the functionality of their applications, building progressively more complex vocabularies and languages of design. We (Eisenberg and Fischer, 1994; Fischer, 1993b) have only scratched the surface of what would be possible if end users could freely programme their own applications (Nardi, 1993). DODEs will be equipped with an end-user programming language (such as Visual AgenTalk). This, in turn, implies certain desiderata for that language: interactivity, learnability, and expressiveness within the domain of the application.

Potential Challenges or Pitfalls. We are currently exploring several approaches to end-user empowerment including: creating more powerful substrates, enriching existing languages with domain specific elements (Eisenberg, 1995), designing new domain specific languages (Repenning and Sumner, 1995), and developing self-disclosure mechanisms (DiGiano and Eisenberg, 1995b) within DODEs. Each of these solutions presents its own characteristic advantages and disadvantages as we apply them to end-user modification and programming.

- *Hypothesis 5: Supporting a range of expertise.* Systems supporting lifelong learning will be employed over long periods of time by their users; hence, these systems must be able to accommodate users at progressively different levels of expertise.

Implications for System-Building. The notion of expertise is twofold, implying both expertise in the particular domain and expertise in the use of the system itself. For a DODE to support wide levels of expertise among its users, it must permit beginners to start with a learnable but expandable set of building blocks for design (Fischer and Lemke 1988; Soloway, Guzdial and Hay, 1994). To the extent that a design environment can represent to itself the level of the user's expertise, background knowledge and interests, it can tailor interaction and learning material to the appropriate level.

Potential Challenges or Pitfalls. Within design environments, modelling the user's expertise is especially delicate because these domains and the artefacts developed in them are not amenable to simple evaluations. The primary opportunity in developing ideas of making DODEs adaptive and adaptable (Fischer, 1993b) and in supporting task and user modelling is to exploit the domain orientation and the integration of the different components of these systems.

- *Hypothesis 6: Promoting collaboration.* Systems supporting lifelong learning must include means for collaboration between users.

Implications for System-Building. Designers do their work within a community of practice (Arias, 1995; Brown and Duguid, 1991; Lave, 1988), in which collaboration may take many forms: large-scale projects may involve close ongoing collaboration among numerous designers, whereas smaller-scale projects may be better viewed as a matter of individual work followed by collective evaluation and critiquing (Rittel, 1984). Design environments must be structured to permit productive and flexible collaboration among users. The World Wide Web offers promising new means for providing such collaboration (Brown et al. 1993; Bruckman and Resnick, 1995; Scardamalia and Bereiter, 1991) as in our Remote Explorium project (Ambach, Perrone and Repenning 1995).

Potential Challenges or Pitfalls. Problems designing and maintaining collaborative environments include: the difficulty of allowing multiple users to keep track of distinct versions of projects and recording the rationale for the decisions of multiple users. The development of Visual AgenTalk and other Web-based mechanisms within our group for sharing self-contained pieces of end-user programmes offer new avenues for facilitating group design.

8. Applying our Theory to SimCity

We will illustrate our theoretical framework by applying it to a commercial software package, SimCity 2000, by Maxis, Incorporated. We have selected SimCity because it is one of the outstanding educational games available (as rated by educators (Miranker and Elliott 1995)). It allows players to understand the possibilities and limits of simulation and the concepts of indirect causality by immersing them in a complex construction environment. It is evocative-players of the game are immediately engaged to the extent that they soon try to model cities and city planning issues that have direct, personal relevance. Doing this, they quickly run up against the limitations of the game environment. By analysing SimCity, we wanted to understand how our envisioned environments could support this kind of enjoyable, engaged, self-directed learning experience while, instead of playing a game, users perform real, personally meaningful design tasks.

H1: User-directed and supportive. SimCity allows users to build a city within the framework, object sets, and constraints provided. The construction mechanisms are quite rich and include support mechanisms such as, reactions based on the simulation model, visual, budgetary, and newspaper feedback. Despite its features, SimCity fails when applied to real city-planning problems (such as the Boulder HOP design, a real problem for the city of Boulder that is explained in our scenario below) because, with the exception of the SimCity Urban Renewal Kit (SCURK) -an add-on module to increase user control- it is a closed system. Players must interact with a fixed set of objects at a particular level of detail that does not necessarily provide the capabilities that allow them to construct models they are truly interested in. The system offers no explanations, and causal relationships among simulation objects are hidden.

H2: Contextualised presentation. In SimCity, the task at hand is the construction situation; there is no way for users to specify high-level goals such as limited growth, or a preference for mass transportation. The game includes pre-modelled city scenarios, however, there is no support for task-based indexing to enable users to identify those most relevant to current tasks or interests. For instance, public transportation affects the success or decline of a city in many ways (Dargahi, 1991). This information is hidden from a user who might find it helpful in a planning context.

H3: Breakdowns as opportunities for learning. Breakdowns are likely in SimCity, but the support for reflection is insufficient. Breakdowns are presented to the user in scenario form, as disasters, or simply diminishing population and dwindling city revenues. When something is going wrong, there are no explanations of what simulation mechanisms are causing problems. Possible solutions must be provided and implemented by the user with little support to explore the worth or applicability of each one to a particular situation. Therefore, contextualised learning is limited.

H4: End-user modification and programmability. SimCity provides users with a very broad but fixed functionality. A user cannot explicitly examine the system model to see how the developers of SimCity have framed certain fundamental issues nor can they make modifications that extend the functionality of the system. For instance, if the crime rate is too high, we can (with substantial effort) infer which of the many components in the game that affect it, such as zoning, education, ordinances, property values, population density, police stations, and the level of police funding. Users cannot develop and introduce innovative ways to prevent crime, by the addition of social services, for example. SCURK allows existing graphical depictions to be edited and new cities to be constructed outside of the simulation. One can change the look of most objects but not object behaviour. Therefore, SCURK would not help to model the Boulder HOP. The simulation is a black box, and users are only permitted to paint the box.

H5: Supporting a range of expertise. Depending on their level of expertise, users can turn disasters off, vary the amount of money they have available at the start, and adjust the speed of the simulation. The explanations given and the tools offered are not adapted to the perspectives, goals, needs, and background knowledge of users with varying degrees of skills within the domain.

H6: Promoting collaboration. There is a multi-user version of the SimCity game that provides similar functionality to the single-user version, except that mayoral decisions can be made by a committee that votes on them. It does not include support for a community of users, including the ability to share reasoning and argumentation or the ability to share simulation components.

The above critique of SimCity illustrates how our theoretical framework can be used to assess computational environments supporting lifelong learning and the integration of working and learning. Because of the weaknesses we have identified in SimCity, it is unlikely to be used to model real problems. We have confirmed this in discussions with members of organisations such as the Boulder City Council, the Transportation Committee, and the Boulder County Healthy Communities Initiative.

Domain-Oriented Design Environments (DODEs). Over the last 8 years, we have created and evolved DODEs (Fischer, 1994a) as a new class of computational environments (Winograd, 1995) to overcome the limitations and to address the challenges identified by our analysis of SimCity. We have developed process models supporting the creation and evolution of DODEs (Eisenberg and Fischer, 1994; Fischer et al. 1994) and a component architecture including construction, specification, and argumentation components, catalogues serving as case-based libraries for the representation of domain knowledge (Willams, 1992), and critiquing and simulation components (Fischer et al. 1991) to help users to identify breakdowns (Fischer, 1994b) and integrate reflection and action (Norman, 1993; Schön, 1983).

9. The Seeding, Evolutionary Growth and Re-seeding (SER) Model - Information Spaces Developed and Evolved by Distributed Constructionism

Most intelligent systems (including systems in support of learning such as Intelligent Tutoring Systems and Expert Systems) of the past have been developed as closed systems. The basic assumption was that during design time, a domain could be modelled completely by bringing domain experts (designers) and environment developers (knowledge engineers) together and the knowledge engineers would acquire the relevant knowledge from the domain experts and encode it into the system. This approach fails for the following reasons: (1) as argued before, much knowledge is tacit and only surfaces in specific problem situations; and (2) the world changes, and intelligent systems modelling this world must change accordingly. In our research, we have developed a process model to address these problems (see Figure 6). It postulates three major phases:

A seed will be created through a participatory design process between environment developers and domain designers. It will evolve in response to its use in new design projects because requirements fluctuate, change is ubiquitous, and design knowledge is tacit. Postulating the objective of a seed (rather then a complete domain model or a complete knowledge base) sets this approach apart from other approaches in intelligent systems development and emphasises evolution as the central design concept.

Evolutionary growth takes place as workers and learners use the seeded environment to undertake specific projects. During these design efforts, new requirements may surface, new components may come into existence, and additional design knowledge not contained in the seed may be articulated. During the evolutionary growth phase, the environment developers are not present, making end-user modification a necessity rather than a luxury. World-wide communities of practice can participate in this process, named distributed constructionism (Resnick, 1996) if the WWW becomes an information environment for collaboration and sharing rather than one for information dissemination.

Reseeding, a deliberate effort of revision and co-ordination of information and functionality, brings the environment developers back to collaborate with domain designers to organise, formalise, and generalise knowledge added during the evolutionary growth phases. Organisational concerns play a crucial role in this phase. For example, decisions have to be made as to which of the extensions created in the context of specific design projects should be incorporated in future versions of the generic design environment. Drastic and large-scale evolutionary changes occur during the re-seeding phase.

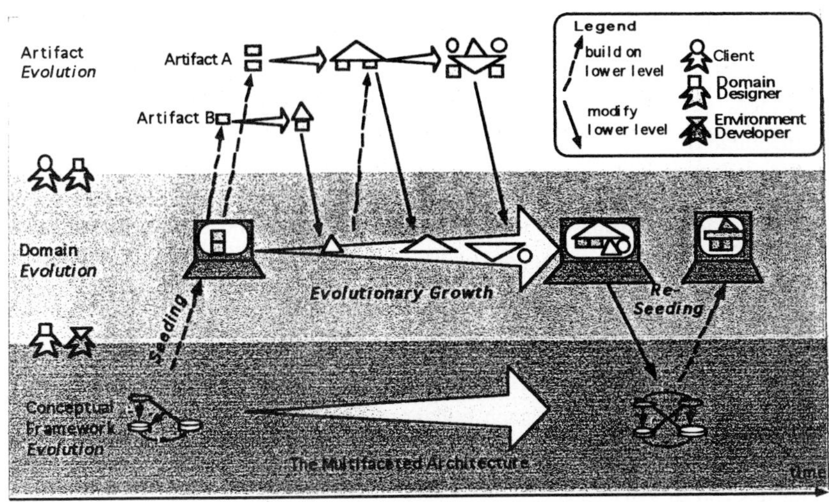

Figure 6: The SER Model: A process model for the development and evolution of domain-oriented intelligent systems

10. Building Interdisciplinary Investigation of Lifelong Learning

Building successful interdisciplinary investigations is not a small task in a world in which specialisation necessarily increases and the days of the universally educated 'Renaissance Scholars' belong to the past. C.P. Snow, in his famous book *The Two Cultures* (1959), identified the difficulty of literary intellectuals and natural scientists communicating successfully with each other. He claimed to have found a profound mutual suspicion and incomprehension, which had damaging consequences for the prospects of applying technology to the alleviation of the world's problems. Many more different cultures exist today, for example, novices versus skilled workers, software developers versus software users, industry people versus academics, and committed technophiles versus determined technophobes.

Experiences. At CU Boulder we have tried for the last ten years to build bridges among different cultures (the most relevant ones will be briefly mentioned):

1. The Institute of Cognitive Science at CU Boulder brings together researchers from the humanities, the social sciences, the natural sciences, and engineering, acknowledging that problems the scientific community needs to address do not always fall neatly into the structures of established departments.
2. In the context of university/industry relationships, we have tried to reinvent the purposes of such collaborations (and have explored research issues in detail in our close collaboration with NYNEX University and NYNEX Science and Technology).
3. By working with the Boulder Valley School District and with several specific schools, we have tried to understand the problems of empowering teachers to become lifelong learners and of introducing and sustaining technology in school settings.
4. Acknowledging that learning is desired and takes place outside formal institutions, we have recently started a collaboration with the Boulder County Healthy Community Initiative, a group of several hundred concerned citizens, which reflects on the future of our county.
5. In our L^3D Centre we have brought together researchers and students from various parts of the world to understand different perspectives about how people think about our world.

Our focus on lifelong learning and design has served as a forcing function to create these interdisciplinary investigations and they in return have been of critical importance to our understanding of the challenges of learning and intelligent systems.

Challenges: The building of successful interdisciplinary investigations faces the following challenges:

1. To regard the existing symmetry of ignorance (a concept articulated by (Rittel, 1984), who argues that among all the carriers of knowledge for any real problem there is nobody who has a guarantee that her or his knowledge is superior to any other person's knowledge) as an opportunity rather than as a limitation or an undesired obstacle.
2. To overcome the boundaries of creating divisions between basic and applied research by doing basic research on real problems.
3. To find ways and to develop means to allow different cultures to talk to each other and to engage them as active participants in inventing the future (for example, to liberate social scientists from their passive consumer and Cassandra role, and to make technologists aware that technological changes and innovations do not happen in isolation but in existing social networks involving people).

11. A Set of Challenges for Lifelong Learning

'Making Learning a Part of Life' creates many challenges, requiring creative new approaches and collaboration among many different stakeholders. For illustration, just a few of them will be mentioned here.

1. *The educated and informed citizen of the future: 'super-couch potato' consumers or enlightened designers* – The major innovation that many powerful interest groups push for with the information superhighway is to have a future where everyone shows her or his creativity and engagement by selecting one of at least 500 TV channels with a remote control. The major technical challenge derived from this perspective becomes the design of a 'user-friendly' remote control. Rather than serving as the 'reproductive organ of a consumer society' (Illich, 1971), educational institutions must fight this trend by cultivating designers, that is, by creating mindsets and habits that help people become empowered and willing to actively contribute to the design of their lives and communities. This goal creates specific challenges for computa-

tional artefacts, such as the support of end-user programming and authoring.

2. *The 'basic skills' debate* - If the hypothesis that most job-relevant knowledge must be learned on demand is true, we have to ask ourselves: what is the role of basic skills? If, for example, the use of software packages dominates the use of mathematics in the workplace, should not a new function of mathematics education be teaching students to use these mathematical artefacts intelligently? Another important challenge is that the old basic skills such as reading, writing, and arithmetic, once acquired, were relevant for the duration of a human life; modern basic skills (tied to rapidly changing technologies) will change over time.

3. *Can we change motivation?*-As mentioned, there is substantial empirical evidence that the chief impediments to learning are not cognitive but motivational (Csikszentmihalyi, 1990b). This raises the challenge of whether we can create learning environments in which learners work hard, not because they have to, but because they want to. We need to alter the perception that serious learning has to be unpleasant rather than personally meaningful, empowering, engaging, and even fun. In our research efforts we have developed computational environments to address these motivational issues; for example, our systems have explored making information relevant to the task at hand, providing challenges matched to current skills, creating communities (among peers, over the net), and providing access to real practitioners and experts.

4. *School-to-work transition* - If the world of working and living (a) relies on collaboration, creativity, definition, and framing of problems; (b) deals with uncertainty, change, and distributed cognition; (c) copes with symmetry of ignorance; and (d) augments and empowers humans with powerful technological tools, then the world of schools and universities needs to prepare students to function in this world. Industrial-age models of education and work (based on Skinner and Taylor, as illustrated above) are inadequate to prepare students to compete in the knowledge-based workplace. A major objective of our lifelong learning approach is

to reduce the gap between school and workplace learning. Our research addresses some of the major school-to-work transition problems and develops answers to the following questions:

- How can schools prepare learners and workers for a world that relies on interdependent, distributed, non-hierarchical information flow and rapidly shifting authority based on complementary knowledge?
- What basic skills are required in a world in which occupational knowledge and skills become obsolete in years rather than decades?
- How can schools (which currently rely on closed-book exams, the solving of given problems, and so forth) be changed so that learners are prepared to function in environments requiring collaboration, creativity, problem framing, and distributed cognition?
- To what extent will lifelong learning and new approaches to learning and teaching-such as learning on demand, learning while working, relations, and the involvement of professionals in schools-prepare learners for work?

12. What's Wrong With Current Universities

We consider the self-application of our theories a critical element (and a unique opportunity) in the assessment of our research efforts. Universities as institutions need to be in the middle of rethinking the future of working and learning-applying their findings not only to other institutions, but to themselves. Using the previously developed framework causes us to critically examine our own work as university faculty members in the following ways:

- Understanding learning as active knowledge construction rather than passive knowledge absorption questions the dominance of lectures.
- Allowing learners to engage in authentic, self-directed learning activities is at odds with micro-managed curricula.

- Acknowledging that problem solving in the real world includes problem framing calls into question the practice of asking students to solve mostly given problems.
- Recognising that most interesting problems in the real world do not have right or wrong answers, but instead must be solved by satisfying objectives that are most important for that situation.
- Acknowledging that the individual human mind is limited and that outside of schools people rely heavily on information and knowledge distributed among groups of people and various artefacts (distributed cognition) questions the value of closed-book exams, and requires a much greater emphasis on collaborative learning and communication skills.

13. Conclusions

Research in lifelong learning, especially if we want to move beyond the gift wrapping approach of technology, will have fundamental long-term societal impacts. It will force us to reinvent how we think, work, learn, create, and collaborate. It will change

1. institutions, for example,

1.1. universities (as argued above) (Noam, 1995)

1.2. companies will have to become learning organisations (Senge, 1990)

2. individuals, for example,

2.1. who will have a desire to become independent of high-tech scribes in personally meaningful and important activities

2.2. who would like to contribute to their (computer-enriched) reality rather than merely interacting with it

3. mindsets, for example,

3.1. teachers should see themselves not as truth-tellers and oracles, but as coaches, facilitators, learners, and mentors engaging with learners

3.2. breakdowns (Fischer, 1994b) and symmetry of ignorance (Rittel, 1984) need to be understood as opportunities

4. connections and collaborations, for example,

4.1. connecting in new ways (for example, distributed communities of practice and interest) will go along with disconnecting in old ways (being physically together, increased specialisation)

4.2. organisational learning supported by organisational memories will complement individual learning (Fischer et al. 1996).

This research will provide us with opportunities to explore fundamentally new possibilities and limitations of computational media as they complement existing media. It will force us to think about new concepts such as sustainable communities of practice. It will pose the question of how large complex information spaces can be evolved over long periods of time, not by their professional designers but by their affected users. It will enrich the notion of distributed cognition, allowing us to draw different lines between what humans should do and what machines should do.

One may argue that our current thinking does not address the potential magnitude of the change. Have we arrived at a point where the change is of a similar magnitude to the time when our society moved from an oral to a literary society (and Socrates and Plato were arguing about the trade-offs associated with this change) or when Gutenberg's printing press eliminated the scribes and gave everyone the opportunity to become literate? The fact that societies have often overestimated change in the short run and underestimated it in the long run suggests that we should make every effort to understand the long-term societal impacts of learning and intelligent systems.

As argued at the beginning, the future of how we live, think, create, work, learn, and collaborate is not out there to be discovered, it has to be invented and designed. Computational and communication media (firmly grounded in a deep understanding of theories and prescriptive goals) will be a critical force in shaping this future.

References

Ambach, J., Perrone, C. and Repenning, A. (1995), Remote Exploratoriums: Combining Networking and Design Environments, *Computers and Education*, Vol. 24, No. pp. 163-176.

Arias, E. G. (1995), Designing in a Design Community: Insights and Challenges, in Proceedings of DIS'95, Symposium on Designing Interactive Systems (Ann Arbor, MI), New York, pp. 259-263.

Brown, A. L., et al (1993), Distributed Expertise in the Classroom, in Salomon, G. (ed.), *Distributed Cognitions: Psychological and Educational Considerations*, New York, Cambridge University Press, pp. 188-228.

Brown, J. S. and Duguid, P. (1991), Organizational Learning and Communities-of-Practice: Toward a Unified View of Working, Learning, and Innovation, in Organization Science, *The Institute of Management Sciences*, pp. 40-57.

Bruckman, A. and Resnick, M. (1995), The Media MOO Project: Constructionism and Professional Community, Convergence, Vol. 1, No. 1, pp. 94-109.

Collins, A. M., Brown, J. S. and Newman, S. E. (1989), Cognitive Apprenticeship: Teaching the Crafts of Reading, Writing and Mathematics, in L.B. Resnick (ed.), *Knowing, Learning, and Instruction*, Lawrence Erlbaum Associates, Hillsdale, NJ, pp. 453-494.

Csikszentmihalyi, M. (1990a), *Flow: The Psychology of Optimal Experience*, New York, Harper Collins Publishers.

Csikszentmihalyi, M. (1990b), Literacy and Intrinsic Motivation, *Daedalus,* Vol. No. Spring, pp. 115-140.

Dargahi, N. (1991), *SimCity Strategies and Secrets*, Sybex, Inc, Alameda, CA.

Dede, C. (1995), Integrating Learning and Working, NSF Workshop Document (unpublished), September 1995.

DiGiano, C. and Eisenberg, M. (1995a), Self-Disclosing Design Tools: A Gentle Introduction to End-User Programming, Symposium on Designing Interactive Systems, DIS'95, pp. 189-197.

DiGiano, C. and Eisenberg, M. (1995b), Supporting the End-User Programmer as a Lifelong Learner, Department of Computer Science Technical Report #CU-CS-761-95, University of Colorado at Boulder

Eisenberg, M. (1995), Creating Software Applications for Children: Some Thoughts about Design, in diSessa, A., Hoyle, C., Noss, R. and Edwards, L. (eds*.), The Design of Computational Media to Support Exploratory Learning*, Heidelberg, Springer-Verlag, pp. 175-196.

Eisenberg, M. and Fischer, G. (1994), Programmable Design Environments: Integrating End-User Programming with Domain-Oriented Assistance, Human Factors in Computing Systems, CHI'94 Conference Proceedings (Boston, MA), pp. 431-437.

Fischer, G. (1991), Supporting Learning on Demand with Design Environments, International Conference on the Learning Sciences 1991, pp. 165-172.

Fischer, G. (1993a), Beyond Human Computer Interaction: Designing Useful and Usable Computational Environments, in People and Computers VIII: Proceedings of the HCI'93 Conference (Loughborough, England), Cambridge, Cambridge, University Press, pp. 17-31.

Fischer, G. (1993b), Shared Knowledge in Co-operative Problem-Solving Systems - Integrating Adaptive and Adaptable Components, in Schneider-Hufschmidt, M., Kuehme, T. and Malinowski, U. (eds.), *Adaptive User Interfaces - Principles and Practice*, Amsterdam, Science Publishers, pp. 49-68.

Fischer, G. (1994a), Domain-Oriented Design Environments, in Automated Software Engineering, Boston, Kluwer Academic Publishers, MA, pp. 177-203.

Fischer, G. (1994b), Turning Breakdowns into Opportunities for Creativity, in Knowledge-Based Systems, Special Issue on Creativity and Cognition, Butterworth-Heinemann, pp. 221-232.

Fischer, G. and Lemke, A. C. (1998), Construction Kits and Design Environments: Steps Toward Human Problem-Domain Communication, in *Human-Computer Interaction*, pp. 179-222.

Fischer, G., et al (1991), The Role of Critiquing in Cooperative Problem Solving, in *ACM Transactions on Information Systems*, pp. 123-151.

Fischer, G., et al (1996), Informing System Design Through Organizational Learning, International Conference on the Learning Sciences 1996, pp. 52-59.

Fischer, G., et al (1994), Seeding, Evolutionary Growth and Reseeding: Supporting Incremental Development of Design Environments, Human Factors in Computing Systems, CHI'94, pp. 292-298.

Fischer, G. and Nakakoji, K. (1991), Making Design Objects Relevant to the Task at Hand, in Proceedings of AAAI-91, Ninth National Conference on Artificial Intelligence, AAAI Press/The MIT Press, Cambridge, MA, pp. 67-73.

Illich, I. (1971), *Deschooling Society*, New York, Harper and Row.

Landauer, T. K. (1995), The Trouble with Computers, Cambridge Ma, MIT Press..

Lave, J. (1988), *Cognition in Practice*, Cambridge, Cambridge University Press.

Miranker, C. and Elliott, A. (1995), *The Computer Museum Guide to the Best Software for Kids,* New York, Harper Collins Publishers, Inc.

Nakakoji, K. and Fischer, G. (1995), Intertwining Knowledge Delivery and Elicitation: A Process Model for Human-Computer Collaboration in *Design, Knowledge-Based Systems Journal,* Special Issue on Human-Computer Collaboration, Vol. 8, No. 2-3, pp. 94-104.

Nardi, B. A. (1993), *A Small Matter of Programming,* Cambridge, MA, The MIT Press, Cambridge.

Noam, E. M. (1995), Electronics and the Dim Future of the University, Science, Vol. 270, No. pp. 247-249.

Norman, D. A. (1993), *Things That Make Us Smart*, Reading, MA., Addison-Wesley Publishing Company.

Otala, L. (1993), Lifelong Learning Based on Industry-University Co-operation: A Strategy for European Industry's Competitiveness, Helsinki University of Technology.

Petroski, H. (1985), *To Engineer Is Human: The Role of Failure in Successful Design*, New York, St. Martin's Press.

Popper, K. R. (1965), *Conjectures and Refutations*, New York, Harper & Row, San Francisco, London, Hagerstown.

Repenning, A. and Sumner, T. (1995), Agentsheets: A Medium for Creating Domain-Oriented Visual Languages, in Computer, IEEE Computer Society, Los Alamitos, CA, pp. 17-25.

Resnick, L. B. (1989), *Knowing, Learning, and Instruction: Essays in Honor of Robert Glaser*, NJ, Lawrence Erlbaum Associates, Hillsdale.

Resnick, M. (1996), Distributed Constructionism, International Conference on the Learning Sciences 1996, pp. 280-284.

Rittel, H. (1984), Second-Generation Design Methods, in Cross, N. (ed.), *Developments in Design Methodology*, New York, John Wiley & Sons, pp. 317-327.

Scardamalia, M. and Bereiter, C. (1991), Higher Levels of Agency for Children in Knowledge Building: A Challenge to the Design of New Media, *Journal of the Learning Sciences*, Vol. 1, No. 1, pp. 37-68.

Schön, D. A. (1983), *The Reflective Practitioner: How Professionals Think in Action*, New York, Basic Books.

Senge, P. M. (1990), *The Fifth Dimension – The Art & Practice of the Learning Organization*, New York, Currency Doubleday.

Snow, C. P. (1959), *The Two Cultures*, Cambridge, Cambridge University Press.

Soloway, E., Guzdial, M. and Hay, K. E., Learner-Centered Design, *Interactions*, Vol. 1, No. 2, pp. 36-48.

Sullivan, J. (1994), A Proactive Computational Approach for Learning While Working, Ph.D. Thesis, University of Colorado at Boulder.

Williams, S. M. (1992), Putting Case-Based Instruction Into Context: Examples From Legal and Medical Education, *The Journal of The Learning Sciences*, Vol. 2, No. 4, pp. 367-427.

Winograd, T. (1995), From Programming Environments to Environments for Designing, in Communications of the ACM, pp. 65-74.

Section 5

Gender and Adult Continuing Education

Christiane Schiersmann

Advanced Continuing Education for Women in the Transformation Process. An Empirical Analysis.

The political, economic and social transformation occurring in the new states of eastern Germany is having a major impact on the lives of women. In the former GDR they comprised half of the labour force, and were able to plan their lives on the assumption that employment and family responsibilities could be combined without difficulty. However, the gender-specific division of labour continued to operate, with repercussions for women both within the family, where they bore primary responsibility, as well as in the labour market, which was segregated along gender-specific lines. Although highly integrated in the labour market in quantitative terms, this did little to mitigate the substantial income disparities between men and women, the limited degree of occupational choice for women or their restricted opportunities for promotion and advancement (Nickel 1994a).

Gender inequalities were reinforced by the transformation of east German society. Women comprised about two thirds of those made redundant, and it has become much more difficult for them to return to the primary labour market than is the case for men (Engelbrech 1994). This situation is further exacerbated by deteriorating conditions for combining work and family duties. In view of the high orientation to employment they continue to have (Böckmann-Schewe et al. 1994), women are correctly seen as the 'losers' of the political changes that have occurred since unification. They have lost the gains in equality achieved under the GDR regime and instead have become vagabonds with risk; laden or 'patchwork' biographies' (Nickel, 1994b).

Major importance was and still is attached in political debate to continuing education and training as a means of mastering the transformation process. In the research debates of recent years, there has been much controversy about the real function of continuing education in the context of changing individual biographies and socio-structural conditions. However, in contrast to the rather more optimistic assessments of continuing education by policymakers who believe that it performs a 'bridging' function in the transition from the centrally planned to the market economy, social scientists tend on the whole to be more critical. They see the rapid expansion of the continuing education sector first and foremost as a manifestation of strategic social policy (Meier, 1993), condemn the compulsion to participate in continuing education (Geißler, 1994), and emphasise the need to resist any kind of 'compulsory' continuing education (Bolder, 1993).

To prove these hypotheses an empirical research project, completed towards the end of 1994, concerning the continuing education situation in the new Länder from the perspective of women (Ambos & Schiersmann, 1996) has been conducted.

1. The function of continuing education

The continuing training programmes that were launched with astonishing speed after the political turn in 1990 enjoyed a high degree of acceptance in all sectors of eastern German society at first, even if there is now general acknowledgement that they were not always of adequate quality. The interviews we conducted in 1993 and 1994 with women who had taken part in such schemes in the eastern German states confirm that women indeed attached considerable value to continuing education, although, in addition to the social pressures to respond in a certain way, this is qualified by the fact that women who actively participated in continuing education assessed the need and potential benefits in more positive terms than non-participants, that is, we can assume an additional positive distortion of the results.[1]

If the survey results are attributed to different combinations of motivations, it turns out that efforts to obtain continuing vocational training were directed primarily at the individual improvement of women's chances on the labour market. More than half (56%) of all the women in the survey (N=736) and more than 93% of those seeking work at that time wanted to improve their chances of being reintegrated into the labour market. Furthermore, a major

1 It was not possible within the scope of our study to interview non-participant women.

motivating force for 37% of the women[2] was the need to adapt to new demands in their particular occupations; especially for those in employment and those holding higher qualifications. After all, almost one in ten (almost 20% of those in employment) stated that one reason for participating in continuing education was to minimise the risk of becoming unemployed. What is striking in this context is that, according to expert assessments, continuing education was primarily started through the initiative of the participants themselves, and less in response to external pressure or demands. Of course, the question is raised whether participation as an unemployed person or as somebody under threat of unemployment can really be seen as 'voluntary' participation in the classical sense, or whether there is not a latent 'compulsory' aspect to continuing education (Bolder, 1993).

The more apparent it became that training does not necessarily lead to employment (Faulstich 1993) the dilemma of unemployed women who came to realise that 'continuing education gets you nowhere' the more the policy function of continuing education emerges, that is, the financial aspects such as securing a living in the form of maintenance grants, or extending or delaying unemployment benefit or retirement benefit, obtained increasing importance for participation in continuing education funded under the AFG (Employment Promotion Act). Social communication aspects also played a key role in this connection; filling in time while unemployed or until the transition to (early) retirement, the need to escape the isolation of the domestic environment, the need to have personal contacts and feel part of a 'collective'. More than one third (36%) of all the women and 56% of the unemployed women in the survey referred to 'making good use of time while unemployed' as one of their reasons for taking part, and one in six or seven (four fifths of them unemployed) specified the need to have contact with other women as a reason. The significance of these aspects is probably attributable not only to the importance of social relationships within the work context in the GDR, which declined in the course of the transformation process and in many cases disappeared altogether, especially for unemployed women, but also to the fact that participation in continuing education

2 Multiple responses were possible.

conferred a certain social status that was more acceptable than unemployment.

Even if, in the estimation of the experts, the latter functions of continuing education gained in importance for certain sub-groups (for example, unemployed women), they were still secondary on the whole, at least for the period reviewed in our study.

The repeat interview we conducted with the women participants enabled us to address the question whether the general attitude to continuing education had changed as a result of experiencing it. Comparing the answers of those women who participated in the second interview phase (N=173) with their responses in the first interview when they were participating in continuing education programmes, one finds that their attitudes have become somewhat more critical. At the same time, the contradictory nature of their attitudes to continuing education has become more conspicuous. On the one hand, the proportion of those who considered continuing education in general to be necessary increased by 12 percentage points (from 50% to 62%). On the other, agreement with the statement that continuing education is an important way to improve one's own chances on the labour market fell slightly (from 82% to 78%), but remained high. This is all the more astonishing when one considers that our survey also revealed that the employment situation of the women at the time the second interviews were conducted had improved only very slightly, even though there were various changes in status as employee in the first or second labour market or as unemployed. Similarly, there was increased agreement with the statement that 'many people only take part in continuing education because it is expected of them' (from 8% to 15%) and with the statement that continuing education was a kind of 'occupational therapy' in many cases (from 21% to 28%). This clearly indicates a decline in the initial optimism that chances on the labour market can be improved through continuing education. Several experts emphasised that, during the period immediately after unification, this positive attitude towards continuing education was based on a underlying optimism towards structural transformation as such.

An interesting aspect, especially for the subgroup of unemployed women, was whether they were hoping to use the prospective training to return to their original occupations, or whether their plans were to re-orient their careers instead. In the opinion of the experts, the women generally intended, especially the older ones, to build on the work experience they already possessed. However, this turned out to be impossible in many cases, both for those with lower and those with higher qualifications, and in greater proportions than for men, because many vocational qualifications, especially in the industrial sector, were not recognised, because the occupations no longer existed (for example, partially skilled workers), because there was no longer any demand (for example, in textiles or agriculture), or because men were preferred (for example, in the industrial-technical field). Furthermore, it was also pointed out that deficits in the regional spectrum of continuing education opportunities made it more difficult for unemployed women (for example, from the engineering field) to obtain further training in their original professions.

However, as well as emphasising the real compulsions to engage in occupational reorientation, the experts also observed that a number of predominantly young women tried to actively exploit the restructuring of the labour market and the new continuing education opportunities to put their careers on a new footing, thus taking corrective action against previous decisions that in many cases were more the result of state control than individual decision making.

Readiness to take part in continuing education was often accompanied, in the estimation of the experts, by willingness to retrain for less demanding occupations, that is, to accept deskilling. Differing opinions were expressed in response to the question whether the tendency towards deskilling was a problem encountered specifically by women. There was a majority consensus among the experts, however, that on account of the more restricted range of jobs available and the perceived displacement to lower-skill positions, women were more often prepared 'to sell themselves below value', that is, to undergo continuing education at a level below the qualifications they had previously possessed. On the other hand, some experts pointed out that anxiety about deskilling was also a factor preventing participation in continuing education. The benefit of retraining at a level below the initial one was assessed by interviewees in different ways: some considered that university graduates would have better chances on the labour market by acquiring an additional vocational qualification, whereas others considered the over-qualification this implies to be more of a handicap.

Regardless of whether occupational reorientation was forced on women by the labour market situation, or was a voluntary decision, the experts identified a basic underlying tendency for women to choose typical women's occupations, especially in the commercial and social fields. The fact that women tended to concentrate on a narrow range of training goals, especially on a few less attractive areas in the services sector, must be seen as an indicator for the growing gender-specific segmentation of the labour market compared to the situation in the former GDR. The primary factor behind this trend was considered to be the better labour market chances in these areas compared to the industrial sector. This on the one hand is a very realistic perspective, but on the other reinforces gender segmentation in the labour market.

It is particularly noteworthy with respect to gender-specific aspects that the majority of experts we interviewed expressed the opinion that women in the eastern German Länder were more motivated than men to take part in continuing education programmes, were more ambitious and were more committed to the realisation of their continuing education interests.[3]

These assessments are congruent with the results of the study carried out by Infratest Social Research (Kuwan,1992a, p. 40), which revealed that a greater proportion of women than men in the east German states (in 1990) were actually putting their continuing education intentions into practice.

The high degree to which women were willing to participate in continuing education should be interpreted against the background of their unbroken

3 Only a minority of the experts accorded men in the new *Länder* a more pronounced willingness and motivation to participate in continuing education programmes than women. This was related above all to the traditional role of men as breadwinners, or reference was made to the comparatively better labour market chances as a motive for taking part in continuing education.

orientation to employment, an attitude that persisted throughout the political changes and despite the severe labour market problems that existed. Further, the experts explained the greater motivation of women, and this is where the indirect gender-discriminating effects take hold, in terms of the anticipation of different labour market chances; men were more likely to rely on employment prospects alone, even without further training. Women, on the other hand, viewed participation in continuing education schemes as an important way to counteract the threat of marginalisation, to stop oneself ending up 'with one's back against the wall'.

In the estimation of some experts, this situation led to some women attending further or retraining programmes in a comparatively haphazard fashion. However, in view of the uncertainty surrounding the future development of key economic sectors and the jobs they provided, on the one hand, and the change to gender-specific recruitment policies on the part of employers, on the other, it is not surprising that such attitudes were common.

2. Structural factors specific to women that prevent their participation in continuing education

Having looked at the subjective and individual determinants of participation in continuing education, I shall now address the 'objective' factors that influence the likelihood of participation, that is, the 'opportunity structure' of continuing education. What we find is that gender-specific differences result from two main factors; from the specific life situation of women pulled between employment and family responsibilities, and from their specific situation with respect to education, training and the labour market.

The fact that women in the east German states assume the bulk of responsibility for domestic labour and especially child care is operating increasingly as a block on continuing education. Combining work and family is particularly problematic for the relatively large group of single mothers. Reference should also be made in this context to the deteriorating provision of day-care facilities, especially in rural areas. These disadvantages relating to the life situation of women and the problems associated with the 'dual burden' are further compounded by women's comparatively lower mobility, which experts consider to be a serious obstacle above all for women living in the country who would be interested in taking part in continuing education.

Other factors that experts see as preventing or obstructing the participation of women in continuing education are related to shortcomings in the supply of, access to and promotion of continuing education, and which need to be interpreted in the context of the deteriorating labour market situation for women. Examples referred to by the experts include the lack of relevant AFG courses and schemes for particular target groups. For example, there were very few courses catering for university and polytechnic graduates. It was pointed out in this connection that the labour administration tended to reject the idea of retraining such people at a level below their qualifications, even when those concerned were willing and motivated to do so (see above). Secondly, the experts identified and emphasised the restricted range of training courses for women with low skilling levels, that formal entry requirements were either lacking entirely in some cases, or were too high in others (usually 10th grade and completed vocational training as a skilled worker), thus constituting a hurdle for the people in this category, who are predominantly women. Finally, the experts identified a lack of continuing education schemes for women in industrial-technical occupations.

Confining AFG support to those schemes and programmes which the labour administration believed would offer good prospects of job placement also entailed discrimination against women. The rationale behind this strategy was that many typical 'women's occupations' offered relatively weak opportunities on the labour market and already featured an excess supply of labour, with the result that continuing training schemes in such fields received grant support much more rarely. Even though it makes sense to link continuing education to subsequent job prospects when deciding on what supportive action to take, the implication of this particular strategy was a systematic exclusion of lower-skilled women from continuing education, thus cementing the segmentation of continuing education familiar in west German states. This means that worsening labour market prospects for women restricts even further their participation in continuing education, that is, another vicious circle is set in motion, added to which women are given virtually no chance to retain their level of qualification.

3. Conclusions

As we combine all these findings, the dominant impression they create is that women use continuing education more intensively than men in order to compensate at least a little for the gender-based discrimination that operates against them on the labour market. In doing so, they display a kind of instrumental optimism.

The positive assessment of continuing education and training by women that is expressed in our research results continues a long tradition that dates back to the first women's movement in the 19th century. Women have always displayed a greater interest in education and training, but to this day have not succeeded in translating their intensive educational efforts into adequate positions on the labour market. What women in eastern Germany are now faced with is a new deterioration in their social position compared to the one they enjoyed in the former GDR.

However great the motivation among women to participate in continuing education may be, there is an obvious risk that the new and enhanced gender discrimination now operating against east German women in the field of continuing training and education, and the increasing extent to which such training produces little tangible improvement, especially among the unemployed and women in rural areas, are also leading to demotivation and resignation.

The demands that ensue are, firstly, that stronger links be forged between continuing training and employment prospects. There are indications that a regionalisation of continuing training could perform a supportive function in this context. Education, labour market, social and structural policy must be interlinked, with special consideration given to gender-specific aspects. Secondly, it is becoming clear once again that the function of continuing training should not be exaggerated: the only jobs it creates are for the educators themselves. On the other hand, if continuing training is to be given responsibility for conserving skill potentials (Knöchel & Trichter, 1995), then both the support frameworks and the content of continuing education must be subjected to radical rethinking, taking into account both the specific living conditions of women and their precarious labour market situation.

Our study reveals a need to make the terminology used in research on the motivational aspects and the functions of continuing training more precise, to base it on current empirical findings and thus to link the individual and institutional levels with each other in order to put the definitions of continuing education functions by the research community and the political sphere on a more solid footing. The intentional and unintentional effects of continuing training must be subjected to more intensive analysis than has been the case so far (see Gieseke, 1994, Meier, 1993a). Such analysis should work on the basis that the new states in eastern Germany are a kind of crucible where the problems that will apply to the entire country in future are currently concentrated.

References

Ambos, I., Schiersmann, C. 'Wir lassen uns auf keinen Fall unterkriegen!' Die Bedeutung von Weiterbildung für Frauen in den neuen Bundesländern (forthcoming in 1996)

Böckmann-Schewe, L., Kulke, C., Röhrig, A. (1994), 'Wandel und Brüche in Lebensentwürfen von Frauen in den neuen Bundesländern' in *Aus Politik und Zeitgeschichte*, supplement to *Das Parlament* B6/94, 11 Feb. 1994, pp. 33-44.

Bolder, A. (1993), Kosten und Nutzen von beschäftigungsnaher Weiterbildung' in Meier, A., Rabe-Kleberg, U. (eds) *Weiterbildung, Lebenslauf, sozialer Wandel. (Grundlagen der Weiterbildung)*, Neuwied, pp. 47-60.

Engelbrech, G. (1994), 'Frauenerwerbslosigkeit in den neuen Bundesländern. Folgen und Auswege' in *Aus Politik und Zeitgeschichte*, supplement to *Das Parlament* B6, 1994, pp. 22-32.

Faulstich, P. (1993), *Weiterbildung in den "fünf neuen Bundesländern und Berlin"*, Hans-Böckler-Stiftung, Graue Reihe - Neue Folge 55, Kassel.

Geißler, K. A. (1994), 'Vom Lebensberuf zur Erwerbskarriere. Erosionen im Bereich der beruflichen Bildung' in Negt, O. (ed.), *Die zweite Gesellschaftsreform. 27 Plädoyers*, Göttingen, pp. 105-117.

Gieseke, W. (1994), 'Erwachsenenbildung in den neuen Bundesländern' in *Hessische Blätter für Volksbildung*, 1994, 4, pp. 311-321.

Knöchel, W. and Trier, M., *Arbeitslosigkeit und Qualifikations-Entwicklung*, published by Waxmann Verlag GmbH, Münster.

Kuwan, H. (1992), *Berichtssystem Weiterbildung 1991. Ergebnisse der Räpresentativbefragung zur Weiterbildungsbeteiligung in den alten und neuen Bundesländern*, (Bildung-Wissenschaft-Aktuell 12/92), Bonn.

Meier, A. (1993), 'Die Probe aufs Exempel: Weiterbildung im sozialen Strukturwandel Ost-Deutschlands' in Meier, A., Rabe-Kleberg, U. (eds.), *Weiterbildung, Lebenslauf, sozialer Wandel. (Grundlagen der Weiterbildung)*, Neuwied, pp. 183-198.

Nickel, H. M. (1994a), 'Mit dem DDR-Gleichstellungsvorsprung in die bundesdeutsche Modernisierungsfalle? Deutschlands Frauen nach der Wende' in *Berliner Debatte: Initial. Zeitschrift für sozialwissenschaftlichen Diskurs*, 1994a, 4, pp. 3-14.

Nickel, H. M. (1994b), 'Die Ankunft der Ostdeutschen in einer verdampfenden Gesellschaft', *Frankfurter Rundschau*, 30.11.1994b.

Anne Ryan

Adult Continuing Education: Empowerment or Containment

This paper investigates the potential of adult continuing education for either empowerment or containment within the context of a specific project that targets severely disadvantaged women. The paper argues that these women's experience of social and economic disadvantage is particularly acute and as such necessitates an a priori response that focuses on alleviating their immediate poverty and isolation, but must additionally address fundamental structural issues relating to gender based roles, relationships and access to power. The paper goes on to point out that interventions which do not tackle gender related oppression further compound the problems these women face.

The *empowerment* versus *containment* role of adult continuing education is debated within the context of the Mullingar Women's Community Project. Mullingar is a midlands town with a population of 11,000 approximately one hour from Dublin. The Project was established in 1985 by a Parish Sister working with women in the town who were experiencing economic and social hardships due to unemployment within the family, an inability to manage the tight family budget, debt, loneliness, isolation, low self esteem, depression, and violence in the home. In the past ten years the Project has grown to encompass basic training, a comprehensive childminding service and enterprise and employment related activities.

This paper asserts that it is imperative for the Project to promote a democratic, participative management structure in which the target group is directly involved in decision-making. This would serve to articulate the empowerment aspirations of the Project and further the participants' capacity for independence, self-actualisation and self-advocacy in all aspects of their lives. The paper also asserts that any future developments that *exclude* the target group from meaningful involvement at management level will not only miss an opportunity for empowerment but will *actively* serve to disempower these women further. In so doing the Project itself will become a mechanism for containment and domestication.

The Project Review

In May 1994 the Management Committee of the Mullingar Women's Community Project commissioned the Centre for Adult and Community Education, Maynooth College, to review the Project[1].

In undertaking this review the Centre opted for a research methodology which would itself reflect an Adult Education commitment to dialogue and democratic participation. A series of meetings were held with former and present participants on the programmes led by an experienced adult education facilitator. Participants were encouraged to be completely open in all matters regarding their experience of the Project. No staff members of the Project were present at the sessions.

This methodology attracted a high level of approval from the participants. They recognised the openness of the methodology, the freedom it conferred and the way in which it validated their individual and collective experiences.

A short questionnaire was administered to each individual who took part in the consultative process with a view to constructing a personal and socio-economic profile of the Project participants. A total of 50 completed questionnaires were returned.

Detailed interviews were conducted with the staff of the project and with 17 key individuals within the wider community who were familiar with the Project.

The review noted the growth of the project, the unique partnership of statutory and voluntary organisations reflected in the initiative, the socio-economic profile of the target group, the impact of the project on the well being of those participating and the nature and extent of that participation. The findings are briefly summarised below.

1 Collins, T. and Ryan, A. 1995. *Mullingar Women's Community Project: An Evaluation*. Centre for Adult and Community Education, St. Patrick's College, Maynooth.

Project Background

In describing the origins of the project in 1985 the founder noted that the impetus stemmed from a realisation on her part that short-term solutions that alleviated the women's immediate hardships were not appropriate. The women became dependent on help and were not in fact any better equipped to cope with the everyday problems they faced.

The founder's primary aim in bringing the women together was to alleviate their loneliness and depression. The project began with an initial group of six women who met three mornings per week. Child minding facilities were organised to cater for pre-school children. As other women in the community saw the positive results achieved by their friends and neighbours the numbers attending grew to twenty by the end of the first year.

By 1986, statutory and voluntary bodies were approached to support the project. A Home Management and Personal Development course, sponsored by FAS, was offered with the local Vocational Education Authority (VEC) providing inputs on numeracy and literacy.

On completion of this course, a follow up Project was requested. This led to the establishment of the Women's Education/Learning Project. The funding and organising of this project was undertaken by the Lion's Club, and was part-sponsored by the VEC, the Department of Social Welfare, the Society of St. Vincent de Paul and from parish funds.

A survey, conducted in 1987, indicated that there was enough work in the Mullingar area for 100 people in housework and caring for others. Based on these findings, the Home and Family Care Training Project was developed to provide training in house keeping and care of children and elderly people.

By 1988 rooms were rented and thirty women undertook a Training Project in Knitting and Sewing from which the Lakeland Enterprise was set up. This initiative developed into what is today the Uniform Boutique. These training and enterprise activities led to greater self-confidence and independence on the part of the participants. It was noted that those attending the courses:

- were unlikely to request financial or material assistance
- became more confident and ambitious to improve the quality of their lives and that of their family
- appreciated the value of companionship of other women with whom they shared their experiences
- were open to new ideas
- approached problems with a more positive attitude
- encouraged others to participate in the training courses
- were likely to become involved in Resident Associations or other community organisations

In 1990, a Money Management Service was set up to respond to the need for financial advice. This aspect of the project is designed to enable people to take responsibility for their own money management. It focuses on overcoming problems associated with debt and provides education and training on budgeting and financial management.

Today 12 staff are employed in the Project. The number of women participating in the activities varies, from 50-60 in the Learning Project, 25-30 in the Home and Family Care Project and an indeterminate number availing of the Money Management Service. There are 120 women registered with the Home Care Service. Similarly, the number of children taken care of by the childminding facilities varies with the time of the year, the timing of the courses and other demands, such as the availability of other members of the family to provide child care.

Funding

Apart from the obvious direct costs associated with the employment of staff there are many other needs such as accommodation, heat, light, office and administrative overheads, food and materials. The project receives no direct or ongoing statutory funding though there is a major statutory involvement on a programmatic basis, most particularly FAS, VEC and the Health Board. Additionally requirements are met through the Parish Community Centre.

Maintaining this project requires a substantial financial commitment. In the absence of secure, ongoing statutory funding this commitment can only be met by a great deal of enthusiasm, optimism and voluntary effort. Fund-raising events are organised to keep the costs for those availing of the service low.

In the course of the review funding emerged as the least satisfactory aspect of the Project. The ad hoc nature of funding support was seen as the major obstacle to future expansion. Long or medium term plans cannot be made because of the present funding arrangements. The need to constantly fund raise was seen as a drain on personnel whose energy could be better utilised in service provision. While the voluntary, hands-on localised nature of the present provision was recognised as contributing to the present lack of financial security it was also lauded as crucial to the programme's success to date and therefore one which should be maintained.

The Partnership Reflected in the Project

Essentially the project represents a unique partnership between voluntary and statutory sectors in the town and indeed an unusual partnership between the different statutory bodies themselves. Key individuals from the relevant organisations contributed to the review. All were unanimous in their praise of the Project. Participants were seen to have gained a great deal particularly in terms of personal development and skill acquisition. Evidence of personal development was referred to in terms of:

- heightened self-confidence
- openness to new ideas
- greater capacity for independence
- assertiveness
- sense of dignity

- improved family relationships.

Skills were seen to have been acquired mainly in the areas of:
- financial management
- communication
- negotiation
- parenting.

The seven staff members who took part in the review were also liberal in their overall praise of the Project in terms of the achievements of participants in the areas of self and skill development and the support and friendship which the women offer each other.

The need for the present Project to build on the adult education model by promoting a democratic, participative management structure which would enable those who take part to play a greater role in decision-making was recognised. Staff also noted the need to provide opportunities for participants to get directly involved in implementing the programmes and proposed courses in leadership to provide participants with the skills necessary to enable them participate in this way.

Because the Project plays such an important role in providing learning opportunities and because so many individuals, both men and women, have not had their educational needs met through formal systems a number of respondents remarked on the necessity to expand the Project not only to include more women but also to reach men in similar situations. Those who refer clients to the Project were particularly keen to see a similar project set up for men who lack confidence and skills.

Participant Profile

The participants in the Project are mainly seriously disadvantaged particularly in educational, economic and employment terms. The impact of these disadvantages are frequently compounded by gender role expectations whereby these women are regarded as the primary child rearers and carers within their immediate and extended family.

Invariably the respondents alluded to the contribution of the Project in tangible areas such as income generation and child care and more intangibly in areas such as personal confidence and self esteem.

Child Rearing Responsibilities

The age profile of the participants in the project indicated that almost 80% are in the twenty to forty age group. Given that such women are most likely to be involved in taking care of their children the availability of affordable and dependable child care within the Project is a key factor in enabling them to participate. This is borne out by the fact that all but two of the respondents were mothers. On average the respondents had three or more children. Many of these women had married young and started families early in life.

In the course of the review it emerged that half of the respondents moved to the town as adults. The data did not indicate when individuals arrived or why they chose to live in the town. Whatever the reasons it is significant that 50% of the participants in the Project were apparently not brought up in Mullingar and are therefore unlikely to have immediate access to the support provided by the extended family networks generally available to those whose family of origin live close by.

Educational Experiences

Data relating to the educational background of respondents indicated that 34% left school at 15 or younger.

By comparison with the pattern nationally, the respondents are significantly disadvantaged in terms of formal educational attainment. This is particularly evident in the high proportion of respondents who have no formal second level educational qualifications. At 46% compared to the national figure of 28% this sector is well represented among the project participants.

One woman described her experience of school as follows:

> *'I left school illiterate...I was always put at the back of the class and forgotten about. If something went wrong those at the back were blamed and brought up in front of everyone, you were the laugh then. If you're told often enough that you're stupid then you think they're right, I am stupid. I'm only learning now how to write since I came in here'.*

In the course of the discussions the women spoke of the many positive experiences afforded them by the Project. When they undertook courses they found that unlike their previous learning experiences in school, they could relax and not worry constantly about appearing stupid. They basically felt respected and respectful of each other.

Employment Experiences

Data relating to the first job participants held and their present employment indicates that those taking courses or those who are unemployed account for 64% of the respondents. Despite the fact that such a high percentage are thus not involved in paid employment proportionately more of the women (36%) are now engaged in domestic work, home or hospital care and catering than were at the time of their first job (26%). As such the range and variety of occupations has narrowed significantly for respondents in the period between their first job and their current one. Not only have the opportunities narrowed but so too has the nature of the work in which the women are engaged. The present employment profile is wholly within sectors which tend to be largely low paid, part-time, lacking in job security and opportunities for career advancement.

Self Esteem

Respondents were asked to describe the impact of the Project on themselves. Their responses were extremely positive and focused predominantly on their personal development. Before joining the Project most had spent their time in the home taking care of their families and many expressed feelings of isolation and low self-confidence. In describing the benefits of the Project they focused primarily on the extent to which it gave them a sense of self worth and esteem, enhancing their relationships within the family and providing opportunities for them to make new friends. The following quotations provide a flavour of the high level of enthusiasm which characterised these responses:

> *'It changed me and gave me confidence. I can express myself more and am able to stand up for myself. I can get out now to work and feel confident calling to the door of houses where I work.'*

> *'It gave me more confidence in myself, getting out of the house and my own independence for the first time in my life.'*

> *'The quality of my life improved dramatically. Apart from gaining new skills I have become more assertive and more confident. I have acquired new friendships and have become more independent. My kids have benefited from the excellent care of both nursery and pre school - giving each of us a much needed break. In my opinion it should be compulsory for any woman who felt as I had to give it a go.'*

> *'It made me very independent and it made me realise that I was worth something other than just having kids and getting no thanks for it. I look forward to meeting people everyday. I have made a lot of new friends. When I come home in the evening I look forward to the kids*

telling me about their day and I telling them about mine. It makes me feel important.'

The reasons articulated by the participants for joining the Project could be explored in terms of 'push' factors and 'pull' factors. Push factors refer to those aspects of the participant's social and economic circumstances which contribute to a desire for change; pull factors refer to aspects of the Project which enhance its attractiveness.

Overall it would appear that push factors predominated over pull factors in setting the conditions for the decision of the participants to join the Project, but particular pull factors were required before the decision was realised. Invariably the women identified the need to get out of the house as the primary factor in their decision to join the Project:

'I was in the throes of post-natal depression at the time and it saved my sanity...

I was just out there dying away.

I needed some kind of stimulation outside of the kids and house and tranquillisers.

My three kids had started school. I was getting into a dreadful rut...going back to bed all day till five to three...getting more and more depressed.

I was going out of my mind. I was cleaning the whole time...two kids full-time at school...there on my own cleaning.

'Before I came in here I could never look people in the face or say anything, no way'

'Before coming here I couldn't talk to you (i.e. facilitator) knowing your education'

On their own, however, such push factors would not have provided sufficient impetus for the women to join the Project. Few of them, especially the least resourced members, simply 'walked on to' the Project. In general they were recruited on a one-to-one basis by friends or relatives who had themselves been on the Project, the staff of the Project or other professionals. The Project's capacity to reach out to these women through individualised, face-to-face contact, was a crucial factor in bringing the women into the Project. Without such a proactive approach it is unlikely that many of the women would have had the necessary confidence, self-esteem or motivation to join the Project on their own. However, even if they had wished to join or were ready to do so, they could not do so in the absence of child care. The provision of child care was the final ingredient which enabled them to become participants.

Notwithstanding the positive benefits of participating in the Project's activities the focus on homemaking or traditional skills such as cookery, sewing and knitting was seen as limiting. While keenly aware of the strides the Project and they as individuals had made they expressed a willingness to tackle new barriers, to strive for better conditions and to keep growing as a group and as individuals. A sense of wanting to continue with the process initiated in the Project was echoed repeatedly.

Summary of the Review Findings

Perhaps the most noteworthy aspect of the Project is its ability to reach a severely deprived sector of the population. The profile of the participants that emerged in the course of the study indicates profound social, economic and educational disadvantage. Most of the women have young families and the Project's main contribution lies in combating the stress, isolation and monotony associated with family related tasks in the particular circumstances in which these women find themselves. In an adult education context, this is a target group which can easily be overlooked in the distribution of adult education resources, just as they were overlooked in the formal education system earlier. The great achievement of this project is that it focuses exclusively on this group and caters for their specific domestic circumstances particularly their need for child care facilities.

Restrictive funding arrangements and poor facilities have constrained the Project from expanding or developing a strategic long term plan. While the participants have a wealth of experience in overcoming financial difficulties and a wide range of problems in their personal lives this experience is largely unharnessed within the Project itself to date. The future of the Project may depend on finding a mechanism to enable these women play a meaningful role in overcoming the problems it faces.

More fundamentally the Project has failed to engage the women in any educational initiatives that investigate the causes of their hardships, the division of labour within the home, or the general invisibility of women within decision-making forums.

The Future of the Project

In looking to the future the main concerns for the Project are of two types; administrative and philosophical. The purely administrative issues are concerned with:

1. Long-term security.
2. Retention of the voluntary, innovative nature of the Project.
3. Expansion of the current range of courses.
4. On-going support to former participants.

A more profound choice revolves around the task of enabling the participants to become directly involved in Project management, a democratic process of collective decision-making and action while enabling them to identify the structural constraints of gender and class which circumscribe their life chances at a personal level.

1. Long-Term Security

Everybody consulted in this review bemoaned the short term and ad hoc nature of the funding provided towards it. They were also concerned at the high levels of energy which were expended in fund raising.

As stated earlier the Project in its structure has pioneered a unique local partnership of voluntary and statutory bodies in the town, collectively targeting their respective resources on the participants in the Project. This partnership needs to be reflected in the funding arrangements.

The project is of immense personal and social value to the participants, their children and the community. The case for secure core funding is an imperative if the project is to continue. Ultimately no project such as this can expect to survive indefinitely on the personal energy of a small core of enthusiastic promoters. Turnover and tiredness will undermine this enthusiasm.

Essentially, the project should receive core funding, not simply because it deserves it, but because it represents a good investment in community development and community welfare. If one was to identify one core impact area in this regard, it would be that of personal well-being. As stated, participants repeatedly referred to the positive impact of the Project on this area of their lives. First and foremost, the Project is an investment in good health, both physical and mental.

In terms of Adult Education, the programme's success lies not only in the contribution which it makes to the participants but in its extraordinary success in targeting a population which has heretofore gained little from the education system. The fact that many of the women are the mothers of young, school going children is a further aspect of its potential contribution within the educational area. Undoubtedly through this Project these women are better equipped to participate in the education of their children and thereby break the cycle of disadvantage.

Training for employment is a further aspect of this Project. While one senses that this issue is more a vehicle for other forms of educational and training provision, employment is nonetheless a fully legitimate aspiration of all the participants and one which ultimately can make a significant contribution to the economic and social well-being of the women and their families. However, the type of employment offered has poor career prospects and reinforces gender specific occupations.

The project also provides valuable insights into approaches to the delivery and targeting of social services to women and children in disadvantaged circumstances. Perhaps equally impressive is its developmental approach to this task as opposed to a simple service delivery one. Commentators are increasingly concerned today that welfare provision should not only be adequate but that its mode of delivery should be one which does not 'colonise' the client, but rather one which enhances the person's capacity for self-direction and for taking personal responsibility.

2. Retention of the Voluntary, Innovative Nature of the Project

The success of the Project to date is due in large measure to the voluntary and innovative nature of the provision. The close relationship between staff, management and participants has fostered information flows and ensured the on-going appropriateness of the project. Developments throughout the history of the project have been in direct response to the needs that have emerged. This level of responsiveness to the target group has ensured that the training and employment opportunities are relevant and likely to attract participants. However, the future of the project depends on its capacity to involve those women who have gained confidence and self-esteem in the management process.

3. Expansion of the Current Range of Courses

The successes of the Project have prompted those involved to seek ways to expand the provision to reach greater numbers of women and to also target men. The focus has tended to be on providing a wider range of courses which would meet the needs of these individuals. It is worth remarking at this point on the fact that much of the programme's success has depended on its capacity to provide opportunities for participants to build friendships and give support to each other. If the project were to become very large this may no longer be possible. It is also noteworthy that the inclusion of men in the present project might serve to shift the focus from the specific needs of women who are particularly marginalised.

Bearing in mind these considerations it may be more appropriate for those involved in the Project to encourage other bodies or agencies to replicate their success rather than attempt to meet these needs directly through expansion. Such initiatives should develop within the ambit of a broader community development and education initiative whereby each project would have its own separate management team.

Notwithstanding this suggestion it would be desirable for the project to consider broadening the range of courses offered to the target group it reaches at present. A number of women felt that the focus on domestic skills was not adequate in increasing their own skill levels or in enabling them to explore less traditional employment opportunities which would generate greater financial rewards.

4. Ongoing Support to Former Participants

Adult education activity tends to be self generating and, at least presently, to be somewhat circular in structure. On a Project such as this, people who are introduced to the possibilities offered through adult education are naturally enthusiastic to maintain an ongoing participation.

Invariably, people who become involved in adult education rarely feel that they have arrived at an end point in the process. In many instances the process is the end point and to be cut off from the process may well leave the participant more frustrated than was the case before becoming involved. In that sense therefore there is something of a moral imperative regarding the provision, once started, of ongoing opportunities for learning and social development.

Empowerment

The concept of empowerment is a central tenet in the adult education philosophy. Right through the Mullingar Women's Community project, participants refer to their empowerment by ongoing reference to self-confidence, self-esteem and feeling good about themselves.

The project should continue to explore the possibilities of an empowering process. It can do this in several ways; in terms of Project content, Project methodologies and Project management.

Ultimately empowerment should result in meaningful involvement on the part of the project's participants not only in the project, but in the democratic process at local and national levels. The project has undoubtedly provided a valuable learning environment whereby women who are largely voiceless have been afforded opportunities to share their experiences and draw strength from the group. The task then is for the project to equip these women with the *skills* and *confidence* to make their voices heard in a wider context and with a *heightened awareness of how society is structured* so that they can understand such a context. Learning in each of these three areas can be initially stimulated within the project.

Skills

The goal of an empowering process is that the affected population becomes the active population. The project, if it is to achieve this goal, should aim for a community of adult learners in which all involved, but particularly the women, have access to resources of decision making, planning and overall management. This would help shift the project from an early formative service delivery stage to a more assertive, independent and self creating one.

These skills are in essence the same as those needed to participate in the broader democratic process.

Confidence

The second area, namely that of confidence building and increasing self-esteem have to date been the hallmark of the project and the outcome most noted and lauded by all connected with the project. This is the kind of personal development which individuals need to enable them participate in the wider community. It is also an ongoing process which continues throughout one's life.

Understanding the Broad Social Context

Finally, understanding how society is structured and gaining access to groups, agencies and organisations which impact on such structures can also be initiated within the project.

The project emerged from a realisation on the part of its founder that simply helping women, at an individual client-based level, to overcome each crisis that they confronted offered at best a short-term solution and at worst led to dependency. As such the project began by seeking to find sustainable long-term solutions that would restore or enhance the women's capacity to perform better those roles assigned to them.

Since its foundation the project has successfully brought together statutory and voluntary agencies and efficiently utilised the resources they have to offer. In so doing the project has demonstrated its awareness of the local and national contexts in which it functions. As such the greater involvement of the participants in the running of the project can provide a most fertile learning environment in terms of understanding structures within the wider community and effectively demonstrating how such structures can be utilised to create change.

Working towards a situation whereby the women can acquire the skills, confidence and understanding necessary to participate in the broader democratic process will ensure that their concerns are put on agendas which have not to date taken cognisance of such issues. Through participation in such a forum the issues pertinent to the project's participants can be dealt with in ways that highlight the material conditions that affect these women's daily lives and also confront the fundamental gender based divisions within society.

One would have to say that in its present format the Project performs well as an induction or foundational intervention to engage with a severely disadvantaged sector of the population. It provides a forum for women to support each other and begin to recognise their potential and worth. It gives the participants access to affordable child care and some opportunities for part-time employment.

However, were it to remain as it is the Project could at worst be seen as one which merely taps this sector of the population as an amenable source of domestic labour within the town, does little to involve the target population in the planning and management of the Project and generally perceives the impact of the Project in terms of the individual woman and her family.

The following check list[2] which focuses on the project's objectives, the participants involvement in initiatives undertaken within the project and the overall impact of the project on the social system or status quo would serve to enhance the project's capacity to further women's development by ensuring that the impact of the project on individual women, their family and the community as a whole is maximised.

Project Objectives

1. What *direct results* is the project expected to bring for those women who participate?

   (i) How will it influence their *activities* (e.g. will other members of the household increase their share of domestic duties?)

   (ii) How will it influence their *income*? (e.g. will it create employment opportunities for women? Will it help them to increase their control over the disposal of their own sources of income? Will the dependence of women on the income of their partners/husbands for household expenditure be lessened?)

   (iii) To what extend will new *skills* be developed and if so what skills?

   (iv) Will it increase their *self-confidence* and if so how?

   (v) How will the project promote a *change of attitude* among the women?

2. How will the project make it easier for women to gain access to *sources of help?* (e.g. will they find it easier to make contact with other women and with organisations and agencies?)

3. How will the project help women to gain access to *information and knowledge?* (e.g. ways of organising themselves and on their legal

2 adapted from a check list on Women and Development used by the Netherlands Government and published in *A Wealth of Women* Irish Commission for Justice and Peace pp 34-35.

rights, on the nature of their problems and on possible solutions; knowledge in caring for their children, their health and that of their family).

4. How will the project influence the participants *access to power, structures and decision-making?* (for example, in the household, in the community, in organisations, in religious and administrative structures and in government?).

Participants Involvement in Initiatives during the Preparatory Phase

(i) Are the participants directly involved in the preparation of initiatives?

(ii) Are the needs and wishes of the women sufficiently defined and taken into account? If so, what procedures are used to enable this to happen?

(iii) If no women are involved at this stage, why not? Can they be involved at a later stage?

(iv) If participants in the project are involved at the preparatory stage what proportion of those so involved are project participants?

(v) Are non-participants involved in the preparation and decision-making process? If so, are they staff members or those in positions of authority within the project or in the community? Do they belong to the community? Are they familiar with the life styles of the project participants? Are they genuinely committed to the project's goals?

Participant's Involvement in Initiatives during the Implementation Phase

(i) Do participants take part in the decision-making process as initiatives are implemented? If so, what structures are in place to enable this to happen? If not, why not?

(ii) Can the women exercise any influence on the progress of the initiative/activity? If so, how?

(iii) Are the participants passive in the sense that services or information are offered or are they active? Are the participants encouraged to provide services and information to each other? If so, how?

(iv) Is the project as a whole flexible enough to adapt to the changing needs and circumstances of the participants?

The Impact of the Project on the Social System

(i) How does the project influence women's range of choice? Can women use the skills acquired through the project in other activities? Does the project have an adequate bearing on anticipated social changes? If so, how?

(ii) What consequences does the project have for existing man/woman relationships? (e.g. role patterns, relationships of power and ownership, divisions of labour). Will it improve the status of women? (in the eyes of men, of women?). Do these consequences create problems and if so, what are they and how can they be addressed?

(iii) Will women in any way be discriminated against or exploited in the longer term as a result of participating in the project? (for example, by lack of payment or inadequate payment for women's work, by giving women work which carries a low status or by not giving them the skills to influence the environment in which they work).

(iv) Can the project have a favourable influence on the attitudes of local and national authorities towards better legislation and better implementation of existing legislation relating to women?

Gerda Siann

Gender, Generations and Generativity

'... we are in the middle of an historic change in the relations between men and women: a shift in power and values that is unravelling many of the assumptions not only of 200 years of industrial society but also of millennia of traditions and beliefs.' (In the preface to Wilkinson, 1994).

In this paper I consider this assertion, and its implications for gender issues and lifelong learning in the context of some recent Scottish research. The paper is written from a British perspective but I think the trends that I discuss are probably characteristic of other European countries as well.

While there is no doubt that gender relationships have been altered by the direct action of feminists, there is also little doubt that recent changes in economic and social factors have also impinged directly on these relationships. I would argue that four factors have been particularly salient in this respect.

The first of these is the recent *changes in the nature of employment* in Britain which have affected males and females differently but in a way that interacts significantly with social class. At one end of the social class continuum the decline of the industrial sector has created relatively high levels of unemployment in the ranks of unskilled and semi-skilled male workers. This has been accompanied by a rise in the part-time employment of lower paid women largely in the service sectors. As a result, in many families, women are the chief or sole breadwinners. At the other pole of the social class continuum, in dual career families, professional women are increasingly likely to earn as much or more than their partners. Across all sectors the notion of a job for life is disappearing and there is a decline in long-term employment with the related benefits of fixed and relatively generous pension benefits. Thus the historic advantages of men in employment, which was their far greater likelihood than women of holding permanent pensionable posts, has been very much eroded.

The second factor lies in changes in legislation. *Anti-discriminatory legislation* has outlawed sex discrimination in education and employment. This has not eroded sex differences in pay but is beginning to have an impact in that it now appears that the pay gap between men and women is largely a result of family responsibilities rather then of gender *per se*. Whereas the overall gender gap in Britain is in the region of 20% with women earning around 80% of male earnings, in the case of single childless women the gender gap in comparison with single childless men is only 5% (Innes, 1995). In the recent in-depth interviews I have been conducting with graduate engineers of both sexes (9 males and 17 females) it is very clear not only that the women are acutely aware of this legislation and that they are prepared to take advantage of it if necessary but that men are also keenly aware of its implications in their own relationships with the women they work with.

The third factor is that *advances in medical technology* notably in the area of family planning but also in areas such as AID have given women far more control than they had in the past of their fertility. As a result, a substantial number of women are now making decisions about being mothers in a very autonomous manner and their new found confidence in controlling their maternal destiny is reflected in the number of women electing to rear children on their own. Notable examples are, of course, Madonna and Sharon Stone. Madonna, talking about her desire to have a child without any long term commitment to its father put it this way 'My biological clock is ticking so loud, I may run an advertisement for a suitable father' (Lee, 1996). Celebrities such as Madonna and Stone mirror an increasing tendency in the UK and the USA for career women to postpone childbirth and then rear their children, when they do have them, on their own.

This new found trend to elective single parenthood is also reflected in Britain in the number of unemployed or poorly paid women who choose either to become pregnant with little commitment to their children's biological fathers or to leave/divorce their children's fathers if they consider that as one young women put it 'they are more trouble than they're worth'. It is also confirmed by the fact that women are more likely than men to initiate divorce proceedings (Innes, *ibid*).

And, finally, *greater openness about sexuality* has freed both sexes from the constraints of the conventional family dynamics. While the great majority of women are heterosexual, younger women are aware of choices, and therefore agency with respect to their sexuality, in a way that is very different to the experience of their mothers and grandmothers. Research on sexuality consistently shows that women are now more proactive in their attitude to sexuality and that the sexual stereotypes of active males and passive females is rapidly being eroded (Siann,1994).

I would argue that these four social forces, employment patterns, legislation, medical advances, and the increasing openness about sexuality, have contributed to changes in a number of important areas that impact directly on gender relationships. For example, in surveys of the social and personal values of 2,500 representative members of the British population conducted by *Demos* there has been evidence of a general shift in the population away from security, authority, and rigid moral codes towards the valuing of balance (valuing quality of life rather than success), risk, excitement and hedonism and androgyny. These shifts have been more pronounced for female than for male respondents (Wilkinson, *ibid*). In education girls have started to outperform boys at school and females have achieved parity in entrance to the elite professions previously dominated by males (Siann, *ibid*). Finally, women are both more prominent in the media and also found in areas previously dominated by males, for example, political and economic journalism and even in reporting from war zones.

It has been argued, however, that these changes are only cosmetic and that at the structural level women are still disadvantaged in the most central aspects of national life; in earning power, in senior management, in the judiciary and in the legislature (see, for example, Wilson, 1995). While I accept these current limitations on the progress of women, I contend that it is not possible at this stage to predict whether such limitations will continue or indeed increase, or whether, as the critical mass of women in the professions and in the labour market advances, the disadvantages women currently still suffer from will be further eliminated. My position is that the jury is still out in the area of permanent and increasing changes in senior management, earning power, the legislature and the judiciary but I am convinced that there are massive changes in the psychological sphere. I see these in three areas, in generational differences with respect to gender, in the convergence of the sexes in attitudes and values and in the balance of power relationship between young men and women.

That there are substantial generational differences with respect to gender should not be surprising and the survey conducted by Demos to which I referred to above showed large differences between their respondents in the 18-34 year old age group and those older. Referring to the younger group as the 'first post-equality' generation, Wilkinson, utilising a phrase coined by Naomi Wolf, suggested that it is this generation who have been most affected by the 'Genderquake' which has transformed the relations between men and women.

In Britain this post-equality generation has grown up in a period which saw a strong female prime minister as well as a number of other formidable female politicians. While it could be argued that the media sometimes still projects very sex stereotyped images, there can be no argument that there have been massive changes in the way women are portrayed in advertisements (for example, motor and insurance adverts directed to the female consumer), in situation comedies (for example, by strong confident figures like Roseanne), in documentaries (frequently produced and presented by women) and, as I have already noted, in the use of women for hard news reporting and as experts in fields ranging through finance, economics, the law and medicine to the arts.

Growing up in such different times as their mothers and grandmothers has created a cohort of confident young women who take for granted that in their education and careers they will be treated as equals. My own research has consistently shown that young women take for granted what their predecessors fought for and, not surprisingly, many see feminism as irrelevant (Siann and Wilkinson, 1995). My research also indicates that the great majority of young men also consistently endorse gender equality though it does seem likely that such endorsement is correlated with education and social class (Wilkinson, *ibid*).

Other research (Banks *et al*, 1992) also shows a tendency for gender convergence on social issues among young people. For example, there tend to be stronger variations between occupational and interest groups than between genders. Furthermore, there is far less gender segregation in adolescence than there was in the past. By this I refer to the growing tendency for young people to socialise in mixed groups and to have intimate friends of both sexes. This is in marked contrast to friendship patterns of the past where with the exception of boyfriend-girlfriend couples the sexes tended to socialise separately.

This tendency towards gender convergence in social attitudes and behaviour amongst younger people has been very obvious in my interviews referred to above with 26 young scientists. During these interviews I explored their perceptions of gender relations particularly with respect to childcare. Gender differences in this regard were minimal. In general, both sexes took the position that domestic and childcare should be shared in dual career families and that men could care as competently for children as women. My interviewees tended to believe that personality attributes were more related to individual differences than to gender. For example, they did not see male and female managers as having different management styles.

I am aware that the young scientists I interviewed were a highly selected group and Fiona Wilson and I are now replicating this research with a large body of students and also with office workers and with shop floor industrial workers. Following on from some of the findings of the *Demos* survey referred to above we anticipate that the gender convergences in social attitudes and values which I am describing will be affected by social class and by educational level. The *Demos* survey found that it was the less well educated groups in their sample who showed the most gender divergence in attitudes. We also expect our larger sample to confirm our hypothesis that gender convergence in attitudes decreases with age.

In these interviews I was struck by the optimism and confidence displayed by the young women I interviewed. They confirmed my impression from teaching at both the undergraduate and the postgraduate level that educated young women in Britain are in many ways more sure of themselves than their male peers. Their approach to life seems more positive and their levels of what I have termed 'generativity' seems higher. They appear more productive and, as a result , I would expect this generation of women to be more likely than their male counterparts to take up the challenges of lifelong learning. My impressions in these areas resonate with Wilkinson's conclusions that women are adapting better to the changing social and economic circumstances than men.

During the period I have been conducting these interviews the media in Britain have been very concerned with gender relations, particularly from the perspective that it is men rather than women who are faring badly as a result of the social and economic changes that have been occurring. The term 'crisis of masculinity' is often cited in the media. Defining what is meant by masculinity is, of course, fraught with methodological problems (Cornwall and Lindisfarne, 1994 Edley and Wetherell, 1995). Nevertheless, however masculinity is defined, there is no doubt that in recent years a vociferous and impassioned stream of books have been published which argue that currently men are being sidelined and discriminated against in comparison to women and that as a result men are suffering as a group from an identity crisis (Brod, 1987, Fekete, 1994, Farrell, 1993, Kimmel, 1990, and Thomas, 1993).

I explored these issues in my interviews and found that most of my interviewees felt that overall the change in employment patterns in Britain had disadvantaged men relative to women and a number felt that in general men, particularly men with little education, were coping less well with the world than their female peers. Some men felt that in recruitment interviews for scientific and engineering staff women were more likely to be appointed than men because the company concerned took the position that employing women technical staff was seen as confirming its leading edge position. In general, the interviews tended to confirm the position I have been developing in the area of gender relations which is that at the personal and psychological level young women have the edge on young men.

Demographic trends in Britain would seem to confirm this in three areas. The first two of these have already been mentioned; the increasing trend for girls to outperform boys academically at school (Darling and Glendinning, 1996) and the fact that female students have achieved parity in entry to those elite professions which used to be dominated by males; medicine, the law , accountancy, etc. The third factor is the fact that the gap in the suicide figures, with men more likely than women to commit suicide, is widening (Charlton, 1995).

As should be obvious from the discussion above, my conclusion is that young British women are faring better than young men, are more confident and are therefore more likely to be more productive and generative. This may only be a temporary phenomenon and I would certainly not wish to see it reversed. I believe, however, that it is important that policy makers seek to redress some aspects of this trend, in particular the growing exclusion from mainstream British society that appears to be characteristic of many young men, particularly those who are not well-educated and who live in inner city areas. One of the major tasks of conferences such as this should be to seek to illuminate methods of drawing groups such as these into the mainstream of lifelong education and learning.

References

Banks, M., Bates, I., Breakwell, G., Bynner, J., Emler, N., Jamieson, L. and Roberts, K. (1992), Careers and Identities, Milton Keynes, Open University Press.

Brod, H. (1987), The Making of Masculinities: New Men's Studies, Winchester, Mas., Allen and Unwin.

Charlton, J. (1995), Trends and Patterns in Suicide in England and Wales, International Journal of Epidemiology, 24, pp. s45-s52.

Cornwall, A. and Lindisfarne, N. (1994), Dislocating Masculinities: Comparative Ethnographies, London, Routledge.

Darling, J. and Glendinning, A. (1996), Gender Matters in Schools: Pupils and Teachers. London, Cassell.

Edley, N. and Wetherell, M. (1995), Men in Perspective: practice, power and identity, Hemel Hempstead, Harvester.

Farrell, W. (1993), The Myth of Male Power, London, Fourth Estate.

Fekete, J. (1994), Moral Panic: Biopolitics Rising. Quebec, Robert Davies.

Innes, S. (1995), Making it Work: Women, Challenge and Change in the 90's, London, Chatto and Windus.

Lee, V. (1996), Going it Alone, The Guardian, 21-8-96, 2, p.6.

Kimmel, H. (1987), Changing Men: New Directions in Research on Men and Masculinity. California, Sage.

Siann, G. (1994), Gender, Sex and Sexuality: Contemporary Psychological Perspectives, London, Taylor and Francis.

Siann, G. and Wilkinson, H. (1995), Gender, Feminism and the Future, London, Demos.

Thomas, D. (1993), Not Guilty: In Defence of Modern Man, London, Weidenfeld and Nicolson.

Wilkinson, H. (1994), No Turning Back: generations and the genderquake, London, Demos.

Wilson, F. M. (1995), Organisational Behaviour and Gender, London, McGraw-Hill.

Bettina Dausien

Education as Biographical Construction? Narration, Gender and Learning - a Case Study

Introduction

I should like to begin my paper with a number of questions that have occupied the social and educational sciences again and again ever since the dramatic acceleration of social modernisation processes began, let's say a good hundred years ago.

How do people manage to find their way in a social world that is undergoing increasingly rapid change? On what do they base their actions, if there is little in the experience and rationality of preceding generations that they can make use of? When the old calculations and maxims no longer apply, such as those which help us to further our careers or which govern relations between the sexes? When familiar social milieus are left behind and unknown regions of the social space are explored? How do women, for example, find their bearings within their biography, when they no longer wish to lead either the 'traditional housewife' lives their mothers led, or the dubious model represented by the 'career woman', when they are confronted with the fact that society provides virtually no support for a life plan in which professional career and family are combined? How do people manage and cope with processes of upward social mobility in which they remove themselves from their milieu of origin, for example, by taking a university degree and then finding themselves in a new and alien cultural milieu? Finally, how can individuals design their biography and plan their future when they have to assume that the rationalities currently in force, such as those of vocational education and the labour market, will change and transform in the course of their own lifetimes? What are the individual and social skills or resources that enable people to achieve this, and how can they be given targeted support through educational processes? What 'key qualifications' and competencies should be conveyed by institutionalised learning processes?

We all know that questions like these surface primarily in situations of crisis and upheaval, when 'self-organisation' by the members of society and hence social integration as a whole no longer functions as efficiently as it did in the past. The times we are living in are quite obviously a period of such upheaval and change. The recent debates on 'lifelong learning' should thus be seen in the context of the wider debate on individualisation and modernisation.

In the following I should like to focus specifically on the question of how individual subjects engage in 'self-organisation' within this process, or, more precisely, on the *biographical construction* that people perform when they make plans for their entire biographies and recapitulate for themselves the life they have already lived, when they organise and reorganise their activities. These aspects of biographical theory can be linked rather congenially to social constructivist concepts that are currently being debated in the field of adult education theory. Greatly simplified, the basic principle of constructivism is the realisation that education should not be conceived of as mere *input* within a simple input-output model of teaching and learning, but more as *'intakes'*, that is, as active constructions on the part of biographical subjects.[1]

I shall refrain here from any deeper analysis of the theoretical benefits and drawbacks of this approach[2], but would like instead to make use of, and link it, with the notion of *biographical construction* of social reality that we developed in many years of empirical research.[3] The issue centres on how subjects 'process' and 'reconstruct' their experiences in life, and how this process of individual life history influences both institutionalised and non-intentional learning processes.

1 This approach is based on advances in the field of biological systems theory and cognition research, according to which our brain is to be seen as an autopoietic, operationally closed system that does not image or mirror reality, but 'produces' it, so to speak. The biological and social significance of such constructions of reality is their *viability* for the subjects concerned. This does not imply that we are unable to reflect on or communicate with others about these 'second order' products of consciousness. We are quite capable of 'observing how we ourselves observe the world' (Siebert 1995, 50).

2 For more detail, see Alheit & Dausien (1996b).

3 See Alheit & Dausien 1985, 1990; Alheit 1994; Dausien (1996).

My paper, which is based on an article that I wrote with Peter Alheit[4], has four sections. In the first, I would like to outline the theoretical approach and deal briefly with the narrative structure of biographical constructions. I shall then elaborate the concept in more detail with reference to an empirical case study we conducted. In the second section I will portray a specific female biography, in order, in the third section, to go into more detail regarding the significant role played by education in this case study. I shall conclude with some implications for theory.

1. The narrative structure of biographical experience

The process of 'biographical construction' and reconstruction of social experiences is not performed 'intrapsychically' by an isolated individual. It does not occur in empty social space, but is characterised in particular by the linking of individual reconstructions with collectively shared experiences and constructions of meaning. This is the essence of 'biographicity' (*Alheit*). Peter Alheit uses the term to refer to 'the ability to link modern knowledge bases to biographical resources of meaning and to reassociate oneself with this knowledge' (1995: 292). This ability is based on the biographically structured knowledge acquired through experience[5]. Biographicity is not, therefore, a skill that is acquired once only and retained unchanged, but is a *processual structure* instead. Biographical knowledge not only about one's own life history, but also about unaccomplished plans and unexplored options, changes throughout a lifelong process that can be interpreted as a complex biographical *learning process*. The manner in which people 'socially assimilate' and reconstruct their own experience, in other words, the way in which learning processes are actually enacted, is crucially

4 Alheit & Dausien (1996a).

5 This knowledge is predominantly implicit and functions, as 'practical consciousness' (Giddens) in a largely pre-reflexive way; it is rendered an object of conscious reflection only in critical situations, when it stands out against implicit background knowledge in a specifically reconstructed shape and form (on the operation of this process as a function of experience, remembering and narrating, see Rosenthal 1995).

dependent on the unique biographical structure within which such experience is 'organised'.

How to gain access to such biographical constructions is a key methodological issue for both the research community and practical educational processes. The concept of 'processually structured' biographical experience relates to a specific *narrative structure*. Put more simply, we do not organise our experiences primarily in the form of *static* categories, self-descriptions and interpretational patterns, but in the form of narrated histories.

Narration is a mode for the reconstruction of reality, not a 'copy' of reality. Narrated life is not 'life', and of course biographical narrators construct their own reality of experience in their own specific ways[6]. Social reality only exists as *interpreted reality*, but our interpretations are by no means arbitrary.[7] Narrative (re)constructions, in particular, are based on a complicated system of rules that we apply unquestioningly in everyday life. Impromptu narratives, at least in our cultural world, obey certain compelling rules of interaction[8] that make it impossible to totally dissociate the *narrative flow* from the flow of events or experiences[9]. Unlike other modi for reconstructing reality, such as argumentation or description, narration leads us back into the compulsions governing the sequencing of actions and requires from us the sequential ordering of the recollected event. The 'raw material' of narrative reconstructions thus determines the active construction to a considerable degree. Reality is not only 'constructed'; it is also 'constituted'.[10] By analysing narratives, it is possible to a certain extent to ascertain the conditions and events of the story being told: an unusually important aspect for educationalists.

Narration, as a specific communicative act, also refers to the very social framework into which the individual stories and histories are woven. A nar-

6 For more detail, see Alheit 1990, especially pp. 15ff, 116ff.
7 The accusation that narratives are nothing but illusory (Bourdieu 1990) or mythologised (Osterland 1983) versions of the 'real' life course can be refuted both theoretically and empirically (see Rosenthal 1995; Schütze 1984, 1995).
8 Cf. Kallmeyer & Schütze 1977.
9 Cf. Schütze 1984.
10 See the theoretical writings of Fritz Schütze (especially 1981, 1984, 1995) and Peter Alheit (1990, especially p. 125ff).

rated life history is never just the hermetic output of a self-referential system; it is rather a form of communication that relates itself to others and which embraces other social actors as well. Jürgen Habermas has expressed this aspect of narration with great clarity: 'Actors base their narrative presentations on a lay concept of the 'world', in the sense of the everyday world or lifeworld they can develop personal identities only if they recognise that the sequences of their own actions form narratively presentable life histories; they can develop social identities only if they recognise that they can maintain their membership in social groups by way of participating in interactions, and thus that they are caught up in the narratively presentable histories of collectivities' (Habermas, 1981: II, 206). Narration means more than just the construction of subjective worlds, but also the integration of self into a collectively shared lifeworld.

This 'latent' meaning in a narrative recapitulation, can also be 'decoded'. The procedure for such decoding is not a 'technique' in the instrumental sense, of course, but a methodically controlled *reconstruction* of the construction principle operating in the respective narrative.

Without wishing to deal in any more detail with the methodological aspects, I should like in the following to present a case study as an example for how the narratively structured and recapitulated construction principle of a specific biography, if you like, the individual 'logic' of the life history, shapes and determines biographical learning. The focal point of the case study involves *adult educational processes*. It thus illustrates the thesis put forward at the outset, namely that learning processes should be thought of more as biographically structured 'intakes' than as reactions to organised educational 'inputs'.

First, I shall present you the life history in the form of a 'biographical portrait' of the women narrator[11], and then go on to sketch the biographical 'logic' in rough detail.

11 This 'portrait' is not an arbitrary 'regurgitation' of and commentary on biographical 'facts', but a 'condensed description' acquired through analysis. It is based on the detailed reconstructive case study and highlights the way in which the educational process is woven into biography (see Alheit & Dausien 1990; Dausien 1996).

2. Gisela Schwarz: biography as 'self-education' - a woman's life plan oscillating between family and career

Gisela Schwarz was born in the late 1930s as the first of three children in a small town in southern Germany. Her mother was a kindergarten teacher, but she no longer worked in her chosen occupation. The father was a precision mechanic, a skilled craftsman who was an active trade unionist at his place of work and involved in various social activities. Despite their limited means, the children grew up 'free' and received all manner of stimulation and ideas from their parents, for example through country walks, collecting berries, story-reading in the evening, and narrating.

Gisela's school career was dogged by material constraints. Despite her good performance and interest in learning, she was unable to go to the local grammar school because her parents were unable to afford the monthly school fees. When she left the 'Volksschule' (elementary school), Gisela wanted to become a nurse, but she was still too young at that time. Finding a suitable apprenticeship was difficult in the mid-1950s, and it was not until more than two years has elapsed, a period in which Gisela acquired various kinds of work experience and explored where her own interests lay, that she finally entered a regular apprenticeship as a cook. Her choice of career has 'crystallised' during the intervening period. The apprenticeship itself was dominated by the rigid hierarchical structures that were typical in the catering trade at that time, and extended from sexual harassment to tight control on her private life and physical beatings. Despite this, Gisela stuck to her chosen career and acquired skills and self-confidence. This was the basis on which she gained her apprentice's certificate and, as is typical in this sector, started seasonal work and gathered further experience in various hotels and restaurants.

A striking feature of Gisela's vocational training was that she developed a pronounced 'double' outlook from childhood on. She describes retrospectively how her parents shared the typical gender role expectations of the time, according to which their daughter would marry and start a family: *'We were sort of inoculated with the idea... it was virtually automatic, like being programmed - you just got married, that's all'.* Although this orientation is passed on *'automatically'*, that is, it stems from a deeply rooted social consensus and is supported by a variety of norms and everyday codes, her parents gave their daughter an explicit order: *'Apart from that - I get told 'you gotta learn a trade, right, I mean you've got to get your apprentice's certificate, so's you can always say later on: listen, I've got a trade. Then you can make something of yourself'.* Gisela received special support from her father, who was a model for her to follow and a man to whom she had strong emotional ties, but the example set by the mother probably contributed as well to Gisela's developing her own career perspectives as a matter of course. She was expected to and wanted to *'get somewhere'*.

If we inquire a little deeper about what kind of 'pretentious ambition' this was[12], which could well have been the exception rather than the rule for a girl from a skilled worker's family in the 1950s, we find, of course, that economic rationale played an important role - especially after the experience of war. It was vital that she earnt a livelihood, independently of marriage if need be (*'leaving that aside'*). Furthermore, her occupational orientation is linked to an explicit notion of education; the perspective of 'getting somewhere', of 'having a trade'. Education and career have become an object and a medium of biographical plans and aspirations. This is shown in the phase when she chooses her career, where the issue is not only the idea of getting a job, but the actual work that she would like to do. Her parents did not entertain any exaggerated hopes of their daughter rising through the social ranks, but they wanted to ensure that she would have a solid basis of skills and a social position as defined through her occupation (the *'apprentice's certificate'*) within the familiar milieu (skilled workers).

Gisela herself fills out the option presented to her with her own biographical imagination. Supported by her parents, family and career are both aims in life that appear in a positive light for her, and are linked to a wide spectrum of ideas for what she can do with her life and what things she would like to

12 The term 'pretentious', in the broader sense in which it is used here, refers to any form of 'pretension' (see Bourdieu 1983) or anticipatory planning as a form of biographical investment that pays dividends later in life. The pretension relates more to the individual's *biography* as such, and less to the upward social mobility that Bourdieu describes.

achieve. 'Occupation' for her means developing skills and interests, an option to a piece of 'self-realisation', a biographical plan in other words.[13] As with her parents, her primary aim is not upward social mobility. 'Getting somewhere' for her does not mean 'becoming somebody better', but 'becoming oneself'.

This perspective determines not only her vocational experience, but also the starting of a family. When, at the age of 23, Gisela marries Peter Schwarz, also a cook whom she got to know through her work, she ratifies the societal 'programme' that had been communicated to her, but she turns it into a self-willed part of her biography. She stays in her chosen career and answers 'no' when her husband expresses soon after his desire to have children. When their first child is born two years later, she makes a deliberate decision to stop working for as long as her children need her (her second child was born three years later).

For Mrs Schwarz, having a family of one's own involves a responsibility to shape and give form to life. She discharges this responsibility with a wealth of activities and ideas, drawing on childhood experience and the self-assurance gained in her vocational career. The family plays an integral role in the realisation of her own biographical plan. On the other hand, real-life conditions impose definite constraints: Mr Schwarz had to change his occupation in the early 1960s and became a shift worker in a large factory. The family's financial resources are very limited and their accommodation is cramped. Mrs Schwarz suffers from her isolation as a housewife. Her mother-in-law lives in the same town and tries to meddle in the marriage. However, organising day-to-day life with a shift worker in the family is a particularly oppressive burden. Co-ordinating the diversity of interests is particularly hard when the children are toddlers, but remains a problem, in the long run as well. Mrs Schwarz must solve this problem anew every single day.

13 One example for the restricted scope for designing such a life plan is the process by which people choose an occupation. Lack of money and training opportunities compel Gisela to take more time over this process, in the course of which she adapts her aims to the realities of the labour market, without, however, abandoning them altogether. She works out her own vocational direction and puts it into practice. All in all, choice of occupation is an explicit decision-making process for Gisela, and one that is intimately linked to her own identity. The fact that she sticks to her apprenticeship as a cook until final success is achieved, despite the tough conditions, is evidence for the enormous biographical importance that her chosen occupation has for her, not least as a result of the preceding search.

The 'family phase' lasts a total of 15 years, after which Mrs Schwarz succeeds in returning to her old trade. She finds a full-time job in a factory canteen and likes the work, especially the contact with colleagues and managers. The new opportunities for social contacts and the recognition she gains in and through her work help her to win back her previous self-confidence and self-assurance, as well as an 'action-schematic' attitude[14] in her life.

With the benefit of hindsight we might think that Mrs Schwarz succeeded in putting her 'double life plan' into practice and combining work and family, but this was neither plannable[15] nor predictable as regards its specific biographical 'dynamics'. We should therefore examine the biographical process in greater detail as it appears from the protagonist's forward-looking, 'lived-out' perspective.[16]

The family phase, interestingly enough, is highly ambivalent. The action plans implicit in her self-assured decision to adopt a role as wife and mother[17] are quickly met with constraints in everyday family life, and they disintegrate or get lost sight of among the privations and the compelling reality of everyday life. The longer this condition lasts and repetitiveness predominates, the more her biography loses any pretence of subjective freedom to decide and act as she would like. Initial conflicts within the marriage and deliberate efforts to oppose being tied down by the family role soon give way to a more resigned attitude. Her individual project in life turns into that standardised biographical 'programme' in which the woman is expected to dedicate herself to the marriage and the family. Adaptation, day by day, to this new scheme of things has eaten away at the biographical perspective she once held. Her original plans, based as they were on learning and per-

14 Cf. Schütze's theory of processual structures of biography (1981, 1984), in which he distinguishes between four basic attitudes that subjects adopt vis-à-vis their own biography.

15 'Plannable' as regards the specific duration of the 'family break' and the chance to return to her occupation. The fact that Mrs Schwarz succeeds in this endeavour, making her one of a relatively small group of women who actually put the ideological three-phase model into practice, is more an indication of 'coincidental' conditions and the subject's resistance to social pressures that of any applicability of the model (see Dausien 1996, pp. 358-404 for more detail).

16 On the temporal dimension in biographical narratives, see Alheit 1990 and Fischer-Rosenthal 1995.

17 It has already been pointed out that these plans involve more than the mere adoption of gender-specific norms, and that they are active biographical constructions based on the experience amassed by subjects, and on their potential for implementing such plans.

sonal growth, are gradually 'put on ice' once she stops working. Mrs Schwarz displays considerable powers of self-reflection when describing this experience:

'Yes, but somehow as the years went by - I didn't realise, I mean I wasn't really aware of it myself until I was living in East Street - that I just wasn't working any more. All my self-confidence had been dying away. I was getting more and more dissatisfied somehow, more depressed. I mean, I didn't like anything that was going on... Doing the washing, for a start - I didn't like ironing, and after I'd washed everything, I just left it in piles. Peter's always saying, 'You and your piles of stuff everywhere. Put a shroud over them or something.'... We had a lot of arguments about it. It probably all came from that - first of all, I didn't have so much around me any more, the child didn't keep me on the go as much as it used to. The flat was two rooms, kitchen and bathroom. Not a lot. And we didn't have much money either...'

Here Mrs Schwarz is describing how her biographical perspectives go into decline, a process of *unlearning*. Her experience in the family is obviously not enough to give her self-confidence and the feeling of personal growth. She cannot derive this through the relationship with her husband either. At the end of her biographical narrative she is quite realistic in saying, *'Basically, Peter can never give me the self-confidence I need. That's something I have to work for all by myself.'* She is therefore evaluating her biography as a process of *working on oneself* - a process of becoming self-aware, as was already discernible at the beginning of her biography in the form of a pretentious life plan. The fact that Mrs Schwarz succeeds in reversing this trend, returning to her chosen trade and picking up her life plan where she once left it, can be described in this sense as a process of 'self-education'. Let us take a closer look at how she does this.

3. Self-willed learning processes - the other side of adult education

What is interesting for us is that this biographically important step is accompanied by organised education: after years of dissatisfaction with her family situation, Mrs Schwarz hears, quite by chance, about a course in the mornings organised by the local church community. In retrospect, that was the day when a new development was launched: '*... that's when I started to do a bit of thinking about myself*'. In the years that follow, Mrs Schwarz attends various evening classes, where she experiences things that gradually help her to develop a new feeling of self-confidence and self-assurance. Not until this basis has been established does she feel up to the difficult process of returning to the labour market and a steady job - with adult education functioning as a kind of impetus towards social autonomy.

A closer look reveals that the process was much less straightforward, and that in no way can it be interpreted as the result of organised courses on the adult education market. What is astonishing is that Mrs Schwarz does not go to the kind of courses specifically addressed to people like herself - courses for housewives and women returners to the labour market. Mrs Schwarz describes several 'stages' that her continuing education went through.

The first course: Mrs Schwarz's first course is an 'Introduction to Marxism'. Nothing unusual for the early 1970s, of course. More than likely, the tutors were aiming to achieve a certain degree of political enlightenment and convey a body of knowledge, perhaps even instigate an emancipatory learning process. But what did Mrs Schwarz 'learn' in the course?

Her narrative contains no reference to the actual course content, but instead a detailed description of how she experienced these changes in her life. Starting with the parish leaflet in her letterbox, which at a time of great dissatisfaction she sees as an '*opportunity to do something*' and escape the isolation of her housewife existence. As far as the course itself is concerned, she can remember the anxiety she felt towards the strange social surroundings, and especially '*saying something in front of so many people - there were twenty-five members in all*'. She feels inhibited by her dialect and on top of that is confronted with '*an awful lot of foreign words*'. Mrs Schwarz does not attend the whole course, but is there long enough to learn one important new thing - *'I just noticed that there were other women there as well who had just as little self-confidence as I did'.* The fact that, despite finding the actual course content somewhat daunting, '*something stuck*' in the end, such as her interest in current affairs programmes and greater openness towards new and foreign words, is largely attributable to this basic experience with other women. By comparing her situation with that of other women, Mrs Schwarz starts to gain self-confidence and '*do some hard thinking*' about herself.

From the perspective of organised education, learning experiences such as these may seem 'external' or 'extrafunctional', but they do have something to do with the 'inner logic' of the biographical process, and that is by no means a matter of coincidence.[18]

The second course. Thus encouraged, Mrs Schwarz signs up for her second course. She decides on 'Introduction to 19th and 20th century painting', one of a wide range of adult education courses offered by the 'Volkshochschule'. She relates this to her own biography by reconstructing a 'family tradition' - her grandparents on the mother's side *'had a bit to do with painting'* and her grandfather had been a teacher. For Mrs Schwarz, this is an adequate basis for explaining the actual content of her learning process, which she describes otherwise as a somewhat passive process in which 'something is bound to stick': *'I thought, you see, well - get some education - know more about painters, styles of painting and so one - after a while something's bound to stick, right?, you recognise what they are and that.'* As with the Marxism course, the real learning process is occurring at a different level than the actual content might suggest.

Mrs Schwarz is very taken by the teacher of the course - *'The woman could talk for two hours non-stop - my goodness, she sure was an amazing talker'.* The men and women on the course are actively involved as well, however, visiting the municipal art gallery and talking about how they

18 Prior to the first course, Mrs Schwarz took on a cleaning job in an active attempt to establish social contact. In her own words, she hoped she might find '*someone to talk to for half an hour*'. When she realizes that '*that wasn't what I was really looking for either*', she continues her search until she discovers the evening courses.

respond to the pictures there. In a different vein, but no less interesting, is Mrs Schwarz's recollection that one had to get the key off the teacher if one had to go to the toilet during class. This was so embarrassing for her that she used to drink very little before the course. However banal this anecdote might sound, it shows how Mrs Schwarz experiences herself and feels tested in new social spaces.

In an attempt to share and communicate these new experiences, Mrs Schwarz motivates her husband to go with her, but this is soon stopped by his shift work. It is a source of regret for Mrs Schwarz that so few men participate. The course represents a particular aspect of public life, and is bound up with the positive experience of meeting other women. But at the same time there is the threat that it could be devalued socially as soon as it consists 'only' of women.

The trip to Amsterdam. Mrs Schwarz sticks to the subject of 'art' and - after another course dealing with the topic of modern art[19] - she registers for her third course, this time involving a weekend trip to Amsterdam. This, for her, is another big step forwards into unknown territory: *'I went on my own, can you believe that, with all these people I'd never seen in my life before? I was different then than I am now, I mean I was really scared, honest'*. For Mrs Schwarz, the journey involves a whole series of tasks and problems that are not planned by the organisers, indeed probably not even perceived by them in the first place: going away on her own for the first time in ages, together with people she had never even seen before, behaving 'properly', establishing contact and communicating with others. Mrs Schwarz overcomes her fears and advances her learning process by yet another step, one that is more important than any knowledge she acquires about art and artists.

She also has her own peculiar way of interpreting their visits to Amsterdam museums, the 'educational objective' behind the whole trip. She establishes a personal connection to the pictures she sees and looks for those she

19 The works they discuss are obviously so provocative that Mrs Schwarz talks this time about the actual content of the course. Adopting a somewhat bemused yet interested attitude, she mentions a number of experimental works.

became acquainted with in the seminars.[20] In this way, she constructs her participation in separate and disconnected courses as an interconnected and ongoing development process, as *part of her biography*. She is disappointed at not finding some of the pictures she was looking for. But in taking this approach she is asserting her own criteria against the expertise of the course tutor, which she qualifies as mere 'book knowledge'. This bolsters her self-confidence.

Mrs Schwarz opens up new areas of experience for herself through the trip. She explores hitherto unknown regions, sees landscapes and cities, meets people and stays with a Dutch family. She is impressed by a tower that has been converted to a youth centre. The self-service restaurant in the Van Gogh Museum and the snack bar she lived over are all just as important to her as the pictures in the museums. The trip as a whole is full of biographical significance - breaking out of the everyday routine in which Mrs Schwarz sees herself, and is seen by others, in terms of her role in the family unit. Now she can be active and experience things of her own accord - 'all by herself' - in social contact with others. In short, she 'explores' her world and in this way explores her self.[21]

New self-confidence. Mrs Schwarz attends yet another art appreciation course, this time on 'critical painting'. Almost as if she were following a secret 'inner syllabus', she exploits a public situation to test out her growing self-confidence. More precisely, she firstly creates such a situation with others: the participants on the course invite the director of the art gallery where they had been on a guided tour, to come into the class and discuss the exhibition they had seen. Mrs Schwarz criticises the 'highfalutin words' that the expert uses and insists quite self-assertedly on her right as a lay person to think and talk about art.

20 The educational goal she set herself was to *'get to know the painters'* and to *'recognise who a painting is by'* (see above).

21 The quality of this experience is underscored again when the Amsterdam story is finished - Mrs Schwarz returns home from the trip and finds her parents on a spontaneous visit. The contrast as she describes it could hardly be starker - on the one hand, her lively, emotional narration of the trip and the self-experience it denotes for her, on the other, the static image of her parents waiting shivering on the sofa, reminding Mrs Schwarz of her caring role in the family nexus - a role that is determined 'externally', with precedence over the individual's own experience.

This is another clear indication that education is functioning for Mrs Schwarz as an authentic dimension of public and social life. It is no coincidence that she addresses once again the presence (or rather absence) of men in the courses. But she also emphasises that some of the women participants were in employment or were 'incredibly brainy' thanks to their educational experience. She views herself and some of the others as 'small fry'- but not in a denigrating way. Full of self-confidence, she summarises her own learning process thus: *'But all the same... we tried hard and didn't let ourselves get put down. We stuck it out to the end'.*

She is referring here to the discussion they had with the art gallery director, but the same principle applies to the way she appropriates new action space in general. The educational situation enables Mrs Schwarz to compare herself with others, to establish relations, to 'locate' herself in a public social space and thus to step beyond the confines of the private family nexus. The various seminars she attends can be reconstructed as 'stages' that are only linked as an educational process when the subject performs 'biographical labour'. The effects intended by the educational body are irrelevant in this context.

'Education' instead of 'work'? If it is really the case that the courses in Mrs Schwarz's biography function primarily as 'participation in society', independently of all other learning aspects, we have clear evidence for the limits to organised education. 'Education' cannot substitute for 'work' in the long run. After Mrs Schwarz has found a job that matches her vocational qualifications, she stops going to courses. Her occupation guarantees her active participation in public life, personal recognition and self-esteem, on a day-to-day basis and in a socially acknowledged manner. In this respect, the courses were nothing more than a 'bridge' - indeed an individual biographical 'bridge construction'. This is built of specific 'material' - it is no coincidence that Mrs Schwarz makes use of the courses available, rather than going to a self-encounter group for housewives, for example. She is forging links with educational outlooks that existed at an earlier point in her biography, described in the foregoing as her life plan for 'self-education'. The

'bridge' joins various strands of experience within her life history that must be reconstructed in terms of their individual significance.

On the other hand, her educational process is more than a (flawed) substitute for employment. It fails to close the 'gap' that ensued as a result of the family phase. By attending the courses, Mrs Schwarz is drawing on biographical perspectives that she was unable to live out during her previous employment years before. She finds scope for social activity and self-reflection, for gaining autonomy and reappropriating biographical perspectives in a way that was not possible for her before. Her experience with education is imbued with a logic of its own that does not simply vanish when she starts back to work. Mrs Schwarz is a different person when she returns to work after 15 years caring for her family. Even though she no longer attends courses, she is 'continuing' her 'education' in new social domains, both within her occupation and beyond it. She continues to 'work' on her biographical project of self-development and personal growth. She makes new acquaintanceships, goes out, starts up a lobby group in her local community with her husband and neighbours. She develops an interest in trade union activities, and she supports her children's education in such a way that she, too, learns from their experiences.

4. Education as a biographical construction?

I would like to summarise some of the conclusions we can draw from this case study.

(1) When we compare Mrs Schwarz's 'self-education' with the learning objectives of the official educational bodies offering the courses she attends (and these objectives are easy enough to reconstruct), we discern a glaring discrepancy. The thing that makes her personalised construction of an individual, vocational and even political learning process possible is her individual life history - her 'double' life plan and the specific experience she has of

work and family life. In this sense, we can conceive of learning as a form of biographical construction.

(2) Although this 'construction' is only ever activated in concrete interactive situations, it is not a merely situative act. It must be conceived of theoretically as a *temporal structure* that encompasses her entire life up to that point and beyond - as a complex process of biographical learning in which the individual's specific linking of experience - social conditions, events and interactions - determines and shapes the 'logic' of subsequent biographical development. Using appropriate methods, the latter can be reconstructed as a narrative structure. However, it can only be decoded in 'reverse' mode, because biography is an open-ended structure. We always have more options open to us than the spatial and temporal limitations on biography actually permit us to utilise.

(3) This means that biographical learning processes are non-linear in nature. Biographical perspectives that are actively pursued at one moment can suddenly collapse as a result of everyday experiences, with loss of biographical sovereignty and 'unlearning' of social knowledge, the ultimate result. Or the reverse can also occur: long-suppressed potential for education and autonomous shaping of one's life can be reactivated 'out of the blue' as a result of particular events. The course leaflet in her letterbox does not have an automatic impact, but is turned into an impulse for further learning only through the specific biographical structure.

The limitations endemic in any causal model of education are discernible here. Lifelong learning should be thought of more as an 'organic' structure, in which experiences are superimposed on one another and shaped into self-willed constructions and movements through interaction with the surrounding 'environmental' structure.

(4) Finally, the case shows that the logic of biographical construction is not a purely individualist one. It is embedded, particularly in its concrete ramifications, in specific 'environmental' frameworks that themselves obey supra-individual patterns in time and social space. Mrs Schwarz comes from a lower-middle-class/proletarian milieu, is a member of the post-war generation, and she is a woman, so her biographical construction is not arbitrary.

She is not 'free' when she engages in biographical labour. The educational history we have been reconstructing exhibits above all the structural conditions imposed by *social gender* - by entertaining a 'double' life plan, Mrs Schwarz has fallen into the unavoidable dilemma faced by all women in our society, namely that career and family can *not* be combined as a matter of course. Instead, she must live out some kind of 'solution' to this problem, involving the postponement or 'freezing' of a key element in her life plan throughout extended phases of her biography. The reconstructed educational process is a remarkably active achievement on the part of the subject, who asserts and expands her own perspective on life *against* gender-specific restrictions.

(5) Subjects are well capable of reflecting on and 'steering' the construction and constitution of biography, and actively using the opportunities for 'learning processes within transitions' (Alheit, 1993). Adult education could perform an important function here, (a) by providing participants with opportunities for 'biographical work' at individual and collective level and (b) by making it possible to link continuing education and biographical learning processes. Such outlooks would be particularly important in the field of continuing education for women, because women's life plans are up against a social 'ecology' that tends to operate more as a 'counter' than a supportive structure.[22] Mrs Schwarz's biography, and many others besides, are living proof that a specific learning potential can nevertheless ensue from precisely this situation.

References

Alheit, P. (1990), Alltag und Biographie, Studien zur gesellschaftlichen Konstitution biographischer Perspektiven. Forschungsreihe des Forschungsschwerpunkts 'Arbeit und Bildung', Bd. 4. Bremen, Universität Bremen, erweiterte Neuauflage.

Alheit, P. (1993), Transitorische Bildungsprozesse: Das 'biographische Paradigma' in der Weiterbildung, in Mader, W. (ed.), Weiterbildung und Gesellschaft, Grundlagen

22 Cf. the idea of 'counter structures' in the work of Born 1995 and Krüger 1995, which relates more to life course aspects.

wissenschaftlicher und beruflicher Praxis in der Bundesrepublik Deutschland, Forschungsreihe des Forschungsschwerpunkts 'Arbeit und Bildung', Bd. 17. Bremen, Universität Bremen, 2., erweiterte Aufl., pp 343-418.

Alheit, P. (1992), The Biographical Approach to Adult Education in Mader, W. (ed.), Adult Education in the Federal Republic of Germany, Scholarly Approaches and Professional Practice, Vancouver, The University of British Columbia, pp 186 - 221.

Alheit, P. (1994), Taking the Knocks: Youth Unemployment and Biography - A Qualitative Analysis, London, Cassell.

Alheit, P. (1995), 'Biographizität' als Lernpotential: Konzeptionelle Überlegungen zum biographischen Ansatz in der Erwachsenenbildung, in Krüger, Heinz-Hermann and Marotzki (eds), Erziehungswissenschaftliche Biographieforschung, Opladen, Leske und Budrich, pp 276-307.

Alheit, P. and Dausien, B. (1985), Arbeitsleben, Eine qualitative Untersuchung von Arbeiterlebensgeschichten, Frankfurt a. M., New York, Campus.

Alheit, P. and Dausien, B. (1990), Arbeiterbiographien, Zur thematischen Relevanz der Arbeit in proletarischen Lebensgeschichten: Exemplarische Untersuchungen im Rahmen der 'biographischen Methode' Forschungsreihe des Forschungsschwerpunkts 'Arbeit und Bildung', Bd. 2. Bremen, Universität Bremen, 3., leicht überarbeitete Aufl.

Alheit, P. and Dausien, B. (1996a), Bildung als 'biographische Konstruktion'? in Report 37, Literatur- und Forschungsreport Weiterbildung, Juni 1996, pp 33-45.

Alheit, P. and Dausien, B. (1996b), Die biographische Konstruktion der Wirklichkeit. Überlegungen zur Biographizität des Sozialen, in Hoerning, E. (ed), Biographische Sozialisation, Stuttgart, Enke (at press).

Born, C. (1995), Modernisierungsgap - Angleichung im Wandel geschlechtsspezifischer Lebensführungen? Unpublished Paper, given at the Symposium 'Lebenslaufpolitik - Institutionen und Statusmanagement', University of Bremen, 21./22 September 1995.

Bourdieu, P. (1983), Ökonomisches Kapital, kulturelles Kapital, soziales Kapital in Kreckel, R. (ed), Soziale Ungleichheiten, Soziale Welt, Sonderband 2, Göttingen, Schwartz, pp 183-198 .

Bourdieu, P. (1990), Die biographische Illusion, in BIOS, Zeitschrift für Biographieforschung und Oral History, Jg. 3, H, 1, pp 75-81 .

Fischer-Rosenthal, W. (1995), Schweigen - Rechtfertigen - Umschreiben, Biographische Arbeit im Umgang mit deutschen Vergangenheiten in Fischer-Rosenthal, W. and Alheit, P. (eds, unter Mitarb v. Hoerning), Biographien in Deutschland, Soziologische Rekonstruktionen gelebter Gesellschaftsgeschichte, Opladen, Westdeutscher Verlag pp 43-86.

Habermas, J. (1981), Theorie des kommunikativen Handelns, Band 2, Zur Kritik der funktionalistischen Vernunft, Frankfurt a. M., Suhrkamp.

Kallmeyer, W. und Schütze, F. (1977), Zur Konstitution von Kommunikationsschemata der Sachverhaltsdarstellung, Exemplifiziert am Beispiel von Erzählungen und

Beschreibungen. In: Dirk Wegner (ed.), Gesprächsanalysen. Vorträge, gehalten anläßlich des 5, Kolloquiums des Instituts für Kommunikationswissenschaft und Phonetik, Bonn 14.-16. Okt. 1976, Hamburg, Buske, pp 159-274 .

Krüger, H. (1995), Prozessuale Ungleichheit, Geschlecht und Institutionenverknüpfung im Lebenslauf, in Berger, P. and Sopp, P. (eds), Sozialstruktur und Lebenslauf, Lebensläufe und soziale Ungleichheit im gesellschaftlichen Wandel, Opladen, Leske and Budrich, pp 133 - 153.

Osterland, M. (1983), Die Mythologisierung des Lebenslaufs, Zur Problematik des Erinnerns, in Baethge, M. and Essbach, W. (eds), Soziologie, Entdeckungen im Alltäglichen, Hans Paul Bahrdt, Festschrift zu seinem 65. Geburtstag, Frankfurt a. M., New York, Campus, pp 279-290 .

Rosenthal, G. (1995), Erlebte und erzählte Lebensgeschichte, Gestalt und Struktur biographischer Selbstbeschreibungen, Frankfurt a.M., New York, Campus.

Schütze, F. (1981), Prozeßstrukturen des Lebensablaufs in Matthes, Hans-Joachim, Pfeifenberger, A. and Stosberg, M. (eds), Biographie in handlungswissenschaftlicher Perspektive, Kolloquium am Sozialwissenschaftlichen Forschungszentrum der Universität Erlangen, Nürnberg, Verlag der Nürnberger Forschungsvereinigung, pp 67-156.

Schütze, F. (1984), Kognitive Figuren des autobiographischen Stegreiferzählens, in Kohli, M. and Günther, R. (eds), Biographie und soziale Wirklichkeit, Neue Beiträge und Forschungsperspektiven, Stuttgart, Metzler, pp 78-117 .

Schütze, F. (1995), Verlaufskurven des Erleidens als Forschungsgegenstand der interpretativen Soziologie, in Krüger, H.-H. and Marotzki, W. (eds), Erziehungswissenschaftliche Biographieforschung, Opladen, Leske und Budrich, pp 116-157.

Siebert, H. (1995), Konstruktivistische Aspekte der Erwachsenenbildung, in Derichs-Kunstmann, K., Faulstich, P. and Tippelt, R. (eds), Theorien und forschungsleitende Konzepte der Erwachsenenbildung, Dokumentation der Jahrestagung 1994 der Kommission Erwachsenenbildung der Deutschen Gesellschaft für Erziehungswissenschaft, Beiheft zum REPORT, Frankfurt a.M.: DIE, pp 50-54.

Heiner Barz / Rudolf Tippelt

The Influence of Social Milieus on Attitudes and Activities of Women in Lifelong Learning

Introduction

This paper is based on the following thesis:

(1) A leading and classic empirical study by Strzelewicz, Raapke and Schulenberg (1966) which points out that adult education has for a long time ignored issues of social class and social inequality.

(2) In target group analysis of adult education this deficiency becomes apparent and also in the general discussion about the modernisation of society. As a result our interest in the social fabric of society has been revived.

(3) The discussion about the social structure in modern society, concerns itself with an individual's circumstances (to be understood as external conditions for decision-making), that is, housing conditions, working conditions, opportunities for leisure-time, financial resources, prestige, etc., as well as with life-styles. Also taken into consideration are the more or less freely chosen typical social patterns of every-day behaviour which are often clearly and recognisably set aside from other life-styles.

(4) People who share a common set of core values and beliefs constitute social groups which are called 'social milieus'. Each social milieu is composed of persons who tend to agree with one another about the basic realities of their everyday lives: work, leisure, tastes, relationships, hopes and dreams. Simply stated: a social milieu can be seen as a group of like-minded people.

1. Multiplicity of interests in adult education

In the last decade, within Education and Social Science Departments, there has been a growing recognition that an analysis of social structures based on a class or stratification model has become an increasingly inadequate representation (Hradil, 1992, Beck, 1983: 35, Barz and Tippelt, 1994). In the current debate on social structures these are seen as multi-dimensional and not depending entirely on occupational status (Müller, 1992, 1995: 17). Entering the debate in the last few years was the idea that socio-cultural structures, such as milieus and life-styles, partially chosen by individuals, should become part of what we understand by social structure (Vester et al, 1995, Ueltzhöffer and Flaig, 1993).

As an indicator for the desire for a socio-cultural differentiation, one can take the general acceptance of differentiation as described by Bourdieu (1982), German educationalists and social scientists, and also the positive response to Schulze's (1992) study of the 'Erlebnisgesellschaft' (an analysis based on people's experiences). Besides Schulze's description of five socio-cultural milieus, the SINUS Institute has worked out a model encompassing nine milieus of socio-cultural divisions in society (in Western Germany). The initial impact in the discipline of political education was described in a study commissioned by the Friedrich-Ebert-Stiftung (Flaig, Meyer and Ueltzhöffer, 1993). It was possible to show the relevance of the analysis by milieus for adult education in terms of milieus determining the factors relating to actual attendance at courses and the willingness to participate in political education. Equally relevant to practice are the apparent differing demands as to the content of seminars. There were clear differences in relation to desires for leisure-time activities, for acquiring knowledge and for artistic experiences (Flaig, Meyer and Ueltzhöffer, 1993). However, one can so far only make assumptions about a correlation of interests in adult education, educational careers and social milieus. It was for this reason that we initiated this study researching milieus and adult education in Freiburg.

2. Social milieus as reference groups in adult education

The milieu specific framework we chose can be said to follow the established theory on social class by Max Weber (1972) which adheres to four classes; the working class, the petit bourgeois class, the intelligentsia without capital and specialists, as well as capitalists and the educated class. The milieu model, developed by Sinus since 1979, now encompasses nine milieus in Western Germany[1]. In the following pages they will be outlined briefly (Flaig 1993, Ueltzhöffer and Flaig 1993).

Upper Conservative Milieu (8%, trend static)

Aim in Life: Superior life-style, material success and a recognised position in society, aspirations and time for self-realisation and satisfaction in one's private life, harmonious family life.

Social Position: Higher than average formal education. Many executives and civil servants as well as self-employed and those working on a freelance basis, a high proportion of recipients of a (superannuation) pension. Frequently on high or the highest income bracket.

Life-Style: Traditionalism, closeness to nature, rejection of everything exaggerated, artificial and superficial, demanding high quality standards, and good tastes in commodities etc.

Petit-Bourgeois Milieu (21%, trend decreasing):

Aim in Life: Establishing oneself in all spheres of life, particularly achievement in one's work, ordered family life, own one's home, permanent, conservative values.

Social Position: Predominantly with secondary school qualifications and a completed vocational training. Many employees and lower civil servants, as well as self-employed and farmers. A high proportion of pensioners and recipients of superannuated pensions. Mostly smaller and medium incomes.

[1] Meanwhile the SINUS Institute has worked out a typology of milieus in the five new lands of the federal republic. Because of the different structure and history of society there, there are not only different results in terms of frequency and distribution, but a different declination in terms of values, life-styles, aesthetics and consumer demands (see Flaig 1993).

Life-Styles: Conventionalism, conformity, maintenance of the status-quo. To be like others, thriftiness, restraint. Preference for solid products not subject to change of fashion.

Traditional Blue Collar Milieu (5%, trend decreasing):

Aims in Life: Satisfactory standard of living, material security, safe job, security in old age, recognition amongst friends, colleagues and neighbours, related to the traditional working class culture.

Social Position: Predominantly secondary school and vocational training, high proportion of pensioners and recipients of a superannuation pension, more than average skilled workers, semi-skilled and unskilled workers mostly small to medium incomes.

Life-Style: Pragmatic sober view of one's own social position; no exaggeration of consumer demands. Preference for solid and lasting products.

Uprooted Blue Collar Milieu (12%, trend increasing) :

Aim in Life: To keep up with the material standards of the broad middle-class.

Social Position: Little formal education, left school without qualifications, high proportion of the unemployed, many unskilled or trained workers, lower income brackets.

Life-Style: Mostly living for the present, looking to the future is repressed, limited financial opportunities, impulsive consumption.

Progressive No Collar Workers Milieu (6%, trend increasing):

Aim in Life: To arrange one's life in as pleasant a way as possible, to be able to afford what one likes; combined with a flexible approach to wants (reality related hedonism).

Social Position: Relatively young milieu, at least qualifications equivalent to 'O' level (Realschule), many school children and students; skilled workers, employees with qualifications, those in public services.

Life-Style: Openness to new experiences, no closed world-view, prepared for change, tolerance of different styles of living, concentration on leisure-time.

Social Climbers Milieu (25%, trend increasing):

Aim in Life: Advancement in one's job and socially, to work one's self up the ladder, to show success, to enjoy recognition.

Social Position: Mostly equivalent to 'O' level qualifications, many skilled workers and employees in medium positions, smaller self-employed and those working on a free-lance basis, mostly medium to high incomes.

Life-Style: Looking to the standards of the higher strata's. Desire for prestige, high value of status symbols.

Technocratic Liberal Milieu (9%, trend static):

Aim in Life: To be successful; a high standard of living, planning one's career and private life, one can make one's own luck.

Social Position: More than average medium to advanced formal education ('A' level equivalent (Abitur) or Degree), high proportion of students, more than average number of employees of a higher status and Civil Servants medium to larger self-employed, those working on a free-lance basis, high and the highest income brackets are over-represented.

Life-Style: Strong desire for self expression (advantaged style, good tastes), open to new trends, easy approach to life (not to take it too seriously).

Hedonistic Milieu (12%, trend increasing):

Aim in Life: Rejection of conventional life, divide oneself off from the 'squares', freedom, independence, desire for enjoyment, to live intensively, breaking out of the demands of everyday life.

Social Position: Little formal education, but also isolated cases of high qualifications. Main age-group between 15 and 30, a high proportion of unemployed, semi-skilled workers, ordinary employees, those with a job mentality, mostly small to medium incomes.

Life-Style: Live for the here and now, little by way of formulating a life-plan, to be distinctive, and original. Genuineness in relation to aspirations as to style; fascination with luxury and consumption; impulsive consumer style.

Alternative Milieu (2%, trend decreasing):

Aim in Life: Development of one's personality, self-realisation, building a humane world, harmonisation of the private and social life, intensive personal relationships.

Social Position: Over-representation of those with the highest level of education (those with 'A' level equivalent (Abitur) and graduates); high proportion of students and pupils, more than average higher civil servants and employees, as well as people working free-lance; while there is an over representation of small incomes there are also frequently those in high and the highest income brackets.

Life-Style: Rejection of material requirements, stylish simplicity, asceticism in consumption, naturalness, genuineness in values, that is, environmentally conscious living, making one's own clothes and furniture, retreat into the alternative ideal.

Quantitative changes in the structure of the milieu have been delineated by the use of the milieu indicator which encompasses 46 items and has been used in 400,000 cases up until now.

More interesting than the quantitative changes in the proportion of the population belonging to a particular milieu is to position the milieus into a two dimensional space whose co-ordinates for the traditional socio-economic strata's on the one hand and value identification on the other are to be represented (see illustration 1).

Using this approach the traditional blue collar milieu, for instance, is situated at the lower end of the strata and is also identified by the largely basic traditional values ('to preserve') which this group holds. The upper conservative milieu shares the same basic values, but finds that it recruits people who are more privileged in terms of socio-economic position. While the social climbers, the technocratic liberal and the traditional blue collar milieu occupy a middle position on the scale of changing values to post-material and post-modernistic identification, the alternative and the progressive no collar milieu, as well as particularly the hedonistic milieu, have internalised fully such values.

3. The Freiburg Study 'Social Milieu and Adult Education of Women'

3.1 Initial Considerations:

Despite the advantages in using the milieu model into research on adult education there has only been one attempt to do so. This particular research looked at political education and adult education (Flaig et al, 1993). It empirically examined the milieu specific experiences, motives, expectations and interests in regard to adult education in Germany. The findings of that project prompted this research study. Hopefully our study will offer an empirical foundation for this field. We will start off with some background information:

(1) The key focus was the identification of milieu specific attitudes and patterns of behaviour in regard to (further) education and the nine social milieus established by SINUS for our sample

(2) Additionally demographic factors were taken into consideration. This related a person's interest in further education to a particular stage in life and the nine milieus. This gives rise to a second criteria for differentiation of our subjects; their age and the stage in their lives they have reached.

(3) We found the method of in-depth analysis useful for access to an understanding of the milieu, people's specific expectations and experiences, hopes, fears and inhibitions. Interviews were, therefore, more suitable than the use of a standardised questionnaire.

(4) A further vital underlying hypothesis for our research plan was that people's attitudes towards adult education were formed by their first contact with institutionalised teaching and learning in childhood and adolescence. In this context questions about the individual's biography of initial education, the memories of learning experiences at school and outside seemed indispensable.

(5) One has to go back a long way, namely to the 'Göttinger Studie' (1958) and Strzelewicz, Raapke and Schulenberg (1966) as well as the follow-on study by Schulenberg et al 1978, to look for a wide ranging study of the problem of 'adult education and inequality'. This pioneering work, still the standard study (Brödel 1995: 10), was based on a model of stratification. We, however, today prefer a milieu model. A strict replication was therefore not our intention. However, we took inspiration from this group of researchers, using some of the ideas and approaches, and even some of the formulations used by them.

(6) As in other research projects we had to work within the limits of time, financial and personal resources. As we had decided to combine a milieu perspective with specific attributes in the stages of one's life in our sample, we had to conduct a relatively large number of interviews, even when considering exclusively only one sex. We chose, therefore, in this first phase of our research to concentrate exclusively on female interviewees because

women are the main participants in general further education. For example, they represent 75% of those attending the Volkshochschule (community adult education centres) (Dohmen, 1994: 410).

(7) In relation to the different large providers of adult education we also had to make an informed choice. We decided to study the institution that provides most further education, the 'Volkshochschulen' (community adult education centres). It registered 8,654,000 participants in 1993. In comparison the relative figures by the Church Institutions for the same year were; Protestant adult education 3,148,000 and Catholic adult education 5,880,000. The number of teaching hours showed an even greater predominance in terms of the Volkshochschulen (BMBWFT, 1994).

(8) In order to be able to make a statement about specific urban situations, our research stretched throughout the region of Freiburg. The inclusion of the surrounding areas does allow comparison on attitudes towards education by participants in urban and rural areas.

3.2 Sample for Analysis

Following the above initial considerations, we set ourselves the goal to consider all nine milieus as described by SINUS. Further, within each milieu, women of differing ages and from different stages in their lives were to be represented. Research into participation so far suggested the following divisions:

Women before they had families:

Those in work, the unemployed, those in training or studying, without children, between the ages of 20-40.

Women with families:

Mothers, without regard to age, with children aged up to 15 years old.

Women after they brought-up families:

Older women over 45 years of age, who had no more children to care for in their own household ('empty-nest-families').

Our decision to concentrate our research on the Volkshochschulen (VHS) allowed us a further differentiation; to look at the VHS-experience. We differentiated, therefore, between women with or without recent VHS experience. We, therefore, looked at VHS experience operationally by specifying that these women had to have taken part in at least two classes in the last two years. The group without actual experience of the VHS include some who in earlier years had attended a VHS class. Illustration 2 shows the final distribution of participating interviewees in our sample (desired ideal distribution put in parentheses).

Two modifications that arose during the course of our research need to be mentioned. The search for hedonists and no collar workers over the age of 45 soon had to be abandoned as these milieus are exceptional to the young between the ages of 20 and 30. Secondly, the criteria for 'experience with VHS' for women from the uprooted blue collar milieu was altered in such a way that we included women who had participated in one VHS class only. The VHS represents for women from this milieu something so far removed from their every-day experience. As a result they have a lot of hurdles to overcome before even entering the institution. They mostly attended a remedial class or sought to catch up with their Hauptschulabschluss (secondary school qualifications).

We took on board suggestions made in the 'Göttinger Studie' which also had taken as its focus the way the Volkshochschule was perceived. We also took from Strzelewicz, Raapke and Schulenberg (1966) the concept of 'the cultured person' and the question about 'what one had missed out on at school.' Finally, we also incorporated, in a carefully modified way, their process for looking at the most important tasks of schools and the Volkshochschule. For example, the suggested responses to the questions of the main tasks of the VHS were enlarged to incorporate 'health promotion', 'spiritual studies' and 'intercultural relationships' while 'relationships with human beings in search of themselves' was replaced by 'ways to self-discovery'. In addition to this approach we listed the responses our interviewees gave when asked to explain their understanding of the concepts 'education' and 'Volkshochschule'.

In our interviews, in line with the expressed aims of our study, we covered the following areas:

PART A:

Here important information for the diagnosis of the milieu was collected and the initial questions to warm up our interviewees, covering the description of their day-to-day lives, leisure pursuits and the description of social relationships. However, the most important insights determining the milieu clarification were gained by encouraging our interviewees to describe what in their view are the most important things in life (philosophy of life) and what is or would be the most important thing in the upbringing of their children.

PART B:

Besides taking a history of the interviewees schooling and educational experiences we also invited an assessment of the value or the uselessness of the institutions they had experienced. We also enquired into the expectations of the tasks schools performed, into the effectiveness of vocational training and social learning (the hidden curriculum). We also explored ideas for improvement such as 'imagine you are the Minister for Education...', and expectations for the future and relevance of the concept of an educated (cultured) person. by asking 'do you know a person who you would call well educated?'.

PART C:

Here we looked at the individual's personal experiences of adult education. We gave emphasis to experiences gained and the images held by participants of the Volkshochschule. We also asked what are the assumed and desired tasks of a Volkshochschule. Questions about the individual's willingness to participate in further education and the possible use of advice about courses in further education were also asked. We also wanted to know whether or not the vocational and general courses on offer in further education met the expectations of adults, such as the time of classes and the type of programmes offered. Finally we also enquired whether or not people were aware of other providers of further education, for example, the church, 'Bundes- und Landeszentrale für Politische Bildung', political foundations, esoteric provisions and other private providers.

4. Results

We will first give an overview of the 'milieu specific interests' in adult education but will later focus on three milieus in particular.

4.1 Classification of interests in adult education (an overview)

The Working-Class Milieus 23 %

Traditional Blue Collar Milieu (5%, trend decreasing)

- looks for involvement and security,
  - participation in trade unions
- job security and responsibility in work
- obstacles to learning from school-age, but education is a human right

Uprooted Blue Collar Milieu (12%, trend increasing)

- little integration into further education, fears of the hurdles to overcome, ignorance
- small financial budget, spa's and health education
- VHS is for others, but 'education' is to be curious

Progressive No Collar Milieu (6%, trend increasing)

- 'learning is like rowing; if one stops one goes backwards'
- lifelong learning (computer courses, rhetoric, compensation for deficiencies)

- vocational courses at the VHS (i.e. languages in one's job) but also private providers

The Middle Milieus (58 %)

Petit-Bourgeois Milieu (21 %, trend decreasing)

- trust in the established providers, eager for culture
- personal bond with Church providers, but also important target group of the VHS
- deep desire for harmony, to find one's identity
- adult education in order to achieve social and vocational integration
- further vocational trade training; to establish oneself

Hedonistic Milieu (12%, trend increasing)

- disassociation from political education and a rejection of established providers
- boring, dogmatic; rejection of lifelong learning
- adult education seen as a social and youth orientated cultural event

Social Climbers Milieu (25%, trend increasing)

- no particular aspiration, culturally and intellectually. Ambivalence to higher education
- further vocational training in order to achieve vocational and social advancement, visible success
- conscious of the prestige and status of the providers. Reservations: 'some of the courses on offer are not up to standard'
- interested in VHS - (Qualification orientated, health education and creativity)

The Higher Elitist Milieus (19%)

Technocratic Liberal Milieu (9%, trend static)

- broadly based interests: creativity, art, politics (not to be passive and become apathetic), condemnation of television

- planning further education (one can make one's own luck), planning one's career
- private providers, but also VHS, not only recipients but providers
- one's own arranging and implementation of adult education

Upper Conservative Milieu (8%, trend static)

- interests in culture (history of civilisation, literature). Satisfaction in the private sphere of one's life
- against anonymity, against too much schooling, 'VHS in the vocational field to achieve qualifications is good for others'
- but a lot of older people attend intensive courses at the VHS (creativity, language, art, environment, politics)
- high expectations as to quality
- 'information about further education is good for others'.

Alternative Milieu (2%, trend decreasing)

- action orientated, political and creative interests
- health education mostly from private providers
- open for methodological and group dynamic innovation
- multiplicity of adult education, interested in VHS

4.2 The assessment of the value of further education seen from the perspective of selected milieus

In order to give a more detailed example of our findings, we looked at the assessment of further education. We, therefore, selected the perspective of the petit bourgeois, the progressive no collar and the alternative milieu. The three milieus examined in more depth had in common the realisation of the necessity for lifelong learning.

In the petit bourgeois milieu we found approval for lifelong learning, but they also had a diffused eagerness for education. There was a demand for a higher recognition for adult education in society. The importance of meeting new people was emphasised in order not to be limited as a person. The compensatory role of adult education as a counter-balance to increasing specialisation was viewed as important. For instance, the kind of value given to education and knowledge by the petit bourgeois as described by Bourdieu (1982: 518), was also found to be relevant to this milieu in our study (and also to the traditional blue collar milieu). However, tentative thoughts about self-realisation were also found.

One could describe the specific attitudes found amongst our interviewees from the progressive no collar milieu as being ones which stressed the practical application of knowledge and learning materials. This is the group most likely to demand vocational further education courses leading to qualifications in computer studies, accounting and business studies. This group also has an emerging interest in self-realisation (development) which is viewed as being highly relevant to vocational advancement (see the case below). There is a rejection of group dynamics: 'to learn French, I do not need an arm-chair'.

In the alternative milieu we found that interests are predominantly directed towards creativity and self-realisation. Also in the study courses for language learning and other vocational courses, group dynamic components and excursions are welcomed. It is also considered important that, in relation to time and venue, thought is given to opportunity for relaxation and for meeting other course members. Course attendance figures show an emphasis on the preference for subjects of relaxation and the experiencing of one's body (Tai Chi, Qigong, Yoga, the Alexander Technique, Feldenkrais Method, Bioenergetics). The belief in learning as a means of educating oneself as a 'need in order to achieve happiness' by the human race, also emerges here. Education amounts to independence and it therefore needs to be accessible to all. Therefore, one of our interviewees demanded that television should be made more expensive and the money thus acquired used to invest in or provide more adult education.

In all the milieus there are visible differences in attitudes towards vocational further education and those programmes that arose from private initiatives. However, there is evidence that attitudes are increasingly merging especially amongst the progressive no collar and the alternative milieus. Vocational further education is described as being more serious, more disciplined, more productive, more effective, more exhausting and more closely related to work and application. In contrast, general further education is associated with play, fun, social life, hobbies and leisure time. All these concepts imply that such education is 'not to be taken too seriously'. On the other hand there are some negative attitudes associated with vocational further education, such as examinations, tests, and the pressure to succeed. While some criticised the lack of commitment and seriousness in general further education, it was also appreciated that there is room for fun, interest and initiative. In terms of our question whether internal or external leaders of courses are to be preferred, almost all expressed a preference for external educators. The latter were seen to be better, often more specialised, more competent, more independent and less prejudiced as they were distanced from institutional politics.

4.3 Thoughts about the firmly established concept of 'lifelong learning' entering the 'everyday life world'

The conviction that 'lifelong learning' is indispensible has largely been accepted by all social groups. This is apparent in the overview of our findings about the importance of adult education now and in the future. The views our female interviewees expressed about what represented the best education, and the characterisation they gave of an educated cultured person support this trend. In their comments people from all milieus stressed the necessity and the willingness to look at education as a lifelong process. It was repeatedly emphasised that existing knowledge and skills had constantly to be added to and expanded. We found particularly revealing the fact that the concept of lifelong learning had obviously become part of the every-day use in language. Many interviewees from all milieus used the term 'lifelong learning' quite spontaneously when explaining their individual understanding of education and further education, that is, without the interviewer having introduced it. An openness to new things, flexibility and the willingness to adapt were repeatedly cited as the qualities generally required in our modern industrial society. These were felt to be indispensable for advancement in one's work, even for meeting the changing requirements of the position one presently occupied. Technological change and developments in data-processing were cited as key areas where updating is needed. The second important factor in today's work environment which demands a constant willingness to engage in lifelong learning are the increasing number of jobs which require competence in languages and intercultural learning, as economic relationships, administration and tourism become progressively international. These changes in conjunction with the development of a world-wide net of transport, information and communication, result in the redundancy of some occupations and in the creation of new ones and the need to modify and to newly define some fields of work.

Across the milieus, the improvement and expansion of social competencies is seen as very important, particularly in relation to working life in the future. In fact it is noticeable that the economic perspective is predominant in regard to the necessity for further education. Most of our interviewees viewed education, because of the demands of the labour market, first and foremost as a means and not as an end in itself. A widespread willingness to change one's orientation and to learn new things does, however, also assist in the development of an individual's personality in order to negotiate successfully relationships in our private, family and social life and to cope in crisis situations.

As well as the dimension of the professional/vocational verses social/personal competence, a second dimension is, according to our findings significant: that is the way a person believes in the indispensability of further education. This is strongly influenced by the milieu to which they belong. The individual's attitude to further education can be said to be somewhere between the opposites of 'further education as a pleasurable pursuit' and a 'pressure to engage in further education'.

Members of the more modern milieus, the technocratic liberal, the alternative and progressive no collar milieu, together with the upper conservative milieu, see themselves as the active creators of change, taking the initiative in respect of ambitions to engage in further education. It is obvious for members of the upper conservative milieu, that one 'keeps oneself up-to-date' both at home and by attending courses well into one's old age: 'because if one stagnates, one gets old'. Often examples of such 'youthful oldies' are given from within the person's own family. In the progressive no collar milieu and, particularly in the technocratic liberal milieu, equal importance is attached to the development of one's personality and the realisation of professional know-how: 'Learning is like rowing; if you stop then you go backwards', a secretary from the progressive no collar milieu told us.

A 63-year old woman from the technocratic liberal milieu put the same idea differently: 'You always have to want to learn and not think. Now I am finished and I know everything'. Interviewees from this milieu stress the necessity to fundamentally rethink at particular stages in one's life: 'One had to say now I enter a phase in my life where I have to put order into things, where I have to look and see, what I can discover, rethink and experience afresh, where I have use of human creativity'. In the alternative milieu 'lifelong learning' is decisive and part of one's holistic personal realisation. It is seen as a basic human right: political and artistic education are given much emphasis in this milieu. Also the notion that 'education is seen as a pleasurable pursuit' is predominant, for instance, one of our interviewees confessed euphorically that she would really love to 'enrol on 15 courses'.

In contrast the 'pressure to participate in further education' is most keenly felt by members of the traditional blue collar milieu and even more in the uprooted blue collar milieu: 'Well, one had to if one is not to be detached from social and economic development'. It is quite typical of those in the uprooted blue collar milieu to have a somewhat detached attitude to further education. This is expressed in utterances like 'actually one should'. Further education also tends to be seen as a kind of undesirable pressure by members of the hedonistic milieu. Whilst members of this milieu do express that they have many interests, the intentions to pursue them rarely result in enrolment. The middle groups, the social climbers milieu and the petty bourgeois milieu, also take the middle ground in relation to the 'reactive verses active understanding of further education'. Lifelong learning is, at the present time, not only pleasurable and self-motivating, but also more of a duty. However, it is not purely motivated by a fear of going down in the world.

The petit bourgeois milieu understands education mostly as a widening of one's horizon and also as acquiring knowledge about cultural traditions. Further education functions to increase knowledge about art and the history of civilisation.

In the social climbers milieu, vocational and pragmatically orientated interests predominate but further education is also regarded as a means to develop one's personality and to cope with conflicts.

References

Barz, H. and Tippelt, R. (1994), Lebenswelt, Lebenslage, Lebensstil und Erwachsenenbildung, in Tippelt, R. (eds), Handbuch Erwachsenenbildung/Weiterbildung, pp 123-146.

Beck, U. (1986), Risikogesellschaft, Auf dem Weg in eine andere Moderne, Frankfurt a.M.

Bélanger, P. (1994), Lifelong Learning: The Dialectics of 'Lifelong Educations' in Internationale Zeitschrift für Erziehungswissenschaft, Special Issue: Lifelong Education, pp353-382.

Bourdieu, P. (1982), Die feinen Unterschiede, Kritik der gesellschaftlichen Urteilskraft, Frankfurt a.M.

Brödel, R. (1995), Teilnehmerforschung im Überblick - Deutschland als Fallbeispiel, in Meyer, T. (eds) Teilnehmerforschung im Überblick (Jahrbuch 1995 der Akademie für Politische Bildung der Friedrich-Ebert-Stiftung), Bonn, pp 7-19.

Bundesministerium für Bildung, Wissenschaft, Forschung und Technologie (eds) (1994), Grund- und Strukturdaten 1994/95, Bonn.

Dohmen, G. (1994), Volkshochschulen in Tippelt, R. (eds), Handbuch Erwachsenenbildung/Weiterbildung, pp 407-413.

Emmerling, D. (1988), Dynamische Strukturen für die Weiterbildung in Bundeszentrale für politische Bildung: Zukunft der Weiterbildung. Eine Standortbestimmung, Bonn pp103-117.

Flaig, B., Meyer, T. and Ueltzhöffer, J. (1993), Alltagsästhetik und politische Kultur, Zur ästhetischen Dimension politischer Bildung und politischer Kommunikation Bonn.

Flaig, B. (1993), Wohnwelten in Ostdeutschland, Alltagsästhetik, Wohnmotive, Wohnstile und Gärten in den Neuen Bundesländern, Ein Forschungsbericht der Burda GmbH, Offenburg, und Sinus, Heidelberg, Offenburg.

Hradil, S. (eds) (1992), Zwischen 'Bewußtsein' und 'Sein', Die Vermittlung 'objektiver' Lebensbedingungen und 'subjektiver' Lebensweisen, Opladen.

Müller, H. P. (1992), Sozialstruktur und Lebensstile, Der neuere theoretische Diskurs über soziale Ungleichheit, Frankfurt a.Maine.

Müller, H. P. (1995), Sozialstruktur und Lebensstile. Vom Menetekel Klassengesellschaft zur Schönen Neuen Welt, Von Risiko- und Erlebnisgesellschaft - und zurück? in Derichs-Kunstmann, Faulstich, K., Tippelt, R. (eds), Theorien und forschungsleitende Konzepte der Erwachsenenbildung, Dokumentation der Jahrestagung 1994 der Kommission Erwachsenenbildung der DGfE. Beiheft zum Report, Frankfurt a.Maine, pp 13-28.

Schulenberg, W. (1978), Soziale Faktoren der Bildungsbereitschaft Erwachsener, Stuttgart.

Schulze, G. (1992), Die Erlebnisgesellschaft. Kultursoziologie der Gegenwart, Frankfurt a.Maine.

Strzelewicz, W., Raapke, H. D., Schulenberg, W. (1966), Bildung und gesellschaftliches Bewußtsein, Eine mehrstufige soziologische Untersuchung in Westdeutschland, Stuttgart.

Tippelt, R., Eckert, T. and Barz, H. (1996), Markt und integrative Weiterbildung, Zur Differenzierung von Weiterbildungsanbietern und Weiterbildungsinteressen, Bad Heilbrunn.

Ueltzhöffer, J., Flaig, B. B. (1993), Spuren der Gemeinsamkeit? Soziale Milieus in Ost- und Westdeutschland, in Weidenfeld, W. (eds), Deutschland, Eine Nation - doppelte Geschichte, Köln, pp 61-82.

Vester, M., Hofmann, M., Zierke, I. (eds) (1995), Soziale Milieus in Ostdeutschland, Gesellschaftliche Strukturen zwischen Zerfall und Neubildung, Köln.

Weber, M. (1972), Wirtschaft und Gesellschaft, Tübingen.

Margarita Tereseviciene

Changing Women's Role in Lithuania: an Aspect of Continuing Education

According to the data of the Department of Statistics of Lithuania, in 1994 women constituted 52.7 % of the inhabitants of Lithuania. Their psychology, attitudes and life experiences differ from those of men, and it is important to take this into consideration in relation to the welfare and comfort of the whole society. Urgent problems of modern life should be solved by men and women equally.

According to the law of Lithuania equality of gender exists de jure, however, de facto it is often violated. A United Nations (UN) Bulletin published in Lithuania points out a number of problems concerning the status of women, such as, abuse and sexual harassment, unsatisfactory health care, and a higher unemployment rate than men. Some of these problems are closely related to education.

Education. There is no formal discrimination in our schools between boys and girls. Their numbers in secondary schools is almost equal (50.1% of girls in primary schools, 60.6% in high schools and 55.2% at universities). Inequality begins in higher education both in terms who gets degrees and academic appointments in the institutions. Men domination of men in both areas (Fig 1).

The number of men and women holding academic degrees

Fig.1

Academic degree	Total number	From total Men	From total Women	Part of women in %
Doctor of Science/ Humanities	2685	1856	829	31
Doctor Habilitatis of Science/ Habilitatis	395	344	51	13

Only 31% of women have a degree in the 'Doctor of Science/Humanities' while 13% are the holders of the highest degree of 'Doctor Habilitatis of Science/ Humanities' in comparison with men.

A similar situation is to be found among employees of educational institutions, see Fig. 2.

Employees of Educational Institutions

Fig.2

Educational institution	Total number	From total men	women	Part of women in %
Schools employees (primary, compulsory, high)	44394	6470	37924	85
Teachers	41052	5420	35632	87
Principles of primary schools	174	13	161	93
compulsory schools	581	304	277	48
high (secondary)	712	455	257	36
Higher schools	3136	1014	2122	68
Universities	8069	4970	3099	38

More women than men work in schools while more men work in the university sector than women. A similar relationship can be found concerning principles of schools. Only 38% of women are employees at universities; all presidents of universities are men. Such disproportion is the result of social and economic conditions and traditions of the patriarchical society.

Women and decision-making. Notwithstanding good education and active participation in the labour market only a few women have positions on governing bodies. Women constitute 7% of the members of Parliament and there is only one female minister. Women's duties, such as those of mother, wife, householder make it more difficult for women than men to participate in a political or academic career. On the other hand, the negative attitude of society towards career women makes their efforts to achieve decision-making positions extremely painful: 'women are worse in governing', 'women are too emotional to be leaders' are the clichés we can hear all the time. The very fact that women's issues are put forward as part of society's problems which need to be solved is met unfavourably by men as well as by women. Women need to be much more competent and work much better than men if they want equal evaluation or to achieve in politics. Gender discrimination is flourishing both in attitudes and in remuneration for work. Our attempt to have an Ombudsman or an independent advisory body at the government level is still fruitless. The only progress we can talk about is the position of an Adviser to the Prime Minister on Women's issues. (Ms Giedre Purvaneckiene is the person at the moment). After the Beijing Conference an Information Centre for Women's Organisations was established to bring women leaders closer together, to consolidate the women's movement, and to put forward national goals of the women's movement.

Women and family. In 1990, after independence in Lithuania was restored women were asked to 'return to the family'. However, only a few families can live on one salary. Women have to concentrate their efforts on bringing up their children, to be the bread-winners for the family and to take the responsibility for the welfare of their children's future. Let us consider some figures. There are 1,025,000 two-parent and about 100,000 thousand single-parent families in Lithuania. In 15% of families the children are raised by the mother alone. The 15% stands for more or less 110,000 children; another ten thousand children are brought up by single fathers. The divorce rate is now close to 4 per 1,000 of the population. In the future it is quite likely that about half of all children will be raised without one of the parents.

The figures suggest these women have neither the time nor the possibility for study. It is quite lucky if they have graduated school or university before their first baby is born. Otherwise, their studies are interrupted, postponed for the future or cancelled forever.

Feminisation of the poor. The majority of those living in poverty are women. The average rate of their income is 1.4 times lower than that of men.

Last year the Labour Exchange Bureau registered thirty thousand and one hundred unemployed people. Women outnumbered men 1:4 times. Most of them had previously been office employees, engineers, or philologists. As the statistical data indicates it is very difficult for the women to find a job according to their speciality; most of them take any job available. This group of women is generally well educated.

In our newspapers you can find a lot of advertisements for a company secretary. The requirements are usually a university education, fluent English, German, Russian, computer skills, and to be aged between 25-35. It is impossible to imagine men in such positions as the salary is usually not adequate for the qualifications.

Women and continuing education. In 1991, when the Concept of National Education was discussed in the mass media, great emphasis was put on developing a continuing or lifelong education system in Lithuania. The result was that a number of higher education institutions, state institutions and private enterprises delivering in-service training courses or courses for re-qualification sprang up. However, having received no support from the state budget, most of them died out.

Today the universities and university-type institutions of education happen to be the best functioning institutions for continuing education. However, their efforts seem to be quite sporadic and lack co-ordination. Other educational centres are either supported by private foreign charity funds or, in very few, cases by local private funds.

In order to get to know what possibilities women see in lifelong training and what stimulates women to participate in the system of continuing education some investigation was carried out in the largest cities of Lithuania, Vilnius and Kaunas.

164 women took part in the research and filled in a questionnaire. For a comparison two groups of women were interviewed: 82 of them participat-

ing in lifelong training and 82 not participating. The women were of different education and marital status and the age varied from 18 to 59. The women were chosen accidentally, trying to include as many social groups as possible.

According to the results of the questionnaire, most of the women would be interested in participating in continuing education. 72.5 % of women answered positively to the question 'If you had the necessary conditions would you be interested in continuing your education? (see fig. 3).

Women's attitude to further studies

Fig.3

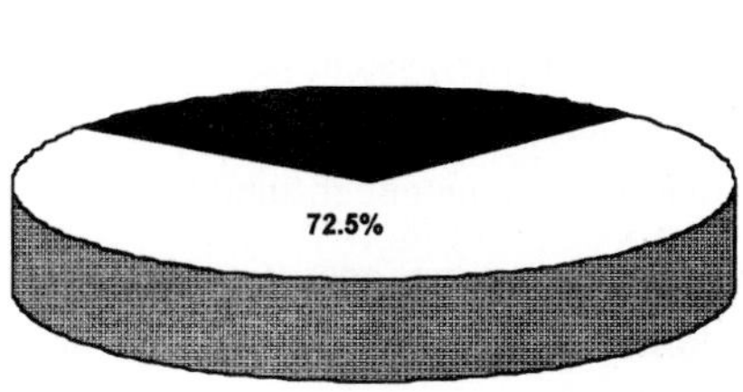

The positive answers were distributed into groups according to the women who were studying and those not studying, their education and marital status. In all groups we can trace an equal distribution of the positive answers.

The question about the what stimulated them to return to study was answered by those studying as follows (fig. 4):

1. 'I want to improve professionally' - 65%
2. 'It is easier to find a job' - 28%
3. 'I want to change my occupation' - 4.8%
4. 'It will be useful in my private life' - 35. 3 %
5. 'It is interesting' - 36. 5%

Reasons stimulating studying

Fig. 4

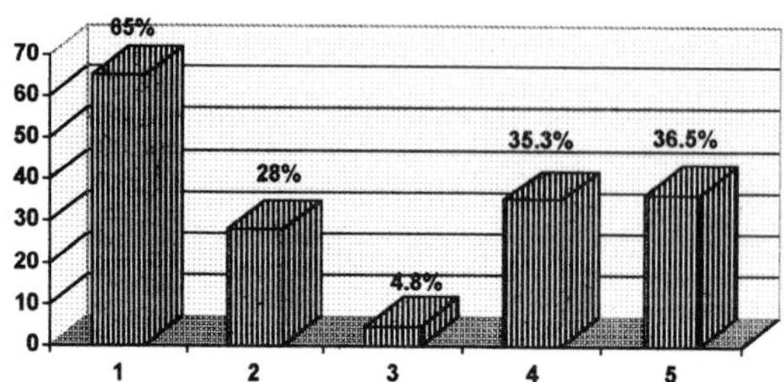

The answer 'I want to improve professionally', I suppose , is related to the women's situation in the labour market and unemployment. The main reason stimulating women to participate in the system of continuing education is their wish to improve professionally, for it would help them not to lose their current employment in a situation of economic instability.

Pointing out the problems of continuing education both groups mostly picked out two answers 'studies are too expensive' - 58.5% and 63.4%, ' there is no choice' - 28% and 21.9%.

Most private institutions of adult education are profit-making organisations. They are established and operate in educational fields of the greatest demand, for example, foreign languages, computers, commerce, bookkeeping. These courses are paid for by the students themselves. As we already know, the largest potential audience is women but the fee of the course is too high for them. Most women cannot take such an amount from their family budget.

13.4% studying and 9.7% non- studying women said that 'universities are closed to the society' and regretted that the age limit (40 years old) is still valid in the majority of universities. When the children have grown up and some professional experience has been gained, women would like not only to increase their professional knowledge, but also to get some different forms of education, however universities are not waiting for them.

Evaluation of insufficient choice of possibilities to study by both studying and non- studying women looks as follows in fig 5:

1. 'few desirable courses' - 28% (studying), 21.9% (non- studying);
2. 'lack of information' - 10.9%, 7.3%;
3. 'studies are too expensive' - 58.5%, 63.4%;
4. 'universities are closed to society'- 13.4%, 9.7%;
5. 'lack of time' - 4.8%, 3.6%.

Insufficient choice of possibilities to study

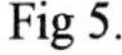

Fig 5.

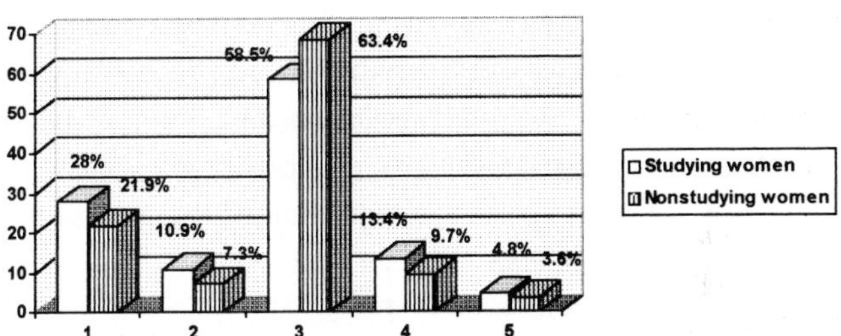

Only 4.8 % women mentioned lack of time, and 10.9% lack of information. In reality we know that most of them learn about the possibility of, let us say, studying English or upgrading their teaching skills from their friends or an accidental advertisement in a newspaper as there is not enough publicity of educational events in the country. It limits women's participation in the system of continuing education.

Conclusions

In the period of change, a major factor to reduce the number of unemployed women in Lithuania would be a wider choice of courses for re-qualification or in-service training. Private institutions can hardly cover the great need of training for market-dictated new skills: they are profit-making and thus expensive, small, uncoordinated and ineffective.

The results of the survey discussed above clearly suggest that universities and university-type schools in Lithuania should open up to adult education and, specifically, for the education of women. The inflexible attitudes of the old-type institutions expressed in terms of age constraints, as well as the small variety of courses taught, should be substituted by the modern-type school policies offering a wide choice of courses for different groups in society.

It is understandable that every new initiative requires some initial investment. This probably is one of the main reasons why adult education is not given deserved attention by the government and the local authorities: Lithuania is still in a deep economic crisis. However, it is important for the well-being of more than a half of Lithuanian citizens. The possibility of continuing education for the most vulnerable members of the society, women in their productive age, calls for a reconsideration of the present position of universities and other institutions of higher education.

References

Dvylika Lietuvos moteru problemu, Lietuvos aidas, (1996m.) birzelio 16d.

Zemaitaityte, I. (1995m), Moteris nuolatinio mokymosi sistemoje: galimybes, motyvacija, nuostatos, .magistro tezes, vadove M. Tereseviciene), VDU Kaunas,

Kanopiene, V. (1995), 'At the threshold to unemployment', Woman's World, March, pp 5-6.

Linden West

Intimate Cultures of Lifelong Learning: on Gender and Managing Change

Learning that none of us is, or ever will be, the grand figures we so often imagine men to be is not a recipe for disaster. It may be the only way forward (Janet Sayers, The Man Who Never Was)

Perhaps for the first time, a category called 'men' can be said to exist...in the past it has been men who defined all the other categories that there might be; men themselves were simply part of the intellectual furniture. Now, men are looked at in the way in which they have historically looked at everything else (Andrew Samuels, The Political Psyche)

Introduction

The starting point for this paper is the conviction (which many in this Conference may share) that lifelong learning is most often considered in narrow and constraining economistic, labour market terms. More fundamental questions surrounding, for instance, people's struggles in late capitalist modernity - to negotiate biographical discontinuities, to cope with frightening changes and uncertainties as well as feelings of powerlessness in the face of global and market forces - have been marginalised. Lifelong learning has become part of a rhetoric of individual adaptability to economic imperatives: of the need to upskill oneself, constantly, in a fiercely competitive, fast moving labour market. The point is to fit into the established order rather than change it.

I want, in this paper, to focus on deeper questions of managing change, of acquiring some greater sense of agency and more authentic voice, however fragile, in contexts of biographical and cultural fragmentation; and to connect this analysis to issues of lifestyle, emotional life and the construction of gendered identities. Lifelong learning can, in contexts of economic and cultural fragmentation, provide an important space for men and women to experiment with identities, selves, relationships and more diverse lifestyles as part of rebuilding. The analysis and conclusions are informed by research into adult student motivation in specific communities. I became interested in how and why particular people rather than others in communities in crisis, women rather more than men and in spite of oppressive experience, were open to learning and new biographical possibilities. There might, I hypothesised, be wider lessons in their experience to inform the development of learning in the lives of others.

The research focused on 30 students (working and middle class; black and white, men and women; younger and older) all of whom had enrolled on Access to higher education programmes, specifically designed to offer alternative entry routes into university for older learners (West, 1995; West 1996b; Lea and West, 1995). The students live in two communities, the Medway Towns and Thanet in the county of Kent in the South East of England. These are localities in severe crisis, struggling to cope with major economic and social dislocations: in the collapse or precariousness of main and traditional sources of employment; in patterns of social deprivation and exclusion and personal despair; and struggling too with the consequences of the New Right political experiment of privatisation, deregulated markets and the dismantling of the welfare state. The research involved a series of reflexive conversations over nearly four years, beginning at their point of entry into higher education. The conversations considered, in an empathic, dialogical relationship, intimate as well as wider experience; past, present and future; and the meanings people themselves gave to experiences over time.

I will use a kind of cultural psychology, consisting of feminist, sociological and psychoanalytic frames of reference, to explore, socially as well as psychologically, how particular women and men keep on keeping on even in the worst of times and can exploit some of the opportunities of late capitalist modernity; I have recently developed these ideas in a book[1]. My basic contention is that women, even in the worst conditions, are often better able to manage change and dislocation, in all their dimensions, better that is than many men: and that this is to be understood as part of a culturally induced adaptiveness. Within this is an acknowledgement, on the part of many women, of vulnerability and an openness to the support of others. Many men, in contrast, in contexts where biographical linear certainties have disintegrated, are frequently trapped in a pretence of coping and psychological defensiveness. This connects in turn with traditional constructions of masculinity involving the neglect of feelings and alienation from inner emotional life; where feelings have often been constructed as other and threatening (Seidler, 1994). This presents a critical problem for learning and managing change at times of severe dislocation.

Wider contexts of change

There are, I am suggesting, new opportunities, however limited, for men and women to experiment with who and what they are in the fracture of older certainties, and in the challenge to essentialist ideas of gender and identity. Sociologists like Giddens, and psychologists such as Frosh, have portrayed a paradoxical contemporary cultural context which constantly precipitates crises of, as well as opportunities for, the self. As tradition loses hold, individuals are forced to make choices among diverse, competing options and what Giddens calls a 'reflexive project of the self', consisting of sustaining a coherent, yet continuously revised, biographical narrative becomes an imperative if we are to make informed choices and construct a coherent life (Giddens, 1991). Stephen Frosh suggests that modern states of mind are forged in cultural instability of a 'cataclysmic kind' but there are opportuni-

[1] The case study material in the paper is reproduced by kind permission of Taylor and Francis; see West L (1996), *Beyond Fragments; adults, motivation and higher education, a biographical analysis*; London, Taylor and Francis, especially chapters 6, 7 and 8.

ties among the fragments if we can grasp them, not the least to experiment with what it means to be a man and woman (Frosh, 1991).

In these perspectives, older, rigid certainties associated with masculinity and femininity have been replaced by ideas of their contingent qualities and a new politics of identity. Feminism and psychoanalysis, in their differing ways, have destabilised the sense of confident, ahistorical, coherent, rational, essentialist and clearly gendered selves. The old certainties, or hegemonies, have been replaced by dispute and uncertainty surrounding what it means to be a man and woman, how s/he is constituted and the extent to which gender, as with other aspects of identity, may be open to a variety of different and diverse expressions. Boundaries and perceptions surrounding gender are in a state of flux. The only certainty is that we are no longer confident about what we mean by masculinity and femininity, and what it might mean to be a man or a woman.

However, there are dangers in this kind of argument. Selves and identities are not commodities simply to be donned or rejected in a kaleidoscope of endless, unlimited possibility, as in some postmodernist accounts. Composing a life, and self, however contingent, is more problematic than that. Past emotional/relational patterns, however destructive, are not easily jettisoned while some degree of biographical continuity appears to be essential to psychological well being; to know in other words something of where I come from, what I am and where I might want to go to and for these to have some clear relationship one to the other (Frosh, 1991). There is also the danger of ignoring the material and structural constraints on choice of lifestyle: in the poverty and despair of many working class communities. Edward Luttwark (1994), among others, has observed how structural economic change has evoked considerable consequences and at such speed that men must abandon what he calls *'lifetime proclivities, self-images and work place connections'* to acquire new skills. It is difficult to survive let alone experiment when worlds disintegrate so quickly; moreover, the alienation precipitated can be a fertile breeding ground for fundamentalisms of many kinds.

Yet it is also true that even the most frightening changes and discontinuities can provide opportunities for risk taking. Resources may be scarce but there can be creative possibilities in the economic and cultural rubble of older social formations. As Alheit (1994) has noted, traditional forms of work within capitalism, while offering status and material reward, most of all for men, brought severe constraints too. The worker was often alienated from the product, from time, from planning the work process and from emotional aspects of himself and intimate relationships. The crises of communities, and the crisis of masculinity within them, present new and positive opportunities too.

Women and change; case studies

It is interesting that many feminist writers argue that educational participation, for many women, may be an expression of a learned adaptiveness over time and a capacity to adjust to uncertainty and changing demands without psychologically fragmenting. This is because, in the dislocations of many marginalised communities, women have needed, and been increasingly expected to adapt to a range of roles and demands, including finding paid work, while continuing to carry prime domestic responsibility. And women had less at stake anyway, by way of status, identity and material reward, in the older division of labour. There was less to lose.

Crucially, many feminist writers suggest, that the construction of feminine identity has, in contrast to dominant forms of masculinity, emphasised co-operation, mutual support and the importance of emotional life. Women, it is argued, have needed each other to cope with multiple, shifting identities and to keep different parts of a life and selves together. The metaphor of a quilt has been used to capture such adaptive qualities in managing diversity and weaving some meaning and integrity from fragmented and frequently oppressive experience (Sellers, 1994; Aptheker, 1989). Bateson (1990), from a socio-biological perspective, suggests that improvisation holds the key to women's lives. She argues that *'the physical rhythms of reproduction and maturation'* create sharper discontinuities in women's experience than in men's. Yet *'the shifts of puberty and menopause, of pregnancy, birth and lactation, the mirroring adaptation to the unfolding lives of children, their departures and returns, the ebb and flow of dependency, the birth of grandchildren....the ability to shift from one preoccupation to another, to divide one's attention, to improvise in new circumstances, has always been important to women'*. Learning and education can, in these perspectives, be considered a form of improvisation in the need to rework roles and relationships. Women, in conditions of fracture, may find transitions easier because they have been used to improvising and managing uncertainty. Lifelong learning, however constrained, has been a constant feature of many women's lives.

I want to use three case studies[2] to focus on the differing responses to crisis and fragmentation in the lives of women students and their partners; and to consider the experience of one male working class student whose identity collapsed in the recession of the early 1990s. This was a man who, despite materially struggling to get by, managed, nonetheless, to reconstruct a life and renegotiate relationships. This narrative, I believe, provides clear clues as to what may be necessary, relationally, emotionally and educationally, for men to transcend painful transitions. There are important lessons in what I have termed the 'poetics' of fishing for the lifelong educator.

Both of the women in the case studies entered higher education for many reasons, among them acute difficulties in their husbands' careers. It was the women, in the two situations, who held families, futures and, to an extent, their partners together. June and Hilary[3] talked, over three and a half years, of the difficulties their husbands were experiencing and how these had shaped their own motives. For June, her husband's business was in serious trouble due to recession on the Medway and she desperately needed a

---

2 I am well aware of the problems of generalising from single case studies to wider constituencies, from particulars to the general. The criteria used in this research were those derived from hermeneutic, illuminative as well as biographical research in which the depth of analysis, and the richness of material, provide insights into complex particulars often lost in more quantitative methods. Such particulars can be used to enrich an understanding of wider social processes and the development of theory (see Evans, 1993). The validity of any study lies not in statistical criteria but in its meaningfulness to other sense making practitioners struggling with similar questions in related contexts.

3 The names are fictitious. All the material used is with the permission of the learners concerned. It has however been anonymised and certain details have been altered to protect the identities of the people concerned. The essence of their narratives has however been preserved.

secure and lucrative job to enable him to retire. For Hilary, economic restructuring and a new management culture in a privatised utility had undermined her husband's career, confidence and health. She was looking to develop her own career to help them cope with a possible redundancy or early retirement. These intimate struggles, in both cases, have to be located in the wider political economy of the last two decades.

June is in her early 50s and lives in the Medway Towns. She enrolled on an Access programme in 1992 and has recently completed the second year of a degree in European Studies. She had thought extensively about which programme to follow: she was good at languages and hoped that this, and a multi-disciplinary European degree, might enable her to find a job as a translator or teacher of languages. She needed a job for financial reasons but could find nothing that suited her or offered any security without a degree. She considered, over the period of the research, the complex and demanding patterns in her life, including combining part-time work, managing the finances of her husband's business, dealing with her children and money worries as well as coping with her husband's disintegrating morale. And how she was able to keep some, at least, of these diverse fragments together.

June described, in an early interview, some of the problems of her husband, Ted's, business, and the consequences of its fragility and decline on them both. Business difficulties were crucial to her decision to enrol on an Access programme:

> *Well, basically I think it's got a lot to do with the recession, my partner has got his own business which I was helping him with - I still do the books for it. What he does - he's a retailer and '88 was a boom year certainly....But the last 2 years, year and a half it's got really bad, really, really, bad and I had applied for jobs, I thought well, I'd better work as well but my age is a lot against me - they'd rather employ a younger person and invariably I was overqualified for a lot of jobs anyway and they'd say, look you're over qualified you don't really want this job, you'll be bored. And I used to say well I know I'm over qualified but the reason I'm applying for jobs is because I have to*

work. So in the end I thought well, let's go about it properly and I thought well, I came across this Access thing....So I thought I'll slide into this slowly. I'll go into an Access course to get back into education cos' it's changed an awful lot since I was in it, certainly since I was a child....I sort of discussed it with my husband and I said 'well, what do you think?' and he said 'well, I'm getting a bit old,' because he does the markets you see, cos' the reason he went into was because aircraft engineering went down obviously. Contracts finished and the Americans have the hold on it anyway and he looked around and got into that job 'cos it was easy to do and he worked for himself, so he said I'm getting a bit old I don't want to keep doing this....I think he probably just thinks that approaching 60 he ought to be able to have a rest now.

The decline of the local economy had severely affected Ted and the viability of the business. The prospect, as he saw it, was of working harder merely to stand still and this was not what he wanted. He needed a change and some respite from the pressure and like many men, as well as women, felt trapped.

At the end of the first year of the degree and the second year of our conversations, June elaborated at greater length on Ted, his morale and her worries about his health. Ted was losing heart. It was not that he was working any less, rather the business was going nowhere. At the time of a subsequent interview, a few months later, the business had improved slightly but the sense of disillusionment for Ted was still strong. June had become, by this stage, heavily involved in managing the business accounts; she worked weekends as well as weekdays in what had become a life of unmitigating pressure. She managed this and a home alongside studying for the degree, as well as a part-time job in a local supermarket. June described this existence, and Ted's, as a matter of '*squeaking by*'. It was difficult if not impossible to consider herself a student in higher education in such circumstances; she was many things to many people and found herself pulled in contradictory directions.

We met for the seventh and last time after she had completed her third year in higher education. June once again referred to her need to keep going and adapt as a way of helping Ted through his continuing difficulties. She could not afford to let go because he and others depended on her. She ruminated on men, women and change, and apparent differences between the sexes in their ability to cope. She felt far more adaptable than Ted and thought this was like women in relation to men more generally. She had noticed that some of the male students in College struggled, like her husband, to cope with the loss of traditional roles and expectations. Unemployment, for example, was provoking questions that many seemed ill-equipped to address. Men had to reinvent themselves in such situations, June insisted, something women have had to do for most of their lives:

> *Oh yes, I think women are more adaptable. I can think particularly of two men who are in the class, ex policeman and one an ex, I think he had been in the navy originally, and then worked in some employment that he had obviously lost. And I think it has been very difficult for them, extremely, and they do tend to be a bit shy and reserved because of it. I think they feel out of kilter, out of the fact that they have lost employment. But I think women do adapt, they have to adapt, far more easily. I think it is in their nature anyway. They are able to and I notice that in the classes, most of them are mothers.... and they cope.*
>
> *....I think you have to be, I think a woman has to be, because, well it still is but it always has been a man's world and in order to achieve anything, in order to get anything and also to have a family and home and children you have to be adaptable to deal with circumstances as and when they arise. Because unlike going to work, a 9-5 job, all right problems do arise and you deal with them, but you know generally what your schedule is, what you are expected to do, your parameters, your guidelines are there. But I think being at home and by the very nature of children there are so many disasters, things go wrong, you have to cope or you just go under and I think you just become more adaptable. But I think women in their nature are more adaptable, they have to be.*

June needed to be adaptable because others depended on her to be so. She had little sense of choice in this and there was minimal time to think or agonise about roles or the fairness of situations. Problems had to be resolved and it was more a matter of crisis management than ethics or feminism. She was the emotional and, increasingly, the financial hub of the family and without her it would have ground to a halt.

In the last interview June also described taking greater responsibility for Ted's family, including dealing with grown-up children and other relatives. His children were better able to communicate with her about their problems than with him. Ted was struggling at all levels, economically, socially and emotionally. June felt many men could barely cope with the emotionality of change and crisis in a place like the Medway:

> *I don't think they manage them, I think they just don't admit they are there. But men do get emotional. I have seen men very emotional....*
>
> *That is what I mean, if they don't manage them, if they don't... men often talk about managing emotions, they don't, it is a silly word, they don't manage emotions, what they do is submerge them, keep them capped, so if at any time they show emotion they can't control it, they control them that is what they do, they don't actually manage them. I think it is a slightly different word, they keep them submerged, so when there comes a point when they are out of control, there is nothing they can do, they do tend to erupt like a volcano, whereas I think women probably deal with emotion all the time.*
>
> *....They (men) don't survive because the whole meaning of life is taken away from them and that is why women tend to survive more, or for longer periods, or longer years after because they are used to adapting. There is more to life than just a job, coming home from the pub, or whatever, golf, or whatever men do, and home is just a station really on their journey. Whereas for a women it is everything, it is their life, everything they have to do, it is their experiences, it is what they do all the time.*

June talked of the large number of males who were unable to deal with the collapse of traditional employment and lifestyles; of the brokenness to be seen on most street corners in the Medway Towns. The sense of depression and defeat in these communities made it difficult to continue at times. On occasions she hated the place and wanted to run away.

Quilting a life

Moreover, June's life, during the period at college, had been in perpetual crisis. Her daughter had tried to commit suicide in the middle of the first year of the degree; her 18 year old son disappeared at the end of the second. June also described losing her part-time job at a local supermarket which exacerbated already severe financial difficulties. She wove, in the course of the research, a patchwork of a life in a part-time casualised, non-unionised work place as well as at home and college. Nothing was permanent in these contexts and livelihood depended on the whim of powerful others including managers. Her son had probably gone abroad, she thought, as he tended to wander off for long periods but she was still concerned for his welfare and had been trying to discover precisely where he was. As for the daughter, the suicide attempt, June believed, was more a gesture than a serious effort at self destruction but she was desperately concerned for her well-being nevertheless.

June was finding it hard to keep going and was surprised at her own resilience, most of all at continuing her studies. She often felt guilty about neglecting other parts of her life and the people in it, because of the degree. However, despite the perpetually contingent quality of June's life, the depressions and the multiplicity of demands on her, she talked of feeling strong and relatively secure in her self. She attributed this to her parents as well as her ability to relate well to other people, including the students at College:

> *....yes it has been marvellous in finding me again I think.*

> *....I suppose in a way I have felt selfish doing this, because it is just purely for me and it is me that is gaining by it. I hope it isn't just me in the end, but I feel it is like that. Well the two particular lecturers, have been very good. They are extremely good, very patient, and most of the students, there is quite a few students, there is a small group obviously, but we tend to gel as a whole class, which is quite good....I have had a lot of help from one or two, particularly one student, Mandy, who did a course at a lady's college....and she was very genned up on all sorts of things. I wouldn't have known where to start looking or to find out or even know about. She has been a great help and Nicky as well, who is a staunch Labour Party member. Both a bit younger than me, but we have been great buddies, great personalities, very strong and marvellous to talk to, lovely to get information from and all sort of things.... which has been very good, helped me an enormous amount.*

Particular teachers were important in the struggle for self belief and learning because they recognised and respected her. This was the story across the research as a whole: students stressed the importance of teachers, and other learners, who found time to relate and support fragile, uncertain attempts to compose essays or participate in a discussion; teachers who were sensitive to the material and psycho-emotional frailties of individual lives, as well as being able to communicate ideas effectively (West, 1996a). The basic question is how such inter-subjective processes are best theorised, and provide the means to survival and more effective transitions.

Hilary and Keith

Hilary's story covers the period of new right hegemony in which markets, the privatisation of public utilities and the development of a strong profit orientated and individualistic culture were dominant. The idea of public service was devalued, even disparaged, in a climate which privileged acquisitiveness and individual competitiveness as the mainsprings of human action

(Hutton, 1995). In Britain, the Thatcherite years produced major changes in the welfare state and in the ownership and culture of public corporations. Public authority was deemed bureaucratic and inefficient in comparison to private, commercial sector practice, underpinned as this was by the disciplines of the market and competition. The changes intruded into the careers and securities of countless public sector workers, including Hilary and her husband Keith. She worked as a nurse in the Health Service, he as a manager in a public utility.

Hilary had just begun a two year Access programme in English Literature and Social Studies when we first met. Over the period of the research, Hilary constructed a detailed account of the painful impact of change on her husband and his role; of the death of a close brother-in-law, Sean; and of education as a crucial space which allowed her to explore what was best for herself and for her husband. She decided eventually in favour of work in a Hospice and that higher education should be set aside for the present. But Access had given breathing space and support to consider options - to experiment in other words - in a period of deepest uncertainty.

Public lives, private pain

Hilary described, over time, what had been a disturbing and unsettling experience. Keith, like Ted, was finding it difficult to cope with change and his self-esteem had plummeted. Hilary elaborated on changes in Keith's work. Until recently he had felt valued in his job and he had been achieving important results in what was a public service. Staff were now being shed, however, from all levels and his situation was perilous. Keith became very depressed and there were psychosomatic symptoms of disease in a chronic back pain. He felt it his duty to support his family but he was giving way, literally and figuratively, under the pressure:

> *....Keith had a lot of trouble physically with his back and in fact, was quite ill with it and in retrospect we both decided that he was probably*

depressed. He'd probably had a period of depression. Not serious depression and it never got to the...it was only afterwards that we thought it was a physical manifestation. I mean, it's a vicious circle depression anyway. He'd got physical problems and of course, that makes you depressed but if you've got other mental worries that makes the physical problems worse....I did feel at one point that this is hard, this is difficult, having two young children, not a lot of money and Keith in retrospect, obviously buckling a bit and I went on a bit longer before I started to buckle....Because when we discussed it afterwards he felt overburdened with responsibility. Having to keep us all and well, he said he had worries of 'My back's going to get really bad' he got really depressed about it 'Oh, God, my back, my back, does it mean I might not work? What happens if I don't work?' and all those kind of things and that was hard then and since then things have just not got easier. So much...we had...a what's the word...we both felt devastated, about Sean's death last year and that has certainly had a knock on effect but to a...we both feel the same way about it. We both feel a similar effect of what happened and what then it might mean for us, you know, when you contemplate your own, 'what if?'

The 'what ifs' were becoming overwhelming. Old securities - material, occupational and psychological - were evaporating as Sean died from cancer and Keith was suffering the severest stress. Like many public sector workers, he was carrying a cultural revolution on his back and it was breaking. Hilary later reflected on the times in which they lived. Both she and her husband were uncomfortable with the politics and values of the Government. Keith hated the new culture of management and the loss of the old ideals of public service:

....I mean, they are, um...budget, budget bound really. They're a very American style management techniques that have been brought in. Whereas yes, when he joined...it was more of a service. He saw it as more as a service industry, but now their monopolies been taken away, they've lost their monopoly but in actual fact they're almost subsidising other networks that are setting up. They're having to help them to sup-

posedly make the playing field more level. So yes, it's very hard and difficult times for them I think, all round and morale is generally really quite low....

Six months later, towards the end of the research, he was offered redundancy and he accepted. His performance rating was poor and years of committed service counted for little in the new climate:

.... I just feel very sorry for him because I think he is quite right to feel angry and in fact, when he was saying he felt a failure and whatever, I said well, I don't think you should feel like that because to a large extent, you're a victim of circumstances like a lot of people. There have been such a...I suppose he's...suffering the effect of technological industrial revolution that really has happened since the '80s in that people are more redundant, for a start and that's just the way it's happened. The other thing that from his own point of view I think he feels cheated, he does feel cheated because last year, their performance ratings go from one, which is the best, down to six and last year he had a three, which was considered up to standard, good, you know, great. This year he had four, he dropped to four but he was in a new area of work and I think I read the report that he had and he had mostly threes I think nine threes on his appraisement and a couple of fours and one two, so he challenged his boss and said 'Well, why is it overall four when I had so many threes'. She said 'Well, the two fours were in key areas of your work,' but she said 'Don't' worry you're on learning curve, because you haven't really been properly trained.' He's had a couple of days training on the work that he's doing which is this internal auditing and quality business, whereas the other people he works with had two weeks intensive training and really they just chucked him in at the deep end and unfortunately...I mean, his boss said 'Oh, next year, you'll get a three because you're on a learning curve' and he's thinking 'Well, that's not much good to me now!' Because they're looking at...that's part of the selection as to who they want to stay and who they want to go, is the performance rating, so that's where he thought. 'Well, I think I'm going to be asked to go'. So, yeah, it's unsettling, it's

very unsettling but we've just got to wait really and...then see and just hope he gets something he enjoys doing, that's the crux.

Managing change and crisis

Hilary thought, at the end of the research, that getting a part-time job at a Hospice, alongside the experience of higher education and being successful academically, were crucial in managing these problems. She had *'a brain'*, after all, while the Hospice enabled her to work flexibly and increase her hours if she wished. She was fulfilling, she felt, a crucial function in the role and it gave her satisfaction and purpose. She was considering doing a counselling course to increase her qualifications and options at work. She had been able to keep going because she had learned how to manage emotions more effectively:

Yes....and...well I have always felt that...or people have told me as well that I am a good listener and that people will...do ask...friends as well will ...talk to me about things and say well I thought I would come and tell you.... so I think I have a good ear in that way, and I have always found that with the work, even prior to the Hospice, I feel that I'm quite good with people ... I am not inhibited about discussing emotional subjects in an unemotional way, and I think that is something that I have just learnt from having nursed for so long I have had to do difficult things and talk about difficult subjects with people...and I don't find it preys on my mind unnecessarily, I can get involved but not to the point where it has a negative effect... I don't get too involved. I get involved without... I can step back... I mean working at the Hospice you can have particularly traumatic experience or very emotional relatives .... But also talking about the counselling, I would like...most of what I do is on instinct, I have never had any formal training and I think common sense obviously helps a lot and personal experience helps a lot, but I think that there is a lot more to it .... as I say I think I probably do it a lot better and also I feel referring back to Sean's death, it's

> *given me another...a completely different insight, it really has...as to what people are going through.*

Hilary, for all her pain, was a successful innovator and good at managing difficulty and supporting others in their struggles. She was the rock on which this family, most of all her husband, depended. There are threads, I suggest, linking these two stories together: of women adapting psychologically better to change; and of this being a function of diverse lifestyles and the greater capacity of many women to give and receive emotional support; in short, to form good enough relationships in which positive inner dynamics are reinforced.

Evidence from different communities, I think, supports the idea that women are psychologically more adaptable, less constrained by traditional expectations, and better able to respond, flexibly, to change and upheaval. In the mining communities of South Wales, for instance, women have led the struggle for community regeneration and the expansion of educational opportunities in difficult times while many men have found it harder to cope (Humphreys and Francis, 1995). In one mining community a major community educational project, the University of the Valleys, developed from the energies of a miner's wives support group founded during the 1984 Strike. The women's group seem to have been a main driving force behind a number of community and educational initiatives. Campbell (1995) has drawn similar conclusions from mining villages in the North East of England. It is the women who most often appear to be showing leadership when the old ways have fragmented while many men seem emotionally paralysed in the collapse of older biographical certainties. There are echoes here of processes at work in the women's movement more generally. This provided supportive yet challenging transitional space to experiment with new stories and possibilities: in which women supported each other in the struggle to resist and to compose different stories about the personal being political and oppressive. The crisis of the present has yet to provoke an equivalent men's movement. This appears relatively uncertain and restricted to middle class groups. Yet such a movement - for mutual support, for admitting vulnerability and uncertainty and for better and more equal relationships - is sorely needed (Samuels, 1993). And it need not take the reactionary form of some American movements in which men are being urged to be more like men and women to know their place (see, for example, Bly, 1990).

Psychoanalytic perspectives

I believe that psychoanalytic theory can explain some of these processes and how inner and social life are connected: how it is possible, for example, for particular people like June and Hilary to keep on keeping on. Object relations theory stresses the role of 'good enough' relationships and a supportive environment in the creation of confident and stronger inner states. The development and expression of self, most of all in conditions of fracture and uncertainty, are intimately dependent on others and, by extension, on wider patterns of relationship and power. Feminists, as Jane Flax (1990) has observed, were initially antagonistic towards considering women's struggles in any psychological terms at all. A founding mother of feminism, Simone De Beauvoir, located women's pain in the social construction of the other, in a culture privileging men's experience and public roles while disparaging and marginalising women's experience. Feminists gradually discovered and developed more psychological and intimate perspectives within an overall cultural critique of gendered oppression. They began to integrate object relations within a constructivist model of human development and identity formation (Shaw, 1995). In object relations theory, suffering and its transcendence emanate from the interplay of different parts of a self - good or bad objects, loving or hateful and envious feelings - in interaction with others. A capacity to recast an identity and to compose a more authentic subjectivity depends on the constant support of and mirroring of a new experimental and confident self (or 'selfobject') in others' eyes; one that can be slowly appropriated and made part of one's internal mental structures. We are made, and remade, of each other, for better or worse, over a lifetime.

These ideas can be applied to learning too. Like many feminists, radical educators have often been suspicious of psychologising learning and experience. They have reacted against the strong essentialist and ahistorical tendencies in both mainstream psychology as well as traditional Freudian psychoanalysis. The consequence has been a lack of any real theory of subjective life at all: of reducing psyche to an epiphenomenal status within largely structural forms of analysis. Educators have lacked a language to explain how the social, such as Courtney's (1990) supportive social milieu and significant others, becomes internalised into stronger and more confident subjects willing and able to learn.

(Of course, I recognise there is a problem in adopting a set of theories such as object relations given that their existence cannot be 'proved' in any conventional, experimental way, only hypothesised. This is one reason why mainstream psychology, with its naturalistic inclinations, has eschewed any real interest in how selves and subjects come to be. But the difficulty is that central aspects of human experience and inner life are therefore left unchartered. Mainstream psychology has focused more on phenomena which can be directly observed and/or modelled empirically. As Stephen Frosh has written, *'Psychology takes as the object of its discourse the already-constructed individual 'subject' and asks, 'How do her or his psychological parts work?' Psychoanalysis looks at the fragmented neonate and questions, 'How does this one become a 'subject' at all?'*

There is also the question of deciding the validity of any one theory of becoming a subject as against any other. This has, I think, to be decided on the grounds of pragmatic utility: how helpful is it in making sense of early and subsequent experience? In the present context, for instance, do these ideas provide a useful framework for considering the interplay of culture, relationships and psyche in the building as well as subsequent interpretation of a life? Many of the learners in the research considered such ideas to be meaningful in making greater sense of aspects of their life histories, including educational experience).

Men and change

I want to use the case of Jim to expand on the argument of how the social and external may become part of a self, for better or worse; and to use the story as one exception to prove, perhaps, a more general rule about the problems of change and emotionality in men's lives. His narrative provides compelling evidence of the construction of a more 'feminised' lifestyle and good object relations; and the importance of these to successful transition, however contingent this might be. In the research as a whole, he was the most successful at change management although a number of the other men succeeded in working through some of their emotional traumas, mainly due to empathic and sympathetic teachers (West, 1996b).

Jim is a young middle aged, working class man from Thanet, with a wife and two sons who was made redundant from the building industry in 1992. His working life has consisted of insecure employment, periods out of work, followed by a relatively secure time as a painter and decorator which came to an abrupt end with redundancy. His biography is shaped by these insecurities and uncertainties but the narrative contains surprising elements of creative activity too. At the centre of his story is a self and momentum, maintained in certain respects at least, through a love affair with fishing. For Jim it is a source of companionship (most of all with his sons), the deepest personal satisfaction and the strongest sense of achievement. Fundamentally, fishing has been one of the main means by which Jim has managed some of the most difficult periods of his life. And in the process of rebuilding his life, he negotiated a new relationship with his wife in which there is a more equitable division of emotional labour. She eventually took the plunge into education herself by registering on an Access programme.

At one level Jim's story is about drifting from one job to the next, feeling alienated in work and depressed out of it. Having been made redundant, he was trying when we first met, to build a new career by training as a radiographer. This was a radical step but it was perceived as necessary when little else was available. He enrolled in a Science Access programme at a local college and eventually moved to study for a degree at a College of Higher

Education. There the story might have ended, except, later, Jim's narrative raised basic questions about the role of creative activity as well as relationship in managing change and, ironically, (given the tendency to disparage informal as against vocational forms of learning) in constructing a new career.

The poetic object of fishing

We talked almost accidentally about fishing in the final two sessions. I asked him if we had missed any aspect of his life and he spoke of his children and the impact of his studying on them:

> *....I do my best, not always easy, but I do my best to involve myself with them, you know, what they want to do, their interests. I try to take an interest and do things together. I take them fishing, play football with them, not there's the ball, there's the park, go and find your friends, sort of thing which a lot of parents tend to do.*

> *....Fishing, angling, fresh water. Something I think about probably more than anything else, any one other subject, it is a passion. I like to go at least once a week, and when I go I like to be there for as long as possible. I try and get as much time fishing as I can. I consider myself to be good at it, but that comes back to what we talked about before. When I do things I like to do them well. Otherwise I would rather not do them.*

> *....I have friends who fish and we go together most of the time, so it becomes a social thing as well. Not all about just taking your rod and sitting on the bank alone. Can be and that can be great as well. There is also a technical side of the fishing which I enjoy as well. I am not a traditionalist when it comes to fishing. I like new methods, like gadgets. If it was all split cane rods and centre pin reels I don't think I would have taken it up, like it used to be. Obviously there is an art to it still but I like to develop as many different approaches to it as I can....*

The art, difficult to put your finger on what is artistic about fishing, very loose term when it is applied to fishing....

Yes, there is a feel for fishing. Some people just haven't got it, you can give them all the right equipment, sit them in the best places and they still couldn't catch a fish. There is something there that you can't describe what it is within a person that makes them capable or incapable. I suppose that would be the art, not anything you actually do, just something within the person.

....I used to fish when I was about 10 or 11 when I was at school. It was a friend who introduced me to it. I didn't do a lot when I was at school, mainly because I didn't have the equipment and the only places we could go to were on our bikes, because parents weren't involved. Just between me and a friend. The fresh water fishing stopped really when I started sea fishing for a living. The two things didn't go together and I didn't have the time anyway. I didn't take up coarse fishing again until about 3 or 4 years ago. And as soon as I started doing it again I just couldn't believe how I had ever stopped doing it. Unbelievable that I had managed to live without it considering that I had already experienced it.

....I look forward to it from one week to the next. I count the days until I next go. It is a love without a doubt. If I go just for a day's session I have to get there whilst it is still getting light. There is something about that time of day. There is a feeling about it. It looks nice, you look around, mist on the water, sun coming up, all the wild life jumping out of wherever they come from. There is just a magic about that time of day that is worth being there for even if you don't get your fishing tackle out for another hour, it is worth being there at that time of day. And then there is an excitement every time you go, even if I am going 2 or 3 times a week which I was probably doing in the summer last year, sometimes. Feeling of excitement, get your gear out, can't get it out fast enough, can't wait to get started. A strange thing. To talk to people who haven't fished, or maybe who have fished and didn't enjoy it, you can't get across your feelings for it properly.

....Still makes me shake when I catch a good fish and I have caught a lot of good fish, but it still gives me the shakes still. Strange, but I am not alone, there are a lot of people like me.

....I feel when I am out there that, yes that is what I feel, almost feel like putting it down on paper sometimes, but never bothered to try because I think I am not all that good at it.

There was no stopping Jim on the subject; previous conversations had often been hesitant and brief but on this matter time slipped by. This was an artist enjoying his work and a creative magical passion which belied the intensely practical tone of earlier interviews. A lively, enthusiastic and committed man emerged from behind a screen:

Only time I leave the house other than for College or hospital is to go fishing and more often than not at least one of them [the boys] is with me then. So I am there a lot of the time.... I am doing mainly, well I say mainly it is all carp fishing now, I don't really worry too much about any other species of fish now. That involves longer sessions, overnight sessions, very difficult to do more than 24 hours in one stint obviously. We get Fridays off whether I am at College or Hospital, so that leaves me free Friday afternoon to Saturday late lunch time and we usually take that time out. So it is a very very important part of my life.

....Yes it is specimen hunters territory. You are looking for bigger and better fish basically, stepping up tackle wise. It has cost a little bit but I have dealt with it quite well, finding second-hand bargains and stuff, but it is more rewarding to catch a nice big carp than half a dozen small tench sort of thing. We have done very well considering we only actually converted to that at the beginning of last season, we have had some good results....Me and my eldest son mainly I am talking about, but then I have two nephews who are heavily involved with fishing and they tend to follow my lead and they have both gone on to carp fishing as well, and they usually come with me as well. So there is quite a group of us.

....What my son, Michael my oldest son, he is still very very keen on fishing, he loves his fishing. He hates not going fishing if I am going and occasionally if I get a day off in the week I take a night over at the lake then and it drives him wild. He asks for a day off school and he very rarely gets it. Yes it is a nice thing for us to do together. It gives us something very much in common that we sort of build a relationship on and he's very mature in his attitude towards fishing. The patience side of it, the fish care side of it, looking after his own tackle, he is very mature in that respect whereas you quite often see the younger kids are not so. Kids older than him are not so responsible as he is, so he is learning a lot through it as well.

It is just, I feel that almost like a release when I can get out, away from it all, and can be myself entirely, it is a release of everything else that has built up during the week, it is a period to relax, a period to reflect, it is a period that I can,....this is the fishing and I can just be myself and I don't have to worry about anyone watching me, judging me for what I am doing, it is a complete reversal really of the other extreme and that is nice, it allows me to turn round at the beginning of the week to start afresh and have something to look forward to at the end of the week as well.

I feel that the fragments of my life are quite varied, like my fishing, if you just take the two extremes I suppose, when I am out fishing or when I am in the hospital, very different sort of worlds, but it all revolved quite smoothly. It is the differences that make your life more rewarding....It is my space, it is very important to me. And that is not just the pure fishing aspect of it, it is my time, I feel that is quite important to me. I would feel that maybe I would have less of a claim on having that time if I spent more time socialising, going out, drinking with friends, what have you. But I have cut that aspect out of my life more or less altogether now and so I regard my time at the weekend when I go fishing as my time and nobody can say that I am not entitled to it.

Fishing was what he was good at, as well as, increasingly, radiography, and the balance composed his life. Fishing connected him to his sons and created the kind of relationship he had never known with his own father. Fishing was where he felt most himself, a place where no-one could label him stupid. His descriptions could easily have sounded trite but instead were energising, self evoking and compelling. The language sang, like poetry. This was language constituting a vibrant self as well as representing a creativity which had sustained him over the last four years, from the time of his redundancy.

Jim talked more of his family and relationships too, including his wife, in the closing phases of the study. She had educational qualifications and was deeply frustrated at home and in her job as a part-time waitress. They were continually negotiating their relationship which had recently improved. She was, by this time, taking an Access programme too and he was sensitive to her difficulties and frustrations and wanted to help. And he was enjoying his family more as he felt better about himself. He was making a conscious effort to strengthen the relationship with his children at this time. Higher education and fishing encouraged more, not less, equality in the emotional distribution of labour. Jim wanted a new career to provide meaning, purpose and money. Yet this was only one element in composing a more balanced lifestyle.

Selfobjects: people and symbolic experience

Individuals, I suggest, need good enough objects, in the form of people or more symbolic interactions, to evoke and maintain a self, emotionally, most of all during periods of transition. As Wolf argues: '*As an adult, one still needs selfobject experiences...When my own self-esteem is low, I can usually find enhancement by listening to music or by reading.*' Purposeful activities provide '*a sustaining selfobject ambience*' to make it possible to keep on keeping on (Wolf, 1988). Fishing appeared to fulfil this function in Jim's life. By 'objects' Wolf means, significant people, or symbolic experiences, to which an individual is attached. Early as well as later relationships, symbolic or with specific people, shape an inner emotional dynamic, in which different aspects of a self, or objects, interact. The primacy of loving feelings, for example, and a capacity to cope with hatred and anxiety, provides *'structural cohesion'* and *'energic vigour'*; or, if anxiety and rage predominate, a self is depleted and, at an extreme, feels meaningless and empty, like life as a whole.

The idea parallels Winnicott's facilitating environment which encourages creativity and the expression of a truer self. What may be important is the capacity to 'let go' and surrender conscious ego functions and controls in such activities as fishing and the creative moment. Winnicott calls this a *'relaxed self-realisation'*, which in creative moments involves the individual in enjoying what is being done and to feel alive in the process (Winnicott, 1965; 1971). Paradoxically, a self may be most itself when forgotten, absorbed and uplifted by experiences which provide primitive emotional sustenance as well as intellectual satisfaction and practical achievement (Gordon, 1987; Cartwright, 1994). Such moments of recreation - creatively and emotionally - have always been at the core of good, informal adult learning. What has been missing is a conceptual language to understand and explain the inter-subjective and subjective dynamics involved (West, 1996).

Intimate cultures of learning

I am arguing that women are often better equipped than men to manage change and dislocation, to 'quilt' a life from diverse elements partly because they have been better at managing their feelings, with the support of others. Or to put it slightly differently, their object relations have been better managed. The cultural construction of masculinity, on the other hand, seems to involve the fear of relatedness, intimacy and a terror of vulnerability in male development (Samuels 1993; Sayers, 1995). The crucial point is that such terror can be transcended and that lifelong learning - informal as well as formal - provides a means for men to do so. Fishing and/or the good relationship with teachers, students and, perhaps with other men, can provide the creative, imaginative, intellectual *and* emotional means to a stronger, less defended self. I believe that an awareness of the primitive, emotional roots of successful change management; and, underlying this, of the vulnerability and perpetual contingency of human subjectivity in fragmenting times, needs to be at the centre of the present debate about lifelong learning.

I am not, in suggesting the emotional as well as intellectual roots of learning and effective agency, denigrating the importance of rationality and the intellect, merely locating them in a broader and more integrated frame of reference. Other students in my research illustrated the inter-related nature of intellectual and emotional development for oppressed people (West, 1995). Brenda, for example, was abused in childhood and as a wife, has felt subjectively fragile and illegitimate from earliest times and yet found intellectual *and* personal meaning, and greater emotional security, through literature and the connectedness this provided with the biographies of other oppressed women. The point I am making is that we need more a diverse, comprehensive but also integrated cultural psychology, connecting mind and emotions, intellect and feeling, creativity and agency, one person with another.

These are deeply paradoxical times, involving profound dangers and distress (expressed, for instance, in the growth of fundamentalism) alongside opportunities to learn and develop in different and more diverse ways. We need, in such contexts, to connect discussions of lifelong learning with these wider processes, struggles and possibilities. There are forces, under the guise of lifelong learning, which seek to domesticate, manipulate and reduce human possibilities to commodities in the service of the market and the corporation. An emotional literacy, combined with critical intelligence, can help people to fight back, on more of their own terms, and construct more pluralistic, developing biographies which include continuing experiments in what it means to be a man and a woman; and in building better and more equal relationships and communities.

References

Alheit, P. (1994), 'Everyday Time and Life Time, on the problems of healing contradictory experiences of time' in Time and Society, California, Sage pp 305-319.

Aptheker, B. (1989), Tapestries of Life, Boston, University of Massachusetts.

Bateson (1990), Composing a Life, London, Penguin.

Bly, R. (1990), Iron John: a Book about Men, Shaftesbury, Dorset, Element

Campbell, B. (1995), Communities in Crisis, Paper to the Universities Association for Continuing Education, April, Swansea.

Cartwright, A. (1994), Notes on Psychoanalytic Psychotherapy, unpublished paper, Canterbury, University of Kent.

Courtney, S. (1992), Why Adults Learn; Towards a Theory of Participation in Adult Education, London, Routledge.

Evans, M. (1993), 'How the Personal might be Social', in Sociology, 27, 1 pp 5-14.

Flax, J. (1990), Thinking Fragments; Psychoanalysis, Feminism and Postmodernism in the Contemporary West, University of California Press

Frosh, S. (1989), Psychoanalysis and Psychology, Minding the Gap, London, Macmillan

Frosh, S. (1991), Identity Crisis, Modernity, Psychoanalysis and the Self, London, Macmillan.

Giddens, A. (1991), Modernity and Self Identity; Self and Society in the Late Modern Age, London, Polity.

Gordon, R. (1978), Dying and Creating: A Search for Meaning, London, Society of Analytical Psychology.

Humphreys, R. and Francis, H. (1995), Taking Higher Education to the People: The Case of the University of the Valley, Paper to the Universities Association for Continuing Education Conference, April, Swansea.

Hutton, W. (1995), The State We're In, London, Jonathan Cape.

Lea, M. and West, L. (1995), 'Motives, mature students, the self and narrative' in Swindells, J. (ed), The Uses of Autobiography, London, Taylor and Francis pp 177-186.

Llewelyn, S. and Osborn, K. (1990), Women's Lives, London, Routledge.

Luttwark, E. (1994), 'Why Fascism is the Wave of the Future', London Review of Books, Vol 16, No. 7, April.

Samuels, A. (1993), The Political Psyche, Routledge, London.

Sayers, J. (1995), The Man Who Never Was, Freudian Tales, London, Chatto and Windus.

Seidler, V. J. (1994), Unreasonable Men, Masculinity and Social Theory, London, Routledge.

Sellers, J. (1994), 'Quilting a Life History' in Hoare and others (eds), Life Histories and Learning, University of Sussex pp 136-140.

Shaw, J. (1995), Education, Gender and Anxiety, London, Taylor and Francis.

West, L. (1995), 'Beyond Fragments: Adults, Motivation and Higher Education', in Studies in the Education of Adults, Vol 27, No 2, October pp 133-156.

West, L. (1996a), 'Access to what and on whose terms?' Paper to the ESREA Access Conference, Leeds, April.

West, L. (1996b), Beyond Fragments; adults, motivation and higher education; a biographical analysis, London, Taylor and Francis.

Winnicott, D. (1965), The Maturational Process and the Facilitating Environment, London, Hogarth.

Winnicott, D. (1971), Playing and Reality, London, Tavistock.

Wolf, E. (1988), Treating the Self; Elements of Clinical Self Psychology, London. Guildford Press.

Bettina Dybbroe

Qualifying Unskilled Women in Caring Roles through Adult Education: Gender Experiences that clash with Modernisation

The intention of this paper is to focus attention on some important problems in adult education concerning women who have a low level of educational attainment. One way of presenting the problem is to look at the conflicts inherent in the *learning processes*, both in everyday life, and when the women enter into adult education. This point of view suggests that the learning process is a continuous effort by individuals to understand and construct their own lives subjectively. Another way of presenting the problem is to question what role adult education may have for women with low educational attainment if they are human service workers, for example, in caring roles. What possible consequences can adult education have for women's qualifications both in human service work and in coping with their own lives.

My work has been informed through many years of educating women who have received little or no education since leaving school. My ideas have been sharpened by an empirical analysis I recently made concerning the qualifications of registered childminders in private day-care in Denmark. The childminders in Denmark are women who work for the municipality in caring for small children in their own homes (there are approximately 22,000 women in this field of work taking care of approximately 70 % of children from 0-2 years who are in public care. 50% of Danish children at this age are in public care, and more than 80% from 2 years and up).[1] This study has now become a pilot study for my PhD thesis.

The background for the project is primarily an interest in comprehending the *possibilities of developing qualifications for women in human service work with low educational attainment. The 'radical modernisation' of life and modernisation of the public sector especially, must be included in this comprehension.*

---

1 Bettina Dybbroe, OPUS: Private erfaringer - offentlig service,('Private experiences-public service') Arbejdsmarkedsstyrelsen 1996.

The study of childminders in private day-care has given me the possibility of researching a group of unskilled women doing human service work and who have worked many years solely on the basis of *experiences of life and gendered experiences in the family.* In recent years they are becoming acquainted with education through different types of adult continuing education. It has also been possible to see the areas of conflict in gendered experiences accentuated here, because of the unity of family life and working life, and the womens′ choice of this as their strategy for life.

This paper represents some initial interpretations of the empirical data, and an attempt to suggest possible use of theories in relation to the way the problem is presented. It does not represent any concluded analysis as it is work in progress.

The 'wave' of adult education in Denmark

Denmark has a long tradition of adult education in the form of popular enlightenment and general, liberal, adult education. The tradition has its roots in the Danish 'folk-highschools', initiated in the 18th. century with the aim of improving self-development and qualifications amongst the rural population. The societal and national intentions were related, at least indirectly to the needs of the labour market. This tradition is still alive today, and a large number of the Danish adult population participate in different forms of popular enlightenment, for example, summer folk-high schools.

The general agenda for adult education has changed radically. Education of adults remains central on the political agenda in Denmark in the nineties. It is evident through an annual growth of 30% in adult continuing and general education (measured by the number of year-long pupils). It is a central instrument used by the state in order to solve problems of society, for example, new ways to be retired, how to minimise unemployment etc.[2]

2 Undervisningsministeriet :Uddannelse og arbejdsmarked 1985 til 2021, Danmark 1996.

Adult education is also seen as an instrument to create changes in attitudes, for example, a way to break down attitudinal barriers to acceptance of the breakdown of the public sector and the introduction of quality management etc. It is also a way to influence lifestyles in relation to the value of work and education, and their place in lifecourses. Today labour market policy has penetrated all educational reforms and initiatives.

The national intentions are twofold: an attempt to increase the number of youths with vocational education experiences, and the number of adults who take part in adult general and continuing education. The trade union movement in Denmark has always been a strong motor in the policy-making of adult education, and has played an important role in the success of adult education. The majority of the trade-union movement also see adult education as being part of labour market politics. This has led to the development of many new vocational education programmes being offered to young people and many vocational qualifying courses for adults with low educational attainment. One consequence, however, is that the unskilled jobs disappear.

The policies have not been completely successful. The Ministry of Education concluded (February 1996) that the ten year effort to eliminate the residual group of youths who only obtain a lower secondary school education has failed. Close to one third of all young people still do not obtain a vocational education qualification after leaving lower secondary school. In opposition to what was expected the tendency is that those with the most educational qualifications get more education, and the unskilled are the most difficult to integrate into adult education. Half of the adults with low educational attainment, unskilled workers etc., have never participated in any type of adult general or continuing education. This is not due only to economical and political barriers but is also due to the fact that the desire to participate in education is not generally present. For example, 40% of unskilled workers in Denmark do not want to participate in any type of education.[3]

3 Udviklingscenteret for Voksenuddannelse og Folkeoplysning, 1995.

The disinclination to participate in adult education

A number of different educational research projects have tried to discover the possible reasons for this lack of desire to participate in education. Research into the culture and attitudes amongst the unskilled adults with low educational attainment provides an insight.[4] The characteristics are:

1) people, who have suffered failure in the education system, and who want to avoid meeting with anything, that reminds them of school later on in life.

2) People with completely different strategies of life, where education holds no special value, because other ways of integrating into society have been chosen.

3) People who feel that their qualifications are sufficient to be able to cope with their jobs and their lives, and who do not feel attracted by the perspective of personal development through education. Whether these attitudes are 'rational' for the people in question, or whether their experiences are 'true' or not, they do contribute to the understanding of subjective attitudes to adult education.

This disinclination raises a number of questions which are also relevant in looking at those that do participate in adult education. How is the intentionality of adult education experienced by the lower educated? Do they feel that they can express and implement their own intentionality in adult education, and make it hold reason in respect of their own living and working conditions? Is it possible to include informal qualifications into adult education, and can they be 'opened' or will they be displaced[5]? Numerous evaluations of the effect of adult education in Denmark show, on the one hand, that the lower educated are immensely satisfied with adult education, and on the

4 The most important of these includes 3% of the members of the Central Confederation of Trade Unions in Denmark:Henning Jørgensen m.fl.:APL-projektet, CARMA,Aalborg Universitetscenter, 1992-94.
5 'Displaced' is the phrase I use in this paper to describe, that problems are made tacit in not having existence in the language. A more saying phrase would be 'ex-communicated', which literally describes what takes place. Because of the religious connotations I have not put this into the text however.

other hand, that the effect both in relation to labour market policy and individual development of qualifications is very unclear.[6]

The satisfaction is largest amongst women as they are more likely to participate in adult education than men. A recent analysis by Kirsten Weber[7], concerning women workers in the internal trade union educational programme in Denmark, has suggested some ways of posing the problems and has describes some coherence. These educational programmes are a special area of adult education, but I think the analysis has more general relevance for women with low educational attainment. A connection is established in the analysis between the subjective meaningfulness in participating in adult education, and the central areas of conflict in the social learning of female workers. The analysis shows how the women′s educational satisfaction is independent of whether the women have had the possibility of including their own experiences included in the education process, or whether they have directed the learning process. It is also independent of whether their strategies of life and living conditions are reflected in education. None-theless these educational courses give meaning to the women, and provide a social framework upon which they can they build an identity.

Participating in adult education evidently provides a lot of pleasant experiences, good treatment, 'dignity' etc., which are often missing for the unskilled and lower educated. On a psychological level the satisfaction builds on the social qualification of women in denying the undesirable, and in a very reality oriented way cope with contradictory living conditions. Some women take on an educational identity in relation to a worker's and family identity. Other women get themselves involved with education precisely because the painful experiences of womens' life and work can be discussed and conflicts, thereby, can be avoided. Other women use education to move away from their own painful reality to look at other people's lives.

6 E.g. Aarkrog m.fl.:Uddannelsestilbud til langtidsledige, Danmarks Lærerhøjskole og Udviklingscenteret for folkeoplysning og voksenuddannelse, 1991, which is one of the biggest evaluations in adult education in recent years.

7 Kirsten Weber: Ambivalens og erfaring, EVU-gruppen, Roskilde Universitetscenter 1995

Conclusions have not been drawn. Progressive learning processes amongst women with low educational attainment may or may not take place in adult education today. The important thing for me here is to emphasise that the greatest satisfaction with education for lower educated women does not imply that learning processes take place which contribute constructively to the women´s development of identity and qualifications in working life and in their own lives in general. The women can accept an intentionality in education that is not their own, and still find education meaningful. So I wonder if, we know too little about the dynamics, that can displace the gendered experiences of women workers with low educational attainment, from the educational space?

In whose perspective does education take place?

When people with low educational attainment enter into adult education, they do so with a great deal of life experiences, and almost regardless of content, education will remain a very little part of their whole life-course. This contrasts with people who participate in education frequently and continuously throughout their life-course, and where a practice of education can be as important to them as their practice of work.

Most often they also come from fields of work, where the quality and know-how is a *tacit knowledge*, deriving from the creative handling of their work, and from a vast formation of both individual and collective experience.[8] The division of labour, wage-labour and hierarchical structures at work make it difficult to draw on all life experiences. Part of this is a necessary practical knowledge, or reflection in action (Schön)[9], that can remain unexpressed, tacit or implicit knowledge. A very common example of this is the knowl-

8 Donald Schön: The Reflective Practitioner - how professionals think in action, Arena 1995

9 Donald Schön has developed his theoretical work on the knowledge and reflection of practitioners, in relation to professionals with a high or medium level of education. Therefore his discussions on professional knowledge versus reflection in practice does not apply for people with short educational attainment. None the less I find Schöns work very relevant in describing the way tacit knowledge is produced and how reflection in action takes place with practitioners.

edge of how to handle affectively conflicts inherent in human service work. As tacit knowledge this formation of experiences seeks to avoid 'external' structuring. But 'the subjective formation of experiences does not take place uninfluenced by the broader societal and cultural context, but becomes influenced by it, as described in the theory of 'the consciousness of everyday life'. By this is meant a form of consciousness, that is active in the adult individual, when s/he perceives and reacts to modern everyday life."[10]

For the individual there is a reason to maintain a tacit, implicit knowledge and strong psychological dynamics at play. On the other hand it is this tacit knowledge that must be openly reflected in order to construct subjectively constructive learning processes. In the educational setting, which the lower educated perceive as a continuation of an 'external' or 'top-down' structuring, the 'silence' or displacing of knowledge of practice and experience is allowed to continue. When at the same time taking into account, that adult education is being instrumental to labour market policy, it is possible to conclude that the lower educated can be objectified in adult education, under the structuring and intentionality of others.

For many years experiential learning has been the progressive answer in Danish educational theory and practice for adults, but the tendency has been to largely look at experiences as something on the operational level, something technical, and has not been understood as a question *of intentionality in adult education*. The living conditions and attempts at defining one's own life have remained in the background of the education for the lower educated. In spite of the expression of other intentions, the effect of education is most often measured by criteria's of success, that fit into current labour market policy. Therefore a completely different intentionality, than that of the participants, is not only a hidden expectation of the lower educated, but most often reality in adult education schemes.[11]

10 Peter Ø. Andersen : Pædagogens praksis, s.96, Munksgaard 1995. The theory of the consciousness of everyday life, see e.g. Thomas Leithäuser : Formen des Alltagsbewusstseins, 1977, Campus,Frankfurt.
11 Henning Salling Olesen :Education and Training in Labour Market Policy - a theoretical and methodological Challenge. Paper for the Conference on Labour Market Research, Roskilde Universitetscenter, nov. 1991

Today this is being criticised through biographical approaches in an effort to hold on to the adult-educational way of posing the problem, which is just as important today, as when it was first expressed: 'The problem is not to find out how the experiences of the participants become fruitful in education, but to find out, how adult education can become fruitful to the experiences of the participants.'[12] Adult education possesses the possibilities of contributing to the learning processes of the lower educated when these are understood as ongoing learning processes in a continuing life-course, and when education contributes to a subjective construction of the individual life.

This is an important point. It is asserted by the theorists of the 'modern project' (Giddens, Baumann, Ulrik Beck), that people's life-courses change and the development of identity no longer follows traditions. It puts the individual construction of people's lives on the agenda. Biographical theorists preoccupied with adult learning and people with low educational attainment, also predict this. Nobody is left untouched by certain life-changes and the *detraditionalising* process: 'Class, gender and generation are still important, as biographical resources, but their value as a prognosis regarding specific life-courses has diminished measurably'.[13]

On the other hand Peter Alheit has, through empirical studies, criticised this and tried to moderate the notion of 'the modern project' by pointing out, that the 'thesis of individualisation' is greatly exaggerated, and that the detraditionalisation looks very different according to social milieus. While some are successful under modern living conditions, others become losers in the process: 'It would be a mistake to believe that all traditional social milieus are equally affected by such dissolution processes (that is, the individualisation thesis). Instabilities are certainly evident in that 'opening corridor' of the social space. This is the location for a clear separation and differentiation of classical proletarian and petit bourgeois milieus - the background milieus for

12 Henning Salling Olesen: A biographical Approach to Adult Learning , in: Olesen et Rasmussen: Theoretical Issues in Danish Adult Education, Roskilde Universitetscenter 1996

13 Peter Alheit: The biographical Question as a Challenge to Adult Education, in: International Review of Education no. 40, 1994

social climbers.'[14] How modernisation penetrates everyday life is far from being clear to me, but I find that there are good possibilities in gaining a framework of comprehension through biographical research.

The picture is contradictory when you look at the life-courses and life-expectations, the values and the attitudes, of Danish women with low educational attainment.[15] The youngest women are attracted to a certain extent by the perspective of individualisation and the construction of one's own life and their life-courses do change to a certain extent. At the same time traditional values (such as solidarity and care for the family) are highly valued and the life-qualifications are inherent herein.

Childminders and gendered experiences

Registered childminders in private day-care, the focus of my empirical material, fall into the category of poorly educated women who hold these new perspectives of life, giving expression to the changed living conditions of women. However, they are also women who are deeply rooted in traditional life patterns. They possess a lot of experience, partly because their work draws on life-experiences (and 14 days of education/training in a working life of maybe 25 years). They also have a lot of 'human experience' gained from the private sphere of life, that gives them very relevant informal qualifications for the job.

Private day-care is a job that can be obtained without any formal vocational education, and predominantly attracts working-class women (and a few men). The economical and social demands on the framework of the day-care home mean that the women are in stabile family relations with mainly skilled

14 Peter Alheit: Changing basic Rules of biographical Construction : Modern Biographies at the end of the 20th. Century, in Arbejdstekster til voksenpædagogisk teoriudvikling nr. 10, Roskilde Universitetscenter 1993.

15 The APL-project(note v) shows how limited the extension of 'the modern project' is amongst the shorter-educated. While other investigations,e.g.Birgitte Simonsen: Unges forhold til familieliv og kønsroller,EVU-gruppen, Roskilde Universitetscenter 1994 show some signs of untraditionalization and individualization among young women in general. And e.g. Hansen m.fl.: Liv i voksenundervisningen, EVU gruppen, Roskilde Universitetscenter points to contradictory tendencies.

husbands, and live in good houses. The job is typically chosen after ten years on the labour market, and after their own children have entered day-care institutions or school. The women are early school leavers, but more than 50% also have a vocational education qualification mostly in office and commerce work. The women chose the job 1) in order to mind children, which they feel is a strong personal qualification. 2) To unite work and private life, and to brign more coherence to their lives, and 3) to gain independence in their work in relation to the much stronger influence of a wage-labour structuring on the 'big labour market'.

The very conscious choice of day-care work was a surprise to me. Before my research I had two views about such work: 1) its low status in society and on the labour market, and 2) the isolated and traditionally gendered framework that it situates women in relation to 'the modern project'. I made a big mistake in overlooking the need of the lower educated women to actively use a very large part of their qualifications, derived from gendered experiences. The interviews enlightened the way the women had moved from work and vocational education they had been in because of financial factors, parents` expectations, tradition, experiences in their youth etc. Most held an instrumental attitude to their job and saw it as a precondition for life in the private sphere or for others it highlighted the dilemma about priorities in life. As a contrast to this there was a much larger satisfaction with their own qualifications in day-care work. The empirical material also showed an observable and expressed 'desire' for the job.

In my preliminary hypothesis I underestimated how strong the wish was to create harmony in the conflicting management of family and work and to eliminate or displace the undesirable in both. The choice of day-care work was for these women such a strategy. Day-care work is a way to earn a living, but at the same time the private sphere mixes so deeply with the work, that I was inclined to conclude in the pilot study, that it was an attempt to develop a female strategy of life.

This does not go to say that the women in day-care achieve harmony, free of conflicts. The undesirable aspects of the work were expressed by the older day-care workers. The women discovered how vulnerable they are in relation to the structure of wage labour and that this is reflected in their own homes. The women stay in day-care work so that they can embrace the conflicts in both work and home, and the conflicts between them, all taking place in the same space- and this somehow unites the private and the public wage-labour. The burn-out syndrome is not a rare phenomenon with the more experienced childminders who reflect upon these conflicts The conflicts contain both resistance (acting out as suppressed anger) and a reaction to the desire and the commitment. To become burnt-out you must have been burning.

A possible theoretical explanation of the dynamics that reflects the situation of the childminders, I think, can be found in Regina Becker Schmidts theory[16] about the *social learning of women*. It derives from the idea of continuous double work of women, in the family and in the job, and the ambivalent feelings derived from family and work and the logic which women have to cope with. Both spheres have both desirable and undesirable meaning to women which they learn to live with and this creates their most important social learning. Women achieve new and stimulating learning through coming into contact with the feelings they have invested in these ambivalences: 'Women survive because of their tolerance of ambivalence, but they gain experience only when the emotions and psychodynamics invested in ambivalence are brought into motion.'[17]

I have tried in a very preliminary way to reflect upon the empirical data from my Danish pilot study using the theoretical concept of social learning and ambivalence. On the subject of 'the choice of day-care work', which I have chosen to draw on here, I find the reflection relevant. The shift from 'other work' to day-care work, seemed to be an important step for all the women, a

16 Regina Becker Schmidt und Gudrun-Axeli Knapp: Geschlechtertrennung-Geschlechterdifferenz-Suchbewegungen sozialen Lernens, Dietz Verlag 1989. Regina Becker Schmidt has developed the theory of social learning through investigations of the lives of unskilled women workers in Germany. Women with a low level of educational attainment. The culture, the values, the attitudes and learning processes seem very much the same as with my empirical material. There is one criteria though, that Becker Schmidt used, which is special. Her material were all single mothers. Motherhood and the family identity must thus be somewhat different from the group I am investigating. But I do not find that this outrules the basic concepts of social learning and ambivalence with other women workers.

17 Interpreted by Kirsten Weber in: Experiencing Gender - A Psychodynamic Approach to Adult Learning - and a Case of Masculinity and Social Work, in Olesen et Rasmussen: Theoretical Issues in Adult Education Research, Roskilde University Press 1996

way of constructing a life in a special way, where they 'did something' with the ambivalences. They expressed having been very affected by the strongly undesirable sides of wage labour before taking their decision. The choice was for some women very conscious, for others more affective at the time, taking several years, but resulting in a new learning about themselves and their lives. Working in a day-care practice the ambivalent feelings remained, but structured in a new way. From the point of view of education, it was very evident that a lot of learning had taken place, and also that some of the women became more and more affected with the new ways the ambivalent dynamics were at play. This group were in need of support to go through with the new constructive learning processes. However, in the educational context these ambivalences and this type of learning was absent as themes. Neither on educational courses nor in supervision etc. were these gendered issues picked out as a central theme. The painful experiences of engendered in caring roles as childminders were not treated.

Bettina Dausien[18] has pointed out in an analysis of German women, that I find comparable, that on the level of attitudes, orientation and values women today have a problem that they lack *patterns of interpretation and pictures to express their life practice between family and work through*. There is no golden solution to the contradictions of double work, and no described 'normal course' on how to live your life as a woman. This analysis connects with the thesis of detraditionalisation and modernisation, but focuses even more, I think, on the empirical reality with the recognition of different social milieus. For example, the traditional image of women and the logic of the family is still extensively being held as valid as patterns of interpretation by the unskilled and lower educated women themselves. This matches the findings of my empirical study.

This orientation is contradictory to women's experiences and results in a lack of language. It creates a taciturnity from the women, a taciturnity about their life and practice. (This is of course related to context, and is not unaffected by being on the level of practice or on the level of reflection on practice, or in an everyday intimate context or a public representative context.)

18 Bettina Dausien: Biographie und Geschlecht, Donat Verlag, Bremen 1996

My empirical data signalled that either the childminders participating in education treated their work very technically, and used wage labour instrumentally (for example, relating everything to a time schedule, but at the same time in practice this schedule would not function). Or they treated other personal problems and subjects, than those directly involved in day-care practice.

To interpret it as plainly a result of inhibitions, unconscious repression and suppression would be absolutely wrong within the concept of social learning. It must rather be seen as, what might be called 'the guts to hesitate', and an expression of the very reality bound way women relate, because of the social learning they bear. 'Hesitate, that is what many women actually do. The understanding, that this is the only logical way to react to the structural double bind between family and wage labour, does not make the ambivalence, the psychological approaching of it, or the empirically observable hesitation that is its expression into experience, neither for the women in general, nor for the researcher, who chooses this problem as a challenge for her. But it does expose on ambivalence as a potential of experience....'[19]

From the perspective of adult educational this interpretation of women's attitudes in education are important. At the same time my empirical work shows that the lower educated women are in great need of having their experiences and knowledge expressed, and their informal qualifications used to their own intentions in constructing their lives.

Childminders and qualifications of care

Through the building of a large public sector, a number of human service and educational tasks have been drawn out of the family sphere and put into an area of the state, which is by definition neutrally gendered. The experiences and qualifications belonging to the family sphere, are not automati-

19 Kirsten Weber: Ambivalens og erfaring, see note vi

cally possessed by the people who work with these tasks professionally. The rationality itself and the values attached, are broader and different than those of the family sphere. This leads to assumptions of a functionally gender neutrality in both the educational and the human service sector. On the other hand a democratisation between the sexes is taking place where women's experiences are being carried into the public work places by women who teach, participate in education, act as nurses, mind children etc. The nature of this type of work is becoming visible and extended into society to reach more people through democratisation. This leads to assumptions of a feminisation of society.

Numerous empirical and theoretical analyses imply that the traditional gendered patterns are being continuously recreated, so that female authority and female values do not establish themselves on a general level of society. In this respect the 'gender neutrality' can be perceived as an effort (also from the professional organisations, such as the teachers union, the nurses union etc.) to demasculinise for the purpose of democratisation. At the same time it can be seen as an effort to defeminise in the sense of drawing away from the patterns of the family. It may be seen as existing contradictory tendencies, where the 'functionally gender neutrality' is dominant, and gendered practice exists alongside it.[20]

Most institutions of adult education understand themselves as functionally neutral. The childminders, on the other hand, stand in the middle of the gendered practice that human service work is evidently full of. Day-care practice is very gendered. The logic of the family, gendered values and attitudes cannot be avoided; they are maintainers of what goes on. As an example of the neutrally gendered way of thematising day-care work is the demand that childminders must act 'professionally' in relation to the customers, the parents. The significance is: to put at a distance, to disengage, to be impersonal in contact, to follow a wage labour time schedule and not the natural rhythm of the children. At the same time the care must be 'successful'. In contrast to this stands the experiences of the women from their own families and the

20 Karen Borgnakke:Udviklingstræk - Teser, tolkninger og analysekategorier, Danmarks Lærerhøjskole, 1996

experiences created through everyday practice of work. This meeting between different logic and structures can often be very painful for the childminders, because the result is dissatisfied parents, children who cry a lot, and deprived children's needs that must be 'dropped'.

This demand for professionalisation, which I define as a demand for gender neutrality, is at the political level a result of the 'reconstruction and modernisation' which the public sector is going through in Denmark. It signifies, among other things, that the individual human service worker must learn to balance between the necessary distance and a demanded engagement. Rather than being professional by holding professional knowledge, you must be professional in representing the rationality of state institutions. Adult and continuing education is in Denmark an important part of this, as it is very often used to modernise public institutions.

The modernisation of the public sector in Denmark has put the problems in public human service work on the agenda. An investigation into the relation between the education of nurses and the practical qualifications in care in the health sector by Tine Rask Eriksen shows some tendencies that can have significance also for the education of childminders. It shows how the *caring qualification* is a qualification connected to gendered experiences, in the family and from the mother-child relationship, and pre-verbal ways of communication. Orientation towards needs, community and close relations are the most important values.

In educating young women in nursing schools and in practical training a new and different structuring comes in, determined by the relations of production, the division of labour and the structuring of time. It has a fatal importance for the qualification of care. Eriksen expresses this illustration of the typical nursing student: 'When Sophie is at the beginning of her education, her gendered qualifications are a socially determined 'impulse', and she will in the caring space determined by the system, continually try to reactivate these caring practices. Over time these forces of production will be chained to the conditions of production and the logic of the system. In this way Sophie's practices of care will immediately be transformed into a tacit knowledge of care. The same knowledge will over time undergo a dialectical transformation towards partly enchainment (dequalification) of the gendered practices of care because the relations of production determined by the system 'counteract' Sophie's qualifications of care in relation to social relations.'[21]

Childminders and adult education

In 1996 the Ministry of Education in Denmark decided to launch a vocational education programme of one and a half years years for childminders, and all working childminders. The majority of women do not want this education but can now look forward to more programmes of adult and continuing education. Up until now education has played a small role for day-care workers because of tradition, where their parents have had little education and because of the described disinclination to education from the lower educated. It is also because many have experienced vocational education courses which they did not find useful, and on the other hand have had a job as childminder with no education, and found their life qualifications sufficient.

Day-care workers have learnt mainly from their own experiences, secondly from other childminders and human service workers and only very partly from supervision by educated childminders. The picture held by the educated and educational planners is quite different. For example, it is assumed that professional knowledge and professionally educated childminders are very important as role models for the 'unskilled' childminders. The most remarkable aspect about the learning processes in the empirical data is that nearly all important learning processes for the individual childminder have taken place outside of an educational and formal workplace framework. The catalysts and the helpers in a process of reflection for the learning process of the individual has typically been another childminder (the intimate girlfriend) or a member of the family of the childminder; people in a familiar relation. It has taken place in the family space. At the same time a lot of very difficult

21 Tine Rask Eriksen: Kvindeverden - og offentlig sektor, in Social Kritik nr. 3, 1989, s.14. See: Omsorg i forandring, Munksgaard, 1992, which is a presentation of the investigation.

happenings and practices have been left unreflected upon: 'it just so happened', and thereby many necessary learning processes have not taken place.

Education is valued by the childminders not as a need to develop practice, but much more in order to confirm practice. The chat with other childminders, often in breaks on educational courses and seminars, is what gives the feeling of 'being like the others.' Thereby education is much more seen as a response to an isolated job situation. Although it also touches on the lacking 'professional' identity as workers in childminding. When the childminders ask for adult education, they do not have the expectation, that their experiences will have a great influence. Their educational experience is most often that their practices are somewhat unwelcome in the educational space; the other side of the coin, when considering the described taciturn attitude of the childminders. They like participating in seminars etc., and they want more adult education as long as it does not interfere with their practices. Just as soon as there are signs of interference with action, there is a reaction, interpreted by teachers as inhibition and resistance against change.

The temporary theoretical explanation I am focusing on is: when human service work in caring roles is threatened by the structuring of wage labour and the tightening grip of the modernisation of the public sector and when women with a low level of educational attainment are positioned so relatively far away from the detraditionalisation and opening of social space, education does not possess a force of attraction, as development and learning. It may be seen as an external element, and even seem threatening. When the childminders at the same time have mixed the family and working sphere so much together, as a source of identity, then so much is at stake for them personally. At the same time the possible strain through the presence of the ambivalent feelings will double. The way the women relate to adult education can therefore be understood as a very marked, and to them necessary and reality orientated 'hesitation'.

Section 6

Social Movements and Adult Continuing Education

Agnieszka Bron

Social Movements and Adult Continuing Education

Introduction

As a rapporteur for Section 6, Social Movements and Adult Continuing Education, I have three sets of comments to make. Firstly, I will present the subject area by explaining the concepts discussed. This approach helps to explain the choice of topics for the papers presented at the conference. I will also introduce the papers by structuring them by contexts under three headings. Secondly, I will summarise the main issues of our discussion, and finally share my own views and concerns about the lack of research in this field among adult educators/educationalists, and look for a possible explanation of this situation.

Introduction and papers' content

The section's theme formulated as *social movements and adult continuing education* gives an opportunity for various interpretations and accordingly different papers. Therefore, we should not be surprised that the papers differ.

Let me start with writing a few words about the main concepts of our theme:

The notion of *social movements* historically means an organised effort by a significant number of people to change (or resist to change in) some major aspect or aspects of society. Nowadays we are talking about new social movements and refer to groups of organisations which previously were situated outside the mainstream of the political system, such as, for example, environmentalist movements who have moved more towards the centre of mainstream. They are however different than the 'old' movements as they do not correspond to the forces characteristic of the 'old' ones. Thus the concept invites both historical and contemporary contributions.

Even *adult continuing education* can be interpreted differently, especially in non-English speaking countries. Adult continuing education means learning undertaken after a break from completed initial education. In some countries, however, adults never started initial education when they were children or they have not completed it, so we can only speak about adult education, as in a paper by Liam Kane concerning popular education in Latin America. Moreover, we can only speak about 'reparatory' education when adult learning is concentrating on how to recover from damages done by initial schooling. Thus, it could be difficult to use the term continuing education in such cases. Because the level of education in the Western countries is rather high, continuing education can also mean more advanced education at the tertiary level. But even in Western countries we deal with adults who do not participate in adult education, or with minority groups who may lack initial education.

At last we have a conjunction *and* which might denote two things at least:

- that the two phenomena new social movements (NSM) and adult continuing education are treated on the same level, thus not necessarily dependent on each other, that is, having an equal status; or
- that the two phenomena are related to each other. NSM can require/demand adult education/learning or vice versa adult education is dependent, needs a support from NSM, for example, to increase participation. Thus as a point of departure we can study NSM and the role of learning within them, or starting from adult education and investigate the significance of it upon NSM (that is, goals, content and methods). Taking the first position we probably concentrate more on informal learning; taking the other more at a formal level or both.

The topic of the section thus made it possible to include papers which do not necessarily take the second position, that is, the relationship between adult education and social movements, and because of this it directs discussion towards other issues.

We know that the history of early European adult education is just a history of social movements. This was the situation in Britain, the Netherlands and Sweden, to name just a few countries. Old social movements had a close relationship with adult education by using it as a means for reaching their goals. 'Knowledge is power' was their slogan. One can say that adult education's significance as a field of study and practice developed from the movements. Today the old movements have lost their membership and their role both in society and adult education. In NSM a relationship with formal adult education is rather vague, or our knowledge about it is too limited. So there is a place for speculation and missionary thinking by adult educators. We need more research to find out how, and in what sense, informal learning takes place within the NSM, and among individual members. Actually some research findings are testing that (Field, 1991). There is an abundance of good empirical research into NSM, as well as some interesting theoretical analysis, for example, the work inspired by Habermas (1987) and Offe (1985). Interestingly enough, both of them see NSM as 'learning movements'. What stops adult educationalists/educators to do research on learning and NSM? To be able to answer this question is an investigation in itself.

Altogether there were eight papers in our section, representing four countries: UK, Germany, Spain and Finland. One of the UK contributions dealt with issues concerning Latin America. Papers from Central and Eastern Europe were unfortunately absent (this was a pity because there is much going on in the sphere of new social movements on a local and regional level, which needs to be investigated). At Wroclaw University there are some researchers, for example, Ewa Kurantowicz, who study such issues. There is also in Poland educational and cultural work connected with the issue of little homelands, when people look for their roots. The topics of the papers presented could be grouped according to the following structure:

(1) papers concerned with the description of new social movements and the role formal adult education can play or plays for them

This includes the following four papers:

- by Steve Morris on *Recent language protest movements in Wales: adult learning of a new kind?*, where adult education is treated as a tool for the language movement and the remains of the role education played for old social movements.
- by Angela Franz-Balsen on *Just talking? Learning processes in intersectional alliances for local environmental activities*; Adult education role is seen as a facilitator for environmental activists and officials on the local level, and
- by Martin Ryle on *Adult education, environmental education, and the green movement: possible futures?*, where in a normative, future and missionary way a relationship between departments of continuing education and NSM is advocated. Adult education at the university should according to the author facilitate and give a theoretical framework for NSM.
- by Jenny Parker on *Adult Education and Local Agenda 21 – Linking Regional Development on the 5th Action Programme – 'Towards Sustainability'*, where the practical role of adult education in helping New Social Movements in meeting their challenges is presented. An example is based on ACET, a county-wide service and social movement sector initiating projects on adult environmental education. The course organised by ACET, is directed towards adults from the community. This paper can be placed at a borderline between the first group and the second because there is not real linkage between NSM and this special adult education activity. The only similarity is in the topic of interest: sustainability.

(2) papers concerning adult education more distinctly, which eventually can serve/help social movements: (also descriptive)

Two papers are in this group:

- by Maria del Mar Herrera Menchen on *Adult education outside formal education. Another option for social training*. Paper deals with training animators for socio-cultural animation by Public Schools run by municipalities in Spain. The goal of this training is to create and mobilise social movements. Here the clear influence from above, that is, from adult educators is advocated.
- by Liam Kane on *Popular education beyond the conventional institutions: lessons from Latin America.* This paper is based on experiences, concept, methods and philosophy of popular education as a vision for non-formal adult education, outside formal British adult education. Latin American popular education is treated here as a social movement. Again the role of adult educator/facilitator is crucial.

(3) Finally papers concerned with research into social movements, and learning, changing of membership/participants/activists.

Here two papers can be included:

- by Klaus Körber on *From social movement to professionalisation – new tasks and new institutions between market, state and communities*. The paper deals with development of alternative movements in Germany towards professionalisation and institutionalisation. It takes up the role informal learning is playing for individual members.
- by Ritva Lindroosone on *Citizenship as an environment for lifelong learning.* Two out of three projects described in the paper can be included here: one dealing with Environmental protection organisation (Finland) and lifelong learning of the participants; another a research project on small-scale enterprises, a networking enterprise, and could be compared with the Klaus Körber project. Research projects are presented very superficially so it is hard to make any conclusions about their quality and relevance to the topic discussed at our session.

Discussion during the section's sessions

The diversity of papers enabled us to have an interesting discussion, which every time was introduced by the same discussant, David Browing, who in a analytical and concluding way presented his comments. He also related the relationship and linkages between the papers helping us to find a wholeness in a variety of issues and topics.

The discussion could be characterised and summarise by one sentence: From new social movements to adult education, back to social movements and the role of informal learning. Discussion, thus, focused on adult educators' role in facilitating and supporting social movements and civic society at large. Participants had a strong belief in the intervention role of adult education, but unfortunately were unable to look critically at the role of the adult educator. They talked in terms of visionaries, missionaries, animators and those providing expertise and concepts. To act as 'old' adult educators did, that is, invisibly as organic intellectuals was the interesting comment of a Chairperson: Hywel Francis. We cannot blame the presenters and some of the audience for this type of discussion, because most of the participants represented adult education profession, engaged and committed adult educators, practitioners, but having very little to do with research and evaluation of their own and others practices.

Some questions discussed were as follows:

(1) Is it possible to transfer specific cases of New Social Movements (for example the Welsh language movement or environmental movements in Britain) into new contexts? Thus, are we able to generalise and learn from specific/single experiences?

(2) Is it too much optimism to consider the adult educators role of helping in finding consensus when antagonistic forces or views meet? For example working within local Agenda 21.

(3) Why do we not talk about the content of our work but concentrate on methods?

(4) What is a role of NGO, social movements and adult education to bring people together and concentrate/work on important issues, like for example, the sustained development?

Comments

This section deals with my evaluation on the role of adult educators *are playing* as researchers into the topic: new social movements and adult education.

Interestingly we dealt in our session *only* with two papers based on research, which included the analysis of new social movements or alternative movements and learning issues. Why there are so few research contributions? Our discussion concentrated on interesting but, nevertheless, practical solutions, and we did not take research topics and issues into consideration.

Are social movements and learning, though, an area which is more relevant for speculation, polemic and hopeful thinking, than research? Or, is it that most adult educators do not include research in their professional work? This needs to be investigated. It raises an interesting issue of adult educators/educationalists employment obligations at the university and the lack of research within continuing education departments, especially in the UK. Contributors to the section presented an interesting field of reality which could be easily investigated. Thus they had inside knowledge/first hand knowledge, which often is needed to do research but which also limits them; one stays as a good practitioner and visionary.

The papers which are not based on research, do not contribute either to theory building. I am missing theoretical approaches to analyse NSM and learning and the discussion about which of the theories, for example, 'resource mobilisation theory' or 'identity-oriented' theories are most suitable to understand the relationship between the movements and learning/education (Zald, M, .N, and McCarthy, J,D, 1985). Or perhaps those of Habermas and Offe which lead to experiment with solutions to the challenges of 'risk society'. The last one could imply research on communication and those of historical analysis. Treating NSM as learning movements could be an interesting issue to explore by adult educationalists. Even the questions we asked directed us to interesting research problems: for example, what happens with those adults who leave organised adult education? What process initiates such learning?

The theoretical framework Klaus Körber is using, that pointing at social mediation and the role of alternative movements as intermediary institutions, can be of interest in future study, and especially the non-traditional role of learning/education in the movement. Our understanding of learning/education influenced by research results could change if we study similarly another movement. Moreover such understanding and research gives us the possibility to a new conceptualisation of adults learning. This also is needed to go further and developed as an reflexive practitioner.

So, the question remains for all of us: why are adult educators not engaged in research on learning and NSM? Is it because of their own engagement (engagé) in NSM as activists or sympathisers, that makes them 'blind' to do any research, and to play a role of 'expert researchers', or is it that NSM rejects any ideas of the outside research expertise, as they are aware of their own role in knowledge-creation, which does not need to be tested by so called 'objective' scientists? Our engagement as Hywel Francis, rightly pointed out, gives us both a strength and a weakness.

References

Field, J. (1991), Adult Education and the new Social Movements. International Journal of University Adult Education.

Habermas, J. (1987), A Theory of Communicative Action, Cambridge, Polity.

Offe, C. (1985), New Social Movements: Challenging the Boundaries of Institutional Politics. Social Research 52, 4, pp 817-868.

Zald, M. N. and McCarthy, J. D. (1985), Social Movements in Organizational Society: resources, mobilization, conflict and institutionalisation, New Brunswick, Transactions.

Steve Morris

Recent Language Protest Movements in Wales: Adult Learning of a New Kind?

The main focus of this paper is to review the reasons behind the creation and influence of language protest movements in Wales during the last four decades with particular emphasis on (i) the learning processes acquired within the language movement (in particular but not exclusively *Cymdeithas yr Iaith Gymraeg* – the Welsh Language Society) (ii) the ways in which more formal, traditional adult learning institutions have responded to these changing linguistic pressures and (iii) how the Welsh language movement has related to other social movements. A historical overview of the background to the formation of the movement and its various protests leads to an examination of its contribution to the status of the Welsh language today and, in particular, in the field of education.

Developments in the field of language protest over recent decades in Wales are viewed in the wider context of the redefining of Wales as a nation and Welshness as a concept. This has been the subject of much discussion here during recent years. An examination of the role of adult education within this process and within the wider processes of, for example, language restoration, literacy for native speakers of Welsh and addressing the needs of a changing demographic cross-section of Welsh speakers follows. In conclusion, possible indicators for a future role for adult education as a facilitating mechanism within language policy formulation in Wales in the light of the 1993 Language Act are investigated.[1]

1 For a complete and thorough discussion (in English) of the Welsh language census returns from 1961 - 1991, including many useful maps, see Aitchison and Carter, *A Geography of the Welsh Language 1961 - 1991* and see Carter, *Dirywiad yr Iaith Gymraeg yn yr Ugeinfed Ganrif* for a general overview of the mains reasons for the decline in the language during the twentieth century.

Census, decline and response

At the beginning of this century, when the idea of *Prifysgol y Werin*[2] had been realised at the colleges of the University of Wales, almost 50% of the population of Wales were Welsh speakers and unbroken swathes of the country, stretching from parts of the industrial South into rural west and north Wales including the slate quarrying areas of Gwynedd, had more than 80% of its people speaking Welsh as their everyday language: the language of their community, the language of their work, the language of their religion and the language of their home. Fifty years later, by the time of the 1951 census, only 28.9% of the country recorded themselves as Welsh speakers signalling an unparalleled decline in both the percentage and number of people able to speak Welsh in Wales[3]. It became evident that with a continuation of rural depopulation/English immigration, lack of status for the language in education (from primary to university levels) and in any other public domain, increased world prestige of English (the idea of the English language as the '*language to make your way up in the world*' and find better employment prospects) and demographic factors which meant increasingly that Welsh was becoming the language of the more elderly members of society in some parts of Wales, that action either had to be taken to counterbalance these trends or the language would continue to shrink together with its heartlands and face the inevitable possibility of extinction by the turn of the century.

By the beginning of the sixties, it was generally accepted that the 1961 census returns would again show a further decline in the numbers of people speaking Welsh and it was during the period (1962) prior to the release of these figures that the eminent Welsh language dramatist and nationalist,

2 The nearest translation of this would be 'the university of the people' - this was how the future University of Wales was envisaged by its founders. See Kenneth O. Morgan 'The People's University' in Elliott and others (ed.) *Communities and their Universities* pp. 1-9 for an account of how the University of Wales subsequently developed away from this ideal.

3 Aitchison and Carter summarise thus: '*...a whole nexus of socio-economic changes had reacted with domain limitation and status loss to produce a fifty-year period of catastrophic decline, all the more hurtful since it had followed so closely on what had been perceived as a golden age of renewal and opportunity.*' (op cit p.41).

Saunders Lewis[4], was invited to deliver the annual BBC Radio Saint David's day lecture. The title of this lecture was *Tynged yr Iaith* (the Fate of the Language) and in it, Lewis spelt out in no uncertain terms that '*I shall ... presuppose that Welsh will end as a living language, should the present trend continue, about the beginning of the twenty-first century* (and with a chilling reference to global concerns of that period) *assuming that there will be people left in the island of Britain at that time.*'[5] Although this apocalyptic scenario had been discussed and aired many times before this particular lecture, here at last was a man of great academic and national standing publicly stating for the first time the fears of many. He further lays much of the blame for lack of action on this front, and others,[6] on the inertia of Welsh people themselves: '*There is nothing in the world more comfortable than to give up hope. For then one can go on to enjoy life.*'[7] Finally, whilst urging Welsh speakers to become more assertive and to start to demand services through the medium of Welsh, he concludes that '*It will be nothing less than a revolution to restore the Welsh language in Wales. Success is only possible through revolutionary methods.*'[8] This lecture, in which Lewis had graphically highlighted the plight of a minoritised Celtic language on the peripheries of Western Europe and next door to the home of one of the world's most powerful languages, became extremely influential in the creation of *Cymdeithas yr Iaith Gymraeg* (the Welsh Language Society) which in turn inspired a generation of language activists whose influence and protests have shaped the development of language policy (such as it is) in Wales up until the present day. This was to such an extent that the Welsh historian John Davies described the period that followed as '*...the Welsh*

---

4 For a comprehensive treatment of Saunders Lewis' political views together with essays on aspects of his work, politics and theatre (including a translation of *Tynged yr Iaith* and other essays, poems and plays) see Alun R. Jones and Gwyn Thomas (eds.) *Presenting Saunders Lewis.*

5 op cit. p.127

6 The lecture was written after the drowning of Tryweryn to supply Liverpool with water despite immense opposition in Wales and during the time of building nuclear reactors in Gwylfa and Trawsfynydd to, as he states, '*...feed Lancashire with electricity*'. The link between environmental desecration and the demise of the language is one that surfaces again in the campaigns of the eighties.

7 op cit. p.139

8 op cit. p.141

version, perhaps, of the unrest prevalent in those years among young people throughout the Western world'[9].

Status and Equal Validity

At the time of Lewis' lecture, there was virtually no public status for the Welsh language in Wales which would often result in the absurdity of fluent Welsh speakers in positions of responsibility (for example, court clerks, council employees, councillors etc.) using English with other Welsh speakers, frequently because that was the language associated with official business and the state. It was natural, therefore, that some of the first protests held by *Cymdeithas* were aimed at achieving either some level of public visibility for the language, for example, the campaign for road signs to be erected bilingually (a campaign which aroused considerable animosity in many areas and dire warnings of motorists taking too long to read the signs and crashing as a consequence!), being able to register children's' births in Welsh (something that is still impossible only in Welsh in the Swansea area), bilingual car tax disks etc. or were campaigns aimed at certain specific areas, for example, the campaign for more Welsh in the colleges of the University of Wales (students were very prominent in the initial years of *Cymdeithas* and throughout most of its campaigns since then) and the start of a campaign for more Welsh in the mass media which was to mushroom during the seventies. It was agreed at a fairly early stage that the methods of *Cymdeithas* would be those of non-violent direct action and by the end of the sixties, several members of the movement had already been arrested and imprisoned for their parts in protests and direct action. At the same time, gradually at first, the authorities, however hostile their initial reaction, began to capitulate to some of the demands: some colleges agreed to implement bilingual policies, bilingual cheques and car tax disks were allowed and permission was granted to register births and marriages bilingually[10]. Indeed, the government had established a committee - the Hughes-Parry Committee,

9 John Davies, *Hanes Cymru*, p.626

10 For a comprehensive account of the first twenty five years of *Cymdeithas*, see Gwilym Tudur (ed.) *Wyt ti 'n cofio?*

as early as 1963 to 'clarify the legal status of the Welsh language and to consider whether any changes in the law ought to be made'. The authors duly recommended equal validity for both languages when they reported in 1965 but as so often has happened before when the British state endeavours to legislate on the Welsh language, the ensuing Welsh Language Act of 1967 fell far short of the aspirations of not only the activists but also the committee it had established to advise it on the bill. The campaign for a fair and just status for the language therefore continued apace well into the eighties.

The language movement was not only involved in campaigns of direct action and protest during this time. It endeavoured to solve some of the problems facing the language itself, in particular as they affected young adults. It spawned a Welsh language pop industry headed by one of the most popular protest singers at that time Dafydd Iwan whose songs deal with many of the political issues facing Wales such as the investiture in Caernarfon, the drowning of Welsh (speaking mostly) valleys for water for England, the lack of Welsh language education in schools, and in later years, more international issues such as oppression in Chile, apartheid in South Africa and the peace movement thereby presenting these issues to Welsh speaking youth in their own language. Impetus was given to publishing. One of the most successful presses in Wales today *Y Lolfa* was set up by an early activist with *Cymdeithas*, Robat Gruffudd and much of its output was devoted to issues connected with the language campaign but with a distinct Welsh, anti-establishment voice.

The issue of language was forcing many in Wales, both English-speaking and 'establishment' Welsh speakers, to reassess their ideas of what constitutes Wales, how far should status for the language extend, should non-violent direct action be condoned or condemned, was it worth fighting for a language which by 1971 was spoken by only 20% of the population and could Wales still be Wales without the Welsh language? *Cymdeithas* itself established an annual *Ysgol Basg* (Easter School), an educational forum used well by Plaid Cymru since the early twenties, which would debate issues and hear speakers often from other countries with similar minoritised language situations. Activists could gather together and exchange/compare ideas and plans for future campaigns as well as assessing the success of those of the past. This in turn led to a deeper examination of the place of the Welsh language in Welsh nationhood and in turn, the place of Wales in a world context. In particular, the writings of the professor of philosophy, JR Jones, on nationhood and nationality and Alwyn D. Rees, Director of the Extra-Mural Department at Abersytwyth, offered a public forum and rationale for the motivations behind the campaigns. In addition, information was disseminated to *Cymdeithas* members through *Tafod y Ddraig* and a general meeting was held every year to elect officers. It succeeded in remaining a democratic, yet radical movement, not losing the fire which had sparked its very first protest on the Trefechan bridge in Aberystwyth in 1963. These open processes of debate and discussion which thrived in the language protest movement and had been cultivated and sustained by proponents such as JR Jones and Alwyn D Rees, continued to generate new ideas and ways of approaching the linguistic situation of Wales[11].

The challenges facing the language, although some success had been achieved notably in the field of bilingual signs and limited degrees of bilingual publicity in some of the larger public bodies such as the post office, the utilities and some local authorities, continued and intensified during the long years of Thatcherism in the eighties. Other organisations had by this time emerged such as *Mudiad Ysgolion Meithrin* which promoted and organised Welsh medium nursery provision to feed into the growing number of schools providing bilingual education (especially in the more anglicised areas of south and north-east Wales) and many of those earlier activists were now working in posts in the 'establishment' (albeit a more Welsh-speaking 'establishment'). The idea of protesting for the language had become less of a 'shock' in the eyes of the public, indeed, many parents were now protesting to establish more and more Welsh medium primary and secondary schools for their children, parents who very often were unable to speak Welsh themselves but wished their own children to be able to grow up bilin-

11 Cynog Dafis, for example, was amongst the first in Wales to apply the study of socio-linguistics and the sociology of language to a Welsh context, Gareth Miles actively campaigned for a more left wing approach within the language movement and Emyr Llewelyn emphasised the importance of maintaining the *bro Gymraeg* or Welsh-speaking heartland as a priority.

gually. However, the exigencies of life under Thatcher and her free market economy demanded new tactics and approaches.

Wales soon provided the new prime minister with one of her first opportunities to execute a U-turn. Following a previous commitment in the Tory manifesto to establish a Welsh television channel on the new Channel Four network, the home secretary of the time, William Whitelaw, reneged on this promise much to the consternation of activists who had been campaigning vehemently during the seventies for such a channel in Wales. The president of Plaid Cymru at the time, Gwynfor Evans, an avowed pacifist and not a man known to make rash decisions, announced at the Lliw Valley National Eisteddfod in 1980 that he would fast to death unless the government changed its decision. In due course, the government announced a further change in policy and in 1982, S4C began broadcasting with two to three hours of Welsh every night during the peak viewing times. One television channel with a few hours of Welsh every night is obviously not going to save a language but it was nevertheless an important step in offering a growing mass medium to the people of Wales in Welsh and has created a huge industry in television around Cardiff and to a lesser extent in the Welsh-speaking area of Caernarfon in the north thereby offering the prospect of work for Welsh-speakers in their own language and country. It was also the culmination of a campaign begun by *Cymdeithas* back in the early seventies.

It could be argued that *Cymdeithas* became the first real language planners in Wales in the eighties. During the time of the miners' strike (in which *Cymdeithas* played an active role in supporting communities and campaigning with the miners) and the subsequent economic upheavals of the time, it came to be realised more and more that language campaigns could not be divorced from campaigns for jobs (one of the many factors in the decline of Welsh-speakers during the twentieth century has been the constant need to look to England and beyond for employment), for stable and supportive communities, for sensitive planning policies[12] and opportunities not only for

12 During the eighties' property boom, there was not only a huge increase in inmigration to rural areas of Wales from wealthy areas of England but there were also several proposed holiday home developments almost always in areas with high percentages of Welsh-speakers and unemployment. The issues of

newcomers but for non-Welsh-speaking Welsh people to learn the language. Involvement with other campaigning organisations whose aims reflected the kind of society and conditions necessary for the language to flourish increased, notably CND (many *Cymdeithas* women activists took part in protests at Greenham Common), the anti-apartheid movement, the women's movement in addition to forging further links with organisations with similar aims in other parts of Europe and the world, sometimes creating controversy[13]. Towards the end of the eighties, a campaign for real status for the language and a new comprehensive Welsh language act resulted in the government creating a non-statutory Welsh Language Board and in 1993, a new Welsh language act and a statutory Welsh Language Board (with an ex-Plaid Cymru MP and new member of the House of Lords, Dafydd Elis-Thomas as its chair). Many of those activists, who fought so vigorously for this Act, remain deeply sceptical of the ability of the Board and the Language Act to 'deliver' a bilingual Wales in the new millennium especially as the Secretary of State for Wales[14] retains the power to veto any plans proposed by the Board and the principle of equality of treatment for Welsh and English embodied in the Act '*wherever appropriate in the circumstances and reasonably practicable*'. They point out that the 1993 Act falls far short of similar language acts passed by the autonomous governments of the Basque Country and Catalunya in Spain, for example. What is, however, indisputable is that there has been a sea-change in public attitudes in Wales during this thirty year period with a recent NOP poll[15] indicating that 83% of the population (Welsh and English-speaking) feel that the Welsh language is something to be proud of and 83% saying that public bodies should deal with people in both languages. The 1991 census also showed that for the

affordable local accommodation and holiday homes became prominent during this period with *Cymdeithas*' '*Nid yw Cymru ar werth*' [Wales is not for sale] campaign of non-violent action contrasting to the burning of holiday homes by more shady organisations such as *Meibion Glyndwr*.

13 For example, the visit by members of *Cymdeithas* to Belfast and Sinn Féin to observe developments in the field of education through the medium of the Irish language in the city.

14 The then Secretary of State, John Redwood, fuelled fears in this respect by refusing to sign letters which had been translated by the Welsh Office's own translators and only signing the English copies.

15 The poll was actually commissioned by the Welsh Language Board and can be accessed through their internet site at http://www.netwales.co.uk/byig

first time this century, the biggest increase in Welsh-speakers is amongst children aged between 3-15.

Continuing Education in Wales: serving bilingual communities

Saunders Lewis in his radio lecture berated the University of Wales and its colleges as '*...an ironic and bitter tragedy*'[16] as far as the Welsh language was concerned. '*It was Welsh Wales which created it, supported it, doted upon its honorary degrees, and is satisfied that its diploma of honour is a token of the degree of the language's degradation.*' The University was, indeed, an early target of *Cymdeithas* with some of its members refusing to accept its degrees because of its attitude to the language and its anglicising influence upon the education system[17]. Nevertheless, the old extra-mural departments, together with the WEA in Wales, had a long tradition of providing classes in their communities through the medium of Welsh with emphasis on Welsh literature, culture and history. Many well known and respected figures in both Welsh literature and Welsh language campaigns have been lecturers in the extra-mural departments of the University of Wales, for example, Alwyn D. Rees, Ifan ab Owen Edwards, Meredydd Evans, Hywel Teifi Edwards to mention a few. Despite the recent changes in funding emphasis, this tradition of liberal community based Welsh medium teaching continues today (although as Gruffudd has argued[18], proper account needs to be taken of the generational and societal changes which have occurred in the demography of the language's speakers and, therefore, potential students, by the nineties).

One of the departments of continuing education in Wales' main contributions to the language campaign during the last twenty years, under the leadership of Chris Rees in Cardiff, has been the organisation and development

16 Jones & Thomas, op cit, p.133

17 A full analysis of the University, the Welsh language and its communities was presented in a paper by my colleague, Heini Gruffudd, to the UACE Conference held at Swansea in 1995: '*Cymuned, Iaith a'r Brifysgol*' and more recently in the Welsh language monthly *Barn*:'*Prifysgol Saesneg Cymru?*' The main thrust of the two pieces is that the University of Wales remains a factor in what socio-linguists call the language shift towards English in Wales and is failing to respond to the substantial increase in young people who have persued pre-higher education schooling through Welsh.

18 op cit (*Barn*) p.36

of an effective system of intensive second language programmes for adults based on the Ulpan system used in Israel to immerse its people in the Hebrew language[19]. Unlike many language programmes for adults, the system developed within the CE departments in Wales had as its primary objective that of enabling students to become fluent in Welsh as soon as possible and assimilating into the Welsh-speaking community. It has been particularly successful with students whose children receive Welsh medium education, those who have needed to learn the language for reasons of employment and those who have moved to Welsh-speaking areas (whether they be born in Wales or England) in addition to the many students who attend classes simply because they are Welsh and feel that they should speak their own language. Many successful students have consequently made valuable contributions themselves to the wider language campaign either by becoming tutors themselves, through their work, through contributing to their community through the medium of Welsh (thereby ensuring that it remains the language of that community) or by being able to aid the intergenerational transmission of language through using their acquired language with their own children. The learners' movement, as it is sometimes called, has contributed substantially to changing the stereotype of those who speak Welsh and where (if such a stereotype ever existed) and it has in turn enriched and infused Welsh culture with ideas which do not spring from a shared linguistic, and to a lesser extent, cultural background[20].

More recently, in response to the need for public bodies and business in Wales to respond to the Welsh Language Act, courses in literacy skills for first language speakers have been established. The situation in Wales is similar to that, for example, in the Basque Country where increased demand for competent speakers has been to some extent thwarted by the lack of native speakers with the necessary reading and writing skills in the minoritised language. According to the 1991 census, just over two-thirds of Welsh

19 For a review of the development of this provision and a student profile and motivation analysis see Morris, S. in Elliott, Francis, Humphreys & Istance (eds.) *Communities and their Universities* 'The Welsh Language and its Restoration: New Perspectives on Motivation, Lifelong Learning and the University' pp 148-163

20 Several of the officers of *Cymdeithas* during the past fifteen years have been learners, a learner has won one of the main poetic competitions in the National Eisteddfod and many successful learners currently hold posts where their command of Welsh is in daily use.

speakers are fully literate and able to read, write and speak the language. There is, therefore, a big potential for these courses and they also provide a fairly quick and cost-effective means of creating competent workers in public bodies and industry who are able to operate in both languages of Wales. Departments of CE have, however, been much slower to respond to the other important changes in the demography of the language during the last fifteen years. The 1991 census has shown that the percentage of young people speaking Welsh is growing and not just in the Welsh-speaking heartlands but also in the more anglicised south and north east of the country. There will therefore inevitably be a growing demand for vocational and continuing education courses of a varied and multi-curricular nature in all kinds of communities throughout Wales now and even more so in the future. As so often before in the course of the language's development, demand often follows supply and departments need to be reacting to this situation. There has been some headway on this in the further education sector but, to date, CE departments have been mute or lukewarm in their response to this challenge[21].

A future role for Continuing Education in a bilingual Wales

The potential for CE to respond to and initiate change is well documented and understood. The Welsh language has, and will always make, CE in Wales different to the rest of Britain. Ironically, the situation in Wales is often much better appreciated in other parts of the world such as Catalunya, the Basque Country, Belgium or Quebec than by its neighbour, England. Bilingualism is the norm in many other parts of the world and responding to the challenge it presents is a normal process of educational planning. For too long, the response by those with the power to be able to make a change in Wales has been to ignore one linguistic strand of national life entirely in favour of what has often been perceived as the more 'international' and economically beneficial allure of English. CE has frequently been a counterbalance to these trends in Wales but its role needs to be re-assessed in the light

21 Gruffudd, op cit. p.36

of the changes which have occurred in the Welsh-speaking cohort during the past thirty years. In particular:

- the already strong and effective contribution to intensive teaching of Welsh to adults needs to be strengthened and 'ring-fenced' in the current financial climate of higher education. The aim must be to facilitate the development of even more intensive courses (such as those offered in the Basque Country) of 2,000 hours a year as part of a national language policy which would encourage day-release from work or benefit allowances for those not in work.
- similarly, the already established programmes for Welsh language literacy should be expanded and made more available either in places of work or within communities. The role of CE in realising and facilitating the implementation of any language policy formulated to enhance these opportunities should be acknowledged.
- university CE also has an important role to play in carrying out research in these fields and informing language policy makers of potential areas for development in addition to assessing the success of the provision already offered. Valuable opportunities for joint research work exist within the European Union and further afield and much can be learnt from similar linguistic situations in other countries.
- serious consideration and developmental work should be initiated into the CE needs and potential in many other vocational and academic fields through the medium of Welsh, *in* the community. One approach might be through co-operation with colleges of further education and local language agencies (*mentrau iaith*). There are obvious financial and staff implications here but until this area of work has been seriously addressed and not ghettoised to those members of staff who happen to speak Welsh, a substantial cohort of students is being denied educational opportunities.

The last thirty years of language protest and campaigns in Wales have without doubt produced many successes which many today take for granted. They have directly, and indirectly, resulted in a change in the make-up and distribution of today's Welsh-speakers and like any other healthy culture/ language in the world, change is vital to the welfare and continuance of the Welsh language. The lessons learnt during this period have produced a language movement which is generally outward-looking and progressive[22]. The challenge for CE in Wales is to respond to these changes and create a Welsh medium programme in the communities of Wales worthy of the name *Prifysgol y Werin*.

References

Aitchison, J. and Carter, H. (1994), A Geography of the Welsh Language 1961 - 1991, Cardiff, University of Wales.

Carter, H. (1990), 'Dirywiad yr Iaith Gymraeg yn yr Ugeinfed Ganrif', Cof Cenedl V, 147-176.

Davies, J. (1993). The Welsh Language, Cardiff, University of Wales.

Davies, J. (1990), Hanes Cymru, Harmondsworth, Penguin

Morris, S. (1996), 'The Welsh Language and ist Restoration: New Perspectives on Motivation, Lifelong Learning and the University'

Elliott, J., Francis, H., Humphreys, R. and Istance, D. (eds.) (1996), Communities and their Universities: the Challenge of Lifelong Learning, London, Lawrence and Wishart.

Gruffudd, H. (1995), Cymuned, Iaith a'r Brifysgol, paper given at the UACE Conference, Swansea.

Gruffudd, H. (1996), 'Prifysgol Saesneg Cymru?'. Barn, 399, April 1996, pp 34-36

Herbert, T. and Jones, G. E. (eds.) (1995), Post-War Wales, Cardiff, University of Wales.

Jones, A. R. and Thomas, G. (1983), Presenting Saunders Lewis, Cardiff, University of Wales.

Thomas, N. (1991 new ed.), The Welsh Extremist, Talybont, Gwasg y Lolfa.

Tudur, G. (ed.) (1989), Wyt ti'n cofio?, Talybont, Gwasg y Lolfa.

Williams, G. A. (1985), When was Wales?, Pelican.

22 One example of this would be the National Union of Students in Wales who classify their Welsh language campaign as a *liberation* campaign i.e. similar to the womens campaign and has in its constitution a clause including language as one factor where discrimination is not acceptable.

Angela Franz-Balsen

Just Talking? Learning Processes in Intersectorial Alliances for Local Environmental Activities.

Introduction

Unconventional fast learning processes have been observed in the broad field of environmental communication for more than fifteen years (Peters 1993, Franz-Balsen, 1996). Normal citizens acquired in very short time detailed knowledge about environmental risks, they learned to organise themselves in protest against official planning etc. At the same time industrialists and government officials have learned to pay respect to public opinion, before they take decisions of environmental impact (Slovic, 1996). As the concept of mediation gained ground, it became more and more accepted by all the parties involved in environmental activities that an open dialogue can be more constructive than fighting.

All this is nowadays analysed in the new transdisciplinary scientific field called 'Risk analysis' or 'Risk research' (University of Surrey, 1996) but has been paid relatively little attention from the field of adult education. In the nineties, however, environmental adult education cannot overlook any longer the relevance of informal processes, by which both the citizens as target group of environmental communication and the communicators themselves acquire knowledge and abilities to push environmental activities in their locality.

The *'Clearinghouse of Environmental Education' in the 'German Institute of Adult Education'* (DIE - Deutsches Institut für Erwachsenenbildung, Frankfurt) has been observing and is still studying this shift to informal life-long-learning of individuals, which goes hand in hand with a shocking decrease in interest for institutionalised environmental adult education (Apel, 1996). The results of our observations indicate, however, that environmental adult education is now adapting to these changed conditions by exploring methods of furthering lifelong learning and participation of the target groups. This process of reorientation and reorganisation of environmental adult education implies that the multipliers themselves undergo learning processes (Franz-Balsen/Apel, 1995, Laube, 1995).

'Local Agenda 21' as a chance and framework for lifelong learning

Positive impacts on environmental communication/environmental education in this sense can be observed at the community level in the context of *'Local Agenda 21'*. As a result of the World-Conference on Environment and Development (Rio de Janeiro, 1992) a programme for action, the so-called *'Agenda 21'*, provides detailed information on how to organise a broad public discourse about Environment and Development and how to achieve participation of all public sectors before measures are taken. Chapter 28 of 'Agenda 21' was well received in most European countries. This addresses the community level. It proposes a consultation process between the local authorities and all relevant groups in order to work out a plan of urban environmental management, the so-called *'Local Agenda 21'*. The fascinating aspect of this chapter is that it focuses on pure communication, on *'just talking'* between different sectors as the first step towards understanding and achieving 'sustainability' at the local level.

The role of adult education

In a constantly growing number of German cities and towns intersectorial alliances between local authorities, NGOs, private enterprises and institutions were/are formed in order to put this into practice. All kinds of debate groups and round tables have to be formed and thematic work groups to be established. Only few of the cities and towns nowadays have funds to finance such extra-activities necessary for an Agenda-process. In this situation the municipal institutes of adult education and other institutions involved in environmental education offer manpower (moderation, organisation) and infrastructure (rooms and other facilities) for these meetings and events, thereby documenting a new understanding of what environmental education for adults can mean: just talking. The best known case is the

Volkshochschule München which serves as a model for other places (Agenda Transfer, 1996).

In co-operation with partners from municipal units, non-governmental organisations, private enterprises, religious and other associations a variety of arrangements for talking about 'Local Agenda 21' are now being tested from Hamburg to Munich, from Dresden to Aachen:

In some places, usually when it is a top-down initiative, the Agenda-process takes place behind closed doors. The broad public is not directly involved. The citizens are represented by delegates and other relevant parties. However, it does mean that there is a new combination of people brought together in round-tables, meetings and thematic workshops and regularly meeting working groups, that would probably not have gathered without the framework of 'Local Agenda 21'.

In the majority of cases, however, 'participation' is taken seriously in the sense that communication with the public is aimed at; press conferences, radio or television interviews, panel discussions, talk-shows or cultural events as the means to inform the citizens, workshops and other activities in towns as a means to involve them. Some of these new ways of environmental communication are a real challenge, both for the representatives from the local authorities and for the environmental educators and protagonists from environmentalists groups. Well-established barriers of communication have to be torn down. There is not the same distance any more, neither between conflicting parties nor between decision-makers and the public. Of course this is not at all easy to handle: one has to find a common language, confidence has to be built up, success has to be shared. The difficulties however result in the most effective learning processes for all the persons and sectors involved.

What is the new quality of learning through intersectorial communication ?

Analysed from the point of view of a theory of adult education, the new alliances which 'Local Agenda 21' generates at the community level, are a chance to put into practice 'old' aims of adult education like community-orientation and participation, and relatively 'new' aims like lifelong learning. They give us the opportunity to observe and evaluate learning processes of adults, which cannot be strictly ranked under the category of 'adult continuing education' in the sense of professional training, but which are increasing the competence of professionals and citizens in the environmental field and increasing their personal communicative abilities.

Using a kind of arbitrary division, one could analyse these learning processes as follows:

- *learning from each other*

At the community level the relations between citizens, environmentalists (including environmental educators), members of other non-governmental organisations, members of the municipality, politicians and industrialists have so far been characterised by an imbalance of power. Even if in the last years confrontation has generally been making room for dialogue, the communication and co-operation that is initiated within the framework of 'Local Agenda 21' is of a different quality in that it gives the different parties a similar rank. Hierarchical structures are blended out, at least temporarily. Experts are not defined by position, but by the real expertise of people, shining through in their contributions. So it might well happen that citizens or environmentalists are teaching administrators and decision-makers, coming up with information from other places or other countries not known before. There is also a transfer of professional methods and terminology taking place: on the one hand unconventional creative methods of working together or towards the public are shown to members of the municipal administration by the representatives of various associations and institutions. On the other hand the non-professionals in the field of urban affairs get an idea of professional urban or industrial management.

- *learning about each other*

Competing groups, as for instance ideologically different environmental or third-world -groups, or different units and departments within the municipality, cannot ignore each other in the context of 'Local Agenda 21' and have to think about joint projects. People, who did not talk to each other before, get personally acquainted and in many cases get rid of old prejudices. Womens' organisations, for instance, hope to finally find more acceptance for their experiences and ideas in local authority policies and practices (Life, 1996). The competence of others has to be acknowledged and used for this work. New contacts and alliances between institutions and persons generate new ideas and help to finance and realise projects which would have been declared illusory before.

- *learning together*

Even three to four years after the Rio-conference in 1992 the concept of 'sustainable development', which is the great aim of all the measures recommended in the 'Agenda 21' is still widely discussed and far from being understood. Also working out what 'Local Agenda 21' really means, how to organise the process in the community and to give it a structure is a complex task; even more if a newly formed group of people has to do that. It has been reported from many places that the people involved in 'Local Agenda 21' (from citizens to the mayor) invested many hours to study and discuss the new concepts in seminars, workshops, lectures or panel discussions. Of course people complain about these time-consuming activities, but at the same time admit that these learning arrangements have been very stimulating.

If the consultation process in a place has already reached the stage where citizens and their initiatives are involved in decision-making processes, still another quality of learning together appears: the 'fast learning processes' of lay people that want to inform themselves about issues that directly affect their everyday life or their future quality of life.

- *learning about oneself*

It is obvious that men or women actively involved in 'Local Agenda 21' have trained their personality in various respects. A normal citizen will have to develop other abilities than a professional, for instance self-confidence.

The communicative abilities the Agenda process teaches are of advantage for everyone.

- *learning to develop new professional perspectives*

For the professionals within or without the municipality the interdisciplinary work opens up new professional perspectives. These will be different in each case, but a common feature will certainly be that there will be more awareness for the political responsibility that everyone has in his/her job.

I want to specify this only for the field of adult environmental education/communication: environmental educators have since long been asked to offer less theory to their clients and to get more involved in local environmental issues (like the TU WAS-Projekt near Munich, Häusler 1996). It is their task to back up citizens in their wish to participate in urban planning and in other fields of local decision-making. 'Local Agenda 21' gives the communicators the opportunity to try out co-operation with new partners and to experiment with new communication channels, such as cultural events.

With the (good or bad) experiences of a consultation process as demanded by 'Local Agenda 21', environmental educators perhaps will shift their professional perspectives more towards the local level and closer to other social movements. Not everybody is fit for this kind of work. Therefore it is not surprising that quite a number of seminars and even longer qualification projects for multipliers are being offered, and there seems to be demand for them.

Perspectives of Investigation

The described intersectorial alliances are too young to have been thoroughly analysed and evaluated. The first studies, for example, the comparison between 'Local Agenda 21' in different places of Germany; the roles of certain actors; the importance of adult education, which we are investigating ourselves, have only just begun. As a result the 'state of the art' is mainly documentation and observation of what is happening. Both in the context of 'Lifelong learning' and in the context of 'sustainable development', the communication processes at the local level should be of interest to investigators from, for example, environmental sciences, adult education, sociology, psychology. The experiences of individuals will be as worth investigating as the systemic processes in the cities and towns as entities.

References

Agenda-Transfer (1996), München steigt ein, Stadtgespräche 00/96, pp 3-4.

Apel, H. (1996), Umweltbildung an Volkshochschulen, In: Internationales Jahrbuch der Erwachsenenbildung, Band 24, pp 103-119

Franz-Balsen, A./Apel, H. (1995), Professionalität und Psyche, Einsichten aus der Klimabildung, Deutsches Institut für Erwachsenenbildung, Frankfurt.

Franz-Balsen, A. (1996), Informationsvermittlung in der Umweltbildung oder, Über den Umgang mit Nichtwissen in Nolda, S, (ed), Erwachsenenbildung in der Wissensgesellschaft, Bad Heilbronn, Klinkhardt Verlag.

Häusler, R. (1996), Das TU WAS-Konzept als Antwort auf die traditionelle Erwachsenenbildung, (unpublished).

Laube, M. (1995), Umweltbildung vor der Neubestimmung, Hannover, Stiftung Leben & Umwelt.

Life, E. V. (1996), Frauenblicke auf die Lokale Agenda 21, Frankfurt, Tagungsdokumentation.

Peters, H. P. (1993), In search for opportunities to raise 'environmental risk literacy'. Toxicological and Environmental Chemistry, Vol. 40, pp 289-300.

Slovic, P. (1996), Wissenschaft, Werte, Vertrauen und Risiko in De Haan, G. (ed), Ökologie - Gesundheit - Risiko, Berlin, Akademie Verlag.

University of Surrey (1996), Risk in a modern society: Lessons from Europe. Conference Proceedings, Guildford.

Martin Ryle

Adult Education and New Social Movements: Teaching/ Learning Environmental Politics

My focus is on a specific question: how, in Britain[1] today, can we envisage future relationships between university adult education and environmental social movements? I aim also to offer a general view of relations between formal education institutions (especially their adult education departments) and 'new social movements'; and thus to contribute to the broad analytic enquiry, and policy debate, which this strand of the conference pursues.

University extra-mural education in Britain has offered a space within which excluded and marginalised groups have both sought access to existing educational provision, and attempted to challenge and redefine dominant knowledges and curricula. This experience of developing educational partnerships offers a basis for future educational collaboration between adult educators and environmental (and other) social movements. I argue that this aspect of *partnership*, already important in earlier interactions between educational institutions and social groups which sought or demanded participation, will become central in the future. Given the contested, socially differentiated and dispersed nature of 'knowledge' about environmental questions and policies, educational provision in this sphere cannot be seen as the delivery of knowledge. Indeed neither 'provision' nor 'delivery' are quite appropriate terms (though they are favoured terms in current educational policy discourses in Britain).

In conclusion, drawing on these reflections (and against the background of discussions with a number of groups and people engaged in environmental politics and environmental education),[2] I make some suggestions about possible future activities.

---

1 There are in fact significant differences between the situation, and the history, of university adult education as between England, Northern Ireland, Scotland and Wales. In this paper, which is cast at a general level, I use the term 'Britain', though some of the argument refers more especially to the English context.

2 I have discussed some of the questions this paper addresses with environmental activists in the Brighton area (Richard Welsh, a consultant developing the Brighton and Hove Community Environment

Adult education, social movements and civil society

The term 'civil society' denotes forms of association and collective practice which, while they exist within the public sphere, are distinct from the agencies of the state. Indeed their role, as represented (for instance) in some of the essays in John Keane's influential *Civil Society and the State*,[3] is precisely to guard against the over-extension of formal state power, and to preserve and extend the space for autonomous, critical discourses and initiatives. The 'new social movements' that have arisen in western Europe, complementing the established political parties and trade union movements, exist and seek to be effective within the space of civil society.[4] Their involvement in formal, state-sponsored political activity is usually limited (the Green Parties provide a significant exception to this rule: many of the internal difficulties that have beset them arise precisely from the tension between their participation in electoral politics and their autonomy as 'social movements'). Operating within the public sphere, they do not themselves seek authority even to implement reformist policies, let alone to 'seize power'. They must rely, then, on a long-term process of *education*, which would issue in new political majorities to take effect by way of the institutions of representative democracy.

By mounting campaigns and direct actions – to defend abortion rights, to highlight the presence of short-range nuclear missiles at Greenham Common, to delay or prevent the building of new roads, or to impede the dumping at sea of toxic wastes – the movements seek to affect public perception of the issues which they address. Direct actions may have an immediate concrete objective (unlikely, in many cases, to be successfully attained), but

Project; and activists involved with the production of *SchNews* - see the final section of this paper). I have corresponded, and talked informally, with fellow academics at Sussex with interests in environmental politics and new social movements: Luke Martell, Peter Dickens, and in particular Jenneth Parker, who teaches environmental courses to graduate and undergraduate students as well as in adult education. None of these people has seen this paper, however, and the views I express are my own.

3 Keane, *Civil Society* .

4 Martell and Melucci both emphasise the location of 'new social movements' within civil society and see this as a criterion for differentiating them from 'old' movements. Different definitions and emphases would be needed in any account of civil society and social movements in Eastern and Central-Eastern Europe. My focus in this essay is on social movements in western European societies with post-1945 traditions of representative democracy.

they aim primarily at modifying opinion. Shell altered its policy of disposing at sea of oil-drilling rigs not because the initial actions of Greenpeace made this physically impossible, but because they generated publicity which in turn led to a consumer boycott. This educational and cultural activity, whose importance is stressed by theorists of 'new social movements',[5] involves diverse agents and media, outside and within the movements. Campaigns and actions, reported and discussed in the press and through broadcasting, are 'texts' which inform the public and become the object of subsequent political discussion.The movements make the provision of information, and the stimulation of debate, a part of their own purposes. The well-established national and international organisations (Greenpeace, Friends of the Earth, the Worldwide Fund for Nature) appoint campaigns and information officers, but communication and publication, by words and through actions, are also essential activities for the informal, anarchistic grassroots eco-action networks at the other end of the spectrum.

New social movements, and perhaps especially the environmental movements on which this paper focuses, are already 'educational agencies'. Their characteristic mode is to challenge official governmental policy and/or established commercial practice. Formal institutions of education which sought to collaborate with the movements would be involving themselves in an existing project of critical and political education. This raises questions about the social production and use of knowledge, and the changing role of formal institutions within it, which I turn to shortly. It also raises, as earlier forms of political education have done, questions about the accountability of educational institutions and about academic objectivity. Is the formal 'academic freedom' of universities a real guarantee of autonomy, or does their dependence on public funding limit their ability to engage in critical projects: that is, are educational institutions part of civil society, or are they organs of the state? From another point of view, how can academic values of objectivity and impartiality be sustained once we enter these contested

5 See A. Melucci, 'Social Movements and the Democratisation of Everyday Life', in Keane (ed), pp. 258ff. See also Keith Jackson, 'Popular Education and the State', in Mayo and Thompson, esp. pp 195f.

areas?[6] In the British context, university adult education has been a sensitive terrain for the working out of such tensions. It has been one site, important just because it has been 'marginal', for struggles not only about the social accessibility but also about the content of higher education.

The contradictions I mention, between a culture of academic objectivity and a culture committed to political education, between institutions' claims of autonomy and the reality of government funding for HE, will nowadays be sharply felt in any project of environmental education. At a certain level of public policy, 'education about the environment' is no doubt agreed to be a 'good thing', in Britain as in Europe generally. However, 'the environment' is not a 'single issue' (even if many environmental campaigns focus on specific local or sectoral questions), and political ecology engages concerns and anxieties about the whole direction of contemporary societies, including fundamental moral and political questions about the nature of development and under-development. At the same time, certainly in Britain, there has been within the political establishment (and specifically the Parliamentary Labour Party, which no longer accommodates seriously dissenting voices) a general closing down of utopian and critical imagination. Explorations of alternatives to the capitalist market seem to have been driven beyond the margins of what is sayable even by social democratic politicians. A 'common sense' stress on economic competitiveness, growth, and what is 'best for Britain' is more dominant than at any time since the early 1960s.

In the field of education, this is registered (as many commentators document)[7] in a more and more vocationalist discourse: a stress on accreditation and 'progression' for individual learners, and on the economic (rather than cultural/social) purposes of education. Environmental education, especially insofar as it presents students with critiques of economic rationality, is part of a project of education for democratic citizenship rather than educa-

6 In their contributions to Taylor et al, *University Adult Education,* Roger Fieldhouse and Richard Taylor grapple with some of the tensions which arise in radical educational projects where practitioners seek to avoid one-sided teaching: see especially Chapters 3, 4 and 8.

7 See Mayo and Thompson, passim, especially the chapters by Marjorie Mayo, Tom Steele, David Alexander and Ian Martin, Wilma Fraser, and Keith Jackson (a particularly thoughtful contribution). For the earlier 'radical moment', see Thompson, *Adult Education for a Change.*

tion/training for work. It runs against both the micro-ideology of 'education for capability' and 'transferable skills', and the wider 'common sense' of established political discourse. For this reason, as well as because it should involve collaborative relationships with social movements 'outside the walls', environmental education fits well within the radical traditions of British university adult education.

Work with social movements must be integral to any attempt to contest the currently dominant redefinition of 'education' as preparation for merely *economic*, as opposed to social, participation. As Keith Jackson (1995) argues, 'there might be a concept (and associated practice) of an integrated education and training for civil society rather than the market, the outcomes of which would be seen in social development and democratic processes'.[8] In this wider concept, working with social movements would not simply provide space for particular 'movement' perspectives and policies; it would recreate and sustain possibilities of debate and argument between *dissenting* voices (including the quite diverse voices of the different cells/campaigns/organisations *within* the green movement). The 'old' radical project of advancing the claims of a particular social actor (or 'revolutionary subject'), which was problematic both politically and in terms of academic values of impartiality, would be complicated and qualified by its inclusion within a more 'neutral' and open-ended project of education for social participation and citizenship. I touch on these questions again, and suggest how in practice some of these tensions might be managed, in my concluding remarks.

Radicalism in British adult education

While I have no space to sketch a history of radical initiatives and projects in British university extra-mural education, it is worth isolating, and emphasising, some general points that emerge from that history.[9]

8 'Popular Education and the State', in Mayo and Thompson, p. 200.

9 I draw especially on Taylor and others, *University Adult Education*; Lovett (ed), *Radical Approaches*; Thompson (ed), *Adult Education for a Change*; and Elliott and others (eds), *Communities* For a contem-

We can distinguish two aspects of previous 'radical encounters' between extra-mural educators and social movements. One aspect has had to do with *access*: the right of excluded groups and individuals to obtain what was offered to their more privileged contemporaries. The other has had to do with *ownership*: the challenge which excluded groups might make to the curricula, disciplinary boundaries and cultural hierarchies embodied in dominant academic knowledges. Both aspects have been to the fore in the engagement of universities with those excluded from the mainstream, whether by class (workers' education, in which collaboration between the Workers' Educational Association and extra-mural departments was centrally important)[10] or by gender (in women's/feminist education, where adult education has played a perhaps less crucial but still significant role).[11]

Summarising, and simplifying, a complex history, it seems reasonable to observe that in its dominant twentieth-century institutional form, the partnership between extra-mural departments and the Workers' Educational Association (WEA), the participation of universities in 'workers' education' in Britain only partially and unevenly succeeded in raising issues of 'ownership' of the HE curriculum generally. Some recent commentators repeat the oft-voiced criticism that the WEA/extra-mural project amounted essentially to a 'missionary' endeavour: to dispense to the working masses the enlightenment of a largely unmodified middle-class culture.[12] Others argue that

porary overview which attempts both to evaluate and to sustain the radical project, see Mayo and Thompson. For developments in England in the first half of the twentieth century, see Blyth, *English University Adult Education.*

10 See Dobbs, *Education and Social Movements* ; and Richard Johnson, 'Really Useful Knowledge: Radical Education and Working-Class Culture, 1790 - 1848', in Clarke, Critcher and Johnson. For some of the later controversies, see the balanced survey by Geoff Brown, 'Independence and Incorporation: the Labour College movement and the Workers' Education Association before the Second World War' (in Thompson (ed), *Adult Education for a Change*).

11 See Jane L. Thompson, *Learning Liberation*; M. Owen and M. Price, 'Sitting Pretty? Women's Studies and the Higher Education Community', in Elliott and others, *Communities*; and the chapters by Julia Swindells and Jane Thompson in Mayo and Thompson.

12 Some of the relevant criticisms are cited in my chapter on 'Cultural Studies and Adult Learners' in Preston (ed), *Literature in Adult Education*. See (for instance) Ellwood, p. 48; Crombie and Harries-Jenkins, esp. pp. 59ff; and S. Westwood, 'Adult Education and the Sociology of Education: an exploration', in Thompson (ed), *Adult Education for a Change*.. The image of 'missionaries' (and 'cannibals') is in Raymond Williams, 'Adult Education and Social Change', published 1983, reprinted in McIlroy and Westwood (pp. 258 ff.).

these critiques are overdrawn.[13] The experience of 'extra-mural work' did have a cumulative impact in modifying the assumptions and disciplinary frameworks of the higher education mainstream: Raymond Williams, himself the single most influential figure in the post-war academic redefinition of 'culture' in Britain, argues that 'the birth of Cultural Studies', which registered a secular 'shift of perspective about the teaching of arts and literature and their relation to history and to contemporary society', 'began in Adult Education'.[14] Nonetheless one can suggest that the workers' movement, at least until the post-war expansion of secondary and higher education gave working class students – such as Williams himself – some (still limited) mainstream access to the prestigious formal institutions, remained in a deferential relation to 'education': the confidence to raise questions of ownership was limited.

In terms of the wider conceptual framework I am seeking to establish, we can note that unlike earlier movements (such as that for working-class education), the 'new social movements' tend to draw on the expertise of activists who possess a high level of formal education.[15] This was an important aspect in the post-1960s development of feminist teaching and scholarship. Second-wave feminism, paradigmatically a 'new social movement' in its orientation towards changing consciousness and culture, was also paradigmatic in that its founding 'organic intellectuals' (de Beauvoir, Greer, Millett, Firestone) possessed, and made use of, formally accredited knowledge. Feminist academic work from the start broached fundamental questions about the content of 'knowledge': 'work done from feminist perspectives challenged the theoretical frameworks, key assumptions, epistemologies, methods and findings of the patriarchal establishment'.[16] This challenge was mounted partly from *within* the institutions that produced and validated knowledge. But the knowledge that feminists within the academy have pro-

13 See Geoff Brown, cit. (note 10 above); and Kenneth O. Morgan, '*Y Brifysgol a'r Werin*: the People's University', in Elliott and others (eds), *Communities*, p. 5.

14 Williams, in McIlroy and Westwood, p. 260.

15 See Martell, *Ecology and Society*, p. 116, p. 127 (and see his chapter 4, 'The Green Movement', for the sociology of environmental movements). Scott notes that the new movements tend to be based in the 'new middle class' (p. 155). Melucci claims that 'militants and activists in social movements are typically recruited from those who are highly integrated into the social structure' (*Nomads*, p. 35).

16 Owen and Price, in Elliott and others, p. 165.

duced continues to validate itself at least partly through the conviction that it can benefit those 'outside the walls'. The relationship between women's education as a broad political project and the development of academic feminism is by no means straightforward: in recent years, Jane Thompson argues, under the baneful influence of postmodernist theory, feminism in the academy has moved 'away from being a subversive social movement' and is becoming 'a cerebral, inward-looking elite activity'.[17] Nonetheless, despite these tensions, feminist knowledge and scholarship must continue to hold themselves accountable to a political constituency (or social movement) as well as to the institution. Thus while feminist education continues to seek to overcome the historical exclusion of women from higher education, this aspect (*access*) has been intertwined inextricably with the aspect of *ownership*.

Beyond 'provision' and 'delivery': spaces for environmental education

Feminism has been one, particularly powerful, agent in a more general social-cultural process, which must replace the notion of a centre which owns and diffuses established knowledge with the notion of a cultural space within which knowledge is created though contestation. At the same time, the proliferation of 'information', in the whole range of media, spells the end of any idea of a comprehensive, once-for-all repository of knowledge, within *any* set of walls. Academic specialists are no longer able to keep track of (let alone read) publications even in their own specialisms. Within the sub-culture of eco-politics, quite marginal movements and campaigns have been quick to set up e-mail addresses and Internet home pages,[18] complementing the established presence in print and broadcast media of mainstream organisations such as Greenpeace or Friends of the Earth. Thus both social and technological changes have created conditions in which what was once a

17 'Feminism and Women's Education', in Mayo and Thompson, p. 133.

18 For instance, the campaign against the Newbury bypass can be contacted at *roadalert@gn.apc.org*. The British radical monthly *Red Pepper* lists (in its 'paper' edition) electronic addresses and sites for a range of campaigns, and has its own home page which gives information about many more.

radical educational-cultural project – the 'decentring' of formally established education, the dispersal of knowledge to a host of social actors – is in some senses a *fait accompli*.

This is not, of course, to claim that 'everyone', or even any kind of majority, now has access to the full range of educational opportunities. 'Access' is still an item on any radical continuing education agenda. In my own view, however, work with 'social movements' nowadays is *not* primarily, if at all, about access. Adult education with the actors who work within and around the edges of the new social movements will differ from as much as it will resemble earlier partnerships. The 'potential students' (to use the standard term) will almost certainly not feel themselves to be deprived of education, or cultural capital, in general. In many cases they may well be especially engaged with and knowledgeable about the topic of the 'course' they are taking. In this setting, the role of educators must lie in offering a space, and some tools, for making that knowledge useful. This is what Alberto Melucci (1989) envisages when he speaks (in *Nomads of the Present)* of 'public spaces': asked to elaborate on his claim that new forms and institutions of representation are needed in complex societies, to complement formal political processes and offer openings for social movements to work democratically, Melucci notes that 'among the most important [of these public spaces which need further development] would be knowledge-producing institutions, such as universities, cultural foundations and research institutes'.[19] As well as offering literal and metaphorical space (a meeting place, but also public funding and formal accreditation of learning), educators will, one hopes, have expertise and experience in proposing conceptual frameworks and discursive procedures by which to organise, understand and debate what is at stake. Of course the procedures and frameworks are themselves contestable and it will be part of an appropriate pedagogy to encompass that contest too.

In the development of this kind of work, there are both practical and political reasons for thinking that continuing education (CE) has a particular role to play.

---

19 *Nomads*, p. 228.

Practically, even now that CE in Britain is subject to quite cumbrous procedures for course approval, student registration and 'quality assurance', CE programmes are relatively easy to set up, and offer flexibility in modes of 'delivery' (part-time and short courses, run in various locations and outside conventional timetables). Politically, the notion of partnership, in which the institution collaborates with other agencies, is well established in CE. The reality of a diverse and plural economy of knowledge, in which the university is not so much the source of information as the agent for its contested and problematic social (re)production, can be reflected in the explicit practice of CE departments more readily perhaps than in mainstream undergraduate programmes. CE work can offer an interestingly different setting for academic social scientists and political theorists interested in and sympathetic to environmental and other new social movements: one in which the latter are explicitly and actively involved not as 'objects of knowledge' but as agents of its creation.

Some conclusions

From a personal, and departmental, point of view, the opportunity to reflect on these questions has also been an opportunity to begin exploring the possibilities for developing more substantial on-the-ground provision of environmental education. Both in its extra-mural programme[20] and in some undergraduate and postgraduate courses, the University of Sussex is already active in this area; and in the region (as elsewhere) there is a range of environmental activism. This ranges from grass-roots, eco-anarchist direct action (in preparing this paper I had interesting conversations with people involved in producing *SchNews*, Brighton's 'do-it-yourself campaigns' newsletter) to educational/community initiatives supported by the local authorities. The role of adult education, in that context, begins with identifying the network of common interests, inside and outside the academy, and providing opportunities for dialogue. Out of that, educational work may develop. I conclude

20 See the paper (in this strand of this conference) by my colleague Jenneth Parker,

by noting some guiding principles which should inform future work, and which reflect both the practical possibilities that exist, and the underlying educational/political orientation that is needed.

1 Even though in important respects we may need to break with the notion of 'courses delivered to students', environmental CE should be offered within the 'mainstream' framework of CE provision. This will ensure that it attracts resources, is of assured quality, and offers participants a properly demanding and appropriately accredited educational experience.

2 The role of the University will be to activate and co-ordinate a *network*. This will comprise interested academics; activists from various parts of the broad environmental movement (such as eco-campaigners, conservation and wildlife bodies, development charities); other public educators; and also, local enterprises and employers, especially those whose activities have a clear environmental focus or impact.

3 On the basis of discussions within the network, programmes of general public education can be offered. There may also be possibilities for developing the expertise of the network itself, within a programme of accredited learning – for example through the establishment of regular seminar meetings.

4 The CE department will need to appoint teachers – *conveners* is perhaps a better word – to develop specific programmes, and (by facilitating sessions/seminars/classes) to ensure that the modes of debate and learning allow for serious academic work: in particular, by pressing for underlying concepts and questions to be fully articulated. A further responsibility will be to seek the representation of a wide and diverse range of opinions and social positions. The expertise of the department, and the convener, needs to include an element of 'knowledge about the environment', but is above all an expertise in the facilitation of good and appropriately balanced debate.

5 It would be good to develop and sustain a wider, revitalised CE project of 'education for social participation', both as a context for this and other particular collaborative developments, and as a much-needed, explicit challenge to narrowly conceived vocationalism. 'Society, not

just the market' is a slogan of vital importance to the future both of education and of the environment.

References

Blyth, J. A. (1983), English University Adult Education 1908 - 1958, Manchester: Manchester U.P.

Clarke, J., Critcher, C. and Johnson, R. (1979), Working-Class Culture: Studies in History and Theory, London, Hutchinson.

Crombie, A. D. and Harries-Jenkins, G. (1983), The Demise of the Liberal Tradition, Leeds: University of Leeds Dept of Adult Education.

Dobbs, A. E. (1919), Education and Social Movements 1700 - 1850, London, Longmans Green.

Elliott, J., Francis, H., Humphreys, R. and Istance, D. (eds) (1996), Communities and their Universities: the Challenge of Lifelong Learning, London, Lawrence and Wishart

Ellwood, C. (1977), Adults Learning Today, London, Sage

Keane, J. (ed) (1993: first publ. 1988), Civil Society and the State: New European Perspectives, London, Verso.

Lovett, T. (ed) (1988), Radical Approaches to Adult Education: a reader, London and NY, Routledge

McIlroy, J. and Westwood, S. (eds) (1993), Border Country: Raymond Williams in Adult Education, Leicester, NIACE.

Martell, L. (1994), Ecology and Society: an Introduction, Cambridge, Polity.

Mayo, M. and Thompson, J. (eds) (1995), Adult Learning, Critical Intelligence and Social Change, Leicester, NIACE.

Melucci, A., Keane, J. and Mier, P. (1989), Nomads of the Present: Social Movements and Individual Needs in Contemporary Society, London, Hutchinson Radius.

Preston, P. (ed) (1995), Literature in Adult Education: Reflections on Practice, Nottingham University Dept. of Adult Education.

Scott, A. (1990), Ideology and the New Social Movements, London, Unwin Hyman.

Taylor, R., Rockhill, K. and Fieldhouse, R. (1985), University Adult Education in England and the USA: a reappraisal of the liberal tradition, London, Croom Helm,

Thompson, J. L. (ed) (1980), Adult Education for a Change, London, Hutchinson.

Thompson, J. L. (1983), Learning Liberation: Women's response to men's education, London, Croom Helm.

Ritva Lindroos

Citizenship as an Environment for Lifelong Learning

My research project involves three main investigations, all focusing on the problematics of individuals and communities. The communities of my research are (a) the workplace, (b) the home district and (c) the network of small entrepreneurs.

The role played by the citizen in my research is interesting because it is associated with activities endeavouring to clear a space for autonomy and freedom under circumstances which are experienced as ordained from without and based on necessity. This applies at least to the investigations of mental violence in working life and of the social impact of nuclear power. The broad theoretical-philosophical framework of my research is communicative activity with reference to the theory of communicative activity of Habermas (1981). When the systems of understanding and symbolic activity forming the vehicle of the living world of the individual are no longer adequate for the powers of economy and administration, state bureaucracy and publicity, then they begin to break down and the living world of the individual begins to contract. The 'authentic' areas of the living world are reduced. This line of development contains the danger that the minimisation of real individualism will not suffice to produce the sense and motivation potential needed for the democratic and enlightened development of society. It is interesting and important to do research in the fields of human autonomy and authentic activity. If aims of this kind were to be imposed, then there would also be discussion of the educational objectives of adult education and of its organisation (lifelong learning). An increase in autonomy in the sphere of adult education might be held to be necessary on account of many factors (structural changes in the economy and production, unemployment and the need for new jobs, environmental pollution and degradation, the protection of human rights). The tasks of education would not, therefore, be exclusively technical-economic but would also exert a communicative-rational influence.

Adult education should be a science with an interpretative and enlightening capacity. In the research programmes and pedagogical activities of adult education basic problems of education ought to be thematised, the conditions for reflexive self-control by the individual ought to be investigated and developed, expert input and the everyday behaviour of individuals ought to be brought together in research and in pedagogy. It should also be possible to achieve communicativeness and common definitions of situations. I hope to be able to combine these various demands in my research.

I The Fields of Investigation

1 My first project investigates communities as the environments of the individual from the perspective of special problematics. This investigation, which has been completed and is awaiting publication, deals with mental violence in communities and working collectives. The investigation is to be annexed to the broader trend of research into violence in working life.

In this investigation I have been able to construe empirically the adult traditionally striving to develop her/himself and her/his work and the contradictions to which such individuals have been driven in communities where those who study are neither esteemed nor supported and in which they have ended up on the fringes of the workplace. Interpreted in the Bourdieu manner, they have, in the area of work, become embroiled in a struggle for symbolic, cultural, economic and social capital in which, on the basis of their experience, competing cultures would appear to have been other kinds of cultures of participation. When there is also a stratification battle going on simultaneously for economic sectors, there is a concentration on competition for those forms of dominance whereby the field may be controlled. The competing cultures easily develop scapegoats, the lynching of whom purges the culture (Girard 1977). It is my impression that my research subjects as individuals are bearers of rather traditional values such as honesty and diligence. In its present form their choice of mode of life and of lifestyle values is representative of advanced culture (Schulze 1992). Their modes of life have, on average, involved studying and higher cultural pursuits. They are living a biographical tradition which, in adult education, is called self-development. In Finnish fashion these are traditional values, as children from worker and peasant homes have traditionally moved both geographically and socially within society by means of education (Antikainen, Huotelin 1996). For them, studying has also had a considerable lifestyle-value. The significance of studying has thus not been limited solely to the instrumental. Talent combined with biographical traditions has undoubtedly been important in the formation of modes of life. In working communities they have been set on opposing sides due to their educational pursuits. Those who participated in my research appear to have hit upon cultural contradictions of a kind in which the content is composed of their own lifestyle materials (self-development as a biographical tradition) and the other kinds of rules of community convention in which, on the basis of reports, their mode of life is at least not esteemed. On the contrary, it has become the object of open derision, envy and challenge. Those who develop themselves are turned into scapegoats who have criticised the working community and done other kinds of things. Thus one is able to preserve one's own status and to resist the symbolic, or perhaps even real, threat of one's own exclusion.

I have conceptualised community processes using the idea of the uniformity of a community in which the discussion of authority and of cultures of dependency in a postmodern society (Giddens 1991) comprise the principal content. In this kind of theoretical and qualitative context I describe how the rules of operation in a community are turned into principles in communities. The most important thing in the formation of principles appears to be the investing of disputes with authority. On the basis of the material the greater part of disputes in working communities seem to be merely apparent conflicts for which no factual solution is desired. In my interpretation the investing of matters with authority explicitly emphasises the exercise of power, on the one hand as enabling status and on the other as enforcing character. In the collapse of the structures of working life, the increase of flexibility and, on the other hand, the delineation of permanent and temporary employment there is, besides the criteria of objective definitions, an emphasis on criteria which are subjective and based on agreement. The struggle for benefits becomes, in the end, a contest of natures. The participation cultures of communities may be constructed on necessities which are maintained artificially and discursively by violently inhibiting the personal growth of individuals and, on the other hand, in a manner stressing uniform adaptation to communities and to society. I have considered these matters as issues for the individual and for citizenship while on the other hand also for the expert.

The research is a participatory operational investigation in which I have arranged joint meetings in order to acquire information about progress in the research and in order to discuss interpretations. With the completion of the research begins an operational phase including efforts to discuss the problematics of the research with a broad public and to influence political decision-making in matters of legislation.

2 The second subject of my research is the social impact of nuclear power. The concrete environment of the investigation comprises the coastal area of east Uusimaa to the east and west of the town of Loviisa. The area has long been populated by Swedish-speaking Finns to whom the nuclear power industry has brought newcomers from elsewhere in Finland. At the end of 1970 the town of Loviisa had a population of 6984 (53% Swedish-speaking). By 1979 the population was 8895 (42% Swedish-speaking), rising to 8694 (41.5% Swedish-speaking) in 1986 and 7758 (40.6% Swedish-speaking) in 1996. The largest single factor in the change of language proportions was the arrival of the nuclear power industry in the area. The nuclear power station is the largest single employer in Loviisa (presently 460 jobs). The distribution of livelihoods (by places of work) is as follows: 0.8% agriculture and forestry, 35.3% industry, 3.8% construction operations, 60.1% service sector. The present rate of unemployment is high at 20.9%. According to statistics for July 1996, unemployment in the rural districts falling within the Loviisa Manpower Services District varied between 14% and 17.5%. The arrival of the nuclear power station in the area has had a negative impact on its traditional fishery business.

The operational environment of my investigation comprises the Miljoringen Environment Association, a voluntary environmental protection organisation. The association maintains an information service on the effects of nuclear power. It has about sixty members, most of whom are Swedish-speaking.

On the basis of interaction and experience gained so far I have begun to analyse the activities of the association as a local movement. There are a few activists working in the association who are specialised in nuclear power issues. The majority are involved out of a sense of local solidarity. Two kinds of research perspectives into the association are possible: (1) the local movement as the regenerator of traditions and (2) as activity opposed to nuclear power. The latter of these includes the evaluation of individual and biographical effects as well as the social and regional effects of the activity.

The research materials have been gathered in part.

3 The third subject of my research is small-scale enterprise. The investigative perspective is a culturally organised enterprise in networking and in vocational education. I have earlier published a work comprising biographies of entrepreneurs and vocational endurance (1995). In that investigation I considered, on the basis of empirical materials, individual, social and regional departure points for enterprise, endurance as an entrepreneur, the acquisition of vocational skills and approaches thereto and the networked economy as an environment for enterprise as well as the relationship of transition in society and working life and of training as a theoretical interpretation.

In my doctoral research (1993) I considered unemployment, albeit chiefly from the participant's viewpoint and experience. In my research into enterprise, I am indirectly dealing with the conditions for new jobs or new work. The investigation of the person, individual, social and vocational behaviour of the entrepreneur is a central element in my research. In connection with this I am investigating the conditions for successful enterprise. According to my interpretation, new enterprise is a matter of shifting from traditional (sole) trading to networked enterprise. A successful small enterprise is thus also interested in environments and networks, local, regional, national and international (export enterprises). In what way do education, networks and other matters form layers in success?

The investigation is located geographically in eastern Uusimaa.

The economist Paula Kyro (1995) has evaluated the significance of my earlier entrepreneur research in the following terms:

> 'As was stated earlier, a common way is to classify scientific approaches to enterprise into the investigative points of view offered by economics, sociology and psychology ... These three approaches are now being joined by a newcomer, a pedagogical approach. Perhaps the adult education business which has taken off in the current social situation has also begun to annexe the examination of enterprise in connection with unemployment. Tales and careers of enterprise have also begun to interest this group of researchers as an option for the future.'

During the remainder of 1996 I shall concentrate on compiling material.

II Materials and Modes of Conceptualising

Biographies. The basic materials in these various investigations are those of biography and accounts of working life. Building on Fritz Schutze's methodological foundation (1981, 1984, 1987), I have developed the methodology of biography-based research in my doctoral thesis (1995). The research interviews are of narrative character and I also employ the idea of Schutze's life process theories as an analytical tool, even though I make no direct investigation of life processes. Biography analysis yields analyses of the biographically mediated terms of individual activity as a citizen, an individual and a professional.

The network: my research into violence in working life has partially progressed within the networks of those studied. On the basis of old social relationships an activity has developed for this in which new concepts are created and a new environment is formed. New members have joined the network from outside through spontaneous contact. A network has operated in the investigation, the members of which function or have functioned in widely varying environments, have served in very different occupations, moved around through various kinds of education and status representing differing linguistic and cultural groups (Finnish and Swedish-speaking Finns). As a community, the network enables various people to work together in a quite surprising manner.

In the investigation into the social impact of nuclear power the basic network comprises those working within the association. The network is not limited to a single geographical district; a few publicly-known figures are involved in its activities.

No enterprise research network has yet formed for my investigation.

The networks are communities of participants and I also study them as communities. For the individual participant, activity in the network may be the realisation of a life policy (the term comes from Giddens 1991) which becomes an operating strategy.

The basic communities: the participants have their roots in the basic communities or in the old communities. Workplaces and the local district (the tribal lands) are typical old communities. Individuals have learned to live in stable social organisations or hierarchies.

Discourses and publicity: when new important issues are discussed on the networks an effort may be made to bring them to public attention. This gives rise to published materials such as press articles, the argumentational structure of which I shall analyse. The discussions which go on within the networks are the everyday material of my research and may be conceptualised as discourses.

Lifelong learning: my research as analysing lifelong learning and producing theory.

III Lifelong Learning in the Regeneration of Traditions

My principal interpretation of lifelong learning in the context of my own research is that lifelong learning is the regeneration of traditions. The conclusion arising from this is that traditions may teach us something about lifelong learning (a) as biographical traditions and (b) as social, societal, cultural and economical traditions. The aims of my research are pragmatic and theoretical to produce a theory of lifelong learning.

Based on my first investigation, the object of inspection is the Finnish tradition whereby the children of peasant and working class homes have become geographically and socially mobile through education. In my research (1996) I have found a principle in which studying has become a biographical tradition. Considerable subjective significance has been vested in the scholarly way of life. This observation is interesting from the point of view of lifelong learning because they have been caught up in the tradition of self-development and continue it. On a theoretical interpretation, with their biographies they confront modernised biographies which are more devoid of tradition and which repeat dependencies more characteristic of compulsion (Giddens 1991).

From characterisation to activity

In my research I have considered the question of the disappearance of the individual in the original individualistic sense (Saul 1993). In the human characterisation of adult education individualism is regarded mainly as a humanist concept of the individual. Individualism is a heterogeneous concept but may be associated, for example, with the following value extensions: the dignity of the individual, privacy, autonomy and self-improvement. Privacy is an absolute condition of liberty. The autonomy of the individual is the capacity to be free. Self-improvement is an ethical imperative (Hautamaki, 1996: 21-27). I would consider that the subjects of my research have sketched a very powerful humanist model of the individual for this investigation, in which the individual has free will and sense is the instrument thereof. However, the person her/himself is not 'empty' in the behaviourist sense, as the product of circumstances (in the sense of being governed by dependencies). On the contrary, this is the characterisation from which they have sought to distance themselves. The opposite of the completely free and open is the deterministic, the predetermined. One may flee from fate or it may be confronted and an effort may be made to change it. Self-improvement is an obligation from the cultural point of view and, for the individual, represents spiritual growth: the refinement of one's own authenticity.

As opposites, I characterise the person who is 'independent' and the one who is 'dependent on circumstances'. The 'independent' subjects of my research have got into difficulties: those who seek self-improvement and those who go along with the old tradition of education have been excluded at work and in life generally. At the same time the significance of studying and self-development has been called into question in (working) communities. This contradiction is of theoretical interest and is challenging in many ways, even though it is not yet theoretically possible to generalise from its empirical basis. Are we already living at the end of the educational project, when we should re-evaluate the foundations of (adult) education and make decisions about (a) deliberately abandoning the project or (b) re-embarking upon it and regenerating it? At least at the present stage my ideas of lifelong education are bringing about an interpretation of adult education as a regenerator of traditions. Because of this, my concepts are functional and pragmatic: biographies, discourses, basic communities, networks, activity. At the same time I am seeking to construct each of my own investigations as a participatory and participating investigation of activity.

Competencies in activity

A scholarly way of life as subjectively significant has not flourished along with the growth of education and participation, even among the educated. Finnish research into lifelong learning (Antikainen et al. 1996) has shown that rather the opposite is generally true.

'The development of an ideal into something self-evident follows the generation line of Finnish society. It may be concluded on the basis of this line of development that an increase in the 'objective' (institutional) importance of education has not been followed by an increase in its 'subjective' significance. On the other hand, the principal categories indicate a change in society from the scarce educational opportunities and struggle for a material experiential environment of the war years all the way to the symbolic experiential environment of the young educated cohorts, in which the personal self and its pursuits have become the core of what is significant' (Kauppila 1996: 47).

I also noticed this point in my doctoral thesis, even if I did not at that point investigate the generation importance of education. In my research I analysed such matters as operational competencies as an aspect of functional orientation and socialisation. Hurrelmann (1986: 14) has defined socialisation as a lifelong process of development of the personality which is realised by individuals when certain material-social terms prevail.

Hurrelmann's view is basically operation-theoretical. The individual integrates into her/his activity the terms provided by the environment. Hurrelmann describes socialisation as the relations obtaining between operational competencies and activity. Hurrelmann's concept of activity is one of deliberate, autonomously dirigible, objective-oriented, planned and intentional activity (ibid. 1986:171). Broadly understood operational competencies are abilities and capacities which are available to the individual and adaptable, and which may be used to conceptualise an external reality (ibid., 160). The individual encounters challenges in the social world which s/he understands in linguistic, moral-ethical, social, cognitive aesthetic and emotional ways.

'The cognitive operational competencies' turned out for the most part to be subordinate to the instrumental significance (of work). If the instrumental values (of work) are, for one or another reason rejected, then the development/use of intellectual-cognitive abilities will also not be felt to be of particular importance. The qualities of the knowledge relationship were (1) the acquisition of knowledge is not felt to be significant, (2) it is confined experientally by what is beyond the limits of our own opportunities, (3) knowledge has a problem-centred importance in the construction of everyday practices (academically trained housewives), (4) knowledge is functional from the point of view of working life, and (5) knowledge has a significance which is exclusively its own. The last of these alternatives would seem to be realised only in those lives which are constructing knowledge projects, that is, in those of scientists.

Amid the biographical interviewees of my thesis, those who had experienced unemployment or through illness came to be excluded from working life, the ethical-moral, aesthetic and social operational competencies were felt to be of greater significance than the cognitive operational competencies. The basis for several biographies was in a fundamental Finnish story, in ideology, in religion, in political or even in kinship stories. The ethical-moral values arose from this foundation.

This may also be interpreted as traditionalism. The basic stories of the more successful were social and the social competencies were emphasised (see also Hurrelmann 1986). These stories brought out their own abilities and opportunities as well as their efforts to govern social relations as a means of success. They also did not thematise the absolute significance of matters, but rather their flexibility. In my thesis the ethical and social were opposing strategies and were contained in different modes of life management. The ethical-moral dimension was dominant in institutional living processes and in those realising processes of social change (Schütze 1981).

'Social' life management could be regarded as central to the so-called project of the emancipatory reflexive self which is currently the principal and dominant theme in Finnish adult education. The community is a necessary condition of subjective identity in the modern organisation. At the same time an entirely egotistical individual is required. The development of the community is a rational intelligible self-interest for individuals and is a means for them to survive. The individual decides whether and how s/he will rest on the available solidarity (Lohmann, 1996: 6). The social character of the agent is that of the 'gambler' (Bauman, 1993 and 1995).

The significance of knowledge, activity and learning.

Finnish society has traditionally valued education and knowledge. There is general anxiety about cultural degeneration but it is probably also appropriate to take an interest in educational life management. It cannot be presumed that knowledge in the postmodern everyday practice will be based on the rules of scientific reasoning, for example, on a striving for truth. On the other hand, some of the sciences have also begun to live in textual forms forming their arbitrary significance with no effort made to get at any reality external to the text. The growth of mass media orientation has ushered in increasingly superficial and arbitrary meanings for things. The point of view known as social constructionism has become one of the dominant methodological positions in research in the social sciences. The investigation of discourse is thus a natural approach to the rules of knowledge formation and the significance of knowledge. In my own research I seek to investigate the argumentation contained in discourses and to compile argumentational analyses in which newspaper writing forms the basis. The share of this kind of material has a central status beside biographical materials, especially in my research into nuclear power. A symbolic environment for operation is created by discourses. Commitments to action are undertaken or not undertaken on the basis of the significance of the action.

Biographical orientations have been constructed at the individual level in order to realise orientations which could, on the basis of the characterisation of general phenomenological sociology, be termed an assimilation of time, place and social factors (Schütz, A., and Luckmann, P, 1979). Depending on their life histories, people live with various self-evidences. Various time orientations have also been constructed in biographies (Voges 1987, Brose 1985). It has been observed that they realise success-modernity; future-orientations in different ways. While people are nowadays living a success orientation, it may also be characterised as a traditional time perspective which realises stability (success) or instability (failure) in its efforts at continuity or to the continuation of a successful tradition (continuity at work or in other social relations, a career in one enterprise, a life in one locality). This takes the form of a basic model of traditional life in the community. The power of traditional biographies lies in their ability to reform a tradition or traditions; to maintain their vitality. The departure points and goals of adult education would correspondingly lie in the reform of the individual and the social living world.

References

Antikainen, A. and Huotelin, H. (ed) (1996), Oppiminen ja elämänhistoria. Aikuiskasvatuksen 37. vuosikirja. Kansanvalistusseura ja Aikuiskasvatuksen Tutkimusseura.

Bauman, Z. (1993), Postmodern Ethics, Oxford, Blackwell.

Bauman, Z. (1995), Life in Fragments. Essays in Postmodern Morality, Oxford, Blackwell.

Brose, H. G. (1985), Die Bedeutung der Zeitdimension für die Analyse des Verhältnisses von Arbeit und Persönlichkeit in Hoff, E. H., Lappe, L. and Lempert, W. Arbeitsbiographie und Persönlichkeitsentwicklung, Stuttgart, Verlag Hans Huber, pp 142-153.

Giddens, A. (1991), Modern and Self-Identity, London, Polity Press.

Girard, R. (1977), Violence and the Sacred, Baltimore and London.

Habermas, J. (1981), Theorie des kommunikativen Handelns. Band 1 & 2, Frankfurt am Main, Suhrkamp Verlag.

Hautamäki, A. (1996), Indidualismi on humanismia. Teoksessa: Hautamäki, A. & Lagerspetz, E. & Sihvola, J. & Siltala, J. & Tarkki, J. Yksilö modernin murroksessa. Helsinki, Gaudeamus, pp 13-44.

Hurrelmann, K. (1986), Einführung in die Sozialisationstheorie. Uber den Zusammenhang von Sozialstruktur und Persönlichkeit. Weinheim und Basel, Betltz Verlag.

Kauppila, J. (1996), Koulutus elämänkulun rakentajana in Antikainen, A. and Huotelin, H. (ed), Oppiminen ja elämänhistoria. Aikuiskasvatuksen 37. vuosikirja. Kansanvalistusseura ja Aikuiskasvatuksen Tutkimusseura.

Kyrö, P. and Nissinen, H. (1995), Yrittäjyys markkinarakenteessa. Helsingin kauppakorkeakoulun julkaisuja.

Lindroos, R. (1993), Työ, koulutus, elämänhallinta. Elämäkertatutkimus työllisyyskoulutukseen osallistuneiden työorientaatioista. Tutkimuksia 136. Helsingin yliopiston kasvatustieteen laitos.

Lindroos, R. (1995), Yrittäjien työelämäkerrat ja ammatissa selviytyminen. Työministeriö. Työpoliittisia tutkimuksia 103/1995.

Lindroos, R. (1996), Kiusaamisen kurjuus yhteisöissä ja työyhteisöissä. (julkaisematon)

Lindroos, R. (1995), Yrittajien tyoelamakerrat ja ammatissa selviytyminen. Tyoministerio. Tyopoliittisia tutkimusia.

Saul, J. R. (1992, 1993), Voltaire's bastards. The Dictatorship of Reason in the West. New York, Vintage Books.

Schulze, G. (1992), Die Erlebnisgesellschaft - Kultursoziologie der Gegenwart. Frankfurt, Campus Verlag.

Schütz, A. and Luckmann, T. (1979), Strukturen der Lebenswelt. Band 1. Frankfurt am Main, Suhrkamp Verlag.

Schütze, F. (1981), Prozesstrukturen des Lebenslaufs. In: Matthes, J. & Pfeifenberger, A. & Stosberg, M. (Hrsg.) Biographie in handlungswissenschaftlicher Perspektive. Nürnberg: Verlag der Nürnberger Forschungsvereinigung e.V.

Schütze, F. (1984), Kognitive Figuren des autobiographischen Stegreiferzählens. In: Kohli, M. & Robert, G. (Hrsg.) Biographie und soziale Wirklichkeit. Neue Beitäge und Forschungsperspektiven. Stuttgart: J.B. Metzlersche Verlagsbuchhandlung.

Schütze, F. (1987), Das Narrative Interview in Interaktionsfeldstudien: erzähltheoretische Grundlagen. Teil I (Merkmale von Alltagserzählungen und was wir mit ihrer Hilfe erkennen können). Fernuniversität Hagen (Studienbrief).

Voges, W. (1987) Zur Zeitdimension in der Biographieforschung. In: Voges, W. (Hrsg.), Methoden der Biographie- und Lebenslaufforschung. Opladen: Leske + Budrich, pp 125-141.

Maria del Mar Herrera Menchen

Adult Education Outside Formal Education

Introduction: The concept of Animación Sociocultural

The Animación Sociocultural (sociocultural mobilisation) is a participative methodology of working with groups and communities. The term came from France in the seventies and referred to cultural activities in free time. It was also practised in Spain, with a strong influence from South America. The concept includes a social theoretical basis and diverse techniques in order to get to know and understand the community and how to work with it in a participative way. The concept has developed from the Popular Education movement (education for and to the people) in France and Latinoamerica; from the 'Animation Socioculturelle' (cultural activities in free time) in France; and from community development in the United Kingdom. In addition, it has a certain parallelism with the 'Sozio-kulturelle Anregung' (free time occupation and continuing social education) from Germany and the Agology from Belgium (de Miguel Badesa, 1995).

The Animación Sociocultural is 'the process of organising people in order to carry out projects and initiatives from their culture, with the intent to achieve 'social development' (Cembranos, Bustelo, and Montesinos, 1989). The main characteristic is that the process has to be participative. Angel de Castro (1990) says that when we talk about Animación Sociocultural (ASC) we mean 'to understand ASC as a stable process of participation and creativity'. From this process the individual finds the possibility to become an active protagonist of his/her own development as well as the development of his/her own community.

The Animación Sociocultural is an individual and community process in which the individual learns to know what is going on in his/her own community, to recognise what he/she can do in order to change those situations which are seen as problems, and to organise him/herself with other people in order to achieve their common goals.

Animación Sociocultural Process and its role in Social and Economic Development

Andalusia is a very poor region in comparison with other parts of Europe but not in comparison with other parts of the world. In any event, we have one of the highest rates of unemployment (32,39% in the second half of 1996 in comparison with 22,27% in Spain as a whole). This is due to the rapid change from a rural and agricultural society to an industrial and services society. The Andalusian cities are like other parts of Europe: they have good services in the centre but very few in the periphery. The main burden of changes is carried by the villages and rural areas. Therefore, although the lifestyle and quality of life in general are good, there are people who really need to be helped in order to have a worthy and decent life.

At local level, the process of development can be encouraged by the Municipalities trying to create processes of social mobilisation through economic, educational, and/or cultural projects. Unfortunately in Andalucia many of these projects are disconnected at local level. The Escuela Pública de Animación Sociocultural de Andalucía (EPASA) wants to collaborate with professionals and volunteers. By starting from their experiences, culture and resources is it possible to organise a training process that can indeed achieve social change. For that it is essential that the animador (the professional or volunteer that facilitates the process) learns the necessary techniques:

1. to motivate the community to be willing to change unpleasant situations
2. to provide for open discussion to come up with possible solutions
3. to show them how to organise themselves to achieve their goals.

The origins of the Public Schools of Free Time and Animación Sociocultural in Spain.

Artillio and de la Riva (1996) have defined four stages in the recent history of the Public Schools of Free Time and Animación Sociocultural. I think it is important to know them in order to understand the work of EPASA today.

First stage: The Creation of the Democratic Town Hall (1970-1979).

In the 70s social groups and associations started to talk about Animación Sociocultural (ASC) but the Public Administration did not carry out any initiative that can be defined as being ASC. In the middle of the seventies the Ministry of Culture published the first documents where Animación Sociocultural and Cultural Democratisation are mentioned. The small social groups, neighbourhood associations and Christian groups begin with adult education experiences as well as with leisure groups. The training is not formally organised but there are courses at group level. Authors such as Paolo Freire began to be known among the social groups. The church movement is in this period was the real protagonist of the training. They directed the training activities to 'natural animators' and the leaders of the associations. The methodology at this time was imported from experiences in France, Belgium and Hispanoamerica (Freire, Ander Egg, etc).

Second Stage: The Beginning of the Democratic Town Hall (1979-1984)

The left parties gained power in the Municipalities and in the Regional Governments (Comunidades Autónomas). They have committed themselves to fulfil the social and cultural needs. The goals of the new government agencies are social participation and the empowering of the social movement, with the Animación Sociocultural being the general guiding principle. Cultural houses, popular universities, adults schools, citizens centres, etc. appeared at this time. However, the movement was characterised by a lack of cohesion and the improvisation of initiatives and professional jobs. The Public School of Animación Sociocultural began in some Regional Governments and Town Halls. There was an increase in the number of conferences, courses, and seminars. The main protagonists of the training activities were the professionals of the public institutions. The first curricula for the animador was created by the Regional Governments, but the models of France and Belgium as well as the Latinoamerica continued without any reflection upon the context and reality of Spain.

Third Stage: The Official Recognition of the Professionals and their Formative Programmes. (1985-1992)

The Socialist Party gained a majority in Parliament. This allowed the consolidation of many programmes at local and regional level with an increase in the budget, and a creation of facilities as well as new human resources. The Animación Sociocultural is now an active process with the possibility of creating new jobs, especially in the youth and unemployment programmes.

The Cultural Management replaced the Animación Sociocultural. The new goals are the effectiveness and profitability of the programmes. The creation of the Welfare State opened new avenues to the ASC: minorities, social pathologies (drugs, alcohol, delinquency), women, youth, senior citizens, etc. The Animador has many fields and a great range of tasks. The confusion about his/her role is now greater.

In this period the Public Schools were consolidated. The curriculae and programmes became official. There was an increase in the number of conferences and courses, and an effort to make the programmes and diplomas of all Public Schools in the Spanish State equivalent began.

The University and the Educational Administration began to show an interest in this subject. Private Schools reappeared, strengthened by funds even though they are constrained by legal restrictions.

The students are the professionals and volunteers from the institutions and associations but a new group has appeared: the professional of the specific field such as minorities, women , youth, etc, and the unemployed with university degrees (social worker and primary teachers) who consider ASC and social and cultural action in general as a possible job.

This period was characterised by a dispersion and confusion of the methodological proposals. Nevertheless, there is an increase in the number of places to debate and reflect upon the social and cultural fields and the kind of training that is needed.

Fourth Stage: The crisis of the Welfare State (1993 till present)

There has been a reduction in the budget and programmes of social and cultural action. Staff numbers have been decreased and the contracts are now precarious. The labour field has been narrowed down even though the functions of the professionals have not been clearly defined.

Nevertheless, as a reaction, a high number of non-governmental organisations have emerged in order to take care of the needs left by the professionals. It is a period of stagnation and reformulation of the programmes.

The University organises careers and degrees related to ASC, for instance the social education three-year degree. At the same time the Public Schools are experiencing a crisis because of the competition with the Ministry of Education, and because the crisis of the Welfare State has begun to question its role. Nevertheless, the Health Schools, the Centres for Infant Studies, the Social Services Schools and the Centres for Resources of the Cultural Management have been created.

The University maintains its hegemony while the Public Schools of ASC are now less important. The social movement and associations have acquired more strength. They promoted new initiatives of training together with the Public Administration. The formative private sector gained importance and now offers a new range of courses.

The new students of the Public Schools of ASC are volunteers and those who have finished secondary studies. The training activities are more formal now perhaps because of the participation of the University in this sector. This has the disadvantage of a less flexible curricula and methodology as well as the difficulty of being close to the practical field. On the other hand, the courses are now more rigorous, and the social acceptance of Animadores has, therefore, increased with the result that the programmes are being considered equivalent to other professional ones in the field.

This period is also rich in research and new creative processes of training: self-training, training of social leaders, training in the field, etc. In addition, the evaluation and the revision of programmes of the previous yearsallows for reflection upon the experiences.

The Public School of Animación Sociocultural of Andalusia (EPASA)

One of the main tasks of the EPASA is the training of volunteers and professionals working at local level. The area of work is the eight provinces of Andalusia, a region with 7,314,644 inhabitants and an area of 87,232 square kilometres.

This institution, which depends on public funding (Regional Ministry of Culture), is a school in charge of continuing education for professionals working in the social and cultural field. It concentrates on:

1. providing free time monitors and Animadores with a certificate.
2. organising training for people working in this field: social workers, cultural workers etc.

The certificates are official. They are issued by a public institution. However, since the training is not organised by the Ministry of Education but by an agency of the Ministry of Culture, this causes problems of acceptance at professional and labour level. Nevertheless, the Municipalities are increasingly asking for people with a degree from EPASA.

EPASA tries to be aware of the needs and works closely with the Municipalities as well as with associations working at local level. The theoretical and ideological background is very important to EPASA, but more important is to profit from the experiences and the practice of professionals and volunteers.

Half of the students of the EPASA have a three-year university degree, and 14% of the participants have a five-year degree. We believe the school complements a university degree in two ways:

a) many of our students come when they finish at the university level in order to have a different type of training, one more practical and close to the field.
b) others are professionals who are working in local institutions and are in need of training in certain areas for which they have not been previously for.

EPASA teachers are people working in the field who collaborate with us when needed. This situation allows the student the possibility to be near to real working conditions.

The content of the training for the social and cultural professional

In EPASA's experience there are certain contents which are basic for all community workers:

1. principles, method and techniques of the social research and field analysis
2. principles, method and techniques for planning and managing of the programmes implementation.
3. principles, method and techniques of communication and mobilisation of groups.
4. principles, method and techniques of social information and communication.
5. principles, method and techniques for the systematisation and evaluation of the experiences and programmes.

The following table shows the main area of contents that has been worked on in EPASA.

Areas of Work of Epasa

1. Sociocultural Animation:
   - Social and cultural planning
   - Participative methodologies
   - Evaluation of programmes and projects
   - Techniques of study of the territory
   - The dynamics of groups

- Community development
- Ecological education
- Infant and /or youth mobilisation
- Rural tourism

2. Cultural Management:
   - Cultural marketing
   - Design of cultural activities
   - Cultural policies
3. Social Mobilisation:
   - Promotion and mobilisation of different groups: women, seniors citizens, minorities, prisoners and drug dependants
4. Associations and Volunteers:
   - Management and mobilisation of the associations
   - Programming and implementing activities in associations
5. International:
   - Youth exchanges
   - European programmes
   - European social fund
6. Intercultural Education and Education for the Development
   - Intercultural learning
   - Intercultural relationships and conflict resolution
   - International co-operation

The methodology of work: From the practice and/or the experience to the improvements of that practice

Although it is possible to talk about many, I want to emphasise the following characteristics of the methodology of work of the Animación Sociocultural and EPASA:

1. Participative: that is working with people, building up from their pre-existing experiences, ideas, and knowledge in order to improve their practical abilities.
2. Co-operative: these professionals work in groups and with groups; therefore teamwork during the learning process is essential to our teaching methodology.
3. Reflexive: students will learn not only about theoretical concepts but also how to evaluate their work (the feasibility of projects with the existing resources, making sure the projects are really participative). We encourage students to think about what they are doing in their job, projects and to analyse the real possibilities and limitations. This allows the practitioners to focus on their specific communities.
4. An important feature is that the training has to be adequate to each concrete reality, meaning that the training has to be practical and useful. This is the most difficult part of our work because it requires to know in depth the programmes and the needs of the professional and volunteers working in Andalusia. As it has been said, the region is large geographically and the number of staff in each province is small except in Seville, the capital. Our main goal is to improve our knowledge of social and cultural action in Andalusia as a whole.
5. The variety (the diversity of the instruments and type of formative activities), the friendliness (the use of method and techniques that are creative, diverse and adequate to each subject) and the flexibility (the capacity to adapt to the different groups of students and their specific evolution) are features that strengthen the motivation and reinforce the learning.
6. Finally, the learning has to be done as a progressive process, a continuing training built up step by step. To learn what is needed each moment and what each student needs for his/her special situation does not mean individual learning. It means a kind of learning that gives possibilities to each student to discuss what is really important for him/her. Also we have to take into account the variety of EPASA students. We have

unemployed people, professionals from different universities and backgrounds, students from the universities, people from associations, etc. Therefore the training will have to be organised and varied in order to meet the need of such a heterogeneous group.

References

Artillo, J. I. and de la Riva, F. (1996), Aproximación a la formación del Animador. EPASA, Sevilla, non published.

Artillo, J. I. and de la Riva, F. (1996), Aproximación a una propuesta para la formación, de agentes socioculturales, EPASA, Sevilla, non published

Castro, A. (1990), La tercera edad, tiempo de ocio y cultura. Proyecto y experiencia de Animación Cultural. Madrid, Narcea.

Cembranos, Bustelo y Montesinos, (1989), Animación Sociocultural: una propuesta metodológica, Popular, Madrid.

De Miguel Badesa, S. (1995), Perfil del Animador Sociocultural, Madrid, Narcea.

Klaus Körber

From Social Movement to Professionalisation - New Tasks and New Institutions Between Market, State and Communities

This contribution is based on an empirical study that I conducted with Herbert Effinger[1] in Bremen from 1990–1992 on the development of new tasks and responsibilities and of new forms of professionalisation and institutionalisation in various 'person-oriented' services ('*personenorientierte Dienstleistungen*'). The service-fields we investigated were: health promotion and self-help, social work and counselling, training and employment in the second labour market, child-rearing and adult education, art and cultural work, environmental and political organisation and counselling services. The demarcation lines between the various fields are rather blurred in many cases. In all the fields we investigated, continuing education and training services are provided to clients in addition to the more specific professional activities. In other words, although adult and continuing education is not the central purpose or specific goal of the fields we studied, the spectrum of activities involves a significant proportion of formal continuing education work and of informal learning everywhere. To that extent, the sections that follow have an implicit bearing on adult and continuing education, even where it is not expressly referred to.

In the first part of this paper I shall briefly in a idealtypic manner describe common aspects shared by person-oriented services and, in a first, provisional approximation, I shall attempt to define these activities in terms of the sociology of work. The people we interviewed consider themselves members of the alternative movement and alternative economy of the 1980s. When we conducted the survey in 1990-1992, most of them were still working in small nonprofit organisations that emanated from 'self-governing projects', either from initiatives and self-help groups, or from cooperative

1 The study entitled 'Work and Education in the Intermediary Sector (ABIS)' was conducted in the framework of the 'Work and Education' Priority Research Programme at the University of Bremen. It was preceded by studies on the same complex (see Effinger/Schlake/Sosna 1988 and Effinger 1990). I am especially grateful to Herbert Effinger. Without the substantial body of work he carried out beforehand, this paper would never have been written.

enterprises within the alternative movement. These autonomous organisations are legally and economic independent, and still differ today from functional units operated by the state and quasi-state organisations, and from other enterprises and companies (for-profit organisations) operating in the same person-oriented service fields.

Nevertheless, much has changed for the interviewees. In three sections under the general heading of 'From social movement to professionalisation', I shall describe their history since the initial evolution of their self-governed work environment, the changes they underwent over time, and the gradual transformation in their political and professional self-understanding.

The history of the West German alternative movement has shown that the new social movements of the 1970s and 1980s were relatively short-lived historical phenomena. However, I shall try in the concluding section, using the keywords 'social mediation' and 'intermediary institutions', to identify in a more systematic way of looking those functions and structural features that have emerged from the alternative movement and which have survived their demise. The societal functions, occupational activities and institutional structures that I label 'intermediary' are in my view of lasting significance for the modernisation of modern societies. From a systematic and social-historical perspective, they have implications beyond the alternative movement and the many minor organisations which succeeded it. In the third section, I specify some starting points for developing a theoretical reference frame within which such deeper interpretations of our research results and wider issues can be treated.

Finally, I shall very briefly look out on some implications for adult and continuing education.

1. Person-oriented services - a tentative definition

At first glance, person-oriented services perform a wide variety of different functions. They support physical reproduction and regeneration, cognitive and emotional development, psychosocial stabilisation and the socio-cultural integration of people. Their 'products' vary extensively: health, orientation, identity and meaning, skills, qualifications, education and training, social recognition, group membership and belongingness, and solidarity. Traditionally, at least in Germany, they are therefore allocated to different social systems and fields of professional involvement. The thing that leads me to consider it nonetheless meaningful to group them all under the common label of 'person-oriented services' and to view them throughout the following as representing *one* professional context, is the common core that is shared by these professional activities and which distinguishes them from other professional contexts: namely the direct orientation of professional work to the client or participant as an individual person ('client orientation'/'participant orientation').

This orientation determines not only the meaning and purpose of involvement in all the fields we studied; it plays an integral role in the structuring of work processes. A whole bundle of competences and personal qualities are required to carry out these kinds of work, which in essence involves the same for all the various fields. The systematic demarcation and professional closure of the various fields vis-à-vis each other is made harder as a result; conversely, the exchange of responsibilities, mobility and switching between them is facilitated in practice.

Direct communication and cooperation between different people is a precondition for the 'production' of a person-oriented service; this normally occurs in the form of a face-to-face interaction between professionals and clients, for example between adult educators and participants. On the one hand, success of work depends pends on the professionals being able to relate to the problems, needs, situations and individual competences of other persons and trying to understand them, rather than trying, like engineers, to identify and solve objective problems in a distanced manner. On the other hand, success requires that clients or participants do not view and accept a course option, a professional form of help or a counselling session only like some kind of commodity, but that they themselves *take action* of their accord, as independent persons taking responsibility for their own actions.

New 'service' theories attempt to label the active and co-responsible role of clients or participants in the cooperative production of person-oriented services that is essential for such work processes to succeed with new concepts and terms such as 'co-producers', 'active consumers' (Gartner/Riesman 1978) or 'prosumers' (Toffler 1980). Such new terminology is an expression of the fact that neither the strict separation of producers and consumers or customers, nor the temporal, economic and technical pre- and superordination of production, and the subordination of consumption, cannot be upheld in the field of person-oriented services.

The interlocking of production and consumption (the 'uno actu' principle) only holds true for person-oriented services. Services geared to the production and distribution of goods, such as the work done by architects and consultant engineers, bank employees and insurance brokers, saleswomen and waitresses or by repair men, always contain person-oriented elements, but neither the purpose, outcome and success of such work is ultimately dependent on the individual person receiving the service, nor can this have any significant influence on the overall work process itself. In such cases, the separation of producers and consumers remains a structural prerequisite for the subordination of the work process to the rule-bound nature of commodity economics and capital production. It is not just the in-company work process that is kept controllable and predictable as far as possible through formalisation and rationalisation, but also the relations to consumers, by virtue of the fact that there is no relationship to the complex nature and subjectivity of the specific Other and that action is reduced to a specific customer-related role behaviour. Person-oriented services, in contrast, can never completely ignore the complexity of the other person and reduce it to an simple object of manipulation. The service operations could not be performed successfully, if the person would be completely reduced to the role of a customer or completely alienated to an anonymous target on the market.

Person-oriented services rely instead on an indispensable minimum of closeness, empathy and mutual trust between all those involved in the work process. There is empirical evidence to show that the degree of mutuality and participation far exceeds what is otherwise normal in the largely depersonalised, formally rationalised producer-consumer relationships in the production and distribution of goods. Educational staff are constantly endeavouring, when shaping the specific teaching-learning situation in a continuing education course, to create and maintain subject-subject relationships with the participants that are based as far as possible on partnership and the promotion of cooperation and collaboration. Because the conditions on which the success of the programme and any real educational advance on the part of the participants really depends are not created solely through the participants' intrasubjective motivation, readiness to cooperate and individual capacity to learn, but through active cooperation and participation in the situation itself.

The principles of individual focus, participant orientation and self-determined learning are inadequately formulated as long as they are conceived of exclusively, as is still mostly the case, as normative didactic postulates; instead, they are functional requirements and preconditions of success for professional involvement in continuing education or in other person-oriented services. However necessary these conditions may be, they are insufficient in themselves. Person-oriented services are ultimately based on *inter-subjectivity* and successful interaction between at least two, usually several persons. Any subject-oriented conceptions that concentrate solely on *one* side of the interactive relationship or on the isolated learner (self-determined learning) - and this is the case with certain didactic concepts in adult and continuing education - are inadequate from the outset. Besides the subject-related prerequisites just mentioned, a number of complementary factors providing for inter-subjectivity must also be present - such as opportunities for all those involved to participate, as well as active cooperation between them, and, to say it once more, a certain minimum of mutual trust and respect. They are equally indispensable for the establishment and successful operation of a shared process of work and education.

2. From social movement to professionalisation

2.1 From social-liberal and social-democratic milieus to the alternative movement

Our survey sample was comprised predominantly of people who have been working for a long time in these specific fields in the city of Bremen. We surveyed a total of 149 using a standardised questionnaire which the subjects filled out themselves; 31 people in the sample were then questioned in intensive interviews about their professional biographies, their current activities and forms of work, their professional experiences and orientations, and especially on their ideas of professionality and appropriate institutional forms for the work they do, and on their conception of further professional training. The interviewees were almost all born in the 1950s, with only a few people younger. Apart from a few exceptions, they all studied in the 1970s, most of them at Bremen Polytechnic or Bremen University. Some took a second degree in Bremen, others started at the polytechnic and graduated from the university. Ninety percent of those interviewed took social science or education degrees.

These are the very degree courses that were reformed in the early 1970s, or first set up when the new 'Reformed' University of Bremen was established, in a move to train and select skilled personnel for new or 'reformed' professional services in state or quasi-state facilities in the fields of education, culture and health and social work. The decision to take precisely these degrees in precisely this city, at precisely these institutions at precisely that time was a very conscious one on the part of our interviewees.

Three motives and explanations for this decision are predominant. The first motive was social advancement away from the milieu of origin or from previous occupations. Most of the interviewees are from Bremen, the majority from the lower middle classes, the minority from working class milieus; the remainder were mostly from the country, especially from small-town petty-bourgeois milieus. The hopes they placed in their studies, in a large city at that, related to upward social mobility and at the same time the abandonment of the narrow confines, everyday routines and compulsions of their milieu of origin. Many saw their studies as a chance to escape from their first occupation, traditionally chosen by family and milieu, in order to seek a profession that matched their individual skills and inclinations to a greater extent.

The second motive related to 'a different way of working'. For most of the interviewees, the very choice of degree subject and place to study already provided for precisely determined career and employment prospects. Almost all were disciplined and ambitious. They worked during their studies and wanted to enter their chosen profession as soon as possible after graduating. But in a different way than they were familiar with from home. Most of them can say quite precisely what factors and aspects they wanted to change in their work at that time. Above all, they wanted to 'work with people' and 'do something for others'; they hoped for more self-determination, less alienated relations with others and more holistic and democratic structures at work. This is largely congruent with what I described earlier as the special features and distinguishing aspects of person-oriented services. One might object that current experience and orientations will be superimposed upon and will influence the retrospective description of earlier options and decisions in their professional biographies. But there is no denying the fact that they wanted and strove for a different way of working; the evidence is spread throughout their entire professional biography from then to today. The choice of these degree courses at the 'reformed' tertiary education institutions in Bremen, which at that time were geared programmatically to new forms of professional work and the ultimate aim of changing society from within, are also evidence for this attitude. It was precisely this reform programme and the 'alternative' practice of their studies that held out the promise of fulfilling their wishes.

The third motive related to the creation of an alternative, reformed society. The interviewees associate their individual desire for social advancement and escape from home milieus, and their option to work in a different way, with wider perspectives beyond their individual activities and workplaces. Their hope was that their professional activities would contribute towards the reform and democratisation of society itself. Unlike the preceding student and protest movement of the '68 generation, they did not base their hopes and reformist ambitions on abstract, theoretically constructed models for an alternative society as a whole, such as socialism; nor are these hopes and ambitions focused on the state and party politics. They have nothing to do with any high-falutin utopias grounded on philosophy or social sciences, or with far-off problems in the Third World. Instead, their notion of social and societal reform meant experimentation and gradual diffusion of alternative forms of work, living and political activity into more and more areas of society, starting quite practically in the immediate nexus of their own everyday world of work and life. Their own everyday 'workworld', was the area of person-oriented services that we focused on in our study.

In the third complex of motives, there are already signs of a collective pattern of 'alternative thinking'. Still in retrospect, the interviewees locate their former wishes and ambitions for professional work and their first steps in what for them was a new world of work almost exclusively in a socio-political context. For them, the fields which they wanted to and later did work in were not areas of 'person-oriented services' (such a term would have been rejected with outrage in those days), but areas in which a different form of society could be experimented with. They are first and foremost experimental fields for 'alternative work', 'alternative economy', 'alternative living', for a different understanding of and for a different engagement in politics as 'politics of everyday life'. From this perspective, they raise the small, alternative projects in which they gained their first professional post-graduation experience, although those have little significance beyond the local level, to the stature of alternatives with relevance at the political level and for all of society. They themselves are not always subjectively aware of doing so. The fact that economic problems, especially rising unemployment, and biographical problems relating to choosing and getting started in a career were the main factors leading to the establishment of these projects is hardly referred to at all.

Of course, all this does not necessarily mean that the interviewees themselves were members of the alternative movement at the time. Collective patterns of interpretation in which one's own everyday activities are accorded societal and political significance are component parts of a mode of thinking that began to spread in West Germany from the late 1970s onwards, particularly among academically educated members of the post-'68 generation we investigated, when hopes for the great societal alternatives and reforms were already fading away. In the centres of social-democratic reform politics, which in those years became strongholds of the new social movements as well (Bremen being a classic example), such thinking had impacts beyond the confines of the 'alternative' scene for some years.

The people we interviewed were certain to have belonged to the alternative movements after finishing their studies in the 1980s; they themselves say that they were members of said movement. However, our research results do not permit us to say from what point onwards they felt themselves to be members. Some were members when they started studying in Bremen. Others, and probably the majority, were at that time still members of traditional political-cultural milieus and organisations. For most, this was the mainstream socio-liberal or the social-democratic trade union milieu - both milieus with a pronounced orientation to performance and social advancement - and their relevant organisations. They continued to base their notions of societal reform and alternatives on the reformist perspectives and strategies of the social-democratic/liberal coalition then in power, and on the trade unions, which at that time wielded cultural hegemony in the political culture of West Germany, and especially in Bremen.

In the 1970s, when most of our interviewees decided on the degree they wanted to take, deliberate efforts were made to attract students to the social science and education degree courses and the associated professional fields. This was the case in Bremen, a traditional social-democratic stronghold and the home town of a relative majority of those interviewed, as well as in the neighbouring *Länder* ruled by the Social Democrats - Lower Saxony, Hamburg, Hesse and North-Rhine Westphalia, where the bulk of the remainder originated. The framework was provided by the social-liberal reformist perspective aimed primarily at expansion of the welfare state, democratisation of society and the expansion and reform of public administration and the public services. Within this framework, reformist projects acquired an unprecedented level of prestige and importance, above all in the policy fields relating to the labour market, social welfare, health and the environment, and especially education policy.

The social systems and professional fields that we focused on in our study as core areas of person-oriented services were redefined in those days as publicly recognised fields of policymaking, areas in which the state had responsibility to take action. In this way, social science and educational degrees and the professions in these fields quickly gained not only in social prestige and recognition, but also in strategic political importance. They were supposed to operate as agents of change and as new functional elites in order to achieve reformist objectives through practical social action. Scientific forecasts of labour market needs and trends in these fields, changes in legislation and political planning programmes, and above all the provision of substantial state funds for these policy fields and professions, made it look in the 1970s as if they had a rosy future ahead of them. In the mid-1970s, these factors led to a state-driven boost in the institutionalisation of person-oriented services; the consequence was a wave of recruitment for social scientists and educationalists in the public service and related fields. For the very first time, continuing education seemed to provide promising career opportunities and a new labour market segment.

When the people we interviewed completed their studies in the early 1980s, this wave of recruitment had long since ebbed away. They were now standing before the closed doors of the labour market; zero recruitment, rationalisation and privatisation in more and more areas of the public services and cuts in public expenditure have dominated developments since then. The service fields that were promoted during the reformist period to fields of societal involvement and for which the state assumed a management role and financial responsibility, rapidly lost their newly-acquired prestige and public recognition. As a result, their influence and ability to assert themselves in the mounting competition for dwindling state resources and funds declined rapidly. This had obvious repercussions for the professions based on the social sciences and education: their recently acquired social prestige and their influence on the formulation of policies plummeted. The consequences were even harder for the individuals themselves: they lost access to job resources in state and quasi-state institutions. The critical, elitist and vanguardist attitude that led them to believe they were at the forefront of social reforms succumbed to a deep crisis.

Many of the politicised 'social actors' who did not see themselves as professionals until that time remained deeply insecure in their political and professional identity for a long time after (Thomssen et al. 1994). This sense of insecurity intensified in the 1980s, when the strategic perspectives offered by official policymaking were subjected to radical change: Instead of nationalisation and 'democratisation of society' from above by expanding and refining the welfare state into a 'socialisation state' (Böhnisch/Schefold), and the creation of a service-oriented state, the real outcome was crisis and restructuring, even dismantling of the welfare state through increased market orientation and privatisation of state tasks and facilities. Particularly hard-hit were those areas of person-oriented services, such as continuing education and training, which had been institutionalised with the support of the state only a short before in the 1970s.

During the 1980s, the interviewees in our study withdrew somewhat involuntarily to the 'social islands' of the alternative movement and alternative economy. However, they readily established a presence for themselves in these domains. When the survey was conducted in the early 1990s, most of them were still working in 'self-organized' facilities or enterprises that grew out of the 'initiatives', 'self-help groups' and 'cooperatives' of the alternative movement. These nonprofit organisations are small, legally and economically independent, and work autonomously. They are quite distinct from both state and quasi-state facilities, as well as from profit-oriented enterprises operating in the field of person-oriented services.

2.2 From the alternative movement to professionalisation

In the first generation of projects of the alternative movement during the 70s a major role was played by the conscious ideological demarcation from the political culture and from the industrial and bureaucratic work culture in West Germany. The first generation founders were in critical opposition to the corporatist forms of institutionalisation in the social welfare state and, as a result of that, to the bureaucratised forms of work in the field of person-oriented services. 'Capitalist' production and marketing of person-oriented services within the framework of profit-oriented companies, which in those years had not yet attained any significant size compared to today, was totally rejected by the actors of the alternative movement at that time. The mission, objectives and structures of the alternative organisations and their own self-understanding and approach to work were primarily expressed at that time in political and moral terms, not professionally and task-related (Effinger 1993). They took their cue from the traditions of self-governing worker enterprises and the idea of cooperatives and utopian designs of a unity of non-alienated labour and life, as was experimented with in previous periods in anarchistic or religious communities, or in the 'grassroots revolution' movement (Bookchin u.a. 1981; 'Graswurzelrevolution' magazine). If one looks at self-portrayals (Das alternative Adressbuch 1977; WestBerlin 'Stattbuch' 1978; v.Gizycki/Habicht 1978; Arbeiterselbsthilfe Frankfurt 1980; Connexions 1984) and theoretical self-reflection of the alternative movement at that time (Kurz 1979; Müschen 1982; Schwendter 1986a/ 1986b), such tradition-based interpretation patterns had considerable importance and binding force within the movement then for the collective self-understanding and identity-formation process within the movement.

The establishment phase of the second generation of alternative organisations included in our investigations (see Effinger/ Schlake/ Sosna 1988 and Effinger 1990) was at the zenith of the new social movements in West Germany in the first half of the 80s. According to the oral and written self-assessments of the second generation founding fathers and mothers we interviewed, the qualifications and skill profiles needed in the work process and the specific expectations of clients do not yet play a significant role for their self-understanding and for the definition of their mission in this phase. Nevertheless, there is already a primitive form of professional orientation that is expressed in a reverse sense in the critique of institutions and professions. This is closely aligned with the theoretical critique of empirical professional practice and normative concepts of professionalization that the interviewees had been exposed to during their studies (see Lüders 1989; Sturzenhecker 1994). They orient themselves explicitly, but negatively, to the organisational structures, work patterns and 'products' of person-oriented services prevalent in the various fields of work organised by state or quasi-state agencies. They assess them using the tools of scientific critique against abstract, purely theoretical standards and utopian models; the result of this assessment is not surprising: their performance is 'poor'.

The differences that exist to their own alternative ideas regarding organisation, forms of work and cooperation are dramatised and suffused with ideological importance, reflected in terms like 'anti-institutional' and 'anti-professional' and in counter-concepts to existing professional practice such as *Betroffenenorientierung* (oriented to those emotionally affected) or *Basisdemokratie* (egalitarian-democratic 'grassroots orientation'). These terms and concepts perform a double function: firstly, they legitimate their own demarcation from the outside world and from other institutions and forms of work in their professional context, secondly, they help to stabilise internally the collective identity of the alternative movement, the self-assurance of living and working in a fully alternative way. These delimiting and excluding functions relate primarily to ensuring and protecting collective identity within a political reference framework. For an appropriate understanding of one's own work and the social, economic and institutional environments associated with it, the concepts mentioned above soon proved to be dysfunctional. They are totally unsuited for identifying the expectations and needs of clients or participants; and they are just as useless when it comes to rational and proper handling of statutory regulations, funding options and competitive conditions in the professional field (see Beywl 1987; Dudek 1987; Sosna 1987).

In the late 1970s and early 1980s, a time when most of the projects we investigated have just been set up, there is already a growing realisation within the movement that such concepts and orientations are inappropriate for ensuring the continued existence of the projects; they obstruct their economic and social survival. But because these were central concepts that seemed indispensable for the identity of the movement and for membership within it, they could not be abandoned without further ado. This dilemma threw the West German alternative movement into crisis and unleashed a controversial debate on its very identity (see Hollstein/Penth 1980; Schülein 1980; Huber 1980 and 1984; Grottian/Kück 1983; Schwendter 1986a/ 1986b).

For most of our interviewees, however, this conflict was much less dramatic than it was for those who had already been involved since the earlier 1970s. The interviewees are 'second generation founders'; they joined the movement as latecomers not until the time when it was beginning to change its basic character and functions under the impact of structural crisis and long-term unemployment. They themselves were not socialised during the 1960s and 1970s in the anti-authoritarian 'Sponti' (spontaneous action) sub-cultures that emanated from the '68 movement, nor were they in dissident or drop-out communes, or in anti-capitalist and anti-industrial 'counter-economy' projects (see for example Schwendter 1973 and the magazines 'Autonomie' and 'Pflasterstrand'). They no longer needed to identify with the more grandiose designs of earlier years for an alternative society: the autonomous counter-society and counter-culture these called for (see Brand/ Büsser/Rucht 1983), or with any form of 'Ecotopia' (Callenbach 1980). In times of permanent crisis, in which intellectuals are affected, too, on a large scale, the cardinal issue in alternative projects of the second generation is more and more to secure an adequate economic basis for survival. 'Dropping in', be it in second labour markets, or 'grey zones' of relatively insecure alternative employment (Effinger 1990), is from now on a central motive, as opposed to 'dropping out' to economically risky experiments of alternative working and living.

Nevertheless for the first time the interviewees adopted some of the utopian-ideological ideas of the alternative tradition, such as eradicating the division of labour and creating grassroots democracy in everyday working life; as shown above, they also accepted some central concepts of collective anti- and demarcation strategies. But among those we interviewed, these traditional elements of alternative consciousness were supplemented and corrected from the outset with very pragmatic and innovative orientations and motivations for action. It was this, and not ideological awareness that formed the crucial subjective framework for their sustained achievements and successes. The institutions and employment relations that have meanwhile developed from the alternative projects still suffer from inadequate financial resources, but there is still a relatively large amount of institutional and organisational scope to cater to the subjective competences and motivations of the workforce in each case. The fact that so many are still working in such institutions after ten years and more is partly attributable to this factor. Here they can test out their individual strengths more freely than they could in public administration, quasi-state facilities or private-sector enterprises, and pursue their specific professional inclinations.

Most of the interviewees exhibit a high degree of social curiosity and sensitivity; they are quick to identify social responsibilities and new needs on the part of their clients and participants. The former alternative projects or the 'new self-employed' relationships to which many have now switched generally allow them considerable scope for dealing with these challenges. Many combine a basic pragmatic attitude with a lively interest in new activities and a will to innovate; the alternative economy provided them for years with an experimental field for new tasks and responsibilities and for new forms of work and organisation. Virtually all the interviewees have a well-developed interest in hands-on social practice, combined with a desire to test and to prove themselves in it; daring and willingness to take on risks are evident among many in the sample. Without these qualities and competences on the part of their staff, the institutions that have grown out of alternative projects would not be viable today; after all, they are still very risky undertakings. The critical requirements that must be met if the projects are to keep going over longer periods with very limited resources, despite setbacks and against all manner of opposition, are endurance and strategic adaptability. Until today these conditions are clearly met by the 'social entrepreneurs', those with responsibility for a project as a whole.

A critical factor behind their sustained success has been their readiness and ability to consciously abandon the rich tradition of normative ideological expectations and utopian visions of alternative living and working, which led to less and less achievable and sustainable demands on themselves and on the collective involved in the respective project. Some needed years until they were able to accept that the 'communitarian' structures in their projects, especially the strictly egalitarian forms of symmetric working and the grassroots democracy governing decision-making procedures and distribution of responsibility, would have to change on the long and stony road to permanent institutionalisation. Despite this, it was they themselves who ultimately acted as the motors of institutionalisation and professionalisation, because they wanted to preserve the essential core and social meaning of their work.

2.3 The 'alternative kids' grow up - six reasons for their switch from anti-professionality to professionality

The interviewees advance six main reasons for their switch from an anti-professional and anti-institutional attitude to their explicit insistence today on what they themselves call 'professionality' (Körber/Effinger 1995). These reasons are described in the following.

The first reason they advance is subject-related. They have a consciously chosen self-definition of professionality that demands from every individual a concentration on his or her specific qualifications and activities. All the interviewees think that this narrowing of focus provides for greater efficiency, in that it relieves them from the excessive and incalculable burdens imposed by the traditional alternative demand for all-round responsibility according to the anti-professional principle of 'everyone can do everything;

everyone does everything'. Today, they welcome a division of labour and distribution of responsibilities and skills because in that way, particularly in cooperative set-ups, the special individual competences and the different individual capacities and capabilities can be taken into consideration more. This is experienced as a confirmation of self-esteem, and enhances job satisfaction.

The second reason advanced in favour of more professionality arises from the insights they have gained into the diffuse complexity of skill profiles for person-oriented services. What I described earlier as structural features of these activities is repeated by the interviewees as self-description of professional standards and the competences and qualifications that these require. On the one hand, they describe competences related to other persons: to colleagues in cooperative work situations, but above all to the clients or participants. Some of those we interviewed speak in this context of 'key qualifications', using the term to refer to specific social and communicative competences. On the other hand, they describe competences relating to their own person. Many speak here not of qualifications, but of 'personal qualities', because these could not be learned in a formal way in formalised training programmes and courses of study. However, many interviewees experience the fact that these self-referential competences cannot be delimited in professional terms, that they overlap with everyday and semi-private domains, as a dilemma. This situation could be ameliorated, they suppose, if definitions of these competences were generally recognised within the profession and institutionally ratified.

A third type of reason reveals the extent to which the ex-members of the alternative movement continue to deviate from prevailing patterns of definition and strategies of professionalisation. They consider a core set of specialist qualifications and intellectual competences to be of some importance. But most attach minimal significance to their formal academic education, and the scientific background of that, as far as the qualifications they can really use in their current activities are concerned; they consider professional experience and informal learning-by-doing in concrete everyday work to be more important and more effective. In addition, a major role is assigned to 'experience of life' and a certain talent - 'either you've got it, or you haven't', or informal lifelong learning in the widest sense. The reason they put forward is that the qualifications for person-oriented professional involvement are based first and foremost on competences that are relevant not only for professional work, but also for the lifeworld beyond the work context and for the 'whole person'. The manifestly low estimation in which academic education and training are held may have generation-specific reasons in their case, and may result from particular experiences in their professional biographies. Their university or polytechnic degree was geared at the time to employment prospects and workplace structures in the public services in particular. But there were no jobs for them there; instead, they had to create other work structures themselves. This called for other qualifications and orientations towards their professions that those referred to during their studies and in the theoretical critique of professional practice. One aspect that has to be taken seriously is that most of them, even today, stubbornly oppose the moves towards professionalisation that have emanated since the 1970s above all from the universities and which are substantiated in terms of the need for scientisation of professional practice. The guiding principle of the 'scientifically trained practitioner' (Lüders 1989) that long dominated the professionalisation debate in the educational sciences in Germany with respect to the fields of activity of social workers and adult educators is absent in the professionalisation concepts entertained by the long-serving practitioners that we interviewed.

A fourth reason relates to clients and participants. The latter expect a competent and reliable service of good quality, and these expectations must be lived up to. It is for precisely this reason that the majority of the interviewees plea for rational work organisation and 'professional reliable' performance of their work. However, this presupposes that standards of work, agreements on working hours and binding cooperative plans are really complied with by all those working in the field. The professional claims of person-oriented service agencies of being there for others when they need or ask for counselling, assistance or educational opportunities calls for minimum standards of work discipline and social reliability. I have mentioned this aspect already: person-oriented services require a core of high moral standards, beyond any superimposed norms of a political or ethical nature. Mutual responsibilities and obligations are an integral part of the cooperative and participatory relations between the professionals and their clients or participants. In the work process itself, this requires a unique mixture of self-discipline and sensitivity towards others from the professionals. This is known and accepted now by the people we interviewed.

The rather contradictory high standards implicit in these profiles can turn into a trap, however. This explains why, in a fifth reason for greater professionalisation, many of the interviewees place particular stress on the ability to strike a careful balance between intimacy and distance, compassion and demarcation, which is seen as a core element of professional competence in their own person-oriented activities. But they are addressing a much wider issue here; after all, work in person-oriented services is full of these difficulties. There is a need also to strike a balance and mediate between self-reflection and understanding others, between emotionality and objectivity, between the conflicting demands of ego and alter, and to mediate between clients' responsibility for their own actions, their own competences and everyday knowledge, on the one hand, and the specific professional knowledge and expertise of the professionals, on the other hand. The counter-concept of client-centredness (*Betroffenenorientierung*) did not perform this mediation function, but simply denied it by demanding political and moral identification with the persons affected, and replacing the professional competence of 'experts' with lay competence along the lines of 'they themselves know best what is good for them'.

The basic orientation among the people we interviewed has long since reversed. Today, they strive more for professional distance and demarcation vis-à-vis their clients. This stems from experience with excessive emotional proximity and common ground, and is directed against de-differentiation and the permanent confusing of work and private life required by alternative ideology. They experienced and practised such approaches themselves for years. The consequences were painful: the 'tyranny of intimacy' (Sennet 1983) became unbearable in the long run; for some, the result was premature burn-out. A professional barrier against over-identification with clients and their problems is essential if one is to survive in a job that demands, through its very nature, constant empathy with and compassion for others. For some, being affected by and coping with the same problems as their clients may have had benefits for their future professional biography when starting in person-oriented work. Today, they all wish for more professional distance. Their hope is that the collective dimension of the profession will help to find and stabilise the various kinds of psychosocial balance I have been referring to.

The last reason we need to mention concerns joint responsibility for the overall management of the organisations we investigated. Professionalisation and professionality are no longer rejected by the interviewees because they are now recognised as essential to the economic viability of the organisations in question, and as critically important for securing existing and creating new jobs. Even if it were the case that this change in attitudes has been forced on them through adaptation to the very capitalist and state-bureaucratic frameworks that were previously combated, the readiness to consent at the subjective level to this change is widespread today. Some even view the compulsion to operate with economic efficiency as 'curative' because it helps to eradicate 'dawdling', 'dilettantism' and obstacles to decision making arising from 'grassroots democracy'. These interviewees, who have been involved in such work for many years and who mostly perform management functions - we borrow their own terminology and call them 'social entrepreneurs' - see professionalisation as a way to strengthen the feeling of joint responsibility of all staff for the whole enterprise. The basis for this responsibility is thought to be the realisation, stemming from self-interest, that the quality of work and of the services provided depend on the professional competence and a professional attitude to work, thus helping to protect one's own job and those of others.

To summarise, the new professionalism calls for self-discipline with respect to one's own hopes and 'exuberant ambitions', as one of the interviewees expressed it, as well as distance from the romantic and utopian dreams entertained by the alternative movement of development of all-round competence and non-alienated work. Their psychological foundations are cool emotions and ideological sobriety. This reorientation process is interpreted by some as evidence of a 'growing up' or 'becoming adult' process on the part of alternative projects and people. The transformation in the underlying attitude towards work and profession is seen as a decisive factor in the process of individual maturation. They interpret their past lives in the cooperatives of the alternative movement in retrospect as a youthful and sub-cultural phase of 'seeking', finding one's orientation and acquiring education. The desire to submerge oneself in the quasi-familial 'intimacy of the collective', the avoidance of conflict, and the compulsion to engineer apparent harmony that lay behind the old conceptions of unity and identity, not to mention a tendency towards missionary zeal and moral over-taxation of self, are now interpreted as manifestations of extended adolescence. Through the 'self-government' of the alternative cooperative, they had effectively established their own moratorium on becoming adult (Effinger/Körber 1994).

This self-interpretation of the ongoing professionalisation process in terms of developmental psychology shows one thing quite clearly: the issues of professionality and professionalisation are addressed by almost all our interviewees not, as is usually the case, primarily in terms of labour market opportunities or professional policy, but firstly in a biographical context. From the moment they begin to narrate their biographies as various individual educational and professional histories, rather than as integral part the *one* story of the movement, it is the chosen profession, and not the political collective, that serves as a medium of self-presentation and that provides a basic understanding regarding their personal and social competences and their individual identity. At the same time, they try to use the professional context to form a new social identity, now that the communal identity of the alternative movement has ceased to have any meaning.

The reverse side of the coin is not overlooked, of course. Some regret that, as a result of this shift towards professionalisation, the scope for autonomy, solidarity and spontaneity has become restricted, and that all radical, critical and political commitment has been 'smoothed down'. Nevertheless, they have not abandoned all the political and moral ambitions they used to associate with their work. Three quarters of the interviewees would still like to see a 'democratisation of work and more self-government', not only for their own organisations, but also for all other enterprises and facilities in society. However, the professional pragmatism that now dominates is more modest as far as moral demands are concerned, but at the same time more relevant to professional practice. Social-moral demands like mutuality and participation are still seen as collectively binding. Provided that they are grounded in those inter-subjective patterns of relationships which are considered as necessary prerequisites for the cooperation between professionals and clients or participants in person-oriented services. And provided that they can actually be fulfilled in their professional activity.

There is, of course, a certain over-emphasis on subjective aspects in what has been said so far. But there are objective reasons for that. In the various fields we investigated, professionality is something that has to be accomplished in the first place and for the first time ever. The critical factors are the professional self-interpretations and self-definitions of the people involved. Success then depends on whether these subjective interpretations are socially accepted and taken into account on a regular basis in everyday action within the work context. This is a clear indication that profession is a social construct, a result of subjective options and identifications, and inter-subjective understanding. Such a construct relies on common interpretations and interactions between the various people involved within the specific field of work, and between the social reference groups and institutions relevant for their work in the wider social context.

One aspect that is totally absent in the fields we investigated, is stable social agreements similar to the institutionally recognised occupational profiles and career patterns in other sectors. If these were to be made legally binding, as is traditional in the German occupational system, these could provide the employees with secure career orientations and stable professional identities on a long-term basis. In this way, they could be relieved of the burden of having to constantly define their own professions themselves and to campaign for their own recognition. There are no signs yet of any formal and legally valid definitions of profession for the fields of person-oriented services we have investigated.

3. Social mediation and intermediary institutions - starting points for wider issues and theoretical interpretations

3.1 The need for social mediation and integration, and the response of person-oriented services

In the current theoretical debate and in social science research analysing the modernisation process in western societies, a central issue running through the most diverse contributions is what Honneth and Peters have termed 'disintegration' (Honneth 1994, 10) or the 'destructuring of the social' (Peters 1992, 14). The terms embrace all those contemporary theses and findings behind which stands the following socio-historical pattern of interpretation: the unity of a social order with centralist and hierarchical social structures, which was still existent and valid in the 'modernity of industrial society' (Beck 1986) of the 19th century and first two thirds of the 20th century, is now dissolving in today's 'reflexivey' or 'radicalized modernity' (Beck 1993; Giddens 1990). It is being replaced by a multifarious side by side of differentiated and demarcated social systems, and socio-economic spheres, by different social milieus, lifeworlds and communities, and by competing cultural systems of values, orientations and knowledge. In this nascent complex framework, the structuring and integrating effects of specific social systems on society as a whole are diminishing in strength. According to recent political theories (see Willke 1992), this is particularly the case with the democratic political system and the state itself, which is no longer superordinated to society and thus no longer its central control system. The binding force and obligatory nature of the various systems and lifeworlds for individuals is declining, and their scope for action is increasing as a consequence. Membership of social groups and social relations are increasing in variety, but are also becoming more transitory; change is an accelerating process, and problems, decision-making needs and opportunities for self-realisation in everyday life are increasing. Most social scientists assess these processes and their impacts as ambivalent in character; they see them as harbouring both risks and opportunities. Public debate, on the other hand, tends to focus primarily on anomic and pathogenic manifestations of these processes – the acute threats to the cohesion of society as a whole, the progressive loss of values, meanings and sense of community, large-scale crises of orientation and identity, with pathological implications for the individual[2].

I shall not be discussing these theories and theses on functional differentiation, cultural pluralisation, individualisation and subjectivisation, economic globalisation, flexibilisation and segmentation; this is beyond the scope of this paper. Nor is it the point I wish to address. I am simply assuming that if analyses of the current age, which are widely divergent in their theoretical foundations and in their normative implications, are surprisingly congruent in their basic empirical conclusions, then a social fact is being referred to that is of central significance for societies like Germany. Regardless of all theoretical differences, I consider the empirical evidence for the destructuring-thesis as an important starting point for further analysis.

The problematic implications of the expression 'social destructuring', which suggests a one-sided and negative interpretation of the empirical findings, are something I do not confer with. Instead, I assume that processes of social differentiation and destructuring are accompanied by processes of social integration and the formation of new social and personal structures. My thesis is that we are going through processes of social mediation, social integration and restructuring that are accompanying, *contemporaneously*, the dismantling and reconstruction of the 'traditional' industrial society and welfare state structures, institutions, role patterns and normative orientations. In Germany we can observe how the need for social mediation, social integration and communitarianism is growing, parallel to the manifestations of social destructuring, disintegration and social isolation. In response to these changes, a range of institutions and activities has been developed for years now which process these needs and satisfy them by and large. Of course, this occurs nowadays in different forms and by different means that in the past. Only if one considers the interrelation of destructuring and restructur-

2 As an example of the dramatising contributions to a new journalistic and literary criticism with public impact, see the manifesto entitled 'Weil das Land sich ändern muß' ('Because the country must change') (Dönhoff et al. 1992) and H.M. Enzensberger's essay 'Aussichten auf den Bürgerkrieg' ('The prospect of civil war') (Enzensberger 1994).

ing, the thesis of social destructuring becomes a suitable starting part for the theoretical interpretation of our research results.

Fundamental social tasks of reproduction and mediation, such as the physical and psychosocial reproduction of the individual person, social integration, cultural mediation and community-building[3], are increasingly the object of reflexive activity on the part of individuals (Giddens 1995, 143f) - and of professional activities aimed at supporting this process. In other words, they are becoming a focus of formalised work, and an issue in lifelong 'biographical learning', both formally and informally. Societal reproduction and mediation, and the formation of new social and personal structures are now supported to an increasing extent by the professional work in the various fields of cooperative person-oriented services. This is the thesis I put forward on the basis of our research results, and another starting point for their theoretical interpretation. Even communities receive professional assistance, guidance and supervision; communitarianism is increasingly initiated and 'staged' by professionals (Puch 1988 and 1991).

In putting forward this thesis I am not disputing that traditional social institutions for reproduction, integration and mediation, such as the family, the church and religious communities, or local and symbolic communities, which social theory has already written off as pre-modern, continue to perform their functions for many individuals in an effective way. However, this no longer applies for as many as it did 40 years ago, and for most it is only true for a limited time. Nor do I wish to ignore the fact that modern organisations and institutions are a constant source of social integration and collective communitarianism, or political and cultural mediation. Examples included shared housing and communes, but extends via sub-cultural scenes and milieus, social movements and political networks to associations, federations and parties, and even applies to the mass media and their changing publics. For all that, social memberships and collective identities, socio-moral orientations and motivations, and socio-integrative competences and patterns of action cannot be acquired solely through informal lifelong learn-

3 The concepts are still somewhat vague. I borrow from Habermas (Habermas 1981) and Peters (Peters 1993), but deviate from them in some respects. Space prohibits a closer analysis of the theoretical conceptions referred to, or a more precise definition of my own. This has been done elsewhere.

ing, 'on the side', so to speak, and anchored sub-consciously in the person in the form of habitus. Such easy everyday socialisation is counteracted today by the contradictory demands of distinct and competing social reference systems and reference groups, and by the accelerated transformation of cultural interpretations, meanings and orientations within pluralist lifeworlds.

Most of the person-oriented services we investigated originated in a situation in which, for a growing number of people, there are simply no permanent and stable given and stabilising personal relations of trust in their day-to-day lives; these have to be created on a regular basis by such individuals themselves, either alone or with others. Very few are able to escape the pressure exerted by the constantly changing demands and burdens resulting from ongoing social processes of differentiation and from the accelerated processes of social and cultural destructuring and restructuring. And very few are able (or want) to face these processes in the long run without professional support. Our research results corroborate this thesis in a quite paradoxical manner: The people we interviewed commenced their histories in the alternative movement with the collective will to achieve 'unity and simplicity of life'. Their programme for de-differentiating life, work and political activity, including de-institutionalisation and de-professionalisation of work and politics, is aimed at nothing other than social destructuring, although in the opposing direction to current modernisation processes. This means that they deliberately attempted to withdraw from the modernisation process into a 'counter-world' in which they were protected from that self-same process. Despite this objective, they, too, became drawn into the general pull of modern differentiation and restructuring. In the end, it was they themselves who pushed forward the modern differentiation and restructuring process by transforming the unitary 'alternative' context of their own 'holistic' person-oriented activities into specialized professional labour.

Viewed in this way, the people in the alternative movement appear initially as deviants and as 'drop-outs' from modernisation, and ultimately as late-comers. This analytical perspective[4] is too superficial and undialectical,

4 This is the perspective taken by social scientists who adopt a rather more critical stance vis-à-vis the alternative movements. One prominent position is that taken by Habermas, who sees the new social

however, in that they were always in fact agents of modernisation and restructuring. They have already made key contributions to social restructuring and modernisation – they have drawn attention to new social problems and needs; have discovered and become involved in new fields for person-oriented services, and have experimented with and developed new cooperative methods and practices as well as participatory relations in the work context. And they are developing the requisite personal competences, qualifications and professional identity patterns. Their contribution to modernisation goes further than this, however. They invent, test and develop new institutional social structures as well. The next section focuses on this aspect.

3.2 New intermediary organisations and institutions between the state, the market and communities

Organisations, institutions and communities performing social integration and mediation functions are termed 'intermediary' in a specific social theory context with a long tradition - especially in France (Montesquieu, de Toqueville, Durkheim). The basic assumption in this tradition is that modern societies are a differentiated unity comprised of many smaller social units. Individuals do not confront the large-scale units of national society, national culture or the nation-state directly; the manifold smaller social units or collective communities in which they are integrated through social morality act as mediators. A modern variation of this theoretical tradition relates the term 'intermediary' to the corporatist arrangements of modern welfare states. It is used, firstly, for organisations such as political parties, associations and trade unions, as well as for social movements, because these function as mediators of social and political interests between the individual citizen and the state (Streeck/Schmitter 1985; Streeck 1987; Roth 1992 und 1994). Secondly, the term is applied, especially in Germany, to welfare agencies, sick-

movements of the 1970s and 1980s, with the exception of the feminist movement, only as 'resistance and withdrawal movements' with 'defensive character' (Habermas 1981, vol. 2, 578), with an 'unrealistic' and broken, hence non-viable relationship to modernity and modernisation.

ness funds, health organisations and their various facilities, which operate as quasi-state, corporatist organisations and institutions in the German system of welfare and health care, mediating between the individual clients or patients and the welfare state (Bauer 1987 and 1991; Evers 1990).

A further definition of intermediarity has recently been added to the rather traditional definition. In the context of recent international research on the 'nonprofit sector' or the so-called 'third sector' (see James 1989; Salamon/ Anheier 1992; Anheier/Seibel 1990 and 1996; Anheier/Priller 1995), and the debate over the concepts of welfare production and the 'welfare mix' (Evers 1990; Evers & Winterhager 1990), there are also attempts to redefine what is 'intermediary' and to introduce a new concept of the 'intermediary sectors' into scientific debate (Evers 1992; Effinger 1993). The traditional definition still proceeds from a conception of society as a hierarchic social order, with the state at the top level in the form of the actively interventionist or 'preceptory welfare state' (Willke 1992); in this conception, intermediary organisations and institutions mediate in a certain sense in the vertical dimension between individuals and the state. The modern definition, in contrast, assumes the parallel existence of different, distinct and demarcated socio-economic spheres and social systems; the sphere of the state and public service agencies has theoretically equal status alongside the sphere of market and profit-oriented economy and the community sphere comprising families, private households, informal networks and 'expressive communities' (Peters 1993). Intermediary organisations and institutions operate between these various spheres; they mediate horizontally between the state, the market and communities. In terms of organisational structure and work methods, they represent dynamic hybrid forms in which organisational elements, rationales and regulation mechanisms, but more especially financial and personnel resources from the various spheres can be combined with each other in different ways. Such innovative hybrid structures are typical features of the organisations and institutions in our study. In this sense, we can define and classify the organisations and institutions we investigated as intermediary organisations and institutions. Viewed in this way, they form a small segment in a comprehensive social network of intermediary organisations and institutions of greatly varying size and structure, to which the term 'intermediary field' is sometimes applied (see Effinger 1993).

The more recent definition corresponds to the more recent theoretical notion, briefly referred to above, of a modern complex society in which there is no longer any legitimate structural superordination of the sphere of state vis-a-vis the society. This society has since long begun to restructure itself, in that the rather strictly demarcated socio-economic spheres and 'operatively autonomous' social systems (Luhmann 1984) now enter into contact, competition or cooperation with each other at the same level. Of course, this process is not going on without contradictions. There are constantly attempts to establish again conditions of super- and subordination through exclusion, as well as attacks, 'inequitable dominance' or monopolies of specific spheres or systems towards others (Walzer 1983) - for which global capitalism provides sufficient current examples. But also new networks or even innovative social structures with new personal structures can thus develop. The intermediary organisations and institutions in the fields of person-oriented services that we investigated embody, in my interpretation, such innovative social structures. They establish new kinds of structural mediation between the spheres of state, market and community. They also mediate in a specific manner, depending on the specific tasks and activities, between specifically differentiated social systems or sub-systems, or between different social lifeworlds and competing systems of cultural orientation and knowledge. Intermediarity in this sense is another theoretical concept on which my interpretation of our research results and further research is based.

Institutions in the public service sector or quasi-public service also obtain intermediary character in the course of accelerated modernisation: They are transformed into legally and economically independent nonprofit organisations, the number of which is constantly growing. Their structures and methods of operation distance them from the state and quasi-state organisational forms and procedures within the corporatist-welfare state arrangements that have a tradition in West Germany, especially in the fields of person-oriented services, also in core areas of continuing education and training. Just as in the small, alternative projects that were independent from the outset, institutional structures and methods of operation are being recombined here, too, with what were previously separate social spheres of state, market and community. The internal organisational restructuring that leads to an as yet unusual institutional mix of market-oriented, managerial, legal and welfare-state bureaucratic and person- and community-oriented procedures and work methods, is intended to enable these institutions to assert themselves in future within their specific environments more independently of the state, of traditional governing bodies or of business enterprises.

If this is a trend within social modernisation, and there are indications that this is the case, the people who used to be members of the alternative movement might then become the subject of historical and social re-evaluation: instead of being the outsiders they were previously held as and wanted to be thought of, they would become pioneers of institutional restructuring. The new forms of institution, work organisation and professionality they invented could become models for the modernisation of traditional state or quasi-state service administrations, institutions and facilities, especially in the field of person-oriented services. Whether or not this will actually occur is still uncertain, of course. The competitive struggles going on in this field between new models for market mechanisms and enterprise management originating from the profit-oriented sector of the economy, and intermediary models from the nonprofit sector, have not yet been resolved.

For this reason, the existing concepts and strategies for restructuring the welfare state (Flora 1986; Heinze/Olk/Hilbert 1988; OECD 1988; BMWI 1993; EC-Commission 1993) provide a starting point for further inquiries subsequent to our research results. I should like to deal with this aspect briefly. We are observing at present how, parallel to the social restructuring processes I have been referring to, and partly interacting with them, that the structures, responsibilities and procedures of the relevant policy fields are changing. They are distancing themselves, more and more so in recent years, from the model of the actively interventionist, centrally planning and managing welfare state that provides comprehensive and lasting care. Instead, they are being realigned to perform functions and tasks such as general framework-setting and monitoring of certain minimum standards (management policies/*Ordnungspolitik*, recognition procedures and quality management), or initiative strategies (incentive systems, support programmes in the form of projects) and support measures (infrastructures). The traditional function of the welfare and interventionist state as an agent of redistribution and care provision is being confined to particularly needy sections of society and at a lower level than was previously the case (regional structural support, unemployment and social welfare benefit, local and regional policies to compensate for labour market and other social deficiencies, including programmes for continuing education and training). The state and its official policymaking levels are withdrawing to a 'mere' coordinating role in more and more areas. Willke has proposed the term '*Supervisionsstaat*' to describe the counselling and assisting role now played by the state (Willke 1992). In numerous policy fields, including continuing education and training, they no longer operate as actors with all-round responsibility, but also as actors within the framework of intermediary networks. However, this can only function if there are also sufficient intermediary institutions and fields of responsibility besides political actors and enterprises to ensure that the social functions, tasks and problems referred to in this paper are not to be abandoned solely to market mechanisms and for-profit organisations.

4. Outlook: What are the implications for adult and continuing education?

Adult and continuing education as a complex of specific person-related services reacts in a particularly sensitive and flexible way, as well as more rapidly than other social systems and organisations to new individual-subjective and social problems, demands, burdens and needs. It therefore has a special aptitude, as some more recent empirical studies have shown (Kuwan 1992; IfEB 1995), for acute, socially necessary mediation tasks.

Adult and continuing education pays an institutional price for this capacity, however: It has not developed into an independent system or sub-system within education, as was the intention in the West German 'Structural Plan' in the early 1970s, which envisaged a new 'quaternary institution system' for continuing education (Deutscher Bildungsrat 1970). At best, it has attained in Germany a 'middling degree of systematisation' (Faulstich u.a. 1991); even the latter only exists at regional level, and only in some core areas at that, such as state-recognised adult education or professional training geared to social policy or labour market policy. Adult and continuing education would no longer be able to assume the manifold tasks of social mediation and integration that comprise its particular social service function if it were to attain a significantly higher degree of systematisation and become a self-referential, operatively closed system or sub-system. The lower degree of systematisation is not a deficiency, but a functional prerequisite for its specific efficiency, and a factor on which its success with respect to social mediation functions depends.

Instead, adult and continuing education is an open intermediary network, or, more precisely, a network of networks, to which the most diverse participants and professional actors, not to mention different social systems, organisations and institutions have access. In this way, it is open not only to intervention and instrumentalisation on the part of other systems and actors, but also to cooperative arrangements and new combinations of tasks and functions, wishes and interests that in many cases would not come into more intensive contact with each other without the medium of continuing education. Intermediary institutions and networks that perform such functions are indispensable in modern societies, both for the identity and living together of individuals, as well as for the cohesion of society as a whole, and for the interaction of its sub-systems and socio-economic spheres (Berger/Luckmann 1995).

References

Alber, J. (1989), Der Sozialstaat in der Bundesrepublik 1950 -1983. Frankfurt a.M.

Alheim, K./Bender, W. (Hg.) (1996), Lernziel Konkurrenz? Erwachsenenbildung im 'Standort Deutschland'. Opladen

Anheier, H.K./Priller, E. (1995), Der Nonprofit-Sektor in Deutschland: eine sozial-ökonomische Strukturbeschreibung. Wissenschaftszentrum Berlin

Anheier H.K./Seibel, W. (eds.) (1990), The Third Sector. Comparative Studies of Nonprofit Organizations. Berlin/ New York

Anheier H.K./Seibel, W. (1996), The Nonprofit Sector in Germany. Manchester

Arbeiterselbsthilfe Frankfurt (Hg.) (1980), Anders Leben - Anders Arbeiten. Frankfurt a.M.

Bauer, R. (1987), Intermediäre Hilfesysteme personenbezogener Dienstleistungen in zehn Ländern - eine Einführung. In: Bauer, R./Thränhardt, A.-M. (Hg.): Verbandliche Wohlfahrtspflege im internationalen Vergleich. Opladen

Bauer, R. (1991), Intermediäre Instanzen im Strukturwandel der Sozialpolitik. In: Österreichische Zeitschrift für Soziologie, H. 1/1991

Beck, U. (1986), Risikogesellschaft - Auf dem Weg in eine andere Moderne. Frankfurt a.M.

Beck, U. (1993), Die Erfindung des Politischen - Zu einer Theorie reflexiver Modernisierung. Frankfurt a.M.

Berger, P./Luckmann, Th. (1995), Modernität, Pluralismus und Sinnkrise: die Orientierung des Menschen. Gütersloh

Beywl, W. (1987), Alternative Ökonomie - Selbstorganisierte Betriebe im Kontext neuer sozialer Bewegungen. In: Roth, R./Rucht, D. (1987)

Bookchin, M. u.a. (1981), Selbstverwaltung. Die Basis einer befreiten Gesellschaft. Reutlingen

Brand, K.-W./Büsser, D./Rucht, D. (1983), Aufbruch in eine andere Gesellschaft. Neue soziale Bewegungen in der Bundesrepublik. Frankfurt a.M./ New York

Brumlik, M./Brunckhorst, H. (Hg.) (1993), Gemeinschaft und Gerechtigkeit. Frankfurt a.M.

Bundesministerium für Wirtschaft (BMWI) (Hg.) (1993), Zukunftssicherung des Standorts Deutschland. Bonn

Callenbach, E. (1980), Ökotopia. Berlin

Connexions (1984), Das Addressbuch alternativer Projekte. Klingelbach

Das alternative Adressbuch (1977), Hg. v. Initiative Projekt Gruppengemeinschaft. Klingelbach

Dettling, W. (1995), Politik und Lebenswelt: vom Wohlfahrtsstaat zur Wohlfahrtsgesellschaft. Gütersloh

Deutscher Bildungsrat (1970), Empfehlungen der Bildungskommission: Strukturplan für das Bildungswesen. Stuttgart

Dönhoff, M. u.a. (1992), Ein Manifest: Weil das Land sich ändern muß. Reinbek

Dudek, A. (1987), Selbstorganisierte Bildungsarbeit im Wandel. In: Roth, R./Rucht, D. (Hg.) 1987

Effinger, H. (1990), Individualisierung und neue Formen der Kooperation. Bedingungen und Wandel alternativer Arbeits- und Angebotsformen. Opladen

Effinger, H. (1993), Soziale Dienste zwischen Gemeinschaft, Markt und Staat. In: Effinger, H./Luthe, D. (Hg.): Sozialmärkte und Management. Bremen

Effinger, H. (1993), Von der politischen zur professionellen Identität. Professionalisierung personenbezogener Dienstleistungen in Kooperativen des Intermediären Sektors als biografisch gesteuerter Prozeß. In: Journal für Sozialforschung, H. 1/1993, 31-48

Effinger, H./Körber, K. (1994), Zeit zum Erwachsenwerden - Zur Verberuflichung und Professionalisierung in Kooperativen des Intermediären Bereichs. In: SOCIALmanagement. H. 4/1994

Effinger, H./Schlake, S./Sosna, J. (1988), Vom Ausstieg zum Umbau. Forschungsbericht zum Projekt Arbeit und Leistung in lokalen Beschäftigungsinitiativen in der Region Bremen. Bremen

Enzensberger, H.M. (1993), Aussichten auf den Bürgerkrieg. Frankfurt a.M.

EU-Kommission (1993), Weißbuch zu Wachstum, Wettbewerbsfähigkeit, Beschäftigung. Brüssel

Evers, A (1990), Im Intermediären Bereich. Soziale Träger und Projekte zwischen Haushalt, Staat und Markt. In: Journal für Sozialforschung, H. 2/1990, 189-210

Evers, A. (1992), Soziale Bewegungen und soziale Ordnung im Konzept des Wohlfahrtsmix. In: Forschungsjournal Neue Soziale Bewegungen, H. 4/1992, 49-58

Evers, A./Winterhager, H. (1990), Shifts in the Welfaremix. Their Impact on Work, Social Services and Welfare Policies. Contributions of nine European Countries. Frankfurt a.M./New York

Faulstich, P. u.a. (1991), Notwendigkeit einer 'mittleren Systematisierung' der Weiterbildung. In: Faulstich, P./Teichler, U./Bojanoowski, A./Döring, O.: Bestand und Perspektiven der Weiterbildung: das Beispiel Hessen. Weinheim 1991, 42-59

Flora, P. (Hrsg.) (1986), Growth to Limits. The Western European Welfare States since World War II. Berlin

Gartner, A./Riesman, F. (1978), Der aktive Konsument in der Dienstleistungsgesellschaft. Frankfurt a.M.

Giddens, A. (1990), The Consequences of Modernity. Oxford (dt. Konsequenzen der Moderne. Frankfurt a.M. 1995)

Gyzicki H. v./Habicht, H. (1978), Oasen der Freiheit: von der Schwierigkeit der Selbstbestimmung. Berichte, Erfahrungen, Modelle. Frankfurt a.M.

Grottian, P./Kück, M (1983), Modell Berlin: 10 000 neue Arbeitsplätze im Selbsthilfe- und Alternativbereich. In: Bolle, M./Grottian, P. (Hg.): Arbeit schaffen - jetzt! Reinbek

Habermas, J. (1981), Theorie des kommunikativen Handelns, 2 Bde. Frankfurt a.M.

Heinze, R.G./Olk, T./Hilbert, J. (1988), Der neue Sozialstaat. Analyse und Reformperspektiven. Freiburg i. Br.

Honneth, A. (Hg.) (1993), Kommunitarismus: eine Debatte über die moralischen Grundlagen moderner Gesellschaften. Frankfurt a. M./New York

Honneth, A. (1994), Desintegration. Bruchstücke einer soziologischen Zeitdiagnose. Frankfurt a.M.

Hollstein, W./Penth, B. (1980), Alternativprojekte. Hamburg

Huber, J. (1980), Wer soll das alles ändern. Die Alternativen der Alternativbewegung. Berlin

Huber, J. (1984), Die zwei Gesichter der Arbeit. Ungenutzte Möglichkeiten der Dualwirtschaft. Frankfurt a.M.

IfEB Institut für Erwachsenen-Bildungsforschung (Körber, K./Kuhlenkamp, D./Peters, R./Schlutz, E./Schrader, J./Wilckhaus. F.) (1995), Das Weiterbildungsangebot im Lande Bremen - Strukturen und Entwicklungen in einer städtischen Region. Bremen

James, E. (1989), The Nonprofit Sector in International Perspective. Studies in Comparative Culture and Policy. New York/ Oxford

Körber, K./Effinger, H. (1995), Zur Professionalisierung von personenbezogenen Dienstleistungen in intermediären Organisationen. In: Grundlagen der Weiterbildung Zeitschrift, H. 6/1995, 347-352

Kurz, G. (1979), Alternativ leben? Zur Theorie und Praxis der Gegenkultur. Berlin

Kuwan, H. (1992), Berichtsystem Weiterbildung, hg. v. Bundesminister für Bildung und Wissenschaft. Bonn

Lüders, C. (1989), Der wissenschaftlich ausgebildete Praktiker. Weinheim

Luhmann, N. (1984), Soziale Systeme. Grundriß einer allgemeinen Theorie. Frankfurt a.M.

Mouffe, C. (ed.) (1992), Dimensions of Radical Democracy: Pluralism, Citizenship, Community. London/New York

Müschen, K. (1982), Lieber lebendig als normal! Selbstorganisation, kollektive Lebensformen und alternative Ökonomie. Bensheim

OECD (1988), The Future of Social Protection. Paris

Puch, H.-J. (1988), Inszenierte Gemeinschaften. Gesellschaftlicher Wandel und lebensweltliche Handlungsstrategien in der sozialen Arbeit. Frankfurt a.M./Bern/New York/ Paris

Puch, H.-J. (1991), Inszenierte Gemeinschaften - Gruppenangebote in der Moderne. In: neue praxis, H. 1/1991, 12-25

Peters, B. (1993), Die Integration moderner Gesellschaften. Frankfurt a.M.

Roth, R. (1994), Demokratie von unten. Neue soziale Bewegungen auf dem Wege zur politischen Institution. Köln

Roth, R. (1992), Jenseits von Markt und Staat - Dritter Sektor und neue soziale Bewegungen. In: Forschungsjournal Neue Soziale Bewegungen, H. 2/1992, 12-20

Roth, R./Rucht, D. (Hg.) (1987), Neue soziale Bewegungen in der Bundesrepublik Deutschland. Frankfurt a.M./New York

Salamon, L.M./Anheier H.K. (1992), In Search of the Nonprofit Sector. Working Papers of the John Hopkins Comparative Nonprofit Sector Project. Baltimore

Schülein, J.A. (Hg.): Auf der Suche nach Zukunft. Alternativbewegung und Identität. Gießen

Schwendter, R. (1973): Theorie der Subkultur. Köln

Schwendter, R. (Hg.) (1986a), Die Mühen der Berge. Grundlegungen zur alternativen Ökonomie, Teil 1. München

Schwendter, R. (Hg.) (1986b), Die Mühen der Ebenen. Grundlegungen zur alternativen Ökonomie, Teil 2. München

Sosna, J. (1987), Netzwerk Selbsthilfe: Eine Idee koordinierender Projektarbeit verändert sich. In: Roth, R./ Rucht, D. (Hg.) (1987)

Streeck, W./Schmitter, P.C. (1985), Gemeinschaft, Markt und Staat - und die Verbände? In: Journal für Sozialforschung, H. 2/1985, 133-157

Streeck, W. (1988), Vielfalt und Interdependenz: Probleme intermediärer Organisationen in sich ändernden Umwelten. Wissenschaftszentrum Berlin

Sturzenhecker, B. (1994), Wie studieren Diplom-Pädagogen? Studienbiografien im Dilemma von Wissenschaft und Praxis. Weinheim

Thomssen, W./Henschel, R./Körber, K./Tutschner, R./Twisselmann, J. (1994), Politische Kultur und Sozialwissenschaften. Zum Aufklärungspotential sozialwissenschaftlichen Wissens in der Praxis von Volkshochschulen. Bremen

Toffler, A. (1980), Die Zukunftschance. München

Walzer, M. (1992), Sphären der Gerechtigkeit. Ein Plädoyer für Pluralität und Gleichheit. Frankfurt a.M./New York

WestBerliner Stattbuch 1 (1978), Berlin

Willke, H. (1992), Ironie des Staates. Grundlinien einer Staatstheorie polyzentrischer Gesellschaft. Frankfurt a.M.

Zahlmann, C. (Hrsg.) (1992), Kommunitarismus in der Diskussion. Berlin

Liam Kane

New Social Movements and Popular Education: Lessons from Latin America

This paper will argue that a study of the recent history of popular education in Latin America has much to teach about the possibilities, and limitations, of popular education 'outside conventional institutions'. It will begin with a brief discussion of the relationship between education and New Social Movements (NSMs), describe the salient features of Latin American popular education and go on to consider what specific lessons could be learned.

New Social Movements and Education

Even among educators working for social change, it is important not to assume uniform, unquestioning support for all New Social Movements. Different political perspectives will affect our understanding of how education can be of benefit to NSMs. In turn, this understanding will be the lens through which we view other experiences in the field of comparative education, in this case that of Latin America. It is important, then, that my own understanding of New Social Movements is made clear from the start.

As a socialist, in general terms I personally see New Social Movements as a good thing. They provide an alternative route to political activism and draw into their ranks many who would not otherwise participate in the political process; they allow people to challenge energy into real concerns and bypass the bureaucracy of conventional politics; they encourage the view that politics is not just the business of politicians but that ordinary people can become subjects of change. Moreover, evidence of their impact on society is all around us, from the everyday language we use, to equal opportunity policies, to both governments and businesses striving to appear ever greener than grass. Though the extent and duration of their success is open to debate, I certainly see New Social Movements as an important and positive force for change.

In my view, however, there are other aspects of New Social Movements which should caution against according them wholehearted, unqualified approval. The first of these is that not all social movements (or currents within Social Movements) are necessarily progressive. Environmentalist groups who campaign against global deforestation (or in favour of population control) but do not challenge the *economic* oppression experienced by Third World peasants, for example, are inherently reactionary. In this vision, peasants, not the brutalities of capitalism, can end up being blamed for deforestation and what may pass as progress in purely environmental terms can have terrible social consequences: I think of impoverished coffee growers in the Dominican Republic who have been jailed for violating 'green' legislation though their daily survival depended on cutting down trees for fuel. Arguably, depending on the definition used, it could even be possible to include overtly racist organisations in the category of European social movements: they are widespread, they feel passionately about a political issue which affects them, they create a collective sense of identity and through conventional political channels they take action to bring about their idea of 'progress'. This is an extreme example, of course, but it makes the point that social movements are diverse, each should be judged on its own merits and this judgement will rest to a large extent on our own political values.

Another key issue is the way in which NSMs relates to wider issues of injustice and oppression outside their immediate concerns. From my perspective, there is a real danger that in the fragmented, autonomous nature of their struggle, groups engaged in 'identity politics' make it easier for capitalism to survive unchallenged. A tendency to see problems in terms of men, white people, heterosexuals or car owners, for example, means that not only are different oppressed groups not united, they can end up blaming each other for their oppression. The real oppressors, I would contend, are happy to deal with the compartmentalisation of protest and fan the flames of disunity. In her essay on 'mistaken identity', though I think she fails to appreciate their value in encouraging initial engagement in political activity, Sharon Smith makes a powerful case for concluding that with the identity politics of Social Movements 'the veneer is radical, but the substance is not' (Smith, 1994:47).

Popular Education in Latin America

A detailed account of Popular Education in Latin America would require a book to itself. In this article I will simply focus on a few areas which I think can best inform our thinking on the relationship between education and New Social Movements in Europe. In particular, this will relate to the methodological framework of popular education and the ways in which provision is organised. I will assume some familiarity with the ideas of Paulo Freire.

Two preliminary points ought to be made: firstly, in Latin American Spanish and Portuguese the word 'popular' has connotations which do not exist in the English equivalent. It means 'of the people', the 'people' being the working class, the unemployed, peasants, the 'poor' and sometimes even the lower middle class: it excludes and stands in contradistinction to the well-off middle class and the rich. Trade unions, neighbourhood associations, peasant associations, co-operatives, human rights groups - all would be referred to as 'popular' organisations, collectively known as the popular movement. Popular education is committed to serving this movement and though it rejects out of hand vanguardist attempts to impose supposedly objective truths, a class analysis of society is clearly at its heart: 'the practice of popular education has as its objective the strengthening and consolidation of class-based organisations' (Jara, 1989:56). It is a central feature of my analysis that while a popular movement is, per se, a social movement, the converse is not necessarily the case and with the term 'popular education' gaining global currency, it is essential to reassert its commitment to the most exploited sectors in society.

Secondly, it is important to highlight this symbiotic link between popular education and popular organisations. It means that alongside encouraging higher levels of political awareness and activity, popular education necessarily addresses key issues related to effective organisation: the role of leaders and activists, how to encourage participation, collective analysis and systematisation of experience, for example. This is something which I think is often missing from 'first world' attempts to put 'Freirian' education into practice.

The Methodology of Popular Education

Though the two are often confused, the methodology of popular education is quite distinct from the pedagogical techniques that may be used in a classroom-type situation. The former is a set of principles guiding how to approach the educational dimension of any aspect of popular, transformatory practice; the latter a set of tools which enables these principles to be practised in one particular context. The Central American popular education network, Alforja, has been particularly critical of this confusion and in its attempts to clear it up has developed some theoretical concepts worthy of examination. In all its work in training educators and activists throughout the region, whether they work in urban or rural settings, with women, Indians or youth, whether the theme is land, housing, human rights or community development - Alforja promotes what has come to be known as the 'Conception of a Dialectical Methodology' (CDM). Let us briefly dissect and examine what Antillon (1991) calls the 'essential elements of the CDM'.

At the heart of this '*Conception*' is the view that the politics of domination lead to the creation of oppressed and exploited classes and that popular educators have a political commitment to the oppressed - classic Freire, in fact. In addition, however, this commitment requires an organic link with the popular movement in its many different expressions of political militancy.

In the experience of Alforja, '*Dialectical*' thinking can help strengthen the popular movement in at least three crucial areas. The first is when considering the relationship between (social) theory and practice: this is based on the belief that 'social practice is the source, test and ultimate end of the process of knowing, the principle which invalidates all those programmes emanating from preconceived theories and whose application to reality ends up becoming mechanical and laboured' (Antillon, 1991:3). The second is to see history as a process in which the actions and practice of social subjects interact with the historical context (time, place, political conjuncture) of which they are part. The third is that while reality exists as a totality, it is also multiple, complex and contradictory. Human relationships take place in many contexts (at work, home, church, in struggle, for example) and the identity of any given society is never equal to the sum of its parts.

A dialectical '*Methodology*' seeks to enable educator/activists to operate in a manner consistent with these principles in all aspects of their work with popular organisations. Firstly, it means that the 'project of liberation' should constantly be developed from the particular social practice of the organisation, the latter expressed in its political, economic, ideological, cultural, routine, interpersonal (etc) activities. The continual confrontation between what the organisation does (practice), what it thinks it is doing (conception) and the circumstances in which it is operating (context) means it is possible to start the process of 'theorising from practice'. Secondly, in aspiring to an 'internal consistency' with these principles, the educator should conduct him/herself in a manner which promotes democracy and participation: a project cannot work for liberation if key activists reinforce values produced by the system of oppression. Accordingly, workers should develop appropriate styles of leadership and for occasions given over to deeper reflection and analysis (that is, the 'workshop'), become competent in the use of a wide range of pedagogical tools. Thirdly, unlike the functionalist practice of those who parcel up reality into professional specialisms, while popular education will be explicit about which thematic line is being explored, dialectically, educators will endeavour to relate the particular to a wider, integrated reality.

There are additional features inherent in this Conception of a Dialectical Methodology (a concern with the question of culture, for example, the need to encourage participation) but space prevents further elaboration. In summary, then, the CDM 'gives life to the organisational processes, generating a style of working, a vision of the world and the appropriation of new values and theoretical knowledge which are then expressed in a new way of being. The CDM applies globally to all processes of social transformation and is not restricted to strictly educational events' (Jara, 1989:58). Bearing in mind the importance of this overall methodological orientation, it is now time to look briefly at the pedagogical tools characteristic of popular education.

Tools of the Trade: Participative Techniques

A wide variety of participative techniques have been developed to enable a popular education methodology to be put into practice and Bustillos and Vargas (1992) bring together an impressive selection for all occasions, a rich reserve, in fact, for pedagogical predators of any discipline. Discussion techniques, drama, artwork, allegory, song - the whole of popular culture is imaginatively exploited to enable groups to assess their relationship to political and social reality. Among those I personally find useful is 'statues', where someone in a group 'sculpts' other participants into a human statue as a codification for whatever issue is being explored. In debating whether or not this is an accurate representation, other participants step in, explain their dissent and change the statue accordingly. The statue becomes the focal point of discussion and makes it easier for those who are less erudite to participate. Importantly, it is also fun to do and the final visual image can be photographed for future reference.

In the same vein, sociodramas, or what Boal (1992) calls 'Forum Theatre', are also widely used in popular education. A few participants re-enact a scene relating to whichever aspect of the organistion's practice is being examined. This can then be repeated with other participants stopping the sketch at any point, stepping into the role of any of the actors and acting out what they consider would have been a better course of action. The sociodrama then unfolds in an unpredictable fashion with the various options being analysed later in an 'out-of-role' discussion. The sociodrama is a versatile codification allowing people to take a step back from reality and engage in what Boal calls 'a rehearsal for life'.

Straddling the two areas of 'methodology' and 'techniques', Alforja have developed an extended activity called the 'Triple Self-Diagnosis' which, in keeping with their 'Conception of a Dialectical Methodology' and the desire to start from practice, not theory, is seen as a useful tool for initial contact work with organisations. In the first step of this activity the group diagnoses its own *Conception* of what it is trying to do: here a typical technique used would be a 'card brainstorm', where, in groups of 4-6, on separate cards, participants anonymously write down their three main objectives in being part of the organisation. All cards are brought together and each group discusses and categorises these objectives. The educator then co-ordinates discussion between groups, and tries to synthesise the proceedings. Step two would be an examination of the *Context* in which the organisation operates (whether this is primarily local, regional or national will depend on the organisation's perceptions). Typically, small groups codify and present their understanding of the context in the form of a song, rap or drawing. The third step concerns the *Practice* of the organisation. Individually, people write down all the things they actually do and groups then present this information to the plenary in the form of a sociodrama. Having conducted the triple-self diagnosis, the educator then encourages deeper analysis, looking for inconsistencies and contradictions in what has come out. Discussions would be focused on attempts to construct a three-columned chart under the headings of '*Consistencies*', '*Inconsistencies*' and '*Knots*' (that is, issues which have to be straightened out). When the activity is completed, organisation members (and the educator/activist) should have a clear picture of the multiple, complex and contradictory aspects of the organisation's practice: this will be the basis for subsequent theorising on what can be done to bring about social change.

But an important point has to be made regarding these techniques and Bustillos and Vargas give a clear warning that 'on its own, the use of Participatory Techniques for Popular Education gives no guarantee whatsoever that popular education is actually being practised' (1992, Tomo 1.1). Isolated from a methodological orientation seeking to empower the oppressed, the techniques in themselves are not only not radical, they can actually be used for reactionary purposes: even the CIA tried to order copies of the Bustillos & Vargas collection. This is, in fact, symptomatic of a wider phenomenon in Latin America, the attempt to co-opt popular education into conservative political projects.

The Organisational Structures of Popular Education

Popular education takes place in such a wide variety of settings and with such varying degrees of intentionality that no simple picture of its organisation emerges. However, I find it helpful to think in terms of three different levels of practice.

First and foremost, at the grassroots, there is the popular education which by design or default necessarily takes place within popular organisations themselves. As these organisations engage in the struggle for change (whether focused on issues of land, services, women, Indians, human rights etc.) an educational process is set in motion. The advantage taken of educational opportunities will depend on the abilities of the members themselves, their key leaders and activists and any support given by outside bodies.

Also at the grassroots, though initially independent of the popular movement, are the thousands of small-scale 'development projects' funded by charities and Non Governmental Organisations to improve the economic status of poorer communities. While some NGOs never emerge from an assistentialist position, others understand the political nature of poverty and the importance of concurrently promoting community organisation. In this context, with its experience of starting from immediate concerns (such as water, health, housing, income generation etc.) and relating these to wider issues of politics, power and organisation, popular education has an important role to play. By 1986 it was such an integral part of its work that an NGO such as Oxfam UK, for example, felt the need to organise a week-long seminar on popular education for all its staff in Latin America.

Crucially, at an intermediate level, independent of the state and funded by NGOs, there is a vast array of 'support centres' which exist to give different kinds of assistance to different types of popular organisation. These are staffed by professional educator/organisers, most of whom have come to popular education via left-wing politics, liberation theology or the study of social sciences. These centres of popular education come under a variety of names and guises: 'Women's Network' in Brazil, for example; 'Integral Corporation for Social and Cultural Development', Colombia; 'Ecuadorian Institute of Popular Education, Research and Promotion' (CEAAL.1992. 133-134). The centres may vary in size (from two to up to thirty full-time staff) and have expertise in a specific area; some work with many different organisations and some may even only work with one, operating, in effect, as the educational wing of that particular organisation.

The specific support provided can vary but a key element is the training of activists in the principles and methodology of popular education. To take one example, the Mexican Institute of Community Development runs a 'School of Methodology' attended by activists from popular organisations throughout the country. Four times a year they participate in a week-long workshop, going back to their organisations in between to test out the methodology in practice. Not only does this enable key activists (and their organisations) to become more effective, the act of bringing together different organisations itself contributes to the strengthening of a wider popular movement.

Though structurally separate from the centres, another group operating at intermediate level would be the many radical priests, nuns, catechists and religious who, through the theology of liberation's 'option for the poor', involve themselves in popular education within the specific context of Christian Base Communities.

At a higher level still are the various networks of all those working in popular education, where centres can come together to share resources and expertise. Again, a by-product of such collaboration is the strengthening of links between organisations. This networking takes place at both national and regional levels, the aforementioned Alforja being an example of the latter. At the highest level of all, practitioners, centres and networks from all over Latin America come together through the Latin American Centre for Adult Education (CEAAL). CEAAL organises working parties on different aspects of popular education (the training of educators, for example, 'popular communication'), encourages research and co-ordinates debate on educational issues through a regular newsletter (La Carta) and a weightier, termly journal on education and politics (La Piragua).

Other Issues

Popular education is now so widespread in Latin America that it can be properly called a 'social movement' in itself. As might be expected, there are different currents of thought within this movement and given the range of political and economic contexts involved, the actual practice of popular education is more varied and complex than could have been described in this essay. A fuller investigation would also look at such areas as participatory research, communication and self-management; it would examine research into problems such as the gap between rhetoric and reality or the difficulties in being effective at macro level (CEAAL. 1993); it could usefully compare the performance of popular education in different political contexts, from military dictatorship to revolution; it might also explore the tensions between popular education and ideology (Marxism and Christianity, for example) and the relationship between popular education/organising and conventional politics.

In the context of the late 1990s, there are also new challenges to face and to some extent popular education is currently undergoing a fundamental review of its practice. One concern is to ensure that the specialist sub-divisions remain part of a wider movement with an integrated view of reality. Another is the relationship with the state and the formal educational sector. Historically, popular education has normally existed in opposition to the state but with the apparent triumph of neo-liberalism in the late 90's, revolutionary change is no longer seen as being just round the corner and there is currently debate about whether more work should be done within the system. As elsewhere, certain political paradigms are also in crisis and the influence of postmodernism is starting to grow. However, as Carlos Nuñez, secretary of CEAAL, argues, since popular educators have always promoted a political practice 'from and with the people...this has been our insurance against disaster' (Nunez, 93).

Lessons for European Social Movements

The social and political context in Europe is obviously different from that of Latin America. Here, in the UK at least, adult education is dominated by formal state provision while in Latin America there is a large vacuum in which non-formal, popular education can flourish; the paucity of state-provided services in Latin America gives heightened importance to popular and social organisations though some would argue that with European governments generally trying to 'roll back the state' here too, an increasing importance should be attached to this 'third sector' (Jacobs, 1996:96-104); it has also been argued that 'new social movements in Europe mainly represent a response to post-industrial contradictions, and those in Latin America primarily arise in response to clearly material demands' (Hellman, 1992:53). Bearing all this in mind, what can New Social Movements in Europe take from the Latin American experience?

I think that the Latin American experience challenges all New Social Movements to articulate their conception of political and educational practice, particularly as this relates to wider issues of social injustice. Popular education will be relevant to European NSMs in so far as they can make connections with the political vision on which it is based: this, as I argued at the outset, will vary both within and between NSMs. Latin America too has NSMs which are far from radical, even reactionary (cf Crummet's study (1994) of 'Women's Power' and the overthrow of Allende in Chile), but these have nothing at all to do with popular education. In Europe, for NSM organisations inherently and conscientiously conservative, then barring co-option of a few pedagogical tools, I would suggest that Latin American popular education has nothing at all to offer.

If we can assume that there are many currents within NSMs which could have some affinity with the politics of popular education in Latin America, what could they actually learn from this experience? Firstly, I would say, an awareness that in all aspects of their practice, activists and organisers have a key educational role to play. In Latin America, popular education pays close attention to matters of organisation; to styles of leadership, publicity, how to conduct meetings and public events and how to involve members in the production and systematisation of new knowledge. It does not simply address the technical aspects of these functions, however, but seeks to find ways of carrying them out which are consistent with such underlying principles as democratisation, participation and empowerment. Materials such as Equipo IMDEC's 'It Isn't Easy Being A Leader' (1994), for example, would provide NSM organiser/activists with useful points for discussion.

In constructs such as the 'Conception of a Dialectical Methodology', the concise articulation of a methodology of social practice is a useful reference point for debate; if activist/organisers connect with the underlying values, then the distillation of complex philosophy, ethics and social science into a recognisable modus operandi is of great practical help. As it stands, however, the direct importation of the CDM into Europe would have problems. When translated into English, for example, the language is obtuse and activists would need considerable training before it could be taken seriously: how, when and where this training could be provided is another matter. Moreover, as the CDM has clear echoes in the dialectical materialism of Marx, it may not be well received by anyone holding superficial, stereotypical ideas about Marxism. This would be ironic as the principles of the CDM itself are often invoked against supposedly Marxist vanguards imposing their version of reality on the 'people'.

If and when NSMs have the opportunity to organise specifically educational events, then the participative techniques of popular education are not only pedagogically appropriate, they have the potential to galvanise a boring obligation into a dynamic attraction. Again, in their raw state, some of these may be culturally inappropriate and need adapting to suit but they do provide a rich source of inspiration and have been successfully tried and tested in the 'first world' context too (Arnold/Barndt/Burke, 1983/1994). However, as the Latin American experience warns, participative techniques in themselves do not constitute popular education and arguably, in fact, management theories in Europe have already co-opted the concept of 'participation' to a different project from that envisaged by popular education.

The organisational structure of popular education in Latin America provides a vision of what is possible outside the conventional institutions though given the much higher degree of formal adult education in Europe, I cannot see non-formal education assuming the massive importance it has in Latin America. It seems to me, however, that this vision could inspire several developments in the practice of NSM organisations. Firstly, there is a need to take education seriously, commit resources to it and develop an educational strategy which will impact on the whole organisation. The most ambitious strategy would be to work towards creating a popular education movement based around centres which could lend educational support and training to as many organisations as possible. In the UK, in fact, the 'development movement' comes close to this model as many development organisations jointly fund Development Education Centres which are staffed by professional educators whose allegiance belongs to the movement rather than to any particular funding body. DECs remain independent from the state and do a considerable amount of adult education, including the in-service training of teachers in the formal sector. If funding were available, an expansion of DECs into the field of popular education would make sense and currently, in England, an attempt to do precisely that looks extremely encouraging (Kane, 1995). While there are potential problems with this arrangement, as popular education is likely to attract political hostility and charity laws constrain the activities of NGOs, it is at least an encouraging example of how in a European context, independent education centres can flourish. The idea of multi-agency funded centres would also ensure that the interests being pursued were those of popular education, not individual agencies, wasteful competition would be avoided and as in Latin America, joint, co-operative projects might also play a role in developing and strengthening a movement.

In Easterhouse, an area of multiple deprivation on the outskirts of Glasgow, a group of prominent community activists have recently set up a body called Popular Democracy and Educational Resources, known by the acronym PODER which in Spanish means 'power'. This developed from a visit to Nicaragua by one of the activists in which she was inspired by what she saw of popular education. Operating, in effect, as a popular education centre, PODER provides educational support to the many small but isolated groups trying to bring about change in Easterhouse. It also tries to create opportunities for these groups to interconnect and gather strength in unity. The members of PODER keenly participate in any available training modelled on Latin American popular education and while it is still early to evaluate the wider significance of their project, and its long-term funding is in no way secure, it is another manifestation of European groups looking to Latin America for a different way of working.

In the absence of a network of centres (or even a single centre), if a nucleus of NSM personnel were committed to popular education, a practical interim step would be a joint project to set up a 'methodological school' for activists - of the kind run by IMDEC in Mexico. This idea is currently under discussion in Scotland and will hopefully start to take shape following the launch next year of a book on Scottish popular education. As in Latin America, an important offshoot of such a school would be to develop networks of mutually supportive organisations: it is telling that visiting activists from Latin America often comment on the isolated nature of Scottish 'development projects' and the need to integrate these into a popular movement.

Finally, though popular education in Latin America grew in response to the needs of the popular movement, at times it has also been proactive and has itself played a role in the creation of new organisations. With this in mind, those of us formally working in adult education with NSMs could usefully consider whether we might have a contribution to make. Despite the contradictions inherent in working for social change while employed by the state, within Gramsci's concept of a 'site of struggle' there is much which can still be done. I am happy to say that the ranks of those currently promoting popular education in Scotland include many (state-employed) community education workers and, surprisingly enough, even the odd academic!

Conclusion

I have no wish to put Latin American popular education on a pedestal. It might even be argued that some of what I describe is simply good educational practice which has existing parallels in Europe. However, due to the particularities of the Latin American context, non-formal education has gained a central role in attempts to promote social change over the last forty years: the richness of this experience makes it an obvious source of ideas on ways of doing education with conventional institutions. I have tried to draw attention to aspects of this experience which I think are particularly relevant but the real test lies in the extent to which 'popular' and 'social' concerns are able to converge. It is to those who perceive the need to bring about such a convergence that the Latin American experience of popular education will have most to offer.

References

Antillon, R. (1991), ¿Cuales Son Los Elementos Esenciales de la CMD? Guadalajara, Mexico IMDEC

Arnold, R., Brandt, D., Burke B. (1994), A new Wave: Popular Education in Canada & Central America Ontario CUSO & OISE

Arnold, R., Burke B. (1983), A Popular Education Handbook Ontario CUSO & OISE

Boal, A. (1992), Games for Actors and Non-Actors London Routledge

Bustillos, G. & Vargas, L. (1992)Técnicas Participativas para la Educatión Popular. Tomos 1 & 2. Guadalajara, Mexico IMDEC

CEAAL (1992), Desde Adentro: La Educación Vista Por Sus Practicantes Guadalajara, Mexico IMDEC

CEAAL (1993), Nuestras Prácticas: Perfil y Perspectivas de la Formación de Educadores Populares en Ltinoamérica Mexico CEAAL

Crummet, MA (1994), El Poder Femenino: The Mobilisation if Women Against Socialism in Chile in Dominguez, Jl Social Movements in Latin America: the Experience of Peasants, Workers, Women, the Urban Poor and the Middle Sectors (pp 169-180) New York Garland

Equipo IMDEC (1994), Ser dirigente no es cosa fácil: métodos, estilos y valores del dirigente popular' Guadalajara, Mexico IMDEC

Hellmann, JA (1992), The Study of New Social Movements in Latin America and the Question of Autonomy in Escobar, A The Making of Social Movements in Latin America (ppa 52-61), A & Alvarez, S Oxford Westview Press

Jacobs, M. (1996), The Politics of the Real World St Ives Earthscan

Jara, OH (1989), Aprender Desde la Práctica: Reflexiones y Esperiencias de la Educación Popular en Centroamérica San José, Costa Rica Alforja

Kane, L. (1995), Mid-Way External Evaluation of ODEC's Exchange Project Glasgow Department of Adult & Continuing Education, University of Glasgow

Kirkwood, C. & G. (1989), Living Adult Education: Freire in Scotland Bury St Edmonds, OUP in association with SIACE

Nunez, C. (1993), América Libre 2 (pp 46-61) Buenos Aires Liberarte.

Smith, S. (1994), Mistaken identity - or can identity politics liberate the oppressed? pp 3-50 International Socialism No. 62 London International Socialism

Jenneth Parker

Adult Education and Local Agenda 21

Linking Regional Development and the 5th Action Programme - 'Towards Sustainability'

'*...the public is considerably lacking in essential information ... a comprehensive strategy will be required to inform the public at large*'

(European Union 5th Action Programme 1993)

This paper proposes that, in addition to informing the public *about* Sustainable Development (SD), adult education should seek to *involve* the public in SD at the local and regional levels through links to the Local Agenda 21 (LA21) process. In this paper I review concepts of Education for Sustainable Development (ESD) and distinguish this from Environmental Education. I then discuss social movements in relation to LA21 and the relevance of LA21 to regional development. I introduce two examples from my own work linking adult education with LA21 and conclude with some recommendations for adult education in relation to the sustainable university.

Education for Sustainable Development

This paper is primarily concerned with Local Agenda 21 in relation to adult education. However, as LA21 is concerned with Sustainable Development, education focused on LA21 is Education for Sustainable Development (ESD). It is, therefore, necessary to focus briefly on ESD and in particular to highlight the differences between ESD and Environmental Education.

One definition of ESD is as follows:

'Education, training and awareness for sustainable development (ESD) is a process which:

- enables people to build understanding of the interdependence of all life on earth, and of the repercussions their actions and choices have on resources and the local and global community, now and in the future;
- increases the awareness of the economic political, social, cultural and environmental forces which foster or detract from sustainable development;
- develops the skills, attitudes and values which enable people to be effective agents of sustainable development on a local, national and international level, and work towards a more just and sustainable future. In particular it enables people to integrate environmental and economic decision-making'.

(McCloskey and others 1991)

...... a fairly ambitious programme!

ESD entails a re-orientation of Environmental Education, stressing its interrelations with many other aspects. Some of these additional aspects are traditionally included in Development Education such as: justice, equity, trade, debt and global relations. ESD is currently being invented and reinvented by combining the transmuting elements from both Environmental and Development Educations together with many other elements; a commitment to interdisciplinarity and a focus on participatory education. One extremely important (and we hope evolutionary beneficial) mutation to Development Education is that it is beginning to consider 'development' in its widest sense - not just the 'problem of underdevelopment' but the problems of 'appropriate development' in already developed countries (Sachs, 1993). This aspect is, of course, particularly important in relation to European Regional Development and adult education, our main theme for this conference.

Local Agenda 21 and Social Movements

The Rio Earth Summit of 1992 brought together 178 world governments to agree an agenda for the 21st Century; Agenda 21. The summit identified a range of 'Major Groups' to carry forward the aims of the conference, one of which was Local Authorities[1]. Local Authorities were mandated to 'undertake a consultative process with their populations and achieve a consensus on 'a Local Agenda 21' for the community' (UNEP, 1992). Guidance for this process stresses the role of local civil society and organisations as well as that of business and the local authorities themselves.

Social movements have been central to the Rio process from its inception. It was in fact the initiative of the civil associations of the UN, its United Nationals Associations throughout the world which campaigned for the Earth Summit and also helped structure its workings. Perhaps the greatest achievement of the conference was the extremely high degree of participation by Non-Governmental Organisations (NGOs) from all parts of the globe plus the continual emphasis on democratic participation, ownership and the use of local knowledge in Rio follow-up processes. The ways in which social movements have been able to participate in LA21 would be worthy of a full study; here it will suffice to summarise the opportunities for participation provided by LA21 but also to note the challenges to social movement structures and modes of operation.

Local Agenda 21 has been structured in very different ways in different places but there are areas of commonality in the kinds of topics covered. Where I live in Hastings on the south coast of England we have developed the following summary of LA21 themes:

Over-Consumption - reducing energy use, waste and pollution and promoting efficient transport

Nature - looking after the variety of species, habitats and landscape

Health - ensuring a healthy environment for ourselves and our children

1 The educational community was not included as a major group at Rio - UNED-UK, together with the UK Education for Sustainability Forum, are currently lobbying for this to be rectified. It would help ESD greatly to have government commitments.

Work - developing economies that meet people's needs

Community - renewing neighbourhood in our towns and villages

Justice - making sure that costs of the changes we need to make are shared fairly

Future - ensuring the well-being of future generations

(Hastings Local Agenda 21 NGO Forum)

Themes thus include opportunities for the following kinds of social movement groups:

- a wide range of environmental groups and NGOs campaigning on specific issues
- a wide range of community health groups and NGOs
- self-help local economic alternatives
- residents and tenants associations
- charities and churches campaigning on global justice and fair trading issues
- local nature trusts and urban wildlife groups
- groups promoting the interests of specific sectors, e.g. the elderly
- community architecture and urban studies groups
- community organised leisure activities and NGOs such as scouts and guides.

I will outline the challenges to social movements in relation to their main characteristics as theorised by Touraine (1988), Melucci (1989) and Cohen and Arato (1992)[2].

Firstly, social movements are distinguished by their lack of totalising theory. They are very often single issue movements and thus they are able to unite

2 Social Movement theory has been very ethnocentric to date and consequently fails to cover the impact of some of the most exciting and widespread environmental social movements in India and Latin America, for example.

individuals from disparate social groups. The challenge of LA21 is to come together and develop a common agenda under the umbrella of Sustainable Development. In my experience this challenge to the community and social movement sector is just as severe as its counterpart challenge to local government to develop cross-departmental co-operation and policy analysis. (This point applies equally to national NGOs and social movements and to national government).

Secondly, social movements are held to have a 'self limiting' nature in that they do not aim for political power in the traditional sense and they certainly do not aim for state power. This relates to the lack of totalising theory explored above in that social movements typically do not develop an overall political analysis (though this does not unproblematically apply to the women's movement) or an overall political strategy. This can lead to a kind of political opportunism which according to the stance of the commentator is viewed either as disempowering or conversely as empowering. This characteristic of social movements, although variable, can lead to a political naiveté resulting in a lack of a basic analysis of the political requirements of demands made. In the case of LA21 and Sustainable Development an analysis of the *restructuring* of the state is required as I argue more fully below.

Thirdly, social movements are characterised by a high degree of reflexivity in that they tend towards an open model of organisation ('transparency') and encourage reflection on their own modes of operation. It has also been suggested that they act within the larger society as debating fora to analyse the consequences of modernity. This aspect of social movements renders them particularly well placed to engage in promoting open and dialogical processes of change and development of which LA21 (and Sustainable Development in general) is a prime example. However, the NGO part of the social movement sector (as they are by no means identical) has a tendency itself to become centralised and hence to be less effective at a local level. Again, in my experience, hardly a single UK NGO has really tried to enable participation and action at the local level in LA21. Thus, for example, the information provision to members has supported national campaigns rather than enabled members to understand and participate in LA21.

Lastly I will mention the value base and orientation of social movements: it has been one of the effects of social movements to bring back ethical discourse into politics. Local Agenda 21, as outlined above, rests upon certain values which it is hoped may be held in common and this aspect of social movements is very much in tune with LA21. The challenge is to unite and make explicit the value aspects of LA21 in the process of consensus building. The crucial discussion is around the concept of 'quality of life'. I have argued elsewhere (Parker, 1995) that this requires the construction or expansion of a range of local fora where political discourse can be created and revived and the existence of skilled individuals who are willing to facilitate such a 'community of enquiry'. The debate will be extensive and no doubt highly contentious but, if we are to develop any kind of rational consensus on *democratic* forms of Sustainable Development, it is absolutely essential.

I will highlight below some of the ways in which I see adult education as aiding social movements in meeting these challenges but before I do so I would like to briefly return to the regional development theme.

Sustainable Regional Development

The publicity for this conference stresses lifelong learning in relation to 'development and competitiveness'; in this sense the conference organisers are responding to the emphasis within European Regional Development Programmes. However, different European programmes often seem to be pulling in different directions. This is particularly true when we look at programmes to do with the environment verses programmes to do with development. If, indeed, the crux of Sustainable Development is to harmonise these two aspects then to consider, however briefly, questions of *Sustainable* Regional Development and adult education will make some contribution. In order to tackle this question and demonstrate the specific relevance of LA21 I will now outline some consequences of applying the concept of sustainable development to regions.

Sustainable development must be concerned with the *real* economy which includes, but is not identical with, the money economy. The real economy includes all those processes which keep life in being; natural life support systems but also unpaid work (there are gender issues here) of all kinds. Not only is the money economy 'a wholly owned subsidiary of the environment' but it is also dependent upon all those unpaid activities that keep human society in being. In this sense adult education geared towards helping people growing their own food, for example, contributes to Regional Sustainable Development. I am sure that we can all think of a host of other examples of educational activities that help to keep parts of the real economy functioning.

Sustainable development must also be linked to the other Euro 'S' word; subsidiarity. Briefly 'subsidiarity' invokes a presumption in favour of decision-making at the level nearest the grass roots. Sustainable development, because it must involve local knowledge and commitment, necessitates a complete re-thinking of exactly where the best level of governance may be in respect of a huge variety of different decisions. This is a major political undertaking, and one for which social movements may be particularly ill-equipped (as we have seen above). Suffice it to say in relation to LA21 that to be effective this requires a massive shift of power back to the local level: the implications for regional development are similar[3].

Uniting the considerations of the real economy and local/regional decision-making, some 'New Economists' have proposed that the relationship between different levels of the real economy should be seen as 'nested' from local to regional to global (Robertson, 1989). Within that pattern it is seen as vital for relatively stable and sustainable development that each level maintains a core economy that is independent of the wider level. In this way local

3 Existing political boundaries do not always reflect common environmental realities (e.g. boundaries that cross river systems) the debate on these issues is formulated under the heading 'bioregionalism'. Some educational institutions have recognised their duty to serve across boundaries, e.g. the 'Bioregion Baltic' course at Stensund Ecological Centre, Stensund Folk College, S-61900, Trosa, Sweden.

economies should have a degree of autonomy relative to regional economies, which, in their turn should have a degree of autonomy relative to the global economy. As economic autonomy means political control, this view has major implications for the necessity of participation by informed and active citizens at local and regional levels.

Examples of Adult Education and Local Agenda 21

I will deal briefly with these examples as I have brought exhibitions to illustrate both of them together with some free material for distribution.

1 Gloucestershire's Adult Continuing Education and Training (ACET) and VISION 21

Gloucestershire is an English county which has maintained a county-wide service for adult education - ACET. It is acknowledged as one of the best services in the country in terms of quality and outreach work: ACET has well developed networking systems throughout the County which already link it into the community and social movement sector. VISION 21 is the Gloucestershire LA21 process which is being run from the social movement sector by a charity known as the 'Rendezvous Society'. VISION 21 is a flagship LA21, is a pilot project of the UK United Nations Environment Programme (UNEP-UK), and has succeeded in involving quite a large section of the population of Gloucestershire in the LA21 process.

I have been involved in a project to design and carry out a strategy to 'green' adult education in Gloucestershire which has been linked to the VISION 21 process. The project so far has thus concentrated mostly on adult environmental education although the links with VISION 21 and ACET's community programme have imparted some development aspects. We are now looking to the possibilities of extending this work to include more aspects from development education in association with the UK Development Education Association[4].

2 Community, Locality and Environment Course

This course was run on a partnership basis between the Centre for Continuing Education (CCE) at Sussex University and the Hastings branch of the Worker's Education Association (WEA). The course was intended as an opportunity to critically explore central concepts behind LA21 and to link into the Hastings LA21 process. The course ran for 20 weeks, was part of the accredited CCE programme and attracted a good cross section of students. Although experiencing some attendance problems partly due to commitments of activists the course was successful in achieving its objectives: contributions were made to LA21 working group reports and a well attended public meeting was held where some of the course perspectives on LA21 were discussed.

Recommendations

The following recommendations could be made for Adult Education for Sustainable Development in relation to working with social movements in their broadest sense. I will informally illustrate these with examples from my work in my presentation.

1 Adult education could help facilitate social movements' common agenda under the umbrella of LA21 and sustainable development.

2 Adult education can play a role in exploring and debating the political/citizenship consequences of moving towards sustainable development.

4 'New Economics' in the UK is being developed by associates of the New Economics Foundation, 88-94 Wentworth Street, London E1 7SA, England.

3 Adult education can help in social movements' reflection upon their own values, aims and methods of working.

4 Adult education can help network with local partners who need to develop mutual understanding a common agenda towards sustainable development; that is we can aid in the kind of local knowledge production and networking that LA21 requires to be successful between local authorities, the community and business sectors.

5 Adult education can use knowledge and experience of outreach work in involving marginalised groups to help LA21 become more truly participatory.

6 Adult education should begin to theorise the extent of its current contribution to the real economy and hence to sustainable development and to develop ways to enhance this contribution.

7 Adult education should draw upon expertise in interdisciplinary work and investigate ways to put this to work in sustainable development (Parker, 1993).

The Sustainable University

Adult education within universities can draw upon its strengths to support moves towards the sustainable university. We should develop an analysis of the importance of local and regional studies to sustainable development - focusing on the use, development and networking of existing local knowledge. The kinds of activities suggested above could contribute to delivering the corporate commitments to sustainability and to their communities (Committee of Vice Chancellors and Principals 1994) which for many universities unfortunately remain in the realms of policy.

References

Cohen, J. and Arato, A. (1992), Civil Society and Political Theory, MIT Press.

Committee of Vice Chancellors and Principals, Universities and Communities, 1994.

McCloskey, C. et al, (1991), Education, Training and Awareness for a Sustainable Future, UNEP-UK.

Melucci, A. (1989), Nomads of the Present, London, Hutchison Radius.

Parker, J., Quality Generalists and their role in Education for Sustainability on Life and Education in Finland 3/93.

Parker, J. (1995), Enabling Morally Reflective Communities in Guerrier Y., Alexander, N., Chase, J. and O'Brien, M. (eds), Values and the Environment, London, Wiley and Sons.

Robertson, J. (1989), Future Wealth - A New Economics for the 21st Century, London, Cassell.

Sachs, W. (1993), The Development Dictionary, Zed Books.

Touraine, A. (1988), The Return of the Actor, University of Minnesota Press.

UNESCO-UNEP, Earth Summit, London, Regency Press, 1992.

Section 7

Multiculturalism and Ethnicity

Maurizio Lichtner

Multiculturalism and Democracy. A Comment on the Group Work

How do you define a democratic multicultural society? 'Political emancipation' of society was frequently discussed by Marx. In *Die Judenfrage* he considered political democracy as a situation where lifeforms have lost all political relevance, though they maintain their existence at the social level. People see their 'differences' in society confirmed (income, religion, etc.), while in terms of the ideology of politics everybody holds equal citizenship rights. We may add minority ethnic communities as an example of 'differences' in society that are maintained without preventing the exercise of equal rights. Marx strongly criticised the idea of 'political democracy' which leaves unaltered social and cultural differences. The theme is not so outdated; it might be resumed in these terms: to what extent can citizenship leave lifeforms unaltered?

In particular, lifeforms established in traditional (pre-modern) societies may be incompatible with modern democracy. Perhaps they should undergo a transformation process, so as to become 'compatible', while keeping important aspects of their 'cultural identity'. The problem is not new. It emerged during the Enlightenment era in terms of possible recognition of 'differences'. To become full-right citizens, should the Jews give up their faith and tradition? Mendelssohn's book *Jerusalem* was in defence of cultural differences. He said: we are keen to achieve civil rights, but if the price were the abandonment of our tradition, we should renounce it. He understood that some changes in the traditional lifeform was necessary and acceptable. So the question was about *how much* to change, in order to share common citizenship.

Today in our democratic societies, we profess great 'openness' towards cultural differences held by minority groups, but does this attitude really match with the drive for inclusion and citizenship? Ursula Apitzsch, in her opening address to the group, defined multiculturalism as a 'mixture', an unclear concept which can easily engender misunderstandings. Recognition of insiders' views is essential, when approaching an minority ethnic group, but expressing 'respect' for all traditions can mask a new sort of segregation politics, in that people are denied the opportunity to share new meanings. She expressed a clear-cut neo-enlightenment position, arguing that emphasis on differences can imply refusal of universal principles of morality and politics, and that interest in 'otherness' can turn into a sort of new 'third-world argument' against progress and democracy. So, very consistently, she referred to Habermas' concept of 'constitutional patriotism' as the best foundation for a democratic multi-ethnic society. 'Patriotism' means active consensus about constitutional values. This can hardly be achieved unless civil and political rights, and protection from marginalisation, are really granted to individuals.

Multiculturalism in our societies is linked to a reality of deprivation and social exclusion. That is why 'learning to live' in a multicultural society is so difficult. Haroon Saad, reporting on the experiences of black communities in Britain, has rightly reminded us of the existence of 'structural facts', namely that of a 'special' labour market available for black people, characterised by deskilled jobs and vast unemployment, irrespective of a person's educational capital. Black people are also located in highly concentrated urban areas where social segregation is continuously reproduced. He added that the deficit-model still applied to black students in education. The project for race-equality in Southwark (London), described in the paper, follows two lines of action: (a) meeting individual needs (language, vocational skills) and moving away from the deficit-model and developing positive actions; (b) community development; not 'doing things for people' but enabling people to develop capacity of self-organisation. We might ask, therefore, if the stress is on fostering an individual's inclusion in the larger society or on community action and community progress. But very seemingly, as for other underprivileged groups, community progress is the main condition for individual positive involvement in the larger society.

In the discussion of the paper the general problem of the relation between the individual and community was raised. One aspect of the problem was the process of identity formation among youths who belong to disadvantaged minority groups as their values contrast with those of the wider society. in contrast, the problem might be put in other terms: to what extent is developing a multiple identity (as an minority ethnic community member, a member of a professional group, a citizen...) a viable way ahead?

The main concern in the group work was focused on the issue of relativism. Habermas' and Apel's *discourse ethics* was applied by Jan-Kare Breivik to intercultural relations, as a means to overcome power-relations in society and allow 'true' mutual understanding. *Discourse ethics* has often be considered as utopian and an *ideal speech situation* which has never existed. The paper argues that the tendency towards mutual recognition and continuing dialogue is the basic condition for achieving social inclusion without repression. Conversely, and this is the point, continuing dialogue is impossible, or false, if a relativistic stance is held. What is the content of the dialogue, if we have no values to propose? Relativism, as the 'masochist' attitude towards other cultures, finally implies delegation of the 'other' as a subject. Considering modernity as a value-empty construct, and only finding real, 'solid' values in traditional cultures, entails renouncing any possible common moral and political discourse. Sometimes this masochist attitude really means betraying those who need help for making their way out of an oppressive tradition.

It was right to remind us in the discussion that very often refugees fleeing from their countries do not want to participate in their 'traditions', since tradition is to them an oppressive social system that they want to leave behind. However, their past experiences may be resumed later, and used as an important biographical resource.

Some key issues on multiculturalism and relativism are put forward in the paper by Julia Preece on the difficulties encountered by community educators in England when working with culturally distant groups, such as Asian women, and in particular Muslim Pakistani women in Lancaster. The paper argues that the 'discourse' of community education can be deconstructed, revealing itself as a typical 'western' and 'male' discourse, whose concepts, like disadvantage and oppression, and values such as independence, empowerment, difference, may make no sense to people immersed in other cultural contexts.

The criticism is mainly addressed at the 'taken for granted' spectrum of the dominant politically-correct discourses. The theoretical argument goes further, questioning the concept of truth, in that 'truth' always reflects the 'epistemological privilege' of somebody who holds the power to make decisions about legitimacy of discourses. This is a difficult point: no other criterion or source of legitimacy and 'truth' may be given beyond power. In the case of Muslim Pakistani women the paper emphasises the necessity to acknowledge their culture and tradition as a legitimate perspective. While in our view a Muslim religious identity may imply disempowerment and dependence and oppression for women, the paper declares that it is possible to 'empower through Islam'. Therefore, the point is not only starting 'where people are' in education, but retaining people's values in the development process.

The focus of the discussion was on the concept of 'recognition' of what people are. It should not mean that people are encouraged to maintain their traditions whatever they are and to keep unchanged their form of life. What can be acknowledged as a value, or a 'legitimate' perspective? We should not 'reinforce', through our 'recognition', oppressive power relations in the communities. 'Values' should be consistent, at least, with individual rights and this cannot be overlooked. Pakistani women may not share *our* itineraries toward emancipation and liberation but perhaps they should be actively aided in finding their own autonomous way. Furthermore, the encounter itself, especially when so empathetic, should make people change; the intention to preserve the 'culture' of the other may conflict with the developments of a true exchange with him (or her).

Some other themes were discussed in the group. One is the issue of low participation of minority groups in higher education. Participation may be enhanced through anti-discriminatory actions, which usually are 'quota' systems or 'positive actions'. Quotas should not conflict with recognition for individual 'merit'. Perhaps the criteria for admission should be changed (for all students) in order to take into consideration a wider range of cognitive styles. Positive actions are the main way to build up 'substantial' equality. A point was raised about the value attached to education in different communities. From a relativistic (or 'postmodern') viewpoint, it is neither surprising nor negative that education ranks differently in different preference scales. But is low participation really due to 'cultural' factors, or more trivially to lack of economic resources and to underprivileged social contexts? Moreover, it was remarked that some people do not 'wish' to participate in education and this should be recognised. Equally others should be enabled to participate if they wish to do so.

The Danish experience of teacher training for building 'bridges' between different schools receiving immigrant adult students shows how the cultural or anthropological approach to schools can contribute to intercultural relations. Enabling teachers to interpret the other school habits as a 'cultural difference' may create a detachment, a sort of distance, so learning to view school practices from the outsider's (the immigrant's) point of view. Also the intention to bring teachers to a better understanding of their own national 'culture' means learning to see our world from outside, so making it more easily 'readable' by immigrants. Concerning the inclusion of other cultures and traditions in the curriculum, a point was made in the discussion that those values should really enter the 'discourse' of the teacher, really 'mean' something for her, modify her perspective, otherwise the operation may turn into a patronising practice, which does not produce intercultural dialogue.

A different problem that we encounter (everywhere in Europe) in relation to vocational education is the recognition of immigrants' prior qualifications. Sometimes it seems that the education and training received in their countries are 'forgotten': the reason lays in the general devaluation and loss of confidence which affects immigrant people when they do not perceive any viable way into the job system of the new country.

The paper by Peter Shanahan brings us a different situation: the case of Northern Ireland, where a movement for Irish language revival has been growing in recent years in the context of a community which had to cope with unemployment and heavy social and economic disadvantage. The linguistic return of Irish is not to be seen as an elitist revival or an anti-modern protest. It has a working-class basis and it seems to be functional to identity construction or reconstruction of the community. Putting it in more general terms, we might say that the 'progressive' nature of a movement for community identity should always be verified by its contribution to the struggle for individual civil and political rights.

In conclusion, reflection in the group mainly centred on the relation between 'constitutional' commitment for a democracy viewed as a common moral space, and respect and recognition of differences. Habermas' theory was referred to frequently. I would add a comment on Habermas' concept of political 'socialisation'. Political citizenship, though allowing multiple forms of life, 'requires that all citizens be socialised into a common political culture' (Staatsburgershaft und nationale Identitat, 1991). If we conceive political education as far from being mere acceptance of rules but as a 'socialisation process', and democracy not only as a set of institutionalised procedures for decision-making but as a mentality or a 'culture', we have to conclude that separation between the 'private' space of community life and the 'public' space of larger society is untenable. As far as the individual is caught up in a real, involving process of political 'socialisation', her/his 'lifeform' is in question, and her/his prior community life cannot be preserved unchanged.

Wolfgang Leumer / Haroon Saad

Learning to Live in a Multi-Cultural Society

In 1995 a project proposal was submitted to the newly created Socrates action programme with the support of the European Association for the Education of Adults. The title of the project is: *Learning to Live in a Multicultural Society*. The two European adult education bodies working on the preliminary phase of an emerging 'European Network' project are NIACE and DVV. The Institute for International Co-operation of DVV is the lead agency vis-à-vis the Commission. Besides the Socrates funding IIZ/DVV has obtained for the one-year project co-finance from the German Ministry for Education, Science, Research and Technology.

The general objective of the network which goes far beyond the possibilities of a one-year only project under Socrates will be the description and analysis of adult education practice in Europe concerning minority groups and migrant populations and the development of a comprehensive programme of action based on recommendations of good adult education practice to:

i) highlight and share good models of policy and practice
ii) facilitate the exchange of information and expertise
iii) generate 'good practice guidelines' in respect of specific concrete areas of work
iv) identify specific policies which should be adopted to alleviate and address existing (unmet) and emerging needs.

In short, such a network would act as a kind of *'stock exchange'* for those engaged in addressing the needs of minority ethnic groups and migrant communities. Participants in the network will be trained and improvements of training methodologies will be developed in order to have a cascade effect on network members, who in turn will have to use these skills and new techniques in their own pedagogical and organisational approaches in the respective countries and regions. The network will add to the quality of ongoing anti-racist educational work and promote the standards of quality in this field across Europe.

The integration of anti-racist and anti-discrimination practice into a range of adult education provision such as cultural work, social work, vocational training and in advocacy-work against social exclusion in our societies, is the key distinctive feature of the project. This will be enhanced through a European network project. It is not the issue here, to create a new network that has a mono-concern or a single purpose, but the distinctive characteristic of this network is the fact that anti-racist and anti-discriminatory work should be embedded into the broad life-oriented work of adult education providers all over Europe.

Whilst acknowledging that phrases like 'multi-ethnic' or even 'multicultural' may not be seen as appropriate by some, it cannot be denied that national, ethnic, racial and cultural diversity has become a characteristic feature of European society, particularly in the larger urban agglomerations where most of the newcomers have settled.

The recent developments in Central and Eastern Europe with the introduction of market-oriented economies will undoubtedly bring about patterns of unemployment, reduction of social security and marginalisation, which will in turn bring about a higher degree of economically motivated migration to the richer neighbouring countries and so will add to the growth of a multi-ethnic pattern within the European Union.

It is quite clear that minority ethnic groups and migrant communities have experienced and are experiencing a process of direct and indirect structural discrimination. The overall socio-economic profile of minority ethnic communities and migrant populations depicts this sharply. They face:

- considerably higher levels and longer periods of unemployment.
- higher percentage of employment in unskilled and semi-skilled jobs.
- poorer housing and general living environment.
- higher incidence of poverty and homelessness .
- a general state of psychological /emotional impoverishment among migrants

- mounting dissolution of family ties; women having the sole responsibility for bringing up their children, men living alone.
- higher proportion of men and women 'criminalised' through inappropriate police actions and culturally biased judicial processes.
- spatial and social segregation from their respective 'host' community.
- higher levels of theft, street crime, youth delinquency, violence and drug abuse.
- greater incidence of physical and mental illness.
- continual increase in the level of ethnically or racially motivated attacks against them including murder and arson.

Alongside this bleak social and economic profile there is added marginalisation through inadequate mechanisms whereby minority ethnic groups and migrant communities can participate in the major institutions of the established societies which cater for employment, education, housing, and social services. This lack of participation is linked in part to the barriers of language and illiteracy, but also more substantially due to the institutional routinised discrimination which pervades such institutions. This creates a further problem for ethnic and migrant groups by in effect barring them from the democratic decision-making processes.

This triple problem of social, economic and political marginalisation is being passed on to successive generations among minority ethnic groups and migrant communities. A real 'syndrom' of exclusion and segregation is in the making.

It is, therefore, essential to be proactive from the beginning to tackle these problems seriously. The combinations of social and economic disadvantages and lack of actually exercised political rights is a potentially explosive mixture. Through the creation of a network of interest groups and agencies (governmental and non-governmental) working with and for minority ethnic groups and migrant populations we can begin to try and ensure that the problem is not allowed to be marginalised at a national or European level.

The cost of social unrest and far reaching political disruption of cohesion in society will be severe. Not to treat this problem in a preventive and sensible way will be dangerous. The creation of *European citizenship* will not be realised unless European society is able to develop integrative and concilia-tory forces. Adult education will be paramount for checking and advocating for positive educational programmes for both present and future groups of immigrants.

The Strategic Framework for Antiracist and Intercultural Adult Education

The *Multicultural-Network* adopted at a preliminary meeting before the the approval of the Socrates project a strategic framework. This strategic framework has *three key strands*. Each strand will would be addressed by different groups within the network:

Strand ONE:

Strategies for Organisational Change and Development

The overall aim under this strand will be to highlight good practice and organisational 'repositioning' in order to ensure that public service organi-sations (including NGO's) work collaboratively together to develop holistic strategies which address, express and identify needs of minoritiy ethnic communities.

Initial areas of focus should include:

i) Anti-discriminatory training for managers and front-line staff

ii) Strategies to improve access for specific targeted groups, for example, young unemployed, single parents, etc.

iii) Models for effective consultation and participation by and with minor-ity ethnic communities

iv) Race Equality Policies as part of the personnel practices of such organisations

v) Developing more effective marketing provision through use of multi-media techniques

Strand TWO:

Strategies to achieve equality of opportunity for individuals from minority ethnic communities

The overall aim under this strand would be to highlight specific initiatives being developed in member states which address particular needs of certain groups within minority ethnic communities (for example, older migrants, migrant women, unemployed youth, cultural industries).

Initial areas of focus could include:

i) Guidance and counselling strategies

ii) Vocational training

iii) Language and social skills training

iv) Developing traineeships in areas of governmental and non-governmental employment where ethnic and migrant communities are under-represented

v) Cultural diversity in expression (development of)

vi) Developing routes for the accreditation of prior learning

vii) Developing systems for the recognition of qualifications gained in non-EU countries.

Strand THREE:

Community Development / Capacity Building

The overall aim under this strand would be to highlight good practice and develop curriculum resources which would enable and empower minority ethnic organisations to become more effective and thus enable them to participate in the planning, development and delivery of adult education and training provision.

Initial areas of focus could include:

i) Management and organisational skills training
ii) Urban regeneration and community development
iii) Funding strategies
iv) Models for effective self-organisation

The Socrates Project 'Learning to Live in a Multicultural Society'

As one could imagine this very comprehensive and ambitious programme could not meaningfully be carried out under one Socrates bid alone. The actual Socrates project with the title 'Learning to Live in a Multicultural Society' therefore concentrates on Strand One and will try to produce an *Manual of Antiracist Methods and Materials* designed for people responsible for delivering and improving services to black and other minority clients through training and staff development. The operational aim is to provide an overview of methods and materials that can be used in the delivery of training around racism and ethnic diversity.

The objectives are:

a) to introduce a variety of training methodologies / approaches
b) to provide examples of training resources and materials
c) to identify good training practice and key skills
d) to provide a representative bibliography/database

At the end of the project, around October 1996, we hope to be able to present the outcome in the form of a reader/manual, making the results of the network available to a larger European adult education public. In itself such a work bears a lot of difficulties which stem from diverse political and sociological backgrounds in member states. Even within the network a lot of intercultural understanding has to be created first before a joint understanding of concepts of racism/antiracism and intercultural work can be achieved. It is a thrilling task and entails a lot of new learning even for those of us, who feel quite self-assured in their own national settings. To confront these afresh to a variety of diverse approaches in neighbouring European countries will add to reflective capacities and skills in a larger European framework.

Of course, in the light of much more work to be done as depicted by all the subthemes of the three above STRANDS we are quite sure that after this initial Socrates project a proposal for renewal, will be brought forward to the Socrates selection bodies. These fresh proposals will emphasise the aspects outlined in the strategic framework which were hitherto not dealt with by the network due to a shortage of funding and time.

Maggie Woodrow / David Crosier

Ethnicity and Exclusion in European Higher Education

1. Introduction

This paper draws extensively from the report 'Access to higher education for Under-represented groups' written by Maggie Woodrow and David Crosier on behalf of the Council of Europe. The report was commissioned by the Council of Europe for its project on 'Access to higher education in Europe' and is an outcome of surveys of under-represented groups undertaken in sixteen countries in both central and eastern and western Europe[1].

2. Interpretations of Ethnicity

Since interpretations of ethnicity vary and the categorisation of the term is problematic, this paper begins with a brief examination of its usage in (western) Europe. 'Ethnic group' is not a fixed category in the same way as, say, gender: rather, it is historically contingent, and perceptions of ethnicity differ widely not only between different countries, but also within them.

It is useful, therefore, considering the multiplicity of possible interpretations of the concept, to begin by looking at the origins of the word. Derived from the Greek *ethnikos*, the term ethnic was originally applied to heathens, cultural strangers, and 'outsiders'; it excluded the dominant group. In certain ways little has changed. 'Ethnic groups' are still generally used to denote 'otherness' while the dominant group considers itself somehow to transcend ethnicity.

The difficult question is how this 'otherness' is to be recognised and why. Notions of ethnicity may include, justifiably or not, linguistic, religious and

1 The sixteen countries are: Belgium, Bulgaria, Czech Republic, France, Germany, Hungary, Iceland, Netherlands, Poland, Romania, Russia, Slovakia, Slovenia, Spain, Switzerland, United Kingdom

other cultural criteria, nationality, physical characteristics and parental place of birth.

More recent explanations of the term have focused on the importance of a common history and tradition. Schermerhorn describes an ethnic group as 'a collectivity within a larger society, having real or putative ancestry, memories of a shared historical past, and a cultural focus on one or more symbolic elements defined as the epitome of their peoplehood'. To this notion of a common origin is added that of a distinctive culture. Yinger claims that members of an ethnic group are, 'a segment of a larger society whose members are thought, by themselves and/or by others, to share a common origin and to share important segments of a common culture, and who in addition, participate in shared activities in which the common origin and culture are significant ingredients'. Other distinctive characteristics, such as language, religion and lifestyle are included within these shared activities, so that overall, according to Verma, 'the basic, distinctive attribute of an ethnic group is not physical appearance but cultural values.'

This interpretation does not however help in the identification of ethnicity among those who may for several generations have rejected the common culture of the group, including the religion, lifestyle and the language, to embrace a different culture. This conception of culture may be a matter of environment and, to some extent, choice: ethnicity, it could be argued, tends to be a result of conditioning or labelling.

(The concept of 'culture' is itself of course open to a variety of theoretical approaches. The most appropriate working definition here would seem to be, 'the system of shared meanings developed in a social and economic context which has a particular historical and political background' (Klein 1982).

The use of 'ethnicity' in the survey undertaken was further complicated by its relationship with nationality, or citizenship; several Western European countries refusing to recognise as nationals, those from ethnic groups other than the dominant one, despite several generations' residence. Elsewhere, the formal recognition of nationality is not sufficient, as for example, among the black British, where it was recently found that, 'despite a strong sense of social and cultural commonality with the white British, most Caribbeans found it difficult to lay claim to be British. The difficulty was almost entirely based on the knowledge that the majority of white British people did not acknowledge the commonality and really believed that only white people could be called British' (Policy Studies Institute Survey, UK, 1993).

Rightly or wrongly perceptions clearly play a major part in attributing ethnicity, whether they come from inside or outside a particular ethnic group. Although this concept cannot be explored here in greater depth, for the purposes of the survey it has been important to demonstrate that the category of 'minority ethnic group' has been, and is, subject to considerable interpretation, and cannot be considered as a fixed concept. The cynical use of the term 'ethnic cleansing' as a euphemism for genocidal practices has added a new and sinister association to the vocabulary of ethnicity. In each country studied therefore, the authors have sought to respect and understand local interpretations as the best means of comprehending the data provided. This has not always been easy, where different interpretations clearly reflect different political positions within a single country.

3. Monitoring Ethnicity

Of the eight western European countries studied, only two, the Netherlands and the UK, monitor participation in higher education by ethnic group. In the UK, this data has only been available since 1990, and monitoring is now controlled and co-ordinated by a new national body, the Higher Education Statistical Agency (HESA), which monitors many other aspects of participation in higher education. HESA has established common monitoring fields so that equivalent data is to be collected for all UK higher education institutions. Formerly data related only to participation by ethnic group, and not to students' progress and performance, and thus could be undertaken anonymously. Even so the return rate from students was low. HESA has now extended this process to include monitoring of students' progress and performance, which requires students to be identifiable by name. Fears that this would result in a much lower return from students have apparently been unfounded and the first HESA Data Report (July 1995) records a 77% response rate - more data than has been collected on ethnicity in the past.

The UK process involves self-identification by both students and staff from a provided list of the main ethnic groups, which was used in the 1991 Census. Concerns have been expressed about the choice of ethnic categories for inclusion in the list, particularly in respect of the 'black British', that is, British born black people from second or third generation immigrant families. Despite these problems, there is a widely-held conviction in the UK that some form of monitoring is essential if racism in higher education is to be eradicated.

In the Netherlands, monitoring of participation by ethnic group is undertaken in both schools and universities, but a common national system of registration is only just being introduced. The countries of birth of both students and parents are being registered, and if either is a country other than the Netherlands, then the student is registered as coming from an ethnic minority. This system clearly includes foreign students under the category ethnic minority and is thus based on quite different data from that of the UK. This raises the question as to whether statistical evidence like this, or information gathered from a self-identification process like that in Britain provides the more reliable or acceptable form of data.

Of the six countries where ethnic monitoring is not undertaken, the situation in both Germany and Switzerland is complicated by the non-recognition of locally-born ethnic minority people as nationals. The Turkish community, for example, is long established in Germany, but even those who are second or third generation Turks are classified as foreigners and not recognised as having German nationality. In Switzerland, which has a large migrant population, approximately one sixth of the total, no data is kept on participation by ethnic group and university staff reported that this is, 'a deliberate political decision'. Swiss university records are otherwise detailed and sophisticated, with a wide range of statistical data produced annually. Although ethnic origin is an extremely important criterion for social and employment status, ethnic monitoring in higher education institutions is apparently deliberately avoided, both at national and institutional levels. At the University of Geneva, for example, staff reported that there was, 'an absolute refusal to collect this kind of information'. By contrast, statistics on foreign students studying in Switzerland are collected at institutional, cantonal and national levels.

In the other four countries studied, Belgium, France, Iceland and Spain, no evidence was found of an intention to monitor participation by ethnic group.

Monitoring by ethnic group is additionally problematic in central and eastern Europe. Classification by ethnic group has never in the past been undertaken in the interests of those who find themselves in a minority. In most central and eastern European countries it is clearly felt politically expedient to avoid ethnic identification and instead to emphasise the cohesion of a common nationality. The proximity of 'ethnic cleansing' and religious fundamentalism are effective in reinforcing the view that the possession, or even the process of gathering, such statistical information, could be damaging to social peace and stability.

Those interviewed were therefore keen to emphasise the lack of discrimination against minorities, and it was often stated as a logical sequitur that monitoring was therefore both unnecessary and undesirable. In all the countries surveyed except the Russian Federation, no monitoring of ethnic groups was undertaken and evidence was not therefore available.

The exception to this general rule regarding ethnic monitoring is the Russian Federation. Here, higher education institutions are required to provide the Ministry with annual statistics showing participation of ethnic groups. A quota system is in operation, ensuring that, especially in rural communities, higher education establishments have representative figures of ethnic groups.

For the future, particularly in those countries with new frontiers seeking to strengthen their national identity, the introduction of monitoring participation in higher education by ethnic group seems unlikely.

4. Nature and extent of under-representation

4.1 Central and Eastern Europe

In all the countries involved in the survey it was emphasised that there was no discrimination in higher education on grounds of ethnicity or religion. Several of those interviewed expressed surprise that questions about ethnic monitoring should have been asked. Nevertheless the lack of monitoring in this area and the refusal to identify ethnic groups, but to consider individuals only by their national status, makes it impossible to ascertain accurately the participation of minority groups.

Under the ideology of the Communist system there was an assumption of equal opportunity and a refusal to allow the self-identification of ethnic groups. Rejection of ethnic categorisation may be regarded as being positive - especially if it could be achieved in people's everyday perceptions. However, this non-categorisation could now be concealing patterns of disadvantage and under-representation perpetuated from the former regimes, where ethnic identity was, in many cases, officially suppressed. Moreover a denial of the existence of cultural diversity cannot produce a multicultural higher education with a curriculum which responds to a diversity of needs.

In central and eastern Europe the term 'ethnic group' tends to be considered as synonymous with 'minority national group'. Many national minorities have found themselves as part of new nation states as a result of political remapping, and perceived discriminatory policies have created tension with the majority national group. One field where underlying tensions tend to be expressed is in the demand for mother-tongue education. The central question is whether minority groups should have a right to mother-tongue education or whether the nation state has the right to demand that education should be undertaken in the official national language. A variety of approaches can be taken, but the sensitivity of the question ensures that consequences of decisions will be keenly felt and bitterly resented if they are seen to discriminate against national minorities.

It is noticeable that schemes do exist throughout central and eastern European higher education institutions to tackle the recognised under-representation of the Romany community within the education system generally. Such projects are on a small scale, but are a positive development. It may be argued that schemes are targeted at the Romany community because their education presents no political threat to the status quo, while an assertion of cultural or ethnic identity is more dangerous. Other ethnic groups may perhaps use their education to make greater demands on the political establishment.

Evidence of under-representation created by a desire to strengthen national identities is not hard to find, for example, Romania and Slovakia both have substantial Hungarian populations. In both states the Hungarians are under-represented in higher education, but a large number go to Hungary to study, where access for Hungarians living abroad is encouraged as part of a policy to preserve national identity and culture. The issue of language and culture is a source of debate in both states.

In Slovakia the Hungarian community amounts to approximately 600,000 or 1/10 of the total population, and is concentrated in a geographical region near the Hungarian border. Many Hungarians, having been educated at primary and secondary school level in their mother tongue, prefer to pursue their education in Hungary. There are, however, universities in Slovakia which cater for the Hungarian community by offering courses in Hungarian. The issue of language is clearly unresolved, as many feel that the Hungarian population should be 'encouraged' to adopt the Slovak language, whilst other cultural and political interest groups feel that maintenance of the Hungarian language is essential to retain a sense of group identity and to ensure the democratisation process.

In Romania, where the ethnic Hungarian population amounts to nearly two million people, attitudes are divided on the right to use Hungarian as the language of instruction in schools and universities. The Hungarian community has been actively campaigning for a Hungarian-taught university in Transylvania, while at school level, Hungarian has been used as a teaching language in areas with a large Hungarian population.

The approval of a new education bill in 1995, making Romanian the mandatory language for all levels of education and for all citizens irrespective of their ethnic origin has certainly altered the situation. Removing the legal right to mother-tongue education has not removed the aspirations of the Hungarian community. Repercussions are likely to be felt in other states with a significant ethnic Hungarian minority.

In the Russian Federation, where there are over 200 ethnic groups, accounting for 10% of admissions to Higher Education, not only is monitoring undertaken, but a quota system is used, ensuring representation of different ethnic groups. When asked if any groups were still under-represented, the Ministry identified the nomadic people of the Northern Republics, explaining that these communities were worried about losing their cultural identity and language by sending their children away to study. The response to this situation has been to encourage community education, and at St Petersburg University teachers, actors and artists from these communities are employed for this purpose.

Initiatives to encourage participation of specific groups do exist in several states, but they tend to be on a small scale. A typical example can be found at the social work department at the university of Bucharest, which has provision in the short term for admitting a number of students from the Romany community irrespective of entry qualifications. The scheme is aimed at providing teachers from the community to encourage participation at all levels of the education system. Although operating on a small scale, the results have been very encouraging. On average, after two years of study, there is no difference in the achievement of students recruited to this scheme in comparison with the average intake. It is clear from these results that, given a positive environment, the under-achievement of the Romany community can be addressed, although larger-scale projects are required.

In Hungary, where the Romany community accounts for 5% of the population, additional funding is provided for schools with a high proportion of gypsies, and mother-tongue teacher-training programmes are offered to the Romany population; in the Czech Republic money is ring-fenced for programmes targeted at the Romany population.

4.2 Western Europe

Given the absence of monitoring in most of the countries in the survey, the extent of under-representation can in most cases only be speculative. In the Netherlands, about 4% of the population is drawn from minority ethnic groups, with concentrations of about 15-18% in the four largest cities. The largest groups are Turkish and Mediterraneans, followed by people from Surinam and the West Indies. In 1986 only 1% of Mediterraneans participated in university education and in higher professional education and the figure is still less than 3%. In contrast populations from Surinam and the West Indies are better represented; between 12% and 14%. Although this is considerably greater than the Moroccan and Turkish populations, it is nonetheless far short of the 30% participation of the indigenous Dutch people.

In the UK, the first HESA Data Report (1995) shows non-white ethnic groups 'to be well-represented irrespective of age' and that 'black students aged over 21 years of age are found in larger numbers within the student population than might be expected from the Census figures'. Pakistani women however are the exception to this, forming a smaller than expected proportion, especially among students aged 21 years or over. Overall, black students form a larger percentage among part-timers than among full-timers, although 'the distribution of students among the various ethnic groups does not differ greatly between levels of course'. Research from the Commission for Racial Equality (CRE) has shown however that minority ethnic groups suffer from indirect discrimination in that they are 'over-represented among the least favoured', higher education institutions (CRE 1994). There is certainly some danger in the UK of the ghetto-isation of black students into the new (former polytechnic) universities, many of which are inner-city based. This issue of vertical segregation is one for which, so far at least, no data is available from HESA, nor from any of the Western European countries studied.

The major barrier towards widening participation among minority ethnic groups is the refusal by national governments to recognise that there may be any under-representation. Given the extent and range of other statistical information on Western European higher education, the absence of data on minority ethnic participation is surprising. The possibility cannot be ignored that this is not so much an oversight as evidence of a conscious intention to restrict participation to benefit the dominant group.

There is evidence of direct discrimination against both applicants for places on courses and applicants for staff appointments from minority ethnic groups. In the UK, several such cases have been won with the support of the Commission for Racial Equality, but in some of the countries involved in this survey, for example Switzerland, there is no race relations legislation to provide protection of this kind. Moreover the expansion of extremist right wing parties, especially in France, has inevitably influenced attitudes against increasing higher education opportunities for minority ethnic groups.

Not only the political but also the socio-economic status of many minority groups presents a barrier to their participation in higher education. Ethnic groups with low socio-economic status include those from North Africa, the Dominican Republic, Colombia and the Phillippines living in Spain; Moroccan and Turkish people in the Netherlands; and the Bangladeshi community in the UK; all groups which are under-represented in higher education. Moreover the shift in many Western European states towards fee-paying by students is likely to distance these groups further from higher education opportunities, and encourage access only for those who can afford to pay.

While the desire for social mobility may provide greater incentives for those from minority groups to seek higher qualifications, evidence of discrimination experienced by graduates from these groups in obtaining professional employment and recognition (in for example, the UK and the Netherlands) may serve to discourage them from seeking to qualify. Moreover in higher education itself, the absence of role models from minority ethnic groups among academic staff serves to reinforce feelings of cultural isolation.

Lack of experience of the culture of higher education may also be a significant factor affecting minority ethnic groups. A number of research projects, including a study by Mora based upon a large population sample in Spain, has demonstrated that a major determinant of participation is not only socio-economic status, but parental experience of higher education, and this may often be lacking for first or even second and third generation immigrants.

Moreover the desire of some minorities to preserve their culture against what may be seen as centralising assimilatory processes may discourage participation. The Romany community in Spain for example, which retains its recognised ethnic identity, has not acquiesced easily in official government policy and this has included limited participation in state education, at primary and secondary levels, let alone in higher education. By contrast, the use of the Catalan language in higher education institutions in Northern Spain has succeeded in meeting the needs and reinforcing the cultural identity of this group.

Cultural and linguistic differences are often re-inforced and sometimes created by the ethnocentricity of much of the higher education curriculum in Western Europe. Students from minority groups participating in such curricula may find themselves, in the process of adapting to cultural norms, isolated both from their fellow students and from their own family backgrounds.

5. Policy and practice which may increase representation

There are examples of current policy and practice designed to increase participation among minority ethnic groups, at both national and institutional levels, but in none of the countries studied were they fully comprehensive.

At national level, these include:

- race relations legislation, including the appointment of a statutory body, to provide protection against discrimination in higher education, as in other aspects of society
- a nation-wide system for monitoring participation in higher education, which includes monitoring by ethnic group

- higher education systems and curricula which value and preserve the linguistic and cultural inheritance of minority ethnic groups
- financial systems for student subsistence and payment of fees which ensure that the costs of higher education study are not prohibitive for those from low income groups
- financial incentives for higher education institutions which seek to widen access for minority ethnic groups, and external monitoring of their progress
- admissions criteria and procedures which allow the achievement and potential of applicants from diverse cultural backgrounds to be recognised
- recognition of and quality assurance for alternative entry routes which may make higher education more accessible to those from minority ethnic groups
- support for research into the incidence and causes of under-representation.

At institutional level, these include:

- policy and mission statements with strategies and targets for widening participation
- monitoring of participation by ethnic group
- staff development programmes for awareness raising and to avoid discriminatory practices and the association of cultural diversity with lower standards
- outreach recruitment policies targeted towards students from diverse ethnic backgrounds.
- flexible entry routes which enable applicants from diverse cultural and socio-economic backgrounds to qualify for entry
- a dynamic approach to curriculum development which goes beyond a narrow ethnocentric curriculum offer
- staffing policies which value diversity and recognise the need for role models from different ethnic groups
- research into the incidence and causes of under-representation.

Lis Hemmingsen

Development of Teacher Qualifications According to 'Bridge-Building' for Adult Immigrants and Refugees

Introduction

This paper presents and discusses different models for education and development for teachers' working with the establishment of and teaching on what we in Denmark call 'bridge-building' for adult immigrants and refugees.

As an aspect of 'lifelong learning' common programmes have been established between different sectors in the educational system. These have mainly been courses for adults and combine general and technical qualifications.

During the later years a variant of these programmes has been established for adult immigrants and refugees where the aim has been to build a 'bridge' between language schools and institutions in the vocational educational system. This 'bridge-building' is an attempt to make it attractive and motivating for the target group to choose an education which corresponds with their resources and needs, and to stay in the system for the whole educational period.

In the spring of 1995 a cooperation between The Danish Institute for the Educational Training of Vocational Teachers and the Research Center of Education for Adults, at The Royal Danish School of Educational Studies was established, formulating a research project about teacher development and models for teacher development where teachers from different institutions would cooperate in establishing 'bridge-building' for adult immigrants and refugees.[1]

Teaching of the Danish language for immigrants and refugees has been going on for about 25 years. The teaching is carried out at language schools

1 Vibe Aarkrog og Lis Hemmingsen: Broer og kvalifikationer, DEL og Forskningscenter for voksenuddannelse, 1996

for immigrants and refugees and is based on law nr 355 [2]. The responsibilities for the teaching are settled at county level and are carried out by a number of different schools [3] in the county.

The vocational schools have a long tradition for education of the young people for the technical and commercial professions.

Both these educations are linked to the Ministry of Education but to different departments. Other types of education, however, are linked to the Ministry of Labour.

Background for the project

In planning our project we based it on three types of experience:

The first type of experience comes from cross sector programmes.[4] The last few years cross sector programmes have been set up between different educational institutions across the different ministry sectors. These programmes have had different aims and are made for different types of participants, young as well as adults, but one of the most manifest experiences from these programmes is, that the success of the programmes very much depends on the quality of cooperation between the teachers. Much time must be spent on the cooperation, the cooperation has to start early, there must be a very high frequency of contact by phone, visits, meetings or participation in each others teaching. It is also very important that the teacher who is going to teach in the bridge project participates in the planning of the education from the very start.

The second type of experience comes from the teaching of the adult immigrants and refugees in the vocational schools. The main target group for the vocational schools is young people; most of them come directly from the Folkeskole and are about 17 years old.

2 Lov om undervisning af voksne indvandrere 1986, revideret ved lov nr 455, 1994
3 for instance AOF og Dansk flygtningehjælp
4 Vibe Aakrog m.fl.: Voksenuddannelsespuljen-erfaringer og perspektiver, Arbejdsmarkedsstyrelsen og Undervisningsministeriet 1995

The adult immigrants and refugees at the vocational schools form a group which generally has large difficulties in dealing with both the professional demands and the demands that come from the way of teaching at the schools. The principle underlying the teaching and working form is that they should strengthen the pupil centred and active aspect of learning. The adult immigrants and refugees often have difficulties because of their different cultural background and because the Danish school culture at the vocational schools is mostly defined as a culture for young people[5]. Only recently the schools have begun to build up a learning culture for adults in the vocational schools.

The third type of experience comes from the knowledge that the adult immigrants and refugees have of the vocational educations. Often the adults first meeting with the Danish educational system is through the language schools. At these schools the contents are the Danish language and knowledge of the Danish society. At the schools the adults have to decide if they want to continue in the educational system. This decision is often very difficult because of their lack of knowledge of the Danish labour market and which vocational possibilities there are. Also the vocational competencies the desired job will demand as well as how the adult can acquire these competencies is but sketchily understood.

When cross sector programmes are set up between language schools and vocational schools as 'bridge-building' they demand at least two types of competences of the teacher: to be able to work at the development and to teach at the 'bridge'.

The first type of competence is a personal; the teacher must be able to :

– work in accordance with a multicultural educational aim. This means that the teacher should be able to show his acceptance and respect of different cultures.
– choose different values from several cultures, when setting up aims for the teaching or for a 'bridge-building' programme.

5 Lis Hemmingsen: En undersøgelse af de fremmedsprogede elever i erhvervsuddannelserne. SEL 1990. Lis Hemmingsen:En undersøgelse af fremmedsprogedes elevers opfattelse af erhvervsuddannelse. SEL 1990.

- have and communicate a clarified relationship with his own and the other cultures.
- be a mirror of a multicultural world, so there will be representatives from different cultures both among the participants and among the teachers.
- teach and to differentiate the teaching multiculturaly. This means that the teachers should be able to take an experience from other cultures in their teaching and be able to balance between a cultural differentiation and a positive discrimination.
- handle culturally sensitive subjects both in the teaching and at the staff-room. This also means that he must to be able to work with for instance racism as a teaching subject.

The second type of competence is organisational; it depends on the kind of cooperation according to the teaching. For instance these three models of cooperations for cross sector education have been shown to work.

1. Module Model

In this model the teaching of both the language school and the vocational school are placed in modules and is divided according to time so that the modules are placed one after another. The demand for the cooperation of the teachers here is to arrange meetings between the different modules. During these meetings the teachers can inform each other about what has been going on in their own module.

2. Parallel Model

In this model the teaching from the two kinds of school works in parallel. For instance, the language school can teach its subject in the morning and the vocational school teach its subject in the afternoon. Or the language school can be responsible for the teaching every monday and wednesday and the vocational school every tuesday, thursday and friday. In the parallel model the demands for the cooperation are greater because the teachers need to coordinate often and give each other information of the participants and of the subject they have taught.

3. Integration Model

In this model the teachings from the two kinds of schools are integrated in each other in such a way that it is difficult to see which kind of teaching belongs to which kind of school. This model demands not only that the teachers make the planning together but also that they are able to teach together and to observe or participate in each others' teaching[6]. In the last mentioned model two types of teachers' cooperation can occur: two-teachers and team-teaching.

Demands for the adults in transition from the language school to the vocational school

To get into further research of the competencies necessary for a teacher in a 'bridge-building' we carried out a number of interviews with teachers at the different kinds of schools and with some adult immigrant students at the vocational schools.

The interviews show that the transition from the language school to the vocational schools sets up some important demands to the adult immigrants and refugees. The following demands were found to be important:

From a few subjects to many and often more complicated subjects. At the language school the students are taught very few subjects: the Danish language and the Danish society. At the vocational school however the students are taught many subjects even from the first year. At the commercial school about 8 subjects, at the technical school 10 to 15 subjects depending on the profession. So the students have to be able to keep track of not 2 but many subjects, and this multiplicity can be quite overwhelming.

Another point is that the subjects at the vocational school often demand a vocational terminology, which is not normally learned at the language

6 VUP, erfaringer og perspektiver, Arbejdsmarkedsstyrelsen og Undervisningsministeriet 1995

school. So the students feel that they have to learn a whole new language when they start at the vocational school.

The tests at the vocational school also have a different content from the tests that the students were used to at the language school. The tests at the vocational school focus on the professional terminology and on a more general knowledge. Besides this one of the subjects at the vocational school is a foreign language, at the commercial school often two foreign languages. The learning of the foreign languages is often difficult to the immigrant because the teacher uses the Danish language as a background.

From a few lessons to many lessons. At the language school the students often have 3 to 4 lessons a day. At the vocational school the students have 7 lessons a day. For the adult this prolonging of the school day plays a serious role not only at the time spent at the school but also for his or her responsibilities in the family.

From a few teachers to many teachers. The many subjects at the vocational school necessitate many teachers. At the transition from the language school to the vocational school the students have to get used to many teaching styles from many teachers. Often the speed and the lack of clarity with which the teacher speaks makes the understanding for the students difficult.

From a few students to many students. In classes in the language school the normal amount of students is 10 to 15. At the vocational school there can be up to 30 students in a class. The adult immigrants then have to get used to the many students. Also it will be more difficult to get help or information from the teacher in the large class.

From immigrants and refugees students to Danish students. The difficulties with the many students in the classes at the vocational school become large because the major part of the students in the classes are Danish. This mixture of students also has some influence on the way the teacher teaches. How clearly he pronounces the Danish language and how fast he speaks.

From an adult learning culture to a youth learning culture. The transition from the language school means that the adult immigrant has to get used to function in a school dominated by a youth culture. Results from other researches show that there are more calmness and professional seriousity in the adult class than in the youth class in the vocational schools. Result of this is that the adult typical finds it very important to learn in an adult learning culture[7]

From ordinary language to workshop jargon The adult immigrants in the interviews mentioned, that they were very surprised of the language spoken at the vocational school and especially the language spoken at the workshop. It was both embarrassing and difficult to understand.

From a teaching conducted by the teacher to a teaching conducted by the participants. The language teaching at the language schools normally is a teacher-conducted teaching whereas the teaching at the vocational school is more a participant-conducted teaching. One reason for this is that the teaching at the vocational school during the last years has been focused on the concept 'responsibility for your own learning'. The transition for the adult immigrant therefore means that he has to get used to working in groups and to participate in a more active form of learning. The students at the vocational school are generally used to put forward their own opinions and to argue with each other.

The interviews with the teachers showed that they feel that it is difficult to make the adult immigrants and refugees express their meaning and this is not because of linguistic but because of cultural reasons. The adult immigrant has the opinion that it is the teacher's responsibility that he learns something. The teacher is an authority with whom you do not argue. The experience from some of the cultures the adults come from is, that the teacher is a person you are in some way afraid of and not a person who can be your friend.

An interesting point here, however, is that some of the students in the interview said, that they often felt that the teacher was afraid of the student.

---

7 Niels Henrik Helms m.fl. 'Voksne i erhvervsuddannelse- lærerne kvalifikationsbehov' SEI 1995. Vibe aarkrog' betydningen af deltagerforudsætninger. En sammenlignende analyse af tre voksen HG-klasser 'SEL 1995.

From learning to decide for a profession. The transition to the vocational school means that the adult has to choose a profession. This decision not only means having to speak the Danish language but also to understand the working of the Danish society. This understanding is often lacking, and the choice may not be a good one.

Three different models of 'bridges'.

During the project three different models of 'bridges' were set up.

One 'bridge' was the cooperation between the counsellor at the language school and the commercial school. The main aim in this model is to qualify the counsellor so that he is able to give relevant information to the student at the language school about the possibilities for further education at the commercial school. This information could also be about other possibilities for education in other educational institutions. Another aim was that the counsellor at the language school established cooperation with the counsellors at the VUC[8]. The aim is to set up a 'bridge' which combines the further Danish language education with the teaching in subjects from the commercial school. At this 'bridge' teachers from the VUC also take part in. Another aim was to strengthen the students' competencies in the Danish language and to give them the possibility to get acquainted with subjects in the commercial education and the way the teaching is carried out at the commercial school.

Because of the cooperation between the teachers from the different types of education the counsellors at the language school are able not only to guide their students to the VUC-education or the commercial school but also to programmes where the VUC participates in qualifying the students to finish a commercial education.

At the second 'bridge' model a programme of a duration of 40 weeks, divided into two periods of 20 weeks, was established. In this programme a language school and a vocational school cooperated. In the first 20 weeks'

8 VUC is a adult education center, where the adult can take an education which corresponds with the last part of the Folkeskole, but where the contents and tests are made for adults.

period the students in for the half time of each day should be taught Danish by the teachers from the language school. For the other half of the day the students would get an introduction to three branches of the education at the vocational school. The three branches were metalwork, building and cooking and the teaching was carried out by the teachers from the vocational school. All the teaching would take place at the vocational school.

When the project began the detail planning of the second period was not quite finished. But the aim was that the students should get a deeper knowledge of one of the three branches from the first period. The contents of the second period should also include more theoretical subjects, for instance mathematics, science and the English language. In both periods the teachers from the language school and the vocational school to some extent would take part in each others teaching.

At the third model of 'bridge' the teachers from the language school and a commercial school arranged, that the students from the language school would visit the commercial school to help them with their choice of education. As a part of this information the students were invited to a meeting, where the employers from different companies took part in and presented their enterprises so that the students could get an impression of the job profile in the profession. Another result of the establishment of this bridge was to hold a conference for different education institutions in the local area. The aim of the conference was that the different educations institution could get a better knowledge of the education carried out at other institutions and as an invitation to establish 'bridge-building' at a later time.

Teacher development

According to the different models for 'bridges' the teachers in the interviews were asked to formulate their needs and wishes for the content of their future development as teachers. The needs for the development can be divided into two categories: mutual knowledge of other Danish school cultures and knowledge of foreign cultures.

The teachers and the counsellors felt a strong need to get a deeper insight into each others' school systems. What is a vocational school? What are the different educations at the school and the demands to these? What is the content in the subjects and what are the demands and levels in the subject? How to get a closer knowledge of the teaching methods carried out and the different roles of the students and the teachers? What forms of learning and qualification can the different teaching methods give? How can the teaching be participant-oriented in such a way, that the students feel that they learn something? What are the demands expressed in the tests that the vocational schools uses?

Another wish was to establish a common terminology which would facilitate a better understanding of the different 'local languages' used at the schools.

In these wishes and needs some variations were seen in the groups from the different school systems. The teachers at the language school especially have a need to know more about the different cultures of the immigrant groups and the educational systems in their cultures. What are the immigrants expectations to the subjects and the ways of teaching?

A common need and wish was the formulation of teaching methods which were especially suitable for adult immigrants and refugees.

The structure of the teachers' development program was planned according to the 'sandwich system'. It began with a two-day seminar followed by a local working period back at the schools. In this period the teachers would work with the more concrete part of establishing the 'bridges'. During this work they had the opportunity to get some consultancy from the project leaders. The development program ended with a one day-seminar.

The contents of the first seminar was planned on the background of the interviews with the teachers and the main content was concentrated in two categories 'mutual knowledge of school culture' and 'knowledge of foreign cultures'.

Beside this it was planned to work with the development of a common language between the teachers, and to work with establishment of bridges. But during the seminar it became obvious that the participants' greatest need was for the mutual knowledge of school culture, and in consequence of this the subject of foreign cultures was postponed until later in the development program.

During the local working period at the schools the aim was that the teachers should work to make the 'bridges' better defined both in structure and in content. During this period the working groups got consultancy, and the contents of the consultancy were differentiated according to the structure and content of the 'bridge'. The working group at one 'bridge' had a need for knowledge of foreign cultures, the subject which was postponed from the first seminar. In the other working groups the function of the consultancy was to provoke, to structure and to ask questions about the teachers' work at the 'bridges'.

At the last seminar each working group presented its 'bridge' to the other participants and discussed its work with them. This presentation and discussion were very fruitful for all the participants. Besides this the work at the seminar was concentrated on competence requirement for teachers that worked with 'bridge-building'. Two types of competencies were needed: one dealing with the multicultural work and one with the cooperation as already mentioned earlier.

Conclusions and perspectives

The conclusion from the project of establishing 'bridges' falls in three types of experience.

The conclusion from the experiences with the cross sectors cooperation and the education of adult refugees and immigrants is, that there is a serious need for establishing 'bridges'. This is because the adults meet severe difficulties in the transition from one kind of school to another. There are three types of difficulties; those connected with their being immigrants or refugees, those connected with their being adult in a youth culture and those connected with the different subjects, ways of teaching and learning cultures at the vocational schools.

The experience from the establishment of the 'bridges' is that the efficiency of the 'bridge-building' depends on the former cooperation between the teachers more than the extent of the 'bridges' and the concrete form of the 'bridge'. The more experience with cooperation the teachers have the more concrete the plans for the 'bridge' will be. When the project started the teachers who developed two models of 'bridges' had some experience of cooperation but of different variations.

Another experience is that the teachers feel a great need for knowledge of other schools, their educational system, learning culture and the teachers involved.

Briefly - it is not important how tall or broad the 'bridge' is but it is important that the 'bridge' can carry the load of students from one education to another.

The experience from the teachers' development shows that to structure of the program after the sandwich model is good for three reasons:

The structure supports the teacher who works with the 'bridge'. The support consists of giving feed back to the teacher and to keep him at the work. When the teacher has to present a piece of work for the consultant at the local meeting some serious work has to be done.

Another advantage is that the teachers can inspire each other at the seminars, where they have time to work with the development of their 'bridge'.

The teachers' development should support the establishment of a realistic 'bridge'. This means that the contents of the teachers' development must be different according to the structure and the content of each 'bridge'. This can be arranged best in the local period with some support from the consultant.

Our experience with the project seems to indicate that the program can be improved. To obtain a good knowledge of other education institutions demands much time.

Therefore it is necessary to plan with sufficient time for the teachers to get to know each other and each others institutions. This means that the duration of the program should be fairly long and that it should start before the first seminar at the schools. Before the seminar the teachers should have the task to visit each others institutions and make a description of that institution. This description could be presented at the first day of the seminar. By adding a layer to the sandwich the value of the local cooperation is increased.

These does not mean that the investigation of other educations and educational system shall take place without relation to the main aim of the 'bridge'-building. The teachers development shall show the connection between the adult immigrants' problems and the relevant institutions' special education, subjects, content, ways of teaching and school culture.

An important point in establishing 'bridge'-building is that the structure of the 'bridge' is realistic according to the teachers' and counsellors previous experiences and their resources to participate in the project. But in any case the 'bridge' must include central features of the education and pedagogic policy from the institutions involved.

After the end of this project of teachers' development a question was raised: could the establishment cooperation - the bridge - hold after the closing of the development project.

This question has resulted in a new research project: which kind of teachers' development is required during working and teaching at a 'bridge' so that the cooperation continues in the daily work. This research project is now formulated and will be carried out in the last part of 1996 and the beginning of 1997.

Julia Preece

Deconstructing the Discourse of Community Education and Development for Women of Muslim Pakistani Heritage: Alternative Solutions?

This paper is, for me, a risky one. It is risky on two counts. Firstly, I am a white Westerner, programmed to operate within the dominant ideology of community education as it is theorised in academia. I take the risk of misinterpreting alternative cultural discourses for community and their associated education and development theory by simply re-inscribing my own values on those discourses. Secondly I take the risk of challenging, to only a limited extent, ideologies which are embedded across community work practice in the United Kingdom (and probably across the Western world). I risk doing this because of my own incomplete understanding of alternative knowledge representations, and because of the limited amount of literature on this viewpoint in relation to community education. Nevertheless, whilst community education itself has not received much attention of this nature I can draw more extensively on theoretical positions in feminism and poststructuralism to raise the issue of epistemological difference and the existence of unrecognised or disqualified discourses as the basis for my argument.

With these hesitations, but coupled with a sense that such a debate is long overdue, I start my paper. First, I would like to explain the relevant terminology which I am going to use for my analysis. I shall explore some of the theoretical principles behind community education and development in Britain and some recent comments on these principles. I will then attempt to problematise the dominant practices and goals for community work in relation to the values of one Pakistani Muslim community in the central north of England. In this context I shall describe my university's attempt to reconstruct a community work training course which allows that community to assert itself on its own terms. Comparison of the curriculum for this course with a more conventional programme highlights some of the effects of racism which are unintentional but already inscribed in institutional practice.

The theoretical argument

The theoretical viewpoint behind this paper claims that identities and definitions are multiple and fragmented. Categories such as 'woman', 'community', 'empowerment' only have similar meaning in particular contexts. Knowledge is merely an interpretation of truth and is expressed through discourses whose meanings change according to time, place and social context. Discourse is used here to include the language, behaviours and systems of any one institution or society which together serve to sustain its cultural values and truth. Discourses are legitimised through a constructed logic in order to rationalise and justify why things are done in a certain way. People are positioned within discourses with varying degrees of authority. Their authority proclaims certain values as common sense and more important than alternative values. Notions of justice and equality, for instance become unassailable norms with meanings which everyone takes for granted. It is difficult to break through common sense values because of the power of multiple discourse strategies to maintain their position and because of the authority of those who uphold them. People come to believe ideologically in the value of those discourses irrespective of their own status or position within the discourse. Ideology, therefore, becomes a powerful mechanism for sustaining discourses in different cultures. The nature of a dominant discourse is such that it automatically disqualifies alternative versions of truth or knowledge, particularly if those versions directly challenge the dominant ideology. (Foucault, 1972, Preece, 1996, Sarup, 1993).

Feminist interpretations of this theory have identified how power relations in discourses consistently undermine women's representation of knowledge and the value of women's experience in creating new knowledge. The notion of 'epistemological privilege' enables feminist writers to identify suppressed knowledge; often knowledge based on experience and as a result of oppression by dominant power holders. The concept of difference then, is offered as an antidote to discriminatory practice and an attempt to prevent alternative discourses from being positioned as 'oppositional' or 'other'. (Weiner, 1994, Stanley and Wise, 1993). Differences must necessarily be multiple, otherwise one suppressed discourse will simply claim privilege over the other. Black feminists, for example, question the single category of woman and identify several standpoints, or positions of experience, within and across cultures. Unfortunately differential power relationships across discourses often have the effect that certain discourses are always in danger of re-inscribing their values without knowing it onto communities of difference (Stuart, 1996). Gorelick (1991) describes this as the 'blindness of privilege'. The recognition of difference, then must ensure 'insider' views are not reconstituted as fixed categories, resulting in a form of racism which uses difference as a reason for maintaining discrimination.

Defining the problem

Community education and development now has a discourse pedigree which is predominantly male, white and Eurocentric (Mansfield, 1992). The concept of 'community' is sometimes acknowledged as an ideological construct, with a tendency for community education to be seen as compensatory education for those communities envisioned as 'deviating from the healthy norm' (Martin, 1996: 120). As with other discourses, the purpose of community education is positioned within contemporary politics. It operates across a continuum which ranges from a perception of education as an information resource to one where the goal of education is for development and action (Lovett, Gillespie and Gunn, 1995). Nevertheless, the broad goals of community education and development function in a dominant discourse which pathologises communities under the theme of 'educational disadvantage'. Certain key words reproduce themselves with regard to the professional training of community workers for community education and development. These include: partnership participation inter-agency collaboration, social purpose and empowerment (Martin, 1996, Francis and Henderson, 1992, Lightfoot, 1990, Lovett, Gillespie and Gunn, 1995). The emphasis for community workers is to address inequality, disadvantage and non-participation, by intervening in communities and helping them to address local needs, ostensibly from a grass-roots perspective.

At first glance such goals seem unassailably laudable and, as a work colleague of mine might put it: 'ideologically sound'. The professional goal for community workers is to help local people identify and solve their own problems through a process of critical evaluation, inter-agency collaboration or local action and awareness raising of wider societal contexts (Francis and Henderson, 1992). If such goals are interpreted through their dominant discourses, however, then the marginalised discourses and knowledge of those 'disadvantaged' communities remain excluded and unseen through the blindness of privilege. As Lightfoot suggests:

Merely reproducing existing institutional structures, which are predominantly those favoured by adult white males is inappropriate (1990, p.2).

It is difficult within existing community education literature to find levels of discourse awareness which address this issue. Whilst many writers emphasise the need to understand grass-roots concerns, these are usually addressed from the dominant discourse perspective, often resulting in an obscuring of culturally bound issues. Perhaps the best example of this awareness comes from Northern Ireland, where the discourse of minority Nationalists has long since been misrepresented:

> To simply explain certain behaviour as meaningless ... will not make the behaviour cease and it ignores the problem of ideology (Lovett, Gillespie and Gunn 1995, p.9).

Their concern is to avoid the patriarchal approach of community education and development which interprets difference as a form of prejudice that can be 'cured' through awareness raising within the dominant ideology. The emphasis for Lovett, Gillespie and Gunn is on actively accepting the culture and its values as a prerequisite for progress (p.103). The difficulties of understanding values outside the dominant discourse are not underestimated. Smith, for instance, re-emphasises the 'situatedness of our perspective' (1994:133) and consequent 'undervaluing of other traditions of reflection' as we, the dominant discourse holders re-inscribe our communities as 'other' (p.25). Stuart, too, highlights how difference 'requires a more nuanced analysis than community education theory has often used in the past' (1996: 180). These arguments are particularly pertinent in relation to Western discourse attempts to interface with black cultures or non-Christian religions.

The conflict of discourses between Pakistani Muslim women and Westerners

This point is demonstrated by a recent piece of empirical research into a group of Muslim women's attitudes to adult education. Ten women had been interviewed in 1993 as part of a larger piece of research looking at different discourses in different class and cultural groupings. The women in this sample were primarily from the rural, Mir Pur area of Pakistan. They had all been educated in Pakistan. In spite of this small sample, and its emphasis on 'newly arrived' women, anecdotal evidence suggests that the views held by these women were representative of the majority of Muslim women in their town. Later discussions will also highlight continued evidence of support for the views presented in this paper amongst women who were educated in northern England. The argument remains that whilst actual examples of epistemological privilege may change over time, the principle needs to recognise that insider values remains.

The interviewer for this group, Raana, described, for example, the Pakistani interviewees' contrasting responses to social and physical space compared with English attitudes:

> You always find one fixed term that everybody says when they come from Pakistan about England and its always 'This place is like a prison' ... the English are quite a closed race and the houses are closed ... closed roof tops ... walled houses ... everything is so enclosed ... so it looks like a prison for them

The reality from which these women came had been one where people sleep on rooftops, shops are open markets and where social interaction is sustained by constant enquiry into each other's lives. Space in Pakistan therefore was dynamic and active. Yet the Western perception of Asian women's space is positioned in a reversed geographical power relationship which sees Asian women as cut off and placed behind walled enclosures. The effect of Western discourses regarding women's space appears to reverse values which are highly significant for these Muslim women in particular (Preece 1996). This can have a direct bearing on how Western community education and development, which is often located in Western notions of public space, can be recognised by women who see these same domains as shut off, and whose own public spaces are shut off from the Western view.

Other Western aspects of community education or development can have similar exclusionary effects. A key community development word, 'empowerment', for instance, assumes a single category of identity and oppression which is applied across races, cultures and sexes (Yuval Davis, 1994). For migrant women from Pakistan, however, perceptions of empowerment needs an understanding of different racial, religious and gender power relations and the dynamics that go with that, particularly in relation to the additional tension of living in a foreign environment. Buijs (1993) argues, therefore, that what may seem disempowering to Westerners may be liberating for Asian women. Ali (1992) also argues that the tensions for black people in identifying racism as oppression but religion as liberating rather than oppressive are often misrepresented within the western discourse of empowerment and disadvantage. In contrast to common Western images of Muslim women, Ali points out that Islam is often a means of retaining community identity and protection, whilst allowing personal growth and change through Islamic values. She adds that such a standpoint has particular significance in northern England where British northern conservativism reinforces a retrospective brand of male dominance in white and Asian cultures. Islam can therefore be a means of expression rather than a force of oppression. If Western empowerment discourse challenges power relations by the same descriptors as their white counterparts without recognising empowerment for some Muslim women at least, in their particular context, the result can be exclusion rather than partnership. The role of women in Muslim communities needs to be seen within their cultural role as bearers of religious identity as well as in the context of patriarchal power relations (Yuval Davis, 1992). Rattansi (1992) challenges more explicitly 'culturalist assumptions' about Asian women who are often depicted as a problem and in need of learning the language and customs of Britain. She emphasises the need to 'change the discourse if you want to tackle racism' (1992:29), a discourse which allows for difference and fragmentation within cultures as well as racism (p.36). Whilst opinions amongst Muslims on the value of Islam to empower women are divided, Ali confirms the disempowering effect of anti-Muslim discourse in Britain, which makes Muslim communities insecure and vulnerable. She emphasises the need to 'empower through Islam', rather than make assumptions about starting where people are at. Simply acknowledging the existence of communities and identifying needs, does not mean recognising the values within them. This sentiment echoes the concerns of Lovett and others mentioned earlier in this paper, where 'empowerment' education from the insider view is requested. Starting 'where people are at' is not the same as retaining their values in the development process.

Professional training, encased in theoretical discourses which encourage 'engagement with the social system' and 'cultural forms' (Smith, 1992: 107) rarely require community workers to explore the meaning behind that discourse in different contexts. Indeed Knowles and Mercer (1992) claim the failure of feminist discourses to challenge the particular forms of disadvantage relevant to black women. As Brah says:

> We need to be attentive to the ways in which needs are socially constructed and represented in various discourses' (1992: 129).

It is within this context that the Lancaster University Community Access programme attempted to address the issues of community education in an Islamic context for one community of women in Northern England. Evidence of the requirement to question our own, Western ideologies came from three sources: an article by an educator living within the community we worked with, our own empirical findings from research on differences within adult education discourse and from the attendance profile of an existing training course in community development.

The evidence of need to recognise different discourses in community education and development training

Hartley (1994) recorded a small ethnographic survey of literacy practices amongst a bilingual community in a small town of East Lancashire. Her findings revealed how skills and responsibilities were shared as a collective amongst generations and across families according to need as well as a form of social activity:

> 'Activities are constantly shared, negotiated, shaped by members of the family and the wider community and those who have no direct access to the written word are guaranteed access through family members and friends' (Hartley, 1994:39).

Yet these collective responsibilities are dislocated from the non-Muslim community because their values are not recognised within the Western world of community education. The 'written word' in Western discourse is part of a discourse of power but one which is constructed around Western politics of power which tends to exclude women who share unequal levels of literacy (Rockhill, 1993).

Similar examples of reversed discourses were apparent amongst my own previously mentioned research, using in-depth interviews which explored educational values for Muslim women in the same town. It was evident for this group at least that an inter-related sense of religion, community and education embraced many Western community education words, but in a context of peace, rather than challenge to their own status quo:

> The most important thing was faith and the second most important thing was living in harmony and living together as a community .. we should teach exactly the same things to our children .. and.. education is such an important thing we ought to encourage our children as much as possible. And only then will our children be able to stand on their own two feet (Shazir).

sense value in Shazir's life. Independence, too, was an assumed outcome of increased education. Yet Western perceptions of many Asian families is one of repression and enforced dependence. When such contrasting discourses function alongside each other it is hardly surprising that mutual engagement in training courses rarely takes place. It was necessary for us to interpret 'independence' from the insider view. Educational value, for instance, was intertwined with gendered notions of responsibility for harmony and collective responsibilities which were also inscribed in the women's meaning of independence. As independence alone might lead to a dislocation from the community, religion encourages spiritual community and forms the basis on which all schooling rests (Preece, 1996):

> Islamic education is the way of life. It's not just a religion - Islam is the purpose of my life (Surrya).

Unlike the individualistic, self-seeking nature of education and achievement promoted within the UK education system, education is seen as a community process, to which a variety of people contribute and in which women have a particular role. As Afshar points out: 'women are the perceived transmitters of cultural values and identity' (1994:131). As Hartley had identified in her observations, education, to varying degrees, was seen to offer opportunity within, rather than away from, the extended family community, primarily as a means of returning knowledge and skills to the community. Such discourses in themselves have inscribed common sense, particularly for a community which has uprooted itself from various locations in the Indian Sub Continent. Yet they also refract, rather than intermesh with the more secular, confrontational concerns of Western community development philosophy. Further evidence of active community work within this community was revealed in conversation when interviewees described their practices of teaching Urdu or Arabic to groups of younger generations, but based within the family home.

On the basis of these insights, I and a colleague decided to explore some discourse contentions within Lancaster University's community development training course. The course is funded by the European Social Fund.

Whilst the course was free, it had mixed sex attendance and required some travelling to the course venue. Although these would have been inhibitory factors for women in East Lancashire who might have wanted to participate, we decided the major issue was the nature of our curriculum and its starting point. The course divides into forty hour modules. Our first module explored equal opportunities issues for young people: race, gender and disability oppression. The second looked at non-participation in adult education and how to encourage new learners. We had an assumed common sense expectation that people would come to similar understandings for values such as independence and liberation in relation to these topics because both modules had the appearance of addressing equality *issues*. They were not looking, however, at *values*, or the meaning behind those values. The discussion of non-participation, for instance, assumed that participation should be a goal in itself. The values ingrained in that participation were white, Western values of equality and justice from one perspective. These were frequently garnished with middle class goals of individualism and progression where personal growth would lead away from, rather than engage with the community of origin. By attempting to respect everyone equally, we used a language which failed to respect difference, particularly difference as a term which encouraged evolving, rather than fixed identities. As a result the curriculum and its examples of empowerment made no connection with the lives and daily concerns of people like those in the research sample.

We proceeded to rewrite our theoretical perspectives with a view to encouraging a different form of dialogue. We wanted a dialogue which allowed values to develop, be reconstructed and change in relation to developing concepts in the West and East, but through, rather than in opposition to Muslim qualities. The course therefore has the following objectives:

- to give respect and status to Muslim values
- to offer knowledge which is relevant to Asian community work
- to give credit for work done in the family and local community
- to make links between western community work goals and Muslim goals
- to involve Muslim tutors where possible

– to provide a course with a local study base.

Instead of starting with Eurocentric models of literature and practice, the introductory module for this course explores Muslim and other religious values and compares activities here with those experienced in the Indian Sub continent. The course is taught bilingually to enable both newly arrived and English born women to participate together. Community education notions of partnership, equality and human potential are explored in the context of Muslim family lives and current practices (Preece and Bokhari, 1997, forthcoming). The work placement module, instead of requiring students to seek placements outside of their community, invites students to consider how their existing activities meet community work goals and how such activities might be improved to develop the autonomy and independence they seek for their children or themselves, but within their own discourse boundaries for such words.

The course is only beginning properly next term. It was devised in consultation with local women and Asian heritage teachers who knew and understood the concerns of this particular community. It might be argued that the curriculum has been devised too closely around the needs of one particular group, even though responses from the surrounding communities suggests that such culturally relevant courses have wide local appeal. Ali has already pointed out that Asian communities in northern England are not necessarily typical of communities in the south, as they are also caught up in the patriarchal discourse of white, working class northerners. Such a training programme may have to be adapted to the discourse values of different communities. The theme, however, of exploring 'community' and 'education' from an Islamic, insider-view is a state which sits uneasily amongst mainstream education courses with their Western notions of oppression and pathology for women bearing the label 'Muslim'. By building on reconstructed community education concepts and cultivating difference as developmental rather than fixed, we, the course organisers, hope that this programme is providing discourse tools which can challenge some common sense Western values implicit in structural racism. We hope that by providing a course from an insider Muslim perspective the participants will feel sufficiently able to talk on their terms and give us the evidence to question our own discourses. The resultant goal will be to facilitate social integration on more equal terms than those which are at present available on mainstream training courses.

Conclusion

This paper has tried to demonstrate that community education and development strategies need to recognise different values and meanings within their common sense assumptions. A theoretical perspective needs to draw on theories of deconstruction and feminisms in order to develop academic arguments in favour of difference, but with recognition that difference should not become a fixed identity. The theoretical positions in this paper are just developing. They need to be translated into practice so that structural racisms can be challenged more fundamentally than they have been up to now. Whilst my own paper is only at the beginning of this debate I hope we can learn from our own curriculum development with local communities of difference in northern England.

I am grateful to contributions from the seminar at the Bremen Conference to celebrate the 1996 International Year of Lifelong Learning, in particular Haroon Saad's insights which helped me to clarify my arguments.

References

Afshar, H. (1994), 'Muslim Women in West Yorkshire' in H. A. Afshar and M. Maynard (eds) The Dynamics of Race and Gender, London, Taylor and Francis.

Ali, Y. (1992) 'Muslim Women and the Politics of Ethnicity and Culture in Northern England' in Saghal, G. and Yuval Davis, N. (eds), Refusing Holy Orders, London, Virago Press.

Brah, A. (1992), 'Difference, Diversity and Differentiation' in Donald, J. and Rattansi, A. (eds), 'Race', Culture and Difference, London, Sage/Open University Press.

Buijs, G. (ed) (1993), Migrant Women: crossing boundaries and changing identities, Berg.

Foucault, M. (1972), Power/Knowledge, Harvester Wheatsheaf.

Francis, D. and Henderson, P. (1992), Working with Rural Communities, London, Macmillan.

Gorelick, S. (1991), Contradictions of Feminist Methodology, Gender and Society 5 (4) pp 459-477.

Hartley, T. (1994), 'Generations of Literacy Among Women in a Bilingual Community' in Hamilton, M., Barton, D. and Ivanic, R. (eds), Worlds of Literacy, Multilingual Matters Ltd.

Knowles, C. and Mercer, S. (1992), 'Feminism and Antiracism: an exploration of the political possibilities' in Donald, J. and Rattansi, A., 'Race', Culture and Difference, London, Sage/Open University Press.

Lightfoot, J. (1990), Involving Young People in Their Communities, Research and Policy Paper no. 12, Community Development Foundation Publications.

Lovett, T., Gillespie, N. and Gunn, D. (1995), Community Development Education and Community Relations, CRDC, University of Ulster.

Mansfield, S. (1992, 'Histories of Community Education' in Allen, G. and Martin, I. (eds), Education and Community: the politics of practice, London, Cassell.

Martin, I. (1996), 'Community Education: the dialectics of development' in Fieldhouse, R. and Associates, A., History of Modern British Adult Education, Leicester, NIACE

Preece, J. (1996), 'Positions of Race and Gender: alternative discourses' in Zukas, M. (ed), Diversity and Development: futures in the education of adults, SCUTREA conference, Leeds.

Preece, J. and Bokhari, R. (1997), Making the Curriculum Culturally Relevant, Journal of Further and Higher Education, Vol 21 (forthcoming).

Rattansi, A. (1992), 'Racism, Culture and Education' in Donald, J. and Rattansi, A. (eds), 'Race', Culture and Difference, London, Sage/Open University Press.

Rockhill, K. (1993), 'Gender, Language and the Politics of Literacy' in Street, B. (ed) Cross Cultural Approaches to Literacy, Cambridge, Cambridge University Press.

Sarup,M. (1993), An Introductory Guide to Poststructuralism and Postmodernism, (2nd ed), Harvester Wheatsheaf.

Smith, M. K. (1992), 'The Possibilities of Public Life: educating in the community' in Allen, G. and Martin, I. (eds), Education and Community: the politics of practice, London, Cassell.

Smith, M. K. (1994), Local Education: community, conversation, praxis, Milton Keynes, Open University Press.

Stanley, L. and Wise, S. (1993), Breaking out Again, London, Routledge.

Stuart, M. (1996), 'Working with the Enemy' in Elliott, J., et al, Communities and their Universities: the challenge of lifelong learning, London, Lawrence and Wishart.

Weiner, G. (1994), Feminisms in Education, Milton Keynes, Open University Press.

Yuval Davis, N. (1992), 'Fundamentalism, Multiculturalism and Women in Britain' in Donald, J. and Rattansi, A. (eds), 'Race', Culture and Difference, London, Sage/ Open University Press

Yuval Davis, N. (1994), 'Women, Ethnicity and Empowerment' in Bhavnani, K. K. and Phoenix, A., Shifting Identities Shifting Racisms, London, Sage.

Enrico Taliani

Multiculturalism and Social Conflict in Tuscany: Local Policy and Integration Problems of Non-EU Immigrants ('extra-comunitari')

Introduction

In our analysis we intend to focus especially on 3 strategic issues in relation to a migration policy which considers multiculturalism as a constitutive element of the integration process:

1. The role of 'local policy' in the control and regulation of 'migration phenomenology' as a new form of interaction connected to a continuous acceptance of new orientation patterns on the part of the local population on the one hand and the non-EU immigrants on the other.
2. The role of the 'non-formal system' confronted by the 'migration question' and proposing solutions through collaboration with local government or in a spontaneous way.
3. The social conflict dynamic which emerges in the process of daily life (*quotidianità*).

1. Local policy and migration process

With regard to this first point, three indicators are assumed as guidelines in our discussion: a) the nature and contents of regional laws and their importance for the migration process on a local scale; b) the 'programme of action' focused on the issue of human rights, and c) the question of the gap between the system of legislation and the organisational capability of applying it.

1.1 Nature and contents of regional laws

To understand the 'migration phenomenon' in Italy from a legal point of view, we have to consider the National Law of 30 December 1986 (no. 943). It provides for the setting up of the 'Council for the problems of migrant workers and their families'. Included in its members are four representatives of local governments (*autonomie locali*), two of which are directly designated by the Region, one by the National Association of Italian Town Councils (ANCI) and one by the Union of Italian Provinces (UOL). In terms of the law, it is the duty of the Regions to found 'regional councils' in order to satisfy more directly the needs and requirements of the 'non-EU immigrant communities' living within the country. In addition, the obligation of providing, through social services, for their integration into society by looking for and arranging suitable housing was transferred to the local boards (scala comunale). The 'housing question' is considered one of the most important priorities in attempting to avoid excessive forms of exploitation and conflict with local populations.

In the decrees and laws which follow, the attention of legislators is concerned above all with the legislation which governs residence permits, influx control and seasonal work, regularisation for the offer of work, the illegal employment of foreign workers, the regulations regarding admission and residence, as well as sanctions in the case of non-observance of the laws, etc. Little or nothing is added with regard to social interventions and the delegation of responsibilities to public bodies. However, the great strides made towards direct management of the migratory process on a regional and national scale are confirmed and recognised by the law. The Regions not only have the responsibility of government with regard to immigration, but also the power to legislate by preparing 'plans of action' with maximum decision-making autonomy.

This top-down delegation of functions is interpreted by experts and legislators as a decisive step towards the decentralisation of an act of government that by its very nature speaks for the needs and expectations of *citizens*. (2) Rather, it will be public bodies - Town councils in the first place - who participate in and press for a 'procedure of government' in which all the social components participate, *from below*. The immigrant, from this perspective, is an integral part of a process of democratisation and of the governability of 'social unities' whose logic rests on an axiom which, in juridical terms, is recognised in the principle of 'equal rights'.

The *Town Council*, on an ideal political level, becomes, therefore, the reference point of an action-programme, or rather of a *project*, the carrying out of which requires the participation of all the social services throughout its area of jurisdiction.

An analysis of 'official writing on current public affairs'[1] (2) on the subject offers a cross-section of the process of the *regionalisation* of the migratory phenomenon. In short, with the decentralising of delegations there is a desire to move towards the immigrant, by removing her/him from the blind alley of bureaucratic impediments and by reducing the psychological conditioning weighing on her/him through forms of active participation - as we shall see - in the management of her/his integration into the new social context.

With regard to this it is worth mentioning that Italy, in transforming itself from a country with a high rate of emigration into a country of immigration[2], is compelled to confront more immediately problems of strategic world importance. The relationship with diversity as an axis of reference in the process of globalisation is experienced on a daily and ongoing basis. Scientific culture, in particular, has been shaken to its foundations giving rise to a slow but gradual process of modernisation and deprovincialisation which is continuing.[3] The confrontation with *diversity* means in the first place knowing how to make use of categories of thought that did not belong, until a few

1 i.e. publications in specialised magazines, official documents published in institutions, scientific treatments of the subject, newspaper articles, etc.

2 Apart from migratory fluxes towards other countries, the displacement of consistent numbers of the population of the South to the Centre-North of the country. In many circumstances very widespread forms of rejection and derision have been and are being recorded which are in many aspects worse than those directed at non-EU immigrants.

3 This concerns a cultural aspect of contemporary Italy which demands consideration. But it is certainly true that from the beginning of the seventies, coinciding with the increasing presence of non-EU immigrants, support initiatives for them have multiplied; this has given rise to a body of research on a national and regional scale of great scientific interest, and moreover it creates the conditions to react - as was predictable - to forms of intolerance and of discrimination which develop in the social context.

years ago, in the legal code and of the behaviour of local populations and the ruling class that they express.

The Region of Tuscany, in truth, as many documents testify, understood, even as early as the middle of the seventies, that is, a few years after its institution was established, that immigration constituted an *emergency* and as such was to be dealt with within the scope of a view of things that was inspired by equal rights. Proof of this is in the first legislative interventions for the benefit of immigrant workers and their families in the field of social assistance. The very institution of a Regional Advisory Body for emigration and immigration denotes that the presence of non-EU immigrants was posing problems of a human, social and moral nature that were to be tackled with a new spirit and great commitment. What were lacking, however, in those first deliberations, were references to organised plans of intervention aimed at modifying situations of great hardship, and there was not even a hint at even a minimum strategy of 'rehabilitation' or of 'social assimilation'. Concepts such as 'diversity', and 'multiculturalism' are still not found in political and cultural language. The fear of degeneration on the other hand was very evident, but it is true that the interventions were aiming at finding 'a priori' solutions on two fronts: a local one consisting of non-hostile (that is, 'friendly'), but certainly unprepared and suspicious people, and an 'external' one, consisting, especially at that time, of human beings for the most part 'drifting' who sought by any means to grasp at the first little offers of support that came their way.

From this derives the importance attributed to initiatives which tend 'to protect the rights of immigrants and their families within the ambit of regional jurisdiction', by guaranteeing them 'the effective exercising of their civil and political rights'. And it is certainly not coincidental that the Regional Advisory Body should have defined amongst its essential responsibilities that of 'studying the causes of the phenomenon of emigration and immigration and the effects that it may have on the economy and social life of the Region'. In the deliberation both 'immigrants' and 'foreign emigrants' are placed on the same level. One infers, that is, that a close connection exists between processes which, by their very nature, are developed in spatial and long-term temporal dimensions and that in their way are intertwined. However, it is not clearly understandable what non-EU immigration may imply at a local level, for which reason one sees the necessity of entrusting to institutions and scholars the task of inquiring into the reasons why Italy, and also Tuscany, changed from a 'country of emigration' to a country which imports foreign workers and thus the need to put emigrants and immigrants on the same level. Inquiring means, in this cognitive perspective, raising the level of awareness in order to organise, as will consequently take place, plans of intervention capable of impacting positively on the substance of facts.

Equal rights

With the Deliberation of 13 February 1990, no. 80 the Regional Council approved an initial tranche of interventions directed at the provision of health care to the families of resident non-EU immigrants living in Tuscany. In compliance with State law (no. 943/1986) which guarantees 'to all non-EU immigrant workers legally resident in Italy and their families the same equal treatment and full equal rights as that of Italian workers, including rights to the use of social welfare and health services', the Region of Tuscany has moved to permit their enrolment on the registers of Local Health Authorities, and to guarantee equality of treatment to both unemployed workers and their families, provided that they are registered at the local Employment Office. However, it is with the passing of the Regional Law of 22 March 1990, no. 22, that the Region of Tuscany, fully identifying itself with the principles of United Nations Resolution 40/144 of 1985 on the protection of human rights and of fundamental liberties… 'promotes initiatives aimed at guaranteeing to non-EU immigrants and their families, conditions of equality, in the enjoyment of civil rights, with Italian citizens, and to remove the economic, cultural and social obstacles that hinder their assimilation into the social, cultural and economic fabric of the Region'.

The strong points of the programme of action can be summarised as follows:

a) protection of the right to work, to study, to social welfare and health care for non-EU immigrants and their families;

b) campaign against every form of social and cultural discrimination through the removal of stereotypes and support in the form of associations;

c) maintenance of cultural and linguistic links with the country of origin;

d) working out strategies to encourage the voluntary return of immigrants to their countries of origin;

e) social and cultural promotion of immigrant women, and

f) conducting inquiries aimed at a deeper understanding of the migration phenomenon in all its forms and manifestations.

Procedures of intervention

The Regional advisory body on non-EU immigration, emerging in 1990 and replacing its predecessor, in its function as a consultative body, becomes a means of support in the bringing about of intervention strategies which impact on a regional and local scale. It can not only 'formulate proposals and express opinions relating to initiatives and regional interventions' or to social welfare-health care plans and programmes, professional orientation, professional qualification, right to study, further education, and residential housing provision, but can also enter into the evaluation on merit of any action that has as its objective what can be defined as 'the phenomenology of immigration'.

A few words on the composition and functioning of the Advisory Body. It is worth remembering, however, that the wide representation of social components testifies to the political will to manage the interventions in the name of a broad representative democracy, despite some unnecessary complexities in procedural terms and thus of efficiency.

We would like to focus our attention on two aspects: *co-ordination between the Region and local bodies* - town councils, provinces, mountain communities - which function on the basis of a 'territorial government' which is inspired by principles of an informed and participatory democracy; the *typology of interventions* that more or less constitutes the axis of reference of our enquiry, which aims, in the first instance, to verify, within territorial limits (3), 'the level of efficiency' of the interventions undertaken by the Region of Tuscany in support of non-EU immigrants.

Regarding the first point, the Regional Council, as supreme organ of government, 'determines its interventions on behalf of non-EU immigrant workers and of their families, subject to agreements with interested local bodies, with the object of achieving the co-ordination of reciprocal interventions and the utilisation of the relevant resources' (Art 10, Regional Law 31.3.1990). In the workings of the Regional Council, two lines of thinking prevail which really succeed in establishing themselves at the moment of decision-making: the first gives the idea of a broad-based democracy that aims to involve, besides local bodies, representatives of non-EU immigrant associations, as well as representatives of a voluntary force who show a particular vitality in the social fabric of the region. The second line of thinking seeks to introduce the 'migratory problem' into a discussion on the programming of resources. In fact it is up to the 'Regional Development Programme' to establish 'the objectives, the general direction and the priorities of interventions to be undertaken on behalf of non-EU immigrants and of their families' (Art. II, ibid.). The attempt to reconcile elements of social democracy and economic democracy constitutes the fulcrum of a plan of action that has always characterised the Region of Tuscany since its inception. (E. Taliani ed., Scuola e Professionalità, ETS Pisa 1980).

As far as the 'typology of interventions' is concerned, the axis around which all the socially directed initiatives turn can be identified in 'the institution, on the part of town councils, of reception centres' which, operating on a micro-territorial level, should be sounding posts for the most direct needs of immigrants. Organisational efforts will thus be directed at 'providing information and advice on access to social welfare services'; at 'assisting immigrants who find themselves in conditions of hardship of particular seriousness'; and at 'accommodating the activities of immigrant associations'. Town councils, through the management of Reception Centres, can 'reach agreement with voluntary associations of proven experience in the field of providing assistance to non-EU immigrants'.

The 'typology of interventions', as defined by Regional Law no. 20, is not limited to the institution of reception centres. The legislators intended to discard the juridical bases for a consolidation of essential rights which are meant to make of the immigrant not an impersonal 'beneficiary of services', but an active individual who works consciously at the running of her/his daily life and that of the community into which s/he is assimilating.

There are four cornerstones to the programme of action centred on the safeguarding of essential rights: the right to information, the right to cultural protection, the right to work, the right to social welfare and health care.

a) *The Right to Information*

The activities of information on immigration are intended to have a dual aim:

a) to foster the assimilation of immigrant workers and their families by offering useful and functional information with the aim of, and in the expectation of the utilisation of services which are the responsibility of public bodies, and

b) to explain to resident citizens the migratory phenomenon in its diverse manifestations in such a way as to reduce or prevent incidences of intolerance or prejudice.

To which purpose the Region operates through the proper territorial structures of professional orientation.

b) *The right to protection of cultural identity*

The Region of Tuscany, as official documents confirm, is very sensitive to the safeguarding of the cultural identity of non-EU immigrants. They are convinced that *diversity*, in a system of social relations marked by mutual respect, rather than dividing, can form the basis of a policy of social integration that encourages diverse ethnic groups to participate in a process that requires them to be conscious and responsible agents. The problem of integration and cultural protection of immigrants which is given prominence in

Regional Law no. 20, is tackled largely in pedagogical-educational terms. On the one hand, the aim, through close collaboration with scholastic institutions is 'the linguistic recovery, of literacy and Italian language through enrolment in courses organised for this purpose'; on the other hand the need is emphasised, in the name of diversity, to take account, at the didactic level, 'of the ethno-linguistic identity' of the various groups.

Moreover, the initiatives in multicultural education must further programmes that consolidate linguistic and cultural links with the countries of origin and at the same time to urge institutions and local populations to take responsibility for the dissemination of knowledge regarding migratory problems so as to combat diverse forms of social marginalisation. Particular attention will have to be given to immigrant women who, without doubt constitute with children and 'illegals', the weak link in the whole migratory phenomenon.

Of particular interest, in this context, is what the Regional Law no. 20 provides for 'with regard to maternity, sexuality and the use of contraceptive methods'. Interventions will have to take account of the cultural and religious diversity of immigrant women.

Yet again, public bodies must know how to proceed on the level of initiatives by providing courses of instruction directed principally at administrative workers who carry out functions in close contact with immigrants and by supporting courses of foreign language and culture for students and Italian citizens promoted by officially recognised non-EU immigrant Associations.

c) *The right to professional training and work*

Absorption into the job market represents for the immigrant one of the most difficult things, both on account of the structural weakness of many productive and distributive components of the Italian economic system, and because of the massive presence of non-EU immigrants who live illegally, causing considerable difficulties for those immigrants more firmly settled.

Let us not enter into the merits of the 'regularisation problem' as it would force us to enter into a subject more juridical-penal and ethical than properly sociological. The Region of Tuscany, however, in observance of the laws that regulate migratory influx and those 'softer' regulations governing work, has produced a very clear 'Discipline of interventions with regard to professional training' which provides for interventions of orientation, training, re-qualification, rehabilitation and professional upgrading which are available to 'all non-EU immigrant citizens in Tuscany'. The objective is to promote their assimilation into the job market by avoiding 'friction' with the local workforce and moreover by giving a chance to those immigrants interested 'in their possible permanent and qualified return to the country of origin', and that in line with aid policies worked out during Italian and regional co-operation agreements with developing countries (Regional Law, co-operation interventions with developing countries).

Still, in terms of jobs and employment, immigrants registered at Employment Offices acquire a 'legal status' on a par with that of the local population which includes the right to set up business and thus to undertake autonomous employment activities.

d) *The right to social welfare and health care benefits*

The Region of Tuscany has provided in this regard a programme of social welfare services and of access to social services which puts the non-EU immigrant 'in a condition of parity with Italian citizens'. Through modification of the Regional Law children of immigrant families are entitled to 'pre-school services'.

So that the 'right to welfare' may be guaranteed to all immigrants resident in the Region, the distribution of funds destined for each town council for social welfare-health care services 'will take account of the existence of the non-EU immigrant population' actually present in areas of council jurisdiction. Yet again councils are called upon to undertake responsibilities of great social and programmatic importance with a view to guard, provide for and intervene in defence of every citizen living in their area of jurisdiction. In this extended undertaking of protection, the council can enter into agreements with legally recognised voluntary regional associations who have distinguished themselves in their organisational capability and their level of professionalism.

Finally, the immigrant worker, as long as s/he is resident in a council in Tuscany, is permitted 'to participate, on the same terms as resident citizens, in application procedures within the provision of the Region of Tuscany with regard to residential housing for the acquisition, renovation, construction, and rental of accommodation'.

(Art.17). Public bodies, finally, in the case of an emergency, can intervene to find temporary housing for resident immigrants who find themselves in conditions of particular hardship. In such a case the Region encourages such initiatives. It is up to the Council, however, to demonstrate the will and the capacity to solve problems that demand timeliness and courage in the use of human and financial resources that are not always available.

2. The gap between the legislation and its capacity for implementation

With the empirical inquiry conducted by the Department of Social Sciences[4] it was intended above all to verify the initiatives and activities currently under way on behalf of non-EU immigrants in observance of the policy programmes emerging from the official documents of the Region of Tuscany. Furthermore, from the stock of knowledge acquired through the questionnaire, to reconstruct the role that public bodies perform at the level of strategies of reception and so of the organisation of interventions in support of immigrants.

[4] The research group, led by E. Taliani and O. Barsotti, was composed of researchers in the Department of Social Sciences and Tuscan businessmen. The inquiry was carried out in the 'Leather district', an area in the heart of Tuscany with a high concentration of industry and had as its aim the collection of information regarding the dynamics of the labour market and its social impact. The group consisted of S. Venturi, T. Telleschi, Moreno Toigo, Cristina Bagini and Barbara Simili. cf. The Role of non-EU immigrants in the economy and society of Tuscany, Pisa, 1994. Report sent to the Region of Tuscany. In the text, reference is made to the results obtained in the inquiry on the social impact of labour politics.

As regards the first point, we have compared the texts relevant to the Meeting of 14 December 1993 (504) and of 28 February 1995 (no.99) concerning respectively the 'Plan of interventions' for 1993 and for 1995. Following that we include the types:

of interventions effected in 1993 and 1995 considered and approved by the Regional Council and the regional consultative body.

Plan of interventions for 1993	Plan of interventions for 1995
Initiatives in education for diversity, solidarity, multi-culturalism and development. *Types of financial support* - exhibitions of programmes and in developing countries produced videos or about communities in Tuscany (two); - People's Music show and 'ethno-musical films' for the enhancement of popular traditions (two); - activation of a 'multicultural section' and activation of information services at council and/or provincial libraries (one); - drama presentations for elementary school pupils (two); - book publication for multicultural education for middle school pupils (one).	Integration and cultural protection (Initiatives which refer to education for diversity, etc.) *Types of financial support per sector*: - 1994 Plan: interventions which can be carried out in the field of the 'right to study' and further education. The interventions extend over practically all the provinces and involve a growing number of councils. Activities include organising meetings, educational trips, often in collaboration with universities and other institutions. In particular, as far as further education is concerned, courses in literacy and the teaching of Italian language and culture have been instituted; courses in health education, programmes of scholastic integration, etc. The initiatives pertain particularly to the provinces of Florence, Livorno and Lucca. The intiatives are backed by film projections, shows and art exhibitions, meetings, publications, etc.

Interventions of initial reception

- advisory and reference services for immigrant minors or in war situations
-support for refugees from ex-Yugoslavia
- emergency support for Somalian refugees
- the constitution of permanent 'watchdogs' at reception centres and of accommodation for foreigners intended as a means of
support for the control and development of a housing
policy for immigrants.

Interventions of initial reception

- census-taking in the halting sites of Florence intended for citizens of Romish ethnicity and ex-Yugoslavian refugees
- funeral fund for the repatriation of corpses
- activities of the *housing conditions watchdog*: analysis of projects and aspects of management and on-the-spot investigations in all reception centres established in Tuscany on the initiative of public bodies or volunteers; research into the settlement of the Chinese community;
- organisation of the seminar 'Agency for immigrant housing' for workers in public bodies and in the voluntary sector;
- publication of the monograph 'The limits of the city', dedicated entirely to the theme of immigration.
- a policy of equal opportunity for immigrant citizens regarding the problem of housing as provided for by Regional Law 22/90 does not seem to have been operated.
- the details of educational programmes for cultural diversity and solidarity have been
worked out and managed directly by councils such as those of Florence, Pistoia, Pontassieve, Poggibonsi and Bibbiena; by state middle schools, professional institutes; by the 'G.La Pira' International Stu-

dents' Centre; COSPE;
Fatatrac Publishers; CIES - Tam Tam video project 1994.

Contributions to Associations of immigrant citizens (officially recognised by the Region)

- intra- and inter-ethnic cultural and folklore displays;

- application procedures for funds for the return of deceased compatriots.

Contribution to Associations of immigrant citizens

- intra - and inter-ethnic cultural and folklore displays;

- application procedures for funds for the return of deceased compatriots.

- Radio and television communications

- reinforcement of the broadcaster Controradio contributing to the achievement of a cycle of broadcasting, called 'Babel', containing weekly cultural news bulletins and monthly transmissions on the problems of immigration.

- Information and radio and television communications

- presentation of the feasability project for the initiation of the Regional Information System on Non-EU Immigration which anticipates an intensive effort of collecting and checking information on the migratory phenomenon in Tuscany.

- a series of radio programmes has got under way, rather later than was predicted, that cover the whole of 1995, as follows: *Babel News* (8 minute weekly news bulletin); *Mondo Babele* (Babel World) (weekly musical-cultural programmes lasting an hour); *Interview* (investigative programmes on themes of particular interest to immigrants (monthly, 15 minute duration).

- programming of the *Information*

Bulletin. The first issue will be out towards the end of the year in bilingual copies distributed by delivery and postal subscription and by widespread distribution in places frequented by immigrants.

- the institution of a *Centre of Research, Documentation and Services* with reponsibilities in interpreting, advice regarding relations with public bodies etc. for Chinese citizens (Council of Prato).

1994 - 1995 : Dynamics of Labour Market Initiatives and Social Policies.

(cont.)

Social welfare and Health care interventions

- ordinary interventions for welfare services with financing to the town councils;
- experimental, consultatory activities of the local health authority (USL): special interventions directed at the health care of immigrants and in sexual matters the use of contraceptives. In this field welfare-health care interventions for the benefit of women have been programmed. Such interventions will have to take account of cultural differences and linguistic diversity in such a way as to enable immigrant women to benefit from existing

- Assimilation into the labour market

- intense activities of orientation, training, requalification and professional upgrading; programmes aimed at facilitating the assimilation of immigrants into the employment sector; courses of orientation run by provincial administrations with financing from the European Social Fund; differentiated courses aimed at immigrants of different backgrounds; giving out information through the proper channels about access to the labour market, labour legislation and schools; courses for immigrants under 25 years of age and aimed at repatria-

services, by creating appropriately trained women health workers of immigrant background presenting themselves as cultural intermediaries.	tion; reaction of the 'Extrapico' service in Florence (Centre of information and orientation advice). The above mentioned activities concern especially Florence, Siena, and Livorno.
(cont.)	- courses specifically aimed at immigrants that come under Objective 3 (1994-95 Professional Training Plan) who find themselves in particular hardship or disadvantage risking never to be able to take up formalised work opportunities. - courses for 'migrants, immigrants and nomads' have been organised in all the Region's provinces. -concessions for the creation of new businesses in support of young entrepeneurs (cf. Regional Law 27/93). The criteria are established for an 'equal opportunity' policy for the benefit of the 'extracomunitari'. (Non-EU immigrants).

The points of fundamental importance in the 'Plan of Intervention', on the basis of financial contributions supplied, can be recognised in those activities which are inspired by the culture of multiculturalism and diversity, in support of initiatives undertaken by scholastic institutions in agreement with the cultural programmes of the Councils and with voluntary associations, or by voluntary organisations with particular competence and experience or also with experts from the Ministry of Foreign Affairs, as well as the interregional observer of co-operation or UN agency.

If the plan of intervention, as far as multiculturalism is concerned, has an undeniable qualitative breadth, what emerges is the still limited extent of action. In fact the Councils involved are three: Florence, Pontassieve and

Prato. It is useful to remember though that the highest concentration of immigrants is recorded in those councils.

As for theatrical, musical, radio and television activities and promotion, however, they achieve a much higher consumption which sparks off a process of sensitisation at a local level thanks to the contributions of teachers, lecturers, priests, trade unionists, and civil servants who ‘quietly’, but with widespread effect, keep alive the ‘sense of tolerance’ and ‘understanding’ with respect to non-EU immigrants.

It is necessary besides to note the involvement of prestigious scientific organisations such as The Institute of the Innocents for their work of advising and supporting refugee children from ex-Yugoslavia.

Many of the initiatives we have referred to have a recurrent character. Usually the quality of the initiative tends to be improved by the involvement of various, ever more qualified ‘partners’.

As for financing, the figures included in the table which follows can give an idea of the effort being made at regional level in initiatives which are more directly financed by contributions from the Region.

With a comparative analysis of the interventions provided for in the 1993 ‘Plan of Action’ and that of 1995, a strengthening of assimilation strategies at all levels considered is recorded. Each initiative, in fact, seems to enter into a rights-and-duties ‘scheme of reciprocity’ that aims at a substantial parity of rights between the local population and immigrants. At the same time the need is highlighted of giving to the immigrant the means of developing the greatest possible autonomy of initiative.

Looking at the results of the empirical research into the role the immigrant worker plays in the ‘Leather district’, an area of high industrial potential supported by small and medium scale entrepreneurism, confirms the tendency for a responsible and informed involvement on the part of public bodies and their basic social services in the work of sensitisation and assimilation of immigrants. However contradictions and ‘mistakenness’ remain in the period of time from conception to execution. We summarise them briefly, taking account of fundamental problems:

In the Councils of the District the greatest organisational effort was directed in the years 1989 - 1992 at the renovation and repair of accommodation, to the construction of showers and laundries, to the acquisition and refurbishment of apartments for immigrants. Interventions of the 'initial reception' type - prompt dispatch of bureaucratic red tape, emergency assistance, job searches, literacy courses, etc. - were also intensive. In the subsequent period a greater attention is recorded to the consolidation of 'structures of reception' through the institution of 'Centres', places of worship, the opening of a Counter on the part of USL 17 (local health authority) to provide information regarding health and health care. Courses of 'cultural mediation' got under way, and the first attempts, on the initiative of local bodies, at the sensitisation of teachers and students to the problems posed by the presence of immigrants in the area, can be witnessed. That is to say that an awareness develops of 'ethnic and cultural diversity', which, beginning with scholastic institutions, should filter through to families and the community as a whole.

As far as the 'mistakenness' is concerned, the greatest difficulties, according to our interlocutors are due to a) a basic lack of preparation on the part of the Civil Service in tackling problems which were 'urgent'; b) the lack of a network of communication between Councils which meant that every initiative took effect in the guise of improvisation: 'everyone does what suits her/him best'5; c) lack of financing relative to demands with the resultant political polemics (not inconsiderable) with respect to the Region; d) 'the lack of studies about the problem of immigration at regional and local level' which made it difficult to confront diverse social realities.

With reference to the application of the constitutional imperative of equal rights, mayors and civil servants confirm that 'the current legislation curbs… the disposability of local Administrations to exert greater weight in connection with equal rights.' Two examples: the housing problem, which provokes friction with the local population and family reunions. On the basis of the laws family groups, not parents, are privileged for which reason, in applying a criterion of *equity* and *parity*, the applications of immigrants

5 From interviews with mayors, functionaries and workers of the Social services, June - September 1994.

'would not have enough points to obtain a council house'. Finally, suitable means are lacking 'to facilitate the assimilation of children and women, even though these last show a greater capacity for adaptation'. Certain instances of irregularity, infringement, abuse of power, etc. have been reported, although the phenomenon is limited to a few cases.

In terms of the revision of the laws regarding immigration, it is proposed, almost unanimously, that it is necessary to review both the national and local legislation. The 'emergency phase' having been passed, it is felt that thought should be given to operating in terms of stability. The initiatives, under this proposal, must aim 'to involve immigrants more fully so as to make them more responsible for their decisions and not to wait for solutions found by others. The problem then is how to involve them'. However, there is a general admission of having often made a reductive use of the energies expended. This is due in large measure to the scarce knowledge of the non-EU immigrant as 'cultural subject'.

Therefore on the subject of review and proposal, what is needed, especially on the part of the Civil Service, is greater clarity in the definition of the duties and the norms which regulate the relationship with the immigrant: 'laws which look to concrete application and that offer to local bodies the possibility of creating new conditions of reception and support, marked by an awareness of the long term assimilation of immigrants'.

To emerge from the 'initial reception' phase (primare Solidaritat, emergency aid), the energy of the 'programmierten Hilfe' is indicated and connected to strategies of long term integration. In this context, there are 4 basic issues:

a) the formation of social co-operatives run either directly by immigrants or in joint form in such a way as to sustain their autonomy at all levels;

b) to find solutions for the so-called housing problem producing formulae to reduce friction with the local population;

c) to promote initiatives which have multiculturalism as their aim, entrusting to local bodies and schools the task of co-ordinating actions with this aim;

d) to co-ordinate in an effective manner the initiatives between voluntary organisations and public bodies, between private and public, in such a way as to reduce the incidence of *incomprehension* if not of *friction*.

The 'conflict problem' must be examined on two levels. At the level of initiatives that aim to reduce the incidence of latent conflict through actions of rapprochement between immigrants and the local population, and that more specifically direct, of the real disputes that arise at the moment in which vested interests are affected. In the 'Leather district' both forms of conflict, latent and obvious, exist, though not comparable with what has happened in other parts of the Region (cases in Florence and Pisa) or in the rest of the country. With respect to 'rapprochement strategies', those initiatives centred on multi- or inter-culturalism can be counted as examples of integration and comparison. For example, from musical and culinary evenings, religious celebrations such as the feast of Ramadan, other cultural-folklore initiatives, to topics of debate and of reflection such as Islamic fundamentalism, on respect for diversity, friendship evenings etc.: these can function as a framework for the affirmation of a culture centred on diversity and solidarity. From this perspective the role already played by volunteers as single agents or as 'groups', as well as voluntary associations such as *Africa insieme* (Africa together) and others, contribute to the attainment of an informal network, which can open up the prospect of a full and deeply felt integration for both parties in the achievement of the common objective: to remove the immigrant from a state of isolation and social marginalisation.

With reference to obvious forms of conflict, it is possible to verify that at the level of work the friction with local workers is practically non-existent. Bosses and trade unionists too do not complain of any particular disturbance. Businessmen, however, tend to praise the superior industriousness and reliability of certain ethnic groups over others. The most frequently cited case is that of the Senegalese, who by virtue of a strong identification with rules and clan traditions, seem to develop a rapid integration into the production process. Thus friction is not recorded in the labour market, due also to the fact that the working of leather and accompanying processes demands sacrifices and a strong spirit of adaptation for which reason the local work-force prefers to delegate to immigrants.

Public conflicts are sporadic. It seems that real disputes emerge between the application for and the offer of assistance, for example housing, which Council administrations define as excessive while immigrants consider it inconsistent or completely inadequate, especially when thinking of extending it to close relations or family members. It must be said, in conclusion, that instances of intolerance on a vast scale are not mentioned. That does not mean that, at the level of individual experience, disputes may not have arisen with members of the local community. According to everybody though forms of discrimination or of refusal such as to provoke retaliation one way or the other have not been reported. For example, centres of social gathering, such as bars in small urban centres, have never had recourse to formulae of prohibition or of use under certain conditions. In short, the non-EU immigrant is seen as a 'poor devil who has to make ends meet' or sometimes, partly as a joke and partly out of that typical Tuscan sarcastic irony as the butt of 'little jokes' or of 'derision' that provoke either hilarity or 'spontaneous reactions without comeback' in people of colour. It should be noted that a similar treatment is given to Tuscans of other towns and districts or other Regions of the country. Actually, in this case the reactions or the excesses seem to be in fact greater.

The debate on the so-called 'culture of diversity' follows two methodological orientations. An official line exists with a strong emphasis on the institutionalisation of initiatives that depend on public bodies and schools or on both. The strong point of this approach is that it showed that only through the 'the programming of interventions' on a national level is it possible to raise the levels of consciousness of the local population and so to promote cultural exchanges which aim to involve children, teachers and lecturers through reciprocal visits and common activities to be undertaken 'in loco' and, as far as possible, in the countries of origin of the immigrants; civil servants through visits and formal contacts with representatives of the communities present in the Region and similarly with colleagues who carry out public functions in those countries. On the other hand, still at the official level and, in accord with the new demands of autonomy that the civil service requires of the citizen, the immigrant is asked to act consciously in the new society promoting her/his own contacts or making her/himself as autonomous as possible in forming social and work relations.

The second orientation, conversely, focuses largely on the 'spontaneity of actions', through the creation of 'channels of communication' which seek to operate leaving the more formal initiatives, which are the responsibility of public services, out of consideration. The best way to overcome differences and mistrust is the diffusion and consolidation of a network of relations on a small scale which acts as an intermediary directly with immigrants offering them the opportunity of direct assistance, of social gathering, of prospects of integration ranging from work to the achievement of little projects for their future. For example, the council houses or the social centres in parishes in the Councils in our inquiry have carried out a significant function. There has been a gradual development to closer contacts and to a social and cultural interchange which, according to many, has contributed towards overcoming initial mistrust.

Another form of social gathering which needs examining is the public canteen of the Santa Croce Town Council. From these contacts ideas develop that lead to ever more demanding initiatives. For example, the party organised to celebrate the feast of Ramadan, as already mentioned, represents a point of reference not only for immigrants of the Islamic faith, but also for all the others, including the local population. As, after all, the many summer feasts (*sagre*) and celebration parties of the various (political) parties are a further occasion 'to get to know each other better and to show in any circumstance that we are present and aware of our rights and duties', as indeed a Senegalese person expressed it when asked about the question of social relations with the local population.

It is not possible to cover all the issues in this paper although they are far from being resolved. However, they are tackled in juridical-institutional terms, and we have examined the ways in which juridical norms are interpreted and applied at a local level. It can be said, in conclusion, that in the more industrialised areas of Tuscany where the rates of unemployment and underemployment are not very high, firm and irremediable opposition from the local population has not emerged. Local bodies become promoters of an undertaking, if erratic and uncertain, of integration into the productive and social fabric of their respective areas of government. The discussion changes if the focus of the analysis were to be moved to urban concentrations where the political dialectic between 'right' and 'left' emerges more strongly. But such an analysis goes beyond the scope of our work.

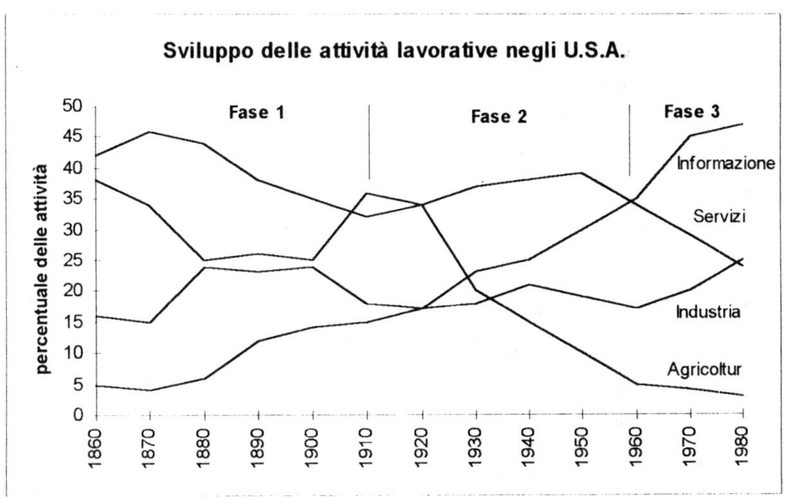

Jan-Kåre Breivik

Morality in a Multicultural Society

Introduction

A multicultural society could be marked by harmony and/or conflict. This essay contains an attempt to explore the conditions and possibilities for mutual understanding and co-operation in Norway. One of the main questions is related to the other`s otherness and how to behave inclusively without repression.

In a world with continuing wars, expanding numbers of refugees and growing racism (1), the need for mutual understanding and the strive for consensus formation on a whole range of issues is strongly felt by a growing number of people. Particularistic tradition-bound moralities are insufficient in meeting these new big problems in this 'scrimping world'. Some would go as far as to say that local moralities destroy or hinder the possibility for the growth of more apt forms of morality which could transcend the limits of the local and national community. On the other hand some versions of more universalistic ethics are felt to be too abstract to offer good enough reasons (as aspects of the good life) for people to be committed to it and too liberally individualistic (meaning too western) to be a real universal alternative. (2)

Discourse ethics places itself in the centre of these differing perspectives. The purpose is to offer a formal, procedural ground, where issues and conflicts can be solved without external (or internal) force, and it is said, without any preference in any particular moral tradition or theory (like Christendom or utilitarianism). Participants in discourse are asked to accept only 'the force of the better argument'. In certain respects such an ethic is transparent. It is often called 'minimal ethics'. This is both its strong side and its weak side.

In this essay I am first going to give a brief view of some of the elements in discourse ethics; communicative rationality, discourse (ideal and actual) and consensus formation etc. I will then discuss the ways in which discourse ethics can offer good input to actual discourse concerning refugees and integration (and a critic of the monolingual tendencies here) and the possibilities of discourse ethics in a multicultural society. I will also offer a few critical remarks on discourse ethics, pointing to some of its limits and its eurocentric blend despite its aim. What the conclusion will be, I do not yet know.

What is discourse ethics?

In this paper I am mainly focusing on discourse ethics in terms of how Habermas and Apel discuss it (3). I have no possibility of going into details, but I will try to make a sketch. Discourse ethics must be understood as an post-war ethics, as an intellectual effort to restore the place of reason and rationality in a modern society where 'the loss of meaning' and the Weberian 'disenchantment of the world' (Entzauberung der Welt) was (and perhaps is) in the foreground. In the literature of modernisation (from Max Weber and unto the present) there has been a strong bias towards viewing the process of rationalisation as a process where rationality means goal-rationality with its companions; strategic and instrumental action. The rationalisation process then has a tendency to be viewed as a destructive force with social disintegration as its outcome and an eroding effect of any version of the good life. Anomie, reification, alienation and the loss of meaning and freedom are some of the namings of these phenomena.

The diagnosis of the modern world from this perspective is too pessimistic, Habermas argues. He claims that the concept of rationality is too narrow in the Weberian tradition. The root of this misconception, Habermas states, is to be found in 'the philosophy of consciousness-tradition, in which the actor is viewed as being isolated. To put it briefly, Habermas means that there has to be a paradigm shift where the social and communicative nature of the human and of human language is put in the foreground. This shift gives room for expanding the concept of rationality to include communicative rationality aiming at mutual understanding and co-ordination of action. In addition this concept leaves an open space for critics from within modernity. The inter-subjective ground for rationality is put in front, and this means that values and validity claims have to lose both their purely subjective status and objectivity.

Within discourse ethics there is an optimistic view of modernity if we look at the rationalisation of lifeworlds as based on Habermas' communicative rationality with emphasis on subject-object relations. The opposite (and in some respect complementary) rationalisation process is the strategic/instrumental rationality which operates mainly on the systemic level of society and in man's relations to nature. When Weber and others talk about 'the loss of meaning', Habermas introduces what he calls 'the colonialisation of the lifeworld' by the system and its means-ends rationality. This represents the negative side of modernity which threatens core aspects of integrated lives. In western social democracies it means the potentiality and danger of being reduced to clients and consumers only.

The source of resistance and alternative ways out of this mess is to be found in the communicative use of language itself. In order to give this idea some kind of support, Habermas points to the 'immanent obligation' contained in the use of language (4):

'...(T)his choice is not open to a rational agent, because an obligation to normative argumentation or justification is already 'rooted' in communicative action itself'(White, 1988:53).

There is then certain presuppositions that have to be taken for granted if we engage in communicative practices. To illustrate this Habermas speaks about 'the ideal speech situation' and Apel talks about 'the ideal community of communication'. This sounds very idealistic and utopian, and it could be so. However, both authors stress that it is not an abstract idealism pointing to some otherworldly situation. It is not meant to be a description of an alternative to actual communication, but rather a 'counterfactual projection' which can turn into operation whenever a validity claim arises It is a way of conceptualising the ideal in the actual, so to speak. It is here that the term 'discourse' fits in.

'Discourse' is in a sense another level of communication where it puts stronger demands on the aim of reaching understanding and consensus (which is already implicit in any communicative action). This means that the shared understanding which communicative action aims at can, if necessary, turn into another level of communication called discourse, 'which is communication in which all non-verbal elements have been bracketed as much as possible' (Brand 1990:19). The centrality of argumentation and verbalising is clear.

When there is a non-agreement situation on the level of communication embedded in specific situations in the lifeworld, the discourse offers a possibility to solve the problem by having different validity claims discussed under more ideal conditions where 'the force of reason' can operate in a more unrestricted manner. Discourse ethics tries to describe (and proscribe) some rules to make the discourse operative and places some constraints on the participants to eliminate other uses of force than the argumentative power (excluding strategic action).

What can discourse ethics offer cross-culturally?

Eriksen (1993) has produced three theses concerning discourse ethics and communicative rationality (5). He suggests that in situations with common aims and ends and a relatively simple agenda, the operation of communicative rationality has its best possibility to succeed. On the level of principles for regulation (law, constitution, rules etc.), the need for rational consensus formation is most precarious. His last and in my case most interesting thesis is as follows; *Where you find great discrepancies in world views and reality conceptions, and where the agenda is most complicated, communicative rationality has its least ability to operate.* The aim of mutual understanding and rational consensus formation does not have to be banned, but the time dimension among other things has to be accounted for.

The growing number of immigrants (includes asylum seekers, refugees and labour migrants) to Norway poses in this respect a problem which discourse ethics can say something about. Keeping Eriksens' third thesis in mind, actual cross-cultural dialogue begs some questions; when does integration turn into assimilation, and when does the ghetto-question turn into an ideology of separation? How can we discuss such and other similar issues through dialogue and in an understanding and seeking way? These questions are not easy, but I think that they go to the heart of some of the debates among Norwegians and immigrants and between the two groups. In what way could these questions be solved through rational consensus formation via communicative action, and when and how could it be turned into discourse?

Before I return to these questions I will try to bring in some aspects from an ongoing debate in the mass-media concerning the relations between Norwegians and immigrants, and what kinds of demands and claims that are legitimate to put on each other. Then I will in part try to answer the questions by relating them to Kettner's (1993) constraints on the participants of practical discourse.

The climatic conditions for debate.

Moving into the area of research and debate on immigrants is problematic in many respects. The area is strongly politically infused and the debate is polarised (Brox, 1991). In the Norwegian research milieu, there has been a debate on how to do research on and write about immigrants. Some argue that a critical distance towards the other could give support to latent (and manifest) racism among Norwegians and others argue that a too accepting (or advocating) attitude could mean a diminishing thrust in this sciences impartiality and objectivity (could mean legitimacy). (6)

The debate I am referring to was initiated by Lien's article 'A good researcher or a good human being?' (my translation from Norwegian) in Nytt Norsk Tidsskrift nr.2/91, which contained an attack on what she thought was a too accepting and positive (relativistic) attitude towards the other and a too critical attitude towards ourselves in research on immigrants in Norway (1991:178). Lien is questioning a central and interesting masochistic tendency in the Norwegian immigrant supporting milieu and she continues:

To write about immigrants is also a way of writing about oneself - as a good or a bad human being. This can represent a great danger for the scientific, truth seeking project when the researchers self-presentation as 'the good, antiracist human being' gets a superior place (Lien, 1991: 183).

The article named several researchers that could be placed under the rubric 'the good ones', and the reactions came quickly. Some of the responses were marked by the named persons feelings of being personally attacked, but some of them, notably Gjertsen, moved towards a more critical attitude towards the concept of science (both self-critical and as a critic of Liens project):

We would all say that the claims of science must be the main focus. What we see as truth must come first. But at the same time we know that what we count as truth is determined by conventions and that our interpretations are culturally determined. ..it is great challenges we stand in front of in understanding our cultural blind spots (Gjertsen, 1991:376).

In one sense this debate is naive, but at the same time it touches upon central points in anthropology and the social sciences in general. As examples of 'doing research at home' we can notice how difficult (and perhaps unavoidable) it is not to take a stance (this corresponds at least to my own experiences). The main question as I see it is not to move towards a stronger scientific position if this means unbiased and balanced research and writing, but to move into a more reflexive research where we in critical ways examine both research and researcher as positioned. If the researchers position drops out of the social scientific discourse, then the main parts of the material from which we generalise will also drop out. Unavoidably this leads to an objective discourse where 'the other' no more are or will be counted as discourse partners.

If Lien's diagnosis of the present research/writing on immigrants is right (an accepting attitude towards the other combined with self-criticism), then I agree with her. But what she does not say is that the opposite strategy is as bad (and even worse). My point is not to argue in favour of the one extreme position against the other (in fact most research is done between these poles), but to see that position as unavoidable anyway and that we have to be reflexive in handling ourselves in our presentations of the other.

Lien is in fact also criticising her own earlier work on immigrants for being too accepting etc. In her new search for a more unbiased and impartial ('upartisk') position, she has tried to attack 'the migrant problem' from another angle. In the following pages I will examine how well done this is, and I will also examine a counter example (Monsen) that fits her criticism of a too accepting attitude towards the other. Both are seen as contributors to what I call 'the Norwegian discourse on strangers' (den norske fremmed-diskursen) and touches upon the relationship between 'hosts' and 'guests' and their claims and responsibilities towards each other).

'When the guests criticise the host'

The actual debate that I am referring to started when the mass media began to focus on some articulated responses from Bosnian asylum seekers at the end of 1992 and the beginning of 1993. Some complaints about the living conditions in the refugee camps were made; its isolated location, its food and the missing mental care. The state representatives reacted one day angrily and another day with a more understanding attitude. As far as I know some of the Bosnian's claims were accepted as legitimate and the conditions were improved. In an incident in the north of Norway, some Bosnians tried to escape from the bad conditions in their new camp, and they said that they would prefer to return to Bosnia. There has since been a debate to try and understand this attitude. Should one take their articulation 'seriously' and let them 'go home', or explain it as being contextual; as an understandable act of despair? (7)

In this context a social scientist, Lien, writes a provocative chronicle in Aftenposten (13.8.93) with the title; 'When the guests criticise the host'. She takes the reports from the media mentioned above as 'empirical material' and starts generalising in a good sociological manner. She uses some concepts from the sociologist Z.Bauman 'Modernity and Ambivalence' (1991) and points to the fact that the refugee's position is ambivalent:

The stranger falls between the two categories 'friend' and 'enemy'. The stranger is suffering from an incurable disease that Bauman labels multi-layered contradictions. It is difficult to determine who this stranger is. Is he an enemy? Is he a friend? Does he take responsibility? Is he willing to be loyal and solidaristic? Does he want to share? Is he willing to commit himself to duties? Is he willing to sacrifice anything himself, or is he just going to put claims and be a free-rider on the host? (the translation from Norwegian is mine)

These questions could be both good and relevant, and they could be a mark of fruitful curiosity on the hosts behalf. The host wants to understand the 'unbidden' guest, and that should be legitimate. The answers from the guest should be guiding in how the host categorises and treats him or her; as friend or enemy (other categories are also available).

The article, I think, is a meta-level discussion on the problems of integration, I think, using a few concrete examples to illustrate some of the problems involved in complex multicultural societies. In general terms she explains that the relation towards the stranger:

...must be handled with care and with consideration. The stranger has a responsibility to participate and to show loyalty with the local community which takes care of him, in the same way as the local community must be inclusive and friendly disposed in their attitude towards the stranger. It is a mutual thrust-responsibility relationship where both sacrifice, and nobody makes excessive demands. (Lien op cit.)

The debate contains, of course, more than this, and the responses on Lien's article have been both many in numbers and critical attitude. I will not refer to this, but use the mentioned inputs in the debate to ask some questions about the communicative aspects of this debate and the possibilities of consensus formation on the bases of principles in discourse ethics.

Before I do this, I will briefly introduce a perspective that represents a contrast to Lien`s point of view, namely the mentioned 'masochist' attitude. This perspective will not be examined as thoroughly as Lien`s, but function as a supplement to the understanding of the Norwegian discourse on strangers.

The 'masochist' attitude

The philosopher Nina K.Monsen wrote recently (Aft.p. 18.7.93) a newspaper article about the relationship between Norwegians and refugees/immigrants. Her perspective is, as I see it, one of the perspectives that best fits Lien's criticism of masochism. She draws an extreme self-critical picture of the modern Norway and the Norwegians, combined with an accordingly uncritical appraisal of the strangers traditional culture. Norwegian society is seen as modern (and in her view with necessary negative values and emptied of old values as; 'togetherness, awe for God, sobriety, moderation, satisfaction in the work and willingness to work'. She continues:

It is mainly this emptied Norway the strangers meet, either they live here for longer or shorter periods. Most of these new groups have themselves brought with them a cultural heritage that look like a reminiscence of the old Norway. They have a strong sense of family solidarity, a clear religious anchoring, clear rules for acceptable practice, they keep their language intact, and preserve their cultural heritage as good as they can (my translation).

Her critic of modernity is as we can imagine strong, and she postulates that '...modernity and wealth has emptied the human communities of the West.' She is not standing alone with such a diagnosis of modernity, and MacIntyre and other communitarians are sometimes close to such a view. But what concerns me here is not the rightness of the diagnosis, but her sharp drawing of outlines and categories that by fundamental means separating 'us' from 'them'. 'We' are modern and rootless, 'they' are traditional with good anchoring. Her description gives an impression of a uniform negative modernity in which 'we' inhabit, and a uniform positive traditional order where we find 'the other'.

In my view this is an unjust categorisation which cuts off all interesting nuances. One of the consequences of this perspective is that 'the other' is effectively cut off from participation in 'our discourse'. The objectification of the other is as effective as a racist categorisation even if the other is described in positive words. As we shall see later on, both positive and negative stereotypes contribute to silence and repression, and that the way out of this non-intended outcome is to allow 'the other' to be represented in her complexity and ambivalence where the dividing line is certainly not tradition verses modernity.

I am now returning to Lien's contribution (but still keeping Monsen's perspective in mind) and I want to see what discourse ethics can offer in these kinds of debate as aspects of 'the Norwegian discourse on strangers'. In order to do this I will introduce Kettner's constraints on participants in practical discourse (1993), and see if they can help us onto fruitful tracks.

Discourse ethical constraints

Kettner's constraints are as follows (8); one constraint is called the 'power-neutrality constraint', which means that the differences among the participants with respect to power have to be neutralised so that it has no bearing on the consensus formation through argumentation. This is of course one of the real difficulties. One actual problem in this respect is that such issues as I have put in front now is mainly left over to the parliamentary system (and its offices).Most immigrants do not have the right to vote. They are not yet citizens and it is not always clear if they are going to be. Asylum seekers are in this respect not 'inside' at all. The Bosnians had at the time of Lien's writing mildly spoken about a highly unclear status. Another problem concerning the debate(s) I am referring to is that in a majority/minority situation the definition of the situation, the formulation of the problem and the access to the debate is strongly biased in favour of the majority (the Norwegians).

Let us say that the issue involved here could be formulated like this; 'what can the host expect and claim from the uninvited guest and vice versa?' I will guess that there would have to be an initial debate on how to describe the problem. Is there not a certain bias in the formulation of the issue? Why use the host-guest metaphors and the word 'uninvited'? The descriptive formula contains as we can see evaluative elements (and there is no way of separating the fact element from the element of value in the statement). This means, I think, that there would be considerable problems of reaching consensus even on the formulation of the problem. Reasons for this could be that there are differences in world views and that the agenda is too complicated.

The same holds for Monsen's description of categories involved, namely 'us, the moderns' and 'them, the traditionals'. A dichotomistic view does not capture even a small bit of the complexity involved, and certainly not 'the other' perspective on modernity and tradition.

It is clear that we have a long way to go to minimise this power bias implicit here. Until then this could be one of the reason why some potential participants dropped out of this 'communication game'. Habermas is aware of this problem, and points to the connection between consensus and compromise. People in a weaker power position, could (and sometimes do) accept compromises even if it means segmentation of unequal relations. In such cases 'the burden of proof' for fulfilment of discourse ethical principles are put on the participants in power and not the other way around.

The second constraint is called the 'role-taking constraint' where the participants '...must be able to adopt a hypothetical stance toward their own interests, values and needs etc., as well as to those expressed by others' (Kettner, 1993:35). I really doubt if this constraint is possible to fulfil totally, especially when the potential participants are very different from each other and when the issue touches deep identity questions. It could be questioned if this constraint contains a bit of the ideological self-image of persons and identities in the western cultural sphere, as separable from the roles they occupy (9). If this is so, I think this constraint could function eurocentrically with the consequence of keeping the other outside 'our' discourse. As part of the communicative dialogical process some of this role taking inevitably takes place. The question is whether this 'pressure' to adopt a 'hypothetical attitude' is too radical or not. If it is seen as a radical thoroughgoing questioning and self-questioning towards the participants' life forms and life histories (identities), it could be a destructive process and a parallel process to the 'colonialisation of the lifeword'. (10)

In this respect I think Lien demonstrates a double problem. In one way she invites the other by formulating questions and claims, in another way she pushes these questions too far and too quickly. In the context of migration refugees very often need a large amount of time both to identity confirmation and adjustment to a new society. I think her willingness to adopt the stance of the other is too weak, with the possible result of blocking further fruitful communication. To be sure I realise that there is a tricky double bind here. If you push, the other could fall off the track or the other will be further confirmed in her belief in non-involvement. If you do not, she will not be regarded as able to step into 'our moral discourse'.

Monsen's contribution (the 'masochist' attitude) fits the last option, and as we have seen with a strong tendency to isolate 'the other' in a fictive traditional order. In her perspective the whole question seems without any interest, maybe because 'the other' is not one to communicate with, but just an archaic character that can remind us about our old lost values and by chance help us on the track back to tradition.

This could mean that the constraints and elements in discourse ethics could be used strategically, with the result of eroding the possible mutual entering into practical discourse. This possibility is ruled out by one of Kettner's other constraints (see note 8 on the transparency constraint). But anyway; the time dimension must be considered and closeness (preferably face-to-face interaction) must also be stressed in handling these kinds of potential identity threatening questions. If we do not do this, I am afraid that the aim of dialogue will turn into a monologue or silence.

The last constraint is called the generality constraint; 'practical discourse over an issue ought to be open to all competent speakers whose interests are or will be affected by regulations adopted to resolve the issue.' (Kettner,

1993:34) This constraint demands, as I see it, that strangers or the 'guests' (also) are invited to an initial formulation of the problems discussed above. But as we have seen, in actual discourse the others are excluded to a very strong degree and perhaps they exclude themselves (there are many reasons for this and some of them we will find in the non-fulfilment of the other constraints). Now, this implies, I think, that one of the main tasks of practical discourse is to define a common ground for these kinds of discussions in an inclusive manner.

From power praxis to good dialogue?

As we have seen in these different contributions to the actual discourse on strangers, there is no easy path towards achieving mutual cross-cultural understanding and perhaps there is no path at all. Lien has not in her perspective demonstrated the necessary openness towards the other, it is mainly one aspect of the Norwegian perspective, using the strong metaphors of 'guests' verses 'hosts', and her willingness to try to see the problems from the other side is weak. However, she asks better questions, and puts more relevant claims on the other than Monsen does. The other as subject is not totally absent. In the case of Monsen, the other is visible but purely as an object. Her treatment of both 'us' and 'them' is clearly part of the 'system of representation' or the 'discourse' Hall calls 'The West and the Rest' (in Hall and Giddens, eds, 1992). By means of 'stereotypical dualism' (Hulme, 1986) she first collapses several characteristics into one unified body representing her vision of 'the other'. Then she does the same with 'us the modern Westerns', and imposes a fundamental split between 'us the bad' and 'them the good'. This 'system of representation' often places the values the other way around, but Monsen's reversal is not uncommon and places her on the level of romanticism which views our past through an idealised picture of 'the other'.

We could conclude this by saying that the actual and possible participants and the central 'issues' are not yet prepared to move into discourse. This would imply a very purified and restrictive view of the concept, and, I think, a kind of misuse. Discourse must rather be seen as a process and not as a product. In actual discourse the community of communication is limited, but we are in and on our way into discourse. It is proper to say, I think that we have no choice in this question. The problem should be formulated like this. Now when we are in discourse (that is, in some kinds of dialogue, including with strangers), how can we look for the latent in the manifest? What is demanded of us to reach a kind of mutual understanding (to avoid the horror of different kinds of separatism)? What kinds of limits has argumentation, and what kinds of differences are in need of being harmonised?

To give some kinds of answers, I think, we have to go beyond the procedural, formal and universalistic aspects of discourse ethics. First, it is necessary to understand what is at stake for people, and what is in fact the values and relations they live by and for. Without pointing to any link from tradition-bound or particularistic lifeworld values to theses new ethics, there will not be good enough reasons to jump into the situation of putting everything under scrutiny. To make these ethics more attractive we have to expand the concept of rationality even more to include more than the cognitivism in present discourse ethics. The quality of argumentation or 'the taste of a good dialogue' must be stressed in addition to an openness to different kinds of practices of dialogue with more space for what we call 'the surrounding elements'; the strong coffee, the food, smell, taste and bodily contact etc. (11) It could mean that some of our rationalistic presuppositions have to be altered, not in the name of 'irrationalism', but in the name of striving for mutual understanding and the good life or the art of living.

It is necessary to keep warm one of the Habermas' insights on 'moral intuitions'; those which 'inform us about how we, in the best way through carefulness, shall act to compensate for persons extreme vulnerability (Habermas, 1988:285) (12). The argumentative power to erode the ground for mutual understanding could otherwise be a possibility and the colonialisation of the lifeworld would be complete. The theory of communicative action and discourse ethics, could accommodate this problem by putting less stress on argumentation and more stress on other integrative dialogue aspects of communication and learning.

Inclusion without repression?

Some last disturbing questions must be raised before we leave the matter. How can we ever know that we are on the right and good track towards mutual understanding? Do we have any means to de-mask the power practices we regularly engage in, and if so where does it lead us? Could it be that the eagerness to include 'the other' by means of, for example, discourse ethics masks the normalising tendency of universalism to the extent that 'the otherness' fades away? And lastly, how can we behave inclusively without repression?

Some of these questions I have tried to answer above, but in the end they remain unsolved and perhaps unsolvable. Anyway they represent problems and challenges that have to be met by any ethical oriented social scientist trying to understand multicultural late-modern societies. The intellectual conqueror will perhaps meet the problems by means of more fine-grained categorisations and improvements of the old systems of explanations. For others, on the other hand, that have recognised the ontological and existential nature of ambivalence, the challenge is more a question of how 'to live with ambivalence' and insecurities in the lines of the writing and thoughts of Zygmont Bauman (1991, 1993).

Without going into Bauman's perspective I will close this essay by means of some open questions for discussion. What is the nature of Habermas' contribution and how can discourse ethics be supplemented (or rejected) to meet the problems described above? Does any tenable ethical alternative exist? And if so, how can this alternative be formulated?

Notes

(1) I am thinking about the Yugoslavian tragedy, refugee-problems in general, the racism in Germany and the racist tendencies and incidents in Norway among endless numbers of other things.

(2) S.K.Withe (1988) summarises some of the critics against discourse ethics in this way; 'it is either empty of ethical content, or, if its prescriptions do have some bite, they are nonetheless so abstracted from concrete traditions as to have no motivational support.'(p69) I can accept some of these critics, but I still see some hope for discourse ethics.

(3) On Apel I am drawing exclusively on secondary sources, mainly on the Swedish translation of Reese-Schafers; Karl-Otto Apel zur Einführung (sw. version 1992). On Habermas the secondary sources are S.K.White: The recent work of Jürgen Habermas. Reason, justice & modernity (1988) and Arie Brands: The force of reason, an introduction to Habermas` theory of communicative action (1990). From Habermas I have used an edited sample of his articles in Swedish; Kommunikativt handlande; Taxter om språk, rationalitet och samhalle (1988), mainly the articles; Moralitet och sedlighet (from Kuhlmanns; Moralitat und Sittlichkeit...1986) and a reply to critics of his theory of communicative action (1986). Discourse ethics` roots in both kantianism and pragmatism is not going to be discussed.

(4) This part of his theory draws heavily on an evolution theory containing 'the linguification of the sacred' and the growth of lifeworld rationalisation where integration is reached trough rational consensus. This theory is problematic in many respects, but it is not going to be discussed in this paper.

(5) The three theses are taken from E.O. Eriksens' contributing lecture 1.oct. 1993 on the seminar 'Discourse ethics' in Melbu (27.9 - 1.10.93). The seminar is one of many courses runned by the Norwegian research council's research program on ethics.

(6) The debate touched serious theoretical-methodological problems in social science; among them questions on objectivity, impartiality, neutrality and relativism. Though relevant, I will not comment much on these questions here. I can just point to other parts of my work (Breivik 1994).

(7) There was also debate on information routines. One of the main questions was whether the Bosnians had got enough information or not. This debate was (and is) typical, in so far as it stressed mainly the instrumental aspects of information, not its communicative and dialogical basis.

(8) I am focusing in the text on three of Kettners five constraints. The other two are interesting, but as a matter of space I will just briefly mention them here. One is called the 'autonomous evaluation constraint' and contains a restriction on paternalism and dogmatism, where such stances rule out alternatives. This is also meant to rule out the possibility of both external and internal coercion (like some of the other constraints). This means that practical discourse should provide every potential participant freely and without coercion to introduce, challenge and express their needs, wishes and interests.

Then we have the 'transparency constraint' which points to the 'incompatibility of practical discourse with purely strategic action.'(s35) The other should not be treated as either limiting conditions nor as means to one's ends. Cover-actions are banned. In one way this means that there must be a considerable amount of thrust from all participants both in the others good will and in the good argument.

(9) I am thinking of the distinction between honour and dignity and the differences in the understanding of what identity means. Berger says it this way;

'In a world of honour, the individual discovers his true identity in his roles, and to turn away from the roles is to turn away from himself.(...) In a world of dignity the individual can only discover his true identity by emancipating himself from socially imposed roles.' (1974:90-91)

Such a view could fit the dangerous scheme dividing us moderns from the other traditionals. I will strongly oppose such an interpretation, especially as a starting point. But as a matter of understanding individual selves such distinctions can be fruitful, but then as different aspects of the same individual sense of selfhood and identity. And of course the weight on the one over the other is differently distributed.

(10) Habermas is aware of this problem both when he speaks about communicative competence and personality;

'By the concept of personality, I understand those competencies which make a subject capable of speech and action, that is able to participate in processes in which shared understanding is reached, maintaining at the same time his or her own identity.' (Habermas 1984b:594-95 quoted from Whithe,1988)

But first you have to take a chance, and nobody knows the outcome; and it could disturb your identity maintenance. Our competencies are never totally secure.

(11) The hierarchy of the senses embedded in western culture is interesting here. 'We' have given sight a privileged position which we tend to think as an universal matter of fact. Stoller (1989) makes reference to other ways of ordering the senses, and in 'The taste of ethnographic things' he is critical to give sight this position. The sight has a tendency to function objectivating and as a distancing device (see also Fabian (1983)). On this occasion I will just point to the predominance of sight-metaphors in 'our' way of understanding through language, and that the sight/language is creative in its drawing of outlines, separating phenomena and in its abstracting capacity. This is neither good nor bad in itself, but it represents certainly not our best 'tool' in creating closeness, thrust and good conditions for mutual understanding.

(12) This is my translation from the Swedish version.

References

Bauman, Z. (1991), Modernity and Ambivalence, Polity Press, Cambridge.

Bauman, Z. (1993), Postmodern Ethics, Oxford, Blackwell.

Berger, P., et.al. (1974), The homeless mind: modernisation and consciousness, Oxford, Vintage Books.

Brand, A. (1990), The force of reason: An introduction to Habermas` theory of communicative action, London, Allen & Unwin.

Brox, O. (1991), Jeg er ikke rasist, men..., Oslo, Gyldendal.

Fabian, J. (1983), Time and the Other: How anthropology makes its object, New York Columbia University Press.

Habermas, J. (1988), Kommunikativt handlande; Texter om språk, rationalitet och samhälle, Göteborg, Daidalos.

Hall and Giddens (eds) 1992, Formations of Modernity, Cambridge, Polity Press.

Hulme, P. (1986), Colonial Encounters, London, Methuen.

Kettner, M. (1993), Scientific Knowledge, Discourse Ethics, and Consensus Formation in the Public Domain in Winkler, E.R. and Coombs, J.R. (eds), Applied ethics: A reader, Cambridge, Blackwell.

Lien, I. L. (1991), En god forsker eller et godt menneske, (p177-185) in Nytt Norsk Tidsskrift, nr 2/91, Oslo.

Lien, I. L. (1993), Når gjestene kritiserer verten, chronicle in the newspaper Aftenposten (13.8.93), Oslo.

Monsen, N.K. (1993): 'Motsetninger og nasjonal identitet' chronicle in the newspaper Aftenposten (18.7.93), Oslo

Reese-Schafer, W. (1992) Karl-Otto Apel; En introduksjon, Göteborg , Daidalos.

Stoller, P. (1989), The taste of ethnographic things; the senses in anthropology, Pennsylvania the University of Pennsylvania Press.

White, S. K. (1988), The recent work of Jürgen Habermas: Reason, justice and modernity, Cambridge, Cambridge University Press.

Peadar Shanahan

Towards an Alternative University Adult Education?

Reflections on University Adult Education Practice with Social Movements

The Problem with UAE: The dominant themes in university adult education (UAE) today might be listed as marketisation, competencies, vocation, mainstreaming, accreditation, progression, lifelong learning, distance learning. Included too are notions of partnership and community accountability. Even these latter notions have been mainly redefined in terms of training for the economy and are operationalised in adult education and training programmes which are, in the main, geared towards individual learning needs and lacking in any, not to mention critical, social analysis. As a senior UK civil servant said some years ago: 'There is no such thing as adult education today, only adults attending classes.' (Quoted in Jackson,1995) University adult education, like adult education generally is 'largely shaped by psychological, individualised, orientations...' and is concerned 'with designing techniques that will change the individual learner's behaviour and inculcate coping skills to make up for what are claimed to be objectively identified deficiencies.' (Collins,1991) There is nothing unusual about this. Like all other state institutions in this globalising world, UAE pays its allegiance to global market values and individualism. University centres for continuing education change their names to centres of education and development to compete with the other business enterprises selling their services. Writers report that more than half of the teaching of UAE is connected with continuing professional training, a third with retraining and a tenth with open university study for a degree. (Kivinen and Rinne, 1994) As Gelpi, Zwerling, Thompson and others have suggested, adult education is mainly for the 'haves' in society. The main beneficiaries are the universities, colleges, consultants and enterprises which serve their needs.

UAE with Social Movements: One of the marginal activities of university adult education is represented by UAE *engagement* with social movements. UAE with social movements is essentially about dialogue: both activists and professional educators bring different contributions to this dialogue and the result is learning on both sides. The result too is that UAE can make a particular contribution to the quality of democratic and cultural life of the constituency of the university.

What UAE with Social Movements is Not: In historical terms, UAE work with social movements is in line with the so-called 'radical' tradition of adult education with its collectivist approaches to societal change. It has its roots in traditions like that of the Danish Folk High schools, the historical trade union education programmes of the UK and the rural cooperative movement associated with land reform in Ireland in the last century. UAE too has been involved in social movements like feminism, environmentalism, ethnicity, disability. It also appears in the 'radical' educational efforts in Third World countries where it has had it origins in the critique of modernisation theory and the search for indigenisation. It is particularly to be seen in the politics of identity as exemplified by Preece. (c.f.-Deconstructing the Discourse of Community Education and Development for Women of Muslim Pakistani Heritage: alternative solutions?, Bremen Paper)

However closely they may be related, UAE work with social movements should not be confused with UAE work with an array of 'community action groups', 'public interest groups', 'neighbourhood and community development groups', etc. In the writer's opinion, this does not constitute adult education work with social movements. While some writers refer to the latter groups as constituting a social movement (for example, 'citizen movement', 'community planning movement' etc.) they do not, in the writer's opinion, constitute a social movement. They may only be called a virtual or potential movement of the 'excluded'. As Marjorie Mayo has argued: far from coming together to press for more radical social change, community groups are tied in closely to the urban planing process and are routinely consulted as part of community politics. (Mayo, 1994). The vast majority of such community development groups in the mid-1990's are teleologically guided and are often organised for the simple purpose of wresting any resources they can from the state (O'Neill,1992). Many of these 'single-issue' self-help service groups are the creation of the free-market, neo liberal, New Right strategies to 'roll back the state'. The 'hollowed-out state' sees these groups of excluded people as a means to 'reduce state spending on social welfare and to promote alternative solutions based upon the private market as well as upon the voluntary...sectors and community-based self-help' (Craig and Mayo, 1995). The state, often as a 'partner', is firmly in control (Curtin and Varley, 1995; Robson,1995). These are often single issue groups that do not feel part of any movement although there is some evidence that this may be changing (somewhat) and that the social policy fora in the EU are beginning to seriously take on board the poverty lobby associated with the 'excluded' (*Working on European Social Policy: Report on Forum*, 1996). Most community-led initiatives aimed at development may be crudely referred to as reflecting, either more or less, a 'statist' tendency in community development education. This is a massive growth area in UK adult education. For instance, it is calculated with figures supplied by the Northern Ireland Voluntary Trust, that there are now 5,000 voluntary and community groups in Northern Ireland (population of one and a half million). These groups, it is calculated (probably exagerated) may have 65,000 volunteers, with about 30,000 paid employees (mostly short term and half-time community employment) and an annual turnover of between £35-40,000,000 (Mostly 'Peace Money' and EU-funded programmes). Having stated this, however, it is important to underline that non-teleological collective responses in the community are not so apparent as they were in the 1960's-1970's and even the 1980's. More than ten years ago, Peter Marris (1983) has offered a thorough explanation of this phenomenon and, more recently, Keith Jackson (1995) suggests that 'a consciousness of being citizens within a welfare state has shifted to that of expendable commodities in the labour market, disempowering people and reducing expectations that our parliamentary democracy is capable of responding to, or even acknowledging, collective action in civil society as appropriate.' The writer's experience in IRL-N would lead him to the same conclusion.

This paper confines itself to UAE with social movements and while it examines this topic within a case study of UAE work in community development, it is not concerned with UAE and contemporary community development groups in general. In particular it reflects on UAE work with social movements throughout the 1980's. More particularly, it reflects on the relationship between a particular UAE project and the Irish language revival movement. The writer likes to think that the paper has common ground with the paper by Steve Morris, 'Recent language protest movement in Wales: Adult learning of a new kind?' (Morris, 1996). The paper divides in two. Part One illustrates UAE practice with social movements using a case study approach. Part Two reflects on this practice and argues for the maintenance of this marginal traditional activity in UAE and the development of imaginative and validated curricula in order to do so. This sanguine advocation, however, is not meant to cloak the arguments and strong forces against this development.

Part One: University Adult Education and Social Movements: A Case Study

1.1 A UAE Project for Social Movements in the 1980's: Local Actions Groping for Global Aspirations?

Many writers in the 1980's drew attention to the potential of locally initiated community education programmes aimed to facilitate collective movements of people seeking to negotiate new personal and collective identities and behaviours (for example, Lovett et al., 1983). These community education initiatives (often called Non-Formal Education or NFE) sought, and seek, to alter consciousness and attitudes with a view to changing the structural arrangements in order to alleviate specific perceived grievances. As such, these community-led initiatives in education were seen as the educational 'arms' of social movements. And as such, these self-starting and internally-motivated educational initiatives were of real interest to those involved in community development, particularly university-led adult education programmes, for community development.

To illustrate how a university-based, validated programme of study might have contributed to social movements, I might ask the reader to consider the experience of the university adult education project organised by the Magee Community Development Studies Unit in Derry in Northern Ireland (IRL-N). The Unit owed its existence to Tom Lovett's work in Derry in the 1970's. As a cross-border initiative in community development, the Magee Unit was initially established in the early 1980's in a situation of militant insurgency and in a political environment in which the absence of legitimacy of the state, and its institutions, was apparent to a substantial section of the population. In such a situation, and at that time more generally, social movements were active: for example, the trade union movement, the womens' movement; the ethnic revival movement; the co-operative and community business movement; the alternative planning movement; the environmental movement; the anti-nuclear arms movement.

Trying to Transcend Sectarianism: In this situation, the Magee UAE Unit set out to explore the contribution which university adult education could make to local expressions of international social movements (Shanahan, 1984; 1995; 1987 a b; 1989; 1990) and to explore how these movements could possibly contribute to community economic development which was aimed at the production of socially useful goods and services, that is, goods and services which were defined by people in disadvantaged neighbourhoods as being needed by them (Course Handbook). By concentrating and focussing on groups which had a 'window' on the international scene rather than those groups myopically focussed on 'the local' only, we argued for a non-sectarian approach and for a global perspective in our local action. The European and global dimension continually provided us (and still provides us) with an 'openness' which we would not have had (or have) had we concentrated and explained ourselves in community development terms only.

During the initial 'Cinderella Phase' between 1982-1987, the Unit was engaged in the development of a number of 'Fora' in the community with local activists involved in various social movements. A number of community seminars and conferences were organised with well-known community activists, the most important of which were: Forum for the Study of Community Crime in Derry (Shanahan,1985); Forum for Community Access to the Media; Forum for the Study of the Relationship between Christians and Capitalism; and Forum for the Study of the Relationship between Social Class and Irish Culture (MacGrianna,S. et al.eds., 1993). During the second 'EU-Innovatory Phase' between 1987-1989 when the Unit received substantial monies, (£303,000 for a two-year, cross-border pilot project) the university 'allowed' the Unit to adopt policies advocated by Walter James in an article in 1982. Following this policy, the university formally employed six project workers most of whom, in their own ways, had substantial credibility with active local groups. Certain of these groups saw themselves as local expressions of international social movements: the womens groups; the alternative planning and community 'business' groups; the trade union and socialist revolutionary movement; the international cooperative movement. The local, ethnic revival movement was also represented in the Unit by one member who was elected as Chairperson of Cairde na Gaelscoille(a fundraising and pressure/organising group for preschool and primary school education through Irish). The Unit made contact with the International League for Social Commitment in Adult Education (ILSCAE) and two members visited Nicaragua in 1988. In 1992, the Unit organised a very successful International Conference for ILSACE in Magee College, Derry, attended by local activist groups and people from around the world. In the early 1990's, the Magee Unit organised a series of well-attended seminars, sometimes with international speakers, entitled: 'The Contribution of Social Movements to Community Re-generation'. Some of these seminars have been the basis of publications. The Unit was supported by Derry City Council, EU funding bodies, ESF, INTERREG and ERASMUS (£1.3 million plus the university's contribution of about 40%).

Assessment: Over this period of about 14 years, there is evidence that the Unit succeeded in contributing to the broad infrastructural development and viability of neighbourhoods and groups in disadvantaged areas of the city and rural countryside (Shell UK Prize, Partnership Awards, 1990; Robson and McClenaghan, 1995). However, there are fewer and more tentative answers to the question: can UAE contribute to the empowerment of local expressions of international social movements? By 1989, we were asking whether UAE does not debilitate such movements through a process of domestication, forcing them to adopt professional manners and changing their aims until they eventually end up as contributing to state voluntarism and neo-right policies of self-help (Shanahan et al., 1989)? However, there is ample evidence available to show that community activists (all of whom were unemployed) involved in social movements in the community used the UAE Unit and programme and developed projects which they judged to be in the interests of 'their' social movements. More importantly, they made the educational and network resources, the cultural capital, of the university available to their movements and added to their own learning and the learning of the wider academic community.

1.2 University Adult Education and the Irish Language Revival Movement: A Case Study within a Case Study

This article mainly reflects on involvement with the local ethnic language revival movement. It is suggested that the European ethnic revival movement is to be recognised in the fifty or so million people in Europe who speak 'home' languages other than those of the official languages of the EU and is seen in the efforts of adult people learning an 'unused' or 'dead' language (for example, 'The Death of the Irish Language' by Hindley) of which they are entirely, or almost entirely, ignorant but which they themselves perceive to be their own, indigenous language. The paper will document the Irish language and ethnic revival movement in Northern Ireland (IRL-N) during the period of community militant insurgency against the state, 1969-1996.

The Irish Cultural Project: By Irish culture we normally mean those features of everyday life and thought that are distinctively native to the Irish consciousness but that consciousness today has four streams with four sources in history and originating in four distinct groups: Gaelic, Anglo-Normal, Anglo-Irish and Ulster-Protestant. Here we confine our definition of Irish culture to the Gaelic Language. This decision is justified by the fact of the enormous importance of language to a people's ability to name their own reality and to a people's feeling of self-worth and confidence. The contemporary revival of a traditional, indigenous language after it seems to have been killed off (Hindley) either by modernisation, colonialism or even Europeanisation is as significant as its loss was poignant.

Concern with culture in Ireland is of recent origin. Three hundred years ago only the Gaelic poets were concerned about Irish culture and their concern was for their own threatened redundancy situation. Even the Irish 'patriots' of the 18th century like Daniel O'Connell and the Fenian revolutionaries had completely internalised their contemporary dominant ideologies of progress and thus, regarded things Irish as inferior. Later, in the early 20th century, Synge was to bemoan the fact that the Irish had accepted 'the Devil's Own Mirror' from the English, a mirror 'which would cast a squint across an angel's brow.' (Playboy of the Western World) and Yeats was to complain that 'they have dug up our rose garden and given us a cabbage-patch instead'. English was regarded in the 19th century as a modernising, progressive force. Only in the last hundred years has the sense of loss been felt among the Irish people and for the masses of people. However different to Wales, this sense of loss expressed itself in nationalism and insurrection and not in language. Movements to preserve the Irish language were always elitist. However, the language, at the beginning of the century, became the justification by nationalists and insurrectionists of statehood. In relation to events at the turn of this century these points have been well-made by O'Connor:

> Reflecting the volkische, neo-medieval, and irrationalist ideas then in vogue in Europe, Irish nationalists of the fin de siecle set out to promote an organic sense of identity, rooted in soil and history. To this end they sought to recover the integral and total culture which Ireland had last enjoyed under Gaelic domination. The imagination of the Gaelic Revival dwelt amongst rural communities, where the last vestiges of a cultural completeness were to be found. If, as Brendan Behan put it, the ascendancy was a Protestant on a horse, the celtic twilight was a professor listening to a peasant. (MacGrianna et al., 1994)

However, such a project was of utmost importance to the mainly English-speaking and 'class-less' Sinn Fein and IRA of the 1920's who 'successfully took up arms against British occupation in the second decade of the century.' 'Class-less Sinn Fein', in the second decade of this century, was the inheritor of, if not the representation of, the new petit bourgeoisie and the class of small capitalists who beat the old landowning class with the weapons of war, but more importantly, they beat them with the weapons of the political and economic philosophy tied in closely with cultural nationalism. After the establishment of the Irish Free State in 1922, this Irish revival project was carried through by the new Irish, but English-speaking, establishment. The divergent dynamics of cultural and capitalist nationalism were accommodated (if unreconciled) in the project of nation building. Finally in the 1960's, the contradictions could no longer be accommodated and in the heady optimism of the day when we thought that science and industrialisation could save all, economic development became its own justification. New consumerist values exposed the contradictions with the Gaelic ideal. Ireland no longer needed an overarching national cultural project to provide it with meaning. Economics was its own justification. And so, the latent anti-indigenous forces always present in Irish society in the form of what was traditionally known as 'West-Britism', came out of the closet and they moved to 'ditch' the Irish cultural project, once and for all, with great earnestness and with the assistance of the media.

The Gaelic Culture ideal then lost its main benefactor, that of the state ideology and, according to O'Connor, there is no class in the Republic of Ireland today which perceives its interests to be bound up with nationalism. 'As the language becomes disestablished ideologically, so it will become marginalised socially' (O'Connor) and eventually this dis-establishment led to the English geographer, Reg Hindley, writing his controversial book, entitled, 'The Death of the Irish Language' (1990). This controversial book stimulated a thorough critique by Eamon O Ciosain entitled, 'Buried Alive: A Reply to Reg Hindley's 'The Death of the Irish language' (1991).

However, there has been and is a growing revival of Irish language in IRL-S over the past twenty years, a revival which has been initiated and led mainly by the middle-classes (It has a strong base in working class estates in Dublin). On the other hand, in IRL-N, after years of bloody war and insurrection, it would appear that it was, and to an extent still is, the unwaged and low-paid working class in disadvantaged nationalist neighbourhoods which has identified with and thrown in its lot with the Irish language.

It is in the most disadvantaged urban neighbourhoods of IRL-N (nationalist working class neighbourhoods have two and a half times higher male unemployment rates than unionist neighbourhoods) , with the highest rates of unemployment, that the Irish language generated fresh enthusiasm, particularly in the early 1980's. This may establish differences between the ethnic revival in IRL-N and the revival of the language movement in IRL-S and perhaps differences to the language movement in Brittany in France where it is reported by O Ciosain, that the ethnic revival movement in the schools is dominated by the children of lawyers, doctors and middle-classes. In those cases, the movement was initiated and is led by middle-class parents who, with other motivation, recognise the advantages of bilingual education, small classes and motivated teachers for the social advancement of their children. The ethnic revival in IRL-N was initiated in the early 1980's solely by, and is still recognisably led by, working-class nationalists. This is changing, of course, with the social mobility of the original families and by new, middle-class involvement, but the evidence seems to indicate that it is not changing substantially. It is still rooted in a working class (nationalist) social environment.

Selection of Projects by Students on UAE Programme: Over the years, the UAE programme attracted on its validated certificated programme, (16 hours classwork over 40 weeks) about 15 unemployed Irish language activists and many more who would see themselves marginally involved in the movement (total certificated population from 1984-1995: 246). The following is a small selection of the projects completed specifically for language revival purposes: two Irish language publishing enterprise feasibility studies; a bulletin for the friends of Irish education; a brochure aimed at parents considering sending their children to an Irish pre-school; a feasibility study of an Irish language video production enterprise; a feasibility study of an

Irish puppet show project; a development study for the Irish pre-schools. Between the years 1985 and 1995, the Irish language speaking families in Derry and Belfast increased substantially. (See Note)

Unemployment and the Irish School Population in Derry and Belfast: The 200+ children attending primary school through the medium of Irish in Derry represent about 100 families and the 700 + children attending in Belfast represent about 350 families. It is calculated that 80% of these families are living in neighbourhoods with male unemployment figures rising to 80%. A reasonable guess is that about 80% of the families represented at the Irish Schools are suffering from unemployment and without a steady income. Thus , this preliminary investigation of Derry and Belfast would indicate that there is a correlation between class/unemployment and involvement in the Irish language revival in IRL-N as indicated by commitment to educate one's children through Irish.

Part Two: An Alternative UAE for Civil Society

Part One of this paper tried to show that UAE can contribute to social movements. It showed this by illustration through a description of actual practice. However, the writer is also aware that such UAE practice is very much a marginal activity, and even an unacceptable one, within contemporary UAE discourse. It is argued here that this present situation is unfortunate and that the UAE goal to advance critical consciousness and new knowledge will be less attainable if the practice of UAE with social movements is not actively encouraged.

2.1 Saving Civil Society: Is Mainline UAE were contributing actively to the Diminishment of Civil Society?

University adult continuing education (UAE) is mainly concerned with people who have sufficient time and resources on their hands to use university facilities in part-time courses to better themselves (economically, socially, culturally and politically) as individuals.

In doing so, it is argued here that UAE reflects and reproduces the structures of advantage and disadvantage of society uncritically; structures of class, structures of gender, structures of race, structures of peripherality, disability, age. The knowledge which UAE produces does not, in the main, challenge and change those structures. UAE perpetuates those structures by augmenting the efficiency of the professions and the bureaucracies and institutions which prop them up and in whose interest it is that they continue. In the main, UAE does not foster a more egalitarian world and a more democratic state but instead contributes to the juggernaut of exclusionary processes which are seemingly inherent in the present developments of capitalism and through which the rich get richer and the poor get poorer. In more sociological terms, the modernising processes of capitalism have led to the further 'encrustment' of the social structures and have not changed the distribution of chances and of risk in relation to those structures. Contemporary, mainline UAE discourse (at least in the UK) may be part of the further 'encrustment' of the same structures.

On the other hand, and in a real sense, we may can say that the personal is political and that UAE may contribute to this politicisation (Alheit,1993). As globalisation increases and tradition releases its hold on us, we are forced back more and more on ourselves as we attempt to grasp control of our circumstances (Giddens,1995). We do so through acquiring knowledge about what we do and, through that knowledge, re-organise what we do in order to survive in a fast and 'reflexive world'. University adult education assists us to adapt and adjust to this world and, perhaps also assists us to act creatively and fulfillingly. In this exercise, we, as individuals often increase our awareness and act politically in so far as our decisions have political implications for policy and financial resource distribution. There is little doubt that for a large section of the population, there is an increase of mobility, an increase of the individualisation of life, and an increase in new chances of participation. UAE contributes to this more pluralistic society.

However, while acknowledging that the personal is political, it is also true to assert that the process of individualisation, so dominant in contemporary society in the 'developed' world, dissipates collective resistance to dominant values and dominant institutions and structures. University adult education practice, like adult education generally, subscribes to and reproduces these dominant values and facilitates the dissipation of collective resistance through the new social movements and, particularly dissipates efforts at the empowerment of the poorest in society. For the latter, detraditionalisation does not mean an increase of mobility and an increase of the variety of chances of participation. For them it means detachment from traditional sources of security and from traditional certainties. For them, globalisation, detraditionalisation, reflexivity elicit disorientation and disintegration. It may lead the excluded towards what has been called 'anti-modernity' (Beck).

One major critique of the dominant discourse in contemporary UAE might be that it has disembedded education from the political and socio-economic interests that are so important in all worthwhile education (c.f. Tawney, 1926 quoted in Jackson, 1996, Polyani, 1957). This belief is accentuated by the knowledge that this new further education UAE system, no matter how rational it might seem at first glance, might reflect the politics of its generators. It seems to deal with people without societal structures, without a community, without a group. Above all, UAE appears to deal with people as if 'collective struggle' did not exit. One is thus reminded of Margaret Thatcher, during whose reign the new further education system was born in the UK, who famously declared that there is no such thing as society. We might also remember John Major's 'classless society'. He followed up Margaret Thatcher by shifting citizens out of the way and replacing them by consumers (Jackson, 1995). Present preoccupations of UAE and its dominant discourse may reflect this political philosophy (Carr and Hartnett, 1996). However, the writer would even go further. I am arguing that the limitations of the present dominant UAE discourse may even be doing actual harm to civil society.

What if mainline UAE is contributing to the diminishment of civil society by contributing in such a direct fashion to the ideological shift from consciousness of being citizens to consciousness of being expendable commodities in the market?

Our Case Study included the Irish language revival movement. Do we find in it an echo of Beck's 'anti-modernity'? I do not believe so. Like Morris (1996) observed in the case of the Welsh language movement which fostered connections with other international 'progressive' movements, the same observation may be made of the Irish language movement in IRL-N. The international dimension to the movement is quite conscious and new technology is adopted enthusiastically. The language revival movement in IRL-N, although locally based and engaged with local neighbourhoods, seems outgoing, modern in its symbols and European in its orientation. Do we not have here a collective, community adult education movement incorporating a different type of adult learning than that found in mainline adult education? Do we not have here a UAE form of adult education different to that of mainline contemporary UAE? Such an example of adult education provides what Steve Morris calls 'adult learning of a new kind'(Morris, 1996). Perhaps the adjective 'new' is too strong. Such adult learning has been around for a long time. Perhaps we have here, instead, an alternative form of adult learning which seems in almost total contradiction to contemporary UAE mainstream adult learning. How can the dominant discourse within UAE conceptualise (not to mind serve) social movements like this? Can competency-based learning contribute to the dynamics of such a movement? Will it debilitate such a movement? How does contemporary UAE contribute to the ailing civic society which has been so well argued by Putnam? Quite obviously, UAE needs an alternative discourse to the present dominant one; an alternative and acceptable UAE discourse ('discourse' here includes practice, 'cognitive praxis'...see later) capable of augmenting collective, consciousness-creation by dissidents who are involved in changing societal structures through cognitive praxis in civil society.

2.2 University Adult Education, Social Movements and Unemployed

The literature on social movements reports that militants and activists in social movements 'are typically recruited from those who are highly integrated into the social structure' (Melucci, 1988). The new social movements seem to be populated by the 'new middle class'. In the case of ethnic language revival movements in Wales and Brittany and certainly in the IRL-S, this observation would seem to stand up. However, in the case of the ethnic language revival movement in IRL-N, the movement is dominated by people with working class origins and it still possesses a strong working class milieu. All the people involved with the UAE Unit from the Irish language movement in the case study were unemployed. The high degree of unemployment in the interest group is arguably due to sectarian and/or post-colonial unemployment structures, practices and traditions as well as their own alienation from the state (See Clayton, 1996 for an alternative view of social relations in IRL-N).

2.3 An Alternative University Adult Education, Social Change and the Creation of New Knowledge?

This last selected argument for an alternative UAE is probably the most important.

Unlike all other categories of adult/continuing education, we are dealing here with an 'alternative' tendency towards the state (Curtin and Varley, 1995). Social movements are born in, and take their continuing life from, protest and struggle. Social movements, as community-based initiatives, (a) protest against the structural arrangement in the status quo as they see them and (b) struggle to alter those arrangements to alleviate their specific perceived grievances. But in the examination of the activities of social movements we should not loose sight of the essential and core importance of knowledge to such movements and hence the core importance of adult education to such movements. Indeed, Eyerman and Jamieson (1991, quoted by

Jackson, 1995) examine 'social movements as cognitive praxis'. Like Tawney, they argue that this 'cognitive praxis' is the social action where new knowledge originates. They are in line with social constructionists like Peter Berger who sees society as being constructed by recurrent acts of new knowledge. Social movements are to be recognised not in terms of their activity nor in terms of their organisation but in terms of the new type of conceptual space they are seeking to make available to themselves and to others. They are creating a new 'cognitive territory' with their protests and their struggles.

This is not to argue, however, that we can look to new social movements for the democratisation of and the transformation of everyday life (Mayo, 1994). Although some have seen it that way (Meluci, 1988). All we are saying here is that social movements are essentially about creating new 'alternative knowledge' and as such adult education is an essential element in such movements.

When we speak of 'new knowledge' we are immediately in a 'conflict mode' because knowledge is power and 'new knowledge' means the disturbance of the status quo. The interpretations of truth and knowledge are dependent on where the promoters of that knowledge are positioned by others, and by themselves, in that society. New knowledge or a new discourse will be resisted or accepted to the extent that it is seen to be constructive or destructive in relation to the dominant power relations in that society. All discourses are ideologically located and their meanings may change over time depending on contemporary power struggles and depending on sites of resistance.

Foucault takes this line of thinking still further (Preece, 1996) and presents discourse as a form of social practice. This means that for Foucault discourse can include activity and systems of behaviour as well as dialogue. By relating discourse to behaviour and systems of behaviour we can now understand how the notion of 'discourse as social practice' links in very nicely with the earlier definition of social movement as 'cognitive praxis': that is, social action, social behaviour, social practice. It is from this praxis that new knowledge originates (Eyerman and Jameison, 1991). Using Foucault, Eyerman and Jameison we can see that the source and spring of really new knowledge resides in 'cognitive praxis': the deliberate creation of knowledge from and through struggle; the deliberate creation of struggle from and through new knowledge. Without collective struggle there is no new knowledge. Genuinely new knowledge by its very nature creates struggle. Without struggle there is no real change. Without the creation of knowledge from struggle and struggle from knowledge there is only the production of mainstream knowledge which perpetuates exclusion and the further 'encrustment' of the social structures. The production of knowledge which is not new in the sense in which it being used here, adds nothing to the system. Mainstream UAE knowledge only increases the determinative power of the structures which have enabled it to be reproduced. Mainstream UAE reflects these structures. Does it not reproduce inequality? The 'cognitive praxis' and alternative discourse which is the essence of social movements does not reproduce nor further the 'encrustment' of structures. Its new knowledge challenges those structures. This new knowledge is only produced in a thriving civil society.

Conclusion: Is UAE an Organ of the State or is it Engaged with Civil Society?

The UAE programme which was the subject of the case study, struggled to find civility and democracy and 'academic understanding' in the midst of what sometimes appeared as an 'ethno-mafia' war (Alheit, 1993) and at other times as brutal, colonial-style state illegality. It is a case study within a university system which reflects the structures of advantage and disadvantage in the community at large in IRL-N (FECNI, 1989; 1990) but which occasionally and, dare I say, admirably rose to its UAE task/challenge of addressing the needs of the turbulent adult education constituency . It is a case study of a university adult education programme becoming involved (engaged) with social movements in which the formal, university selection panel 'allowed' the formal employment, albeit temporary, of community activists in 1987. As a result, this UAE programme avoided the usual role of a confused, academic figure standing aloof from its war-torn constituency and confining itself to 'safe' training of well-controlled, social work and health and other professionals. In taking the decision it did, the university faced up to the central question: is the university part of civil society or is it just an organ of the state? The UAE Unit was allowed (albeit with substantial EU monies directed at the unemployed) to operate and survive in a 'divided community' (Shanahan, 1994). It did so with some 'success.' However, we might also mention that the members involved in the case study struggled with the truth of Kierkegaard's statement that 'Life can only be understood backwards. In the meantime, it has to be lived forwards'. Indeed, decisions were occasionally made by the Unit members in the acute awareness that 'The time for understanding life is in conflict with the necessity to get on with it' (Alheit, 1991). Sometimes we got it wrong.

This paper was critical of the limitations which are seemingly inherent in the dominant discourse in UAE today. It has argued for maintaining and developing a tradition of university adult education in civil society which seeks to facilitate social movements. Its arguments were based on actual practice, not just on theory. It has argued that this alternative and essentially marginal UAE activity and tradition is important to maintain and develop anew because: (a) it addresses the pressing needs of an ailing civil society to which the dominant discourse within UAE seems unable to respond; (b) it addresses the needs of struggling dissidents (although not as apparent as before, they still exist!) who are collectively objecting to various inhibiting structures, structures which they see are preventing the individual from achieving full human potential; mainstream UAE does not even conceptualise such struggles not to mention serving them; (c) above all, the alternative UAE discourse (praxis) facilitates in a very direct way the development of really new knowledge and new power arrangements in society. It thus facilitates social change.

The advocation of this alternative UAE policy is one thing. The actualising of the policy is another. Perhaps social movements are destined to exist outside state-supported systems like UAE? Perhaps they may be better off as a result? Perhaps not. The argument of this paper has been that if traditional UAE engagement with social movements and their learning processes is lost, then it is to the detriment of UAE. Perhaps it is not too pretentious to say that it is also to the detriment of civil society?

One way or another, the flowering of the alternative UAE advocated in this paper will depend to a large extent on some answer to questions facing the contemporary university: will the contemporary university define itself as an organ of the state which is contributing to the diminishment of civil society? The answer to this question will in turn depend on the answer of the contemporary state to the 'predicament' created by the integrating globalising power of the market economy: will the state opt for policy frameworks which are genuinely pluralist or continue as usual; will it extend power directly to people to enable them to direct their own lives or will it continue with the present charade of representative democracy; will it value needs other than those which the global marketeers dictate; will it extend citizenship and, with it, civil society? Is the tradition of adult education so well exemplified in the Folk High Schools to be lost forever?

Note

Derry and Belfast: Some Statistics

Belfast in the east of the Province and Derry in the west of the Province are the two major urban centres of N.I. and constitute about 65 % of the total population of N.I.of one and a half millions. There are other language revival groups in towns like Newry, Armagh, Claudy, Omagh, Limavady and others, but here we will not consider these and instead, confine our observations to the two large urban centres of population.

Derry

Irish-speaking Families (Families in which Irish is used as the primary mode of communication by at least one member)

1969	1985	1990	1993	1996
0	10	60	75	110

All Irish Preschools (For children under 4 years of age)

1969	1984	1990	1993	1996
0	0	3 (70 children)	4 (120 children)	3 (64)

There are three approved, preschool provisions in the City, all of which begun after 1984: Pilot's Row, Shantallow and Creggan. Together, all three constitute an infant population of 64 with seven teachers, most of whom are unemployed voluntary workers, or are on low-paid, one-year, community employment schemes. Until quite recently, all three of the preschools were without any external support and got their funding from the local community by means of door to door collections. These preschools feed into the All-Irish Primary School at Steelstown.

All-Irish Primary School (For children between 4 and 11 years of age)

1985	1990	1993	1996
1 (20 children)	1 (120)	1 (150)	1 (225 children)

The all-Irish speaking primary school was begun in 1985 with twenty pupils and one teacher. Eleven years later, there are 225 children in this school, which is a unit in an ordinary (Catholic maintained school) primary school at Steelstown, a mixed class area and has qualified, professional teachers.

All-Irish Secondary School (For 11-18 year olds)

1995
39

Belfast

Irish-speaking families

1969	1985	1990	1993	1996
10	40	210	220	350

It is calculated that there were no more than 10 Irish-speaking families in Belfast in 1969 when the first efforts to form an Irish school were begun. It is now calculated that there are at least 350.

All-Irish Preschools

1969	1985	1990	1993	1996
0	2 (30 children)	8 (205 children)	8 (300)	9 (420)

In 1982 there was no all-Irish preschool in Belfast . Today, there are 9 with a combined population of over 420 children between three and four years of age and these schools feed into the All-Irish Primary School.

All-Irish Primary Schools

1969	1985	1990	1993	1996
1 (10)	2 (100)	2 (424 children)	2 (450)	6 (700)

The Primary School was begun on Shaw's Road in 1969 when a number of Irish language enthusiasts decided to form an all-Irish-speaking neighbourhood. Assistance from Government was not given until 1984.

All-Irish Secondary School (For 11-18 year olds)

1996

140

References

Alheit, P. (1991), Less Work-More Culture? Has 'working society' come to an end? Voksenpaedagogisk Teoriudvikling, Roskilde, Roskilde Universitetcenter.

Alheit, P. (1993), Changing Basic Rule of Biographical Construction: Modern Biographies at the end of the 20th Century, (Paper *Education* presented to the Third International Symposium, German Sociological Association 31 March-2 April, 1993).

Collins, M. (1991), Adult as Vocation: A Critical Role for the Adult Educator, London, Routledge.

Clayton, P. (1996), Enemies and Passing Friends: Settler Ideologies in Twentieth Century Ulster, London, Pluto Press.

Craig, G. and Mayo, M. (ed) (1995), Community Empowerment, London, Zed Books.

Curtin, C. and Varley (1995), Community Action and the State in Clancy, P. et al. (ed.) Irish Society: Sociological Perspectives, Dublin, Institute of Public Administration.

Eyerman, R. and Jamieson, A. (1991), Social Movements: A Cognitive Approach, Policy Press.

FECNI, Fair Employment Commission of Northern Ireland, Report of an Investigation into the Queen's University, Belfast, 1989; Report of an Investigation into the University of Ulster, 1990.

Giddens, A. (1995), The New Context of Politics, Democratic Dialogue No.1.

Hindley, R. (1990), The Death of the Irish Language, London, Routledge.

Jackson, K. (1995), Popular Education and the State in Mayo, M. et al., Adult Learning Critical Intelligence and Social Change, Leicester, NIACE.

Kivinen, O. and Rinne, D.R. (1994), Adult Education and Universities in an Era of Economic Depression in Parjanen, M. (ed), Outside the Golden Gate, University of Tampere, Institute for Extension Studies, A 3/94.

Lovett, T., Kilmurray, A. and Clarke, C. (1983), Adult Education and Community Action, London, Croom Helm.

Mayo, M. (1994), Communities and Caring, St. Martins Press.

Melucci, A. (1988), Nomads of the Present in Keane, J. et al. (ed.) London, Hutchinson.

Morris, S. (1996), Recent Language Protest Movements in Wales: Adult Learning of a New Kind? (Paper presented at Bremen Conference Life-Long Education).

O'Ciosain, E. (1991), Buried Alive, Dublin, Dail ui Chadhain.

O'Neill, G. (1992), Adult Education, Community Studies: Transformational Themes and Perspectives. Unpublished Report Magee Community Development Studies Unit, University of Ulster.

Polanyi, K. (1957), The Great Transformation: The Political and Economic Origins of Our Time, Beacon Press.

Preece, J. (1996), Historicity Repeats Itself: Power-knowledge games in Continuing Education, in Hill, S. and Merrill, B. (ed), Access, Equity, Participation and Organisational Change, Leamington Spa, ESREA/University of Warwick and Université Catholique de Louvain.

Robson, T. (1995), The State and Community Development in Northern Ireland: The ACE Programme for Social Change or Social Control, PhD Thesis, University of Ulster.

Robson, T. and McClenaghan, P. (1995), Training for Community Development: The North West Initiative, Community Development Studies Unit, University of Ulster.

Shanahan, P. (1984), Trade Unions, Unemployment and Redundancy, in The Industrial Tutors, 3, 10 (Society of Industrial Tutors) (with J. Munday).

Shanahan, P. (1985), Community Crime In Derry in The Irish Sociological Bulletin, The Sociological Association of Ireland.

Shanahan, P. (1987 a), The University and Community Education in AREAS Seminario Internacional, Instituto de Faro.

Shanahan, P. (1987 b), Social Scientists adandon Maidservant Role in The Times Higher Education Supplement, 15-5-1987.

Shanahan, P., McClenaghan, Mulrine, C., Sidwell, H., Robson, T. (1989), Between Popular Movements and Professional Manners: A Transborder Community Economic Development Training Project, Community Development Journal, 24,2.

Shanahan, P. (1990), Le tien culture/économie à travers le renouveau de la langue Irlandaise in TOUDI Culture et Société, Centre D'Etudes Wallones.

Shanahan,P. (1993), Social Movements and the University in MacGrianna, S. et al Essays on Class and Culture in Ireland, Ulster, Community Development Studies Unit, University of Ulster.

Shanahan,P. (1994), Ireland: Serving a Divided Community in Brooks, L. (ed), Serving Communities, Association for Colleges.

SHELL UK Prize for Open Learning, 1990, Council for Industry and Higher Education, CBI, London.

Tawney, R. H. (1926), Adult Education in the Hisotry of the Nation, 5th Annual Conference of the British Institute of Adult Education.